AREA HANDBOOK
for
CEYLON

Coauthors
Richard F. Nyrop

Beryl Lieff Benderly
Ann S. Cort
Newton B. Parker
James L. Perlmutter
Mary Shivanandan

Research was completed August 1970

First Edition

Published 1971

DA Pam 550–96

Library of Congress Catalog Card Number: 71-609-526

For sale by the Superintendent of Documents, U.S. Government Printing Office
Washington, D.C. 20402

Stock No. 008-020-00366-2/ Catalog No. D101.22:550-96

FOREWORD

This volume is one of a series of handbooks prepared by Foreign Area Studies (FAS) of The American University, designed to be useful to military and other personnel who need a convenient compilation of basic facts about the social, economic, political, and military institutions and practices of various countries. The emphasis is on objective description of the nation's present society and the kinds of possible or probable changes that might be expected in the future. The handbook seeks to present as full and as balanced an integrated exposition as limitations on space and research time permit. It was compiled from information available in openly published material. An extensive bibliography is provided to permit recourse to other published sources for more detailed information. There has been no attempt to express any specific point of view or to make policy recommendations. The contents of the handbook represent the work of the authors and FAS and do not represent the official view of the United States government.

An effort has been made to make the handbook as comprehensive as possible. It can be expected, however, that the material, interpretations, and conclusions are subject to modification in the light of new information and developments. Such corrections, additions, and suggestions for factual, interpretive, or other change as readers may have will be welcomed for use in future revisions. Comments may be addressed to:

The Director
Foreign Area Studies
The American University
5010 Wisconsin Avenue, N.W.
Washington, D.C. 20016

PREFACE

Located eighteen miles off the southeastern tip of the Indian subcontinent, Ceylon has long had a strategic importance with respect to the Bay of Bengal and the Indian Ocean. After 145 years of British rule as a British crown colony, Ceylon achieved independence in 1948 in a peaceful transfer of power and has since proceeded toward establishing on a firm footing its unique national culture and economy. In May 1970, during the preparation of this book, Mrs. Sirimavo Bandaranaike succeeded Dudley Senanayake as prime minister. The proposed policies of her government, as outlined in her public statements, have been reported and described to the extent possible.

This book is an attempt to provide a comprehensive study of the dominant social, political, and economic aspects of the society, to present its strengths and weaknesses, and to identify the patterns of behavior characteristic of its members. It strives for unity of interpretation within an interdisciplinary approach and is intended to provide the background and context in which recent events may be understood. It does not, however, pretend to be exhaustive.

Sources used included scholarly studies, official reports, local newspapers, and current journals. A considerable body of up-to-date information exists, although some of the economic data, particularly that for the late 1960s, should be considered as provisional, and the demographic data should be considered as estimates and used with caution.

The authors are indebted to officials of the United States government and to members of the Ceylonese community in Washington. The latter group in particular gave generously of their time and allowed us access to their personal books and documents. Special thanks are also due to the personnel of the Joint Library of the International Bank for Reconstruction and Development and the International Monetary Fund.

A glossary is included for the convenience of the reader. The place names used are those established by the United States Board on Geographic Names as of August 1960. The spelling of words and phrases follows the transliteration used by the Ceylonese government in its official publications or by the more prominent scholars in the field of study.

COUNTRY SUMMARY

1. COUNTRY: Ceylon is an island country eighteen miles from southeast coast of India. British crown colony until its independence in 1948. British monarch titular head of government, with authority delegated to appointed governor general. Capital: Colombo.

2. POPULATION: Estimated 12.5 million in 1970; growth rate estimated to vary between 2.2 and 2.8 percent annually. Birth rate of about 31.6 per 1,000 population; life expectancy for average male sixty-two years of age. *Composition:* Approximately 69 percent Sinhalese (see Glossary); 11 percent Ceylon Tamils (see Glossary); 12 percent Indian Tamils; remaining 8 percent Ceylon Moors, Eurasians, Burghers (see Glossary), Malays, Pakistanis, Europeans, Veddahs.

3. GEOGRAPHIC DESCRIPTION: Pear-shaped mass of crystalline rock and limestone 25,332 square miles in area. Greatest north-south distance 270 miles; east-west, 140 miles. *Topography:* About four-fifths of land flat or gently rolling; one-fifth a mass of hills and mountains located in south-central portion of island. Major and minor rivers originate in these mountains, radiate in all directions across the plains. *Climate:* Warm, humid, little seasonal change. Average yearly temperature from 80°F. to 83°F. Wet zone comprises southwest plain and southwest side of hill country, receives about 100 to 200 inches rainfall annually; dry zone comprises north-central and eastern part of the island, receives 50 to 75 inches annually.

4. LANGUAGES: Sinhala (see Glossary), Tamil, and English; Sinhala and Tamil are official languages, and English is extensively used.

5. RELIGION: Religion of Sinhalese is Buddhism; of Tamils, Hinduism. About 9 percent of population is Christian, and 7 percent, Muslim.

6. EDUCATION: Free, compulsory school for children aged five to fourteen; free secondary, college, and university education. About 84 percent of population aged five to fourteen in school. Four universities graduate total of about 2,000 students per year. Literacy rate for country over 80 percent.

7. HEALTH: Free medical care through government-supported health system. Infant mortality in 1970 estimated to be 53 per 1,000; overall death rate 8.2 per 1,000. Ratio of doctors to

patients in 1966 about 1 to 1,000. No widespread hunger, but dietary deficiencies produce malnutrition. In 1962 daily per capita caloric consumption 2,070.

8. GOVERNMENT: Authority of governor general exercised by prime minister who, with cabinet ministers, is chosen by political party or coalition of parties that wins majority of seats in parliamentary election held at least every five years. Parliament composed of Senate and House of Representatives. Constitution gives prime minister portfolios of defense, external affairs, and others as he sees necessary. In August 1970 new constitution in drafting stage.

9. JUSTICE: Independent; widely respected for its integrity. Consists of Supreme Court; district, magistrate's, and civil courts; rural courts and conciliation boards. Administration of justice guided by Roman-Dutch law, English law, and body of customary codes.

10. ADMINISTRATIVE DIVISIONS: Nine provinces, 22 districts, 133 revenue divisions. Each province headed by government agent who coordinates and supervises administration of districts and the activities of various central ministries within his jurisdiction.

11. ECONOMY: Agricultural. Three most important export crops are tea, rubber, coconuts. In 1968 agricultural sector of economy accounted for about 40 percent of gross national product (GNP), over 50 percent of labor force, 95 percent of foreign-exchange earnings. World's second largest producer of tea.

12. EXPORTS: Plantation exports—tea, rubber, coconut products—accounted for 91 percent of total export sector in 1969. Remainder of export sector composed of minerals, spices, cocoa beans, tobacco, citronella oil, cinnamon leaf oil.

13. IMPORTS: In 1969 foodstuffs, such as rice, wheat flour, sugar, milk products, fish and meat, pulses, onions, chilies, accounted for 38.4 percent of total imports. Fertilizer, petroleum products, transport equipment, machinery, textiles, clothing, and other consumer goods accounted for remainder of imports.

14. INDUSTRY: Mainly engaged in processing of agricultural produce for export and domestic markets. Most important manufacturing industries in 1970 were those processing the primary export commodities—tea, rubber, coconuts.

15. LABOR: About one-third of population in labor force. Agriculture and related activities employ an estimated 48 percent; services, 14 percent; trade and commerce, 12 percent; other unspecified, 17 percent. Unemployment serious problem, as is underemployment; estimates place number unemployed in 1969 at 265,000.

16. FINANCE: Monetary system organized around the Central Bank of Ceylon. Capital market in early stages of development. *Currency:* Standard unit is the rupee, divided into 100 cents. After November 20, 1967, par value of rupee was agreed to be Rs5.95 per US$1, or 1 rupee per 16.615 United States cents.

17. COMMUNICATIONS: *Radio:* Radio Ceylon broadcasts in English, Sinhala, and Tamil on both national and commercial services. Government owned and operated. One radio per 26 persons in 1966. *Telephones:* Estimated total in 1968 about 57,000, or 1 per 200 people.

18. RAILROADS: First railroad built in 1867 from Colombo to hill country coffee estates. By end of 1968 system totaled 925 miles broad-guage track. Switch from steam to diesel engines underway in 1969. Railroads operated some 1,450 million passenger-miles in fiscal year 1963/64 and about 185 million ton-miles in goods in 1964/65.

19. ROADS: Total miles of highways estimated to be 30,000 in 1966, about 70 percent asphalt surfaced and motorable. Network of roads covers whole country. At the end of 1965 motor vehicles numbered about 148,000, bicycles about 350,000; bullock carts still meet widespread need.

20. AIR TRANSPORT: Air Ceylon, government owned, operates domestic flights to five points within the country, a flight to India, and a London-Colombo-Singapore route with British Overseas Air Corporation (BOAC). Ceylon has three international airports.

21. PORTS: Colombo the major port, Galle a secondary one. There are nine minor ports. Colombo handles over 95 percent of Ceylon's shipping, is fueling station on world shipping lanes to Far East and South Asia.

22. INTERNATIONAL AGREEMENTS, MEMBERSHIPS, AND TREATIES: Member of United Nations and its agencies and Colombo Plan. Has a rubber-for-rice barter agreement with Communist China. Mutual defense agreement with United Kingdom.

23. AID PROGRAMS: International Monetery Fund (IMF) and International Bank for Reconstruction and Development (IBRD) assessed Ceylon's economic needs, organized aid from United States and West European countries. Ceylon-Soviet aid agreement signed in 1958 and Ceylon-Communist China agreement in 1957, both of importance in terms of total aid.

24. ARMED FORCES: Voluntary military service. In 1970 about 10,000 men in army, navy, and air force and about 12,000 in internal security force.

CEYLON

TABLE OF CONTENTS

LIST OF ILLUSTRATIONS

LIST OF TABLES

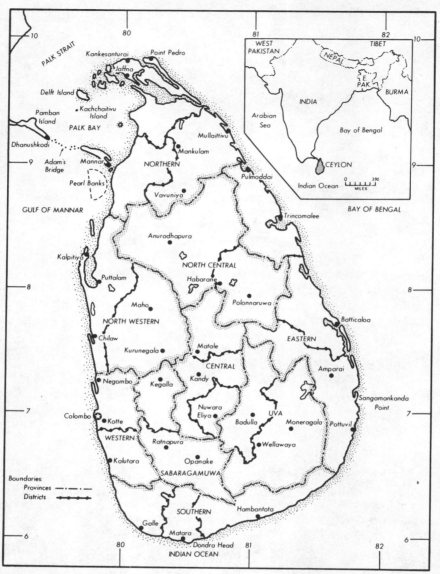

Figure 1. Ceylon

SECTION I. SOCIAL

CHAPTER 1

GENERAL CHARACTER OF THE SOCIETY

Ceylon became independent on February 4, 1948, after nearly 450 years of European domination. The Portuguese, who reached the island early in the sixteenth century, were supplanted in the mid-seventeenth century by the Dutch, who in turn lost control to the British in the last decade of the eighteenth century. During 145 years as a British crown colony, the administration of the island evolved from total British rule to almost complete self-government at the time of independence. The struggle for freedom was for the most part conducted in the context of constitutional and parliamentary maneuvers to determine when, rather than if, the British would relinquish control (see ch. 3, Historical Setting).

The experience gained in this evolutionary exercise in democratic and parliamentary procedures, which were highlighted in 1931 by legislative elections based on universal adult suffrage, has been made manifest by the several peaceful transfers of power from one political party to another of a distinctive and divergent political ideology. The change of government after the May 1970 general elections was the fifth such orderly transfer of power since independence, an achievement that is unique among the newly independent nations and one of which the Ceylonese are proud (see ch. 14, Political Dynamics; ch. 17, Political Values and Attitudes).

The adaptation of the British model to the Ceylonese situation has not been without problems, however. The population, which in 1970 was estimated to be about 12.5 million, is composed of highly disparate language and religious groups. An estimated 64 percent of the population are Sinhalese-Buddhists, and about 20 percent are Tamil (see Glossary) Hindus. The remainder is composed of Muslims, about 7 percent of the total and made up for the most part of Moors, and of Christians, about 9 percent of the total and made up of Sinhalese (see Glossary), Tamils, and Burghers (see Glossary) (see ch. 5, Ethnic Groups and Languages; ch. 11, Religion).

The Sinhalese, whose mythology and folk history ascribes to

1

them a North Indian origin, are over 90 percent Buddhist, and they tend to view themselves and their culture as being endowed with both the privilege and the duty of protecting Theravada Buddhism (see Glossary). The earliest histories, which were written by Buddhist *bhikkus* (monks—see Glossary), return again and again to the theme of the need to maintain the teachings of the Buddha in the face of incursions from the Hindu-dominated mainland of India (see ch. 3, Historical Setting; ch. 11, Religion). As an island people, they developed over the centuries an insular and parochial view of outsiders and intruders from across the seas, an attitude that those from the British Isles soon recognized and, to a degree, encouraged.

During the colonial period an English-speaking elite emerged that, by independence, was in firm control of the civil service and the developing political parties. Members of the group either had been educated in the United Kingdom or had received a British liberal arts education in local schools and universities (see ch. 9, Education). The elite adopted and absorbed British values and mores and in many instances were Christian. In addition, the Tamils and Burghers were members of this elite group in a ratio far higher than their proportion of the total population. Many of them were either unable or unwilling to speak or use Sinhala (see Glossary), the language of the Sinhalese-Buddhist majority (see ch. 6, Social Structure; ch. 12, Social Values).

During the 1950s an upsurge of Sinhalese-Buddhist nationalism, based largely on demands for the adoption of Sinhala as the national language and Buddhism as the national religion, developed a leader in the person of Solomon West Ridgeway Dias Bandaranaike. Although the immediate goal of the Sinhalese-Buddhists was supremacy of their language and religion over the Tamil Hindus, a related target was to supplant the English-speaking elite. The emotions generated by the nationalist movement and agitation were largely responsible for Bandaranaike's success in the 1956 election, for the communal riots in 1958, and for Bandaranaike's assassination in 1959 (see ch. 24, Public Order and Internal Security). By 1970, however, the communal tensions between the Sinhalese and Tamils had eased, and the issues in the 1970 campaign were more economic than social (see ch. 14, Political Dynamics).

The citizenship status of about half the Tamils, however, continued in 1970 to be a major diplomatic issue between India and Ceylon. The Ceylon Tamils, who are descendants of settlers and invaders from South India many centuries ago, were and are considered Ceylonese. The Indian Tamils, on the other hand, are descendants of laborers brought into the island in the late nineteenth and early twentieth centuries, and the vast majority of them continue to live and work on the large agricultural estates. In 1949 the Ceylonese Parliament enacted legislation that granted citizenship to some 134,000 of the Indian Tamils but in effect excluded the remainder from citizenship (see ch. 14, Political Dynamics; ch. 21, Labor).

In 1964 the prime ministers of Ceylon and India concluded an agreement which provided that, over a period of the next fifteen years, 525,000 Indian Tamils would be repatriated to India and 300,000 would be granted Ceylonese citizenship. The formula included the natural issue of the two groups during the fifteen-year period and provided also that the status of the balance of approximately 150,000 Indian Tamils and their natural increase not covered in the 1964 agreement would be the subject of further negotiation by or in 1979. By 1970, however, only about 4,000 Indian Tamils had been granted Ceylonese citizenship, and only approximately 66,000 had been returned to India. Because amicable relations with India are an important aspect of Ceylon's foreign policy considerations, the Ceylonese are desirous of a resolution of the question that is acceptable both to them and to the Indian government (see ch. 15, Foreign Relations).

In 1970 the other two keystones of Ceylon's foreign policy were to remain in the mainstream of Afro-Asian nonalignment in cold-war disputes and to procure significant amounts of economic aid and assistance. The Bandaranaike government in 1970 established diplomatic relations with East Germany, North Korea, North Vietnam, and the Provisional Government of South Vietnam, an action in general harmony with many, if not most, Afro-Asian countries (see ch. 15, Foreign Relations).

In 1970 the national economy continued to be heavily dependent on agricultural exports. Until the 1940s the world market demand and prices offered for tea, rubber, and coconuts and favorable and efficient conditions of production resulted in a consistently favorable balance of payments—that is, export earnings regularly equaled or exceeded import expenditures (see ch. 22, Trade; ch. 23, Finance). From the mid-1940s to 1970 the prices and demand for the major exports declined; tea, rubber, and coconut production became generally less efficient and more costly; the population increased at a rapid rate; and successive governments launched or expanded numerous social welfare projects (see ch. 18, Character and Structure of the Economy; ch. 19, Agriculture; ch. 22, Trade).

Although tea, rubber, and coconuts account for the bulk of the island's export earnings and perhaps three-fourths of the value of agricultural production, most of the people (over 80

3

percent of the total population) live and work on small subsistence farms. The principal food crop is rice, and over 30
percent of the land under cultivation is in rice. During the
late 1960s new seeds and the increased use of fertilizers resulted in significant growths in yields, but in 1970 from 25 to
30 percent of the island's rice requirements had to be imported (see ch. 19, Agriculture; ch. 22, Trade).

The island is located about eighteen miles from the southeastern side of the tip of the Indian peninsula. The terrain is
largely flat and rolling, but it is interspersed with numerous
rivers that flow from a cluster of mountain peaks ranging up
to 8,300 feet above sea level in the south-central part of the
island. There are two monsoons each year—one in May and
another in October and November—and in the southwest and
in some parts of the mountainous region the rainfall is as much
as 200 inches per year. In the northern part of the island there
is a large area known as the dry zone (see Glossary). Because
of the nature of the soil, much of the rainfall is lost to rapid
runoff, and in ancient times huge tanks (reservoirs) were constructed to hold the rainfall for irrigation. During the 1960s
several extensive irrigation projects to reclaim much of this
land for agriculture either had been started or were in various
planning stages (see ch. 2, Physical Environment; ch. 19,
Agriculture).

In 1968 only five cities had populations in excess of 50,000.
The capital city of Colombo, which was also the major port
and commercial center, had an estimated population of slightly
over 500,000. Over two-thirds of the population lived in the
southwestern part of the island—the wet zone (see Glossary)—
where the population density was approximately 700 per square
mile, as opposed to the average density of 483.

The relatively rapid rate of urbanization and the large increase in the number of college and university graduates have
resulted in both a substantial growth in the number of urban,
educated unemployed and in an accelerated change in the traditional social system. The society as a whole was in a tran-
sitory state in the late 1960s and was characterized by seeming
contradictions. Both the teachings of Buddha and national
legislation contain criticisms of, and prohibitions against, caste
exclusivity, but important family rites—particularly marriage—
still largely conform to caste considerations. Unlike other
societies in which caste is of significance, in Ceylon the largest
caste group, the cultivators, is also the most prestigious (see
ch. 6, Social Structure).

Among the Sinhalese and Tamils in the rural areas, formal

caste relationships are still observed, and the extended kin group is the social universe for most people. Marriages are typically contracted by the male members of the family within the kin group. If a marriage is made into an unrelated family, the marriage is between caste equals, and a fiction of kinship ties between the two families is usually established. Within the traditional families, the males are dominant, and among some groups women are considered to be legal minors (see ch. 7, Family).

In the more cosmopolitan urban areas and among the socially mobile university graduates, the traditional family concept has been, and is being, modified. The Burghers, for example, have never observed caste regulations, and their families are largely modern European in structure. Although there is still very little intermarriage between ethnic communities, marriages are increasingly arranged by the prospective spouses rather than by the male head of the family, and among the educated elite there is a lessening, although not an abandonment, of caste considerations.

An increasingly vital consideration in marriage arrangements is the present or future occupation of the prospective bridegroom. The most valued occupation is the civil service or other government service, such as the military. Civil service administrators or clerks, for example, have substantially more social prestige than do administrators or clerks in private industry, even if the latter earn appreciably more than the former. The predilection for government service and the social values attached to owning and cultivating land combine to place a low premium on such occupations as commerce, industry, technical services, and any form of manual labor (see ch. 12, Social Values).

The extensive social welfare activities of the government are by and large an expansion of policies and practices instituted during the British colonial period. In 1970 approximately 80 percent of those fifteen years of age and older were literate, a reflection of an extensive background of free and compulsory education (see ch. 9, Education). During the middle and late 1940s an official antimalaria project was undertaken to complete the work of American technicians during World War II. As a result of public health campaigns of this type and, for all practical purposes, free medical and hospital care, the life expectancy at birth was estimated in 1970 to be over sixty years of age, by far the highest in South Asia. A significant reduction in infant mortality, the elimination of endemic malaria, and a significant decline in the incidence of tuberculosis have contributed to a rapid increase in population. During the late 1960s the annual growth rate was conservatively estimated to be 2.4 percent (see ch. 4, Population).

The island has been confronted with neither a real nor a potential foreign threat to its security since independence. In 1970 the armed forces were composed of about 10,000 officers and men in the Ceylon Army, the Royal Ceylon Navy, and the Royal Ceylon Air Force. The army was basically an infantry force with the primary mission of internal security. The navy performed antismuggling and anti-illicit immigration patrols along the northern and western coastlines, and the air force provided support to the other two services (see ch. 25, The Armed Forces).

The principal task of maintaining internal security fell to the over 12,000 officers and men of the Police Department. The main internal security problem has been communal violence, but by the late 1960s clashes between the Sinhalese and Tamils were infrequent and local, rather than islandwide, in nature (see ch. 24, Public Order and Internal Security).

The Constitution of 1948 placed the armed forces and the police under the Ministry of Defence and External Affairs and specified that the ministry be headed by the prime minister. During the 1960s there were two coup attempts by small groups composed of military and police officers and civilians, and during the 1970 campaign Prime Minister Sirimavo Bandaranaike, then head of the opposition coalition, formally reported to the governor general the coalition's fear of a military coup attempt should the opposition win the election. Shortly after her election, Mrs. Bandaranaike screened several military officers from the service and reinstated several officers who had been involved in the 1966 coup attempt and who had been forced to retire (see ch. 25, The Armed Forces).

In August 1970 the future of the island's economy was bleak, and the nature of its future government structure was uncertain. In compliance with a campaign promise, Mrs. Bandaranaike and her political associates called for, and secured, a vote in the House of Representatives that provided for the transformation of the House into a Constituent Assembly to draft a new constitution. There was believed to be general popular support for a constitutional revision to change Ceylon from a British dominion, in which the British monarch was the head of state, to a republic (see ch. 13, The Governmental System). When the Constituent Assembly was convened, the minister of constitutional affairs declared that the government had not drafted a constitution for the assembly's approval or rejection and implied that the government would not force through a prewritten version.

6

CHAPTER 2

PHYSICAL ENVIRONMENT

Ceylon is an island country in the Indian Ocean, bounded on the west by the Gulf of Mannar and on the east by the Bay of Bengal. It is 270 miles long from Point Pedro, its northernmost point, to Dondra Head, its southern tip, and 140 miles wide from Colombo on the west coast to Sangamankanda Point on the east coast. Colombo is its capital and chief port.

The island is separated from the southeast tip of the Indian mainland by a narrow strait called Palk Strait. At one time Ceylon was geographically a portion of the Indian subcontinent, as evidenced by the continental shelf upon which the island stands. Barely eighteen miles of shallow sea separates the island from India, a distance easily covered by train ferry. An elevated portion of the continental shelf forms a chain of rocky islands known as Adam's Bridge, located just south of the ferry route. Here Palk Strait widens into the Gulf of Mannar, which in turn merges into the Indian Ocean (see fig. 1).

Ceylon's position, about 500 miles north of the equator, assures warm temperatures year round, little seasonal change, and long growing seasons for rice and tea, which are the most important crops. A great variety of fruits and vegetables flourish in the villagers' garden plots. Two yearly monsoons, the northeast and the southwest, bring adequate amounts of rainfall; although violent storms accompany the change of monsoon in the Arabian Sea and the Bay of Bengal, they rarely affect Ceylon. The coastal lagoons and the coral reef surrounding the southern half of the island abound with fish, a potentially important factor in the island's economy. The terrain, natural resources, and climate are all so compatible with human life that the island has been called Resplendent Isle, Isle of Delight, Isle of Gems, and Pearl. This compatibility is reflected in the standard of living, which is one of the highest in South and Southeast Asia (see ch. 8, Living Conditions).

The major geographical regions are the hill country of the central portion, occupying about one-fifth of the island's 25,332 square miles, and the belt of lowland between the

7

hills and the sea, constituting about four-fifths of the land area. The limestone region of the Jaffna Peninsula in the north is identified as a separate entity because of its structure. There are two hyetal regions; the wet zone and the dry zone (see Glossary). Almost three-fourths of the land area is characterized as dry zone, not because of lack of rainfall, but because of the seasonal quality of it.

The natural resources of soil, sea, and forest were being carefully studied in 1970 and their role in the national economy assessed. Graphite, precious and semiprecious gems, mineral sands, clays, and limestones have been mined for years, but deposits of iron ore, peat, and a few other minerals known to exist in workable quantities were not yet being exploited. Potentially valuable timber grows in the jungles and forests. To protect this and the wildlife, many species of which were becoming extinct, the government continued to set aside at intervals acreage for wildlife preserves. In 1968 such lands amounted to about one-fourth of Ceylon's total area.

The culture and economy are predominantly rural; in the wet zone crops can be planted at almost any time of year and are fast growing in the warm temperatures and high humidity. A compact network of roads, cart paths, and footpaths over all but the most remote areas makes garden-to-market transport relatively easy. There are few sections of the island that will not support agriculture of one sort or another. Even in the limestone region of the north villagers manage, through persistent hard work, to grow rice and vegetables. The *chena* (see Glossary) cultivator practices a kind of slash-and-burn agriculture in areas where irrigation is not possible (see ch. 19, Agriculture).

There are numerous and widely varying patterns of settlement. The laborers on the plantations, for example, live in compact, company towns, whereas on the Jaffna Peninsula, because water supply and storage are critical problems, the villages are dispersed along the roadsides and have no easily discernible focal point. In the intensely cultivated and irrigated regions, the villages typically are located above the water level of the tank (reservoir—see Glossary). The coastal fishing villages usually consist of a cluster of houses encircled by coconut trees.

Settlements and urban areas such as Colombo, Galle, Matara, and Ratnapura developed and have remained important as transportation and trading centers. All the major urban areas are linked by railroad and hard-surfaced highways.

8

GENERAL GEOGRAPHIC SETTING

Ceylon's position in the Indian Ocean has for centuries made it an attractive resting and trading place. Rumors of its beauty and wealth and the hospitality of its inhabitants circulated in Europe and Asia in the third and fourth centuries B.C. The Chinese were attracted by news of Buddhism, which so interested them that they sent emissaries to India and Ceylon to gather information about it. By the time of the Chinese explorer-priest, Fa Hsien, Buddhism had been well established in China. Sometime in the late fourth or early fifth century A.D., Fa Hsien undertook a fifteen-year journey by land and sea to India and Ceylon for the purpose of finding original Buddhist manuscripts that could be copied and translated into Chinese in order to preserve the purity of the religion in China. After Fa Hsien's difficult and innovative trip was accomplished, other Chinese Buddhists followed his route to Ceylon on pilgrimages. Chinese merchants, too, had by this time set up a thriving silk trade with the Roman Empire, using the island of Ceylon as an intermediate transfer point.

Around the middle of the first century A.D., the Romans and Arabs had learned to use the monsoon winds to carry them back and forth across the Arabian Sea. Gradually, Arab settlements developed all along the shores of Asia as far south as the island of Sumatra; as they increased their sailing and navigating skills, the Arabs ventured to the coast of China. In Ceylon they entered the gem trade, in which their Muslim descendants are still engaged.

The island was not only a good stopping place, geographically speaking, but was also a hospitable country in which to settle. The uniform climate, fertile soil, long growing season, and regular terrain of the coasts attracted, in addition to Arab settlers, Portuguese, Dutch, and British colonizers in turn. In the interests of trade and religious proselytizing, the European powers gradually conquered the coastal and plains areas. The Kandyan Sinhalese were the last to fall under foreign rule; the dense forests and rugged mountains of their kingdom served as protection from invasion until 1815, when the British finally succeeded in overthrowing the Kandyan king.

During periods of warfare, which occurred from the twelfth century on, much damage was done to the land and the ancient irrigation system (see ch. 3, Historical Setting). Cities were destroyed and abandoned, and tanks were allowed to dry up. But the tea and rubber plantations, on which Ceylon's economy depends, and the system of roads and railroads are among the benefits of the colonial period (see ch. 19, Agriculture; ch. 22, Trade).

LAND, CLIMATE, AND RESOURCES
The Geographical Regions

The island is a pear-shaped mass of crystalline rock on which three levels of ground can be distinguished. The first is a coastal belt that rises from sea level to 100 feet above and is perhaps twenty-five miles across at its widest point. The second is a belt of rolling plain striated with ridges rising to 500 feet in the south. The third is an irregularly shaped mass of hills and mountains having heights over 6,000 feet (see fig. 2).

The coastal belt is ringed with palm trees, both coconut and palmyra. Sandy beaches stretch for miles, indented here and there by coastal lagoons, which are useful chiefly for fishing and for collecting salt. Trincomalee, on the northeast, is situated on a natural rock harbor. Not only is it exceptionally beautiful, but also it is large enough and deep enough to accommodate a modern naval fleet. On the other side of the island, on the southern coast, is the harbor of Galle, also of natural rock but much smaller than Trincomalee. Galle has ancient historical associations, as it was the principal landing for trading vessels on the Arabia-Far East spice route.

A coral reef encircles the southern two-thirds of the island and is rich in sea life. Divers obtain pearls from the famous pearl banks in the Gulf of Mannar, off the northwestern coast. The waters surrounding the island are so deep that Ceylon is almost unaffected by tidal variations. Measurements kept over long periods of time show variations of only 2.6, 2.3, and 2.1 feet at Colombo, Galle, and Trincomalee, respectively. These occur only twice each month; the daily range is only a few inches. The highest tide recorded was under 4 feet. The ebb and flow of tides usually scoop out accumulated silt deposited in river mouths and carry it out to sea, preventing harbors from closing up; in Ceylon, however, because of the near absence of tides, the principal rivers are all blocked by sandbars.

There are many picturesque place names whose derivation can be easily guessed: Foul Point, Elephant Point, Portugal Bay, and Devil's Point, to name a few. Dutch, Portuguese, and British occupation led to such names as Kayts Island, Delft Island, Point Pedro, Back Bay, and Buffalo Island.

Five to twenty-five miles inland from the coastal belt the land changes character. Sandy and saline soil gives way to fertile loams, humic soils and, in the north, limestone. It is land lying 100 to 500 feet above sea level and composes the major portion

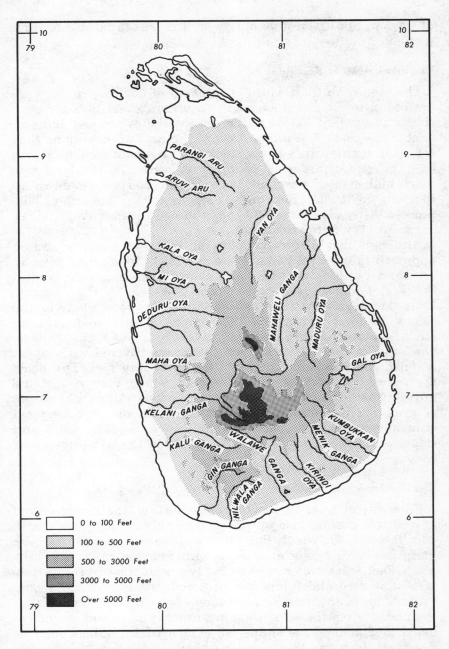

Source: Adapted from Percival Gerald Cooray, *An Introduction to the Geology of Ceylon,* Colombo, 1967, p. 54.

Figure 2. Relief Map of Ceylon.

of Ceylon. For descriptive purposes, it is best divided into three sections.

The Southwestern Section

The area from the Deduru Oya, north of Chilaw on the western coast, to Hambantota on the southern coast is a series of ridges and valleys. Close to the sea the ridges are low and parallel to the coast, but inland toward the central mountains they are seen against the sky as mountain chains, alternating with long, narrow depressions. Millions of years ago the land was much higher in this section, but rain and rivers wore down all rock but the hardest, leaving the ridges as they are today. This process of erosion transferred the top soil to the valleys, creating some very fertile rice land.

Although the hills and ridges of the southwestern section approach the central mountain mass, they are distinct from it, set apart by the plain. The land slopes west and south toward the sea, and the numerous rivers that rise in the Bulutota Hills flow westward through the gaps they have made in the ridges. Around Ratnapura the action of rain and running streams loosened gem-bearing gravel from the rocks and deposited it in the valleys, which then were covered with layers of mud and sand to depths of five to twenty feet. The gems are mined by workers with sieves in which they collect the gravel, washing and sorting out the precious stones. Plumbago, or graphite, is found in veins in the rock and is considered economically more important than the gems. The hills and ridges of this section are collectively called the Sabaragamuwa Ridges.

The Southeastern Section

From the plain of the southeastern section, the mountains of the central portion rise up like a wall, giving the appearance of a fortress, for which that area was used for centuries. The plain is studded here and there with rounded hills. The hills are in fact masses of buried rock. Over millions of years a process of erosion and filling has occurred, the tops of the mountains being worn down and the red, lateritic soil building up the plain. Often the hills are almost totally bare and are of unusual and picturesque shape, as evidenced by names such as Elephant Rock and Westminster Abbey.

The soils of the southeastern section, which is bounded roughly by the rivers Walawe Ganga and Mahaweli Ganga, are good for growing cotton, orange trees, and rice. Most of the area is forest and parkland or *talawa* (an open space with scattered trees). The southeastern section is thinly populated, but dried-up tanks and ruined temples survive from ages past. *Talawa* country is now the home of the Veddahs, who practice shifting agriculture (see ch. 5, Ethnic Groups and Languages).

Toward the coast where the mouths of the Walawe Ganga, the Mahaweli Ganga, and the rivers between them empty into the sea, the plain becomes mostly river basin. As the land is low and flat, flooding can, and does, occur. Because sand and silt have blocked the river mouths, they are navigable only by canoes and small boats.

The Northern Section

Between the Mahaweli Ganga on the east and the Deduru Oya on the west, this section of the plain is very flat, broad at the southern end and tapered toward the Jaffna Peninsula at the northern end. The peninsula is a limestone block, unlike the rest of the island, which is formed from crystalline gneiss and granite. In the wide southern area, near the central mountains, the granite is exposed in long, narrow ridges running north to south. In ancient times the natural caves in these ridges were ancient dwellings for Sinhalese monks who wished to lead an ascetic life (see ch. 11, Religion). Several rivers cross the plain, flowing northward from their source in the mountains, between the north-south ridges until they leave the 500-foot level and turn east and west.

Jaffna Peninsula is the only area in the country having a different composition. The limestone region, of which it is the northernmost part, begins at a line extending from Puttalam on the west coast to Mullaittivu on the east. Only the peninsula and its neighboring islands are of pure limestone, however, as loose stone and the products of erosion cover the larger part of the region to depths of several feet. The surface of the peninsula is dry, since water seeps through into the porous limestone to collect in underground pools or to join the underground streams. The Ceylon Tamils (see Glossary) who live in this area manage to cultivate every available acre and successfully grow tobacco and coconuts.

The Hill Country

This region is remarkably different from the rest of the island, consisting not of rolling hills and plain but of high mountain walls, narrow gorges, deep valleys, and lofty plateaus, in which are about sixteen rivers and innumerable waterfalls. The shape of the highest area has been likened to an anchor, the shank pointing northward, the two arms extending southwest and northeast. Elevations of more than 5,000 feet above sea level are the rule; Adam's Peak at the western tip of the "anchor" rises to 7,360 feet. The remainder of the hill country consists of the Southern and Eastern platforms, the abruptly rising steps by which the area is approached from the south and east; the Uva Basin; the Hatton Plateau; the Dolosbage Group (mountains); the Kandy Plateau; the Knuckles Group (mountains); the Piduru Ridges; and the Matale Valley (see fig. 3).

The Southern and Eastern platforms stand like two giant steps in front of the wall of the southern hill country, which in turn rises sharply and suddenly to over 5,000 feet. The wall extends some fifty miles between the nine peaks of Namunukula, the highest of which is 6,679 feet, to the summit of Adam's Peak. Two tremendous gaps cut the wall; beyond the point where the wall turns to the north, Haputale Gap and Ella Gap allow access through the mountain barrier onto the slopes of the Uva Basin.

Uva Basin is distinctive for its *patanas,* or grasslands. The basin itself is surrounded by mountain walls on three sides; on the north two great rivers, the Badulla Oya and Uma Oya, drain the valley and work their way to the Mahaweli Ganga lying farther to the north in its own valley. The center of Uva Basin is hilly; the grass-covered slopes resemble the "downs" familiar to the British, and hence the name Uva Downs.

The Hatton Plateau is one of a series of high plains of the hill country and lies west of Uva Basin. Its height is between 3,000 and 4,000 feet above sea level. The rivers that flow between its ridges ultimately form the great Mahaweli Ganga. Conditions on the plateau are excellent for growing tea, and nearly all the area is under tea cultivation. Most of the inhabitants are Indian Tamils who live and work on the European-owned and -operated plantations.

Northeast of Hatton Plateau a separate group of mountains, named for its outstanding peak, Dolosbage, is now cleared of its original forest cover and devoted mostly to plantations, especially rubber. The valley of the Mahaweli Ganga separates this group from the central mass of the hill country, the Piduru Ridges. This formidable, nearly inaccessible mountain fortress is composed of peaks reaching 8,000 feet and more above sea level, the highest being Pidurutalagala, 8,292 feet. From this and other high peaks great ridges stretch out in all directions, some of the most important being Great Western, Talankanda, a ridge ending in three peaks over 7,700 feet extending southward, and a ridge extending north toward Kandy. Deep, narrow valleys lie between the ridges and are the principal channels of movement through this rock and forest maze. Four of the main routes lead to Nuwara Eliya, once an English sana-

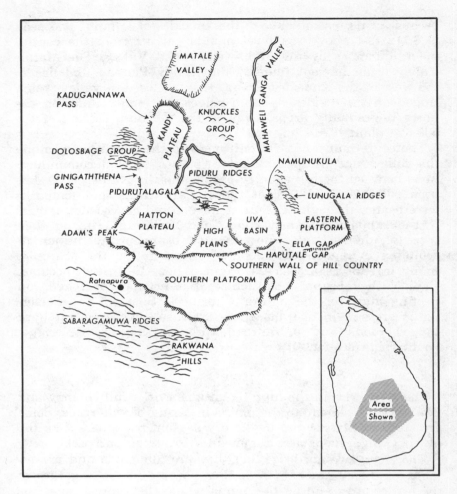

Source: Adapted from Percival Gerald Cooray, *An Introduction to the Geology of Ceylon,* Colombo, 1967, p. 63.

Figure 3. Diagram of Hill Country of Ceylon.

torium, now a thriving tea-producing town, situated in a lofty mountain basin beneath Pidurutalagala.

The Kandy Plateau lies to the north of the Piduru Ridges. It is cut by ridges and valleys and by the Mahaweli Ganga, which here turns in an arc from its northward course to the southeast. In the bend in the river is situated the ancient city of Kandy, above an artificial lake made in 1810 by the last king of Kandy.

The Kunckles Group and Matale Valley are the two northernmost sections of the hill country. The highest point in this group of mountains is Knuckles Peak, so named by the English

15

because of its resemblance to the knuckles of a hand. The peak is 6,112 feet above sea level and is cut off from the central mountain mass by the Mahaweli Ganga Valley. The Matale Valley is an ancient route to the Kandy Plateau and lies to the west of the Knuckles Group. It is a closed-in valley, being ringed on three sides by high ridges and small hills; on the north it gradually drops away to the northern section of the 500-foot plain.

There are many natural entrances to the hill country along the valleys and through mountain passes, so that communications between the hill country people and the plains people has been possible since ancient times. Cart tracks and footpaths were beaten through dense, wet forests and carved out of rock by thousands of Buddhist, Hindu, and Muslim pilgrims on their trips to Adam's Peak, whose summit bears an indentation resembling a huge human foot. This imprint is the source of many legends regarding its origin. When the British occupied Ceylon, they began construction of a network of roads connecting many of the natural entrances. Some of the ancient paths are still in use, but there are also some excellent hard-topped roads and a railroad through this scenic, rugged countryside (see fig. 4).

Rivers

The rivers rise in the high mountains of the hill country and flow over the plateau to the plains in a ring of waterfalls. Some are streams that dry up in the dry season, but others, like the Menik Ganga, have been dammed for irrigation purposes.

The rivers are not large, but they are numerous and are notable for their beauty, both at their sources in rocky gorges of the hill country and on the plains where they spread over the land in shallow lakes. There are sixteen principal rivers; the Mahaweli Ganga is the longest—206 miles. With the exception of the 104-mile-long Aruvi Aru, the other chief rivers range from 97 to 62 miles in length. Although they are not useful for navigation, being too wild in the mountains and too shallow on the plains, most supply plenty of fish to the villages along their banks. The rivers effectively drain the uplands but in the lowlands may divide into several streams and, where the land is flat, water may back up and become an obstacle to land development and communications. In such areas serious flooding may occur. Roads and bridges must therefore be massively reinforced, and people build their houses away from the river's edge. The areas around the cities of Colombo, Trincomalee, and Batticaloa are of this type.

Although Ceylon has few natural lakes, there are 12,000

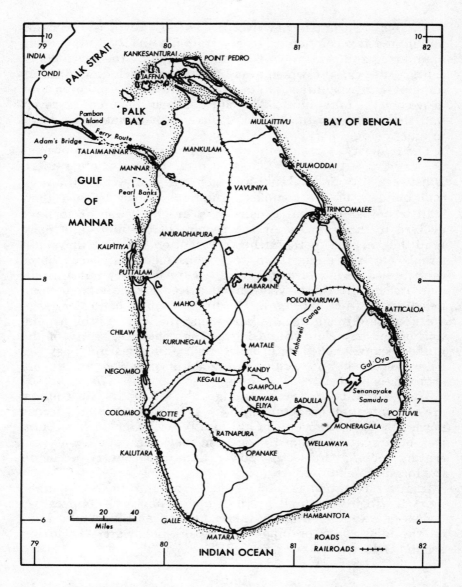

Source: Adapted from E. W. Egan, *Ceylon in Pictures* (Visual Geography Series), New York, 1967, p. 4.

Figure 4. Roads and Railroads of Ceylon.

bodies of water ranging from tiny ponds to manmade lakes several miles wide that are actually reservoirs. The oldest of these tanks, as they are called locally and in much of southern Asia, is believed to be Basawakkulam, built about 300 B.C. to store water for the ancient city of Anuradhapura on the Mal-

17

watu Oya, in what is now North Central Province. Basawakkulam and two companion reservoirs built about 100 B.C. were abandoned and overgrown with dense scrub by the seventeenth century, as was the whole area around and including Anuradhapura. Sources differ as to whether malaria or invasions drove out the inhabitants. The city has been restored, however, and the three ancient reservoirs have been cleaned and made to function again.

The majority of reservoirs are situated in what is known as the dry zone—that is, the north-central region where rainfall is between fifty and seventy-five inches a year. Where the original builders of the complex irrigation system learned their skill is not known, but construction practices appear to have evolved in three cycles. As the people cleared more and more land they needed more extensive irrigation. At first they built simple earthen dams; then they constructed fifty-foot dams that formed bodies of water from twenty to thirty miles in circumference; the third cycle included feeder canals that channeled water from springs in the hills, keeping ponds or reservoirs full and irrigating the land along the way. As the population of the dry zone thinned over the centuries, many of the tanks became choked with underbrush and dried up. They are being restored, and additional modern ones are being constructed as needed.

The waterfalls that ring the high plateau of the hill country are of potential economic value as sources of hydroelectric power. Sixteen or seventeen are locally well known, but countless others are unnamed. Together they are capable of generating more hydroelectric power than the country needs in the foreseeable future.

Inland navigation is made possible by 153 miles of canals, most of which were built by the Dutch. They may connect two bodies of water, such as Puttalam Lagoon and Negombo Lake on the west coast, or may channel off floodwaters occurring around Colombo.

Climate

The island's climate is characterized by a warm, even temperature and a generally high humidity. There is relatively little wind, even during the monsoon seasons, but the heavy rains are often accompanied by thunderstorms. Although there is frequent and heavy cloud accumulation at midday, the nights are usually brilliantly clear.

Temperature and Humidity

The average yearly temperature for the country is 80°F. to 83°F., measured in the shade. The coldest town, Nuwara Eliya, averages 60°F., and the hottest, Trincomalee, averages 92°F. Frost may occur for a few days in January and February at Nuwara Eliya, but otherwise the yearly temperature range is slight. Temperatures in the warmest areas, such as Trincomalee, rarely go above 98°F. Day and night temperatures may vary by five to eight degrees. January is usually cool and May usually hot. Sea breezes, altitude of the land, and moist air combine to keep the island reasonably cool in spite of its tropical location.

The humidity tends to be high, ranging from a low of 61 percent to a high of 90 percent. Seasonal variations occur but are not great. At Anuradhapura, for example, a low of 60 percent is usual for March, which is a dry month for that area, and a high of 77 percent is usual for November, which marks the beginning of the northeast monsoon. Problems associated with high humidity can be annoying; clothing may feel damp, and mildew may ruin stored articles.

Rainfall

Two monsoon seasons affect the island, the first coming from the southwest in May and the second from the northeast in November. Throughout the month of May the southwest coastal region receives fifteen to twenty-five inches of rain, which may fall at any hour, day or night. In June the monsoon moves inland, and the hill country is drenched with as much as thirty-five inches of rain, whereas areas to the northwest, such as Puttalam, and to the southeast, such as Hambantota, remain dry. In August the monsoon weakens but is followed by a period of local thunderstorm activity that produces from two to five inches of rain on the leeward side of the island—that is, on the northern and eastern plains. By October nearly every part of the island is receiving rain, either from the nearly extinguished monsoon or from afternoon thunderstorms.

The northeast monsoon begins to blow in November, bringing considerable amounts of rain to the eastern side of the island. The northern and eastern slopes of the hill country receive fifteen to twenty inches in that month, and areas as far north as Jaffna receive ten to twelve inches. The wind is weaker and drier, however, than that of the southwest monsoon, which blows over the Bay of Bengal, picking up moisture as it moves and releasing it over Ceylon. By February the northeast monsoon has all but blown itself out, and rainfall over the eastern half of the island dwindles to two to five inches per month.

The pattern of rainfall marks three major zones on the land. The dry zone, which comprises the north and central plain and a strip of the southeastern plain, receives from 50 to 75 inches of rain annually. The wet zone, which comprises the south-western plain and the southwest side of the hill country, as well as a small area around Matale, receives 100 and more inches. Two small arid zones stretching from Puttalam to Jaffna and from Tangalla to Pottuvil receive 25 to 50 inches (see fig. 5). In the dry and arid zones a great deal of rainfall is lost through evaporation and runoff, which makes necessary the irrigation and water storage systems in spite of heavy rain over the entire island.

Soils and Mineral Resources

Soil formation in Ceylon has been influenced more by the climate than by the underlying basic material. The type of soil changes with the distribution of rainfall; thus dry zone soil, a reddish-brown earth full of ferromagnesian minerals, differs from wet zone soil, which is reddish-brown laterite, formed by erosion. The coastal areas are mostly sand overlying clay; and where the rivers fan out over the plains, much of the soil is alluvial clay and gravel, carried down from the hill country. The thin soil of the Jaffna Peninsula is sandy and stony, but enough gray loam is present for rice growing on a small scale. Parts of the peninsula lie within a belt of land stretching north from Puttalam, whose soil indicates that the climate of earlier ages differed from that of the present day.

The island is rich in industrial rocks and minerals, such as gemstones, graphite, mineral sands, and several types of clay. Gems, graphite, and mineral sands are mined chiefly for export; kaolin clay, limestone, feldspar, and quartz are used in local industry. No coal, oil, copper, lead, or zinc has been discovered (see ch. 20, Industry; ch. 22, Trade).

The island has for centuries been famous for its gems, since almost nowhere else in the world are so many varieties of precious and semiprecious stones found in such a small area. Within about 800 square miles on the southwest side, centering on Ratnapura, forty-four varieties occur in the rocks and gravel of streambeds. The more prominent gems are blue sapphires, moonstones, garnets, and zircons.

The graphite industry is more than 100 years old and involves extensive mechanized mining procedures. For many years Ceylon was the world's largest producer of graphite, or plumbago, as it is sometimes called. Graphite is pure crystalline carbon. It occurs as plates or needles in the veins and cracks of crystalline rocks, and the major deposits are in the southwest section of the island around Ruwanwella and Kurunegala.

The Kandy, Matale, and Badulla districts are the sites of small deposits of mica found in the limestone as "books." The

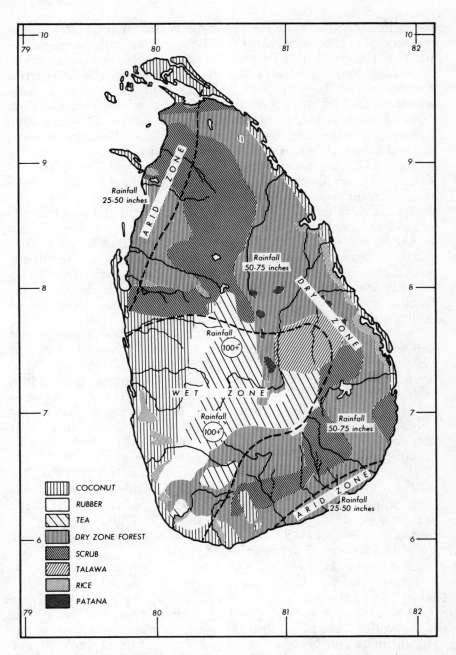

Source: Adapted from *Ferguson's Ceylon Directory, 1966* (108th ed.), Colombo, 1966, pp. 20 and 1299.

Figure 5. Vegetation and Rainfall of Ceylon.

21

demand for mica was high during World War II but subsequently diminished, until in 1970 there was little demand for it. The Kandy-Matale-Badulla area is more important as a source of limestone from which chemical lime is extracted. Further north the limestone changes from crystalline to sedimentary, and the northwest coast and the Jaffna Peninsula are sites of several large cement factories (see ch. 20, Industry). Reserves of limestone from which cement can be manufactured are estimated to be sufficient for many years.

Ilmenite is the source of titanium oxide, used as a component of high-grade white paint and as part of an alloy used in the manufacture of certain airplane parts where its light weight is a valuable factor. Ilmenite occurs in the black sands around the coast; the largest deposit is near Trincomalee and is estimated to be more than 20 million metric tons. The coastal sands, when purified, are also valuable for: monazite, potentially useful as a nuclear raw material; garnet, useful as an abrasive; zircon, from which a new metal, zirconium, is extracted; rutile, a source of titanium dioxide; and quartz, from which glassware and glass bottles are made.

Two types of clay, kaolin and alluvial, are now being mined and put to use in the pottery, brick, paper, tile, and electrical industries. Kaolin, which has great resistance to high temperatures and chemical changes and also turns pure white in the kiln, is located in riverbeds, on reservoir bottoms, and in veins in crystalline rocks. The largest deposit is a few miles south of Colombo, and the Kaolin Refinery there can produce 5,000 metric tons of pure kaolin a year. It is used in making electrical insulators and high-grade pottery and as a filler in textiles, paint, powder, and bricks (see ch. 20, Industry). The alluvial clays are colored and are used in bricks, tiles, stoneware, pipes, and cement. The ball clays are dark but turn white or cream-colored when fired and are used in ceramics. Alluvial clays are found in the valleys of the major rivers in fourteen of the twenty-two districts.

Other potentially important but still underexploited mineral resources are iron ore, peat, gold, and a variety of radioactive and rare-earth minerals. The crystalline rocks and limestones are excellent building stones and are beginning to be widely used for that purpose. A very beautiful green serpentinous marble and a quartz ranging from pink to red in color are cut and polished to a high luster and used as ornamental stones.

Natural and Cultivated Vegetation

Vegetation is tropical, and many species are the same as those found in India. Some are indigenous, however, suggesting that the island's separation from the Indian mainland occurred so long ago that new species have emerged. Soil, rainfall, the quality of the light, and temperature all influence the type of vegetation. Many of the plant forms have adapted themselves to climatic conditions and thrive in areas where nothing else will grow. Hence, much of the island is green most of the time.

Humidity and rainfall are the chief determinants of what grows in the dry zone and in the wet zone and, although there is no clearly marked boundary, there is a distinct difference in vegetation between the two areas. About 50 percent of the land is forest and scrub covered, but only a small portion is left of the original covering. The largest type of forest in Ceylon is the dry zone tropical forest. Vegetation here is affected by the northeast monsoon; plants grow very fast from November to February when rainfall is heavy, and many different species live together in the same area. From March to August rain is scanty, the wind is dry, and growth is imperceptible. Even the soil is dry, lacking humus. Various adaptations to the dry conditions have developed: to conserve water, trees have thick bark; most have tiny leaves, and some drop their leaves in this season; and the topmost branches of the tallest trees often interlace, forming a canopy against the hot sun and a barrier to the dry wind.

About 2 percent of the dry zone forest is economically valuable. Marketable timber is obtained from such species as satinwood, ebony, palu (a species of ironwood), and milla. Some of the wood is exported, and some is used domestically. Reforestation in satinwood and teak is proceeding, as well as research to determine which of the unexploited species might be useful (see ch. 19, Agriculture).

The wet zone forests are of two types, corresponding to the low altitude of the plain and the high altitude of the hill country. The low-country, or plains forests are hot and wet. The trees grow very tall, and their foliage is broad. Dense undergrowth consisting of vines and creepers makes it difficult to work in these forests. Trees of the hill country resemble those of temperate zone countries, and some European species imported to Nuwara Eliya flourish. Rhododendron, for instance, grows all over the hill country.

Early settlers of the dry zone found clearing of the land relatively easy. In the dry season they simply set fire to the underbrush, and in a short time the wind spread the flames, leaving a swath of cleared land that eventually could be planted. For this reason none of the original forest is left in the dry zone. *Chena* cultivators still practice the same method of land clearing, moving on from place to place as the soil becomes exhausted.

The drier zones of the northwest and southeast bear a stunted, thorny growth of cactus in great abundance and small shrubs and trees. There are several varieties of acacias, producing beautiful flowers, which are especially well adapted to arid conditions so that they flourish on the Jaffna Peninsula.

Forest land that has been cleared has subsequently been replanted either in more trees, such as rubber, coconut, and various types of fruit trees, or in rice, tea, *mahna* (citronella) grass, and several cereal grains. *Mahna* grass (from which the growers obtain citronella oil) is native to Ceylon, as are the coconut palm and the jackfruit tree, both of which need human cultivation to increase the quality of their fruit, but other economically valuable species have been imported (see ch. 19, Agriculture).

The occurrence of large areas of grassland on hillsides, in mountain basins, and on the plains results in scenes of great beauty on all sides. Two types of grassland are distinguishable—*patana*, with short, velvety grass and without trees, and *talawa*, with long, coarse grass and dotted with trees. Both types of land may be the result of old deforestation practices. *Patana* would be good grazing land if cattle raising were undertaken. *Talawa* grasses, among them the *mahna*, grow to three or four feet.

Colorful flowering plants and shrubs, many of which have still to be studied and classified botanically, grow in abundance in the forests, in marshes, beside pools, and along streams everywhere on the island. Many of the plants that grow in the forests are valued for their healing properties. There are many types of lily. The lotus is very widespread, its red flower rising from the large circular leaf that rides the water in almost every garden pond.

Wildlife and Wildlife Preservation

Like the vegetation the wildlife shows similarities to that of South India and also has species peculiar to Ceylon. The island is apparently on a large bird migration route, and birds seen in all parts of the world winter in Ceylon. The crow, which is found all over Asia and Africa, is more abundant than the seagull and, in Ceylon, fills the seagull's function of scavenging. The peacock and the hummingbird lend flashes of color to the greenery. One of the more unusual birds is called the Seven Sisters bird, because it seems always to flock together in groups of seven. Species of songbirds are few, but calling birds such as the cuckoo, owl, hawk, eagle, and wild duck, either migratory of indigenous types, are fairly common. A species of fowl has been half domesticated for egg-producing purposes, but the demand for eggs is small in this predominantly Buddhist country so that ventures in chicken farming appear to be confined to government dairies (see ch. 8, Living Conditions). The value of all types of birds in maintaining the ecology has for a long time been recognized by the government, and strict laws are in effect for the preservation of all types of birdlife.

The small animals include: a species of squirrel that is grey in color and has a flat, broad tail; five kinds of monkeys; several types of bat, the largest of which is called "flying fox"; porcupines; and hare. There are two or three species of small deer. The large animals include the Ceylon elephant, water buffalo, leopard, and Ceylon bear; elephants and water buffalo are vitally needed draft animals. Reptiles range in size from tiny house lizards to crocodiles. There are several kinds of snakes, among them the Russell's viper, which is poisonous. All kinds of insects thrive in the tropical climate, as they can breed and lay eggs at any time of year. Butterflies are exceptionally large and brightly colored. There are many species of insect that are valuable as scavengers but also many that spread disease, seriously affecting human and animal life. Malaria, for example, claimed thousands of lives until the anopheles mosquito was practically wiped out in the 1940s, but other insect-borne diseases still affect livestock and make livestock raising hazardous (see ch. 8, Living Conditions; ch. 19, Agriculture).

Unwise and unlimited hunting and trapping of wildlife of all kinds over the past centuries led to the extinction of many species and seriously diminished others. As early as the 1930s the government began to set aside land for the preservation of plant and animal life, and hunting is now regulated by laws. Preserves are classified as: strict natural reserves, of which there exist 234.4 square miles; national parks, 440 square miles; and sanctuaries, 668.8 square miles. The government may declare a designated area a preserve at any time. At present about one-fourth of the total land area of the country is reserved for wildlife protection.

The two national parks, Ruhuna and Wilpattu, are both famous. Ruhuna is located on the coast of Southern Province, on the southeast side of the island. Elephant, deer, and peafowl are abundant. Hunting and trapping and picking or destroying plantlife are strictly forbidden. Wilpattu, on the northwest side of the island in North Central Province, is the habitat of many kinds of water birds, such as storks, spoonbills, pelicans, ibis, and teal. In both parks the public is invited

25

to enjoy the observation and study of wildlife. In the strict natural reserves the public is prohibited, however, and only scientific research is carried on. Sanctuaries sometimes include private land, and any activity except hunting and shooting is allowed.

INTERNAL ADMINISTRATIVE DIVISIONS

The country is divided into nine provinces created by the British from three already existing units. These had been established by the Ceylonese along natural boundaries such as rivers and mountains. Each of the three units was further subdivided into *korales* (districts) and *pattus* (groups of villages). The first Legislative Council of British rule in 1833 created five provinces—Western, Southern, Eastern, Northern, and Central. Later the British subdivided Central Province to make North Western, North Central, Uva, and Sabaragamuwa. The provinces are divided into districts, of which there are twenty-two.

GEOGRAPHY AND SETTLEMENT PATTERNS

The earliest inhabitants of the island are believed to have settled in the north, where they made their living by clearing and planting large tracts of forest land. For reasons not yet clear they left or were driven out, and the area they occupied, which includes Northern and North Central provinces, is now only sparsely populated (see ch. 4, Population).

The Jaffna Peninsula is densely populated by Ceylon Tamils. Although the soil is thin and dry, they manage to grow rice, tobacco, palmyra palm, and vegetables. Many of the fields are watered by hand from wells or streams, as the limestone of the region is not suitable for building tanks. There is a complex network of roads, some of them very old, and from earliest times people have lined both sides of these roads with houses, so that a typical village may be spread out in all directions instead of centering on a square.

The up-country, or Kandyan, Sinhalese are the mountain people of Ceylon. The ruggedness of their territory has insulated them from the outside world, and they are regarded as hard working, proud, and conservative. They are rice growers and have terraced many of the mountainsides, constructing irrigation channels that guide water from one level to the next down the slopes. The Indian Tamils (see Glossary), who also occupy the hill country, live and work in the southeast portion of the hill country around Hatton Plateau. Most of them are employed on the large tea estates.

Low-Country Sinhalese are concentrated in the rich southwest and are regarded as the most cosmopolitan of all the ethnic groups. They are both a rural and an urban people. The land is excellent for growing rubber and coconut. Four important cities are located in this fertile area: Colombo, Galle, Ratnapura, and Matara.

Natural factors in the country's geography have played an important role in the kinds of settlement developing over the centuries. The earliest type is the village built around a spread of good rice-growing land (see ch. 19, Agriculture). The forests behind the village supplied timber, fuel, and ropemaking material, and garden plots supplied vegetables. Rubber and coconut plantations, modern roads and railroads, and other accouterments of progress have broken down the isolation of the typical village and changed much of its life.

The fishing villages, located along the coasts, are usually clusters of houses ringed with coconut palms. A landing for boats is made on the beach, and in some areas poles to be used as fishing perches are driven into the sandy bottom a few yards offshore. Some important market centers have developed from fishing villages located near railroads or highways.

Settlements tended to develop at river crossings, especially if there was some kind of ferry to transport people and goods back and forth. As commerce increased, the settlement grew and often expanded to a good-sized town. Matara, on the southern coast, is a good example of such a town. When the Portuguese found it and named it "Great Ford," it was a crossing place on the Nilwala Ganga. When the Dutch gained control of the maritime provinces, they built a fortress at Matara, and thus it became a good example of a fort town. Today it is an important collecting and distributing center for agricultural produce.

Trincomalee, Jaffna, Kankesanturai, Galle, and Colombo are port towns. This type of settlement is rare in Ceylon, despite its miles of regular coastline. Two factors influence the development of a port, however: it must have a good harbor and must be on or near a good trade route. Thus Trincomalee, although situated at one of the finest natural harbors in the world, is not on the main sea route and has not developed as a commercial port.

MANMADE FEATURES

Man's early attempts to change the land and make more use of natural features around him are evident in the irrigation system. Artificial dams, terraces, and retaining walls that

27

went into the building of the reservoirs and canals became integral parts of nearly every river in the dry zone, changing the character of the land, so that the dry zone is sometimes called the lake country of Ceylon. Men built houses and temples with the native rock and carved stone images representing their gods. Many of the ancient stone structures are overgrown and lost in the jungles, but many others have been restored. By the nineteenth century paved roads and a railroad augmented the paths and trails connecting the villages and towns, and the once impenetrable forests were crisscrossed by miles of scenic drives.

Mining and quarrying operations have produced large holes and scars in the earth and complexes of buildings and machinery on it. Gem mining, because it has not been mechanized, has brought the least conspicuous changes. Refineries for processing raw materials and factories of all types change the products of the land into consumer goods. Modern dams divert the course of rivers. In 1970, for example, Parliament approved a large project on the Mahaweli Ganga that provides for a dam to divert the river's water to supply irrigation to thousands of acres in the dry zone (see ch. 19, Agriculture). Clearing and grading land for airports and housing developments slowly push back the forests, making room for a fast-growing population.

CHAPTER 3

HISTORICAL SETTING

Ceylon was granted independence in February 1948 after over four centuries of domination by the Portuguese (1517–1638), the Dutch (1638–1796), and the British (1796–1948). The colonial experience, especially the nearly 150 years as a British crown colony, transformed the political, social, and economic fabric of the island and provided the framework for the political, governmental, economic, and educational systems operative in 1970. The island was not an effective political entity until 1815 when the British gained control and absorbed the central highland kingdom of Kandy, which had served as a haven for refugees from the European invaders and had functioned as the preserver and conservator of Sinhalese-Buddhism.

The majority of the Sinhalese-Buddhists, who constitute over two-thirds of the population, view the period of European dominance as an unfortunate interlude in the long history of Buddhism in Ceylon (see ch. 5, Ethnic Groups and Languages; ch. 11, Religion). The Sinhalese are conscious of their identity as descendants of Indo-Aryans from northern India. They attach great importance to the legend that late in the third century B.C. a Sinhalese king was converted to Buddhism by Mahinda, a son or brother of the famous Indian Buddhist ruler, Emperor Asoka.

From the viewpoint of the Sinhalese, the major themes in the island's history have been the recurring struggles to protect Buddhism from the incursions by South Indian Hinduism and from the influence of Western modernism, and the establishment of Sinhalese-Buddhist centers of political and military power and artistic and intellectual excellence (see ch. 10, Artistic and Intellectual Expression; ch. 17, Political Values and Attitudes). They are particularly aware and proud of the cultural and economic achievements associated with the Anuradhapura and Polonnaruwa kingdoms.

The Tamils, who constitute over one-fifth of the population, are descendants of invaders and settlers from South India from the earliest times onward and of estate laborers, also from South India, brought in by the British during the nineteenth and early twentieth centuries (see ch. 5, Ethnic Groups and Languages). In addition to the occasional threat posed to the Sinhalese kingdoms by the Tamil kingdoms in South India, the Ceylon Tamils established a flourishing kingdom in the northern tip of the island during the thirteenth century. Because of these historical precedents and because the Tamil Hindus to some extent continue to look to the traditions of South India for cultural inspiration, they are regarded by many Sinhalese-Buddhists as a potential threat to the society and as being outside the mainstream of Ceylonese nationalism (see ch. 12, Social Values; ch. 17, Political Values and Attitudes).

The direct influence of the Portuguese and Dutch regimes was limited to the coastal regions. They introduced Christianity and Western education in those areas, and the Dutch laid the groundwork for a plantation economy, which the British subsequently greatly expanded, and for a Western legal system based on Roman-Dutch law (see ch. 19, Agriculture; ch. 13, The Governmental System).

In 1802 Ceylon became the first British crown colony. With the establishment of British rule, the traditional linkage between Buddhism and the state was severed. The Buddhist *sanghas* (communities of monks—see Glossary), deprived of their former power and influence, provided a focus of discontent with British rule and Western customs and practices that manifested itself in various riots and rebellions, not only against the British rule but also, during the 1950s, against a Ceylonese government believed to be too Western and insufficiently Sinhalese-Buddhist in outlook.

The independence that was achieved in 1948 was the result of peaceful agitation and negotiation in both Ceylon and England by Western-educated politicians. The island also benefited from the granting of independence to the neighboring countries of Burma, India, and Pakistan. Although Ceylon was the first British colony to be granted universal adult franchise, no mass movement developed until after independence.

Political parties began to develop in the 1930s but, for the most part, they represented communal interests. Only the various Communist parties, whose strength lay in urban areas, were intercommunal. There was considerable cooperation among members of the Western-educated elite from different communal backgrounds, but communal tensions smoldered beneath the surface. The United National Party (UNP) that won the first election at independence was chiefly made up of the Western-educated Low-Country Sinhalese and at first took a moderate line on communal issues except to disenfranchise the Indian Tamil estate workers.

In many respects the UNP leaders were alienated from the culture of the majority of the Sinhalese. In reaction, Solomon West Ridgeway Dias Bandaranaike founded the Sri Lanka Freedom Party (SLFP), a political party that appealed directly to those who felt themselves at a disadvantage in a government run on Western lines. In 1956 he campaigned on a platform of Ceylon for the Sinhalese, promising to make Sinhala the language of administration and education and to restore Buddhism to its former glory. He was swept into office but was then not able to control the Sinhalese extremists who refused to accept the use of Tamil in largely Tamil-speaking areas. Riots occurred in 1958 that gravely impaired the unity of the nation, and in the following year Bandaranaike was assassinated by a Buddhist monk. The governments of the 1960s were largely concerned with finding a way to accommodate legitimate Sinhalese interests and at the same time, to protect minority rights (see ch. 14, Political Dynamics).

ORIGINS

Both legend and linguistic evidence suggest that the Sinhalese came to the island from North India about 500 B.C. According to the most popular legend, Vijaya, the grandson of a lion (Sinha) and an Indian princess, was exiled from India with 700 followers and landed in Ceylon the day the Buddha achieved *nirvana* (release from the cycle of life—see Glossary) (see ch. 11, Religion). The prince married a Veddah princess but later discarded her to marry the high-caste daughter of a South Indian king. The Veddahs are thought to be descendants of the original inhabitants of the island (see ch. 5, Ethnic Groups and Languages).

The legend illustrates two essential themes of the Sinhalese view of history—the Indo-Aryan colonization of the island and its associations with both Buddhism and South Indian culture. These themes were formalized in the *Mahavamsa*, a dynastic and religious history composed in Pali (Sanskritic and sacred language of Theravada Buddhism) in the sixth century A.D. Repeated clashes with South Indian Hindu Tamil kingdoms evoked a form of Sinhalese-Buddhist ethnocentrism that continues to be a significant factor in contemporary Sinhalese consciousness. In the second half of the third century B.C., a mission was sent to the island from the court of Emperor Asoka, who had secured dominance over most of India and who was a devout Buddhist. The mission was reputedly led by his son, or brother, Prince Mahinda. When the Sinhalese king, Devanampiya Tissa, converted to Buddhism, the close association between Buddhism and the state began that continued until the nineteenth century.

In 1970 there was no conclusive evidence concerning the date of the first settlements in Ceylon of the other large ethnic group, the Tamils. The Tamils belong to a group of peoples speaking Dravidian languages who inhabit the peninsula of India and whose origins are in dispute. Tamil and other literary sources, however, point to flourishing urban and trading centers in South India in the third century B.C. Early trade between Ceylon and the West appears to have moved through South Indian ports.

Anuradhapura Kingdom: 200 B.C. to A.D. 1000

By the first century B.C. most of the dry zone of the island was populated. Anuradhapura had become the seat of Sinhalese kings and remained the capital until the eleventh century A.D. (see fig. 6). Although King Dutugamunu is said to have unified the island under one rule in the second century B.C., the influence of Anuradhapura was little felt in the southwest, the southeast, and the central highlands.

In theory the king was an absolute ruler, but he was expected to conform to the rules of *dharma* (justice and equity) and give consideration to the counsels of the elders of the Buddhist *sangha* (see ch. 11, Religion). Maintenance of power rested with the army, which was under the king's control, and there was also an advisory council of state composed of the chief administrative officials.

From earliest times the king was entitled to land revenue equivalent to one-sixth of the produce. His subjects owed him free labor, called *rajakaria*, for a certain number of days a year for building roads, irrigation projects, and other public works. The king rewarded his senior officials by grants of land and land revenue, and in time a privileged landlord class developed. The Buddhist monasteries were also given extensive lands and eventually became the biggest landlords in the state. This pattern of landownership and royal revenue changed little until it was gradually disrupted by European rule, starting in the sixteenth century.

The Sinhalese settlers practiced rice cultivation based on simple irrigation, either by village tanks (reservoirs) or building small stone dams across streams. The first major reservoir was constructed in the first century B.C., and by the reign of King Mahasena (A.D. 276–303) the reservoirs and canals had reached extensive proportions, although they reached their greatest extent about the ninth century A.D., with the total length of canals being more than 250 miles. They are a source of great pride to the Sinhalese, as are the architectural, artistic, and literary achievements of the capital cities of

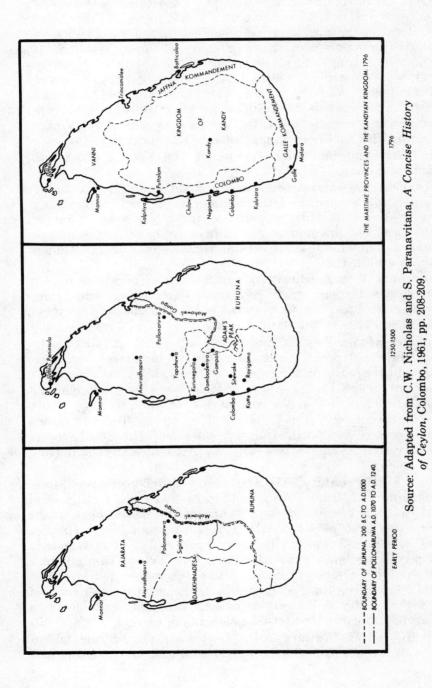

Source: Adapted from C.W. Nicholas and S. Paranavitana, *A Concise History of Ceylon*, Colombo, 1961, pp. 208-209.

Figure 6. The Early Kingdoms of Ceylon

33

Anuradhapura and, later, Polonnaruwa, which the irrigation works made possible (see ch. 10, Artistic and Intellectual Expression).

From its introduction into Ceylon in the third century B.C., Buddhism influenced and molded every aspect of Sinhalese life. Because the missionaries preached in the vernacular, the Sinhala language was enriched and developed (see ch. 10, Artistic and Intellectural Expression). The relic of Buddha's Tooth was reputedly brought to Ceylon in the fourth century A.D. Possession of the Tooth was later considered essential to legitimize the rule of a Sinhalese king. During the several centuries of dynastic wars, the Tooth was moved from place to place. The Kandyan kings became the final repositories of the Tooth and built the Temple of the Tooth, which still stands in Kandy.

Monasticism was introduced with Buddhism. The monastery was called a *vihara*, and the community of celibate monks, a *sangha*. Vows of celibacy could be taken for a short period, and it was not uncommon for princes to spend some time in a *vihara*. The monasteries became centers of learning, both in Sinhala and in Pali.

The only formal education available was provided by the monasteries through their *pirivenas*, or colleges. The *Mahavamsa* and, later, the *Culavamsa* were religious and dynastic histories written by Buddhist monks.

Images of the Buddha and places of Buddhist worship became the focal point for artistic and architectural activities. *Stupas* or *dagabas* (mounds built of earth, brick, or stone as a memorial to the Buddha) were developed with great elaboration. Although the successive styles of architecture, painting, and sculpture were often influenced by Indian models and executed by South Indian craftsmen, the results were distinctively Sinhalese (see ch. 10, Artistic and Intellectual Expression).

By the fifth century A.D. the island had become an important center of trade. Although trade between Ceylon and other trading centers does not appear to have taken place before the first century A.D. except through South Indian ports, the island was well known in the West for its pearls and precious stones. An early name for Ceylon, Tambapanni, is shared by a river in South India where pearls were also found. According to Fa Hsien, a Chinese traveler-monk of the fifth century A.D., commerce was an important factor in the establishment of the first settlements of Ceylon.

By the second century A.D. the topography of the island was well known to Western traders and sailors. At about the same time, contact was established with China, and the Sinhalese sent ambassadors to China in the fifth and eighth centuries. They also sent their own ships to Persia, India, and Ethiopia and, in the eighth century, sent an embassy to the Arab rulers of the Eastern Caliphate. In the seventh century the Sinhalese lost control of Western trade to the Arabs, who called the island Serendib, and a powerful Malayan Empire disrupted trade with China after the ninth century.

The period described as the classical age of Sinhalese culture, from 200 B.C. to A.D. 1000, coinciding with the time Anuradhapura was the capital, was marked by a succession of internal dynastic struggles, wars with South Indian kingdoms, and periods of stability under a strong Sinhalese ruler. The authors of the chief sources for this period, the *Mahavamsa* and the *Culavamsa*, emphasized the role of the Sinhalese Buddhist kings, especially in the building of the great city of Anuradhapura. Special praise was accorded to those kings who repulsed invading South Indian Tamils. King Dutugamunu, who expelled the Tamil King Elara in the second century B.C., was the first of these. Another was King Dhatusena, who drove out a Tamil king in the fifth century A.D. and who is a popular cultural hero.

Dhatusena is also renowned for some major irrigation works and some magnificent religious endowments. He met a tragic death at the hands of his son, Kassapa I, who, in fear for his own life, built a fortress on top of an impenetrable rock at Sigiriya. This walled city is a remarkable engineering and architectural achievement. The palace building contains paintings that have been described as the finest Gupta paintings outside of India (see ch. 10, Artistic and Intellectual Expression).

The proximity of South India, home of the three rival Tamil dynasties of the Pandyas, Pallavas, and the Cholas, was both a threat and a source of aid for the Sinhalese. When one of these South Indian kingdoms expanded, territorial ambition often led them to extend their sway to Ceylon, especially as there were already Tamil settlements on the island. The Sinhalese usually allied with some other South Indian dynasty to drive out the invader. When internal dynastic disputes wracked the Sinhalese kingdom, one of the claimants to the throne often called on Tamil aid. In the seventh century A.D. the Pallavas enabled a Sinhalese prince, Manavamma, to seize the throne at Anuradhapura. His dynasty continued for almost three centuries, during the early part of which the Sinhalese maintained their alliance with the Pallavas. Tamil artisans and craftsmen came to Ceylon, and their influence is especially noticeable in the architecture and sculpture of the period (see ch. 10, Artistic and Intellectual Expression).

In the middle of the ninth century the Pandyas rose to power in South India, invaded the island, and sacked the city of Anuradhapura. They withdrew on the condition that the Sinhalese pay a large indemnity. Twenty years later the Sinhalese king made an alliance with a rebel Pandyan prince, invaded the mainland, and sacked the ancient capital of Madura. In the tenth century the Sinhalese again sent an expedition to the mainland, this time to aid the Pandyan king against the Cholas. The Pandyan king was defeated and fled to Ceylon, carrying with him the royal insignia. The Cholas were determined to recapture the royal insignia, and within fifty years, they had sacked Anuradhapura and attached Rajarata to the Chola Empire. Mahinda V, who ascended the throne in A.D. 982, was the last of the Sinhalese kings to reign in Anuradhapura. The Cholas took him prisoner in 1017 A.D., and he died in South India in 1029 A.D.

Sinhalese historians note that during the earlier periods of Tamil rule in Ceylon, Tamil kings and nobles were generous toward Buddhism, although they also maintained their own Brahmin priests in court. Brahmin rituals, in fact, were incorporated into the ceremony of the Buddhist kings, and a Brahmin was often put in charge of state administration. The Brahmins never attained much influence, however, either in the Tamil or Sinhalese communities at large. The seventy-five years of Chola rule marked the only time Ceylon was ruled as a province of South India. During this period Saivite Hinduism flourished and Buddhism received a serious setback (see ch. 11, Religion). After the destruction of Anuradhapura, the Cholas made their capital at Polonnaruwa, farther to the southeast of the dry zone and near the Mahaweli River. This strategic location enabled them to control the main route to the southern Sinhalese kingdom of Ruhuna.

King Vijayabahu I, who wrested power from the Cholas in A.D. 1070, has been described as the author of Sinhalese freedom: "Had there been no Vijayabahu, there would perhaps have been no Sinhalese in Ceylon today." In order to restore Buddhist strength, Vijayabahu invited monks from Burma and rebuilt Buddhist temples and monasteries. He restored the water reservoirs and irrigation works and, himself a poet, became a patron of literature. Although Vijayabahu regained control of Anuradhapura, he made his capital at Polonnaruwa, beginning the Sinhalese retreat into the southern and central portions of the island.

Vijayabahu I and the kings Parakramabahu I and Nissankamalla are considered the three greatest patrons of Buddhism. Parakramabahu the Great (1153–86) restored Sinhalese civilization to its former glory. He reconstructed many of the *stupas* and ancient temples at Anuradhapura and undertook extensive building in his capital at Polonnaruwa. The religious orders were purged and provided with new monasteries and shrines. He was strong enough to send a punitive expedition against the Burmese for mistreatment of a Ceylonese mission in 1164 or 1165. A few years later he invaded South India to aid a Pandyan claimant to the throne, but the expedition failed after initial success.

Nissankamalla (1187–96), who also was a patron of the arts, reputedly regulated the caste system by the introduction of a modified Brahminical legal system. The highest caste was the *govi,* or cultivator caste, and ownership of a piece of land conferred high status. The occupational castes were hereditary; the members lived in their own section and intermarried within the extended family (see ch. 6, Social Structure). The *chandalas* corresponded roughly to the Indian untouchables. Slavery also continued to flourish, and the social structure corresponded closely to that described by the first European observers. During the Polonnaruwa period it became mandatory for the Sinhalese king to be a Buddhist.

The period 1184–1235 is referred to as that of the Kalinga kings. The Sinhalese had intermarried with the Kalinga dynasty, whose origin is traditionally considered to be Indian. After the death of Nissankamalla, dynastic disputes contributed to the breakup of the Polonnaruwa kingdom and the establishment of a separate Tamil realm in the north of the island. During this troubled period, for which sources are both contradictory and fragmentary, Sinhalese claimants to the throne invited South Indian and other outside aid. The incessant wars virtually destroyed the irrigation system upon which civilization in the dry zone depended, and malaria is believed to have made its appearance at this time. The Sinhalese migrated to the malaria-free wet zones in the central highlands and the southwest and southeast coasts. Those who remained reverted to a slash-and-burn agriculture.

The destruction of the Sinhalese civilization in the dry zone has been popularly ascribed to the incursions of South Indian Tamils. This view provides the modern Sinhalese with a historic rationale for their hostility to South Indian and Ceylon Tamils. Impartial observers have pointed out, however, that disorder within the Sinhalese kingdoms themselves, as well as the depredations of malaria, which is believed to have ravaged the population at this time, were also responsible for their decline.

Decline of the Sinhalese Kings: 1250-1500

After the rule of the Kalinga king Magha at Polonnaruwa in the thirteenth century, a rule that has been described by historians as disastrous, the next three kings ruled from Dambadeniya, and one made his royal residence at Yapahuwa (see fig. 6). The last king to reign in Polonnaruwa was Parakramabahu III (1287-93). Subsequent kings moved to Kurunegala and later to Gampola and Kotte.

Taking advantage of Sinhalese weakness, the Tamils secured control of the valuable pearl fishery and achieved considerable power under a ruler called Aryachakravarti during the fourteenth century. For the first time the Tamils became almost completely separated from the Sinhalese by vast stretches of jungle. The Tamil kingdom was strengthened by refugees, particularly of the powerful Vellala caste from the Muslim sultanate at Madura in South India. The Vellalas eventually became the dominant caste in the Jaffna area, maintaining their position even above the Brahmins. In the fifteenth century the last great Sinhalese king, Parakramabahu VI, captured and held Jaffna for seventeen years, after which it reverted to the Tamil kings of Jaffna.

The separation of the Tamil kingdom from the Sinhalese had important psychological and cultural implications. The Tamils in the north developed a more distinct and confident Hindu culture that looked toward the rich cultural traditions of South India for its inspiration (see ch. 10, Artistic and Intellectual Expression). The Sinhalese, on the other hand, restricted by circumstance to the southern and central portions of the island, developed a minority complex toward the far more numerous Tamils on the Indian mainland. Some Sinhalese historians consider that the arrival of the Portuguese in the sixteenth century prevented the island from being completely overrun by South Indians.

Rule over the rest of Ceylon was divided between Vikramabahu at Gampola in the central highlands and Alakesvara at Rayigama near the west coast. Parakramabahu VI, who earned the epithet Bodhisatvavatara for his patronage of Buddhism, ruled from Kotte, a fort he established near Colombo. He had obtained the throne in 1415 with the help of the Chinese. It was at this time that the coastal areas were cultivated and cinnamon became a major export. The island also became an importer of rice, because the rich ricelands of the irrigated dry zone had been lost.

During the expansion of the Tamil kingdom, the Sinhalese kings sought the aid of Arab trader-settlers. From the ninth century onward, the Arabs had developed extensive commerce and shipping on the East-West trade route. The first trader-settlers from the Arabian peninsula arrived in the seventh century. In the tenth century Indo-Arab colonists from South India took an active role in the island's trade, and Adam's Peak, in the heart of the gem country, became a place of Muslim pilgrimage. After the Jaffna kingdom's naval power declined in the fifteenth century, the Muslims secured a virtual monopoly of trade and established communities in all the major coastal towns.

PORTUGUESE RULE

The first Portuguese contact with Ceylon was accidental. In 1505 Lorenzo de Almeyda, son of the Portuguese viceroy of India, was blown off course into Galle while attacking Moorish ships south of the island. Not until twelve years later did the Portuguese establish a fortified trading settlement.

Portuguese naval power, combined with the continuing dynastic disputes within the kingdom of Kotte, enabled the Portuguese to establish their rule in the coastal areas. The Portuguese at first secured certain trading rights and permission to start a trading settlement. The building of the first fort near Colombo aroused popular hostility and had to be given up in 1518. In 1521, however, the ruler of Kotte requested Portuguese aid against his brother, who had made himself king of Sitawake, part of the Kotte kingdom. From then on the king of Kotte relied on Portuguese aid and, before his death in 1551, obtained Portuguese recognition of his grandson, Dharmapala, as his successor. When Dharmapala converted to Christianity in 1557, his rejection of Buddhism disqualified him from the throne in the eyes of his people. The king of Sitawake mounted an attack but was defeated. In 1580 Dharmapala was induced to declare the king of Portugal heir to the kingdom of Kotte with nominal overlordship over the other kingdoms.

In the north Portuguese missionaries crossed over from South India and, by 1544, had made numerous conversions among the fisherfolk of Mannar and Jaffna. The king of Jaffna reacted by attacking Mannar and killing several hundred of the Christian converts. In 1560 the Portuguese sent an expedition of revenge that was at first successful. The following year, however, they were forced to retreat to Mannar, and not until 1591 did the Portuguese launch another attack. The king of Jaffna was killed, and a Portuguese protegé put on the throne. In 1619 the Portuguese annexed Jaffna.

The Portuguese gradually took control of the major ports on the east coast, including Trincomalee and Batticaloa, and they dominated the island's trade. They failed, however, to take Kandy, the seat of the Sinhalese kings in the central highlands. An expedition through the disease-infested jungle in 1630 ended in disaster.

The Muslim traders were a prime target of Portuguese hostility. In the 1520s the Portuguese ordered the expulsion of Muslim traders from the kingdom of Kotte. Because the Muslims were useful, both as traders and as sailors, the order was never fully implemented, and long-established Muslims were allowed to stay, but eventually several thousand fled to Kandy.

The Portuguese also discriminated against other religions. They destroyed Buddhist and Hindu temples and gave the temple lands to Catholic orders. Buddhist *bhikkus* (monks—see Glossary) fled to Kandy, which became a refuge for those disaffected with colonial rule.

The chief legacies of the Portuguese in Ceylon were the introduction of the Roman Catholic religion, the establishment of a small Eurasian community, and the beginnings of a Western educational system. The Portuguese interfered little with local administration. A Portuguese *dissawa* (governor) was put in charge of each province; otherwise, the customary hierarchy was maintained. In the traditional Sinhalese manner, land grants, called *accommodessan*, were made to Europeans and Sinhalese in place of salaries. The traditional service obligation of *rajakaria* was made use of for military purposes, and some land rents were paid in cash crops, such as pepper and areca nut. The Portuguese prepared a land register, but the chief innovation was in religion and education. In order to convert the masses, a number of mission schools were opened, teaching both Portuguese and Sinhalese or Tamil. Sinhalese converts often took Portuguese names, and the rise to prominence of many families still dominant in 1970 dates from this period (see ch. 5, Ethnic Groups and Languages).

DUTCH RULE

The initial Dutch interest in Ceylon centered mainly on the cinnamon trade. In 1638, taking advantage of Kandyan-Portuguese hostilities, the Dutch agreed to aid King Rajasinha II, in exchange for control of trade and reimbursement of war expenses. The following year Trincomalee and Batticaloa were captured by the Dutch and given back to the Kandyans. In 1640, however, the port cities of Galle and Negombo were not restored to Kandy after capture; instead, because of alleged nonpayment of war expenses by the Sinhalese king, the Dutch kept the cities and began to collect revenue. The Portuguese continued to resist, but Colombo fell in 1656 and Jaffna two years later.

The Dutch attempted, as had the Portuguese, to subdue the king of Kandy, especially after a lowland rebellion in the 1760s that was allegedly incited by the Kandyans. A major Dutch expedition into the highlands failed, but in 1766 a Dutch-Kandyan agreement gave the Dutch control of all of the coastal area (see fig. 6).

Dutch concerns were mainly commercial, and they, therefore, followed the Portuguese pattern of minimum interference with local administration. The governor of each of the three provinces was a Netherlander, under whom were various local officials, the chief of which was the *mudaliyar*. Dutch attempts to alter the land grant and tenure system of *accommodessan* failed, but its abuses among Europeans were eliminated. Dutch settlement was encouraged by land grants, but the Burghers (see Glossary) preferred urban life and became absentee landlords. They did not succeed, however, in replacing the Muslims as the chief trading community.

Because they were unable to capture Kandy, where much of the cinnamon lands were situated, the Dutch began cultivating cinnamon on a plantation basis in the lowlands. They also introduced other cash crops, such as coffee, sugar, coconuts, cotton, and tobacco (see ch. 19, Agriculture). To save on the import of rice, they promoted paddy cultivation. A stipulation that the peasant sell his produce at a fixed price to the state further commercialized agriculture.

Besides the plantation system, the greatest Dutch contribution to modern Ceylon was the judicial system. Wherever possible, customary law was applied; for example, the laws and customs of Jaffna were codified for the first time in the Thesavalamai, and the Muslims were tried under Islamic law. Otherwise, Roman-Dutch law was used and, eventually, a major court was established in each of the three provinces.

The Dutch set up two seminaries for higher education and, in general, continued the Portuguese school system, but they made little effort to convert the people to Protestantism. Nevertheless, their administration further separated the Kandyans from both the Tamils and the Low-Country Sinhalese, who took advantage of Western education. In the last years of Dutch rule the highest local offices were reserved for Christians, thus disqualifying the conservative Sinhalese-Buddhists.

THE BRITISH PERIOD

The Formative Years: 1796-1833

When in 1758 the French nearly succeeded in capturing the South Indian port of Madras during a temporary absence of the British fleet from the Bay of Bengal in the monsoon season, the British became aware of the necessity of an all-weather port to protect their possessions on the eastern shores of the Indian peninsula. In 1762 the British East India Company sent a mission to Kandy in search of trading rights and access to Ceylonese ports, but the mission failed because the British refused to aid the king against the Dutch.

The Dutch, however, permitted British ships to use Trincomalee until the Dutch joined the French in the American War of Independence. The British occupied Trincomalee in 1782 as a defensive measure but were ousted later the same year by the French, who returned the port to the Dutch in 1783. In 1794 the Stadtholder of Holland fled to England to escape the new Dutch republican government, and the British persuaded him to grant permission for British troops to occupy Ceylonese ports as a defensive measure. In spite of resistance by the Dutch governor, the British captured Trincomalee and, in 1796, expelled the Dutch from the island.

In 1795 the British and the Kandyans negotiated a treaty that provided that the British would have control of the seacoast and the cinnamon monopoly in exchange for aid against the Dutch. The Kandyan king refused to ratify the treaty, however, as he was convinced that the British would not in fact aid him against the Dutch.

During the European peace negotiations of 1796 and 1797, the British expected Ceylon to be restored to the Dutch. When the peace negotiations failed, Ceylon was made a dependency of the Madras Presidency in India. The East India Company brought in South Indian revenue officials, replaced the *mudaliyars*, abolished the land grant system, imposed new taxes on coconut trees, and refused to accept payment in kind. Sinhalese riots against the new system were put down by the military. The civilian government in Madras and the secretary of war in Great Britain were alarmed by the riots, however, and a civilian governor was appointed in 1798. The coconut tax was rescinded, and the rights of the local officials were restored. The East India Company continued to be in charge of the collection of revenue, but the civilian governor handled the administration.

The dual system of administration, whereby the governor was responsible to the secretary of state for colonies in England for law and order but subject to the director of the East India Company for financial and commercial matters, proved unsatisfactory. When the Peace of Amiens treaty in 1802 ceded Ceylon to the British, they united the maritime provinces into the first British crown colony. The governing of Ceylon was divorced from that of India, and Ceylon became the prototype for most of the numerous crown colonies that were created within the British Empire. In terms of constitutional development, Ceylon initially derived an advantage from being the first colony, but in the twentieth century, when the colonial office in Great Britain developed a centralized administrative system for all the colonies, Ceylonese development was retarded by the backwardness of some of the other colonies.

In the early years of British rule, the governor exercised extensive and autocratic authority because of the time it took for instructions to be sent from Great Britain. An advisory council was set up consisting of the military commander, the chief justice, the principal secretary to the governor, and two members nominated by the governor. The governor had power to dismiss members at will, however, and he was not bound to take the council's advice, either in legislative or executive matters. A Ceylon Civil Service (CCS) was created that was under the complete control of the governor. The judges, however, were appointed by the British government in London, and the governor was subject both to local and to English courts for infringements of the law. In 1806 an exceptionally farsighted chief justice called for an elected assembly and recruitment of Ceylonese into the civil service but succeeded only in gaining trial by jury. A few years later Roman-Dutch law, which has been introduced by the Dutch, began to supplant Sinhalese law.

By the close of the eighteenth century the cinnamon and spice trade had ceased to be of paramount importance. By 1739 maintainance of Ceylon had already become more expensive for the Dutch than the revenue it produced. The British were committed to the cost of defending Ceylon, but successive governors were urged to develop the island's resources in order to reduce the cost as much as possible. In 1800 Governor Frederick North announced that a cash payment could be substituted for service tenures, but the measure was withdrawn in 1802 because few Sinhalese had availed themselves of it. There was at first a ban on Europeans buying land, but during the governorship of Sir Thomas Maitland (1805–12) the ban was lifted. This was to have far-reaching consequences for the development of the plantation economy when the highlands of Kandy finally came under British control in 1815.

Dissension within the hitherto inaccessible kingdom of Kandy gave the British the opportunity to take possession of it, although the collapse of the Kandyan kingdom, surrounded on all sides by a superior maritime power, was probably only a matter of time. The first Kandyan war in 1803 was precipitated by the intrigue of the king's ambitious chief minister. The British force that marched on Kandy was at first successful, but on the return march it was struck with disease, and the garrison remaining behind was cut to pieces. For the next ten years no further attempts were made against Kandy.

The king consolidated his power but at the expense of the Sinhalese nobles, who were unhappy with a ruler of Tamil descent. The king further alienated the Sinhalese by actions against Buddhist *bhikkus* and temple property, and in 1815 the Kandyan rebels invited the British to intervene. The governor dispatched a well-prepared force to Kandy; the king fled, and hardly a shot was fired. On capture he was sent with all his family to South India. The fact that the Kandyans remained independent for 200 years after the maritime provinces were occupied has meant not only that they were less exposed to Western influences but also the reinforcement of their self-consciousness as the true heirs to the Sinhalese-Buddhist tradition.

The agreement that was signed on March 2, 1815, between the British government and the Sinhalese nobles vested sovereignty in the British crown, guaranteed the rights and privileges of the chiefs, declared Buddhism inviolable, and placed the responsibility for its protection on the British governor. The collection of revenues was to be carried on under the supervision of British agents. Dissatisfaction with the results of the agreement, known as the Convention of 1815, soon appeared among the nobles, however, whose power was in fact curtailed, and among the Buddhist *bhikkus*, who resented rule by a Christian power. An ill-organized rebellion flared up in 1818, which the British put down with some difficulty, but was the last serious threat to British power in Kandy.

The British governor announced that the rebellion had absolved his government from adherence to all the articles of the Convention of 1815 and amended it by the Proclamation of 1818. Its measures were designed to reduce the powers of the nobles and to modify the government's relations with Buddhism. Only those chiefs recognized by the government were acknowledged as having legal power. Their judicial powers were curtailed, and the dues payable to the chiefs were abolished. A paddy tax payable to the state was substituted, and the remuneration of the chiefs was fixed.

The official connection of the government with a "pagan" religion was sharply opposed both by Christian missionaries, who had been arriving in increasing numbers at this time, and by public opinion in England. As a result, the governor modified the special position of Buddhism. To avoid direct official appointment of Buddhist monks in the Buddhist hierarchy, the government certified their election by the Buddhist *sangha*. This separation of Buddhsim from the state was never fully accepted by the *sangha*, and in 1970 certain Buddhist groups continued to agitate for restoration of this connection.

The treatment of Kandy as a separate administrative unit ended in 1833 when Kandy was dismembered and apportioned to the surrounding provinces. The administrative unification of the island was one of the recommendations of the Colebrooke-Cameron Commission, which was sent out in 1831 and 1832 primarily to effect economic reforms. The basic purpose of Colebrooke and Cameron has been described as the imposition on Ceylon of "the super-structure of the laissez-faire state." To encourage free trade, the government monopolies over cinnamon cultivation and trade were abolished; land tenure by *accommodessan* was abolished, as was *rajakaria*, the latter being replaced by an increase in the land tax. To encourage development, sale of crown lands (see Glossary), which the government had inherited from the king, was recommended.

As a form of economy, the CCS was opened to Ceylonese; at the same time salaries were reduced and pensions abolished. A policy that provided for primarily English education was recommended. On the legislative side, a legislative council was established consisting of nine official and six unofficial members. The governor appointed the unofficial members from among Ceylonese and European residents. The official majority and the governor's veto power secured official control. The advisory council became the executive council, which the governor was obliged to consult on all major matters. He could override its decisions only with approval of the Colonial Office.

The Colebrooke-Cameron Report also recommended important changes in the judiciary in an attempt to resolve the considerable confusion in the system that had existed from the time of the first British administration in 1796. Basically, the system had two parts. Criminal jurisdiction was exercised by courts under the jurisdiction of the Supreme Court. Civil jurisdiction over Ceylon was exercised by a system of provincial courts controlled by the governor, but European civil cases were tried by the Supreme Court. A great deal of friction thus ensued between the chief justice and the governor.

Although not all of the report's recommendations were implemented, all courts were placed under the control of the Supreme Court. A permanent court was established in the District of Colombo, and three circuit courts were set up in the Northern, Southern, and Eastern sections. District courts in each circuit were presided over by a district judge and three assessors or advisers on customary law. They tried all civil and minor criminal cases. The Supreme Court handled all major criminal cases with trial by jury and had appellate jurisdiction in civil cases. There was also final appeal to the Privy Council. Cases were tried according to the legal code of the defendant, although the Roman-Dutch and customary law procedures had been modified by English court procedures relating to rules of evidence and trial by jury.

The Colebrooke-Cameron reforms established the pattern of administrative, economic, judicial, and educational development that was followed during the next century. The road-building program that was undertaken in the 1820s, originally for administrative and security purposes, opened up the high land area for development. Poor salaries motivated the civil servants to attempt plantation agriculture, especially after they were forbidden to engage in trade in 1836. The sale of crown lands provided further incentive. In 1825 a regulation had been passed that no tax was to be made on coffee plantations, and in 1829 those working on the plantations were exempted from *rajakaria*.

The opening up of the CCS to Ceylonese and the emphasis on English education fostered the creation of a Western-educated elite, who spearheaded the drive for independence in the twentieth century but who at the same time were alienated from the culture of the average Ceylonese. Agitation for constitutional reform took the path of demands for an official majority on the Legislative Council and control of the choice of unofficial members. The original choice of one representative each from the Sinhalese, Tamil, and Burgher communities signified the jockeying of each of the major ethnic groups for a place in the modern state.

Economic Development: 1833-1900

The foundation of the economic structure that still largely prevailed in 1970 was laid between 1833 and 1900. The imbalance that developed between the plantation economy and the rural Sinhalese was a major cause of political, social, and economic tension in the twentieth century.

The first regular coffee plantation was opened in the Kandyan hill region in 1827, but it was not until the 1830s that a number of favorable factors combined to accelerate the growth of coffee cultivation. Governor Edward Barnes, who foresaw the possibilities of coffee cultivation, deliberately applied various incentives, particularly the abolition of export duties and exemption from the land produce tax. Production of West Indian coffee fell because of the abolition of slavery, and the preferential duties that had benefited West Indian coffee were extended to Ceylon. The problem of land for the estates was solved by the sale of crown lands that the British government had inherited from the Kandyan kings. The land was sold for a nominal sum, and the government even undertook the cost of surveying.

The plantations were confronted, however, with a labor shortage. Because a peasant cultivator of paddy land enjoyed a much higher status than a landless laborer and because of the insufficient wages offered, the Kandyan peasant was not attracted to the estates (see ch. 6, Social Structure). The peak season for harvesting coffee coincided with the peasant's own harvest, and population pressure and underemployment did not become acute until the twentieth century. There was, however, an inexpensive supply of labor among the Tamils in South India. They were recruited for the coffee-harvesting season and migrated to and from Ceylon, often amid great hardships. The immigration of these Indian Tamils began in the 1830s and became a regular stream a decade later, when restrictions on the emigration of labor to Ceylon were removed by the Indian government.

Capital was at first provided by resident British civilian and military officials, and in the 1840s the civil servants in Kandy were described as behaving more like coffee planters than government agents. This led to serious abuses. In 1840 the colonial secretary, Philip Anstruther, who was also a coffee planter, drafted an ordinance that made it almost impossible for a Kandyan peasant to prove that land he considered his own was not in fact crown land and therefore subject to alienation and sale (see ch. 19, Agriculture). In the first three years of the 1840s, over 200,000 acres of crown land were sold.

In 1845 civil servants were forbidden to take part in commercial or agricultural pursuits. By that time the quick profits to be had from coffee had spurred the arrival of capital and entrepreneurs from England. By 1847 nearly 20 million pounds of Ceylon coffee were sold on the English market, exceeding the West Indian supply. The Ceylon Bank was opened in 1841, British firms were established to finance the expansion of the coffee plantations, and financial and commercial power thus became concentrated in British hands.

This rapid development was checked by a world depression in 1846, which caused a steep fall in the price of coffee. The resulting financial disruption in Ceylon highlighted the tensions that were developing between a traditional feudal economy and a modernized commercial agriculture. In order to make up for lost revenue, the government imposed a series of new taxes on firearms, dogs, shops, boats, carriages, and bullock carts, which primarily affected the Sinhalese farmer, who had held his lands tax free. A tax on land was proposed instead of the traditional paddy tax, and a road ordinance in 1848 reintroduced a form of *rajakaria* by stipulating six days' free labor on roads or the payment of a cash equivalent.

Other new procedures were deeply resented by the Buddhist *sanghas*. The colonial secretary in the 1840s had recommended the alienation of some temple lands for coffee plantations, and the governor had received instructions from England to sever all connection with Buddhism. Thereupon, some tenants refused to pay rent on monastery lands because the monks had not been confirmed by the governor.

Riots broke out in 1848 that were severely repressed. After an investigation by a committee of the House of Commons, the governor and his chief secretary were dismissed. All the new taxes except the Road Ordinance were scrapped, and the government adopted a less rigid policy toward Buddhism.

The plantation system dominated the economy to such an extent, however, that one author described the government as an "appendage of the estates." The road and rail system was developed primarily for the benefit of the plantations. The completion in 1867 of the railroad between Colombo and Kandy meant a two-thirds reduction in transport costs. For practical purposes, the traditional peasant economy was left untouched, especially as there was little attempt to increase the indigenous production of rice. Rice for the estate laborers, almost all of whom were Indian Tamils, was imported from Bengal, and capital equipment from England. The growing body of agricultural research was devoted to improving methods of coffee growing or, later, to developing other cash crops, such as tea and rubber.

In 1869 disaster struck the coffee plantations in the form of a leaf disease. By the end of the 1870s, in spite of everything that could be done, coffee had ceased to be anything more than a token export. In search of a substitute, the planters tried other crops, one of which was *chinchona* (quinine). After an initial appearance of success, the market proved unable to support production on a plantation basis; prices fell, and it ceased to be a major crop. Cinnamon, which had suffered an eclipse in the early part of the century, revived at this time to become an important minor crop, and in 1970 Ceylon was still the major world producer of cinnamon.

The first sugar plantation was established in 1837, but sugar cultivation did not become popular. Cocoa was tried for a time and has continued as one of the lesser exports. Tea eventually took the place of coffee, and by 1929 nearly 500,000 acres were under tea cultivation, the bulk of the area being plantations that were British owned and managed (see ch. 19, Agriculture).

Rubber, which had been introduced in 1876, came into its own as a major export during a slump in tea prices in the 1900s. Rubber earnings exceeded those of tea during World War I but suffered severely during the depression of the 1930s. Coconuts, which had always been cultivated in gardens for home use, also developed into a major export. Of these three cash crops, at independence coconut was mainly in the hands of Ceylonese and rubber partly so. Tea, however, continued to be mainly in British hands (see ch. 19, Agriculture; ch. 22, Trade).

Beginnings of Constitutional Reform

Constitutional reform grew mainly out of European planters' desire to have a greater control over the use of the surplus revenues their estates were producing. In 1842 the Ceylon Agricultural Society was formed by a group of planters to agitate for the expenditure of more money for roads and less for defense, on the grounds that defense expenditures were for imperial, not Ceylonese, purposes. In 1848 the secretary of state for colonies responded by promising that public funds would be spent only with the sanction of the Legislative Council. A decade later the unofficial members secured the right to propose bills in the Legislative Council, provided they were not financial, a right formerly reserved to the governor. The principle of election was introduced for the first time in 1853, by which the Chamber of Commerce in Colombo and the Planters' Association elected three unofficial members, although the Colonial Office retained the right of final approval. The governor still nominated the three unofficial Ceylonese members.

In 1861 a bill was passed in the British Parliament providing that the colonies were to underwrite the cost of military garrisons unless the garrisons were specifically for imperial defense

49

needs. An implementing ordinance, whereby Ceylon would pay the whole cost of British garrisons stationed in Ceylon, was passed in the Ceylon Legislative Council in 1864 over the unanimous opposition of the unofficial members. The unofficial members resigned, and a year later the Ceylon League was formed to work for an unofficial majority in the council. Although the league did not obtain an unofficial majority at this stage, a commission of inquiry was appointed to look into military expenditures. The Legislative Council eventually voted a standing order for military expenditures. Satisfied with this, the Colonial Office gave up control of the budget. The agitation for constitutional reform declined, and the last major reform before the twentieth century was the addition of a Kandyan Sinhalese and a Muslim to the council as unofficial members.

Advances were made on the local level, however, that laid the groundwork for self-government. Colombo, Galle, and Kandy were provided with municipal councils in 1865. Although a civil servant headed the councils, the unofficial members were elected by an adult male franchise based on property qualifications.

In the rural areas a government agent was the chief administrator, although the powers of the local village councils, the *gansabhas,* which had been allowed to lapse, were restored bit by bit. In 1871 they were permitted to hear the numerous petty lawsuits that plagued the district courts. The *gansabhas* had also been in charge of maintaining irrigation works, which had fallen into disrepair with the suppression of *rajakaria.* An ordinance in 1856 restored this responsibility and allowed recruitment of unpaid labor.

A widening of the base of government by franchise created a need for more education, and the Department of Public Instruction was set up in 1869. After 1885 more attention was given to vernacular education, and by the early twentieth century it was available to large numbers of the general population. With the introduction of competitive civil service examinations in 1856, the demand for English education grew. Apart from a few seminaries established by missionary societies, the Colombo Academy (Royal College) established in 1836, and the Ceylon Medical School in 1870, higher education was not available in Ceylon in the nineteenth century (see ch. 9, Education).

Buddhist Revivalism and Agitation for Self-Rule: 1900-31

In the first decade of the twentieth century, some associations composed of professional and upper middle class Ceylonese

50

began a modest campaign for constitutional reform. Among these were the Low-Country Products Association, the Jaffna Association, the Chilaw Association, and the Ceylon National Association. At the same time, a Buddhist temperance and social reform movement developed under the leadership of prominent Sinhalese-Buddhists, who appealed to the masses in the coastal areas around Colombo.

Since the 1880s there had also been a Buddhist religious revival, led by Anagarika Dharmapala and Bhikku Gunananda and deriving inspiration from the Theosophist movement. Its first object of attack was the Christian bias of missionary education. Although their ultimate goals were in conflict, both of these groups—the educated elite and the Buddhist revivalists—held the seeds of an independence movement. The Western-educated group wished to succeed to British power, whereas the Sinhalese-Buddhist religious element wanted to do away with Western influence altogether.

The demand for constitutional reform was led by the Western-educated Ceylonese. Governor Henry McCallum (1907–13) opposed the demands of the Westernized elite for election of the unofficial Ceylonese members of the Legislative Council because he believed that, as a result of their Western education, they did not represent the interests of the mass of the people. He considered that the government agents who were in close touch with the villagers were in a better position to represent the Sinhalese villager. In 1910, however, the secretary of state for colonies authorized the election of an educated Ceylonese member on a restricted franchise. The official majority on the Legislative Council was reduced to one, and an undertaking was given by the governor not to execute a program that was unanimously rejected by the unofficial members of the Legislative Council. The first Ceylonese member elected under this proviso was a Tamil, Sir Ponnambalam Ramanathan.

These constitutional changes did not satisfy the Ceylonese leaders, and there was some agitation in the years immediately preceding World War I. A differential increase in the salaries of British officials in the CCS further disgruntled the Ceylonese professionals. The agitation for freedom in India by the Indian National Congress aroused national sentiments among the educated youths, and a militant group called the Young Lanka League went so far as to demand complete and immediate self-government. Leaders in the Buddhist Temperance Movement organized the railway workers into a union, and a direct result was the first major rail strike in 1912 (see ch. 21, Labor). Playwrights and poets began celebrating national Sinhalese heroes, such as Dutugamunu, and in 1915 an issue of a Sinhalese magazine was devoted to the fall of the Kandyan kingdom in 1815.

None of this quasi-political agitation, however, affected the Sinhalese villager. The serious riots in the Kandyan highlands in 1915, for example, were provoked mainly for religious and economic reasons. Of the less than 300,000 Muslims in Ceylon in 1911, about 30,000 who were recent immigrants from South India and were called Coast Moors, had managed to capture much of the petty retail trade in the Kandyan country. They operated the village shops and were the local moneylenders. With their growing wealth they had constructed a mosque in Gampola on the sacred route of the Buddhist procession of Esala Perahera (see ch. 11, Religion). On the annual festival the Muslims complained to authorities that the music and dancing of the Buddhist procession violated their mosque. The British officials vacillated, backing first the Muslims, then the Buddhists. Finally, in the procession on May 28, a riot started between Sinhalese-Buddhists and Coast Moors, which spread to all provinces except the Northern and Eastern.

The fact that a minor religious disturbance could lead to widespread riots suggested a general state of unrest. Recent observers have pointed to the economic causes of discontent. Food shortages resulting from the outbreak of war in Europe led to a rise in prices, which was exploited by the Coast Moors. Both the Sinhalese villager and the urban poor who patronized the Moors' teashops expressed their resentment by damaging the property of the Moors, although for the most part they refrained from personal violence. In Colombo and Kandyan provinces there was resentment of the economic control enjoyed by the Moors; in 1909 the Buddhist journalist Piyadasa Sirisena had urged a boycott of the goods of the Coast Moors, and the Buddhist revivalist leader, Anagarika Dharmapala, had spoken out against the South Indian merchants. Also symptomatic was the fact that the rail workers in 1910 protested the employment of South Indian Tamils to the disadvantage of local laborers.

British reaction at the time was divided between those persons, such as the governor and the government agents, who regarded the outbreaks as a spontaneous expression of resentment against the Coast Moors and others, led by the colonial secretary and the more conservative groups, such as the planters, who feared a general conspiracy against British rule.

The governor failed to act during the first few days of the disorders. He then declared martial law and handed authority over to the military, whose subsequent repressive measures had far-reaching consequences in galvanizing an independence movement. Special courts were set up that were presided over by civil servants, and the more serious cases were tried by courts-martial. In spite of the fact that many Sinhalese leaders in Colombo personally called for law and order, a large number of them were arrested. Among the Sinhalese leaders imprisoned were D. S. Senanayake, F. R. Senanayake, and D. B. Jayatilaka. Local reserve units, such as the Ceylon Planter's Rifle Corps, were called into action, and orders were given to shoot to kill. Of the 140 killed, an estimated two-thirds lost their lives as the result of arbitrary government actions.

Martial law was lifted at the end of August, but agitation for the release of prisoners and for a commission of inquiry into the government's actions was carried on for the next five years. In June 1915 the official majority in the Legislative Council passed a Riots Damage Ordinance, which made all the inhabitants of a Sinhalese village liable for damages to Muslim property. The Sinhalese were confined to their villages, and their firearms had to be given up to government agents. The ordinance was particularly resented because members of other ethnic communities were exempted. District officers regarded the mass of the people as loyal to the British and noted that the few anti-British pamphlets that were circulated came from Sinhala-educated intellectuals, such as schoolmasters and *bhikkus*.

A mass meeting was held in Colombo in September 1915 in which it was decided that two Sinhalese representatives should go to England and present the Sinhalese case to the Colonial Office and to lobby for redress. Although the envoys did not succeed in obtaining a commission of inquiry, they were influential in securing the release of prisoners and in building up a favorable press in England, which served as a check on the actions of the governor in Ceylon. The constitutional reform that followed in the 1920s has been directly attributed to their agitation.

The Ceylon Reform League was established in 1917 and, two years later, combined with the Ceylon National Association to form the Ceylon National Congress. The main platform of the Congress was a demand for self-government, but it was not a mass movement and, in the long run, pressure applied by Ceylonese political leaders through constitutional and administrative channels was more effective in gaining independence than the occasional demonstrations for political freedom on the part of the masses.

An Order in Council in 1920 provided for an unofficial majority in the Legislative Council and introduced the principle of territorial constituencies. Six members of the enlarged council were communally elected, including two Kandyan Sinhalese, one Indian Tamil, two Europeans, and one Burgher (see ch. 5,

Ethnic Groups and Languages). The Ceylon Chamber of Commerce and the Low-Country Products Association were also entitled to elect their own member, and the governor retained the power to nominate four more unofficial members, including a Muslim, to achieve communal balance. Although the unofficial members now had control of the council, the governor could override any important decision. Three unofficial members were allowed to sit in the Executive Council.

The reforms were far short of those requested by the Ceylon National Congress, which had demanded territorial election of fifty members with an elected speaker, fiscal control, and a broader-based franchise. Sinhalese members of the Congress opposed communal representation and only with difficulty were persuaded to participate in implementing the new legislation. The Tamils were also dissatisfied because they could only return three members to the council. In 1921 they withdrew from the National Congress, which thus came to represent largely Low-Country Sinhalese.

Ceylonese dissatisfaction with the new council led to further reforms in 1924. The number of members territorially elected was raised from eleven to twenty-three, with five more elected on a communal basis. This included a Tamil from Western Province, a provision that the Sinhalese in the National Congress had strongly opposed. The franchise qualifications were liberalized but still affected only about 20 percent of the male citizens, mostly in urban areas. The governor's veto of legislation was modified to a recommendation of a veto to the secretary of state for the colonies. The governor retained the power, however, to initiate fiscal measures. Of the nine members of the Executive Council, four unofficial members were nominated, but they could not sit on both legislative and executive councils.

One of the major disadvantages of the 1924 reforms was the complete divorce of the legislative and executive responsibilities. In addition, the limited franchise did not reflect the recent educational achievements. In 1920 it was estimated that there were nearly 3,000 vernacular schools, and 300 English schools, with a combined total of nearly 400,000 students.

A problem facing the colonial administration with regard to constitutional reform was how to retain ultimate control of the island's affairs and at the same time grant enough self-government to satisfy the Ceylonese. The major obstacle, however, was the intensity of communal feeling. In 1927 a Royal Commission, led by the Earl of Donoughmore, visited the island to devise a formula to deal with these problems. The constitution that resulted and was put into effect in 1931 has been described as "an aberration in political development." A new States Council combined the legislative and executive responsibilities of the old legislative and executive councils. The States Council was divided into seven groups, each of which, under the chairmanship of a minister, managed the affairs of a government department. Under Colonial Office officials were the departments of defense, external affairs, and public services; of justice and elections; and of finance. These three officers of state and the elected chairmen of departments constituted the Board of Ministers. Extensive reserve powers continued to be vested in the governor.

The commission concluded that communal representation did not work, and recommended universal adult franchise to men over twenty-one years of age and women over thirty. When the constitution was inaugurated in 1931 the voting age of women was lowered to that of men. Indian Tamils, resident Europeans, and foreigners were included in the franchise, an inclusion that was strongly opposed by the Sinhalese. Eight seats, however, were still nominated by the governor to ensure communal representation.

The Donoughmore Constitution satisfied hardly anyone, but the Ceylonese leaders were given to understand that no further constitutional changes would be forthcoming unless an attempt was made to function under it. On December 12, 1929, the constitution was accepted by a margin of two votes. In the first elections, which were held in 1932, almost 60 percent of the electorate voted. This did not include the Tamils of Jaffna, who refused to take part, and dissatisfied Muslims, who sent representatives to England to plead their case directly to the Colonial Office.

Achievement of Independence: 1931-48

The Donoughmore Constitution provided valuable experience for the Ceylonese political leaders in running government departments. They were also able to focus on the economic problems of the island that had been neglected because of the concern with, and emphasis on, the plantation economy. As minister of agriculture, for example, D. S. (Don Stephen) Senanayake, who was to become the first prime minister, inaugurated a program for the restoration of some of the ancient irrigation works. An increasing number of Ceylonese staffed the administrative posts in the CCS. The principle of Ceylonization of the CCS had been accepted in 1928, and within a few years there were few non-Ceylonese applicants to the service; by the time of independence, British appointees were restricted mostly to the engineering and technical branches. Control of the CCS, however, remained with the government through the Public (Civil) Service Commission.

In 1936 the second State Council was elected. Although the Tamils did not boycott this election, they and the other minorities were angered when the seven elected ministers turned out to be Sinhalese. The Sinhalese argued that there was more chance of constitutional reform if the ministers presented a united front.

Agitation for reform continued, the prime targets being the officers of state responsible for defense, justice, and finance. In 1938 the governor recommended to the secretary of state that the Executive Committee system be replaced by cabinet government that would not include any officers of state, but the outbreak of war in 1939 temporarily halted consideration of these proposals.

The elections scheduled for the early 1940s for a new States Council were indefinitely postponed when the Japanese entered the war in 1941. With the loss of Singapore to the Japanese in early 1942, the harbor at Trincomalee once again became an important strategic post. A War Council was established that included all the ministers, the governor, the military commanders, and the civil defense commissioner. The importance of a loyal population was recognized, and in 1941 the island was promised self-government after the war. Two years later the government officially endorsed a policy of full internal self-government but reserved to the British unfettered control of external affairs, defense, Commonwealth trade and shipping, currency, the rights of British residents in Ceylon, and legislation concerning religious or communal affairs.

In preparation for self-government, the Ceylonese ministers requested the help of Sir Ivor Jennings, then vice chancellor of the University of Ceylon, in drawing up a constitution. In the meantime, the British decided to send a Royal Commission to Ceylon to consult as many interest groups and factions as possible with a view to framing a new constitution. The ministers decided to boycott the commission because their proposals for constitutional reform had apparently been ignored. The commission, which was headed by Lord Soulbury, arrived in December 1944 and, despite or because of the ministerial boycott, consulted the most politically vocal minority groups on the island. While the Soulbury Commission was in Ceylon, a bill was moved in the States Council by S.W.R.D. Bandaranaike to vote on the ministers' draft constitution; it was approved with more than a two-thirds majority.

In April 1945 the secretary of state invited D. S. Senanayake to London to give his views on the Soulbury Commission Report. Senanayake used the occasion to present the ministers' draft constitution, and a period of intense personal consultation between the Colonial Office and D. S. Senanayake ensued. The main features of both constitutions were similar. The Soulbury Constitution recommended the addition of a second house, the replacement of the executive committees by cabinet government, and, in order to safeguard communal interests, the drawing of election boundaries territorially as well as communally. Emergency powers were reserved to the governor, and dominion status was promised in the near future.

The ministers' draft had not reserved to the governor the special emergency powers, which included the right to legislate for Ceylon by Orders in Council, to appoint the judiciary, to control the Public Service Commission, and to reserve the Royal Assent—that is, to veto—certain types of bills.

The 1945 general election in England returned to power a Labour government whose leaders were more amenable to the demands for independence of colonial territories. In August 1945 Senanayake submitted a revised version of the ministers' draft that did away with the governor's emergency powers but provided for special arrangements with the British on external affairs and defense. In October the British government published its White Paper embodying the Soulbury Constitution with the removal of the governor's emergency powers. The governor would have access to limited emergency powers by proclamation if necessary, and the crown would retain the right to legislate by Order in Council. The British refused, however, to transfer Ceylon from the Colonial Office to the Dominion Office. On his return D. S. Senanayake reluctantly recommended acceptance of the Soulbury Constitution, and it was approved by a vote of fifty-one to three. Two of the negative votes were cast by Indian Tamil members.

In May 1946 the Privy Council in London approved the Ceylon (Constitution) Order in Council. The Constitution itself was to become effective in stages. The first stage concerned mainly electoral procedures and a number of transitional matters. Widespread strikes occurred in 1946 during the economic slump that hit the economy after the withdrawal of the Allied forces. In some cases the strikes were led by members of the Communist Party. Senanayake warned the Colonial Office that, if Ceylon were not given dominion status, the island might withdraw from the Commonwealth. In 1947 the British agreed to grant "fully responsible status within the Commonwealth." September was fixed as the date of the elections, and February 4, 1948, as the date of independence. After the election of Senanayake as prime minister, special defense agreements were signed with the British that provided for British use of ports and bases, the stationing of troops in Ceylon, and mutual military assistance. By provision of the Ceylon Independence Act of December 10, 1947, the office of the governor was replaced by a governor general who, as the representative of the British sovereign, acted on the advice of the ministers.

Sinhalese Majority Rule: 1948-58

The United National Party (UNP), which won the 1947 election under the leadership of D. S. Senanayake, was a coalition of the Ceylon National Congress, the Sinhala Maha Sabha (see Glossary), and the Muslim League. Of the ninety-five seats in the House of Representatives, it won forty-two. In addition, five members of the Tamil Congress (TC), the six members nominated by the governor general (for communal balance), and many of the twenty-one independents usually supported the UNP. The UNP itself had been formed specifically to contest the first elections under the new Constitution. Since the 1920s the leadership of the Ceylon National Congress had been almost exclusively Low-Country Sinhalese. In 1934 S.W.R.D. Bandaranaike had founded within the Congress the Sinhala Maha Sabha, which was oriented toward the Sinhala-educated voter and which had held its own annual congresses within the UNP.

The other parties contesting the election were the Lanka Sama Samaja Party (LSSP), or, roughly, the Ceylon Equality Party; the Ceylon Communist Party (CCP); the Bolshevik-Leninist Party; the Ceylon Indian Congress; and the Labour Party (see ch. 14, Political Dynamics). The oldest Marxist party is the LSSP, which was founded in 1935 and first achieved organization and publicity in the fight against malaria in the rural districts in 1936. Its greatest strength, however, was among urban workers and in the trade union movement (see ch. 21, Labor).

Leaders of the various Marxist parties, such as Philip Gunawardena, Nanyakkarapathirage Martin Perera, Colvin Reginald de Silva, and Leslie Simon Goonewardene, were all Western-educated Low-Country Sinhalese. The entry of the Soviet Union into World War II on the Allied side divided the Communists into Trotskyites and Stalinists. The CCP, which in 1943 grew out of the United Socialist Party, fully supported the Allied war effort. When it tried to join the Ceylon National Congress, however, D. S. Senanayake resigned. The LSSP, on the other hand, opposed the Allied war effort and was banned in 1942. Its leaders either escaped to India or were arrested.

The Soulbury Constitution had maintained the franchise for

the estimated 800,000 Indian Tamils, most of whom worked on the tea estates (see ch. 4, Population; ch. 5, Ethnic Groups and Languages). The resentment of the Kandyan Sinhalese against the alien plantation economy in their midst expressed itself in hostility toward the Indian Tamil plantation workers. In addition, other Sinhalese, especially those educated in the vernacular schools, regarded the Ceylon Tamils with suspicion, at least in part because their command of English had given them a large share of the posts in the civil services. When the civil services reached a saturation point in the late 1940s, competition for the limited number of openings became intense. The Sinhalese sought and achieved disenfranchisement of the Indian Tamils in order to reduce Tamil influence in politics.

The disenfranchisement was achieved by the Indian and Pakistani (Residents) (Citizenship) Act of 1949, which required all Pakistanis and Indians to register to become citizens of Ceylon. Until they were registered citizens, they were not entitled to the privileges of citizenship, such as voting rights. The decision on the right to Ceylon citizenship was vested in the commissioner for registration for Indian and Pakistani citizens. In a test case the Supreme Court upheld the discretionary powers of the commissioner in withholding citizenship.

C. Suntharalingam, a Tamil minister in the UNP government, resigned in protest. His place was taken by a leader of the TC, G. G. Ponnambalam, but the citizenship act had split the Tamils, and S. J. V. Chelvanayakam, a Tamil Christian, formed the more radical Federal Party (FP), which demanded a federal form of government.

A more serious defection from the UNP occurred in 1951 when Bandaranaike crossed the floor of the house with his followers. The move was regarded as both personal and political. The UNP had come to be called the Uncle-Nephew Party because Dudley Senanayake, the son of the prime minister, was minister of agriculture and Sir John Kotelawala, the prime minister's nephew, was leader of the House of Representatives. These two families and the Jayewardenes formed a close-knit political group that tended to keep Bandaranaike out of its consultations. The disenfranchisement of the Indian Tamils had given greater weight to the Sinhalese rural voter, and there was now a chance for Bandaranaike to offer an alternative to the powerful UNP.

D. S. Senanayake, however, was able to hold the UNP coalition together by the strength of his personality and because of his prominent role in the achievement of independence. His accidental death in March 1952 as a result of a fall from a horse further weakened the party. His son Dudley took over and immediately called a general election. The UNP was returned to power with fifty-four seats, and Dudley Senanayake was able to form a government with the support of four TC members and a number of independents.

The economic prosperity resulting from the Korean conflict had temporarily eased the economic situation, but by the end of 1952 the market for rubber fell. When Communist China in 1952 offered Ceylon a barter arrangement of rice for rubber, the prime minister concluded an agreement (see ch. 15, Foreign Relations; ch. 22, Trade). This, however, did not solve the economic problem. A report of the International Bank for Reconstruction and Development (IBRD) in 1953 strongly recommended a reduction of the rice subsidies to put the economy on a more realistic footing. The price was raised by nearly two-thirds and, because it followed an increase in the price of sugar and the abolition of free meals for some schoolchildren, there was widespread opposition. Nationwide strikes took place in August, and a state of emergency was declared. Several rioters were killed, and in October 1953 the prime minister resigned.

Sir John Kotelawala, who had resigned from the cabinet when his cousin, Dudley Senanayake, succeeded D. S. Senanayake as prime minister, assumed the office of prime minister and restored part of the rice subsidy. Although the trade pact with Communist China was continued, he took a strong anti-Communist line, especially at the Bandung Conference in 1955. His call to condemn Communist imperialism along with Western colonialism was very unpopular with some other Asian nations, especially India, with whom relations had already been strained by the problem of the Indian Tamil plantation workers (see ch. 15, Foreign Relations).

The 1956 election has been described as a turning point in the history of Ceylon in that the transfer of power from one group of the people to another amounted to a social revolution. The universal adult franchise that was granted in 1931 became fully effective for the first time, and the needs and interests of the Sinhalese rural voter became paramount.

When Bandaranaike crossed the floor of the House in 1951, he dissolved the Sinhala Maha Sabha and formed the Sri Lanka Freedom Party (SLFP). Bandaranaike came from a prominent Low-Country Sinhalese Christian family that was bound by longstanding ties to the British. His father had been a founding member of the Colombo Turf Club, and Bandaranaike himself was named after Governor Joseph West Ridgeway. On his return from Oxford in the 1930s, however, he turned his back on the West and converted to Buddhism. He adopted national dress and began to espouse the causes of the hitherto un-represented Sinhalese—the *bhikku,* the *ayurvedic* (a type of physician), and the rural schoolteacher. As a minister in the UNP cabinet, he had promoted the interests of local areas and of indigenous medicine.

The poor showing of the SLFP in the 1952 election was largely because of its lack of organization. By 1956 its political organization was vastly improved; dissatisfaction with the UNP and events of great emotional significance to Buddhists transformed it from a minor opposition party to one that swept the polls. The 2,500th anniversary of the attainment of *nirvana* by the Buddha and the legendary landfall of the first Sinhalese king in Ceylon was observed in 1956 and 1957. To prepare for this historic celebration, called the Buddha Jayanti year, the Buddhist community engaged in extensive mass organization. A committee of leading Buddhists formed the Sri Lanka Maha Sangha Sabha (literally, the Ceylon Committee of Great Buddhist Communities), and a well-known Buddhist scholar founded the All Ceylon Buddhist Congress. The congress asked the government to initiate a commission of inquiry into the state of the Buddhist religion in the country. The government was willing to provide funds for the celebration of Buddha Jayanti but not to sponsor such a commission. The All Ceylon Buddhist Congress went ahead with a two-year tour and inquiry of its own and published its report just before the elections in 1956.

Among the recommendations of this group were proposals to deny state aid to Christian schools and to create a Buddhist Sasana Council composed of laymen and *bhikkus* for the purpose of fostering Buddhism in the same way Sinhalese kings had in the past. To finance the council, the congress recommended that compensation be paid for the temple lands that had been alienated by the plantations during the nineteenth century. Bandaranaike gave a general undertaking that amounted to a commitment to carry out the recommendations if he were elected; the two Buddhist groups then combined to form the Eksath Bhikku Peramuna (United Front of Bhikkus) to help him fight the election.

The other major issue in the 1956 election was language. After independence it was assumed that English would not long remain the main language of administration and that both Sinhalese and Tamil would replace it. The Sinhala language, however, was closely bound up with the issue of Buddhist culture (see ch. 5, Ethnic Groups and Languages; ch. 10, Artistic and Intellectual Expression). In addition, the language issue intimately affected thousands of Sinhala schoolteachers whose pay was inferior to those who taught English. Sinhala Only became a popular rallying cry for all those who felt that lack of access to English education—there were more English-language-missionary schools in the Tamil north than in any other area of the island—had deprived them of their rightful share of prestige, job positions, and pay. Bandaranaike's adoption of Sinhala Only in his campaign ensured him the support of the disgruntled Sinhala schoolteachers, who had formed themselves into an association called Bhasa Peramuna (Language Front).

On the economic front, Bandaranaike adopted a socialist platform with communal overtones, such as the nationalization of plantations, banks and insurance, and certain essential industries; abrogation of the defense agreements with Great Britain; nonalignment in foreign affairs; repatriation of the Indian Tamil plantation workers; and restoration of trade and distribution into Sinhalese hands. With such a radical platform Bandaranaike was able to unite many disparate groups into the People's United Front (Mahajana Eksath Peramuna—MEP). In order to defeat the UNP, other Marxist parties agreed to a no-contest pact in several constituencies.

This combination was too much for the UNP, which had made little effort to organize a grassroots campaign, relying on the support of wealthy businessmen, many of whom controlled the votes of their employees, the Kandyan gentry, and the powerful Associated Newspapers of Ceylon (see ch. 16, Public Information). At the last minute, the UNP also adopted Sinhala Only, which lost it the support of the remaining members of the TC.

One of the first acts of the new government was to implement the Sinhala Only policy. A language act was passed in June, making Sinhala the sole official language and setting up a Department of Official Language Affairs to translate the law into action. In his election campaign Bandaranaike had equivocated by mentioning provisions for the "reasonable" use of Tamil but only in his English speeches. Passage of the bill touched off riots in the Gal Oya Valley between Sinhalese and Tamils, in which an estimated 150 persons were killed. The newly irrigated Gal Oya Valley had been a source of contention between Sinhalese and Tamils since the early 1950s, when colonists were chosen from both races to settle the area.

The Tamils, who had already expressed their fears in the 1956 election by voting almost exclusively for Tamil Federalists, made plans for a nationwide *satyagraha* (civil disobedience) campaign in August 1957. The FP leader, S. J. V. Chelvanayakam, and Bandaranaike came to an agreement in July, however, providing for the use of Tamil in the Northern and Eastern provinces, thereby averting the *satyagraha*.

62

The prime minister also made good on some of his other election promises. The special defense agreements with Great Britain were abrogated, and British forces left Katunayaka Airport and Trincomalee, which by 1956 had ceased to have the strategic significance they held during World War II. Ceylon, however, remained a member of the British Commonwealth. The two most important economic portfolios were given to Marxists, and both the Ceylon Transport Board and the Port of Colombo were nationalized. The minister of agriculture and food sponsored the Paddy Lands Bill in 1958, which was designed to give the farmer security of tenure and to provide credit through a Co-Operative Development Bank. It aroused considerable opposition among the conservative members of the cabinet and passed only with amendments. As a result of the restricting amendments, the two Marxist ministers resigned in early 1959.

Negotiations continued between Bandaranaike and FP leader Chelvanayakam, while communal tensions over the language issue developed in various parts of the country. In the Tamil north, the Sinhala script was blotted out on the license plates of cars and buses, and in the south, Tamils were subjected to intimidation. In March 1958 Bandaranaike announced that a pact had been drawn up with the Tamil leader outlining provisions for the "reasonable use of Tamil." Immediately the prime minister was pressured by radical Sinhalese groups to rescind the pact and, under the impact of a sit-down strike of *bhikkus* outside his residence in Colombo, he repudiated the pact.

Emotions had been aroused on both sides to such a pitch that it seemed only a matter of time before violence occurred. In May the Tamil Federalists were due to hold their annual convention in Vavuniya in North Central Province. Five hundred Sinhalese invaded the station at Polonnaruwa and attacked the train that was bound for the convention. Violence broke out in other parts of the island. Several hundred were killed on both sides, and a number of atrocities were committed. When the prime minister failed to act to stem the tide of violence, the governor general, Sir Oliver Goonetilleke, the first Ceylonese to hold that position, took charge. He declared a state of emergency, imposed censorship, arranged personally for hundreds of Tamil refugees to sail from Colombo to the north, and reestablished law and order. The state of emergency lasted until March 1959, even though calm was restored in June 1958.

In June the leaders of the FP and more than fifty other party members were arrested. A few Sinhalese extremist political leaders were also arrested. In August the Tamil Language

(Special Provisions) Act of 1958 was passed providing for reasonable use of Tamil, although Sinhala remained the sole official language.

In spite of his espousal of the Sinhalese-Buddhist cause, Bandaranaike was not able to satisfy the Sinhalese extremists. On September 25, 1959, a *bhikku* with a personal grudge shot Bandaranaike. He died the following day, having set in motion a social and political revolution whose control had occupied the main energies of the politicians of the 1960s.

CHAPTER 4

POPULATION

As of mid-1970 the population was estimated to be approximately 12.5 million. Up-to-date statistics on population are based on projections from the 1963 census and are, therefore, regarded as qualified. Estimates of the annual growth rate vary between 2.2 and 2.8 percent. If the population continues to grow within the mean of this range, it will double before the year 2000. The government is concerned about the social and economic strain that this rate of growth will place on the society, and it has utilized assistance from the government of Sweden to launch an extensive Family Planning Programme. The government's aim is to reduce the birth rate from its level of 31.6 births per 1,000 persons in 1970 to a level of 25 births per 1,000 by 1975.

The most conspicuous feature of the population explosion has been a gradual decline in the birth rate in recent decades coupled with a sudden, sharp decline in the death rate (see table 1). The rapid reduction of the death rate resulted directly from the overwhelming success in combating and controlling malaria that was achieved in the mid-1940s (see ch. 8, Living Conditions).

Table 1. Vital Statistics of Ceylon, Averaged by Decades, 1900–69

	Population (in millions)	Birth rate (per thousand)	Death rate (per thousand)	Natural increase
1900–09	3.7	38.1	28.9	9.2
1910–19	4.3	37.8	30.1	7.7
1920–29	4.8	39.6	26.9	12.7
1930–39	5.5	36.7	23.5	13.2
1940–49	6.6	37.3	17.9	19.4
1950–59	8.6	37.6	10.7	26.9
[1]1960–69	11.0	33.1	8.8	24.3
[2]1970	12.5	31.6	8.2	23.4

[1]Figures based on 1965 average.
[2]Estimate as of mid-1970.

Source: Adapted from Donald R. Snodgrass, *Ceylon: An Export Economy in Transition*, Homewood, 1966, pp. 84, 307; and *Demographic Yearbook, 1967*, New York, 1967, p. 271.

Over 69 percent of the population are Sinhalese, 12 percent are Indian Tamils, and almost 11 percent are Ceylon Tamils. The remaining 8 percent of the population is made up of 6 percent Ceylon Moors and 2 percent Eurasians, Burghers, Malays, Pakistanis, Europeans, and Veddahs (see ch. 5, Ethnic Groups and Languages).

The age-sex distribution figures that were derived from the 1963 census listed a ratio of 104 male births to each 100 female births. The median age was approximately twenty years. Life expectancy for the average male was nearly sixty-two years of age, the highest figure for any country in South Asia.

The urban population at the time of the 1963 census was listed as 1.8 million people, or approximately 17.1 percent of the total population. Most of the urban areas are in the southern and southwestern sectors of the country, where the population density is commonly twice as high as the all-island average of 460 persons per square mile.

POPULATION DYNAMICS

The first islandwide census was taken in 1871, when the population was listed at approximately 2.8 million, and registration of births and deaths was begun in 1867. Most experts concur, however, that the figures for births in the early censuses and registrations were underenumerations, particularly the listings of female births. Beginning in 1893, people were subject to penalties if they failed to report births and deaths, and figures since that year are more precise. Some statistical error is still allowed for, however, particularly in those areas where literacy levels are low.

Natural Increase

From the beginning of the twentieth century until 1963, the annual rates of births ranged between 39.7 and 34.1 per 1,000. By the time of the 1963 census the birth rate had reached its lowest point since 1900—34.1 births per 1,000. As a result of the implementation of a more extensive family planning program between 1963 and 1970, the birth rate was estimated to have dropped to 31.6 per 1,000.

The death rate has declined from a level of 27.2 per 1,000 at the turn of the century to 8.5 per 1,000 in 1963. Since 1963 the decline has been fractional, and in 1970 the rate was estimated to be 8.2 per 1,000. The large excess of births over deaths has been the major obstacle to effective population control, and during the 1940s and 1950s the gap between births and deaths widened. Only in the last few years, because of more widespread acceptance of birth control, has the trend been slightly reversed.

A highly successful public health program, especially with regard to the prevention and control of malaria, has dramatically curbed the death rate. Although the population is healthier, as evidenced by life expectancy figures for both sexes, the drop in the death rate has resulted in a much more densely settled population. The strain of increasing population density manifests itself in many ways, among which are overcrowded classrooms, insufficient hospital space, higher unemployment, and more government spending on welfare activities (see ch. 8, Living Conditions: ch. 9, Education: ch. 21, Labor).

The actual population explosion began in the mid-1940s when the use of dichloro-diphenyl-trichloro-ethane (DDT) successfully alleviated a recurrence of the malaria epidemic of 1935 and 1936 that was responsible for nearly 50,000 deaths, or approximately 1 percent of the estimated 1935 population. The epidemic was also responsible for producing an infant mortality rate of 263 per 1,000, a rise of over 90 per 1,000 from the previous year.

The years 1945 through 1947 were most notable for the sudden turnabout in the rate of natural increase. In those three years there was a slight increase in the birth rate, from 35.9 per 1,000 to 38.5 per 1,000, and a dramatic decline in the death rate, from nearly 21.5 to 14, the decline being particularly significant among infants. The estimated 1970 infant mortality rate of 53 per 1,000, for example, is low compared to the rest of South Asia.

In addition to the improved techniques of malaria eradication, more sanitary medical facilities and more sophisticated medical practice have also helped to lower the death rate of children under five years of age. One demographic expert credits 60 percent of the population growth after 1946 to improved techniques of preventing and controlling malaria and the remainder to other causes, such as higher living standards, better public health programs, and improved education.

Unlike most other developing nations, Ceylon has experienced a more rapid growth rate in the rural areas than in the urban areas. Propitious signs for a lowering of the birth rate can be seen in the continuing rise in the average age of marriage and the growing interest in birth control.

Migration and Repatriation of the Indian Tamils

Before the malaria epidemic in 1935, significant changes in the population were often the result of immigration and migration. Since that time, however, migration has had only a minimal effect on population growth.

A population growth rate of nearly 7 percent during the decade 1871–81 was more attributable to employment opportunities created by the new coffee plantations that attracted numerous immigrants from various countries than to any rapid growth in the rate of natural increase. The subsequent emergence of tea as the principal cash crop of the island in the early 1900s and the need for laborers on the tea estates resulted in extensive immigration, which had a significant impact on the growth rate over the next few decades (see ch. 19, Agriculture; ch. 21, Labor).

By the 1940s, however, nearly all of the variations in the growth rate were accounted for by changes in the rate of natural increase. Immigration and emigration statistics for the decade of the 1940s tended to offset each other. In the early 1940s there was a net outflow of migrants, most of whom were Indian Tamils who left because of rising communal tensions; in the late 1940s, when tensions temporarily subsided, there was once again an inflow of Tamils from India (see ch. 3, Historical Setting).

Since 1950 the net flow of migration has been outward; the major reason for this has been that India agreed to absorb a large number of the Indian Tamils. After 1954 the legal immigration of estate laborers from India was further reduced, and after 1957 it all but ceased.

In accordance with an agreement between Ceylon and India signed in 1964, 525,000 of the Indian Tamils, along with their natural increase, would be repatriated to India in a phased program over a period of fifteen years; Ceylon agreed to grant citizenship to 300,000 Indian Tamils, phased over the same period of time. The agreement also stipulated that the fate of the remaining 150,000 would be decided at a later date (see ch. 14, Political Dynamics; ch. 15, Foreign Relations). Ceylonese authorities are aware, however, that some illegal immigration is still taking place.

STRUCTURE OF THE POPULATION

Age-Sex Composition

The median age of the population in 1970 was approximately twenty years of age. The large proportion of the population under ten years of age (nearly 30 percent) threatens to create a great deal of pressure on educational facilities and may severely limit employment opportunities when these people reach working age (see fig. 7) (see ch. 9, Education; ch. 21, Labor).

The sex ratio at birth during the late 1960s was approximately 103 males for every 100 females. The 1963 census listed as male 54 percent of the urban population and 51 percent of the rural population. A 1965 estimation of the urban population listed 1,977,130 urbanites, of whom 1,083,670, or 55 percent, were males. When males are employed in the urban areas, they often cannot afford to take their families with them (see ch. 7, Family). There were 8,592,130 rural inhabitants, of whom 4,419,180, or 51 percent, were males (see table 2).

Mortality of females is higher than that of males during infancy and continuing on through the childbearing period. After the childbearing period, mortality rates begin to even off. The average man lives to the age of 61.9 years and the average woman to 61.4 years. These figures compare very favorably to those of all other countries in South Asia, where the average life expectancy is usually much lower.

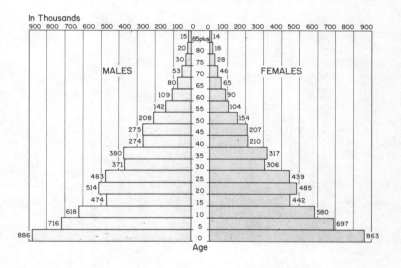

Figure 7. Revised 1963 Census, Age-Sex Distribution, Ceylon.

Source: Adapted from Ceylon, Registrar General, *Report of the Registrar General of Ceylon on Vital Statistics for 1963,* Colombo, 1968, p. H106.

Marital Status

Nearly everyone in Ceylon marries at one time or another (see ch. 7, Family). In a survey taken in 1953, nearly 76 percent of those in the fifteen-to-nineteen age group were single,

Table 2. Urban-Rural Population Distribution of Ceylon, 1953

Ceylon	Urban			Rural		
Province	Males	Females	Total	Males	Females	Total
Western	440,517	326,948	767,465	752,069	712,742	1,464,811
Central	73,122	52,378	125,500	642,557	598,628	1,241,185
Southern	59,951	58,048	117,999	506,145	505,164	1,011,309
Northern	41,278	35,903	77,181	251,225	242,244	493,469
Eastern	25,119	18,676	43,795	168,707	141,908	310,615
North Western	24,683	17,453	42,136	432,934	380,158	813,092
North Central	11,066	7,324	18,390	120,797	90,095	210,892
Uva	12,854	9,228	22,082	233,918	210,896	444,814
Sabaragamuwa	14,200	10,385	24,585	457,588	410,987	868,575
Total	702,790	536,343	1,239,133	3,565,940	3,292,822	6,858,762

Source: Adapted from Ferguson's Ceylon Directory, 1966 (108th ed.), Colombo, 1966, p. 87.

but 65 percent of those in the twenty-to-twenty-four age group were married. By the ages of thirty to thirty-four, nearly 88 percent were married.

The age at which women have been marrying has been rising steadily since the beginning of the century. In 1901 the average age at which women married was 19.4 years; in 1921, 21.4 years; in 1946, 22.9 years; and in 1970, over 23 years. The age at which men marry has leveled off since it reached 28.4 in 1921. In 1946 it was 27.8 years, and in 1970 it was estimated to be 28 years of age. Postponement of marriage to a later age has had the positive tendency of depressing the birth rate and, therefore, increasing the proportion of people in the older age groups.

Ethnic and Religious Composition

The Sinhalese constitute approximately 69.4 percent of the population and are divided into Low-Country Sinhalese and Kandyan Sinhalese. The Low-Country Sinhalese make up roughly 43.6 percent of the population, and the Kandyans form 25.8 percent. The distinction between the two Sinhalese populations is mainly territorial (see ch. 5, Ethnic Groups and Languages). Theravada Buddhism is practiced by 90 percent of the Sinhalese.

Ceylon Tamils, whose ancestors have lived in Ceylon for many centuries, are found mainly in the north and northeast coastal areas and constitute roughly 10.7 percent of the population. Indian Tamils, whose ancestors came only recently to Ceylon from south India as estate laborers, live in the central hills of Ceylon and form nearly 12 percent of the population (see ch. 5, Ethnic Groups and Languages). Nearly 95 percent of the Tamils are Hindus.

Urban-Rural Distribution

According to the 1963 census, the urban areas contained nearly 17.1 percent of the population. Urban areas in Ceylon are defined by the registrar general as "falling within the administrative limits of Municipal Councils, Urban Councils and Town Councils" (see ch. 13, The Governmental System). The estimated total of urbanites at the time of the 1963 census was 1,836,400.

Population density is greatest in the southern and southwestern sectors of the country where agricultural conditions are most favorable. According to the 1963 census, the average density was estimated to be roughly 460 persons per square mile. The areas with the highest population density are in the

Western, Central, and Southern provinces. In the Western Province, where the capital city of Colombo is located, population density is almost 2,000 persons per square mile. In the Central Province where Kandy is located, the density is roughly 600 persons per square mile. In contrast to the southwestern sector of the country, the North Central Province is sparsely populated; around the city of Anuradhapura, the population density is only about 60 persons per square mile.

Colombo is in the most densely settled region of the country. Colombo District has approximately 2,207,420 people and Colombo itself had a population of about 537,900 as of July 8, 1963, the date of the last census. The city is situated on the southwestern coast of the country and is one of the most active port cities in the Indian Ocean area (see ch. 2, Physical Environment).

Jaffna, with a 1963 census population of nearly 89,000 people, lies on the northern tip of the country, nearly 180 statute miles from Colombo. Jaffna has a higher concentration of Tamils than any other city.

Kandy, having a population of about 75,500, lies in the south-central highlands; it was the seat of the native kings for many centuries until 1815 when the British assumed colonial rule of the entire country.

Galle, with a 1963 population of approximately 71,000 is situated on the southern tip of the country; it lies approximately sixty-four miles southeast of Colombo. It is believed to have been known to the Phoenicians, Greeks, and Romans, and legends hold that Galle was once the biblical city of Tarshish.

Trincomalee, with a population estimated at 37,000 as of mid-1963, is located on the northeastern coast of the country. It is the main harbor outlet to eastern Asia and the southwest Pacific region. During World War II, Trincomalee served as a shelter for many of Great Britain's biggest vessels, and only in 1957 did Ceylon assume complete control of the harbor (see ch. 25, The Armed Forces).

FAMILY PLANNING

Formal family planning in Ceylon began in 1953 with the founding of the Family Planning Association. The Family Planning Association is a voluntary organization, but it receives much cooperation from the government.

The government became actively involved in family planning in 1954 when it began administering grants to hospitals and clinics as well as to private organizations set up specifically for family planning. A total of 155 clinics were in operation by 1964, and by 1970 there were an estimated 270 clinics.

An important contribution to the growth of the government's Family Planning Programme has been the cooperation of the Swedish government. The implementation of an agreement signed in 1958 between the government of Ceylon and the Swedish International Development Authority (SIDA) has been cited as a prime reason for recent declines in the crude birth rate and in the fertility rates of specific age groups, particularly among females in the twenty-five-to-thirty-five age bracket.

In 1965 family planning was accepted as part of maternal and child health care and became an integral part of the government's health policy. Before 1968 most family planning activities were carried out by local authorities. In 1968, however, the cabinet acquiesced to the Ministry of Health's proposal to organize a central headquarters for family planning activities. Members of the Bureau of Family Planning in mid-1970 comprised the assistant director of health, representatives of the SIDA and Population Council-Ford Foundation projects, and officials for health, education, and evaluation.

The announced goal of the Family Planning Programme is to reduce the birth rate from its 1970 level of 31.6 per 1,000 to 25 per 1,000 persons by 1975. In order for this to be achieved, family planning experts estimate that an additional 115,000 persons each year must agree to practice some method of birth control.

In early 1970 approximately 60,000 women were taking the oral contraceptive. Ceylonese doctors have given almost unanimous support to the oral contraceptive and, together with government officials, have launched a widespread public information program emphasizing its safety and effectiveness. This program was launched in order to offset fears that had arisen as a result of publicity in Western countries concerning the alleged linkage of thrombosis and cancer to the use of the pill. Ceylonese doctors are confident that the use of the pill by an additional 115,000 women each year will reduce the rate of annual growth to 1.7 percent by 1975.

One factor working against reduction of the birth rate is the growing percentage of women of childbearing age. Of the total female population, 13.6 percent were in the twenty-to-thirty-nine age bracket in 1963; the percentage is expected to climb to approximately 15 percent by 1978. The increase in women of fertile age must be compensated for by a higher age of marriage, by an increase in the number of people who have never married, or by successful implementation of birth control.

In mid-1970 family planning was being viewed as a political as well as a social issue. Sinhalese Buddhist monks and supporters of various political groups expressed the fear that family planning would change the ethnic and religious composition of the population. The reason for the growing Buddhist alarm was their belief that, since the introduction of family planning, the Indian Tamil population had been growing at a faster rate than the Sinhalese.

CHAPTER 5

ETHNIC GROUPS AND LANGUAGES

In mid-1970 Ceylon continued to be a multinational state composed of several self-conscious ethnic communities. These groups are differentiated by language, religion, social customs and, to some extent, racial origin. The numerically dominant Sinhalese (see Glossary), who constitute 69.4 percent of the population of 12.5 million, are primarily agricultural people descended from the inhabitants of kingdoms established in ancient times. The second largest group, the Tamils (see Glossary), who form nearly 23 percent of the population, is divided between the Ceylon Tamils, who are descendants of ancient indigenous Tamil kingdoms, and the Indian Tamils, descended from the estate laborers brought from South India beginning in the nineteenth century. The third indigenous group, the aboriginal Veddahs, whose residence on the island predates that of both the Sinhalese and the Tamils, has largely ceased to exist as an ethnic group and has been absorbed into the general society.

Several smaller but disporportionately influential groups owe their presence on the island to foreign trade and colonization in medieval and modern times. The Muslim community, which functions as an ethnically distinct group, and accounts for about 7 percent of the population, is descended from Arab traders, often called Moors, who settled on the island at various times, and from Malay soldiers brought by the Dutch. The Burghers, a community of Eurasian and European descent and accounting for perhaps 1 percent of the population, are the result of intermarriage of Dutch and Portuguese colonialists with local families (see ch. 3, Historical Setting).

Throughout the 1950s and 1960s relations among the various communities were characterized by rivalry and, at times, open hostility. As a result of colonial policies and historical factors, certain minority communities, particularly the Ceylon Tamils and the Burghers, were granted disproportionate access to the benefits of modernization and so came to occupy a highly privileged position in preindependence society. In addition, British educational and administrative policy fostered the development of an English-speaking elite that was recruited from all communities and that dominated professional, political, and intellectual life on the island (see ch. 9, Education; ch. 3, Historical Setting). The vast majority of the people were cut off from influence and advancement by ignorance of the English language.

Gradually, this majority began to press demands for equality, first against the English-speaking elite and later against the Tamil-speaking minority. This agitation led first to the disenfranchisement of some Tamils and the adoption of Sinhala (see Glossary) as the only official language, and finally in 1958 to open violence and widespread bloodshed between communities (see ch. 3, Historical Setting; ch. 24, Public Order and Internal Security). Throughout the 1960s, however, and especially in recent years, communal relations have been ameliorating, as the government adopted a more conciliatory attitude toward the minorities (see ch. 14, Political Dynamics). In mid-1970 the country appeared to be reaching a new equilibrium based on the replacement of English by Sinhala as the official language and the recognition of Tamil as a secondary national language.

ETHNIC CLASSIFICATION

The ethnic communities are distinguished primarily by language and secondarily by religion, racial origin, and other factors. The Sinhalese and Tamils, who together constitute more than 92 percent of the population, differ in religion and social customs as well as in language, but linguistic factors operate most powerfully to separate them. It is significant that the groups are ordinarily referred to according to language, although their religious division into Hindu and Buddhist communities is nearly as sharp (see ch. 11, Religion).

In the case of the smaller ethnic minorities, other features, such as religion and racial origin, have greater importance in classification, but these also are distinguished largely by language. It is, in addition, the language issue that has most inflamed intercommunal passions. Although other factors are undoubtedly at work, communal tensions are routinely phrased in terms of language differences.

The origins of the groups longest resident in the island are not entirely clear, being known only from legend and archaeological sources (see ch. 3, Historical Setting). It appears most unlikely that racial or genetic exclusiveness was maintained between them; in modern Ceylon they do not form different "races" in a physical sense. Although historic accounts refer to invasions by Sinhalese people, it is improbable that large masses of immigrants arrived on the island in ancient times. Rather, the culture of the invaders was probably adopted by prehistoric people already present, who intermarried with the newcomers. Legend describes the cohabitation of the ancestor of the Sinhalese with a native woman. There is evidence that limited intermarriage between Sinhalese and Tamils took place at various times throughout history (see ch. 3, Historical Setting). Even in modern times it is not possible to distinguish Sinhalese and Tamils absolutely or to think of them as totally distinct racial lines. Some groups, especially certain ones of the Karava caste in the areas of Chilaw and Negombo, use a dialect that is a mixture of Sinhalese and Tamil.

In the case of the smaller minorities whose history and mode of arrival are known from historical documents, linguistic differentiation is also important, although less crucial. The Burghers are differentiated mainly by their pride in European ancestry but also by their English language. The Muslims are differentiated primarily by religion but also exhibit certain dialectal peculiarities.

In modern society the ethnic communities function as mutually exclusive units. The individual owes loyalty to his community rather than to the nation at large; the concept of pan-ethnic Ceylonese nationality is not highly developed (see ch. 12, Social Values; ch. 14, Political Dynamics; ch. 17, Political Values and Attitudes). Since the ethnic communities are, in general, geographically rather compact and each is associated with the particular region or regions where it is concentrated, community consciousness is quite high (see table 3).

A factor contributing to the exclusiveness of the various communities is the high correlation that exists between language and religion. For example, over 90 percent of Sinhala speakers are Buddhists, and a slightly smaller percentage of Tamil speakers are Hindus. Virtually all Burghers, all of whom speak English, are Christians. Muslims are predominantly Tamil speakers. Although small groups of Christians exist among both Sinhalese and Tamils, they constitute a decided minority.

In addition, social organization separates the peoples. Caste, which is recognized by both Sinhalese and Tamils, is organized differently in the two groups (see ch. 6, Social Structure). The Muslims and Burghers do not explicitly recognize caste. There is very little intermarriage. Of a total of 62,103 marriages registered on the island in 1963, only 997, or 1.4 percent, were contracted between individuals of different ethnic groups. As a consequence of these factors, each ethnic community differs from the others in most significant aspects of life and forms

Table 3. *Percentage Distribution of Ethnic Groups by Province, Ceylon, 1953**

Ethnic Group	Province								
	Western	Central	Southern	Northern	Eastern	North Western	North Central	Uva	Sabargamuwa
Low-Country Sinhalese	51.3	3.8	30.6	0.2	0.6	8.0	1.1	1.1	3.3
Kandyan Sinhalese	2.2	28.5	0.3	0.3	1.1	22.3	7.1	10.6	27.6
Ceylon Tamils	10.8	4.5	0.8	58.0	18.4	2.9	1.7	1.6	1.3
Indian Tamils	11.0	50.2	2.4	1.8	0.5	1.8	0.3	17.1	14.9
Ceylon Moors	23.1	15.6	6.1	4.3	28.8	10.2	4.0	2.9	5.0
Indian Moors	43.3	19.7	0.8	6.8	3.4	9.7	2.6	4.6	7.1
Burghers and Eurasians	71.0	10.9	2.6	1.2	6.1	2.5	0.8	2.8	2.1
Malays	63.7	13.6	6.9	0.5	2.5	5.3	0.7	4.9	1.9
Veddahs	....	3.1	....	0.3	3.7	2.7	40.0	46.1	4.1
Europeans	58.7	22.3	2.2	1.4	3.3	1.1	0.4	6.7	3.9
Others	63.1	10.1	1.8	3.1	3.2	6.6	1.2	4.1	6.8

*Latest available official figures; there is no indication of substantial change.

Source: Adapted from *Ferguson's Ceylon Directory, 1966* (108th ed.), Colombo, 1966, p. 81.

a discrete unit. The individual lives most of his life within his own ethnic group. There has traditionally been little common ground between communities.

In addition to the major distinctions based on language, the two largest groups are internally divided into subgroups based on geographic origin and social condition. Among the Sinhalese can be distinguished the Low-Country Sinhalese, who live primarily in the coastal regions of the west and south, and the Kandyan Sinhalese, who inhabit the mountainous region of the former kingdom of Kandy (see ch. 3, Historical Setting). The Tamil population is composed of Ceylon Tamils, who live in the north, primarily in the Jaffna region, and the imported Indian Tamils, who live on estates in the Kandyan hills.

THE PEOPLES OF CEYLON

The Sinhalese

The approximately 8.7 million speakers of Sinhala constitute the largest ethnic and linguistic community. The Sinhalese claim to be descended from a noble line of Aryan invaders who arrived on the island on the very day that the Buddha attained *nirvana* (see Glossary). According to their belief, the truest and purest form of Theravda Buddhism was early entrusted to them; Sri (Holy) Lanka (the Sinhalese name for the island) has always been a special repository of the beliefs and relics of the Buddha and has stood in a special relationship to him. The inhabitants of Sri Lanka, who have for centuries preserved the Sacred Tooth Relic saved from the Buddha's funeral pyre and nurtured a shoot of the Sacred Bo Tree under which he gained enlightenment, believe that Sinhalese culture and the purest form of Buddhism are inextricably bound to Ceylon (see ch. 3, Historical Setting; ch. 11, Religion). These beliefs have been important in shaping modern ethnic attitudes.

The Sinhalese community is divided into groups, based upon geographic and cultural distinctions. The Low-Country Sinhalese, who live primarily in the southern and western coastal regions, constitute 62 percent of the Sinhalese community and 42.8 percent of the national population. The Kandyan Sinhalese, occupying the highlands of the south-central region, form 38 percent of all Sinhalese and 25.8 percent of the nation (see ch. 2, Physical Environment; ch. 4, population).

The vast majority of Sinhalese are agriculturalists, living in villages and raising rice and other crops (see ch. 19, Agriculture). These villages are largely organized according to

79

traditional caste and feudal relationships; widespread education and a modernizing economy, however, are gradually undermining traditional institutions. A significant class in the countryside is the rural intelligentsia educated in Sinhala (see ch.
6, Social Structure). The Kandyan people are substantially
more conservative religiously, economically, and culturally than
the Low-Country population and are more devoted to traditional forms.

The distinction between Kandyan and Low-Country Sinhalese
is largely one of custom and outlook fostered by the conditions
of colonialism (see ch. 3, Historical Setting). Before the
British period, European incursions were largely limited to the
coast. The fact that neither the Portuguese nor the Dutch
conquered the kingdom of Kandy was crucial in the cultural
development of the two regions. The coastal people, being in
contact with travelers and traders from other countries, had
always been more cosmopolitan than the highlanders. When
European colonialists arrived, these coastal dwellers were
quicker to absorb and take advantage of the newly introduced cultures.

The colonialists were largely interested in the products of the
interior. The sophisticated coastal Sinhalese were ideally
suited to be mediators between the foreigners and the inland
peoples. The Kandyans, on the other hand, insulated by their
political independence and the forbidding terrain, never fell
under heavy European influence before the British period. In
addition, as the influence of Christianity and European culture
grew on the coast, many individuals of conservative leanings
migrated to the protection of the Kandyan kings, reinforcing
the traditionalist attitudes of their territories.

The inroads made by Christianity and European culture were
substantial in the coastal area. The Portuguese were determined
missionaries, and Catholic communities are to be found to this
day, particularly on the western coast. During Portuguese times
a limited Western educational system was begun, and many
Sinhalese availed themselves of this education and also of the
new business and commercial opportunities offered by the
colonial trade. This was the beginning of a period of relative
social fluidity and fairly easy upward mobility, since an important new source of wealth and influence had been introduced.
Numerous families of low social origin achieved commercial
and financial success; as the traditional system of surnames
indicated the caste origin of an individual, many upwardly
mobile families took Portuguese surnames, such as de Silva,
Fernando, de Fonseca, and Perera, to disguise their background. The Portuguese honorific title *Don* came into wide

use among the upper groups, as did the custom of European given names. The first prime minister, D.S. Senanayake, for example, was Don Stephen.

The differences between the two regions were further solidified under Dutch rule. Under the British, most of the Sinhalese members of the English-speaking groups that became the political and commercial elite of the country were from coastal families. The immersion of these people in Western culture was quite complete, many communicating better in English than in their native Sinhala. Upon his return from Oxford, Solomon West Ridgeway Dias Bandaranaike, the future Sinhalese nationalist leader, found himself unable to speak Sinhala fluently and never learned to read or write it with facility.

Meanwhile, the relatively isolated Kandyans were continuing within the framework of traditional culture and had little contact with, or knowledge of, the Europeans until relatively late. Consequently, the estrangement between the group in the forefront of colonial adaptation and that preserving the ancient Buddhist literature and tradition was considerable.

The Tamils

The Tamils, who constitute nearly 23 percent of the population, are the largest and longest established minority in Ceylon. They arrived at various times, beginning about 2,000 years ago (see ch. 3, Historical Setting). By medieval times there was a Tamil kingdom established in the north. Unlike Sinhala, which is spoken only in Ceylon, Tamil is also the language of some 50 million inhabitants of South India.

Slightly fewer than 50 percent of the Tamils are of the group called Ceylon Tamils. The majority are the descendants of inhabitants of the Tamil kingdoms of Ceylon and have been established on the island for at least 1,000 years. The Ceylon Tamils are concentrated in the north, particularly around Jaffna, and also in the eastern coastal regions. Although in recent times Ceylon Tamils have scattered widely, if thinly, over most of the country because of their prominent role in the civil service, the Jaffna area is the ancestral home of the Ceylon Tamils and the center of their cultural and intellectual life. Jaffna Tamils dominate the Tamil educational, professional, and intellectual fields. The Jaffna region is densely populated and infertile compared to the Sinhalese regions (see ch. 2, Physical Environment). The Tamils in the Jaffna region, overwhelmingly farmers, have earned their living through diligence, hard work, and thrift. Eastern Province, on

81

the other hand, is rather thinly settled. There Tamils and Moors live interspersed or in small clusters.

Because of the scanty opportunities in farming and the pressure of population in their home region, the Ceylon Tamils have been very eager for formal education, which provides opportunities in other desirable vocations. During British times the Christian missionaries found the Jaffna population so receptive to education that they established most of their schools in that region, giving the Ceylon Tamils a disproportionate share of the English education and, consequently, qualifying them for a larger share of the clerical and professional positions than their numbers would justify.

The remainder of the Tamil speakers are known as Indian Tamils. They were brought by the British during the nineteenth and early twentieth centuries and are primarily workers on the tea estates of the Kandyan highland region. Drawn from the poorest groups of South India and badly exploited by the British tea planters, the largely illiterate Indian Tamils were deposited in self-contained tea estates carved out of forest and village reserve lands among the Kandyan peasantry. No significant communication or interaction developed between these groups; the Tamils retained their language and Hindu religion, obtained their brides from India and, in some cases, returned there to retire.

The Indian Tamils have been largely isolated from the mainstream of life and have been considered foreign by the other ethnic groups. In addition, the Kandyan peasantry came to regard the estate population with considerable hostility as the estates encroached on village lands and population pressure increased. A widespread feeling developed among the Sinhalese that the Tamil laborers lived and worked under more favorable conditions than the surrounding villagers, although the Sinhalese peasants showed neither interest in nor inclination to work on the estates (see ch. 19, Agriculture).

The Indian Tamils were also isolated from their coreligionists in the north. Caste distinctions are of extreme importance in Tamil society generally (see ch. 6, Social Structure). The Ceylon Tamils are mostly of the high Vellala, or cultivator, caste, whereas the Indian Tamils are of much lower caste origin. In addition, the differences in economic and educational standards are great. It has been only since the late 1950s that Indian and Ceylon Tamils have begun to develop feelings of unity.

Before independence the Indian Tamils had political equality with other groups by virtue of being subjects of the British crown, but even at that time they were regarded as intrinsic foreigners by the other communities. Shortly after independence they were declared to be noncitizens because of their relatively brief residence there and their supposed lack of ties to the country (see ch. 3, Historical Setting; ch. 13, The Governmental System; ch. 14, Political Dynamics). Nonetheless, many Indian Tamils were the children or grandchildren of actual immigrants and were not immigrants themselves.

Some Indians who had gone to Colombo and other cities to work as laborers or harbor workers were sent back to India. A small number remains, working in extremely low-caste occupations such as street cleaning and laundering. There was agitation to repatriate the estate workers also, but the tea industry, the mainstay of the economy, could not survive without them. The disposition of the estate population has been a continuing problem; more hours have been spent in parliamentary debate on the status of the Indian Tamils than on any other question.

India refused to admit the total estate population, claiming it was Ceylonese rather than Indian. As of 1964, 134,000, only 10 percent, had applied for Ceylonese citizenship. After years of negotiation, an agreement was signed in 1964 by which Ceylon would eventually accept as citizens some 300,000 Indian Tamils and India would admit some 525,000 (see ch. 15, Foreign Relations). The fate of the remainder was postponed for future determination. Ceylon has accepted the necessity of absorbing a certain permanent Indian Tamil population. By early 1970 well over 200,000 more had put in applications for Ceylonese citizenship; 4,000 persons by that time had been granted citizenship under the pact, including some 595 children born after it went into effect.

As Sinhalese nationalism grew in the 1950s and 1960s, for the first time Indian and Ceylon Tamils began to feel an ethnic solidarity based on a common adversary. Although this movement is not far advanced, overtures toward unity were made by both groups. In addition, the Ceylon Tamils began to show signs of interest in their fellow Tamils in the subcontinent of India; before this time they had tended to identify themselves as distinct from those in India.

The Muslims

The Muslim community, which accounts for 6 to 7 percent of the national population, functions as a separate ethnic community. Although most speak Tamil as a home language, they have not blended into the ethnic Tamil community because of differences in custom and religion. They have remained somewhat aloof from the Sinhalese-Tamil rivalry. Their heaviest concentrations are in the coastal areas of Western and Eastern provinces, although members of the community are to be found in all parts of the island. Muslims gain their living primarily through trade and commerce, especially as small merchants and shopkeepers, although a substantial number are farmers.

The Muslim community is composed of several more or less distinct groups. Most are called Moors, from the Portuguese usage. Like the Tamils, these are divided into groups of so-called Ceylon and Indian Moors. The Moors are descended from Arab traders who arrived at various times during the past 900 years. In addition, there is a small community, under 20 percent of the Muslim population, known as Malays, whose ancestors were soldiers brought from present-day Malaysia by the Dutch.

Before the coming of the Portuguese, the inhabitants of the Arabian peninsula were among the world's leading sailors and dominated trade in the Indian Ocean; Sinbad the Sailor is said to have visited Serendib, as Ceylon was called in Arabic. Arabs are known to have visited the island in pre-Islamic times. As early as the tenth century A.D., Arab merchants and agents were settled in South India. Muslims are known to have visited Adam's Peak, a mountain in central Ceylon that is an important pilgrimage site for Muslims, Hindus, and Buddhists at that time. Shortly thereafter, Arabs began to settle in Ceylon. They controlled the southern ports and were advisers to the kings on commercial affairs. In 1238 King Bhuvaneka Bahu I sent emissaries to the court of Egypt; this mission was planned and carried out by Arabs living in Ceylon.

The Arab community maintained its religion and many of its customs, while intermarrying with Tamils, Sinhalese, and South Indians. By the fifteenth century the character of the Muslim community in Ceylon had changed from purely Arab to Indo-Arab. The Muslims began to adopt Tamil as their home language. As Arab words and sounds were added, the Tamil language took on new forms; new letters were included in it to incorporate Arabic sounds, and the dialect spoken by the Muslims became known as Arabic-Tamil. In modern times the Muslim community retains some special usages in Tamil.

It is probable that the present-day Ceylon Moor community is the result of considerable intermarriage with, and conversion of, Tamils. Some Tamil-like customs are visible in the Muslim community. The Tamil dowry custom, *stridhanam,* has been adopted, as well as certain aspects of the Hindu marriage ceremony (see ch. 7, Family). *Purdah* (seclusion of women) is not stringently practiced. Although Tamil is the language of most Moors, those living in the Sinhalese regions also speak Sinhala, often keeping Tamil as their home language. Since Sinhala became the official language, its use has been increasing among them.

When the Portuguese arrived, they associated the Muslim community of Ceylon with the Moors who were their enemies in Europe and gave it the same name. They persecuted Islam quite severely, and in the early 1600s the Portuguese commander, Constatino de Sa de Noronha, ejected many of the Moors from his west coast jurisdiction under orders of the Portuguese king. The king of Kandy offered asylum to the Moors, and many settled in the Kandyan hills and also in the Batticaloa coastal area, which was under his control. In modern times the Moors have constituted nearly 40 percent of the population of Batticaloa. The emigration of the Muslims probably increased a small Muslim population already present in the area. Most of the Moors on the east coast are farmers, and the community is not very advanced economically or educationally. The Moors were loath to send their children to Christian schools; thus, before the development of the public school system, the community had little secular education and, consequently, little command of English.

The Indian Moors, who are primarily traders and merchants, are descendants of Arab traders who were settled in South India for several centuries and had intermarried there before coming to Ceylon in more recent times.

In the eighteenth century the Dutch introduced a new element into the Muslim group by importing Javanese and other Indonesians and Malayans as soldiers. This group remained somewhat apart, speaking their own language. The Malay community is highly concentrated geographically; over 60 percent live in Western Province and, of these, over 80 percent live in Colombo.

The Burghers

Although quite small, the Burgher community has been disproportionately influential in Ceylonese society for centuries. Because of the rising nationalism and sentiment for *swabasha* (local language) throughout the population, however, the Burghers in recent years have been losing importance and power. The term *Burgher* comes from the Dutch and originally referred to Dutch nationals and their descendants. By extension it came to be applied to all local residents of European ancestry, as opposed to transient Europeans, including Eurasians and Portuguese. Today there is among the Burghers a group called Dutch Burghers; another, rather illogically, is known as Portuguese Burghers.

The original components of the present-day Burgher community were Portuguese settlers, many of whom married locally, and their often Eurasian descendants. Even in Portuguese times this community occupied a very privileged position in society. During the Dutch colonial period a new element was added to the population as Dutch military men and others married into the Portuguese and Eurasian families. With the coming of the British, the Burgher community in general adopted English as its home language, and some Englishmen were added to the population. The Burghers have always been Christians, both Catholic and Protestant, and because of their privileged position and fluency in English they have traditionally been highly educated. Throughout the colonial period they dominated the desirable positions in the civil service, professions, and trade out of all proportion to their numbers in the society.

The Burghers are a heavily urban people. The Dutch East India Company made land grants to Dutch settlers, usually retired military men of the lower ranks, but they were generally not successful farmers, and most settled in cities. Very few European women came to Ceylon in early times, so the majority of the permanent settlers married into resident Portuguese families or took local wives. In modern times a distinction has been apparent between those who claim "pure" European blood and those who have some Asian mixture. The group known as Dutch Burghers claim to have exclusively European ancestors and tend to exclude others from their social circles and clubs.

In recent years the Burgher community has been losing members, since many, particularly Dutch Burghers, have been emigrating to Great Britain, Australia, New Zealand, and other white nations of the Commonwealth. With the adoption of Sinhala as the official language, the position of the Burghers, professionally, educationally, and politically, has become quite precarious. Many fear that they will not be able to maintain their present high standard of living, although they would consider any diminution of it a considerable decline in status.

The Veddahs

The aboriginal population of Ceylon, which in 1970 numbered no more than several thousand individuals, inhabits primitive villages in the backwoods sections of Uva and North-Central provinces. They live by a primitive form of unirrigated shifting agriculture.

Very little is known about the origins of these people, who seem on the whole to have assimilated culturally into the surrounding populations. Anthropologists in the early years of this century noted that it was at that time virtually impossible to find Veddah communities. In modern times their traditional language and culture seem to have fallen into total disuse. In the mid-1950s an anthropologist who traveled extensively in the interior of Uva Province did not encounter a single individual who claimed to speak fluent Veddah.

INTERCOMMUNAL RELATIONS

The relationship between the ethnic communities has always been a significant factor in the life of Ceylon. Colonial policies and historical circumstances upset the precolonial equilibrium and introduced into Ceylonese society certain stresses that had to be worked out before a modern equilibrium could be established.

For two or three centuries before the arrival of Europeans, the two major ethnic groups occupied the island together, yet lived apart in kingdoms separated by uninhabited wilderness and governed under separate systems. There was little communal conflict because the two groups had little contact with each other (see ch. 3, Historical Setting).

When Ceylon was unified by the British into one political unit, the two groups once again found themselves subject to the same authorities. Nonetheless, a sentiment of common nationality did not develop; in modern Ceylon the individual still identified first with his ethnic community (see ch. 12, Social Values; ch. 17, Political Values and Attitudes).

The attitudes of the groups regarding one another have had an important effect on their relations. Although the Sinhalese constitute the overwhelming majority of the population of the island, they nonetheless feel themselves to be a small and isolated group compared to the Hindu Tamils. Sinhala is spoken nowhere else in the world; its approximately 8.7 million speakers feel encircled by their nearest neighbors, the more than 50 million Tamil speakers in Ceylon and South India. Although they outnumber the Tamils of Ceylon by more than three to one, the Sinhalese are, in turn, outnumbered by the combined Tamil population by more than six to one. Even though the Ceylon Tamils have not traditionally shown any interest in allying themselves with the Tamils of India, the Sinhalese nonetheless consider this a possibility.

To the Sinhalese, the culture based on Sinhala has a significance beyond a mere linguistic or cultural value; they feel that there is a special relationship between Ceylon, Sinhala, and Theravada Buddhism. The *Mahavamsa,* the most important ancient historical chronicle, emphasizes the peculiar bond between Buddhism and Sri Lanka; legends hold that the Buddha himself perceived this relationship. Because it was written by *bhikkus* (Buddhist monks), the *Mahavamsa* commemorates and honors those kings and heroes who were loyal to Buddhism (see ch. 3, Historical Setting). The connection between religion, language, and national identity established in the *Mahavamsa* has continued to exert a powerful influence on Sinhalese thought. Furthermore, in colloquial Sinhala, the words *nation* and *race* or *people* are synonymous. Consequently, the concept of a multiracial or multicommunal nation or state is unthinkable in the popular mind. Sinhala-trained intellectuals have been particularly anxious to preserve and strengthen the language in Ceylon, for they feel that if it falls into decay in that country its valuable religious and literary tradition will die. The Tamils, on the other hand, although realizing that they are a minority in Ceylon itself, consider themselves members of a large and significant world culture.

The modern pattern of communal relations started to take shape under the British. Because the majority of English-language missionary schools were established in the Jaffna area, a large number of Tamil youth were prepared for positions in the professions and the prestigious civil service. In addition, the Burgher community has accounted for a strikingly large proportion of the civil servants. From 1900 until the mid-1930s, the Burghers and Ceylon Tamil minorities dominated the services, both in relative and absolute terms.

Because the Low-Country Sinhalese had less access to English education—the only type that prepared the student for government service—their contribution in numbers was smaller. The Kandyan Sinhalese were virtually absent from the rolls of the professions and government services. Geographically isolated and culturally conservative, they did not absorb much of the newly introduced British culture. In addition, during the late nineteenth and early twentieth centuries, the Indian Tamils were imported in large numbers and began crowding the Sinhalese population in the highlands (see ch. 3, Historical Setting).

Meanwhile, primarily on the coast, an important quasi-ethnic group was forming that functioned as an ethnic community. This was the English-educated elite, recruited from all major communities and trained in the British-style secondary schools and often at universities abroad. Drawn primarily from the leading families of traditional society and educated in the Western classics and professions, these men came to dominate political and intellectual life on the island. Their schools were much wealthier than the vernacular schools in the countryside, and the prestige of Western learning was very great. Especially among the Low-Country Sinhalese community, the young men came to ignore or even reject their traditional heritage. Many were more comfortable in English than in Sinhala; in many of these families English was the home language. Although their Tamil counterparts also absorbed English language, learning, and customs, their ties to their tradition were stronger and their rejection of it less complete.

A leading Ceylonese journalist has used the term *brown sahib* to refer to the members of the English-educated elite. They were English in customs, dress, manners, and habits of mind, and their estrangement from their less privileged compatriots increased by the year. Educated in the principles of British liberal democracy, this group began to perceive the indignities of colonial status and led the drive for independence from Great Britain. Nationalism before independence was largely a movement among this elite, the so-called educated natives, who felt they were fully capable of conducting a British-style parliamentary democracy without the tutelage of the mother country. When independence was granted, no mass feeling of nationalism or peoplehood had developed in Ceylon that included all communities such as came about in India during the protracted struggle for independence there.

In the early period of independence, therefore, Ceylon was governed by a moderate coalition of elite members of the various communities. The common people of all communities except the Burghers were effectively cut off from influence in government because all governmental functions were carried out in English and continued to identify with their ethnic communities. In 1946 a government commission studying the language question stated, "The present Government of this country is therefore, a Government of the Sinhalese- or Tamil-speaking 6.2 million, by the English-speaking 20,000 Government servants, for the 400,000 English-speaking public."

Throughout the period of hegemony of the English-speaking elite, parallel developments were taking place in the remainder of the population. Although the most influential people had been educated in English, since the 1880s over 80 percent of the students had been in vernacular schools. Although the demand for English education was great throughout the period, a shortage of trained English teachers prevented many from receiving the desired training. There was growing vernacular literacy throughout this period; in 1953 only one-seventh of the literate persons in the country could read English (see ch. 9, Education). A considerable Sinhala-educated intellectual group had developed, especially among the Kandyans, composed mainly of rural schoolteachers, traditional physicians, and *bhik-kus*. These men were effectively excluded from advancement and influence on any but a local scale.

Among this class a second, very potent form of nationalism began to assert itself about the time of independence. As the political balance of power in the country shifted in favor of the Sinhalese peasantry in the early 1950s, this group began to make its opinions felt on the national level (see ch. 14, Political Dynamics). The Sinhala-educated intellectuals were highly influential in the village scene but had not in the past exerted influence nationally. They believed that they had been unjustly excluded by the English-trained elite; they felt, with considerable justice, that they were better able to speak for the Buddhist villagers than were Christian Oxford graduates or barristers of the Inns of Court. By extension, they also felt that the Tamil community had taken an unfair share of power by virtue of their superior educational opportunities.

In addition, the old fears for the survival of Sinhala, Sinhalese culture, and Buddhism reasserted themselves. The Sinhala-trained intellectuals felt submerged in a sea of Christians and Hindu Tamil speakers. They felt that in its spiritual home Theravada Buddhism and the culture associated with it were not receiving sufficient support or respect. The culmination of these fears coincided with the Buddha Jayanti year, a worldwide celebration in 1956 of the 2,500th anniversary of the attainment of *nirvana* by the Buddha (see ch. 11, Religion). At that time a report by a prestigious commission on the allegedly deplorable state of the faith in Ceylon heightened these fears.

The new power of this Sinhala-trained group of intellectuals was quickly translated into a change in national government and a growing clamor for "Sinhala Only," the establishment of Sinhala as the sole official language, to the exclusion of Tamil and English, in order to guarantee Sinhala its "rightful place" in society. The fears of the Tamil community were immediately aroused, and tensions grew extremely high. In 1958 a series of serious incidents flared into widespread race riots, and hundreds were killed, thousands injured or forced to take refuge, and huge amounts of property destroyed before peace was restored (see ch. 3, Historical Setting; ch. 24, Public Order and Internal Security).

The communal issue continued to be sensitive for some time after the end of the violence. A bill to permit "reasonable use of Tamil" in government operations was passed, but regulations necessary for its implementation were not released until the early 1960s, when another change in government brought about a much more conciliatory attitude toward the Tamil minority. In 1966 Prime Minister Dudley Senanayake, a Sinhalese, went to Jaffna for the first visit by a prime minister in a decade.

During the period of the most fervent Sinhalese nationalism, the Ceylon and Indian Tamils began for the first time to show signs of growing solidarity. In addition, the Ceylon Tamil community has displayed increased interest in the Tamils of South India. Professional opportunities for Tamils have been narrowed to some extent, and there has been a limited migration of the educated of this community to other countries. A treaty was negotiated with India regarding the Indian Tamils. Most were to be repatriated to India, although a limited number of these people would be accepted as citizens and permanent residents of Ceylon. This community, therefore, gained a new legitimacy as a recognized addition to the population.

Although political relations between the two major communities deteriorated drastically during and immediately after the disturbances, the strife was largely confined to the political arena. In most cases the longstanding personal relations between individuals of different communities continued. During the 1958 communal riots, many cases of personal heroism were recorded in which members of one group were protected by members of another at great personal risk.

A significant change has occurred in the position of the English-speaking elite of all communities. Although still occupying a position of importance, this group is no longer receiving new recruits, as nearly all education is now taking place in the vernaculars. When the English school system, which had served as a bond and a channel of communication between the various communities, was switched to *swabasha* and the elite students were divided into language streams, communal consciousness appeared for the first time in this group. In addition, the symbols of English education and culture have suffered a certain loss of prestige (see ch. 12, Social Values). For example, politicians often wear local, as opposed to European, dress to underline their allegiance to the traditional culture; in addition, some elite Sinhalese who were raised as Christians have converted to Buddhism.

It is apparent that the reassertion of nationalist and traditional values in recent decades was the result of strains introduced into the social system by the colonial emphasis on European culture and language. In working out these strains,

91

society seems to be arriving at a new equilibrium that many Ceylonese feel is more suited to the social realities of the nation (see ch. 6, Social Structure).

LANGUAGES

Three languages have occupied positions of importance in the modern history of Ceylon—Sinhala, Tamil, and English. Sinhala and Tamil are both identified with specific ethnic communities and are prevalent in particular geographic regions (see fig. 8). By government action, English, which was once the exclusive governmental language, was replaced by the two vernaculars as the media of administration and education. It continued, however, to be used among the elite and, contrary to government policy, for some governmental functions. For example, the commissioner of official language was quoted in the press in January 1970 to the effect that, in general, the diplomatic missions to foreign countries conduct their business in English rather than Sinhala, although most of the personnel are fluent in Sinhala. Whether this situation is prevalent in other government agencies is not known.

Because of government policy, it is unlikely that English will long continue in a position of importance. Virtually all education now takes place in the vernaculars, except perhaps in the universities, where a lack of advanced textbooks in local languages is a problem. In 1968 the cabinet ordered that university instruction be in Sinhala. Since then there has been considerable agitation for a Tamil university as well. The press reports that the standard of English instruction is deteriorating in the rural schools. The examination system discourages continuation of English studies in the advanced grades (see ch. 9, Education). Therefore, although persons educated in English in decades past occupy posts of importance, the generation of the 1970s, upon reaching the same stage, will probably communicate in Sinhala or Tamil. English has also served as a medium of communication between the various communities.

In spite of these developments, in the past the position of English was extremely high. A nearly caste-like distinction separated those who spoke it from those who could not. In 1911 it was noted that over 2,000 Ceylonese, including 1,700 Low-Country Sinhalese, were literate in English but could not read or write their own language. Since independence the relative importance of English as a language of literacy has decreased. The overwhelming majority of Ceylonese who can read are literate in their native language (see table 4). Those who regularly read the newspapers depend primarily upon the vernaculars (see table 5). Nonetheless, a small, although sub-

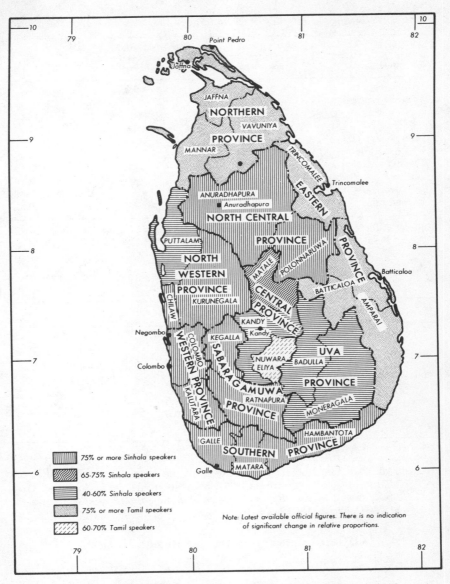

Figure 8. Major Languages Spoken in Ceylon by Districts, 1953

Source: Adapted from Robert N. Kearney, *Communalism and Language in the
Politics of Ceylon,* Durham, 1967, pp. 8-9.

stantial, segment of the population speak and read more than
one language (see table 6). A small but significant number
know both major vernaculars. In urban areas this group includes nearly one person in five.

Table 4. Percentage of Literacy of Ceylon Population, Age Five and Older, 1953

Ethnic group	Literate in native language	Not literate in native language but in another	Illiterate
Sinhalese	68.1	0.8	31.1
Tamils (Indian and Ceylon)	54.9	1.7	43.5
Moors	52.5	3.8	43.6
Burghers and Eurasians	74.2	14.9	10.9
Malays	20.5	47.2	32.4
Others Europeans, Veddahs	47.5	32.5	19.8

Source: Adapted from Robert N. Kearney, *Communalism and Language in the Politics of Ceylon,* Durham, 1967, p. 56.

Table 5. Percentage of Ceylon Population Who Regularly Read Newspapers, 1964

Language of publication	Men[1]	Women
Various (language not specified)	53.0	23.0
Only Sinhala	42.0	16.0
Only Tamil	3.0	1.0
Only English	3.0	4.0
English and Sinhala	4.0	3.0
English and Tamil	0.5	. . . .[2]
Sinhalese and Tamil	. . . .[2]	. . . .[2]

[1]104 males to 100 females, 1963.
[2]Too small a figure to be measured accurately.

Source: Adapted from Robert N. Kearney, *Communalism and Language in the Politics of Ceylon,* Durham, 1967, pp. 18-19; and Ceylon, Registrar General, *Report of the Registrar General of Ceylon on Vital Statistics for 1963,* Colombo, 1968, p. H-16.

Official Government Language Policy

The official language is Sinhala, but Tamil occupies the position of a secondary national language. In 1956 a bill, commonly known as "Sinhala Only," was passed, making that tongue the sole official language of the country. Agitation by the Tamil community brought about the passage of the Tamil Language (Special Provisions) Act of 1958, allowing for the "reasonable use of Tamil" in Northern and Eastern provinces. "Reasonable use" was defined as use in educational instruction, for entrance examinations of the civil service, and for "prescribed administrative purposes." Tamil-speaking persons were given the right to correspond with local and central gov-

94

Table 6. *Languages of Ceylon,*[1][2] *1953*

Language	Number	Percentage of population three years and older
Sinhala only	4,289,957	58.9
Tamil only	1,570,084	21.6
English only	14,066	0.2
Sinhala and Tamil	719,194	9.9
Sinhala and English	307,570	4.2
Tamil and English	146,549	2.0
Sinhala, Tamil, and English	233,567	3.2

[1]Spoken by population, age three and over; speaking is defined as ability to carry out short conversations or answer questions in the language.

[2]Latest available official figures.

Source: Adapted from Robert N. Kearney, *Communalism and Language in the Politics of Ceylon,* Durham, 1967, p. 17.

ernments in their own language. In addition, Tamils already on the civil service rolls were allowed to keep their positions. The administrative regulations necessary to carry out this act were not promulgated until the early 1960s.

Under the authority of the language legislation, the Department of Official Language Affairs was established at the national level to carry out programs necessary to the implementation of the new language policy. Sinhala-language instruction was organized. A study was made of the feasibility of typewriting and shorthand in Sinhala. All government forms were written in both Sinhala and Tamil. In the late 1960s work was proceding on an official dictionary; as part of this project, technical glossaries in Sinhala and Tamil were being prepared for all important scientific and technical fields.

Sinhala

Sinhala is an Indo-European language of the Indo-Iranian group and is derived from one of the Prakrits, or dialectal forms of Sanskrit, in use at the time of the settlement of Ceylon. By the beginning of the Christian Era, Sinhala had sufficiently diverged from Sanskrit through a process of independent evolution and from contact with Tamil to be considered a separate language. Pali, the holy language of Theravada Buddhism, is also a Prakrit.

A classical literary form of Sinhala developed, but in the fifteenth century it began to lose some of its original purity. At that time a written form based on the contemporary vernacular, which differed from the classical form, was also in use. In the eighteenth century a movement began to revive the "pure" classic form; this desire was heightened during the

95

British period as scholars strove to preserve the language and literature. In modern times the high literary grammar has been defended by academics and grammarians as the proper usage for literate discourse and discussions. Alongside the literary written form a more popular written form has developed that more nearly approximates the spoken standard and is used in the popular press and other writing for mass audiences. Throughout the country there exists considerable regional variation in spoken Sinhala and also variation based on class, caste, and educational level.

Tamil

Tamil is a language of the Dravidian family, the linguistic group that dominates South India. Dravidian is unrelated to Sanskrit or the Indo-European languages; some scholars believe it is associated with the Finno-Ugrian languages, which include Finnish and Hungarian. Tamil has nonetheless been influenced by Sanskrit and, in Ceylon, by Sinhala.

In Tamil, as in Sinhala, considerable regional variation exists, and the dialects of Ceylon differ substantially from those in India, especially among the Ceylon Tamils. In addition, there are several styles, often in the speech of one individual, to be used for various occasions. For example, there is a literary form used in formal discourse and writing, as well as a colloquial form used in informal conversation, along with different colloquials for different classes and regions. Sinhala and Tamil are written with different alphabets. The differences between the vernacular and literary forms of Tamil are so substantial that, even for a Tamil speaker, learning to read it, has something of the character of learning a new language.

CHAPTER 6

SOCIAL STRUCTURE

Alone among the world's Buddhist societies, Ceylon has a social structure based on caste. Although the precepts of the Buddha specifically reject caste distinctions, the system is apparently of great antiquity, probably antedating the advent of Buddhism on the island (see ch. 3, Historical Setting; ch. 11, Religion). Both the Sinhalese (see Glossary) and Tamils (see Glossary) are organized in this manner, but their systems differ significantly in detail (see ch. 5, Ethnic Groups and Languages).

Official Ceylonese government policy does not recognize distinctions of caste. The Social Disabilities Act assures all castes equal civil rights. A single pronoun is used for everyone in law courts and in most public meetings. The All-Ceylon Arunathethiyar Association tries to achieve civil rights for the depressed classes. Beginning in 1949, children of the Rodiya, a Sinhalese caste analogous to the untouchables, were accepted in public schools and, in spite of some initial resistance, integration proceeded smoothly. In general, approval of the more derogatory or demeaning traditional customs and terms is lessening, especially among the educated. Nevertheless, caste remains a social reality (see ch. 14, Political Dynamics).

Although the customs of the Sinhalese in the Kandyan region and on the coast are roughly similar, certain castes are locally prominent in given areas, and the greater conservatism of the highlanders emphasizes the importance of caste in that region. The Ceylon Tamil system, which differs from that of the Sinhalese in detail although not in overall structure, is probably a modification of a system brought to Ceylon many centuries ago. Caste among both the Sinhalese and Ceylon Tamils differs markedly from that found in India, primarily in that the position of the priestly Brahmin caste, dominant on the subcontinent, is nonexistent among the Sinhalese and minimized among the Ceylon Tamils. In addition, in both cases, the highest caste is also the most numerous.

The Indian Tamils, relatively recent arrivals from India, represent a variety of South Indian castes, primarily from the lower end of the spectrum. The other ethnic minorities, the

97

Muslims and Burghers, do not recognize internal caste but function as quasi-castes in the larger framework of society.

In mid-1970 the vast majority of the population continued to live in small villages where relationships follow lines of kinship and where families are known and have been resident for generations. In general, traditional social structure remains strongest in the Kandyan and Jaffna regions. A growing number of people, however, reside in cities and towns, where modern industrial and bureaucratic employment is more common. Relationships are more formal, and caste traditions have to some extent broken down. In the urban centers, primarily Colombo, caste is less important. Urban life is dominated by a middle class, largely educated in English-language schools, that staff the civil service and the professions. This group, which forms an influential elite, seems to be losing ground as a result of the emphasis on local languages (see ch. 5, Ethnic Groups and Languages).

The prestige attached to white-collar employment, particularly to the civil service, is very great. Although caste continues to form the basic framework of Ceylonese society, a class system is also developing based on the new occupations introduced by modern technology and bureaucracy. In addition, Western egalitarian views are beginning to erode the foundations of the caste system as lower castes, especially in the north, begin to demand equality.

THE NATURE OF CASTE

Recognition of caste differences permeates social life. In all parts of the country, especially in the rural areas, where the majority of the population resides, important elements of life are embedded in the matrix of the caste system. The matrimonial and family system, for example, can only be understood in terms of caste (see ch. 7, Family). A caste is a closed network of interrelated families occupying a fixed social position in relation to the other family groups in the given locality. Since people ordinarily marry only within their own caste, the proper functioning of the marriage system ensures that over a period of generations the families of a community remain in a roughly stable status relationship to one another. Caste standing is related to ritual purity in a religious sense; persons of lower castes are inherently impure and polluting (see ch. 11, Religion; ch. 12, Social Values). The salient features of social identity are inherited and fixed at birth; status within one's native village community ordinarily cannot be altered by any personal attainments.

On a practical level, caste is a local phenomenon. Although the system may be uniform over large parts of the country, the personal relationships of given individuals tend to concern people of one's own or neighboring localities. Persons from distant areas and, therefore, of unknown antecedents must be confirmed in a relevant caste position within the local system because otherwise they cannot function in village society. In some regions, especially in the dry zone (see Glossary), a sort of caste court rules on the eligibility of newcomers for membership in given castes and, therefore, for membership in the village community. Obviously, such a system is predicated on the relative rarity of strangers.

The castes are most often divided into subcastes and are ranked in general order of social status. Common agreement exists concerning the extremes of the continuum; among the several intermediate castes, however, there is often disagreement about the order of precedence. People jealously guard the prerogatives of status and avoid expressing subordination to another caste group not obviously superior. The order of precedence varies from region to region, and people familiar with custom in one area are not necessarily informed about other regions.

A caste is traditionally associated with a given trade, and the groups are commonly known by occupational titles. Throughout the island the dominant castes are the so-called cultivators—the Goyigama in Sinhalese areas and the Vellala among the Tamils. Other groups, such as fishermen, washers, makers of *jaggory* (a sugar confection made from palm sap), and drummers, are ranked below. It would, however, be inaccurate to suggest that all members of these latter castes earn their living through their caste occupations. Throughout the country the vast majority of families are engaged in cultivation; they may or may not also engage in a caste specialty.

Although it is misleading to suggest that all or even most members of the specialist castes practice their traditional craft, it may safely be assumed that, where those ritual or occupational functions are carried out in the village setting, it is a member of the appropriate caste who does so. In the countryside an individual would not presume to set himself up in the traditional occupation of a caste other than his own. Caste membership does not compel the individual to practice his traditional trade; rather, it provides him with a traditional monopoly opportunity to do so. In urban areas, however, some have entered traditional trades other than their own.

Although on the coast the performance of caste trades most often takes place in the context of purely contractual relations, in many areas the traditional trades are carried out as part of the ongoing relationships subsisting between families. Certain caste functions are tied to important religious rituals. For example, the washerman and his wife play crucial roles in the puberty and marriage ceremonies of the high castes. The tom-tom beaters and the *jaggory* makers are necessary in certain other rituals. The high-caste family is likewise obligated to provide certain fixed rewards for these specific services. Many highland individuals still carry out these services from a sense of caste obligation; they would not think of refusing. The money and other gifts received are more a symbol of mutual reciprocity than a payment for services rendered. Usually the payment made for caste services depends upon the status of the receiver rather than the nature of the service per se. It is generally agreed that working for others for pay is not appropriate to the highest castes.

Even in urban society a strong association remains between a given caste and a given traditional trade, especially those of drumming, fishing, and washing. Clothes washing was traditionally done on a personal basis in the home of the washer, but in 1970, in the urban areas, it was often done in commercial laundries. Nonetheless, the owners and employees of these establishments are almost universally of the appropriate caste. In areas in which specialist castes can sell their services in a money market outside of the traditional caste structures—for example, to Muslims, who do not recognize caste—they have achieved relative prosperity.

In the villages recognized symbols, such as dress, hairdo, ornaments, and family names, indicate an individual's caste or subcaste. Traditionally, the members of the lowest castes of both sexes were not permitted to cover their chests. Women customarily now do so, but some tradition-minded men do not. The right of the low-caste men to wear the *banian,* or sleeveless knit undershirt, was won over the opposition of the high castes. Any supposed presumption of the less privileged to the symbols of higher prestige—for example, the use of tiled roofs, automobiles, or expensive clothing—is resisted and resented.

Names also have important symbolic values and are thought to be inherently elevating or degrading. The Kandyan Peasantry Commission, in discussing ways to improve the condition of the Rodiya, the lowest caste, recommended that the government "remove the word Rodiya by legislation" and in this way automatically elevate their status (see ch. 12, Social Values).

Intimate contact with individuals of lower caste is ritually polluting (see ch. 11, Religion; ch. 7, Family). An elaborate etiquette therefore hedges the inevitable instances of contact between the castes. Both Sinhala and Tamil contain several second-person pronouns expressing superiority, equality, or inferiority. The gesture of salutation, placing the palms of the hands together with fingers up, can be varied depending on the status of the person greeted; the position of the hands in relation to the body indicates the status relationship.

Caste distinctions are most stringently observed in matters regarding the home. One's immediate neighbors are usually of the same caste and subcaste; in some cases whole villages contain only one caste. Multicaste villages are usually divided into separate caste wards or neighborhoods. Intimate neighborly visiting takes place only within the caste. The visit of a person of different caste to the home is a formal occasion. He is either a superior, honoring one's home with his presence, most often on ritual occasions, such as weddings, or an inferior who has come on particular business. In the former case the visitor is treated with elaborate courtesy, whereas in the latter he ordinarily remains on the veranda, occupying a seat reserved for those of inferior rank. Contact in public places, such as in the village lanes, fields, or shops, is less formal among acquaintances. Although the inferior must indicate his subservience through conventional courtesies, the conversation can nonetheless be informal and friendly. It is common to see persons of different castes chatting in the lanes of the villages.

Eating carries many symbolic overtones and is fraught with potential ritual pollution (see ch. 12, Social Values; ch. 7, Family). The etiquette of eating is very strict. Accepting food from a person of lower caste is, with certain specific exceptions, polluting. Although men of various castes working together in the field may take an informal lunch together, each caste ordinarily uses separate cups and utensils. In teahouses members of the lowest castes must stand outside and use their own drinking vessels, often a coconut shell rather than the glass or cup used by higher groups. When the government began a school lunch program, sensibilities were only satisfied by seating the children of various castes separately and using a high-caste cook. Food consumed within the home is subject to the most restriction among all groups, although particular regional customs vary in this regard. In general, there are few food prohibitions directly related to caste. Abstention from meat is primarily related to the devoutness of the individual rather than to caste position (see ch. 11, Religion).

Since the intimate contact of home and family is largely limited to members of one's own caste, the various caste groups resident in a village tend to form separate, self-conscious subcommunities. Nevertheless, community-wide facilities, such as temples and schools, are usually shared by all but the lowest castes.

Although caste represents ritual social standing or prestige, it is not strictly corelated with economic positions. Although more high-caste families are prosperous and fewer poor, on the average they have a standard of living indistinguishable from those of the other castes. The only groups that are uniformly deprived are the very lowest, the untouchable castes that tend to form depressed enclaves apart from the general population. Some individuals of the artisan castes have achieved considerable prosperity, particularly members of the Karava, or fisher, caste. In one case, for example, a man of the blacksmith caste who had amassed a considerable fortune in land employed Goyigama tenant farmers. The tenants, although of a higher caste, occupied a subservient position and therefore treated their employer with the courtesy reserved for a superior except that they did not demean themselves in the presence of others of their own caste.

Because of government policy, it is impossible accurately to estimate the populations of the various castes. The 1911 census is the last one to enumerate on that basis.

THE SINHALESE

The Kandyan highlands and the low country differ markedly in ecological characteristics, in historical development, and in the economic pursuits that characterize them. Consequently, the social structures of the two areas are different, corresponding to local conditions. Both systems are based on a roughly similar outline, but certain castes that fulfill locally significant functions are found only in one region or the other (see table 7). The caste systems of the two regions are roughly analogous; in conservative regions, however, members of a given caste do not necessarily recognize as equal those of castes in other regions who are in theory comparable.

Kandyan Region

Until the arrival of the British in 1815, Kandyan society was organized in a feudal system similar to that found in Europe in the Middle Ages. Robert Knox, the seventeenth-century observer of Ceylon, described the system succinctly: "The country being wholly his, the king farms out his land, not for money, but for service." Individuals of high caste who were

Rank	Caste name	Traditional function
High castes	Goyigama (Govi-vamsa)	Agriculturalists
	Radala	Holders of royal appointments
	Mudali	Popular leaders
	Patti	Cowherds to the king
Subcastes[2]	Katupulle	Royal clerks
	Nilamakkara	Temple servants
	Porovakara	Wood choppers
	Vahal	Domestic servants for the Radala
	Gattara	Goyigama outcaste
	Guruvo[3]	
	Karava[4]	Fishermen
Subcaste	Karava Porovakara	Not known
	Salagama[4]	Cinnamon peelers
Subcastes	Hevapanne	Soldiers
	Kurundukara	Cinnamon peelers
	Durava[4]	Toddy tappers
Low castes	Navandanna (Acari)	Craftsmen, including smiths
	Hannali[1]	Tailors
	Hunu	Burners of lime
	Hena (Rada or Dhoby)	Laundrymen for higher castes
	Vahumpura (Hakuru)	Jaggory (sugar confection) makers
	Hinna[4]	Laundrymen to Salagama
	Badahala	Potters
	Panikku[4]	Barbers
	Velli-durayi[2]	Keepers of the Sacred Bo Tree
	Panna-durayi[2]	Probably grass cutters
	Berava	Tom-tom beaters
	Batgam Berava[2]	. . do . .
	Kontadurayi[2]	Not known
	Batgam (Padu)	Bearers of king's palanquin
	Oli	Dancers
	Pali[1]	Laundrymen for low castes
	Kinnara	Mat weavers
	Gahala-berava	Drummers at funerals
	Rodiya	Beggars (analogous to untouchable)
Not included in hierarchy	Kavikara[2]	Temple (*devale*) dancers and singers
	Demala-Gattara[4]	Tamil outcastes.

[1]In approximate order of precedence.
[2]Found exclusively in Kandyan areas.
[3]Found primarily in North Central Province.
[4]Found exclusively in Low Country.

Source: Adapted from Bryce F. Ryan, *Caste in Modern Ceylon*, New Brunswick,
1953, pp. 93–94.

granted lands in return for specified services to the crown in
turn let their lands to vassals in return for specified services
and shares of the produce. The caste system meshed perfectly
with this feudal organization since each caste occupied a status

103

in the scheme and each social role was occupied by a person of appropriate caste and subcaste.

The social elite consisted of the noble families of high caste who held large land grants and owed the most prestigious services to the king. The lesser castes owed specific services to the nobles. The temples and monasteries had accumulated large parcels of land through donation and thus were also important landowners (see ch. 11, Religion). Temple lands were let to tenant cultivators who paid specified shares of the produce for the support of the *bhikkus* (see Glossary) and also performed specified ritual services, such as dancing, drumming, or providing ritual objects for the temple rituals.

Under the feudal system the Goyigama may not have been viewed as a caste but as that body of citizens who owed service obligations directly to the king. The lower service castes in turn owed service obligations to the Goyigama. The distinctions between the Goyigama subcastes seem to have been based on differing service obligations to the king.

The feudal system came to an end under the British. In 1833 the *rajakaria,* or obligated service of the subjects to the king, was ended, and in 1870 the Service Tenure Ordinance permitted the service tenure obligations to be paid in cash (see ch. 3, Historical Setting). In addition, large stretches of village and crown lands, which had been used as reserve and for shifting cultivation, were sold by the British to planters and speculators, thus introducing the plantation economy to the island and undermining the economic self-sufficiency of the village unit. Because very few Sinhalese wished to work for wages on the new plantations, the Indian Tamils began to be imported at this time to supply labor (see ch. 12, Social Values).

Although the feudal system is largely gone, a residue of social forms and attitudes remains. There still exists a class of leisured landlords, largely the descendants of the feudal lords. Lands are now generally held, and work is done on the basis of contractual relationships; few individuals are still paying old service tenure fees.

Important elements of the feudal system still remain, however, in the disposition of the temple lands. Kandyan temples and monasteries are said to control some 100,000 acres of land farmed ou: to tenants. Because the temples need the traditional caste services for their rituals, some of these tenants still fulfill the old service obligations. Some of the performers in the famous Kandyan Esala Perahera are fulfilling service obligations (see ch. 11, Religion). The chief *bhikkus* of the large monasteries function as important landowners; they tend to be a conservative influence, and most are members of the aristocratic Radala subcaste. The high-caste families who were influential in the feudal system in many cases remain so.

In modern Kandyan society more than half the population are Goyigama. Next in order of size are the Vahumpura, Navandanna, Hena, and Berava castes. Many of the remaining castes are represented by small groups; for example, the Rodiya, the lowest caste, probably number no more than several thousand.

Probably the most influential individuals on the local level are the *bhikku,* the schoolteacher, and the *ayurvedic* (indigeous system of herbal medicine) physician. Within the villages life is organized around the kin group. One authority maintains that probably no more than 25 percent of the heads of families belong to an organized association, club, or society. Most people are infrequent attenders of formal functions or entertainment other than religious observances.

Although there is a large number of castes, most communities consist of one or a few castes. Among the most isolated groups are the Rodiya, who traditionally are not permitted to live in villages with the higher castes. They are generally found in fairly isolated enclaves and have traditionally been institutionalized beggars. Their living conditions are generally inferior to those of the general population (see ch. 8, Living Conditions). Probably fewer than half are literate, and many suffer from unemployment. In recent years, however, attitudes toward the Rodiya have been softening, and many people now favor an improvement in their position, although most probably would not favor close social contact with them.

The Low Country

In social terms, the low country consists of a coastal strip, probably five miles wide, dominated by the Karava, and the interior low country, dominated by the Goyigama. The influence of the port cities, such as Colombo, is pronounced.

The lengthy European influence in the low country and the greater dynamism of the area's economy have produced a degree of social flux and mobility that distinguishes it from the relatively conservative highlands. Several important castes not found in the highlands exploit particular aspects of the low-country environment; prominent among them are the fishermen, cinnamon peelers, and toddy tappers. The elaboration of Goyigama subcastes is also lacking because of the absence of feudal obligations to the king.

The arrival of Europeans in the sixteenth century introduced important new economic opportunities and previously nonexistent channels for social mobility that were exploited by the more aggressive of the coastal people. Ambitious persons of relatively undistinguished standing in the traditional system were quick to respond to the new openings in commerce and government service. The Low-Country Sinhalese, who assimilated much of the European culture and many of whom became fluent in Portuguese and later in Dutch and English, were ideally situated to mediate between the Europeans and the conservative Kandyan Sinhalese who controlled desirable resources. Consequently, low-country castes of respectable but nonelite status were the major beneficiaries of the new conditions.

Under the Europeans the new opportunities were largely limited to Christians. Significant numbers, primarily of the upwardly mobile Karava caste, were converted to Catholicism under the Portuguese. Their descendants are the nucleus of the present-day Christian community. The Karava are divided into two religious groups—Catholic and Buddhist—which, apart from religion, are culturally similar and whose members marry almost exclusively within their own faith.

Although traditional social standing is related to caste, there exists a certain leeway for the rise of upwardly mobile groups. If a large discrepancy develops between ideal caste standing and actual social status measured in terms of wealth, education, influence, or power, a change eventually occurs in popular attitudes if not in the technical precedence of castes. Some authorities suggest that the Salagama, or cinnamon peelers, enjoyed such a rise in the early colonial period owing to the importance of the spice trade to the Portuguese and Dutch. Likewise, the Karava caste has come to dominate much of business and commerce in the low country and counts among its members some of the wealthiest families in the country.

The significance of class or achieved status in the low country is indicated by the structure of the Karava caste. This important group tends to break down along lines of class into three subgroups: village fishermen, who still follow the traditional occupation; tradesmen, artisans, and small businessmen; and white-collar and professional workers. Although blood relations between members of these strata are recognized and visiting occurs, marriage tends to follow the lines of class within the caste as a whole.

Probably three-quarters of the Low-Country Sinhalese are members of high castes, usually defined as Durava and above. Those services rendered by the specialist caste spring from contractual relationships; remuneration is in money, and considerations of caste-based mutual reciprocity are ignored.

THE TAMILS

Among the Hindu Tamils, the caste system is more clearly based on religious precepts than among the Buddhist Sinhalese (see ch. 11, Religion). It follows more closely the Indian scheme of organization upon which it is based. The Ceylon and Indian Tamils in effect form two separate societies and are organized under different caste systems. The Ceylon Tamils of Jaffna live under a caste organization of apparently great antiquity which, although based on Indian antecedents, is unlike that found in the subcontinent. The Indian Tamils are, in caste terms, transplanted members of the contemporary South Indian system. Drawn from numerous locations, they maintain identification with the Indian caste of their forebears. The social organization of the tea estates, however, conforms to the demands of production rather than to the norms of Indian behavior; although still observed, caste customs are not the decisive factor they are elsewhere on the island.

The anomalous position of the Brahmin, or priestly, caste distinguishes the Ceylonese situation from the Indian. On the subcontinent the Brahmins, as ritually the purest and temporally the most influential group, dominate society, despite their small number. In northern Ceylon, on the other hand, Brahmins, particularly the native born, are quite rare and do not occupy a position of secular power. Although ritually less pure, the Vellala, or cultivator, caste is both the largest and the socially dominant caste.

Approximately fifty castes and subcastes are found in the Jaffna region; only seventeen, however, were found in 1967 in more than eleven villages. Most are not numerous and are found in just a few villages. Many villages are composed of only one caste, and most do not include a full range of the castes found in the region. A few villages have representatives of fifteen or more castes (see table 8).

Because of the reverence in which they are held, the Brahmins are at the pinnacle of the social system. They are vegetarians, and nearly all are associated with temples, usually as the employees of the Vellala temple owners. Relatively few Brahmins have received the English secondary education characteristic of the Ceylonese elite, although they are learned in religious subjects.

Apart from religious considerations, the dominance of the Vellalas is nearly complete. They control most of the land and have maintained a virtual monopoly on higher education. It has been estimated that approximately 90 percent of the educated Hindus in Ceylon are of this caste, as are nearly all of the Hindu civil servants, professionals, and political leaders. Although the Vellalas work in white-collar occupations, many retain their

Table 8. *Major Castes Found Among Contemporary Ceylon Tamils[1]*

Category	Caste name	Traditional functions
Clean castes	Brahmin	Priests
	Vellala	Cultivators
	Chetty Vellala[2]	Merchant-cultivators
	Karaiyar	Fishermen
	Muchavar[2]	.. do ..
	Koviyar	Domestic servants to the Vellala
	Panchala	Craftsmen (roughly equal in status)
Subcastes	⎧ Thattar	Goldsmiths
	⎪ Collar	.. do ..
	⎨ Thachchar	Carpenters
	⎪ Sitpar	Masons
	⎪ Kammalar	Brass workers
	⎩ Kannar	.. do ..
	Nadduvar	Musicians
	Vannar	Washers to clean castes
Unclean castes	Ambattar	Barbers
	Palla	Coolies
	Nalava	Toddy tappers
	Kusavar	Potters
	Seneer	Weavers
	Kadaiyar	Lime burners
	Chakkilar	Leather workers
	Paraiyar	Scavengers and funeral drummers (untouchables)
	Thurumba	Washers to unclean castes (untouchables)

[1]In approximate order of precedence.
[2]Ritually equal to caste above.

Source: Adapted from James Cartman, *Hinduism in Ceylon*, Colombo, 1957, pp. 132–133.

lands in order to validate their status in the traditional caste system.

Although Vellalas form a larger percentage of the Ceylon Tamil population than do the Goyigama in the Sinhalese areas, caste distinctions are more strictly observed among the Tamils, and untouchability endures. Members of these deprived groups are politely called "minority Tamils" or "depressed classes." Energetic concern about ritual pollution is widespread. According to Hindu custom, pollution may occur by touch and, in the case of a very high caste person, by passing through the shadow of an inferior. Nonetheless, except in the case of a few devout individuals, the most stringent regulations are not followed, and custom is to some extent giving way to the exigencies of modern life. For example, passengers on public buses are not segregated by caste; only the most pious perform purificatory rites after such contact with strangers. Vellalas, however, observe caste prohibitions on certain foods. The most

108

devout are vegetarians; nearly all abstain from beef, pork, turtle, and certain fishes.

People carefully follow the etiquette of caste relations. The Tamil language contains three forms of the second-person pronoun to accommodate distinctions of rank. In addition, a low-caste person, when speaking with one of high caste, prefaces his remarks with the conventionally respectful "I think." Although the custom is dying out, some tradition-minded low-caste persons do not cover their chest and shoulders. The "unclean" castes are by tradition excluded from the temples. Although members of different castes may eat snacks together outside the home and in informal situations, such as buffets, any meal containing cooked rice is subject to caste restrictions. An interesting exception is found in the status of the Koviyar caste. Although subordinate to the Vellalas, they are apparently ritually their equals, for the Vellalas will accept food cooked by Koviyars and will attend their funerals, which are usually considered to be exceedingly polluting.

In recent years members of the lower castes have begun to rebel against the traditional indignities of their position. Harijans, or untouchables, have for some time been insisting on the right of temple entry. Some temples have been closed altogether to forestall this change in custom. In July 1968 Harijans attempting to enter the sanctum of the Maviddapuram Temple were repulsed by a crowd, and the subsequent rioting was put down by police using tear gas. Through the intervention of a government agent, some temples were thereafter opened to them. In the same year, barbers and restaurant owners refusing service to Harijans were prosecuted under the Social Disabilities Act. Members of "unclean" castes are also demanding the right to cremate their dead rather than bury them, which is considered an unclean practice. Although resisted by some, egalitarian attitudes are gaining considerable ground among the lower castes.

On the estates, which constitute largely self-contained social universes, the Indian Tamils represent a variety of castes. Although accurate statistics are not available, authorities believe that the majority are of low caste standing (see table 9). There is little social contact with the surrounding Sinhalese communities, and the Indian Tamils in no way participate in Sinhalese community life. Because of the nontraditional nature of estate work, most persons do not practice their original trades, although some perform work associated with their former caste specialties.

Even though work does not closely follow caste, traditions are observed in marriage, housing, and other matters. On the

Table 9. *Major Castes Found Among Indian Tamils in Contemporary Ceylon*[1]

Category	Caste name	Traditional functions
Kudianas (clean castes)	Vellala	Cultivators
	Chettiar[2]	Traders
	Retti (or Kapu)	Cultivators
	Kallar	Robbers (now frequently watchers on estates)
	Ambalakarar	Cultivators
	Andi	Beggars
	Panchala	Craftsmen
Subcastes	⎡Asari	Goldsmiths
	⎢Kammalagar	Brass workers
	⎨Kannar[2]	.. do ..
	⎢Thachchar	Carpenters
	⎣Kollar	Blacksmiths
	Ideiyar	Shepherds (now often carters and wheelwrights)
Non-Kudianas (unclean castes)	Kasavar	Potters
	Shannar	Toddy tappers
	Palla	Laborers
	Koravar	Gypsies
	Ambattar	Barbers
	Vannar	Washers
	Paraiyar	Funeral drummers (untouchables)

[1]In approximate order of precedence.
[2]Ritually equal to caste above.

Source: Adapted from James Cartman, *Hinduism in Ceylon*, Colombo, 1957, pp. 133–134.

estates, housing is usually provided for the workers and is assigned along lines of caste, although members of different groups might share a common public water faucet.

URBAN SOCIETY

In a large cosmopolitan urban center such as Colombo, social conditions are not entirely compatible with the social forms of traditional life. The special problems and opportunities presented by city life have altered much of traditional custom. Urban bureaucracy and industrial technology require trades and professions unknown to the caste system, and the introduction of jobs free from caste connotation has dramatically increased opportunities for social mobility. Although loath to enter a field associated with a different caste, persons of all social origins feel eligible for many newer types of endeavor, and the self-made man has become a social reality. There was in the traditional system no caste that corresponded to modern merchant or businessman. Because the members of the dominant Sinhalese caste consider such work demeaning, trade and commerce are largely dominated by Hindu Tamils and Christian Karavas, who took advantage of the opportunities offered by commercial development (see ch. 12, Social Values).

Over a period of several generations the British colonial educational system formed an English-speaking elite that has provided national leadership for most of the twentieth century (see ch. 5, Ethnic Groups and Languages; ch. 9, Education). Membership in this group, in many ways an assurance of privileged social and professional status, depends not on caste origin but on characteristics of education and culture, which could be acquired through proper training. Although the more prosperous members of the higher castes enjoyed certain advantages in gaining this education, persons of various religions and castes have also done so. For example, Sir James Pieris, a Christian Karava, was one of the early national leaders.

The greater anonymity of city life prevents the community intimacy required for strict maintenance of a caste system. It is possible for persons of dubious social background to pretend to higher status; an ironic phrase, "Colombo Goyigama," recognizes this possibility. In addition, caste is a taboo subject among the Western educated; discussion of it is considered somewhat uncouth and old fashioned. Usually strict Jaffna Tamils in Colombo are known to dine with members of other castes, which they would not do in the north. Children of different castes meet in the schools.

Marriages still generally follow caste lines; even the relatively sophisticated city dwellers who place marriage advertisements in English-language newspapers prefer to marry within their caste (see ch. 7, Family). It is only among the city-born slum proletariat, who are cut off from village ties and traditions, that caste endogamy is ignored; this is largely a symptom of the more general breakdown of the family in this group, rather than a rejection of caste per se.

In spite of their great influence, only about 7 percent of the population belong to the Westernized middle class elite. The remainder of the people, including the majority of city dwellers, are guided by traditional cultural values. Many who live in cities maintain strong ties to their native villages and are enmeshed in a social network similar to that of the rural dwellers.

Of the middle class group, not all are well-to-do. The middle class is distinguished largely by values and attitudes; the wearing of trousers and shoes instead of the indigenous dress is symbolic of middle class standing. Some have the requisite education but, because of the shortage of appropriate employment, lack the income to maintain the material side of a middle class life (see ch. 21, Labor). Approximately 4 percent of the population have an income that gives them a solidly middle class way of life. Less than 1 percent belong to the wealthy and sophisticated national upper class.

The middle class occupies the prestigious white-collar positions. Of all careers, government service is considered the most desirable, not only for the security of employment but also for the inherent prestige of the work (see ch. 12, Social Values). Within the government bureaucracy, although traditional caste distinctions are not observed in promotion, it is not common for workers to rise from the ranks to executive positions. Executives have been largely recruited by competitive examinations on liberal arts subjects, and therefore it has been difficult for those lacking elite training to qualify.

Because of the long domination of the Western-educated class, largely alienated from traditional values, considerable resentment built up against them, especially among the vernacular-educated rural leaders, such as *bhikkus, ayurvedic* physicians, and schoolteachers, who were cut off from power by the language bar, and also among urban workers. This feeling culminated in the abolition of English as the official language in the mid-1950s and the subsequent reorientation of national values toward the traditional culture (see ch. 5, Ethnic Groups and Languages; ch. 12, Social Values). As the importance of the elite English-language education diminished, the English-speaking elite became demoralized as a class and was removed from sole possession of power. Thus faced with the need for cultural reorientation and with somewhat straitened career prospects, a significant number of the university educated emigrated abroad. This exodus began in the late 1950s and continued into the 1960s, despite the government's attempts to stop it through travel restrictions.

Although the English-educated elite middle class continues to dominate government and professional life, this group no longer receives new recruits. The change in the educational system precipitated by the new language policy effectively ended the type of education that formed the mid-twentieth-century middle class (see ch. 9, Education). The children of middle class families are being trained in schools emphasizing communal differences to an extent not present under the former system and are forming less of a class consciousness.

The expanding pace of industrialization, the progress of government settlement schemes, and the influence of increasing transportation and mass media year by year uproot more in-

dividuals from the traditional village environment and introduce them to a less personal, more mobile way of life (see ch.
20, Industry; ch. 19, Agriculture). Land hunger is reaching
grave proportions in the countryside, and overpopulation is a
problem on the estates (see ch. 4, Population). Substantial
numbers of people therefore are leaving their native places,
thereby weakening somewhat, although not destroying, the
traditional social structure.

299-639 O - 79 - 9

CHAPTER 7

FAMILY

Social life centers on the family, and the married state is viewed as the natural and respectable condition for men and women. Except in the most cosmopolitan or Westernized circles, there is little social contact with persons outside the boundaries of kinship. Each major ethnic group—Sinhalese, Tamils, Muslims, and Burghers—organizes family life according to its own system, and there is very little intermarriage between communities (see ch. 5, Ethnic Groups and Languages). Marriage, family life, and inheritance within the several groups are governed by a variety of codes. Among the highland Sinhalese, traditional Kandyan law prevails, whereas the Jaffna Tamils follow the Thesavalmai, a code derived from South India. Roman-Dutch law is in force among the Low-Country Sinhalese, and the Muslims are subject to their own customary law (see ch. 13, The Governmental System).

Family life among the Burghers is organized along European lines. There is no caste system or preferred marriage partner. They are monogamous and observe family obligations according to the Western model. In the Dutch Burgher community an important consideration in the choice of a spouse is the alleged purity of European descent maintained within family lines.

In spite of significant differences in family arrangements, however, all groups except the Burghers share significant features of organization. Family interests are the overriding consideration in marriage, and arranged matches are the rule in all groups. Marriage is permissible only within the limits of a specified and circumscribed group that is divided into categories of appropriate and inappropriate marriage partners. Among the Sinhalese and Tamils, the numerous castes and subcastes are endogamous. The Muslims, although lacking castes, marry exclusively within their own religious community.

Among the Sinhalese, the nuclear household (a man, his wife, and their children) is ordinarily the basis of family life; marriage is usually monogamous; although not recognized by the government, polygyny (marriage of one man and several women) and polyandry (marriage of one woman and several men) are known and socially accepted among the Kandyans. The Muslims and Tamils, who more frequently live in extended households, are strictly monogamous. Sinhalese and Tamil households tend to be grouped into larger kinship bodies that lack strong lineal organization, whereas the Muslims emphasize matrilineal descent.

Men are dominant over women in all groups. The woman's primary responsibility is as a housewife, and most husbands do not encourage independence in their wives. Nevertheless, women enjoy legal equality with men and equal property and inheritance rights. They have considerable freedom of movement, except for marriageable young girls, who are carefully chaperoned among the Muslims, Tamils, and Low-Country Sinhalese.

Social change and widespread education have to some extent undermined the functioning of extended family groups in the urban areas. The general outlines of kinship behavior, however, remain unchanged.

FAMILY AND KINSHIP

The caste system, the basic organizing principle of Ceylonese society, is a crucial consideration in the functioning of the kinship system (see ch. 6, Social Structure). In essence, the caste system rests on two functioning requirements: endogamy and the concept of pollution. In accordance with Hindu beliefs, which are widely shared by Buddhists, each caste group is seen as occupying and representing a certain level of ritual or spiritual purity (see ch. 11, Religion; ch. 12, Social Values). Higher ritual levels can be polluted by those lower, and it is incumbent upon each group to protect itself from defiling intimacy with lower ranking individuals.

Superficial pollution may be countered by purifying acts, but serious or permanent pollution renders the individual unfit to associate with members of his caste. The most serious pollution results from the pollution of the internal organs by defiling substances. Consequently, sexual intercourse with a person of a lower caste will cause a woman grave pollution, whereas that resulting to a man in the same circumstances is merely superficial. On the other hand, the eating of food prepared by members of a lower caste will gravely pollute both sexes. The sexual activity of women and the cooking and eating of food are therefore closely tied to caste purity and must take place exclusively within the caste; although men may keep concubines of low caste standing, they scrupulously avoid eating foods prepared by them. In addition, cooking, eating, and marriage are strongly related symbolically, especially among the

116

Kandyan Sinhalese. For example, women commonly refer to their husbands as "the one I cook for." A man's refusal to accept food from a concubine symbolizes that they are not bound in marriage. A Muslim woman does not cook for her father-in-law, who is a forbidden marriage partner.

Marriage ordinarily takes place within a given caste and most frequently between residents of the same or nearby localities. A consequence of local caste endogamy over a number of generations is that local caste groups are extremely inbred and, from the viewpoint of the individual, nearly all members are kinsmen, often related to one another by multiple ties. All relationships of blood or marriage through either parent are recognized. Nearly all potential spouses are therefore members of one's own local kin group. The local caste group may be viewed as a number of related families.

The family system is explicit in its approval of this situation. The systems of kinship terminology and relationships function in such a way as to encourage and virtually require marriage between specified relatives. Although different kinship terms are used in Sinhala and Tamil, the kinship concepts they represent are similar. In common with many systems in South India, the terminology distinguishes cross-cousins (the children of mother's brother or father's sister) from parallel cousins (children of father's brother or mother's sister). The preferred marriage partner is the cross-cousin or anyone who occupies that position by extension of the system (for example, the cross-cousin of a parallel cousin). The parallel cousin is forbidden as a sexual or marriage partner, and such a relationship is viewed with abhorrence. It is believed that siblings of the same sex have the "same blood" and that their children, therefore, are too closely related to be suitable spouses. In keeping with this view, the same term is applied to one's own siblings and to parallel cousins.

As a result of this distinction, all members of one's own generation in one's own caste are divided into two categories: those with whom sexual relations and marriage are forbidden, and those with whom they are allowed and even required. Marriage outside one's own generation is not approved. The terms for cross-cousins, in fact, carry a definite sexual overtone; it is considered extremely lewd to apply them to a person in the class of forbidden partners. This distinction also applies in the senior generation. The parents of all forbidden individuals are called by the same terms as one's own mother and father. The parents of the permissible partners are called by different terms, which imply at the same time, for example, mother's brother and father-in-law. The children of all forbidden marriage partners in one's own generation are called by the same terms as one's own sons and daughters, whereas those of all in the permitted category are called by terms implying nephew or niece and son-in-law or daughter-in-law.

The extended kin group therefore consists of a number of individuals who perpetually stand in relations of blood and potential marriage to one another. It is expected that any future marriage will reinforce the preexisting structure of relationships. The cross-cousins thus have specific and recognized claims on one another. A man in the class of permissible marriage partners (*massina*), who is in fact the mother's brother's son or the father's sister's son, in Sinhala is called by that woman *avassa* (necessary) *massina,* implying that she should necessarily marry him. In Tamil the same concept is expressed as *sonda.* In the Kandyan marriage ceremony a woman who is marrying a man other than her *avassa massina* must ritually ask him to relinquish his claim and gain his permission to leave with her bridegroom. Marriage between the expected cousins causes no alteration in kinship relations within a family group, and many Kandyan Sinhalese omit the wedding ceremony in this case.

Although many marriages take place within the limits of one's own kin group, for various reasons marriages are frequently contracted with other, unrelated families. In such an instance the pending marriage becomes a matter of interest to a wide circle of people and is the subject of elaborate negotiations. A marriage outside the family circle will, in tradition-minded families, be arranged by the parents. Sometimes the initial contacts are made through mutual friends or relatives, or a professional marriage broker.

Among the Sinhalese and Tamils, acceptable marriages occur only between equals; the spouses must be of the same caste and, frequently, of the same subcaste. In Sinhala the word *sambandha,* in addition to being a respectable term for sexual intercourse, also means marriage and equality. Although men may have sexual relations with women of lower caste, women do so only with men of their own or a higher caste. To state that "we do not marry them" is to imply social distance and inequality. Other considerations in a marriage are property or dowry prospects, health, reputation and, possibly most importantly, the congruence of the prospective spouses' horoscopes (see ch. 11, Religion).

Since marriage is embedded in a matrix of kinship relations, which implies that it takes place between kinsmen, marriage between unrelated families produces ties of fictitious kinship between the in-laws. Some observers suggest that a primary motivation in marriages of this sort is the formation of advantageous bonds with new relations in distant localities. The same kinship terms are applied to the new in-laws as to one's own relatives. The new son-in-law, for example, is called by the father-in-law the terms meaning both son-in-law and sister's son. The bridegroom's father, from the point of view of the father-in-law, becomes equivalent to wife's brother or sister's husband, and the bridegroom's other relatives are integrated into the system in congruence with their relationships. It is considered impolite in some regions to refer to the fact that the newly related families have not always been kinsmen. In many cases subsequent marriages occur between the two groups, further cementing relationships.

Among the Sinhalese peasants, marriage is often an informal manifestation of an existing and implicit kinship relationship, and few marriages among them are registered. Among Moors, Tamils, and urban populations, however, registration and wedding ceremonies are much more common. In urban centers, where life is more impersonal, people do not expect marriages necessarily to take place among kinsmen. Nevertheless, caste restrictions, although less rigid, are followed among the English educated, except in the most cosmopolitan Westernized circles, even by Christians.

Marriage arrangements are often more formal in cities, with more use of professional marriage brokers to find a suitable mate. Some people also resort to advertisements in newspapers, both in English and local languages. The advertisements tend to emphasize caste standing, professional prospects or dowry, and religion, indicating the pragmatic considerations that dominate matrimonial arrangements. Romantic love of the Western type is only rarely a factor, appearing primarily in university circles, where young people of diverse backgrounds mingle relatively freely. Although in the vast majority of cases the final decision is made by the parents, the preferences of the young people are increasingly taken into account.

ROLES AND RELATIONSHIPS

The family is the center of social life, and nearly all adults are married. It is dishonorable for a father not to arrange suitable matches for his marriageable daughters or, in the case of the father's death, for their brother not to do so. People usually marry in their later teens or early twenties, although since the mid-twentieth century the tendency has been toward later marriage for young persons pursuing higher education.

Within the family the man is dominant, in spite of the

119

theoretical equality of women. The sexes do not ordinarily take meals together, except for the symbolic meal that man and wife share as a part of the wedding ceremony. Typically, the women wait on the men, and then women and children eat after the men have finished. This is not to imply, however, that the women have no influence in the family.

Although the prospective bridegroom usually can veto an undesirable match, the bride has no such prerogative and is expected to accept her parents' judgment. Likewise, after marriage her wishes are subservient to those of her husband, except insofar as she may exert influence through their personal relationship. In many areas women were traditionally viewed as legal minors. The Hindu wife is supposed to revere her husband as a lord. It is also believed that women are ritually inferior, because of the *kili* (ritual pollution) associated with puberty, childbirth, and the menses. Women in these conditions are "untouchable" and are secluded until purified by appropriate rituals.

The distinction between the roles and spheres of men and women is clear. The man is responsible for the provision of food, clothing, and other necessities, for the construction and maintenance of the house, and for the management of property and finances. The wife's obligations include preparation of food, care of the home and children, and possibly certain specified agricultural tasks. In the Kandyan region she may not, for example, take part in the threshing of rice, which is very pure, for fear she will pollute both it and the threshing floor, harming future harvests.

In tradition-minded families, the distinction between the men's and women's spheres is symbolized by the fact that the husband sleeps in one room and the women and children in another, with the husband "visiting" the wife. In the Kandyan region the wife sleeps in the room containing her cooking place, the symbol of her marriage. The fact that she cooks for her husband is a symbol of their married state, and no marriage is considered to exist without a separate hearth. In Westernized or Christian families, custom follows Western practice in this regard. Households may consist of a single nuclear family, several related nuclear families, or a family and miscellaneous relatives. Each nuclear unit cooks and eats separately.

During the twentieth century women of the middle and upper classes have begun entering the professions and other skilled occupations (see ch. 21, Labor). In 1958, for example, the women entering the University of Ceylon outnumbered the men. In spite of the growing numbers of women in these occupations, however, the ideal woman remains the housewife, not the independent career woman or working wife. Urban men of the educated upper and middle classes generally still prefer a wife with a dowry to one with an education. In the urban working class and lower middle class, some men desire wives who will work when necessary to meet expenses; they prefer, however, that the wife stay home as long as finances permit. Many parents still elect to earmark funds for a dowry rather than for higher education preferring to teach their daughters various accomplishments, such as music, that are thought to make them attractive wives. In some cases the marriage agreement stipulates as a condition of the match that the wife will never work; such agreements are sometimes even made involving university-educated women. Some conservative men resent women driving automobiles as a sign of unseemly independence.

Parents desire sons more than daughters. Although the first daughter is greeted with joy, subsequent girls are less welcome. The birth of many daughters and few sons is viewed as the result of bad *karma* (rebirth according to one's merit) (see ch. 11, Religion). Among the Hindus a son is required to light the parents' funeral pyre, to perform other funeral ceremonies, and to carry out the *tivasham* (a ceremony performed on the anniversary of the parents' death).

During pregnancy the mother may observe certain taboos, depending upon her religion. The exact time of birth is carefully noted, for this determines the child's horoscope, which is important throughout his life (see ch. 11, Religion). During early childhood the family festively celebrates milestones, such as the first eating of solid food, the first haircut, the learning of the first letters and, for girls, ear piercing. As children, the sexes enjoy equal freedom. Children mix freely, but their playtime diminishes, especially for girls, as their responsibilities increase. By the time a rural girl reaches puberty, she has little time to devote to anything other than schoolwork and household chores. She helps her mother in all types of housework and the care of younger children. The burden of work eventually becomes so heavy that many regard birth as a woman as a sign of bad *karma*. Her brother is meanwhile learning the techniques of the family trade from his father, in addition to attending school.

The first menstruation is a major milestone in the life of a female; it marks her transformation from a girl into a marriageable woman. The family and community take note of the occasion with elaborate rites, including seclusion of the girl for periods ranging up to a month, ritual purification, and performance of special ceremonies. Puberty rites are observed in both urban and rural families. When she emerges from seclusion, the young woman is in many areas considered a fully marriageable woman and is sometimes married shortly thereafter. Her chastity and good reputation are matters of concern to the family, which often feels that its women are the repositories of the family's honor. The girl is usually chaperoned until her marriage. Concern for the chastity of daughters is especially marked among the Hindus and Low-Country Sinhalese. Among the Hindus, marriage is a religious sacrament, and the delivery of a virgin bride is a major responsibility of the parents. In both groups the groom's family has the right to inspect the sheet used on the marital bed on the first night for proof of virginity.

Except in the most Westernized circles, such as at the university and in the Burgher community, free social contact between the sexes ends at puberty. In some rural areas girls are withdrawn from school at that time. Often the wearing of the sari, as opposed to the Western frocks worn during childhood, begins at puberty. In any case most Ceylonese women after marriage wear the sari exclusively.

Within the family, relationships are marked by obedience and respect, in addition to love and affection. Children are subservient to adults, women to men and, within a generation, younger siblings to elder. Relations between spouses may be formal, especially in the countryside where men and women rarely mingle socially. Marks of respect, such as refraining from eating or smoking in the presence of elders, are carefully observed. The respect relations observed among siblings are of some importance, and the kinship terms used for siblings indicate relative age. There also exist in some regions conventional joking relationships with certain specified kinsmen. Ordinarily these relationships exist between men, cross-cousins of the same sex, who ideally should become brothers-in-law. Informality and humor, rather than respect, characterize these relationships, regardless of the age of the individuals involved.

SINHALESE

Kandyan Sinhalese

Marriage in the highlands is part of a matrix of kin relationships. It is assumed that all marriage takes place between persons standing in the correct degree of relationship. Since in such cases appropriate relationships predate the marriage, the marriage ceremony is not necessary. A formal wedding is only needed to set up new relationships between previously unrelated families. The Kandyan Law Commission, appointed in 1927 to codify the traditional usage, noted that "In early times the conducting of a daughter by a man of equal caste with the consent of her relations constituted a marriage, particularly in the case of persons of low rank who could not afford costly ceremonies." The report continued, "It must be remembered that when ... writers speak of illegitimate children they refer rather to the issue of a marriage which was considered improper or irregular, in the sense, for instance, that the parties to it were of different castes, than to the issue of a casual connection, the word illegitimate not necessarily implying the non-existence of marriage."

The legitimacy and inheritance rights of a child are determined by the social positions of his parents, rather than by the performance of a ceremony or the lack thereof. Property is held individually under Kandyan law; the spouses do not merge their property into a common estate. The children therefore inherit from each parent individually. Should a person have children by more than one spouse, all the offspring receive an equal share of the inheritance. Since marriage can be begun by an unceremonious setting up of housekeeping, its dissolution is also simple. Divorce and remarriage are common for both sexes.

Marriage takes a variety of forms in the highlands. Two forms of residence are recognized: the *deega* union, in which the woman moves to the man's house, and the *binna,* in which the man lives in the woman's house. The latter, less common form ordinarily involves a wealthy wife and a relatively poor husband; it is a method by which a well-to-do family that lacks sufficient sons induces a man to join the household. The *deega* is the more common type. In many cases, however, the form of residence rule is an academic question, because the family lacks significant property and the marriage takes place within a village or neighborhood. In a *deega* marriage the husband and his in-laws are bound by a relationship of diffuse reciprocal obligations. In the *binna* union the husband works lands belonging to his wife or given him by his father-in-law; he is therefore in a less independent position.

Marriage should take place between equals. All respectable marriages are within a caste; the various castes, however, are divided into a series of levels, sometimes called *wamsa,* according to the relative respectability of the family name and reputation. In addition to its *wamsa,* the family's wealth is also taken into account; these two factors together form its *tatvaya* (level) or relative social standing. Although a woman rarely marries a man of lower *wamsa,* a man may do so, if inequalities in *wamsa* are compensated by a sufficient dowry.

A dowry is given in the highlands only to equalize differentials in social position. The size of the dowry, if any, is up to the discretion and capability of the parents. Families sometimes give the major portion of the inheritance of all their children as a dowry for one in order to establish a connection with a particularly influential or important family.

Dowries are not paid to equals or to kinsmen. People of moderate means most often conserve their resources by marrying their daughters within the local family. Some observers believe that conservation of capital is an important motive behind the system of prescriptive cross-cousin marriage. The dowry, if any, is negotiated formally, is agreed upon before the wedding, and is paid at the wedding. Receipt of a dowry usually disqualifies a girl from further inheritance. The importance of equality between families who contemplate intermarriage is underlined by the fact that when preliminary inquiries between two unrelated families prove promising, the boy's family indicates through the intermediary that they would like to "eat rice and betel" with the family of the girl; as already indicated, in Ceylon society only equals eat together.

Marriage is generally monogamous. In some cases, however, a wealthy man may keep more than one wife, usually in separate households. At times a man of high position keeps a concubine of a lower caste. There is never any question of such unions constituting a true marriage. The children take the inferior caste of their mother and are usually excluded from their father's estate.

Although rare and considered somewhat uncouth, polyandry is an acceptable form of marriage. Polyandrous households often are formed by brothers who induce a woman to keep house for, and cohabit with, each of them. She is considered equally the wife of each, and any children are considered to be of each father; children distinguish between their "older" and "younger" fathers. In this way the men must only bear the expense of one household, and they produce fewer heirs than if each were married monogamously. Family property is therefore conserved, and the risk of the family being left without a breadwinner is lessened.

Polyandrous households may also be formed by unrelated men who agree to contribute their earnings to a common household. The husbands, of course, must stand in an appropriate relationship to one another and to the women in question. Such households can function with little friction if the men get along well, as the relationship between spouses is not expected to be companionate and may be somewhat formalized.

Low-Country Sinhalese

Marriage among the Low-Country Sinhalese is governed by Roman-Dutch law rather than Kandyan law (see ch. 13, The Governmental System). Under this system community property is held jointly and, upon the death of one, the surviving spouse and children inherit. Dissolution of marriage is therefore more complicated than in the highlands, and marriages are accordingly stronger.

The marriage system is essentially similar to that found in the Kandyan region except for the fact that the dowry custom is much more prevalent. It is considered dishonorable to marry off a daughter without a dowry; even the poorer people follow this custom to the extent of their means. Hypergamy, or the marriage of a woman to a man of higher status, is quite general in the lowlands; ideally, the bridegroom should be of slightly higher standing than the bride.

Marriage arrangements and family life among the Low-Country Sinhalese are more patrilineally oriented than in the Kandyan region. *Binna* marriage is regarded with scorn. The chastity of the bride is of great concern to the bridegroom's family, and the sheet used on the wedding night is ceremonially inspected by the bridegroom's mother. In some marriage ceremonies, especially those of the Karava caste, the bridegroom is treated as an honored guest, in accordance with the expectation that he will be of somewhat superior status. Although marriage within the family is considered appropriate, it is less prevalent than in Kandy.

The dowry is collected by the bride's father from his own resources and contributions by close kinsmen, including the bride's mother's brothers, her father's brothers, and her brothers and brothers-in-law. The obligations to help in dowry payments are considered binding debts that can be discharged in no other way. In the future the father of the bride will in turn be obligated to help those kinsmen who contributed to his daughter's dowry.

TAMILS

The Tamils of Jaffna follow the marriage rule of the Thesavalamai, a customary code that is valid in that area (see ch. 13, The Governmental System). Property is held jointly by both spouses. The dowry can only be disposed of by both spouses acting together. If a wife dies without children, her dowry is returned to her parents, who can, however, claim only the particular items of property and money given by them. Some couples therefore sell their dowry property and buy other property of the same value in order to prevent this. All of a parent's offspring, with the exception of women who have received a dowry, inherit equally.

The marriage system of the Tamils is essentially similar to that of the Sinhalese, with cross-cousin marriage the preferred form. Marriage is a religious sacrament in Hinduism, however, and a formal ceremony marks its establishment. During this ceremony prayers are offered to the god of prosperity and the god of fire, symbolizing the domestic hearth (see ch 11, Religion). The *tali,* a gold necklace representing the married state, is tied around the bride's neck by the bridegroom, in a ritual analogous to the exchange of wedding rings.

A dowry is given in all respectable marriages, the amount of the dowry being related to the economic standing and prospects of the bridegroom. Members of the more prestigious professions receive larger dowries than others (see table 10). Ordinarily, the cost of the bride's education must be subtracted from this amount. Young men planning expensive programs of higher education abroad frequently contract marriage before their departure, and the bride's family underwrites all or part of the educational expenses. A civil marriage is performed at that time, and a religious ceremony upon the man's return. The couple do not live together until after the religious ceremony.

Remarriage of widowers is acceptable; men often marry a sister of the deceased wife. The remarriage of widows, although legally permitted, is not considered socially acceptable and is relatively rare.

Adoption is fairly uncommon among the Tamils, and adoptive children are not usually accepted as full family members, often being treated more as domestic servants. The fact that an adoptive child may marry a legitimate or another adoptive child of his adoptive parents indicates that he is not seen as standing in the relationship of a true kinsman. Ordinarily, a child is adopted when his own family cannot properly support or educate him; the true parents and other kin of the child must consent at a public ceremony before witnesses. If a child is formally adopted by a man, he receives his adoptive father's caste; if, however, a woman is the only adopting parent, he retains his own.

MUSLIMS

The Muslim communities of Eastern Province, although using a kinship terminology similar to that of the other communities,

Table 10. *Representative Dowries Received by Bridegrooms in Selected Professions in Jaffna, Ceylon, in 1949*

Profession of Bridegroom	Dowry (in thousand rupees)*
Ceylon civil servant	100
Doctor (British trained, in government service)	80
Barrister at law	80
Advocate	75
Doctor (British trained, in private practice)	75
Doctor (Ceylon trained)	60
District revenue officer	60
Engineer	60
Graduate teacher	50
Proctor	50
English-language-trained teacher	40
Clerical servants (2d class)	40
Subinspector of police	30
Excise inspector	30
Clerical servants (3d class)	25

*Before 1952 the rupee did not have a par value; its relationship to the dollar was maintained through its fixed relationship with the pound sterling. After November 1967 par value was RS 5.95 equal US$1.

Source: Adapted from James Cartman, *Hinduism in Ceylon*, Colombo, 1957, p. 165.

organize marriage around the principle that the husband assimilates himself into the family of his wife. Property is inherited in the female line, and the husband lives in the home of the wife's father. Although property is ostensibly owned by women, as symbolized by the fact that husbands refer to their wives as "the owner of the house," it is nonetheless the men who manage property and finances and dominate home life and society.

The family, or *kudampam*, is seen as consisting of a group of sisters and their daughters. Men born into the family are tangential members who will ultimately owe first allegiance to another house. Nevertheless, men retain lifelong obligations to their own family. Men who marry into the family are "strangers," who gain influence with time. The wife cooks for her husband and also, symbolically, for her father and brothers. A man may never eat at the home of his brother's wife, for her people are "strangers." The marriage ceremony makes explicit the adoption of the husband by the wife's family. The bridegroom accepts a bowl of milk from the bride's mother, exclaiming that it is as good as that he received from his own mother. For the first six months of married life, the mother-in-law, rather than the wife, cooks for the man; within the wife's family he is called *maru mahan* (unborn son), emphasizing that, although a member of the family, he was not born into it. Unlike the customs of the other communities, the wedding procession begins at the bridegroom's house and conducts him to the bride's house.

It would be misleading, however, to equate this form of marriage with the seemingly similar *binna* marriage of the Sinhalese. Under the *binna* system the husband occupies a decidedly inferior position. Marriage among the Muslims, however, includes a sizable dowry paid by the bride's family to the groom; the emphasis is upon inducing a good son-in-law to join the family. The husband negotiates the dowry payment from a position of strength, and after marriage he controls his own property. Marriages in which the couple reside with the husband's family are extremely rare, involving a woman of markedly low status and usually being contracted only in special circumstances.

Weddings are attended by religious ritual and are recorded by the local Palliya Jamaat (Mosque Council), under whose jurisdiction the families live. Marriage is binding, extending even after death. In case of divorce, the husband pays to the wife's family the *mahar*, an amount of money agreed upon during the marriage negotiations, and returns to them the cash part of the dowry. Upon the death of a married man, the eldest son at the deathbed offers to pay his mother the *mahar* in his father's name, giving her the opportunity to dissolve the marriage posthumously. The mother's refusal indicates that the marriage was satisfactory and absolves the dead husband of all obligations to her. Because of the permanent nature of marriage, casual unions are scorned, and unmarried girls are chaperoned.

Although the Muslim custom of *purdah,* or seclusion of women, is not strictly observed, women do cover their heads and faces in the presence of strange men. A ritual avoidance is also practiced between the real, rather than classificatory, mother-in-law and son-in-law. A man rarely visits the home of his son's wife, so that a similar avoidance may be said to take place between daughter-in-law and father-in-law. No woman cooks for for her husband's father because of the strong sexual connotation of exchange of food. Unlike Muslims in other countries, the Ceylon Moors are strictly monogamous; they recognize the Quranic approval of polygamy but believe it inappropriate in their country.

Marriage negotiations are usually initiated by the girl's family, frequently through the good offices of a son-in-law. The cross-cousin marriage is preferred, and the sons-in-law, especially the senior one, are expected to aid in arranging advantageous marriages for their sisters-in-law. As a result, subsequent marriages often take place between members of the same two families who were involved in an earlier satisfactory match. The relationship between brothers-in-law, who reside in the same household as adults, is very significant for the smooth functioning of a family.

299-639 O - 79 - 10

CHAPTER 8

LIVING CONDITIONS

The level of general health and the standard of living were higher in 1970 than the average for South Asia. Famines continued to be practically unknown, and storm damage, except for occasional floods, was rare. The government has been energetic and efficient in conducting antidisease programs, with the result that malaria, cholera, smallpox, and poliomyelitis have been virtually eliminated from the island.

Public health, sanitation, and some welfare services have increasingly been the concern of the central government since the first attempts to control communicable diseases were made in 1866. Since 1931 preventive as well as curative services have been the responsibility of the government at the local as well as the central level. The various types of medical institutions include provincial and district hospitals, rural hospitals, maternity homes, specialized clinics, and health centers. Special medical treatment is free of charge to people whose income is below a certain level; costs are nominal to people above this level. Public medical care is free, as is education.

The government has undertaken the task of relieving an acute housing shortage in the urban areas by building low-rent homes and apartment complexes and by making loans to individuals who want to build their own houses. New government-built homes have running water and electricity, although these utilities had not reached the majority of rural villages by 1970. Rural dwellings were generally airy and uncrowded, however.

There continued to be marked differences in living standards between social classes and between rural and urban dwellers (see ch. 6, Social Structure). The government worker, for example, indicated his generally higher economic standing in the community by his dress and type of housing. If discontent with inequities in living standards was felt, it was not usually expressed in a violent manner. The general attitude appeared to be that it was better to preserve old traditions and values than to sacrifice them for the sake of making more money (see ch. 12, Social Values).

Although many people had adopted Western ways of dressing, furnishing their houses, and using leisure time, tradition

131

still played an important role in the life of people throughout the country in their selection and cooking of food, choice of medical care, dress, and attitudes toward employment, education, and health practices. The *ayurvedic* (indigenous system of herbal medicine) practitioners, who use healing herbs to treat the sick, were still favored by many people and were recognized by the government. Traditional distaste for manual labor manifested itself in an acute shortage of technical and skilled labor. The relationship between good health and good sanitation practices was still not fully understood by all the people.

The government, with the help and advice of the World Health Organization (WHO), the Cooperative for American Relief Everywhere (CARE), and various United Nations agencies, continued efforts to raise the standards of health and living. Local government officials succeeded in gaining the public's cooperation so that islandwide innoculation, education, house-to-house antidisease spraying, and modern sanitation practices could be pursued.

HEALTH AND HEALTH FACILITIES

The infant mortality rate was estimated in 1970 to be 53 per 1,000 population, a figure among the lowest in South Asia. An important factor in the reduced rate has been the increasing popularity of maternity hospitals. By 1970 well over 60 percent of all children were delivered in maternity institutions under professional care and in adequately hygienic surroundings. Mothers and their babies also benefited from instruction in family health given during their stay in the institution.

The major causes of death in infants and young children are malnutrition, parasitic infestations, and gastroenteritis. Male children are preferred over female and are likely to receive somewhat better care. The death rate among boys is lower than that for girls (see ch. 4, Population; ch. 7, Family).

In 1970 the total death rate was estimated to be 8.2 per 1,000. Life expectancy at birth was nearly sixty-two years of age for men and slightly lower for women (see ch. 4, Population). The major causes of death from 1965 to 1970 were, in order of prevalence: diseases of the heart and the circulatory and nervous systems; cancer; parasitic diseases, such as hookworm; tuberculosis, influenza, and pneumonia; anemia and other disorders; gastroenteritis; childbirth; and accidents.

Ceylon was one of the first of the developing countries to undertake massive campaigns against such diseases as malaria and tuberculosis. An islandwide spraying program in 1946, using dichloro-diphenyl-trichloro-ethane (DDT), was successful in reducing morbidity from malaria to 5 per 100,000 population in 1960 with no deaths. The average yearly morbidity rate from 1937 to 1945, before the program was initiated, had been 44,300 per 100,000 population; the average death rate during this period was 112.8 per 100,000. In 1969 there were a few reports of malaria; spraying units visited the areas of infection to conduct house-to-house spraying. No deaths had been reported by the end of that year.

In 1947 the government began one of the first antituberculosis campaigns in South Asia, which proved highly successful in reducing the death rate and preventing new cases. In the five-year period from 1950-1955, for example, the death rate from all forms of tuberculosis fell from 53.3 per 100,000 people to 21.8 per 100,000. By 1963 the death rate had fallen to 12 per 100,000. These results were achieved by mass vaccination programs, such as the one carried out for 1.1 million schoolchildren from 1962 to 1965 and for all newborn babies in ten maternity hospitals. Testing and vaccination continued in 1970.

Hospitals, Clinics, and Health Centers

The number and quality of hospitals and other health care institutions are higher than average for South Asia. The typical Ceylonese regards the hospital rather than the home as the proper place to go for care in the event of serious illness. Many who could be cared for at home enter the hospitals instead, thus seriously overcrowding these institutions.

There are many private hospitals (160 in 1962) and nursing homes, but the majority of all medical institutions, urban and rural, are established and operated by the government through the Ministry of Health. In 1966 government, provincial, district, base, and special hospitals, central dispensaries, and health units totaled 843 institutions; rural health centers were not included in this figure. There were 3.2 beds per 1,000 population. The ratio of doctors to patients in 1966 was about 1 to 4,000.

Outpatient care is provided at special departments in the hospitals, dispensaries, and clinics. Medical attention is available to everyone, and clinic waiting rooms are usually crowded with patients who wait long hours to see a doctor. In 1966 some 3 million people were treated at maternal and child health, tuberculosis, leprosy, cancer, and mental health clinics.

The rural health centers, which numbered 894 in 1962, combine curative, preventive, and educational services. They are located all over the island and are connected by ambulance service. Their primary concern is with maternal and child welfare. The health center usually consists of a dispensary and medical aid station, a small hospital, and a maternity home and is staffed by a pharmacist, a public health nurse, and a trained midwife. The centers' maternity and child welfare services offer routine prenatal and postnatal care, infant care, and care of the preschool child, including treatment of illness, distribution of free milk, and health instruction. The health units of the centers are responsible for environmental sanitation and mass antidisease campaigns.

The sanitation inspectors attached to the health units are responsible for the construction and maintenance of clean wells and latrines in schools, public buildings, and private homes. Health education activities are pursued wherever there are people, through demonstrations, newspapers, radio, and visits by nurses and midwives.

Most medical personnel are trained at the Ceylon Medical School, the Colombo Medical College, the Dental Institute, the College of Dentistry at the University of Ceylon, and the College of Ayurvedic Medicine (see ch. 9, Education). Doctors and dentists are in critically short supply. In the academic year 1969/70 only 69 qualified doctors and 33 *ayurvedic* practitioners were graduated from the University of Ceylon. Although tuition is free at the university level, as well as all other levels, applicants to medical school are few relative to the need. Students prefer government positions for which they can train in two to four years instead of the five required for a medical degree. The only branch of medicine that is exceptionally attractive is nursing, for which some 500 applications are received each year. About 100 nurses are trained annually in schools of nursing or at the hospitals; of these, perhaps half graduate.

Most doctors, upon receiving their degree, join the government medical service instead of going into private practice. To ease the shortage in the private sector, the government recognizes qualified, registered *ayurvedic* practitioners. Qualified pharmacists who have had a complete course in pharmacy and elementary training in medicine and surgery serve as substitute doctors in rural areas, as directors of rural hospitals, and as heads of dispensaries.

Some 4,000 registered midwives were employed by the Public Health Department of the Ministry of Health in 1968. In addition to prenatal care and assistance at childbirth, midwives are qualified to give immunization shots, to assist in family planning and health education, and to give home care to convalescent tuberculosis patients (see ch. 4, Population).

Health and Sanitation

One of the most serious health problems is the high incidence of virus and parasitic diseases, particularly filariasis and hookworm. Few people escape parasitic infestations; from 1.5 million to 2 million people each year are treated for hookworm alone. A large proportion of hospital patients suffer from intestinal diseases, which, although cured through medical attention, often recur after the patients return home.

The primary sources of such diseases as typhoid and of parasitic infestations are impure water and food. Modern antiseptic practices of cleanliness in food preparation, in keeping water uncontaminated, and of adequate disposal of human and other refuse are not widespread (see ch. 11, Religion; ch. 12, Social Values). The rapid growth of the population each year has made it extremely difficult for local and central governments to dig sufficient wells and construct enough latrines to supply adequate water and sewerage facilities. It was estimated that in 1955 one family in three had clean, piped water and a latrine. Furthermore, since the relationship between germs and disease is not readily observable and therefore not widely respected, new wells and sanitation facilities are often allowed to become contaminated. Hence the cycle of infection and reinfection is difficult to stop.

The government maintains an ambitious environmental sanitation program, the goal of which is proper sanitation facilities and pure water for every family. Schools are inspected regularly. The ministries of health and education, in cooperation with the Joint School Health Council and parent-teacher associations, work to provide every school with clean water and latrines and to instill in the children modern habits of sanitation.

FOOD

In 1970 the country was not, for many reasons, self-sufficient in food, and large quantities continued to be imported (see ch. 19, Agriculture; ch. 22, Trade). Fruits, many vegetables, and fish are plentiful, but the food staple, rice, a major import item, is rationed and has been the subject of numerous political disputes. In 1968 the government cut the weekly ration of four pounds per person by one-half, and a factor in the 1970 elections was a campaign pledge by Mrs. Sirimavo Bandaranaike and her followers to restore the four-pound ration (see ch. 14, Political Dynamics).

Although vitamin- and protein-rich foods are plentiful, tradition dominates the average family's choice of diet, and malnutrition, caused by a deficiency of iron and protein in the diet of many segments of the population, is fairly widespread. Many families who could supplement their diet by fish do not do so because fishing is commonly associated with low-caste occupations or because their religion prohibits the consumption of fish or meat (see ch. 6, Social Structure). Beef, pork, and goat meat are sold in butcher stalls in the cities, but prices are high, and the meat frequently does not meet government standards of purity. Early in 1970, for example, stalls in Colombo were closed by government inspectors for selling low-quality beef.

The government operates several dairy and poultry farms and distributes milk, such milk products as yoghurt, and eggs to retailers and cooperatives throughout the island. Authorities hoped to increase the popularity of dairy products by distributing free milk to schoolchildren and to expectant and nursing mothers and selling, through agents, ice cream, ice cream confections, and other milk-based foods. Medical research continued for the prevention of goiter and anemia, which are widespread diseases stemming from nutritional deficiencies. Authorities suggested that, to prevent goiter, all salt for human consumption should be iodized.

Further efforts to improve the level of nutrition are carried out through the Freedom From Hunger Campaign, which is the joint responsibility of the Medical Research Institute and the Ministry of Agriculture and Lands. In 1966 part of the work of the campaign involved recommending specific hospital diets and nutrition for mothers and children. Campaign workers also conducted surveys in two villages, gave lectures and a radio talk, and prepared teaching materials on nutrition.

Food is freshly prepared each day with the exception of the morning rice, which may be left from the previous night's meal. Breakfast often consists of a hot *sambal*, a dish made with ground chilies, onions, fish, and coconut, or of boiled yams and coconut. Most people drink tea. Midmorning refreshment may be tea or coconut milk. The heartiest meal of the day is the noon meal, which may include *pol-hodi* (a coconut-milk soup) and a stew, as well as rice garnished with vegetables or dried fish. Midafternoon tea, with a sweet pastry or bun for those who can afford it, provides some refreshment, and the evening meal is a light supper of rice and curry. Only the middle and upper income groups can afford all of the foregoing, however. It is customary to rinse the mouth before meals and to wash the face and mouth before breakfast and at bedtime.

The standard of living is reflected in the number of meals per day and in how elaborate they are. Some families, for instance, consume European foods and are able to vary their diet by adding French, Dutch, or English dishes. Between-meal refreshment may actually be a fourth meal of the day or may be restricted to a piece of fruit. Besides rice, other imported and native cereals are easily available, as are such vegetables as potatoes, onions, peppers, tomatoes, carrots, and cabbages. Several kinds of nuts besides the coconut, of which no part is wasted, and fruits, such as pineapple, oranges, pumpkins, bananas, mangoes, and papaws, are included in the diet of most families.

CLOTHING

The traditional costume is simple, consisting of the ankle-length sarong for men and the draped sari and blouse for women. Regional and social variations occur; in the north around Jaffna, for instance, the middle class woman will change her sari for a Western-style housecoat before beginning her housework. Businessmen and government workers wear the Western-style shirt and suit at the office but change to a sarong at home.

The sarong is usually made of cotton and most often is white with panels of color, but any basic color is acceptable. It is worn as a kind of ankle-length skirt. Urban middle class men wear a brilliantly colored shirt and, for formal occasions, a white jacket and white shirt. Women wear saris draped in different ways or tight, short-sleeved bodices and *camboys,* which are similar to the sarong in style. Party saris and ceremonial clothes are of costly materials and colorfully decorated. Footwear may be Western-style shoes or fancy sandals. Schoolchildren almost always wear Western-style clothing until they are in their young adulthood, when they adopt one of the Ceylonese styles.

The women's hairstyle appears to be universally the same. It is long, often parted in the middle, and is coiled and fastened at the back of the head with an ornamental pin. Men wear their hair short, except in rural areas where the older men wear it in a bun on the back of the neck. Nearly everyone, from children to old people, wears an ornament, such as a bracelet or necklace. Often the ornament is valued as a charm against sickness and misfortune.

Clothing is bought readymade from the local shop or bazaar, or it may be made to order by a tailor. If a woman can afford a sewing machine, she will often make the family's clothing herself. A shortage of cloth in the late 1960s led many women to set up looms and weave their own fabrics. A person who has three or four changes of clothes is considered financially comfortable. The well-to-do include underwear in their wardrobe.

The typical village has a special caste of laundrymen who, among other things, wash clothes for a living (see ch. 6, Social Structure). Women who do not use this service wash the clothes themselves at the local well, tank, or river, making a social affair of the occasion. In the urban areas, the laundryman comes to the house, or the washing is sent out.

Bathing is a feature of daily life. People bathe together in the rivers and tanks for cleanliness, purification, or simple enjoyment. The homes of the well-to-do, both rural and urban, have separate facilities for bathing.

SHELTER

There are several building materials and styles, but the most common is the mud and plaster two- to four-room dwelling, roofed with pinkish tile or with palm fronds called *cadjan*. The new, government-built houses for the working class are made of rammed earth, which is mud compacted under pressure between wooden building forms. These houses are resistant to rotting, termites, and fires and are much cooler than stone or brick houses, which are also built. Government-built houses have tile roofs and are equipped with electricity and running water.

Village houses usually stand in their own gardens, separated from each other. Urban houses are crowded together, with the garden, if there is one, located in the back. A fence of *cadjan,* extending the length of the street, often separates the houses from the street and gives privacy. Houses are single-storied, sparsely furnished, and whitewashed. Some householders decorate the doors and windows with carving and paint. Houses of the well-to-do are set apart in their own grounds and are of stucco or brick. The architectural style of these and plantation houses is usually European. Public buildings, especially in cities such as Colombo, have a distinctly European appearance.

Overcrowding in the cities is acute, and to alleviate the situation the government has had building and resettlement plans underway since 1954. In the Colombo area, for example, a plan to build 3,100 flats for rehousing was announced in 1966. The project, which was still under construction in 1970, encompassed seventy-five acres of land and would include shops, a school, a college, a post office, and the other facilities of an average town. Another government housing project, New Town, in the vicinity of Anuradhapura, was nearing completion in 1970 and was the result of moving people out of the sacred area of the city. New Town has commercial and residential buildings and modern health and sanitation facilities.

An alternative to building projects is the colonization scheme in which families with farming experience are invited, and given incentives, to resettle in thinly populated areas of the island. Housing is provided, as well as land, in some areas. In others the colonizers are given subsidies to build their homes and are employed on sanitation, electrification, and irrigation projects for their area. Since the colonization plan began in the mid-1960s, about 400,000 people have been settled and employed in the hill country and in Galle, Kalutara, Jaffna, and Vavuniya districts.

MATERIAL COMFORTS

Ceylon neither imports nor manufactures consumer goods in sufficient quantity to provide such items as stoves, refrigerators, cars, and radios for everyone. Except in the homes of upper income families, labor-saving devices are rare. The average village house is lit by an oil lamp, cooking and eating utensils are handmade from coconut shells, and furniture is limited. The families of one village often share a radio. The usual form of transportation is by bicycle or bullock cart or, in the towns, by bus. In the late 1960s there was one telephone for approximately every 200 people.

Such items as transistor radios, wristwatches, fountain pens, cosmetics and toilet articles, kitchen utensils, and Western-style clothing and shoes are sought after as status symbols. Most shops in the cities advertise fabrics, readymade clothing, sheets and blankets, and other household goods and conduct holiday sales, such as those before and after the New Year. Prosperous families own several or all of these items. The women of these families own jewelry set with precious and semiprecious stones.

Statistics were not complete in 1970, but indications were that saving money through such organizations as the post office and the Ceylon Saving Bank was possible for many people and was widely practiced. Savings for the marriage dowry, a larger house, or more furniture is a common goal. Regular saving is encouraged by the National Savings Movement, a government organization that conducts publicity campaigns and forms savings groups. In some businesses and government departments there is a payroll deduction plan. Door-to-door sales of savings stamps are carried on in the villages by women volunteers. In 1966 savings stamps valued at a total of Rs1,036,465 (for value of rupee, see Glossary) were sold throughout the island.

In 1969 the average annual per capita output of goods and services was estimated at the equivalent of US$160. There is an income tax on all personal income over the equivalent of US$50 per month, after deductions and allowances. The majority of families can spend their income on food, clothing, shelter, savings, and amenities such as cigarettes and betel nut.

The cost of living rose each year from 1966 to 1968, but a concurrent rise in per capita income offset rising prices (see ch. 23, Finance). The 1968 cost of living, for example, increased by 5.8 percent over that of 1967, whereas per capita income increased by 6.1 percent. Although a family can live on the equivalent of US$50 per month, according to one Ceylonese, earning that amount is not easy. Unemployment and underemployment are widespread, however, and thousands of college graduates, for example, are faced with the prospect of eventually taking jobs for which they are not trained (see ch. 21, Labor).

LEISURE ACTIVITIES

The Ceylonese use a variation of the Gregorian or Western calendar and a lunar calendar on which religious festivals are based. In the Ceylonese variation of the Gregorian calendar, the days of the week are listed in a vertical column and are read from top to bottom instead of from left to right. The day of rest, Poya Day, is set according to phases of the moon and is therefore not fixed (see ch. 11, Religion). Buddhists, Hindus, Christians, and Muslims have separate religious calendars.

Festivals are occasions for rest from work, for sociability, and for the purchase of extra food and sometimes new clothing. Many festivals are for the purpose of propitiating various gods, driving away sickness, and bringing prosperity. An ancient belief in demons that possess humans and cause illness and bad luck is expressed in the Devil Dance, for instance. In this ritual the dancers wear lacquer masks carved to represent all the evils that befall mankind, and the prayers and games are supposed to exorcise malignant spirits.

The Buddhist festival of the year is Wesak, a celebration of the birth, enlightenment, and death of Buddha. Decorations and lights appear on houses and public buildings, and people crowd into the streets in a holiday mood. The festival occurs in May, and a similar one, the Hindu Deepvali, or festival of lights, occurs in autumn. This is a celebration of, among other events, the return of the Hindu god Rama to India after a long stay in Ceylon (see ch. 11, Religion). The Hindus observe some thirty fast and feast days each year. Hindus and Buddhists observe the New Year at the same time, in early April.

The city of Kandy is the site each year of Perahera, a pageant in which a casket containing relics of the Buddha is carried in a torchlight procession through the city streets. Participants in the procession include brilliantly costumed priests, the celebrated Kandyan dancers, and richly ornamented elephants (see ch. 10, Artistic and Intellectual Expression). The casket is carried on the back of the biggest elephant, called the Maligawa tusker.

Weddings and funerals are always occasions for festive eating and celebrating. Although Buddhism theoretically preaches abstinence from alcoholic beverages, in practice many Buddhists as well as non-Buddhists enjoy drinking arrack, a liquor made from the juice of palm flower stalks. Poya Day is fair day, when people put on their best clothes and go out to shop or to the temples.

The people enjoy many of the spectator sports introduced by the British. Cricket and soccer matches are reported daily in the newspapers. Schoolboys learn to play rugby at an early age. The country has professional teams in these sports that meet teams from other countries. Horseracing, badminton, and tennis are popular sports for Westernized individuals and small clubs. There is an All-Ceylon Women's Hockey Team, and women athletes participate in track meets. In addition to sports, there are contests of skill, ritual games, string games, and games that schoolchildren play as part of their physical training throughout the school years.

Most of the large cities have one or more cinemas that show Western and Ceylonese films. There are also dramatic and puppet theaters and performances of traditional dances (see ch. 10, Artistic and Intellectual Expression). For those families who cannot afford the price of admission to films and sports events, the local festival and Poya Days serve as entertainment.

Attitudes toward work and leisure are set in early childhood. Girls are expected to work longer and harder than boys, and working-class children generally begin domestic chores at an early age, sometimes at five or six years of age. At all social levels children usually defer to the parents in making decisions and adjust their actions according to parental rules. Curiosity, initiative, and experimentation are not encouraged by the average parent or in the school system, so that young adults are reluctant to try new employment ventures and seek instead the security of government positions. Furthermore, hobbies, such as model building and woodworking, that develop manual dexterity are rarely encouraged because of their association with low-caste occupations, such as carpentry and pottery making. Similarly, vocational and technical courses in school are among the least attractive courses of study (see ch. 7, Family; ch. 12, Social Values).

WELFARE

Welfare and public assistance programs cover a wide spectrum of the population, from homes for the aged to temporary aid to tuberculosis convalescents. Both government and private organizations, such as the Lions Club, contribute to relief plans. Public assistance allowances are the basis of social service, which the government sees as the most important form of protection against sickness, disability, and the helplessness of old age. The municipalities of Colombo, Kandy, and Galle administer their own local social service programs, but the central government is responsible for all other public programs. Monthly allowances of Rs10 for a single person or Rs20 for an individual with dependents were given to 155,729 persons in 1966.

In times of disaster caused by flooding, crop failure, or an accident, relief is given in the form of money, food, clothing, and sometimes temporary housing. In times of crop failure the government employs otherwise destitute people on public works. The armed forces are occasionally used in rescue and rebuilding operations, as in late 1969 when severe flooding occurred on the east coast of the island.

The government and various volunteer organizations maintain homes for the aged and for handicapped children. In 1966 there were four state homes for the aged, each accommodating about 240 persons. Each home is staffed by a superintendent, a pharmacist, and others. A revised policy of care for the aged led to the development of the small cottage homes with facilities for 24 people each. Seven such homes had been opened by 1966, and thirty-seven volunteer agencies were operating private homes with government grants-in-aid.

Volunteer agencies provided school and hostel facilities for handicapped children at eleven locations throughout the island. Handicapped adults can obtain vocational training at two centers, which may give them self-sufficiency in some skill or may lead to employment in carpentry, rattan work, or sewing. Training is subsidized for a maximum of two years.

A small allowance (Rs2.76 per day in 1966) is paid each person in the program. The goal is to enable disabled persons to be productive citizens.

In addition to these and other programs, the government pays the full cost of maternity and medical care to any resident of the country, within the limits of available facilities. There is an old-age pension scheme and a workers' compensation plan as well. Although allowances under any of the plans appear to be small, the standards an applicant must meet appear to be fairly lenient.

CHAPTER 9

EDUCATION

Although many aspects of the education system were undergoing change and revision in 1970, free compulsory schooling for children aged five to fourteen, free university education, and compulsory religious instruction had been well established. Nearly 84 percent of the five- to fourteen-year-olds attended school, a large proportion going on to secondary school. After the change of government in May 1970 such longstanding questions as the language of instruction, changes in curriculum and textbooks, and the founding of a Tamil university assumed priority over other problems in education.

There have been essentially two streams of education—private denominational and free public—since the arrival in Ceylon of the Portuguese in the sixteenth century. The missionary schools that were established primarily to teach Christianity were generally small, self-supporting institutions regarded as the responsibility of the clergy. The traditional village schools, open to all village children and providing instruction in the local language in reading, writing, arts, and crafts, eventually were forced to give way before the rising prestige of the European, particularly British, schools. This dual system eventually developed a small educated elite that secured the best jobs and a large number of partially educated people who were underemployed much of the time (see ch. 21, Labor).

The school system was restructured in 1968 to provide seven years of elementary education and five years of secondary. Since the institution of free public schooling in 1946 and 1947, a division of secondary education into two phases has evolved. The first three years are devoted to general education and provide a logical termination to formal education for children who do not plan to go on to college or vocational school. The second two years are spent in preparation for college or in vocational school, after which successful students may continue for two more years before entering a university. There are four universities, all government operated.

The widespread demand for education and the easy access to public schools had led to the development of a high literacy rate of approximately 80 percent by 1970. The definition of

145

literacy used in the 1946 census was "the ability to write a simple letter and read the answer to it." Since there are three major languages—Sinhala (see Glossary), Tamil (see Glossary), and English—the literacy requirement can be met in any of the three.

Government plays a vital role in education, retaining responsibility for financing, curriculum planning, textbook writing, and policymaking. In 1960 the government nationalized most of the denominational schools, which over the years had acquired privileges that the government felt only widened the gap between private and public education. In 1966 the administration of public education was decentralized, responsibility for it being divided among fourteen regional directors of education; each director was accountable to the permanent secretary of the then Ministry of Education and Cultural Affairs.

Education was an important issue in the election campaign of 1970 (see ch. 14, Political Dynamics). After her election Mrs. Sirimavo Bandaranaike proposed changes in the system to bring equal education to all children by ending the disparity between government and private schools. In addition, she stated that elementary schools should have the same curriculum throughout the country and that secondary schools should become comprehensive institutions with less emphasis on the arts and humanities and more on science and technology. Mrs. Bandaranaike promised that the school lunch program would be improved, three new universities would be built, and university students would be granted loans and stipends. The proposed changes will probably not be effected for some time, owing to lack of money and trained personnel and inadequate books and equipment.

HISTORICAL BACKGROUND

Early Indigenous Schools

The earliest known schools in Ceylon were the village (or primary) schools, *pansalas* (temple schools), and *pirivenas* (colleges), corresponding roughly to the modern elementary schools, secondary schools, and colleges, respectively. All learning was Buddhist oriented, and most of the teachers were Buddhist monks; the goal of their teaching was to develop qualities that would lead to enlightenment and good citizenship.

Primary, or village, schools were conducted by the local schoolmaster in his home. The village children learned to read and write their own language by rote method, enforced by firm discipline. The "textbooks" appear to have been traditional poems and ballads and lists of famous towns, mountains, monasteries in the island, and the marks supposed to have been found on the Buddha's body (see ch. 11, Religion).

Many children ended their formal education at the primary stage and went into apprenticeship under their fathers or a village craftsman. Children who showed aptitude continued their education at the *pansala* for one of the professions. The *pansala* was supported and cared for by the village laymen in return for instruction by the monks. Training seems to have differed widely from school to school, but in general the children were taught the principles of Buddhism, grammar, literature, arithmetic, astrology, and some painting and sculpture. Those who learned to read Sanskrit could train for the medical profession or for teaching.

The education provided by the *pirivenas* concentrated on Buddhist culture and learning and attracted young men who wished to become monks. Some taught lay people and clerics in the arts and sciences and provided a general education. The most famous ancient *pirivena* was Maha-vihara at Anuradhapura, where the Chinese scholar Fa Hsien stayed to copy Buddhist writings (see ch. 2, Physical Environment). The *pirivenas* were endowed by the Sinhalese (see Glossary) kings, and education was tuition free.

Although practical knowledge was valued and recognized as necessary for survival, in precolonial ages education was considered worthless if it did not show the way to higher wisdom that came from spiritual enlightenment. Education was essentially religious and based on traditional Buddhism or, in the Tamil areas, Hinduism and, as society changed under the influence of Westernization, the indigenous schools fell behind in organization, wealth, and prestige (see ch. 3, Historical Setting).

Early Western Schools

The first Western schools were those established by the Portuguese shortly after their arrival in Ceylon in 1505. Several of the Catholic orders—Franciscan, Jesuit, Dominican, and Augustinian—set up mission schools wherever possible for the purpose of teaching Christianity. They often dispensed medical aid as well. The schools were supported financially by the Portuguese government, but authority for organizing and administering them was left to the Catholic priests. The method of learning was memorization, and the curriculum consisted mainly of reading, writing, and instruction in Roman Catholicism.

Many of the Catholic schools were established for the children of Portuguese families, and the language of instruction was Portuguese. Ceylonese children who attended these schools thus received a Catholic education in Portuguese. The Jesuits, however, apparently lived among the villagers, learned Sinhala and Tamil, and taught in those languages. Some of the Ceylonese children were allowed to continue their education beyond elementary school at the Franciscan or Jesuit colleges, which by the beginning of the seventeenth century were flourishing in Colombo, Jaffna, Chilaw, Kalpitiya, and other outstations. The Portuguese missionaries are thought to have established a total of 100 schools along the coasts.

When the Dutch conquered Portuguese territory in Ceylon in 1656, they set up a well organized and well supervised system of education designed primarily to convert the population to Protestantism. They also provided hospitals, asylums, and orphanages. In theory and to the extent that enforcement was possible, school attendance was compulsory until the student reached the age of fifteen. Children could leave school at that age but were required to take religious instruction twice a week for two more years. Instruction was in the vernacular by Sinhalese and Tamils, who were supervised by Dutch clergy.

Each village in Dutch territory was provided with a small school, whose headmaster was selected from an important village family. The headmaster was also appointed record-keeper for the village, maintaining school attendance rolls, the registry of births and deaths, property deeds, and the like. The schools were visited regularly by government-appointed inspectors who looked over the premises, listened to the pupils' recitations, and questioned them on their understanding of the subject material. Bright children and children of high-caste families were sent to the Colombo Seminary to be trained as Sinhalese and Tamil teachers; a few were sent to Leyden University and returned to Ceylon as Protestant clergy.

By 1760 the Dutch had established 130 schools with a combined attendance of nearly 65,000 pupils. All but a few of these were forced to close when the British occupied the island in 1796. Teachers' salaries, hitherto paid by the Dutch government, were stopped and, except in areas where the villagers were willing to support the schools, education again became the province of Buddhist monks.

Protestant missionaries from England and the United States set up their own schools and controlled them without interference by the British government. By 1828 European schools numbered over 1,000 and had a total of nearly 21,000 students. Buddhist temple schools also numbered over 1,000, but the enrollment was unknown.

The first of the British "superior schools" was established in Colombo in 1799 by Frederick North, governor of Ceylon. The Colombo Academy was analogous to a college and provided a good education for preparatory school graduates who showed ability and talent. The preparatory schools, set up at about the same time as the academy, were established for the purpose of training the sons of Europeans and a high-caste Sinhalese and Tamil families (see ch. 6, Social Structure; ch. 7, Family). After graduation the students were given posts in the government or were sent to England for further education. There were three preparatory schools, one for each group. English was taught in each one, as well as Sinhalese and Tamil, and grammar, literature, religion, and proper deportment were the other courses of instruction. The preparatory schools charged a tuition fee, but education at the academy was free.

After the British conquest of Ceylon, responsibility for reorganizing a vernacular education system fell to the Reverend James Cordiner and the London Missionary Society. Cordiner became principal of schools, and under his administration a system of government-supported schools was begun. The Dutch schools were reopened in the larger towns, but as education was not made compulsory, attendance was small. Instruction was in the vernacular both by local teachers and by Dutch clergy who had been released from prison. Salaries were paid by the government. The curriculum included reading, writing, arithmetic, and the religious teachings of the Anglican church. The Bible was used in the teaching of reading. The schools were open to both boys and girls.

Although there were many schools, both native and missionary, there was no organized system of education that could remain stable regardless of changes in the office of governor. Until the last decades of the nineteenth century any school could be closed or reopened by a new governor, and changes in personnel and curriculum could be made as he saw fit. From about 1870 on the British government began to take more responsibility for education, and increasing funds from the home government in England made possible not only long-range aid to private schools but also continuing support to village schools. English-language education remained the best, if not the only, avenue to civil service employment, but government-supported schools were also established that provided secular, vocational education in Sinhala and Tamil. Through these schools the government hoped to inculcate principles of

149

religious equality and the dignity of crafts and trades. Western ideals began to penetrate *pansala* and *pirivena* education as well.

By 1900 three categories of schools had developed: government schools, government-assisted schools (Christian mission and Buddhist temple schools), and unaided schools (Buddhist, Hindu, and Muslim) (see ch. 11, Religion). Although statistics collected before 1926 were not conclusive, there were approximately 4,000 schools. Of these, some 2,280 were unaided in any way by the government, about 1,200 were receiving government grants in addition to charging tuition, and about 500 were government-supported, free schools. The model for education increasingly came to be that of the West, including such ideals as specialized teacher training, standardized formal schooling, and the introduction into the curriculum of science, liberal arts, and Western values. Schools that wanted government aid and recognition had to adopt at least some of the Western concepts and, since most of the English-language schools, the mission schools, and the vernacular schools did follow Western-style teaching, the influence of traditional Buddhist education declined (see ch. 3, Historical Setting).

Reforms in Education

Ideals of Western education took root, but during the first thirty years of the twentieth century they became trapped in a rigidly formalized, dualistic system. Children of well-to-do families continued to receive classical English schooling at institutions favored by the government, whereas the vast majority of other children were only partially prepared for useful, productive occupations by inadequately trained teachers. Parents frequently made every effort to send a child to an English school, often incurring debts in order to pay the tuition and travel fees. Others would secure some English-language education for their children by paying a fee for such instruction at the local school.

The curriculum in the prestige schools was geared to the same examinations given to British public school pupils in England and had little relevance to life in Ceylon. The government schools lacked the resources and teachers to provide more than a veneer of Western education. Furthermore, in attempting to inculcate ideals of the worth and dignity of manual labor, the government encountered the traditional caste-based disdain for it (see ch. 12, Social Values). Consequently, there continued to be a critical shortage of trained manpower to fill the country's scientific, technical, skilled, and semiskilled needs.

Growing concern for the quality of education and the availability of opportunity for all led to vigorous and prolonged debates in the legislative councils and newspapers, and several major reforms were eventually undertaken. The first of these was the requirement that all children attend school regularly from the age of five to fourteen. The Compulsory Education Act was passed in 1906. After many years of work and debate it was decided that public education should be government financed, and the Free Education Scheme of 1946–47 was passed. The law abolished fees and tuition in all government schools from kindergarten through university.

Efforts to enable all children to learn English culminated in a policy issued in 1945 that stated that the language of instruction would be Sinhala or Tamil in primary schools and English in secondary schools. Schools lacking the necessary English-speaking teachers would waive the English requirement. In the twenty years after its adoption, the policy was altered several times to accommodate changes in the national language and to allow for shortages in texts and teachers (see ch. 14, Political Dynamics; ch. 5, Ethnic Groups and Languages). In 1966 English was made a requirement for university entrance beginning in 1971, but the government of Mrs. Bandaranaike indicated in 1970 that this proposal would not be carried out. She said that English would be a compulsory language from the third year of primary school on.

In 1960 the denominational schools were nationalized and made part of the state school system. The denominational schools were private, charged tuition, and taught Christianity, and in nationalizing them the government added 2,623 institutions to the state system, bringing the total to 7,562. In addition, the curriculum was standardized, at least in theory, throughout the system. Shortages of books and teachers in some areas meant that some subjects would not be included.

ROLE OF EDUCATION IN MODERN SOCIETY

Private school education continued to have more prestige than public in 1970, although during the late 1960s the government of Dudley Senanayake had done much to close the gap between the two types of schooling. Nevertheless, the expectations of well-established schools, such as Royal College and St. Thomas College, could not easily or quickly be matched. The prestige of these schools is based on their age (they are among the oldest English schools on the island), their teaching staff, and the high tuition fee. Royal and St. Thomas are called "top quality" in Ceylon and are the only two schools in this category. There are other choices of schools available, ranking from "middle quality" to "least good," the former including some fine provincial schools in Kandy, Jaffna, and Galle, and the latter usually including free government schools. The "middle quality" schools have a higher proportion of university-trained teachers, and salaries are commensurate with training.

A family of means will send its sons to Royal or St. Thomas; families that cannot afford these schools will choose other schools above their own station in society but never below it. To send a child to a school below his station jeopardizes his or her future career and dowry (see ch. 7, Family).

In secondary school the liberal arts program is the most popular. Estimates made in 1966, for example, placed 70 percent of secondary students in the humanities, 16 percent in the sciences, and the remainder in vocational technical studies. Graduates from the liberal arts courses look for and expect white-collar positions. Training in science and the vocations is not yet complete, because of shortages in facilities and staff, and does not command the respect of white-collar jobs owing to associations with traditional low-caste occupations. Although the government worked out a program to reduce the discrepancy between graduates in the humanities, sciences, and vocational subjects, the training of teachers remained a major problem in 1970.

The proportion of girls to boys in school has always been low. Until recent years the average family felt that a girl's education should be limited to family life and child rearing and that, in any event, her help was needed at home. Attitudes gradually changed as Western influence increased, and men began to feel they could make a better marriage with a woman whose interests reached beyond the home and who could provide intellectual companionship as well as household and family care. By the 1960s it was not unusual for a middle class young woman to find a job in the city away from her parents. A critical shortage of teachers and nurses provided the incentive for many young women to continue their education beyond secondary school.

LITERACY AND LANGUAGE

Changing attitudes toward education for girls are reflected in the literacy rates for men and women. In 1881, for example, an estimated 17.4 percent of the people over five years of age could read and write a language and, of these, about 3.1 percent were women. By 1953 the rate of literacy for the country had risen to an estimated 64.7 percent; the rate for men was

152

about 75.9 percent and for women, about 53.6 percent. The 1963 census indicated that literacy for men aged fifteen and over was 83 percent and for women in the same age bracket, 62 percent.

Literacy tends to be higher in urban than in rural areas and in nonagricultural occupations than in farming. The literate population comprises those who have received formal rather than *pansala* education and are in the fifteen to twenty-four age group. Although literacy in English is confined to a small proportion of the population (some 10.5 percent in 1953), its importance in modernizing the country's scientific and technological knowledge is conceded by the government and educators. Beginning in 1971, according to announcements by the new government, provisions for teaching these subjects in English would be made, but no details were available.

ORGANIZATION AND ADMINISTRATION

Public Schools

In 1966 the government grouped the 9,555 schools then on the island into the following categories: free government schools; private schools, both tuition and nontuition; estate schools, operated by plantation owners for the children of their employees; *pirivenas*; and night and special schools (see table 11). Although the *pirivena* schools had originally been Buddhist colleges, by the postindependence period the term included all Buddhist schools except *pansalas*. After reorganization in 1968, the elementary school enrollment was about 2,177,600, probably about 83 percent of the total number of children in the five to twelve age bracket. Secondary school enrollment was approximately 497,000, representing perhaps 41 percent of those thirteen to eighteen years of age.

Individual schools have an option to provide kindergarten classes, depending on space, equipment, and teachers. The elementary, or primary, level includes grades one through seven. The children receive instruction in reading, writing, art, mathematics, religion, Western and Oriental music and dance, handicrafts, and physical education. Art, religion, and mathematics are compulsory subjects. In the Tamil areas Hinduism is the required religion, and courses in Islam and Christianity are provided. The study of mathematics begins in the sixth grade. A work program incorporated in the curriculum is designed to link school and community by giving the children agricultural and gardening experience in and around their homes.

153

Table 11. School Enrollment in Ceylon, 1966

Type of school	Number of schools	Enrollment	Teachers
Government	8,361	2,383,968	85,953
Private	103	60,511	2,912
Tuition	(54)	(22,050)	(1,202)
Nontuition	(49)	(38,461)	(1,710)
Estate schools	852	79,911	1,276
Pirivenas	217	29,103	1,715
Night schools	14	1,858	63
Special schools	8	840	62
Total	9,555	2,556,191	91,981

Source: Adapted from *Ceylon Year Book, 1968*, Colombo, 1968, p. 223.

Secondary education is divided into general and technical courses. The general courses are college preparatory in nature and include physics, chemistry, biology, mathematics, religion, and a continuation of the work program. A course in agriculture is required in all secondary schools. Students preparing for university education continue in the general secondary course, which emphasizes the liberal arts. Others prepare for trades, such as carpentry, mechanics, gem cutting, metalwork, textile design, and watch repairing, at one of the junior and senior technical special schools. Preparation for careers in commerce was beginning to be available in 1966 at more than 350 schools. By expanding the facilities for technical and engineering education the government hoped to begin graduating 200 engineers, 1,000 technicians, and 5,000 craftsmen annually to meet the country's anticipated manpower needs.

The school year begins in January. The first term lasts three months, after which there is a month's vacation. The second term is from May to August, and the third term lasts from October to mid-December. School is in session five days a week, and classes are held on either the single or double session plan.

Private Schools

The process of nationalizing private schools, which was finally accomplished in 1960, was long and arduous. When compulsory education was being discussed around 1900, there were 498 secular government schools and 1,328 religious schools registered with, and given grants-in-aid by, the government. The majority (1,117) of denominational schools were Christian, serving some 9.74 percent of the total population, whereas Buddhists, Hindus, and Muslims, who made up some 90 percent of the population, had government grants for 211 schools. Objections were raised, therefore to compulsory education since it appeared that this would also bring about compulsory Christianization. The government found it impossible to build and equip new schools matching in number and quality the established denominational schools, and as a means to an end it granted the private schools the option of secularizing and receiving government support or remaining denominational without government support.

When the policy of compulsory education was effected in 1906, private schools were given deadlines for joining the compulsory scheme, but the issue was so inflammatory throughout the country that the deadlines were postponed several times. Thus by 1966 there remained 103 private, denominational schools. In June 1970 three private Jesuit colleges—St. Alloysius' in Galle, St. Michael's in Batticaloa, and St. Joseph's in Trincomalee—announced that they had decided to follow "the pattern of future education in Ceylon," and on July 1 they became government-operated schools. If Mrs. Bandaranaike's intentions to nationalize estate schools are fulfilled, private, tuition-charging schools will be reduced by 855 sometime in the future.

In addition to the Protestant and Catholic schools, there are the Buddhist *pirivenas*, which in 1966 totaled 224 registered with the government. Buddhist studies are the core of the *pirivena* curriculum, but students may also prepare for entrance to one of the four government universities. The *pirivenas* are classified as junior, senior, and university. Although they are operated by the Buddhist community, they must abide by a government code in order to receive government grants.

Novices and lay people of both sexes attend *pirivena* classes at all levels. The elementary classes are usually small, and the relationship between students and teachers, who are monks, is tutorial. In addition to religious studies, the students are taught reading, writing, and arithmetic and, at more advanced levels, astrology and *ayurvedic* medicine (a system of healing based on homeopathy and naturopathy, with an extensive use of herbs). Vidyodaya Pirivena at Colombo is a large center of Sinhalese studies and *ayurvedic* medicine. In 1958 both Vidyodaya and Vidyalankara *pirivenas* were given university status by the government and in 1970 were fully government supported.

Technical and Vocational Education

Technical education has been slow to develop, and plans to build and equip new schools have frequently been altered or dropped. The announced policy of the government on several occasions has been to place more emphasis on technical and scientific education and less on liberal arts. The United Nations Special Fund offered financial assistance in January 1970 that would complement the building program by establishing standards of apprenticeship, trade tests, and certification of craftsmen and by supervising vocational training. Special programs to train vocational teachers and instructors in industry could also be set up with the US$659,200 from the fund, to which the government would add the equivalent of US$556,000.

There are at least two good technical training institutes—the Ceylon Technical College and the Basic Technical Training Institute. The former trains workers for supervisory positions in industry, and the latter trains skilled machinists, electricians, and carpenters. In addition, junior technical schools give training in the crafts in seven of the larger towns.

Higher Education

The student's training is punctuated by examinations marking the end of one stage and, for the successful ones, the beginning of another stage. The examination at the end of general secondary schooling, after the tenth grade, is supposed to determine the student's fitness for further academic or technical education. The most important is the matriculation examination, on which entrance to a university is based. There are four government universities and several private colleges. The university degree, particularly from the University of Ceylon, carries the most prestige.

The University of Ceylon was established in 1942 but had its origins in the Ceylon Medical School at Colombo, which was opened in 1890. By 1915 popular demand for a university led to an affiliation of the medical school with London University whereby English-trained Ceylonese students at the school could study for degrees at London. World War I made this affiliation impracticable because travel between Ceylon and England was nearly impossible and because examination papers and their results were frequently delayed and sometimes lost in the overseas mail. The Ceylon Legislative Council therefore approved in 1923 the proposed University of Ceylon at Colombo. Several controversies arose to delay the construction of buildings, but ultimately a university was built, located on two campuses, Colombo and Peradeniya, near Kandy. The Peradeniya campus houses the faculties of agriculture and veterinary science, arts and Oriental studies, engineering, and medicine. The Colombo campus is the site of the original medical school and the faculties of law, science, and arts. The two campuses are considered to form two separate universities, and the distinction is always made between Peradeniya and Colombo.

Vidyodaya Pirivena at Nugegoda and Vidyalankara Pirivena at Kelaniya emphasize a liberal arts curriculum, but this includes the social sciences, economics, public and business administration, education, geography, history, and law. The language curriculum includes courses in English, Pali (see Glossary), Sanskrit, Sinhala, and Tamil. Pure and applied mathematics are taught at both universities.

There are six institutions termed junior university colleges, which give two-year courses leading to diplomas in industrial management, commerce, agriculture, technology, and science. The Ceylon Law College trains students exclusively for the practice of law before the Supreme Court.

The universities are corporations composed of a chancellor, pro-chancellor, vice chancellor, board of regents, and senate. The governor general of Ceylon and the minister of education are ex officio chancellor and pro-chancellor, respectively. Some members of the boards of regents, which govern the universities, are drawn from among the university faculty, and others are appointed by the National Council of Higher Education, which has control over all institutions of higher learning.

The government pays student tuitions and faculty salaries and provides residence halls at the University of Ceylon at Peradeniya. Each university has a health insurance plan. Postgraduate courses are taught, and women are admitted to all the universities. The combined enrollment is over 13,000; Peradeniya and Colombo have about 4,500 students each, and Vidyodaya and Vidyalankara about 2,000 each. In 1966 approximately 37 percent of these students were women. Seventy-seven percent of the undergraduates were enrolled in liberal arts courses.

The student's preformance on the General Certificate of Education Advanced Level Examination determines which university he will attend. Those attaining the highest marks are given first preference in the choice of a university, and Peradeniya and Colombo are overwhelmingly the first choice. Students with second highest marks are given their second choice, and so on. One of the hardships arising from this system, which is generally admitted to be unsatisfactory, is that a student living in the Kandy area may be sent to Colombo, thus incurring extra expenses in travel, room, and board. He may also be forced to change his degree program since the university curricula do not coincide. Only Vidyodaya has a degree program in business administration, for example, and only Colombo has a law program.

Sinhala is the most frequently used language of instruction, and for the Tamil-speaking student this presents a further hardship. The need for at least one Tamil university is recognized, but by 1970 such an institution was still in the planning stage. Other universities are planned to accommodate students in Eastern, Uva, Southern, and Sabaragamuwa provinces. Although the government gives scholarships and bursaries (gifts of money not repayable) and grants loans to students for travel, books, housing, and living expenses, the funds available are not enough to go around. It is not unusual for students to be forced to return home without an education for lack of money.

Teachers and Teacher Training

The Department of Education of the University of Ceylon at Peradeniya graduates the best prepared teachers and is the ultimate stage in training in the country. The department is the source of much experimental and innovative work in education since its teaching staff spends periods of study abroad and is able to bring back new ideas and insights. The diploma in education is granted to student teachers who successfully complete a course combining studying, reading, and practice teaching. The department had long advocated a four-year course leading to a bachelor of education degree, and by the late 1960s it was finally able to institute the degree. The number of candidates was 93 and 130 in 1965 and 1966, respectively. An estimated 8 percent of the country's teaching population, numbering about 110,000 in 1970, were university graduates.

University-trained teachers command the best positions and the highest salaries and usually enter one of the "top quality" private schools or remain at the university in a teaching capacity. The majority of teachers, however, either have graduated from one of the twenty-four government teachers' colleges that provide two years of training for secondary school graduates or have completed a one-year course given by the University of Ceylon's Department of Education. Their salaries are paid by the government, which has the prerogative of assigning them to any of the government schools. The government may also transfer a teacher from one school to another, anywhere on the island.

Teachers are allowed to form unions and associations, such

as the National Union of Teachers, University Teachers Association, and All Ceylon Union of Government English Teachers. The Union of Government English Teachers in June 1970 brought to the attention of Mrs. Bandaranaike several of the teachers' problems, including the need for a retirement plan, a pay and promotion scale similar to that of other public services, and the need for faculty housing. In addition, the union requested that hiring, dismissing, and transferring of teachers become the responsibility of a special commission. In the past, government policy had permitted the transfer of teachers from one area of the country to another as the need required; sometimes the transfers separated married couples, both of whom were teachers. The new government's policy stated that such married couples should be given positions in the same area.

Although Ceylon spends about 5 percent of its gross national product (GNP) on education expenditures, the growth of the schoolgoing population and the needs related to it have forced cancellation of some planned expansion. The focus and structure of the education system have altered with changes in government, so that proposals made by one administration have sometimes been abandoned by the next. For example, appropriations made for English instruction have in the past reflected the importance of English in the public schools; when English is compulsory, appropriations are proportionately larger than when English is optional.

CONTENT AND METHOD

Textbooks are prepared and published by the Publications Section of the Ministry of Education, which took over this function in 1964 with a view to raising educational standards through improved texts. Preparation includes editing, revision, and translating. Additional books on science subjects are purchased from private publishers and distributed to school libraries. The Ministry of Education pays the royalties directly to the authors. In 1966 the ministry distributed 2,280,140 school textbooks.

Students at all levels must buy their books at retail prices from government-approved bookstores and cooperatives, of which there were 835 throughout the country in 1966. Special books are required to prepare for the examinations given at the end of the tenth and twelfth grades and for university entrance.

The staff of the Publications Section is small, and there are relatively few editors and translators fluent in Sinhala, Tamil, and English. The number of books published in a year amounts to less than one book per student. Thus schools lack sufficient

159

modern textbooks and must fall back on older books, which a group of university professors criticized in 1970 for inaccuracies, dullness, and subtle racism. The Ministry of Education stated that it hoped to correct the deficiencies within the next few years.

Much of the teaching at all levels is accomplished by reading and listening. The emphasis is less on using acquired knowledge than on memorizing facts. The teacher is the authority in the classroom, and students accept this as they accept the authority of their parents (see ch. 6, Social Structure; ch. 7, Family). There is little opportunity for students to make their own decisions and solve problems. Great importance is placed on the examinations, which over the years have come to be regarded as levels of student achievement rather than measures of his competence to go on to higher levels of education. Thus many of the subjects in the curriculum are relevant to the examinations rather than to daily life.

Although a great deal of research is done in agriculture and related subjects such as animal husbandry, it is confined largely to government farms and dairies. The universities are still in the process of building up research facilities and staff. Traditional education, from the child's early years at home and throughout his school years, does not encourage habits of curiosity, experimentation, and solving problems through reasoning. Interest in postgraduate research for the sake of increasing human knowledge is therefore relatively new.

University faculty members who would like to do research encounter several obstacles. There is an acute shortage of laboratory space and equipment. Financing of research is uncertain and inadequate. There are not enough trained researchers and not enough full-time graduate students to help. The awakening interest in research possibly may induce greater numbers of students to delay their entrance into the already overcrowded job market and to undertake postgraduate study in the future.

CHAPTER 10

ARTISTIC AND INTELLECTUAL EXPRESSION

In 1970 novelists, artists, and dramatists still drew their main inspiration from Buddhism, the religion of the Sinhalese majority, which has largely defined the nature of art and intellectural expression since its arrival in Ceylon in the third century B.C. The Buddhist *sangha* (see Glossary) has favored the individual arts of painting, sculpture, and the plastic arts and discouraged the community arts of music and drama. Most prose and poetry before the nineteenth century was concerned with religious themes or the exploits of Buddhist kings. Little was written of the triumphs and tragedies of the ordinary villager.

Art and architecture in the classical period of Sinhalese history, coinciding with the kingdom of Anuradhapura (200 B.C. to A.D. 1000), achieved great distinction. Temples, statues, palaces, and pleasure gardens were built and adorned with a high degree of technical skill and artistic restraint. The earliest cultural influences came from the Buddhist kingdom of Asoka in North India. The proximity of South India and the periodic influx of South Indian craftsmen also influenced the architecture and sculpture of Anuradhapura and the kingdom of Polonnaruwa (A.D. 1070–1250). South Indian influence was, however, most noticeable during the Kandyan period from 1500 to 1815 (see ch. 3, historical Setting).

The arrival of the Portuguese in the sixteenth century brought Western influences, especially in the sphere of literature and drama. The firm establishment in the nineteenth century of English education for the elite made available English literary forms but, at least partly because of the smallness of the audience, no major literary works were composed in English. The many English-language newspapers and journals, however, became a vehicle for literary criticism of a high standard. The spread of vernacular education in the late nineteenth century created a Sinhala-reading public that favored romantic tales, preferably with a happy ending and the triumph of Sinhalese nationalism. The gap that developed between the English- and Sinhala-reading public was not

161

bridged until the novels of Martin Wickramasinghe in the 1940s. Sinhalese short-story writers have been more successful than novelists, possibly because the *jataka* tale, built around a single incident in the life of the Buddha, has been a popular medium of expression for centuries.

Music and dance were shunned by the Buddhist *sangha* as dangerously sensual arts but were permitted to the royal court and the nobility. The one exception was drumming, which was featured in religious processions. Ritual dances and simple chants in connection with the folk religion of gods and demons have always been an essential part of village life. In the nineteenth century these forms of religious expression were combined with elements of music and dance from Tamil folk drama to become a kind of chanted drama called *nadagama*. A later influence of musicals from Bombay introduced Hindi tunes and elaborate stage sets and costumes, to transform the *nadagama* into operettas called *nurtiya*. In the 1970s the popular Sinhalese film was a direct result of this development. Straight European-style theater is also a feature of city and university life. In the 1960s the Italian realistic style of motion picture making became popular for the first time.

A minor art that developed in the villages was the puppet play. It was adapted from the folk play and was able to hold village audiences after modern and puritanical influences drastically curtailed the live folk plays. In the 1960s government assistance was provided in an attempt to prevent its disappearance.

Modern art in Ceylon has been described as the most significant in Asia. The modern artist draws his inspiration from two sources, the highly developed art of temple and cave painting (the Sigiriya frescoes of the fifth century A.D. are considered among the finest in southern Asia) and European art. Portrait painting was popular in the early part of the twentieth century. Later artists, particularly those known as "the '43 group," introduced impressionist and early abstract styles. Buddhist themes continue to inspire Sinhalese artists.

Original philosophic thought has mainly concerned Theravada Buddhism (see Glossary). Near the end of the nineteenth century a great revival of Buddhism was spearheaded by European and, later, Sinhalese scholars. Since independence there has been increasing agitation for a restoration of the Buddhist *sangha* to a central place in intellectual and political life. In the 1960s a major concern was the adaptation of Buddhist ideas to modern life.

The Tamils, who are the largest minority group on the island, look to South India for cultural inspiration. Literary and nationalist figures, such as Arumuga Navalar, in the nineteenth century contributed to the Hindu revival in both South India and Tamil Ceylon. The Ceylon Tamils have also acted as in intermediary for the inflow of ideas and forms from South India, as in Tamil folk drama.

Unlike literature, philosophy, and the arts, which are closely bound up with language and religion, science cuts across communal lines. Because neither Sinhala nor Tamil has yet developed adequate scientific vocabularies, English is still the language of science. Scientific research has largely been devoted to Ceylonese agriculture, industry, medicine, and archaeology. For scientific research in other fields the student has to go abroad. Increasing attention is being given to archaeological research, particularly as the civilization of Anuradhapura and Polonnaruwa are a source of great cultural pride.

The government actively fosters the arts through its Department of Cultural Affairs with sections on art, literature, and religion. The Art Council, established in 1952, is the institution through which much of the government assistance is channeled. In 1968 the National Science Council was established to advise the minister of scientific research and housing. The council's twenty-one members, drawn from various scientific fields, coordinate the nation's applied-science research.

ART AND ARCHITECTURE

Classical Sinhalese Period

The *Mahavamsa*, the earliest known dynastic and religious history, records that the Asokan prince Mahinda instructed the Sinhalese king how to build the first Buddhist shrines at Anuradhapura (see ch. 3, Historical Setting). The Mahavihara, the first and most revered temple, was to include an open area for the performance of sacred rites, a tank for bathing, an enclosure for the Sacred Bo tree, a dining hall, and a site for the *stupa* (sometimes called a *dagaba*). The *stupa*, a mound or tumulus built over the bones of an ancestral hero, was early incorporated into Buddhism in North India. When the right collarbone of the Buddha was brought to Anuradhapura, it was housed in a special *cetiya* (relic house) called Thurpurama.

All the early *stupas* were built according to a set plan following the Indian originals. The *stupa* itself was a bubble-shaped dome. A square wooden or stone railing, which later gave way to a brick cube, was constructed around the dome.

From this arose a stone pillar that was crowned by one or more umbrellas. Many of the early *stupas* were of enormous size, as much as 200 feet in diameter, and the Jetavana *stupa* at Anuradhapura reached 400 feet in height. The bubble shape has been regarded by some as representing the unreal nature of the world, and the umbrella, as a symbol for royalty. At the top of the umbrella's spire was a precious stone set in crystal.

Some of the early *stupas* are surrounded by pillars, which suggest that the domes were covered by wooden roofs as in the *stupas* of the Kandyan period. Around the base, shrines were built in as many as sixteen places for worshipers to pause and pray. Slabs of stone carved with the images of earth deities or snake kings, reflecting the incorporation of earlier religious beliefs into Buddhism, guarded the top of a flight of steps leading to the base of the *stupa*.

In the second century A.D. *vahalkadas*, or frontispieces, were added to the *stupas* at Anuradhapura and nearby Mihintale. These were elaborate structures facing the four cardinal points, decorated with carved panels and moldings, and standing between two pillars. The origin and purpose of these *vahalkadas* is a matter of conjecture, but from an architectural point of view they have been described as "among the most important features of the Ceylon *stupas*" because they provided the earliest opportunity for the display of the plastic arts. Each frieze was carved with a series of elephant heads, lotus flowers, geese, or dwarfs. The dwarfs in particular were rendered with often grotesque humor. Above a cornice ornamented with a floral design, brackets issue from the mouths of strange creatures similar to medieval European gargoyles. The surface of the pillars also are decorated with reliefs of animals, birds, and flowers, and a three-dimensional symbolic animal crouches on top.

A characteristic feature of Sinhalese sculpture is the moonstone at the base of the steps leading to the *stupa*. Shaped like a half moon and divided into concentric circles, the moonstone is said to represent the various stages in the ascent to truth. Tongues of flame (desire) in the outer circle lead to four animals—the elephant, bull, lion, and horse—which represent birth, decay, disease, and death, respectively. The gradual overcoming of desire is reflected in the geese, the water lilies, and the lotus at the center.

Although the basic design of the *stupas* remained set at Anuradhapura, various features underwent elaboration. Later *stupas* did not match the earlier ones in size, the largest having a diameter of ninety-two feet. Figures of deities embellished the cylindrical supports of the spires, and the gigantic foreparts of elephants were added to the walls of the now square base on which the *stupa* rested.

Another type of shrine was developed in which a number of small *stupas* were enclosed within circular pillars. In the seventh and eighth centuries A.D. the original wooden pillars gave way to stone columns ornamented with capitals carved with dwarves, lions, geese, and other traditional motifs. They are arranged in circles of two or four, with the taller pillars in the center. Many of these pillars survive at Anuradhapura together with molded retaining walls and flights of steps, although hardly any original superstructures remain. The balustrades and the risers of the flights of steps were fancifully decorated by the early stone carvers. In 1970 the only surviving Bodhighara (house for the Sacred Bo tree) was preserved at Nillagama in the Kurunegala District.

Various monastic buildings received the attention of the architects. Baths, both sacred and royal, contain some notable sculpture. At Mihintale one side of the bath is cut out of the solid rock, and on the other three sides stone slabs of lions, dwarfs, dancers, and wrestlers are skillfully carved.

The major influences on sculpture in the early Anuradhapura period came from Buddhist India. Asoka is said to have dispatched several guilds of artists, craftsmen, and painters to Ceylon. A resemblance to the somewhat formal early work in India at Bodh Gaya in Bihar and Sanci in Madhya Pradesh have been detected in the Kantaka-cetiya, and the more graceful poses of the figures of the Jetavana sculptures reflect the Amaravati school of Maharashtra, India. Influences from the Gupta Empire in India (ca. A.D. 330–530) are clearly seen in various Buddha images, in paintings and, particularly, the graceful bas-relief of two lovers at Anuradhapura. Pallava or South Indian influence appears in the rock-hewn figure of a man and his horse at Anuradhapura, attributed to the seventh century (see ch. 3, Historical Setting).

The earliest Buddha images found in Ceylon have been ascribed to the second or third centuries A.D. Upright figures made of limestone, they are considered more impressive than their models at Amaravati. A Buddha figure from the Ruvanveli *stupa* has a rough-hewn stern appearance. The fold of the drapery at the bottom reveals some South Indian influence. Early seated Buddha figures were also carved with great simplicity, partly because of the intractable nature of the stone and partly by reason of the conventions concerning the representation of the Buddha.

Buddha images of the later Anuradhapura period—for example, the well-preserved Avukana Buddha—reached colossal proportions. Another rock-cut image, over fifty feet tall, in the southern kingdom of Ruhuna is ascribed to the eighth or ninth century. Seated Buddha images were also of enormous size, at least partly, it has been suggested, to impress the worshiper with the Buddha's superhuman power. Bronze images are also a feature of this period.

Anuradhapura was, and still is, primarily a sacred city, and its art is mainly religious. The exception is the royal palace and baths. Polonnaruwa, on the other hand, has been described as more of a royal capital. *Stupas*, image houses, and monasteries abound at Polonnaruwa, but more attention was given to secular aspects, such as pleasure gardens, bathing pools, and audience halls. The decoration became more extravagant, and stone was largely replaced by brick and stucco.

The greatest architectural works at Polonnaruwa were undertaken by Parakramabahu I (the Great) in the twelfth century (see ch. 3, Historical Setting). A return was made to the style of the colossal *stupas*, surmounted by a small superstructure, that was prevalent in the early Anuradhapura period. One of these is called the Damila-thupa because it was built by Tamil prisoners of war. A dearth of Sinhalese stonecutters meant the use of South Indian craftsmen, which may account for more elaborate decoration as well as a loss of religious feeling in the treatment of traditional Buddhist themes. The moonstones are considered mere decoration at Polonnaruwa. Some of the most notable structures are the image houses, particularly the Lankatilaka, the Tivanka, and the Thurpurama. Their ground plans correspond closely to those of Hindu shrines in India, and they are heavily carved with images of deities, miniature buildings in relief, pilasters, and friezes. The relic house on a raised quadrangle called the Tooth Relic Terrace at Polonnaruwa, rebuilt by Nissankamalla, has been described as "ornate and elaborate in a way that approaches preciosité."

The remains of a royal palace at Polonnaruwa show a columned hall 102 feet by 42 feet, which originally must have been a storied structure. The audience hall nearby rises in three stages with a portal entrance decorated by a lion. The most impressive achievements at Polonnaruwa are the colossal Buddha images. Of the four rock-cut images at Gal Vihara, the largest is a recumbent figure over 46 feet in length, and close by is a standing Buddha of nearly 23 feet in height. In their simplicity and grandeur, these images illustrate the best in Sinhalese-Buddhist art. Another statue, a stone figure believed to represent Parakramabahu I, holding either a yoke or a scroll, achieves the same power and grace.

Aside from the ancient capitals of Anuradhapura and Polonnaruwa, the most remarkable architecture in Ceylon is the rock fortress of Sigiriya built by Kassapa I in the fifth century A.D. (see ch. 3, Historical Setting). The rock on which the royal palace is built rises 600 feet out of the plain. The city is fortified with a wall of brick and surrounded by a moat and outer ramparts of earth. Part way up, the forepaws of a huge rock-hewn lion form an entrance to a flight of steps. Below, a gallery, which still stands on the western side, wound its way around the rock. On the top a well-laid-out bath, two cisterns, and the walls of many buildings are all that remain of the royal palace.

Sigiriya is most famous for the frescoes that adorn the rock cave above the western gallery. From the time the rock was abandoned at Kassapa's death to the twelfth century, Sigiriya was visited by tourists who came to admire the frescoes, many of whom left their impressions in verses scratched into the rock. The fortress remained inaccessible from the thirteenth to the nineteenth century, when an English expedition into the jungle rediscovered it.

Painting on the walls of caves and temples was an art that the early Sinhalese adapted from Indian civilization. No paintings, however, survive before the Sigiriya frescoes and, of the hundreds of figures painted on the rock fortress, only twenty-one remain. The portraits of voluptuous maidens, alternately light and dark skinned, have been said to represent either royal princesses and their handmaidens or lightning and cloud goddesses because the figures are cut off at the waist. The figures are outlined in black against a lime-plaster surface. The artist preferred reds and yellows partly because they showed up better on the rock surface and partly because blues and greens tended to peel off together with the plaster. In the grace and delicacy of modeling, the frescoes compare favorably with the Gupta paintings of the cave temples in Ajanta, India.

The fragments of paintings that have survived give only a brief glimpse of the extent of ancient painting. The Chinese Buddhist pilgrim, Fa Hsien (ca. A.D. 400), recorded that scenes from *jataka* stories decorated both sides of the highway at Anuradhapura. Ancient painting was largely a narrative art, using symbolic designs, and idealistic in conception, as suited its religious inspiration. At first a mass composition was used with smaller scenes surrounding a central figure. Later the *jataka* stories were illustrated in sequence on temple walls. The Tivanka Shrine at Polonnaruwa contains fragments of what have been described as the greatest "wealth of ex-

167

quisitely painted scenes from Buddhist legend ever presented." Recent discoveries of other ancient paintings have been found in a cave at Hindagala near Peradeniya and in a relic chamber in the Mahiyangana Dagaba in Uva Province.

Kandyan Period

In the centuries after the destruction of Polonnaruwa, art and architecture steadily declined. The successive capitals in the hill country were noted mainly for military fortifications (see ch. 3, Historical Setting). Of the little that remains, such as the gateway of a shrine at Yapahuwa, Dravidian influence is uppermost. South Indian craftsmen sought refuge from the Muslim sultanate in their home country. Dancing girls and figures of Hindu deities appear on the pillars of temples and moldings of buildings. Bronze Buddha statues replace stone and are surrounded by carved images. Temples continued to be decorated with paintings, but the loss of quality has been described as "the difference between literature and journalism."

A favorite theme of the Kandyan period was the Buddha's spiritual struggle, represented by tongues of flame, whirlwinds, and demons. A statue of the Buddha provided the contrast of calm against this fearful background. The story of the Buddha's enlightenment was another common theme. The rendering is colorful and lively but, like the small bronze figures of the period, somewhat rigid and lacking in subtlety.

The early architects and artists were anonymous. The earliest recorded name is that of Silvet Tenne Unnanse, who painted with the assistance of four other artists in the eighteenth century. Until the British disrupted the feudal system that survived in Kandy until 1815, the craftsmen's guilds were under royal patronage (see ch. 3, Historical Setting). In each district (korale) the Kandyan king maintained a department of different types of craftsmen. The craftsmen with the highest status were the painters, architects, goldsmiths, silversmiths, brass repoussers, and ivory and wood carvers. These workers were often imported from the big cities and craft guilds of South India.

The indigenous workers were of lower caste and filled the daily requirements (see ch. 6, Social Structure). They were the turners of wood and ivory, blacksmiths, stone carvers, and inlay workers. Lower still on the social scale were the tailors, embroiderers, leatherworkers, and weavers of coarse cloth. The Sinhalese kings were generous toward their craftsmen, rewarding them with grants of land or the revenue of a village. Upon completion of a special work for a monastery or temple, the craftsman might receive additional gifts of rice, cloth, cattle, gold, and silver. The craft was handed down from father to son, and the son was apprenticed as soon as he was old enough to assist in simple tasks.

In the eighteenth and early nineteenth centuries some fine examples of ivory carving, metalwork, and jewelry were produced, including ivory statuettes, combs, caskets, knife and sword handles, brass areca-nut slicers, betel-nut boxes, drinking vessels, lamps, and jewelry with uncut stones skiillfully set in gold and silver. Lac work was used for adorning knife handles and bookcovers and as inlay for ivory and horn. Painted masks for folk rituals and the folk drama (*kolam*) achieved considerable sophistication. By the beginning of the twentieth century it was estimated that only 4 percent of Kandyan craftsmen were still practicing their craft full time, compared with a probable 10 percent in the eighteenth century.

There have been recent attempts to revive these arts and crafts. The Department of Rural Development and Cottage Industries actively assists the village craftsmen (see ch. 20, Industry).

Contemporary Period

Three major styles of painting have emerged in the twentieth century: the so-called oriental, the academic, and the modern. The sources of inspiration for the oriental school are the cave and temple frescoes. In the 1940s Solias Mendis, a representative of this school, developed his own style in embellishing a temple at Kelaniya near Colombo, which has since been referred to as the Kelaniya style. The academic school was influenced by the realistic landscapes and portraits of the Victorian Royal Academy artists. Portraiture, especially, was popular with the educated middle classes. One of the best known of the portraitists was J. D. A. Perera, who was a student of Augustus John.

The modern school has experimented with impressionist and early abstract Western styles to express both traditional and contemporary themes. This school has been credited by a British critic with producing the most vital modern art in Asia. Known originally as "the '43 group," it included such artists as Justin Daraniyagala, George Keyt, Harry Peiris, David Paynter, and Stanley Abeyesinghe. George Keyt, for example, successfully introduced the Picasso style into Ceylonese painting.

A group of younger artists have carried this development further. Pushpananda Weerasinghe, in addition to painting, has branched out into abstract sculpture. An artist of some achievement—by the age of seventeen he had exhibited in fifty-eight one-man shows throughout the world—and great promise is Senaka Senanayake. Inspired by traditional themes, he uses the impressionist technique with fluency to create a mood or narrate a story.

Sculpture has had fewer practitioners than painting, but at least one is outstanding. Tissa Ranasinghe, a graduate of the Government College of Fine Arts, studied sculpture in England. He won an award at the Sao Paolo Biennial in 1963 for a statue entitled *Penance*. He works in wood, terracotta, plastic, metal, plaster, brass, and stone. Although his style is reminiscent of Giacometti, he often illustrates Buddhist themes. Other sculptors include O. Weerasinghe, A. K. Wijeyasekara, and Prabhat Wijesekera. Wijesekera has been commissioned by a Buddhist Vihara society in southern Ceylon to build a 125-foot bronze standing Buddha. In 1970 he estimated that it would take eight years to sculpt because he holds a position at the Colombo Museum, which will continue to claim most of his time.

In common with Wijesekera, the majority of artists either teach or hold some other job. Buddhist temples are still a major source of patronage. The business community occasionally commissions portraits or sculpture, and the government assists by arranging exhibitions.

LITERATURE

Ancient Sinhalese Literature

As with the visual arts, literary activity was largely confined to the religious communities and the court. The Sinhalese take pride in being responsible for the preservation of the Theravada Canon in the Pali (see Glossary) language long after it was lost in India (see ch. 11, Religion). A feature of Buddhism from its earliest days was use of the vernacular for religious purposes, so that the introduction of Buddhism in the third century B.C. gave great impetus to the Sinhalese language, Sinhala. Commentaries were written on the canon in Sinhala, and these were later translated into Pali in the fifth century A.D. by the monk Buddhaghosa, who came to Ceylon in search of original sources that had been lost in India. The old Sinhalese commentaries themselves did not survive after the tenth century.

As Sinhala was understood in few places outside Ceylon, Pali was often used as a medium of communication. The *Mahavamsa,* a dynastic history by the Buddhist monk Thera Mahanama, was composed in Pali verse in the early sixth century. The earliest Sinhala prose work to survive is the *Siyabaslakara,* a work on rhetoric whose author was reputedly a tenth-century king. Although no early poetry is extant, literary sources men-tion poetic works, such as a poem commemorating the arrival of Buddha's Tooth in the fourth century A.D.

Some early Sinhalese kings were reputed to be eminent poets, and several Sinhalese poets were said to have gathered at the court at the end of the sixth and the beginning of the seventh century A.D. The graffiti on the walls at Sigiriya testify to poetic ability at the time. S. Paranavitana, who collected these verses in two volumes, compared them to the "Japanese *haiku* (unrhymed poem of three lines) in their expression of the emotional reaction to the single incident or the single observation."

After the restoration of Sinhalese power in the eleventh century at Polonnaruwa, there was a resurgence of literary activity (see ch. 3, Historical Setting). Most of it was scholastic and critical, such as the translation of Pali and Sanskrit works into Sinhala and the compilation of grammars and religious commentaries. Poetry was revived under Vijayabahu I, who was himself a poet. The only surviving poem from this period is the *Sasadavata,* which was based on a *jataka* story, written in the twelfth century. The *jataka* story, which deals with events in the life of the Buddha or in his previous births, are the closest approach to popular literature that Sinhalese-Buddhism produced. A noted author of this period was Dhammakitti-thera, who wrote one of the best extant Pali poems and who is reputedly the author of the *Culavamsa,* the sequel to the *Mahavamsa.* A feature of early prose works is the amount of repetition. Books, which were scratched with a stylus on palm leaves, were so expensive that they were primarily used for oral recitation, in which repetition is a necessary device to aid a listener's memory.

Most of the surviving early literature belongs to a period of decline from the thirteenth century onward; this is regarded by a number of present-day observers as unfortunate because many of these works are required reading for students (see ch. 9, Education). A typical example of the style of the period is the *Kavsilumina,* which is described as "highly ornate and artificial in style, and full of striking conceits." Much of the literature continued to consist of translations and adaptations from Pali originals. At this time a major translation of Pali *jatakas* was made that has greatly influenced Sinhalese-Buddhists. A form of poem called the *sandesa,* or message poem, came into vogue. With titles such as *Peacock Message, Parrot Message,* or *Swan Message,* they were essentially a prayer to a god asking for his favor for a royal personage. They were largely descriptive, as were the panegyrics of a king that also became popular. These and the war ballads that celebrate the Kandyan king's victory over the European foreigners are reminiscent of early Tamil poems. A type of love poetry came to be associated with the panegyrics, although it was a love poetry mainly of separation, not romance.

From the end of the fifteenth until the eighteenth century there were hardly any prose works, with the exception of a few historical writings such as *The Lineage of Kings.* A revival took place in the eighteenth century under the inspiration of Valvita Saranankara, who translated some older Sinhalese and Pali texts and prepared some new works on Buddhism.

Modern Sinhalese Literature

The development of modern literature paralleled that of painting. Two distinct kinds developed, one for the English educated, and one for the Sinhala educated. Not until the 1940s did the two streams combine to make a coherent national literature possible. Higher English education became available for the elite in the last quarter of the nineteenth century at the same time that there was a marked growth in elementary vernacular education (see ch. 3, Historical Setting; ch. 11, Religion).

The first work that could be called a Sinhalese novel was published in 1905. It was preceded by important developments in the field of language and the concept of the novel. Most of the early novelists were journalists. Journalists not only played a major role in bridging the gap between the language of everyday speech and that of the scholar, but also newspapers and periodicals were the first to publish short stories and, later, novels. Because of its small population, the then colony could not afford a large book-publishing industry; as a result, most literary activity was confined to the daily and monthly press. Sinhalese journalists were generally bilingual and thus were able to select from English literature that which would appeal to their unsophisticated audience.

The English educated, who had access to the best European literature, developed a critical faculty that was disdainful of the early attempts of Sinhalese novelists. The English educated restricted themselves to literary classification, research and criticism, essays and diaries, and translations of oriental classics. The Sinhala educated, on the other hand, took from European romantic literature its melodrama and translated it to a Sinhalese setting, using either contemporary or traditional themes.

One of the earliest popular works to be translated into Sinhala was *Arabian Nights,* which has been credited with laying the foundations of the Sinhalese novel. Other formative in-

172

fluences were Bible translations, the lives of Christian saints, and a book called *The Family Guide,* which interspersed advice on marriage and medical and family matters with translations of fables and folk tales. A Christian author, Lindamulage Isaac de Silva (1844-1907), used the serial technique for religious propaganda to tell the stories of two fictional families, one happy, the other miserable. The happy family followed all the proper Christian precepts.

Simon de Silva and Piyadasa Sirisena, the first Sinhalese novelists, began publishing in the first decade of the twentieth century. Both novelists were propagandists attacking the denationalized way of life of the Westernized urban middle class, de Silva in *Mina, Terisa,* and *Our Religion* (generally regarded as his best work), and Sirisena in a series of novels beginning with *Jayatissa and Rosalind, or Happy Marriage.* The hero, Jayatissa, is a Christian whose hand the Sinhalese-Buddhist Rosalind refuses until, through a series of events, Jayatissa abandons Christianity and his Western ways. This novel reached a fifth edition in only a decade of publication. Although the novel is mainly set in a Colombo suburb, the couple have adventures in a forest that are reminiscent of *Arbian Nights,* the *Ramayana,* and *jataka* stories. Sirisena was considered a major force in the nationalist movement, and he classed himself more with nationalist propagandists than novelists who had the reputation of writing only frivolities (see ch. 3, Historical Setting).

W. A. Silva, who began publishing in 1909 at the age of seventeen, has been the most prolific writer of the escape novel. Romantic love and the triumph of good over evil, combined with the ability to tell a good story, have made his novels perennially popular. His historical novels, such as *The Assassination of Vijayabahu* and *The Pirate Chieftain,* reach a higher standard, possibly because they are closely modeled on two well-known European works. He did, however, encourage in the Sinhalese public a habit for reading and introduced modern ideas, campaigning against outworn superstitions.

In the late 1960s the novelist most highly regarded by the critics was Martin Wickramasinghe. His portrayal of life in a Sinhalese village, beginning with *Ape Gama* (Our Village) in 1939 and followed by *Gam Peraliya* (Changing Village) in 1944, attracted the attention of the English educated. Wickramasinghe's first novel, *Lila* (1914), was strongly influenced by Sirisena, except that the younger author criticized both East and West. He also introduced the use of everyday speech in dialogue. His realistic approach led him to avoid melodrama and to rely on the drama implicit in the strains of modernization imposed on a traditional society. In *Yugataya* (The End of an Age) in 1948, he conveyed the complexities of social and political life in Colombo in the 1940s. Wickramasinghe is also regarded by Ceylonese critics as the best short-story writer.

No other novelist has equaled Wickramasinghe's achievement, although a number have been successful with the short story. The short-story form is more akin to the traditional *jataka* and folk tales and therefore considered more natural to Sinhalese authors. Translations of Russian stories have also provided inspiration to Ceylonese writers, because of the parallel in the breakup of a feudal system. Hemapala Munidasa and G. B. Senanayaka are masters of the short story. Munidasa, however, has been criticized by some for going too far in his treatment of sex. Sinhalese authors have always had difficulty gaining acceptance from the Sinhalese educated class, particularly the Buddhist community. A positive attitude by authors to change, expecially with regard to women and romantic love, has aroused the hostility of Buddhists.

In 1970 a critic described the themes of novels in the previous decade as "middle class life blended with intellectuality and disconcerting thoughts on social values concerning marriage, love, etc." and as monotonous and boring. He suggested that authors may not have noticed that the reading public has become more sophisticated. Other critics call for more novels of "social uplift." Gunadesa Amarasekara is a promising short-story writer of the 1960s who has moved from adolescent themes to a more mature examination of modern life.

THE PERFORMING ARTS

Drama

Buddhist opposition to music and drama stifled the development of drama. Dramatic elements, however, existed in the rituals of the folk religion (see ch. 11, Religion). In the ceremonies designed to propitiate gods and demons, the exorcist used mime, impersonation, and dialogue. Usually a dramatic story was attached to every ceremony. In addition, the ceremonies, which frequently were nightlong affairs, were interspersed with actual dramatic pieces that became the model for later folk plays.

Two kinds of folk plays developed from the folk rituals: *kolam* and *sokari*. In *kolam,* whose origin is believed to be a pregnancy ritual, the actors wore brightly painted masks of wood and performed without a stage in an open area. They presented traditional folk and *jataka* tales in song, dance, and dialogue that lasted all night. The main element of *sokari,* which also continued throughout the night, was mime. *Sokari* was a specialty of the hill country, as opposed to *kolam,* which in the 1950s was confined to the southern coastal areas. The *sokari* was only performed during the threshing season in connection with religious rites to the goddess Pattini. The story describes the arrival in Ceylon of an Indian entertainer and his wife Sokari and their adventures, in which Sokari elopes with a Sinhalese village doctor. Both *kolam* and *sokari* bear a strong resemblance to Tamil folk drama, or *kuttu.*

At the beginning of the nineteenth century a type of folk opera called *nadagama* became popular in villages and towns on the west coast. Its origin was the South Indian folk drama, which in turn was influenced by the classical Sanskrit tradition. *Nadagama* comes from a Tamil word meaning drama. All the characters sing except the narrator who links the various scenes. The Roman Catholics of the Jaffna Peninsula modified various parts of the Tamil *kuttus* and used them to express Christian and European themes, and it was through these Christian adaptations that Sinhalese *nadagama* arose.

Philippu Sinno, who is credited with the earliest Sinhalese *nadagamas,* was born in 1770. Poorly educated, he belonged to a lower middle class Catholic family in Colombo. He translated Christian Tamil operettas into a mixture of Sinhalese and Tamil. Other Sinhalese Christians followed his example, creating a series of popular *nadagamas* based on Shakespearean plays, Indian legends, and Christian themes. Later on, Sinhalese writers began to tone down the romantic, "lust-provoking" element and introduced Buddhist birth stories. In common with the folk dramas, the *nadagamas* lasted all night, but they were performed on a stage, and admission was charged.

In the 1880s one of the many theatrical companies of Bombay visited Ceylon. The lively Hindi language tunes, the colorful costumes, and the elaborate stage sets of their musicals, which were a cross between a Sanskrit play and a Western musical, made an immediate impression. The Sinhalese writers adapted these new features to the *nadagama* and called it *nurtiya.* The first notable *nurtiya* author was Kaluntantirige C. Don Bastian Bandara Jayaweera. In 1884 he adapted *Romeo and Juliet* from a previous Sinhalese adaptation of the Shakespearean original. The new form divided the performance into scenes and acts and shortened it to an evening's entertainment. Female actors began to take over feminine roles, which had formerly been acted by men. The actors' reputations, always low, declined even further because of the irregular behavior of these actresses, and the *nurtiya* performances were generally shunned by the urban middle classes.

In an effort to raise the level of the *nurtiya,* an English-educated lawyer, John de Silva, took themes from Sinhalese history, such as the story of Dutugamunu (see ch. 3, Historical Setting). He tried to make the music more relevant by adapting the *ragas* (melodies) of North Indian classical music, which correspond to a particular mood, and he introduced some conventions of Sanskrit drama. De Silva formed a theatrical company to perform his many plays. Charles Dias and Peter de Silva, among others, continued composing *nurtiyas* into the 1920s. The songs, however, often had no relevance to the plot.

The *nurtiyas* were succeeded in the 1930s and 1940s by Victorian melodramas and social comedies. These were called Jayamanna plays after two brothers, one the author, the other the chief actor. They satirized upper middle class life in Colombo. The literary language of much of the dialogue and its arbitrary interruption by song kept these plays at an artificial level.

Serious drama entered the Sinhalese stage in the medium of translations. Amateur theatrical groups, particularly the Dramatic Society of the University of Ceylon, put on Sinhala adaptations of Moliere's *Le Bourgeois Gentilhomme,* Oscar Wilde's *The Importance of Being Ernest,* and Nikolai Gogol's *Marriage.* Plays by Bertolt Brecht and Jean Anouilh were also popular. They appealed, however, to only a small educated group.

The production in 1956 of E. R. Sarathchandra's *Maname,* a sophisticated adaptation of a folk play, is regarded as a landmark in Sinhala theater. For the first time song and dance were integral parts of the play, furthering the action instead of interrupting it. It has been equally popular among rural and urban audiences. A Sinhalese critic wrote: "In *Maname* Dr. Sarathchandra created a form that was both popular and capable of serving as a medium of the highest dramatic expression." In later plays his inspiration came from folk tales and *jataka* stories. Other playwrights have followed his lead—for example, Henry Jayasena in *Kuveni.* Jayasena also has used the form to portray contemporary themes, such as the frustrations of youth in *Janelaya.*

The *nadagama* form is, however, extremely difficult to manipulate, and Jayasena and many others have turned instead to adaptations of Western plays. An adaptation of *A Streetcar Named Desire,* called *Ves Muhunu,* has been popular, and Brecht's *The Caucasian Chalk Circle* was the hit of 1967, possibly because it combined both music and drama. There are

176

some critics who consider the degradation of a Southern family in the United States in Tennessee Williams' play as relevant to the Ceylonese situation and others who regard it as an irrelevant play about a nymphomaniac. All deplore the dearth of original Sinhala-language plays and blame in part the fact that writers have to support themselves at other jobs and only have the energy to prepare adaptations. Many authors lack a background in Western theatrical tradition, and those who have it cannot write fluently in Sinhala. The standards of English-language critics are regarded as too high, and the tastes of the Sinhalese public too low.

Puppet Theater

Although puppets are mentioned in Sanskrit literature and marionette performances have long been a feature of South Indian festivals, puppetry as a dramatic art is of very recent origin in Ceylon. It is traditionally associated with Ambalangoda in southern Ceylon, which was also a major center of *nadagama*. A well-known *nadagama* producer, Charles Silva Gunasinghe Gurunanse, produced puppet shows in between his *nadagama* productions. Lack of financial support from the local gentry, other opportunities of employment for the actors, and competition from the cinema had eliminated *nadagamas* from village life by the 1950s. A puritanical movement had also militated against live actors presenting some of the more explicit *nadagama* themes. A greater freedom was allowed the wooden puppet figures.

Although there is evidence that puppetry was popular in a number of southern coastal villages and in suburban Colombo, in the 1960s it was mainly confined to four closely related troupes in Ambalangoda. A troupe also exists near Kandy that claims low-country origin. Each troupe requires singers, puppet operators, instrumentalists, scene changers, and skilled wood carvers. Most puppets are four feet high, but some life-size puppets, which scarcely move, represent royalty and nobility. The clown, the village town crier, the boy player, and the dancing girl are stock characters. Other puppets show a great range of characterization, such as helmeted modern soldiers. The costumes of kings are highly detailed and elaborate.

As an art of the poor, puppetry has had difficulty in surviving, and the jealousy of its practitioners has made it difficult for outsiders to give help. A government attempt to revive the art has been only partially successful. In 1958 the Department of Cultural Affairs gave a grant to the Panel of Low-Country Music and Dancing of the Art Council to set up a school. Two

177

puppeteers agreed to teach, and various new methods and European techniques were introduced. The new puppetry was especially intended for use in schools.

Music and Dance

It is known that instructions in the Gandharva Sastra, comprising singing, instrumental music, and dancing, was given in Sinhalese schools in ancient times, and the *Mahavamsa* records that dancing girls performed at the Sinhalese court. Buddhist monks, however, were not allowed to patronize dance, song, or instrumental playing, so that these arts were developed in spite of their opposition. Royalty, with its South Indian connections, maintained the customs of the *kshatria* (warrior caste), which included the patronage of dancers and musicians, and throughout the centuries kings and nobles, many of whom were skilled in music, fostered these arts. Although the music itself has not survived, there is evidence of it in stone sculptures, such as the friezes of dancers at Polonnaruwa and Yapahuwa, in wood carvings and on ivory combs, as well as literary evidence in the ancient chronicles and the poetry of the fourteenth and fifteenth centuries, particularly the *sandesa*. Although the Buddhist attitude inhibited the development of song and stringed instruments, the art of drumming was not considered so morally dangerous and was, in fact, used in religious processions.

The Veddahs, the original inhabitants of Ceylon, chanted their rituals in a range of only one or two tones, but their dancing was virile and rhythmic. In the Bali, Thovil, and Devil dancing rituals, which coexisted with Buddhism in the villages, the invocations of the exorcist were in chanted poetry, and the folksongs were in a similarly limited range (see ch. 11, Religion). The folk drama of *kolam* and *sokari* distinguished between dialogue, chanted poetry, and occasional songs, but it was not until the development of *nadagama* in the early nineteenth century that the Tamil folksong tradition began to affect Sinhalese songs. On a more sophisticated level, love songs (*viraha*) of probable Tamil origin became part of Sinhalese tradition in the eighteenth century. In the late nineteenth century *nurtiya,* the musicals from Bombay, introduced popular Hindi tunes, which had been influenced by Western music, and this hybrid music has remained popular, especially in films.

Male dancing received a great impetus when the Kandyan king Kirthi Sri Rajasingha in 1775 combined the annual festival of the Temple of the Tooth with the Hindu festivals of the gods Vishnu, Kataragama (Skanda), and Natha (Sakra) and the goddess Pattini. The Buddhist *sanghas* adopted the custom of making grants of land to the dancers in exchange for their services to the temples. From ancient times kings had rewarded the families of dancers with landholdings.

The Kandyan dance bears a strong resemblance to that of Kathakali, the vigorous male dancing of Kerala in South India, with the difference that Kathakali is dance drama and *ves,* the main Kandyan dance, is pure dance, with a great emphasis on rhythm. The *ves* dances center on the legend of the medicine man who came from India to cure a Sinhalese king, Panduva, of a dreadful disease. The legend is associated with the rituals of the Kohomba gods, which were a feature of the Malayarata, or hill country. The distinctive costume of the Kandyan dancer is said to represent that of the royal physician in the Malayarata.

The dancer originally wore sixty-four ornaments, but the modern dancer has reduced this number by half. Typical are the ear ornaments, in the shape of a leaf and a rosette, the headband, the anklets, the flounced waistcloth, and the *inahediya,* made of silk or velvet, adorned with silver bosses and hung from the waist. Later a form of solo dancing developed called *vannam.* There are eighteen of these *vannams,* and they either imitate the actions of various animals and birds, such as the elephant or peacock, or are in praise of the gods and Buddha. Other Kandyan dances that are performed today are the Nayandi Ves Sellama, the Udekki, and the Pantheru. Singing and the playing of musical instruments may accompany the dance.

The Kandyan dancers went through a rigorous training, and the Kandyan style of dancing spread throughout the island, but it was not until the visit of Rabindranath Tagore (1861–1941), who brought Kathakali and Bharata Natyam dance dramas to Ceylon, that modern Ceylonese dancing developed. Seebert Dias made the first significant break with tradition by bringing dancers on stage to perform as interludes in stage dramas. The heavy *ves* costume was modified, and the drumming and dance steps were toned down.

About the year 1945 women began dancing the hill country dances. Formerly, the dancers were considered very low caste, but they have gained a new prestige under government patronage. Chitra Sena, the son of Seebert Dias, has his own ballet troupe, which in 1970 made a successful tour of Western Europe. His Nirthanjali is a balletic rendering of various Kandyan dance styles.

Films

Before the first Sinhala film was made in 1947, Hindi, Tamil, and English films were shown in Ceylon. The earliest Sinhalese directors copied the plots, songs, and even gestures and intonations of the actors in South Indian films. The Tamil film and the Sinhalese *nurtiya* musicals shared the same origin in the Parsee musical and the Sanskrit play, so that the films appealed immediately to the Sinhalese public. From the start, however, English-educated critics have criticized both the style and content of Sinhalese films. A critic in 1970 described the contents of a typical film as "contrived, totally unconvincing fight, a tedious love song, a throw-in ballet or Bombay dance, and embarrassing Singlish dialogue."

In addition to the commercial film industry, the Government Film Unit was set up in 1948 to make documentary and news films. Its first director was an Italian, and he was succeeded by an Englishman, Ralph Keene, whose documentary *Fishermen of Negombo* won a prize at an international competition. The Government Film Unit provided a valuable training ground in Western film techniques. By 1955 all the foreign technicians were replaced by Ceylonese, and George Wickramasinghe became the director. The high standard of the film unit was recognized by awards in international film festivals, including three awards for the film *Kandy Perahera.*

Lester James Peiris, a former assistant director of the Government Film Unit, produced the first successful commercial film in the style of the Italian post-World War II realists. *Rekawa* (The Line of Destiny), his first commercial film failed at the box office in 1956, but his third film, an adaptation of Martin Wickramasinghe's *Changing Village,* was an instant success. Peiris attributes part of his success to the sophistication of the new filmgoing generation, which is demanding more realistic themes, but also to his capturing on film a way of life that is fast disappearing in Sinhalese villages. In common with novelist Martin Wickramasinghe, Peiris avoids the melodramatic, believing that is is "more important to portray the undramatic because in cinema this is where the true drama is." In 1970 he became the third Asian film director to have a retrospective showing of his films at the Museum of Modern Art in New York. *Changing Village* had already won the Golden Peacock Award for the best feature film in New Delhi, India.

Sugathapala Senerat Yapa, a young film director and former government clerk, also won an award in 1970 at the annual Delhi film festival for his short silent film *The Man and the Crow.* In a documentary style, it portrays people's frantic search for a living in the poorer sections of a Ceylonese city. His second feature-length film, *Hatane Katawa,* concerned with university students, was less competent. Siri Sunasinghe, a Sanskrit professor, also makes serious films. A tendency has been noted by some observers in 1970 for the talented young to go in for making films rather than writing novels.

In 1969 the government recognized that the Sinhalese film industry needed protection against foreign competition to survive. The small size of the Sinhala-speaking population (nearly 9 million) means a limited market unless films are made with an eye on the international market. In 1969 it was estimated that only 22 percent of screening time in Ceylon was devoted to Sinhala-language films. The government has recommended legislation to provide a minimum of 30 percent. Special tax incentives were approved in 1970 for newly established film companies, and the government has proposed the establishment of a national film institute to maintain a training school for technicians and artists, hold conferences and festivals, and import high-quality films.

PHILOSOPHIC AND INTELLECTUAL EXPRESSION

Intellectual expression is largely centered on Theravada Buddhism and the preservation of its values. Until the introduction of Western education by the Portuguese in the sixteenth century, the Buddhist monasteries and colleges had a monopoly of learning. Two ways of life were open to the *bhikku* (see Glossary): the life of an ascetic engaged primarily in spiritual exercises or the life of a scholar who studied and commented on the various Buddhist texts. Scholars were responsible for the considerable exegetical literature that developed. Philosophical questions were of lesser importance to the Theravada Buddhists than a practical and orthodox interpretation of the Buddha's doctrines (see ch. 11, Religion).

Mahayana Buddhism, a new philosophical interpretation of Buddhism from India, which acknowledged the validity of the truth of the average man and emphasized the attainment of salvation in the next life, became a serious threat to Theravada Buddhism in the sixth and seventh centuries A.D. Theravada Buddhism officially triumphed in 1165 with the reunification of the *sangha* by Parakramabahu I, but only after certain Mahayana doctrines, such as belief in Bodhisattvas and *bhakti* (devotion), had been incorporated.

By the tenth century Buddhism had ceased to be a major force in India, and Ceylon became the fountainhead of Buddhism. Monks from Burma, Thailand, and Cambodia came to Ceylon in the fourteenth and fifteenth centuries to study before establishing new communities in their homelands.

With the advent of Christianity, beginning in the sixteenth century, Buddhist philosophy and religion were put on the defensive. Vigorous Christian missionary activity in the nineteenth century confronted the *sangha* with the necessity of new interpretations of Buddhist philosophy. In the last quarter of the nineteenth century, newspapers and periodicals were the vehicle for numerous debates on the merits of Christianity and Buddhism. *Bauddha Labdhi Nirakrtiya* (A Refutation of Buddhist Belief) received it own refutation in *Kristu Labdhi Praharaya* (The Blow to Christian Faith) in 1902.

Colonel Henry Steele Olcott, a theosophist, came to the aid of the Buddhists in Ceylon in 1880. He founded Buddhist schools and started two Buddhist newspapers, one in Sinhala and one in English, to further the cause of Buddhism. A young Sinhalese clerk, David Hewavitarne, who was inspired by Colonel Olcott to change his name to Anagarika Dharmapala, in 1886 was elected general manager of the Buddhist schools and took over the editorship of the two newspapers. In 1891 he inaugurated the Maha Bodhi Society and the Maha Bodhi Press. He attacked European dress and customs and is considered the greatest Buddhist missionary of his time.

Dharmapala influenced novelists such as Piyadasa Sirisena, whose novels were a bitter attack on the denationalized upper middle class in the cities. The English-educated elite looked to Europe for intellectual inspiration. Unfamiliar with their own language and heritage, they were unable to make a contribution to their own culture except in politics and science. An exception was Ananda Kentish Coomaraswamy, son of a Ceylon Tamil and an Englishwoman. Educated entirely in England to the doctorate level in geology, he returned to Ceylon at the age of twenty-five and was appointed director of a minerological survey. As a result of his travels throughout Ceylon, he became aware of Ceylon's ancient heritage and eventually became one of the most influential advocates of a national revival in both India and Ceylon. Although a Ceylon Tamil, he was impartial in his work for the recognition of both Buddhist and Hindu culture. He achieved recognition in Western intellectual circles for his brilliant scholarship, although his ideas on the perennial philosophy of both East and West were out of fashion in the twentieth century.

The Sinhalese novelist Martin Wickramasinghe castigates both the English educated who immerse themselves in the European tradition and the Sinhala educated who take an exaggerated pride in their past. In his opinion, both attitudes are inadequate in the environment of modern Ceylon. He regards the rational and critical spirit in Buddhism as a valuable aid in coming to terms with modern ideas. Socialist political ideas have been accepted by Buddhist-oriented political parties (see ch. 17, Political Values and Attitudes). Newspaper articles in

1970 continue to reinterpret Buddhist beliefs in the light of Western ideas—for example, the doctrine of free will and the Buddhist doctrine of nondeterministic causal conditioning. Causality, a central tenet of Buddhism, is linked to causality and chance in modern physics.

TAMIL CULTURE

In 1970 the culture of the Tamil minority continued to be closely interwoven with that of the Sinhalese. Through the centuries artists and craftsmen from South India have been brought or have emigrated to the island. A specific Ceylon Tamil culture developed only after the establishment of the Jaffna kingdom in the north in the thirteenth century, when the ancient kingdoms of Anuradhapura and Polonnaruwa had been destroyed (see ch. 3, Historical Setting). During the Chola conquest (1017–70), a Saivite temple in the Dravidian style was built in Polonnaruwa but with more restraint than the elaborately decorated temples of South India. Several bronze images of Siva, the Hindu god, have been discovered at the site of the temple, but they are presumed to have been imported (see ch. 11, Religion).

The Tamil kingdom of the thirteenth to sixteenth centuries was not rich enough, however, to construct many major temples. Most of the temples were modest versions of the South Indian Madura style built in the period of the Vijayanager Empire (fourteenth to sixteenth centuries), with an elaborately sculptured *gopuram* (tower).

For the most part the Ceylon Tamils have looked for cultural inspiration to South India, and the contributions they have made, especially to literature, have been recognized in Tamilnad in India, rather than in their native Ceylon. At the end of the fifteenth century the Academy of Tamil Literature was founded at Nallur in the Jaffna Peninsula by the Jaffna king. Both literary and spoken Tamil in Ceylon are considered purer than South Indian Tamil and freer of Sanskrit loanwords.

A Tamil scholar, Arumuga Navalar, born at Nallur in 1823, worked both in Jaffna and in South India, establishing schools of Tamil and Saivite Hinduism in Nallur and Chidambaram. Although in his youth he translated the Bible for a Protestant missionary society in Jaffna, he became the leader of a Saivite revival movement in both Ceylon and Tamilnad, establishing a printing press and campaigning for the proper education of Hindu priests and the banning of *nautch* girls (professional temple dancers, sometimes associated with sex rituals) and slaughter of animals in temples. He also edited several Tamil classics.

The development of a modern Tamil literature has confronted many of the same problems that have hampered Sinhalese literature. Among other things the academic tradition has laid great stress on an uncritical acceptance of past literary achievements. The great poetry of the Sangam period in the first centuries of the Christian Era, for example, is the subject of pedantic commentary rather than inspiration to the modern poets. From the fifth to the eleventh centuries a devotional poetry became popular, and a wealth of folksongs and folk tales enriched the lives of the people, but a gap existed between the popular culture and the scholarly tradition. It was the journalists of the nineteenth century who took the first steps toward bridging the gap and developed a modern prose style.

Subramania Bharata (1881-1921), poet, reformer, and patriot, was the major literary figure of the late nineteenth and early twentieth centuries. Another trailblazer was V.V.S. Iyer, particularly in the development of the short story and in literary criticism. In the 1930s a group of writers published short stories of considerable merit in the magazine *Manikkodi*, and in the 1940s there were various experiments with the novel. Mahatma Gandhi, Karl Marx, and Sigmund Freud, as well as traditional South Indian philosophers, have been said to be the chief influences on Tamil writers. The family unit and the struggle of the individual to retain individuality in a traditional communal society have been major themes. The serious writer feels himself at a disadvantage with a newly-literate public that enjoys the escapist literature of magazine serials.

During the 1930s and 1940s there was also a renaissance of Tamil poetry. N. Pitchaimoorthy, K.P. Rajagopalan, and Puthumaipithan were strongly influenced by surrealism. The communication of personal dreams has been more important to them than the clear expositon of a moral, and as a result Tamil poetry has become harder to decipher. A Ceylon poet, Murugaian, having a thorough background in Tamil classical poetry and Western poetry, particularly that of T.S. Eliot, is considered a poet of promise.

The Ceylon Tamils are also heirs to a rich tradition of folk drama, which passed over into Sinhalese culture through the *nadagamas*. Neglect by the Tamil elite has, however, made it almost extinct. In the *nattukuttu* (folk play) there was neither stage nor scenery, except for a circular *mandapam* (platform of earth and sand). The audience encircled the platform. The drama was of two types—*ten modi* (South Indian) or *vada modi* (North Indian)—and was primarily dance. Each type had its own symbolic gestures, music, dress, and dance steps and lasted for almost twelve hours. S. Vithianathan of the University of Ceylon has attempted to create a dramatic unity out of the songs, dances, and dialogue in his version of the Tamil folk play *Karnan Por.* He has expressed the belief that with contemporary themes the folk play could be revived.

SCIENCE

In ancient Ceylon an indigenous system of herbal medicine and astrology were the main sciences practiced. Irrigation engineering reached a high degree of sophistication, although its techniques are not known. In the nineteenth century, with the development of plantation agriculture and health services, modern scientific research in cash crops and tropical diseases began. The Botanical Gardens at Peliyagoda were established as early as 1799. Later they were moved to Peradeniya, where they continue to contribute to agricultural research.

In 1870 the Ceylon Medical School was founded in association with the Colombo General Hospital. Marcus Fernando was one of the first Ceylonese to distinguish himself in medicine. He won a scholarship to University College Hospital in London, and after his return he joined the Government Medical Service. He was the first Ceylonese to hold the post of registrar of the Colombo Medical College and was one of those responsible for the foundation of University College in 1921, which in 1942 combined with he Medical College to become the University of Ceylon. In 1910 he outlined a campaign that would eradicate malaria from the island. Such a campaign was not mounted until World War II, however.

The Ceylon Association for the Advancement of Science (CAAS) was established in 1944. It is divided into six sections: medical and veterinary sciences, agriculture and forestry, engineering, natural sciences, physical sciences, and social sciences. The CAAS is a member of the International Council of Scientific Unions and represents Ceylon at international conferences. At the annual session papers are presented from the various sections. The majority of the papers concern applied research with direct bearing on Ceylon's industrial, agricultural, and social problems. In 1968, for example, research papers were presented on malaria, soils and fertilizers, rice, irrigation, industrial development, meteorology, tropical diseases, contraception, manpower planning, and craft training.

In 1970 there was considerable controversy on the relevance of scientific research. The Ceylonese scientist faces the dilemma of contributing to national development or maintaining his position in the international community through original research. Social scientists, such as Gananath Obeyesekere, have contributed highly technical studies on Ceylonese society, such as *Land Tenure in Village Ceylon*, which some observers consider an invaluable aid in charting development programs. Other Ceylonese observers, however, assert that Ceylon cannot afford the luxury of original research and, for the time being, must limit itself to the adaptation of international research to the Ceylonese situation, as with developing high-yielding varieties of rice.

Other scientific research is carried out by the Tea Institute, the Rubber Research Institute, the Coconut Research Institute, and the Ceylon Institute of Scientific and Industrial Research (CISIR). In 1970 the first Ceylonese to be awarded a doctorate in chemistry at any Ceylonese university conducted his research at the CISIR laboratories after working hours.

Scientists who wish to engage in advanced scientific research are obliged to go abroad. Although the government has discouraged the exodus of scientific talent, it has been unable to halt it. The Ceylonese take pride in the handful of countrymen who achieve international recognition. Cyril Ponnamperuma in 1970 was the chief of the Chemical Evolution Branch in the Exobiology Division of the Ames Research Center in California. A number of others work at laboratories in Canada, the United States, and Great Britain, with little hope of return to a fruitful career in Ceylon.

Archaeological research into the remains of the ancient civilizations of Anuradhapura and Polonnaruwa has received considerable governmental attention. The first attempts to uncover the ancient cities go back to the mid-nineteenth century. H.C.P. Bell of the Ceylon Civil Service, an amateur archaeologist, did preliminary research at Anuradhapura, Polonnaruwa, Sigiriya, and Yapahuwa. S. Paranavitana, head of the Archaeology Survey of Ceylon from 1940 to 1956 and afterwards research professor of archaeology at the University of Ceylon, Peradeniya, has supervised excavations and published numerous papers on the art, archaeology, and history of the island. In 1966 the Department of Archaeology, which had confined its activities to the major sites, expanded to cover the whole island. The preservation of buildings and the chemical treatment of ancient rock paintings are also important features of the department's work.

THE ROLE OF GOVERNMENT

The government takes an active part in the promotion of cultural activities. The Art Council of Ceylon was inaugurated by an act of Parliament in 1952. The council is divided into panels covering a wide range of the arts. For example, there are panels for Sinhala drama, Tamil drama, Islamic fine arts, music, films, publications, paintings, Kandyan dancing and low-country dancing, handicrafts, pageants, and festivals. There is also a government Department of Cultural Affairs, with sections on art, literature, and religion. The Government College of Fine Arts was reconstituted in 1965. Administered by the Ministry of Education and Cultural Affairs, it is divided into three separate institutes. Instruction is given in fine and commercial art, wood carving, light metal work, and other handicrafts. The College of Music provides a six-year course in Oriental music, and traditional dancing is taught at the College of Dancing and Ballet (see ch. 9, Education).

There are national museums in Colombo, Kandy, and Ratnapura. The oldest and largest is the Colombo Museum, founded in 1876 by Governor William Gregory. The museum has specialized in archaeology, anthropology, fauna and flora, etymology, rocks, and minerals. Its collections include some fine early stone sculpture, Hindu bronzes from Polonnaruwa, ivories from the Kandyan period, and Dutch period furniture.

In 1904 the Colombo Museum began publishing a magazine, *Spolia Zeylanica*, which in 1970 was still publishing articles of interest to research scientists throughout the world. Under the National Museum's five-year plan for 1966–71, the cultural section was being reorganized into historical periods. The museums specialized in artifacts indigenous to their areas.

The Colombo Museum, the Department of Archaeology, the Archives, and the Ceylon Branch of the Royal Asiatic Society all contain valuable books and records, but, in most cases, have inadequate funds and trained personnel to catalog and maintain their collections. Libraries have existed in the temples and monasteries since ancient times. The Colombo Museum has a collection of more than 3,000 ancient palm-leaf manuscripts. The government archives department had its origin in 1656, although its present form dates back only to 1899. A report by a United Nations Educational, Scientific and Cultural Organization (UNESCO) library adviser in 1960 noted a tremendous enthusiasm for good libraries at all levels but remarked on the lack of funds and professional training. He recommended the establishment of a national library, which had not been implemented in 1970.

The Department of Cultural Affairs makes funds available for Buddhist, Hindu, and Islamic religious activities and also earmarks a grant for the publication of books of religious instruction for Roman Catholic schools. In the last decade funds have been provided for the preparation of a *Buddhist Encyclopedia*, and some assistance has been given to writers (by purchasing their printed books), libraries, and literary societies, including Tamil literary societies. District art councils receive regular financial support, and the principal ballet and dance troupes are subsidized.

The Art Council provides financial assistance for the first performance of any acceptable drama and has made available a former school hall at a minimal fee for a theater. The only other professional theater in Colombo is the Lionel Wendt, which is expensive and can only seat 400, although plans are underway for expansion. Programs offered at the Lionel Wendt in 1970 included Bharata Natyam (South Indian classical dancing), Shakespearean plays, a guitar recital, an English musical called *The Boy Friend*, Tamil drama, E.R. Sarathchandra's *Maname*, and Chitra Sena's ballet troupe. Only in the 1960s had Sinhala theater been successful at the Lionel Wendt. The Art Council also sponsors an annual drama festival, commissioning plays for it.

CHAPTER 11

RELIGION

Religious diversity characterizes Ceylon; four major world religions have significant followings. One religious community—the Theravada Buddhists — is numerically and culturally dominant, however, and its influence is growing. Approximately 90 percent of the Sinhalese, or 64 percent of the population, are members of this community. Nearly 95 percent of the Tamils, or 20 percent of the nation, are Saivite Hindus. Some 9 percent of the population is Christian; this group is divided among Sinhales, Tamils, and Burghers. The remaining 7 percent are Muslims (see ch. 5, Ethnic Groups and Languages).

Buddhism, which has been present on the island since ancient times, has always been significantly tied to Sinhalese culture; until the fall of the Kandy kingdom to Great Britain in 1815, it enjoyed the official protection of the Sinhalese kings (see ch. 3, Historical Setting). Colonial rule, however, broke its connection with the state, and it lost much of its standing and power. Hinduism, which also has been present for many centuries, was less dependent on organization and governmental support and, consequently, suffered relatively less. Islam was introduced by Arab traders, and by medieval times Muslim communities were established on the island. The Portuguese mistakenly identified the Ceylon Muslims as their Moorish enemies in the West, and many had to migrate to friendly territories to escape persecution.

Various Christian sects were introduced into the island by the Portuguese, Dutch, and British. In time the activities and educational organizations of their missionaries gained great influence and made deep inroads into the indigenous religious communities, especially the Buddhist, undermining their cohesion. Christian communities of several denominations still exist, but their position is declining.

In the latter part of the nineteenth and throughout the twentieth century, a religious resurgence, primarily of Buddhism but also of Hinduism, has taken place on both the religious and cultural level. Combined with Sinhalese nationalism, resurgent Buddhism became, by the mid-1950s, the major political and cultural reality in the country (see ch. 5, Ethnic Groups and Languages; ch. 3, Historical Setting; ch. 14, Political Dynamics).

Although Buddhism has regained much of its former prestige and control of important institutions, modernization, social change, and the needs of a democratic state have altered the relationship between government and religion and have affected the nature of Buddhist monasticism, the backbone of the faith. With the rise of Buddhism in the twentieth century, the Christians have, conversely, lost both standing and members, and some have converted back to Buddhism.

RELATIONS BETWEEN RELIGIOUS COMMUNITIES

Development of Religions in Ceylon

Although the Buddhist religion dominates the spiritual life of the island, the other religious communities have for centuries exercised influence and in 1970 continued to do so. There is no official or established creed, and freedom of worship is enjoyed by all. The cosmopolitan nature of religious life is indicated by the fact that religious festivals of the four major religions are officially recognized and celebrated as national holidays (see table 12).

The original inhabitants of the island, the Veddahs, worshiped animistic spirits, and the early Sinhalese and Tamil invaders brought the Hinduism then prevalent in India. According to Buddhist belief, the Buddha visited Ceylon during his lifetime, accompanied by a number of *arhats* (enlightened beings), and left his footprint on Adam's Peak. He is also said to have known that Ceylon would become a particular bastion of Buddhism. According to the *Mahavamsa,* a dynastic history written by Buddhist monks, the faith was brought to the island in the third century B.C. by Prince Mahinda, the son or brother of the Emperor Asoka (see ch. 3, Historical Setting). The Sinhalese king, Devanampiya Tissa, was converted, and the history of Buddhism in Lanka began.

According to tradition, during the reign of King Vattadamani (89–77 B.C.) a great council of monks assembled in Ceylon, where they codified and reduced to writing the Pali (see Glossary) canon, upon which Theravada Buddhism is based. Sacred Buddhist relics were brought to Ceylon at about the same time as the religion itself. Asoka dispatched the right collarbone of the Buddha, retrieved from his funeral pyre, and also his alms bowl. The sister of Mahinda, Sanghamitta, brought a cutting of the Sacred Bo Tree under which the

Table 12. Religious Holidays Officially Observed in Ceylon

Approximate date	Name	Description	Public and bank holiday	Mercantile holiday
Mid-January	Eid	Day celebrating the end of Ramazan, Muslim month of fasting.	Yes	Yes
..do..	Thai Pongal	Hindu sun-god festival; domestic celebration and *pujas*.	..do..	..do..
February	Maha Sivarathri Day	Hindu festival for Siva's consort, Parvati	..do..	No
March	Hadji Festival	Muslim commemoration of Abraham's sacrifice	..do..	Yes
April	Good Friday	....	..do..	..do..
..do..	Easter	....	..do..	..do..
..do..	Sinhalese and Tamil New Year	....	..do..	..do..
May	Wesak	Buddhist anniversary of birth, death, and enlightenment of Buddha.	..do..	..do..
June	Milad-Un-Nabi	Muslim observance of birth of the Prophet Muhammad.	..do..	..do..
October	Deepvali	Hindu festival of lights welcoming Lakshmi, goddess of wealth.	..do..	No
December 25	Christmas	....	..do..	Yes

Source: Adapted from *Ceylon Calendar of Festivals and Other Events*, Colombo, 1968.

Buddha achieved enlightenment; the ancient tree still stands in Anuradhapura. The relic considered most sacred to Ceylonese Buddhists, the right eye tooth of the Buddha, was brought to the island in the fourth century A.D. It reposes in the Temple of the Tooth in Kandy, having survived numerous misadventures (see ch. 3, Historical Setting).

These symbols, especially the Sacred Tooth Relic, became closely tied to the Sinhalese kingship as its relationship with the religion grew. The Sinhalese state became the protector of the Buddhist faith and especially of the *sangha*. The term *sangha* refers to the total community of *bhikkus,* or Buddhist monks, in the broadest and most abstract sense. The *bhikkus,* although usually called monks, differ from members of Western religious orders in that they need not be associated with a residential community of religious, nor are they under a vow of obedience to superiors. Most *bhikkus,* however, live in residential communities of religious, usually associated with *viharas* (temples) and often called monasteries. The *bhikkus* usually leave the *viharas* daily to seek alms from laymen and carry on spiritual and intellectual activities within their own communities.

It came to be believed that no king could rightly rule without possession of the Tooth, that none but a Buddhist could rule the Sinhalese, and finally that the Sinhalese king was a Bodhisattva, or future Buddha. This belief became so strong that during the British period portraits of the ruler, Queen Victoria, in the guise of a Bodhisattva, decorated temple walls.

In traditional Sinhalese society the influence of the *bhikkus* was enormous. They served as advisers to the king and as spiritual counselors and advisers to the common people; they also controlled education. In most villages the *bhikku* was the most educated individual, often even practicing the indigenous system of herbal medicine called *ayurveda.* A Buddhist gains spiritual merit by giving to the *bhikkus* and the *sangha,* and people of all social positions regularly donated gifts of various kinds. In addition, most *bhikkus* depended on the alms of the villagers for their daily food. The kings in particular made large gifts of land to the communities of *bhikkus* associated with *viharas*, which in time came to be the largest landlords on the island. The land was farmed by peasants and the proceeds delivered to the religious communities in keeping with feudal relationships (see ch. 6, Social Structure).

As the religious communities gained in wealth, they became centers of higher learning and literary culture. Some even ran hospitals. Many branches of knowledge, including astrology, mathematics, and medicine, were pursued by the *bhikkus.* In addition, the erection of temples, shrines, and other religious buildings encouraged the development of fine arts (see ch. 10, Artistic and Intellectual Expression).

During the precolonial period the practice of Hinduism continued, especially in the Tamil north. Because contact with South India was fairly continuous, the religion resembled that practiced by the Tamils of the subcontinent. In addition, some Hindu influence was evident at the courts of the Sinhalese kings. Brahmins served as advisers and also officiated at religious observances. Brahmin priests, for example, were prominent in the ceremonies surrounding the planting of the Sacred Bo Tree. Temples to Hindu gods were constructed from an early date in many parts of the island.

The first Muslims, Arab merchants, arrived in the tenth and eleventh centuries A.D. (see ch. 5, Ethnic Groups and Languages). They established themselves in commerce, especially in the south, and advised the kings on commercial matters. Through intermarriage with the local people, the Muslim community changed in character from purely Arab to Indo-Arab, although it maintained Islamic religious traditions.

Thus, when the Portuguese arrived in the early sixteenth century, they found three religious communities coexisting on the island. The Portuguese came seeking spices to sell in Europe and souls to save for Christianity, and the religion they introduced has been an important feature of island life ever since. Fierce and determined missionaries, they were quite relentless in their suppression of non-Christian religions. In particular, they persecuted the Muslims, whom they identified with their enemies, the Moors, in Europe. Numerous Muslims sought refuge in the territories of the Kandyan king, who offered asylum. The Portuguese zealously sought to destroy the buildings and objects sacred to the other faiths. It is said that the first Portuguese governor of Jaffna destroyed some 500 Hindu temples. The Portuguese claimed to have carried the Sacred Tooth Relic to Goa and there burned and pulverized it; the Buddhists, on the other hand, believe that it miraculously escaped harm and was restored to its sanctuary in Kandy.

The Portuguese made significant numbers of conversions among the Karava, or fisher, caste and other groups on the west coast. The descendants of these converts form the nucleus of the present-day Catholic community. In 1557 King Dharmapala of Kotte converted to Christianity, breaking the tradition of the Sinhalese kingship as defender of the Buddhist faith and depriving the *sangha* in his territory of considerable influence. In the opinion of his subjects, he had disqualified himself as

193

king. He repulsed an attack on his kingdom and, in 1580, declared the Portuguese king his heir. Some temple lands were turned over to Catholic orders at this time.

The kingdom of Kandy retained its independence throughout the Portuguese period, and many devout Buddhists fled there to avoid religious persecution. As the influence of Christianity grew on the coast, Kandy began to take on the role of a sanctuary of conservative Buddhism on the island. The *sangha* there continued in its position of authority and prestige.

The arrival of the Dutch changed, but did not improve, the religious climate. They were less interested than the Portuguese in religious missionizing, although some conversions to Protestantism did take place. Nonetheless, they in turn persecuted the new Catholics, many of whom remained steadfast in their faith. The Dutch did not permit free exercise of religion; neither Buddhism, Hinduism, nor Islam could be practiced publicly during most of their rule. In the Tamil north public worship largely went underground. In many cases Hindus used miniature images and shrines and worshiped in secret, and saivite priests of non-Brahmin castes, known as *pujari* or Pandarams, ministered to the villagers in secret. The issue of cattle slaughter caused conflict between the Hindus and the Dutch; because Hindus revere the cow, some highly placed Hindus either lost their positions or were forced into exile over this issue.

The British, on their arrival, established religious freedom and ceased the official persecution of non-Christian religions. Large numbers of nominal Protestants reverted to Buddhism, which many had practiced in secret during the Dutch period; the Catholics, however, did not reconvert in substantial numbers. In spite of their relative liberality, the British were committed to converting Ceylonese to Anglican and other forms of Protestantism; missionaries from several societies soon arrived and established schools, which later produced an English-speaking, Christianized elite (see ch. 5, Ethnic Groups and Languages).

In 1815 the kingdom of Kandy fell to the British, and the entire island came under their dominion. The Kandyans, who considered their kingdom a bulwark for Buddhism and who had always identified the authority of the *sangha* very closely with that of the state, wanted the new British rulers to discharge the traditional religious functions of the Kandyan kings. The treaty of cession between the British and Kandyans stated that "The religion of the Budhoo professed by the chiefs and inhabitants of these provinces is declared inviolable and its Rites, Ministers, and Places of Worship are to be maintained and protected." But Governor Robert Brownrigg confided to the Earl of Bathurst the next day that he agreed to these conditions only because the Kandyans would agree to cession on no others. As a devout Christian he was troubled by the idea of protecting a "pagan" religion and wished to missionize. But to the Buddhists, state support was an important element of Buddhism.

At the outset the British authority in Kandy did certify some *sangha* appointments and fulfill other functions of the Kandyan monarchy, but pressure from missionary interests caused these activities to cease by the early 1830s. No alternative means of confirming temple authorities was evolved, and the lay trustees responsible for the administration of temple lands often lacked official standing. As the British began to sell temple lands to planters, the temple authorities were unable to make a case in court to prevent the alienation of thousands of acres. The actual extent of temple lands alienated is unknown, but some reports claim up to 800,000 acres.

It was suggested that the *bhikkus* themselves administer the lands, but the Vinaya, or monastic rule, forbids them to deal in temporal affairs. Since Buddhism, unlike Christianity, lacks central authority and each monastery and temple functions as an independent entity, the Buddhist community found itself ill prepared to deal with the organized, resolute missionary groups who had, in addition, official government sanction.

The missionaries were especially aggressive in educational matters. Both in the Hindu north and the Buddhist south, numerous Christian schools were established, which were the only institutions preparing the youth for desirable careers requiring the English language (see ch. 9, Education). The *sangha,* which had traditionally been in charge of education in the Buddhist community, became increasingly alienated from the people.

By 1880 there were some 1,120 Christian schools on the island serving a population of 300,000 Christians. Some 240 foreign missionaries were said to be active in 1888. Consequently, the instutions and observances of the indigenous religion steadily deteriorated for most of the century. Buddhism, depending so heavily on organization, was most affected, but Hinduism and Islam also suffered.

In addition to outright alienation of temple lands, the relationship between the temple landlord and the tenants was changed. As part of the Colebrooke reforms of the 1830s, *rajakyria,* or obligated service, was abolished (see ch. 3, Historical Setting). The tenants on temple lands, however, were excluded and continued to owe service under the traditional system. The temples, therefore, came to be viewed as a reactionary force favoring an outdated inequity. In 1870 the tenants of temple lands in Sabaragamuwa Province agitated for the end of serfdom to the temples; the result was the Service Tenure Ordinance, which provided for payment in place of service, depriving the temples of dependable support. This basic conflict imposed by the system of temple lands continued into the twentieth century. In 1958 the Paddy Lands Bill provided tenant cultivators with secure tenure and a division of the crop that was more generous to the peasant (see ch. 19, Agriculture). The Kandyan temples, which lost considerable income as a result, were thus in the unenviable position of opposing the aspirations of the peasantry.

For several decades in the nineteenth century, the decline in Buddhism was fairly steady; it is estimated that there were 50,000 *bhikkus* on the island in A.D. 450, but the number had dwindled to 2,500 by 1850. A reaction against Christian domination began, bringing a great resurgence of Buddhist and Hindu sentiment in the 1870s and 1880s. There was renewed interest in the study and propagation of indigenous culture and values. By 1901 there were an estimated 7,300 *bhikkus*. The American theosophist, Colonel Henry Steele Olcott, arrived in Ceylon in 1880 and led the drive to resurrect Buddhist culture and education. At the time of his arrival only a handful of institutions, possibly as few as five, taught Buddhist studies.

Between 1880 and 1900, 142 Buddhist schools were founded, including the well-known Ananda College in Colombo, Mahinda College in Galle, and Dharmaraja College in Kandy. At the same time, a similar movement took place among the Hindus, resulting in the founding of Hindu College in Jaffna, among others. Unlike the traditional *pirivenas* (colleges attached to monasteries), these new institutions were meant to compete with the British-oriented preparatory schools training an English-speaking elite. In addition, tracts and magazines were published, and Buddhists publicly debated with Protestant ministers.

The resurgence of religious feeling coincided with a reorganization of the religious groups in the country. In 1886 the Anglican church was granted independent corporate status, whereas previously it had been a department of the government. Having greater independence, it was able to accumulate and dispose of wealth; the single organization now controlled all Anglican schools, churches, and other property and institutions.

In 1889 the government allowed the Buddhists a minimal organization to deal with the problem of the temple lands.

In proposing the Buddhist Temporalities Ordinance, the governor stated, "What is intended is simply to give to the Buddhists as has been given to the Church of England, the means of managing their own affairs, with however this important refined but equally valid religious life that will suit their less several independent governing bodies in the different districts." The Buddhists were denied central organization because of the fear that they would gain sufficient power and eventually pose a threat.

The Buddhist monasteries were still being governed in 1970 under a variation of the Buddhist Temporalities Ordinance of 1889. This bill provided for different lay trustees for each institution, to be directed by district committees. Under the ordinance of 1931 the position of the district committees was taken by a public trustee; in addition, it established the first system for the registration of *bhikkus,* making it a crime to masquerade as a *bhikku.* No one, however, has been punished under this provision.

During the early twentieth century the sentiment in favor of indigenous religions and cultures continued to grow, although the elite remained Christian. During the 1930s, however, a movement began among Ceylonese Christians to convert back to Buddhism. For example, Solomon West Ridgeway Dias Bandaranaike, the political leader, who was raised in an Anglican home, converted to Buddhism upon his return from a university in England. When the Donoughmore Constitution granted universal suffrage in 1931, some ambitious politicians concerted back to Buddhism, giving rise to the sarcastic expression "Donoughmore Buddhist" (see ch. 3, Historical Setting).

Throughout this period the Buddhist community, especially the *sangha,* felt that Buddhism had been deprived of its rightful place in the life of the country, and agitation continued to restore it. This movement gained impetus from the celebration of the Buddha Jayanti year, a worldwide commemoration of the 2,500th anniversary of the *parinibbana* (final attainment of *nibbana,* also known as *nirvana*—see Glossary) of the Buddha. Ceylon celebrated the Buddha Jayanti in 1956 and 1957, and it coincided with a marked increase in Sinhalese nationalist sentiment (see ch. 5, Ethnic Groups and Languages).

To prepare for the celebration, the Buddhist Commission of Inquiry, composed of prominent *bhikkus* and lay educators primarily from the low country, in 1954 began a top-level study on the state of Buddhism in Ceylon. The report, published in February 1956 under the English title *The Betrayal of Buddhism,* was a tremendously influential document. It captured the imagination of the Buddhist masses and led to demands for reform. The report stated that Buddhism was in grave danger of extinction in Ceylon, largely because of Christian missionary activity. It claimed that Buddhism had been ousted from its rightful place as the religion of the Sinhalese, and it suggested specific reforms in education, the organization of a central Buddhist authority, and state support. The Catholic Union of Ceylon replied in 1957 with the *Companion to the Buddhist Commission Report,* a critique that corrected certain factual errors but did not invalidate the Buddhist report's basic arguments. Although the government did not establish direct aid or subventions to organized Buddhism, it did participate officially in the Buddha Jayanti activities.

In recent years the enthusiasm of the Buddhist community has been growing, and the predominance of Buddhist symbols has been increasing. For example, since colonial times the Christian Sabbath, Sunday, has been observed as a general day of rest. Buddhists traditionally observe Poya Days, which mark the phases of the moon, with religious ceremonies. Since the Poya Days conform to a lunar calendar, they are not consistent with the Gregorian calendar but nonetheless fall approximately every seven days. The government of Dudley Senanayake officially changed the national business holiday from Sunday to Poya Days, under pressure from the Buddhist community and on the theory that it would appease all groups. It was argued that the Poya Days fulfilled the Biblical injunction to rest on the seventh day. The Hindus have no tradition of a particular weekly day of rest. The restoration of ancient religious structures was also begun. Government officials, including the prime minister, have participated in an official capacity in the dedication of important restorations.

Common Elements of Popular Observance

Since Buddhism and Hinduism share many basic features and since Ceylon Buddhists were converted from Hindu practice, there has always been a substratum of common belief and worship on the island, especially on the popular level. Buddhist and Hindu practices are not always clearly distinguished; in many cases, professing Buddhists recognize deities also worshiped by Hindus, although often in different rituals. Hindus regard the Buddha as an incarnation of the god Vishnu. Hindus and Buddhists have also at times taken part in the same rituals. The annual Esala Perahera at Kandy, for example, which is the triumphal procession honoring the Sacred Tooth Relic and is one of Ceylon Buddhism's most important observances, originally honored the local gods Natha, Vishnu,

Kataragama Deviyo, and Pattini, who are of Hindu origin. In 1775 the Sinhalese king ordered that the Tooth Relic also be included in the procession.

The festival for the god Skanda held in Kataragama in June and the Vel festival held for the god Murukan (known as Kataragama Deviyo to the Sinhalese) in Colombo are attended by Hindus and Buddhists alike. In many cases Buddhist shrines were built on places sacred to pre-Buddhist gods, and the holy association continued in the popular mind. At one time an image of the Hindu god Ganesha, the son of Siva, stood in front of the Sacred Bo Tree at Anuradhapura and was revered by both Buddhists and Hindus.

Pilgrimage is a common element to the Buddhist, Hindu, and Muslim communities. These groups all venerate as a holy spot Adam's Peak, a mountain located in the southwest section of the hill country (see ch. 2, Physical Environment). Atop the mountain is an indentation in the shape of a footprint, which each group associates with a holy figure. Some Ceylonese scholars suggest that the reverence for the mountain predates Buddhism and results from an ancient cult of a mountain god that continued under a new guise. This possibility notwithstanding, each community has evolved a legend tying itself to the footprint.

The Buddhists believe that the indentation, which they call Sri Pada (Sacred Footprint), is the result of a visit by the Buddha to the island. The Hindus believe that Siva, in one of his incarnations, left his footprint on the mountain; they call it Sivan-oli-padam, or the Sacred Footprint of Siva. The Muslims believe that Adam, when expelled from the Garden of Eden, was further punished by being forced to stand on one foot on the mountaintop. Large numbers of pilgrims of all three confessions visit the spot annually, often accomplishing the climb on foot together. Other pilgrimage sites include important temples and spots thought to be sacred, such as certain rivers and mountains.

Throughout the island there is a strong belief in the influence of the stars and planets and the horoscope generally. The people do not believe that this influence conflicts with the Buddhist and Hindu concept of *karma*, or rebirth according to one's merit, because a person is born under a good or bad horoscope because of good or bad *karma*. It is believed that activities should take place, if possible, at auspicious times and dates. People will go to considerable inconvenience to perform activities at given auspicious moments. In marriage arrangements the horoscopes of the prospective spouses are important considerations. Preceding the New Year and other important events, the newspapers, including the English-language press, carry notices of the most auspicious hours and days for carrying out various activities.

BASIC CONCEPTS OF HINDUISM AND BUDDHISM

Like all the religions that originated in the Indian subcontinent, Hinduism and Buddhism are based on radically different premises from those of the Biblical religions originating in the Middle East. Hinduism and Buddhism are products of a single religious tradition; Buddhism is in fact a development of Hinduism.

The South Asian cosmology is more relativistic than the Western system. The existence of the material world, the functioning of time, and the possibilities of human knowledge are more flexibly construed. The material world as it appears to the unreflecting man, rather than representing absolute reality, is *maya* (illusion, mirage, or a false show). The true reality behind the appearance is knowable to man as special knowledge, attainable through serious and strenuous spiritual exercise. The diligent, fortunate, and spiritually gifted individual can obtain *moksha*, or release from the false notions of the material world. This knowledge, the replacement of false views (*avidya*) with correct ones (*vidya*), involves more than the intellectual faculties; it represents a spiritual achievement and is in fact the goal of the spiritual strivings of religion.

As special capacities and diligence are required to gain release, not all persons can expect to reach this spiritual height; only a small minority of the most advanced may reasonably hope for success and then only through rigorous asceticism. It is believed, however, that although only the most elevated can attain pure release, the less advanced can take part in a less refined but equally valid religious life that will suit their less demanding requirements.

The concept that devotional life should match the capacities of the worshiper is well established; there are believed to be many ways to approach the divine, all with equal validity for their specific situations. All groups hold that the perception of the true unity underlying physical reality leads in some sense to the extinction of the self as an individual entity. Many Hindus view this as a joining or subsuming of the individual soul to the World Soul; the traditional analogy used to describe this is that as salt dissolves in water, so the individual dissolves in the World Soul. Buddhists, on the other hand, deny the concept of a World Soul as useful, or they at least refuse to address themselves to the question of its existence.

200

Central to the South Asian cosmology is a cyclical view of life and the universe. Numerous world systems have existed in the past, will exist in the future, and probably exist at the present, each to be destroyed in its turn by a cosmic calamity, and new ones to be created. The existence of life on other planets or in other solar systems is in many cases assumed. Each world system exists for the period of a *kalpa*, a length of time inconceivably long in human terms. A metaphor is traditionally given to explain it: If a mountain existed as tall as the tallest of the Himalayas and was composed of the hardest possible stone, and if a man visited it once every 100 years and touched it lightly with the finest, sheerest cloth, a *kalpa* would be the period of time it would take him to wear it down completely.

Not only is the existence of universes cylical, but life is also. Man is one of a chain of beings encompassing all living things (including the gods, for theists), which pass through multiple incarnations. For this reason, *ahimsa* (noninjury to living things), sometimes in the form of vegetarianism, is a basic value of these religions. A being who is a man in this life may be reborn as a animal, an insect, or a god in the next. The position one occupies depends on the *karma* established in the previous life.

Karma is the force created by the sum of goodness or badness in a life and determines absolutely both the position and the tendency of the coming life. Although *karma* may predispose a life to be favorable or unfavorable, it does not determine specific actions; the being must interact with *karma*, circumstance, and his own character. In each life, while reacting to the *karma* of the previous existence, one is simultaneously building up the *karma* for the next, so that the causal chain connecting lives is continuous.

Karma differs from the Western conception of divine restitution in that it does not require the existence of a deity to keep accounts; there is no reckoning of sins and virtues by a conscious being. Rather, it is held that *karma* functions as blindly, and is as inherent in the very nature of the universe, as the law of gravity. Therefore, each being is condemned to pass infinitely from life to life, guided by the *karma* established in previous lives. The only possible escape from this dreary round is through *moksha*, or release, which comes to a very advanced being through the accumulation of excellent *karma* over numerous lives. The position one occupies in the hierarchy of beings makes manifest the *karma* accumulated in previous lives and is therefore, in an absolute sense, deserved. The *karma* accumulated depends upon one's reaction

to his particular circumstances; one must well and virtuously
be what he finds himself. There is no absolute standard of
performance for all beings, as the demands of a position
match its supposed abilities.

The practice of asceticism as a means to religious salvation
is an ancient practice in South Asia. At the time of the Buddha this custom had been established for many centuries.
Throughout Indian history the wandering holy man has been
a commonplace figure in society, and there has been a great
variety of austerities and schools that practice them. Consequently, Buddhist monasticism based upon the wandering
beggar represents the incorporation of an ancient tradition
into a new religious system.

BUDDHISM

Life and Teachings of the Buddha

Buddhism was founded by a man born in the sixth century
B.C. in the Himalayan foothills who came to be known as the
Buddha, or Enlightened One. He was born into the chiefly
caste of the tribe of the Sakyas and was named Siddhartha,
with a clan name of Gotama. He is commonly referred to as
Gotama Buddha and, less frequently, as Sakyamuni, or Sage
of the Sakyas.

According to Buddhist belief, the birth of Gotama was surrounded by extraordinary circumstances. His mother, the wife
of the Sakya king, had a dream that was interpreted to mean
she had conceived and would bear a son who would become
either a universal teacher or a universal ruler. When the boy
was born in a grove of trees, he took seven strides and announced that he would have no more rebirths. All the astrol-
ogers predicted that he would be a universal ruler, except
for one, who said that four signs would show him the sorrow
of the world and would convince him to renounce the world
and become a universal teacher.

To forestall this possibility, his father determined that the
boy would never know sorrow and raised him in opulent palaces, shielded from any knowledge of unpleasantness and en-
joying every pleasure. He was a brilliant student and athlete
and, as a youth, married a beautiful cousin.

Nonetheless, the gods had not forgotten Gotama's destiny
and conspired to show him the four signs. One day, while
driving with his companion, Channa, he saw an old and de-
crepit man, who was actually a god in disguise. As Gotama
had never before seen old age, he asked Channa if the man
was born in this repulsive condition. He was surprised and

deeply disturbed to learn that all men must eventually grow old. The second sign was a sick man, and the third a corpse. Gotama's father redoubled his efforts to distract his brooding son with dancing girls and other pleasures but to no avail. The fourth sign was a wandering holy man, not uncommon at that time in India. Upon seeing the peace and serene joy that characterized the beggar, Gotama realized that he too must renounce the world and follow the same path. In spite of whatever luxuries his father could provide, Gotama was not at peace and remained profoundly troubled by the signs he had seen.

One morning he received word that his wife has given birth to a son. Gotama did not rejoice; he named the child Rahula (literally, impediment). He decided that he must immediately give up his life of luxury, and that very night he rode out of his father's palace on his horse, Kanthaka, accompanied by his faithful Indian companion, Channa. Gods lifted the horse's hooves off the ground to muffle the sound. Arriving in the forest, Gotama bid farewell to Channa and to Kanthaka, who immediately died from grief. He then went to study with a noted sage, Alara. Finding that the doctrine of the teacher did not answer his questions, he went to study with another famous teacher.

Finally, dissatisfied with teachers, he decided to seek the truth through ascetic exercises and meditation. He became associated with five hermits who lived in the forest practicing austerity. Finally, having reduced himself to a walking skeleton and still no closer to the truth, Gotama decided that austerity and mortification of the flesh were not enough. To the disgust of his companions, he concluded that, since the body was man's only vehicle, it must be preserved. One must be alive to gain enlightenment. He took solid food and decided to try meditation.

He seated himself under a fig tree and determined not to move until he had gained understanding of the meaning of life and sorrow. He fell into meditation and, for seven weeks, proceeded through higher and higher stages of trance, while the devil, Mara, tried to seduce him with all the pleasures of the world. Sitting under what became known as the Bo or Bodhi-tree (the tree of enlightenment), Gotama achieved *nibbana*, the peace of perfect understanding, when he perceived the Four Noble Truths. When he arose it was as the Buddha, the Enlightened One. Out of compassion for mankind, the Buddha determined to postpone his final *nibbana* in order to preach his wonderful new doctrine to others to spare them from sorrow.

He thereupon returned to his five erstwhile companions, and they became his first disciples. Throughout his life he went about in the guise of a *bhikku*, which is usually translated as monk but literally means beggar. He made numerous converts wherever he went; after a long life his earthly form died and was liberated from the cycle of rebirth, and he went in his *parinibbana* to the extinction that only the enlightened can attain.

The first of the Four Noble Truths which the Buddha perceived under the Bo-tree and which he believed to explain the mystery of existence is that all life is sorrow (*dukkha*). Although men might argue that there is also pleasure and happiness in life, it is probable that in most cases sorrow and pain predominate. Secondly, all sorrow arises from desire (*tanha*) and attachment. Whatever a man desires or is attached to can be destroyed, lost, or taken from him; the separation from a loved person or object invariably causes sorrow. Thirdly, if desire and attachment cease, sorrow will also. Finally, the way to stop desire is through detachment from the world, the self, and the senses, which can be achieved by following the Noble Eightfold Path, also known as the Middle Way, between sensual pleasure and severe austerity. The goal of the Noble Eightfold Path is to free man from earthly attachments, such as possessions, comforts, and even the senses.

The steps of the Noble Eightfold Path are: Right Views, or knowledge of the truth; Right Resolve, or the sincere desire to obtain salvation; Right Speech and Right Conduct, or ethical and compassionate behavior; Right Livelihood, or a means of earning a living that does not conflict with one's spiritual activities; Right Effort; Right Recollection, or training in proper spiritual exercises; and Right Meditation, or the use of proper meditational techniques applied wholeheartedly. Through the application of these steps, man can be liberated from the bonds of self, or personal attachments, and of sensual desires. Man will come to perceive the transient nature of the world and the individual identity.

These teachings form the basis of the Dhamma (also known as Dharma), or doctrine, of the Buddha. His essential teachings are not a religion in the usual sense of including a pantheon. The Buddha did not address himself to the question of the existence of gods or the origin of the universe. He maintained that, since man can achieve enlightenment through the Dhamma, he is foolish not to devote himself fully to it; asking other questions is simple a waste of time. He gave the analogy of a man wounded with an arrow who refuses to have it removed before he finds out who made it, who shot it, where and how it was made, of what sort of wood it was, and so forth.

Buddhism emphasizes that salvation comes not by faith, works, or rituals but by correct knowledge. This is in sharp contrast to Hinduism's emphasis on priestly ritual. An eminent Western theologian has stated that Buddhism is "redemption by insight." Correct knowledge comes not from the senses or from logic but from other levels of consciousness, primarily through meditation. Individual effort is crucial. The Buddha's final admonition to his followers was "be a lamp unto yourselves. . . . Work diligently for your salvation." The *Mahavamsa* tells of the meeting of Mahinda and King Devanampiya Tissa; before preaching the Dhamma to the king, the monk questioned him to test his intellect and reasoning to make sure he would be capable of understanding.

After the death of the Buddha, his teachings and sayings were recalled by his disciples and later codified at several councils of monks. The version of the canon used in Ceylon is written in the Pali language, which is derived from Sanskrit. The Pali canon, the Tripitaka, is divided into three parts called *pitaka*, or baskets; at one time pieces of palm leaf were used for paper and were stored in baskets. The Vinaya (literally, conduct) Pitaka is the rule of the monastic life and also describes the circumstances under which the Buddha made each of the statements. The Sutta (literally, sermon) Pitaka contains numerous sermons; the Abhidhamma (literally, metaphysics) Pitaka is a group of advanced technical works.

During its development Buddhism became divided into several major schools. The Theravada (Teachings of the Elders) branch, also known to members of other schools as Hinayana (Lesser Vehicle), claims nearly all Ceylon Buddhists. It is the most austere form of Buddhism, emphasizing the necessity of individual effort to achieve enlightenment. In the Mahayana (Greater Vehicle) school, which is prevalent in the Far East, the ideal of the Bodhisattva became highly developed. Bodhisattvas are future Buddhas who remain on earth in order to help other beings achieve salvation. They are often prayed to in the manner of saints in the West. Tantric, or magical, Buddhism, formerly prevalent in Tibet, emphasizes mystical means.

The Sangha

In Theravada the only true Buddhist is the person who renounces the world and follows in the Buddha's footsteps as a *bhikku*, depending on alms for his sustenance. Although the layman living with his family can live a virtuous and meritorious life, he cannot achieve enlightenment. The *bhikku* is not a priest, since he has no responsibility for a congregation or for the welfare of laymen, although he may lead laymen in prayer. He is primarily, and sometimes solely, interested in gaining *nibbana* for himself. Although some *bhikkus* are itinerant, most reside in religious communities associated with *viharas*.

The *sangha* is the collective group of *bhikkus*, including the various communities. A man may be admitted to it at any time during his life; a military man, however, must first obtain a discharge. Married men and fathers are accepted. A *bhikku* must try to hew to the Noble Eightfold Path and practice poverty, chastity, and *ahimsa* by harming no living thing. The vows that he takes are not binding in any contractual sense but merely represent a sincere resolve that may be ended at any time. The *bhikku* is not a member of an order and owes obedience to no superior. He is a free member of a community of men who try to be "lamps unto themselves." The senior *bhikkus*, who admit novices to the community, are known by the honorific "Thero" (elder). Each community is also independent. There are, in addition, communities of nuns.

Bhikkus may own only certain prescribed items of property, which include two sets of clothing, usually the saffron-yellow robes of the monk, a tool to cut firewood, a needle, a strainer to remove living creatures from his water to keep from drinking them, and his begging bowl and spoon. On his daily rounds the villagers place what they will in his bowl, and it is considered meritorious to eat this without distinctions of taste. The *bhikku* relinquishes his property and his inheritance and, supposedly, also all caste distinctions. Through gifts to the communities of *bhikkus*, the monasteries in time came to control considerable wealth, and the *bhikkus* often had more than the prescribed items, on the fiction that they belonged to the monastery and not to the monk.

The *sangha* was traditionally probably the single most important group in Ceylon. It controlled education and learning, advised kings on policy, and aided the common people. Most *bhikkus* today live in the country, especially in the Kandyan hills, although growing numbers live in the city. The great influence they still wield was made apparent in the 1956 election (see ch. 14, Political Dynamics). In 1970 there were an estimated 15,000 to 18,000 *bhikkus* in Ceylon. Most belong to one of the three major *nikayas*, or sects.

The Siam Nikaya, the oldest and wealthiest sect, has about 12,000 members. It comprises two main chapters, the Malwatta and the Asgiriya. The most conservative group and the most oriented to Kandyan culture, the Siam Nikaya is limited to men of the Goyigama, or highest, caste, despite the Buddhist proviso against caste distinctions (see ch. 6, Social Structure). The Amapura Nikaya, with approximately 20 percent of the *sangha*, was founded by a monk of the Salagama caste in the nineteenth century to open the *sangha* to other castes. It is open to members of the Karava, Salagama, and Durava castes. The Ramanya Nikaya, with 15 percent, was founded as a reformist splinter of the Siam Nikaya. It is considered the strictest community. The influence of the *bhikkus* in the mind of the traditional villagers cannot be overestimated. A traditional refrain, often repeated by Buddhists, is "I seek refuge in the Buddha; I seek refuge in the *dhamma*; I seek refuge in the *sangha*."

In recent decades, however, the situation of the *sangha* has been deteriorating, as the institutions of traditional Sinhalese society erode under the impact of modernization and urbanization (see ch. 6, Social Structure). With the loss of the temple lands and the erosion of village solidarity, the *bhikkus* have been less able to depend upon the villagers for support. In addition, although most *bhikkus* live in the country, a growing number have taken up urban residence. Many have enrolled in universities. The support of urban *bhikkus* is a particular problem, and some have been forced to accept teaching positions and discreetly adopt other professions or trades that can be to some extent reconciled with the monastic life. Work for pay, however, is contrary to the letter and the spirit of the Vinaya, and many feel that it endangers spiritual growth of the *bhikku*.

The urban *bhikkus* have also been agitating for greater central organization of the *sangha* to help solve the problem of reconciling traditional Buddhist values and practices with urban life. The Buddhist ethic has traditionally been based on rural life and does not harmonize well with the demands of modern urban living. This problem of Buddhism in the cities has yet to be solved.

Popular Buddhism

Theravada Buddhism, if strictly practiced, is a code of extraordinary austerity, requiring the total dedication of the individual and offering no helpful gods to provide solace. The ideal is to become an *arhat*, or awakened individual who has achieved enlightenment through meditation. The teachings of Buddha, per se, offer little to the layman seeking divine assistance and assurance in life's problems.

Consequently, the unsophisticated laymen, although nominally Buddhists, in fact worship a pantheon of local, regional, and national gods. Considerable local variation exists in custom and legend concerning the identity and attributes of the lesser gods, although all who practice popular Buddhism venerate the same higher deities. The supernatural beings of popular Buddhism probably remain from pre-Buddhist times and have been altered to "Buddhists." In addition, a cult of trees existed in pre-Buddhist times, which has continued in the present-day veneration of the Bo-Trees. For some time scholars have noted coexistence of two levels of Buddhist worship. Robert Knox, a seventeenth-century observer of Ceylon, noted that the people have "Budu for the soul, and the gods for this world."

Although the Buddha did not recognize, or at least did not discuss, the existence of gods, he has been transformed into the primary divinity of the popular pantheon. The Buddha is not seen as the Creator, and Sinhalese-Buddhism has no special creation myth to account for the existence of the world. But the Buddha, as the holiest and most divine being, is the source of divine power. According to strict doctrine, on achieving *nibbana*, the Buddha ceased to exist in a temporal sense; according to popular belief, however, the state of Nibbana is thought of as immortality, rather than extinction. The Buddha is felt to be "present," or "immanent," although this offers logical difficulties.

According to popular belief, his divinity is present in his relics, or *dhatu*, and also in those of *arhats*. *Dhatu* of the Buddha and of *arhats* are thought to have *irdhi*, or the ability to travel through the air. It is believed, for example, that the Buddha and Mahinda arrived in Ceylon by means of *irdhi*. A legend states that, when the present world system is destroyed by a flood, the various *dhatu* of the Buddha will come together from various parts of the world by *irdhi*, his body will be reconstituted, and he will preach a final sermon.

In addition to the Buddha, there are other gods, primarily of Hindu origin, each having a given *sima*, or territorial and temporal jurisdiction. The various gods and demons are related to one another by a system of quasi-feudal relationships. Through a process called *varan*, one divinity delegates authority to lesser beings, who in turn owe him fealty. It is believed that the Buddha, during his life, gave *varan* to some gods, who subsequently granted it to others. All gods, therefore, owe ultimate allegiance to the Buddha. The concept of *varan* allows the easy assimilation of new or foreign gods to the pantheon. According to one legend, Mahinda, after converting King Devanampiya Tissa, preached his next sermon to the assembled gods of the island, who immediately were converted to Buddhism and became devotees of the Buddha.

Except for the Buddha, who has been released from the cycle of rebirths, the divinities are all mortal creatures, still subject to rebirth, although their lives are far longer and more pleasant than those of human beings. They occupy their exalted status because of good *karma*. The Sinhalese gods have been described as playful and, like the gods of Greece and Rome, have human-like personalities and frailties. Some gods are recognized as being more virtuous or meritorious than others, and the type of worship rendered reflects this.

At the pinnacle of the pantheon is the Buddha, and directly below him is Sakra, the protector of the worldwide *sasana*, or universal Buddhist church or religion. These two are recognized as representing pure good and the highest moral character. Next comes the group of guardians of the specifically Ceylonese realm, including Saman, Vishnu, Skanda, Pattini, and Natha; these are recognized all over the country. Then comes a group of local, district, and special purpose deities, which vary with localities. Among those recognized are: Murukan, patron of the region of Ruhuna; Aiyana, guardian of forests, lakes, and tanks, who is recognized by the Tamils as Aiyanar; Ganesha, patron of Anuradhapura; Kataragama Deviya, popular in Uva Province; Devol Deryo, worshiped on the west coast; and Devata Bandara, in the Central Province. These gods are recognized as being less meritorious than the higher pair, although still admirable. They are viewed as being "just" gods, in the sense that they reward a man according to what he deserves.

Below the gods is a group of local demons, under their king, Vesamuni, and below the demons is a varied group of spirits, ghosts, and goblins. These two groups represent pure evil. They cause trouble for mankind, usually out of malice. Through the use of *vas*, or *vas-dos*, an evil power that affects people, these beings bring illness, general misfortune, and the like. *Vas* can also be caused by an evil eye (*asvaha*), an evil mouth (*katavaha*), or evil thoughts (*hovaha*).

The different natures of the different divinities require various sorts of worship. Men do not expect the Buddha to involve himself in temporal affairs, and he is worshiped only in a commemorative sense. They do not expect that he will grant favors; rather, they simply revere his exemplary holiness, of-

209

ten with offerings of flowers. The national and local gods, on the other hand, can and do interfere in the affairs of men and thus are propitiated with various offerings so that they will be well disposed toward people. The demons are also propitiated or bribed to keep them from causing trouble. The Buddha and the gods are given vegetarian offerings, to symbolize their purity and goodness. The demons, on the other hand, are often offered eggs and other nonvegetarian foods, emphasizing their low status.

In keeping with the various ways of worship, there are different personnel for each type of divinity. The Buddha is worshiped in a *vihara* and is the concern of the *bhikkus*. The gods are worshiped in a *devale* by special priests called *kapuva* or *kapurala*. The demons are propitiated by exorcists known as *kattandiya* or *yakadura*. One individual will take part in ceremonies in all three systems. When a prayer is to be addressed to the gods, permission (*avasara*) must be sought from those gods higher. The Buddha is venerated first, then the gods. In order to carry out the pilgrimage to Sri Pada to venerate the Sacred Footprint, the worshiper must first seek the protection of Saman, who also functions as the patron of Sri Pada.

In addition to their monastic discipline, the *bhikkus* often participate in ceremonies surrounding important moments in the life of the layman. The *bhikkus* recite *pirit* (protection chants) to mark significant milestones, such as illness or a new home, and to commemorate important events. For example, on March 25, 1970, *pirit* was recited at special ceremonies commemorating the successful completion of a five-year term in office by Prime Minister Dudley Senanayake.

Among the peasants, the more religious laymen, many of them older people, are known as *upasaka*. They observe *sil* (meditation) on holy days and study simplified versions of religious texts and books.

HINDUISM

Hinduism, the religion of the Tamil community in Ceylon, differs from Buddhism in that it has no founder and no unified doctrine. It is a body of ancient tradition that evolved on the Indian subcontinent over millennia and has developed a vast variety of doctrines, creeds, legends, deities, and beliefs. Hinduism ranges from the most subtle religious experience of the mystic or metaphysician to the magical cult practices of the unschooled peasant. At its higher levels, in the form of classical Hinduism, it consists of a system of beliefs derived from ancient sacred scriptures, the Vedas. At its popular level it is a bewildering collection of incredibly diverse local customs and practices that vary from locality to locality, from caste to caste, and from cult to cult. A scholar has said of Hinduism that there is no statement that can be made about it whose contradiction is not also true.

In classical Hinduism the godhead and source of all is Brahman, or Atman, the world or universal soul. The world systems and universes are seen as emanations or manifestations of Brahman. Apart from Brahman, there exists a trinity of the leading gods, who are also thought to be reflections of the single source of the divine. Brahma is the Creator; Vishnu, the Preserver; and Siva, the Destroyer. These gods, particcularly the latter two, assume numerous forms, incarnations, and names. Many Hindus are devoted to either Vishnu or Siva as the principal divinity. The gods are viewed as being mortals, although much longer lived than man, and are thought to have gone through various rebirths.

Ceylon Hinduism does not encompass the whole variety of the Hindu belief. Virtually all Ceylon Hindus are adherents of the Saivite sect and therefore recognize Siva as the leading deity. A small community of Vaisnavites, or devotees of Vishnu, exists in Jaffna, primarily among the weaver caste. There are also Vaisnavite communities on the estates, although most Indian Tamils are Saivites. There is considerable variation among Ceylon Saivites of various locations and castes and between the Ceylon Tamils, many of whom are of the higher castes, and the Indian Tamils, who are generally of low caste.

Three basic elements, common to all Hinduism, find expression in Ceylon. These are the acceptance of the Vedas as sacred scriptures, the veneration of cows, and the caste system. The Vedas are regarded as revealed knowledge of sacred origin. The veneration and protection of cows is the highest expression of the ethic of *ahimsa*. The cow, regarded as a particularly holy and pure being, is not harmed, and its products are believed to embody purifying elements. Among some higher caste individuals, *ahimsa* finds expression in vegetarianism. The caste system, basic to Ceylonese social life, places the individual by birth in a closed, endogamous occupational group (see ch. 6, Social Structure). Nearly all significant experiences take place within the caste, and caste groups to some extent approximate different subcultures as they develop particular customs and traditions.

It is believed that the caste system is related to the *karma* of its members; the castes, therefore, are ranked in order of their ritual purity or worth. The concept of ritual pollution of higher by lower castes is prevalent. Some castes considered unclean, such as the Ambattans (barbers), are not admitted to temples. The members of higher castes ordinarily follow more stringent religious practices than members of lower groups.

In India religious life is largely dominated by the priestly, or Brahmin, caste; in Ceylon the caste is small and exerts minimal influence. The leading caste in the Ceylon Tamil areas is the Vellala, or cultivator, caste, which corresponds to the Goyigama in the Sinhalese areas (see ch. 6, Social Structure). The Brahmins of Ceylon are almost exclusively temple priests and usually are employees of the Vellala owners of the temple. There is also a very low caste group of Kaka (crow) Brahmins, who minister to untouchables. The dearth of Brahmins has been explained as resulting from Portuguese persecution. Others suggest that few Brahmins emigrated to Ceylon in the first place.

Numerous temples do not have Brahmin priests but, rather, priests of other castes known as *pujari* or Pandarams, who will ordinarily be of the same caste as the worshipers who own the temple. *Pujari* are individuals who have rejected their traditional caste occupation to take up a priestly life; some become wandering holy men, begging their subsistence. Although no *pujari* may minister in a Brahmin temple, they perform an important role in the villages and particularly on the estates, where they are the only religious practitioners serving the low-caste Indian Tamils.

To Ceylonese Saivites, probably the most important manifestation of Siva is as Nataraja, Lord of the Dances. Lord Siva, in this manifestation, performs various cosmic dances, and in them he manifests the cosmic rhythm of the universe, which maintains all life. He is usually represented as having numerous arms to symbolize his various powers and dancing before a circle of flame, symbolizing the essentially cyclical nature of the universe. Saivites therefore see him not in his fierce manifestation as the Destroyer but as the Cosmic Dancer who assures the continuance of the universe. He is also represented as Lord of the Beasts; his other manifestations are as a great teacher and as a great ascetic.

Another common representation of Siva is the *lingam*, or phallic symbol, which is worshiped as the creative male essence in the universe. Hindu gods have definite sexual manifestations; this characteristic is indicated by the belief in the *sakti*, or female element of the deity, often represented as the god's wife. Some interpret the *sakti* as being a manifestation of the female creative aspects of the divinity. The wife of Siva is Parvati, a goddess of fertility. She is known by many other names, such as Uma, Minatchi, and Bavani. To symbolize the creative unity of the male and female elements, the *lingam* is sometime surrounded by a circle representing the *yoni*, or female organ.

The two elder sons of Siva and Parvati are also important deities. In fact, there are more temples dedicated to them than to their parents. The eldest son, elephant-headed Ganesha, also known as Pillaiyar, god of worldly wisdom, learning, and prosperity, is very popular. The elephant is a totemic symbol among the Vellalas, and some scholars have suggested a connection between the Vellala clan surname Pillai and the elephant-faced Pillaiyar. The second son of Siva is Skanda, also known as Murukan, often represented as a god of war and often as a handsome youth. His consorts are Devayani, a goddess, and Valli, a Veddah princess with whom he had a celebrated legendary romance. Two other sons of Siva and Parvati, Bhairava and Virabhrada, are less popular. Some of the lower castes have shrines to the former, whereas the latter is very cruel and therefore has few devotees.

Other recognized gods include Aiyanar, Potu-Razu, the popular goddesses Amman and Mari Amman, the goddess of smallpox, and Kannakai, (known to the Sinhalese as Pattini). In addition to the *devas*, or major gods, there are numerous *devatas*, or minor gods. Other objects of worship include distinguished human beings in deified forms, various demons, the sun and planets, certain animals, sacred rivers, mountains, and trees. Hindu worship, which takes place either in a *devale*, a temple dedicated to a given god, of which there are many, or at a shrine in the home, usually involves an icon made sacred by various rituals. It is believed that the god in some sense inheres to, or is present in, the image.

The basic worship ritual is the *puja*, which consists of honoring, venerating, and entertaining the god as one would an honored guest. He is offered food, water, flowers, and incense and is entertained by music and dance. He is believed to eat the "subtle" part of the foods and leave the "gross" or visible part. On festivals the god is sometimes taken for rides in processions. A priest performs the *puja*, and the lay worshipers watch. Like Buddhist worship, Hindu worship is ordinarily not congregational in nature.

Many aspects of Hindu religious life take place within the home, and many rituals involve the family group. The religious life of the devout lay Hindu consists primarily of the performance of a large number of rituals and the celebration of numerous festivals honoring various gods. Every temple has an annual festival, lasting from three to five days. In Ceylon more than thirty festivals are celebrated in the Hindu community (see table 12). Of these, the most important include the New Year, which coincides with the Sinhalese New Year. This entails general merrymaking as well as ceremonial baths and attendance at a temple. Deepvali, the festival of lights, comes at the time of the winter monsoon (see ch. 2, Physical Environment). At this time new clothes are ritually donned; a new accounting year begins in Hindu business, and new books are opened with appropriate religious rites. At Thai Pongal, which comes after the wet season, thanks are given to the sun god, and cows and bulls are honored for aiding in the year's work.

CHRISTIANITY

Approximately 9 percent of Ceylonese are Christians. The majority are Roman Catholics, descendants of converts of the Portuguese. Christians are scattered throughout the country, although very few are found in the highlands; they are also scarce in the high castes among the Sinhalese, in spite of Portuguese conversions of many aristocrats. The greatest concentration of Christians lies along the west coast from Moratuwa to Mannar. They are prominent in Mannar and Puttalam and form the majority in the population on the coast between Colombo and Chilaw.

The Portuguese converted some communities that have remained steadfast in their Catholic faith despite pressure from the Dutch, the English, and the local people. Many of these communities are coastal. Some authorities suggest that the coastal Catholics were largely converted from the Karava, or fisher, caste, who occupied a relatively low position in traditional society, and that their new religion permitted them to discard the indignities of a low caste.

In certain areas traditional cultural elements have blended with Christian elements to form uniquely Ceylon Catholic observances. For example, the Catholic Passion Play, called Pasku by Jaffna Christians, developed in Jaffna and incorporated traditional elements of Tamil village song and dance. In time the Sinhalese also adopted the passion play, and it is performed in Sinhala in alternate years on the island of Duwa near Negombo (see ch. 10, Artistic and Intellectual Expression).

Protestant Christianity has proved somewhat less tenacious in Ceylon. Although British Protestant missionaries exerted considerable influence in education in Jaffna and elsewhere, Protestantism has been losing ground with the rise of Buddhist awareness (see ch. 3, Historical Setting; ch. 9, Education). As the local elite, a main reservoir of Protestants, have become reoriented toward Buddhism and as the Burghers have left the island, the influence of Protestantism has been declining (see ch. 5, Ethnic Groups and Languages). Nonetheless, a community of Anglicans and other Protestants remains.

ISLAM

Islam, the religion of the Moor and Malay communities, which constitute about 7 percent of the population, was founded by the Prophet Muhammad in Arabia in the seventh century A.D. (see ch. 5, Ethnic Groups and Languages). Unlike Buddhism and Hinduism, it is a Middle Eastern religion based on the same Biblical tradition that molded Judaism and Christianity. As such, it rejects the South Asian notion of rebirth and a cyclical nature of the universe and holds that man has only one life on earth and that there was, and will be, only one creation. Furthermore, it accepts the concept of equality of all believers, unlike the South Asian religions, which accept caste.

Islam means "submission" to Allah (God), and a Muslim is a person who so submits. The basic tenet of the faith is expressed in the Shahadah, which states, "There is no God but Allah; and Muhammad is His prophet." Islam is a monotheistic religion. It admits no other gods or godlings or any other manifestation of the one God. The Prophet Muhammad was an exalted messenger but a human being. Islam rejects Christianity's deification of the messenger.

The law of Allah is embodied in the Quran, which is viewed as the final and complete culmination of the Five Books of Moses of the Jews and the Gospels of the Christians. These other scriptures are revered as sacred but incomplete revelations, and the people who believe in them are regarded as "People of the Book," who bear a special relationship to the Muslim community. Other prophets preceding Muhammad are recognized, including Noah, Abraham, Moses, and Jesus.

The practice of Islam revolves about the "five pillars of the faith." These are recitation of the Shahadah in full belief, prayer, almsgiving, fasting during the holy month of Ramazan, and *hadj* (pilgrimage to the holy city of Mecca). All Muslims are enjoined to pray five times during the day at prescribed times, either alone or at the mosque. In addition, the men gather for public prayer on Friday.

In most Muslim communities throughout the world, a salient feature of social life is the practice of *purdah*, or the seclusion of women. In many countries this is practiced very strictly, the two sexes having virtually no social contact with one another. In Ceylon, however, as in the Muslim communities of Southeast Asia, this is not stringently observed.

This departure from traditional Muslim practice probably derives from the compound origin of the Ceylon Muslim community. Although the original founders were Arabs, there was much intermarriage with, and conversion of, local people, especially Tamil women. A number of elements of Tamil religious practice have been incorporated by the Muslim community, including aspects of the Hindu wedding ceremony.

Although Tamil language and culture have been to date the most important indigenous local influence on the Muslim community, the growing prominence of Sinhalese nationalism has encouraged the adoption of Sinhala by many Muslims. Since 1958 the Moors' Islamic Cultural Home has recieved annual grants ranging from Rs5,000 to Rs9,000 (for value of the rupee, see Glossary) to support a project of translating the Quran into Sinhala. In mid-1970 this project was still underway.

CHAPTER 12

SOCIAL VALUES

The society in 1970 was in a state of flux, as a basically agrarian, feudal system continued to absorb and assimilate the successive impacts of colonization, growing modernization, and independence. The circumstances of the colonial period introduced into a previously homogeneous social order a new, influential, Western-oriented urban elite subscribing to a system of values, attitudes, and criteria alien to those of the traditional society (see ch. 3, Historical Setting). A significant residue of the ancient value system presists in the minds of the people, however, particularly among the vernacular-educated and rural populations. On the other hand, certain of the foreign values, not always harmonious with social reality, became associated symbolically and actually with persons and institutions of great prestige. The introduction of extraneous elements undermined the strength of customary practices and caused considerable confusion and alienation throughout the population.

The traditional social structure, which still exerts a powerful influence, was based on a network of feudal relationships and inherited statuses (see ch. 6, Social Structure). An individual was born into the social position he was to occupy for life. Consequently, the universe, including the supernatural, was conceived as a hierarchical organization in which each individual occupied a permanent status (see ch. 11, Religion). Distinctions of social status were viewed as inherent in the nature of the universe and underlie the traditional etiquette and the language. Robert Knox, a seventeenth-century observer, noted that the people "have seven or eight words for Thou, or You, which they apply to persons according to their quality, or according as they honor them ... All these words are gradually one higher than the other." The use of egalitarian as opposed to discriminatory pronouns remains an issue in modern Ceylon (see ch. 6, Social Structure). The word *jati*, popularly used to mean "birth," "rank," "race," or "genealogy," also means in a more general sense "a given type, sort, or kind of." Persons of different birth are, in a real sense, different types of persons.

Modern, independent Ceylon is, nonetheless, a constitutional democracy based on British principles of legal equality (see ch. 13, The Governmental System). The government does not recognize distinctions of caste and birth and is committed to the improvement of living standards through the application of modern technological and administrative techniques. Although not Western in orientation, government policy emphasizes progress, efficiency, popular democracy, and the application of science, all of which are at odds with the static values of traditional society. Although the new values have to some extent been assimilated by all sectors of the population, the dynamic tension caused by the coexistence of two basically inimical value systems has been largely responsible for the unsettled social conditions of the twentieth century (see ch. 5, Ethnic Groups and Languages).

The family was traditionally the core of the social structure and the pivot of the value system. It remains so in rural society. The family is viewed as a composite unit, more important than any individual member. The individual's interests are assumed to be identical with those of his family and therefore subservient to the whole. Authority of the elders and the males dominates, and marriages were, and continue to be, arranged (see ch. 7, Family). Although romantic love exists as an ideal to the young and as a theme of much popular literature, there is no expression in Sinhala (see Glossary) for "I love you" in the romantic sense or for "fall in love."

In rural areas especially, nearly all social contacts take place in a family context. Formal, special-purpose groups independent of kinship ties are not common, and the concept of such groups is scarcely understood. In traditional society there were no such groups; the Buddhist religion, for example, is not organized into parishes or congregations and does not keep membership lists. Social relationship is seen as being tantamount to kinship relationship; the one traditionally does not exist without the other.

As a result of these circumstances, behavior requiring impersonality is not highly valued. Selling at a profit to friends and relations implies outdoing or tricking them; it is nonfamilial behavior. Since most villages are composed of groups of kinsmen, only persons relatively free from the caste system ordinarily engage in retail trade in the rural areas. There was no merchant class in the traditional feudal system; this role was filled by Moors and others outside the local caste and kin systems.

The honor of the individual is intimately bound to the honor of the family. This in turn is tied to the concept of ritual purity, which underlies much of Ceylonese social behavior. Purity and pollution are spiritual concepts, but they have important physical correlatives. The boundary between the spiritual and material realms is more permeable than it is in Western thought. Physical substances not only symbolize spiritual states or values but also inherently embody or subsume them; pollution is not only dirty, it is inauspicious. Certain substances are by their nature either pure or polluting. Blood, the essence of life, is at all times very sacred but also highly polluting.

Contact with these charged substances affects the spiritual state of the creature handling them. Milk givers, such as the cow, and certain trees with milky sap are near the pinnacle of purity. Persons who handle polluting human wastes, such as washermen, sweepers, pallbearers, and midwives, form those castes occupying low positions on the social scale, which parallels the spiritual scale (see ch. 6, Social Structure; ch. 11, Religion). The high-caste individual must guard against excessively intimate contact with the persons or the blood of members of these castes. These less pure castes serve to safeguard the purer high castes from danger. For example, in the puberty rituals, during which time the high-caste girl is spiritually highly charged and extremely dangerous to her own family, a member of the washer caste carries away the pollution contaminating the clothing, jewelry, and personal articles used by the girl at the time of her first menstruation.

In the traditional social system, high status was inherent rather than earned, but within a given stratum an individual could further distinguish himself and his family by meritorious service to the nobles or to the king. The most exalted appointive positions were always held by persons of the highest hereditary castes; these honors tended to perpetuate themselves in families, both in fact and in the custom of handing down a prestigious title in a family line as a sort of surname. For example, the name Bandaranaike means "keeper of the king's treasury."

Government service remains the most prestigious career as traditional values were transferred to the colonial and, later, to the independent bureaucracy. Private enterprise—commerce and business—is much less honorable. The University of Ceylon, for example, only in the 1960s offered courses in business administration or commerce; such courses were not considered proper fields for university study. The most desirable positions are those in the elite Ceylon Administrative Service (CAS), which, in keeping with the British colonial model, only accepts recruits in their early twenties after they pass a rigorous competitive examination on general liberal arts subjects. Higher education in Ceylon has for decades been dedicated to preparing candidates for their civil service examinations (see ch. 9, Education). As a result, skills of memory and verbal expression dominate the educational process, and the most admired students are those who score well on examinations.

Theoretical rather than practical knowledge is highly regarded; even in the medical faculty of the university, students must pass written examinations before being permitted to take practical examinations in scientific subjects. Because the passing of the civil service examinations favorably affects the status of the entire family, many parents view the good child as the one who does well in school. The majority of parents desire government careers for their sons and wish their daughters to marry civil servants. Most university students hope for civil service careers, and many have no more specific ambitions than this.

The fascination of the government career extends beyond the middle class down into the rural population and among the urban workers. Many rural parents hope that their sons will have government careers, if not in the highly selective CAS, then in the clerical services (see ch. 13, The Governmental System). The prestige enjoyed by a government clerk is of a magnitude out of all proportion to his earnings or actual power. Working-class women questioned about their marriage preferences stated that they would rather marry a government clerk than an independent businessman earning several times as much. In the low country two of the most common surnames adopted to perpetuate a family honor are Liyanage (clerk) and Lakkuliyanage (head clerk).

White-collar employment generally has higher prestige than any manual occupation with the possible exception of independent agriculture. Manual work for wages is definitely demeaning; this accounts for the disinclination of the Kandyan peasants to accept wage work on the estates (see ch. 3, Historical Setting; ch. 6, Social Structure). The discrepancy between agriculture and other forms of manual work is entirely in keeping with the traditional feudal system. Under that system the highest caste was composed of agriculturalists, of whom the more aristocratic occupied positions in the king's service. Artisans, laborers, and other manual workers were of a distinctly lower order.

The relatively low status of engineering and other scientific fields among the professions reflects this disdain for manual or technical work. Neither children nor adults show much curiosity about mechanical devices; children are not generally encouraged to tinker, build models, or do experiments, and in many cases adults neither drive nor take any interest in automobiles.

As in the caste system, it is widely believed that the type of work done is intrinsically related to the social position of the individual. The work force is seen as a reasonably immutable occupational hierarchy. In the civil service and in large nongovernment organizations, there is a sharp division between the managerial employee and the rank and file. Managers are ordinarily chosen at a relatively young age on the basis of examinations not directly related to the substance of the work to be done, and there is little opportunity for workers to rise through the ranks. Furthermore it is unlikely that a supervisor would have had experience at the grassroots level of his organization. The board chairman who started as an office boy or the officer commissioned from the enlisted ranks is an extreme rarity in Ceylon.

Professional work for the government carries more prestige than private practice. For example, a government doctor fetches a higher dowry than a similarly qualified colleague practicing on his own (see ch. 7, Family). The extreme respect in which government work is held does not derive from the remuneration, which is not necessarily greater, or from the supposedly greater security, but from the inherent prestige of the position. As a consequence of the derogation of commerce and because of the respect in which agriculture is held, individuals are more likely to invest private resources in land than in business or industry. Most of the large fortunes established in business since colonial times belong to families of less than the most august caste standing, particularly to those of the Karava caste. The old elite considered trade and commerce beneath their dignity.

The traditional Ceylonese social system did not encourage a monetary evaluation of human goals. The British, not understanding the moral universe surrounding Kandyan society, were astonished at the people's failure to react to financial incentives. The Sinhalese (see Glossary) lived in a basically static social structure in which upward mobility was neither necessary nor desirable; they therefore did not share the British concept of "bettering oneself."

The British had expected that the end of *rajakaria* (free labor owed by subjects to early kings) and feudal relationships would produce opportunities for self-enrichment to which the Sinhalese would gratefully and enthusiastically respond. Wealth in Kandyan society had consisted of land and influence over men, currency was extremely scarce, and payment ordinarily took the form of perishable agricultural produce; the people therefore did not possess the acquisitive values that lay at the foundation of the British assumptions. To the traditional Ceylonese, his worth as a social person sprang from his social status rather than from his possessions.

Work in itself is morally neutral in traditional Ceylonese society; there is no concept of an ethical value in keeping busy, nor any fear that idle hands tempt the powers of evil. The Buddhist and Hindu religions do not teach that man is likely to fall into sin unless distracted (see ch. 11, Religion). Although Ceylonese are capable of extremely hard work when required, they do not ordinarily conceive of work as enjoyable or invigorating; it is more often a means to an end rather than an end in itself.

Although hard work and accomplishment are not necessarily valued in themselves, the prestige and perquisites of high status are much sought after. Titles and honorifics command great respect. It is common for authors of books, officials, and other persons to use initials with names to signal degrees, awards, honors, and other marks of distinction. In the 109th edition of the authoritative *Ferguson's Ceylon Directory,* the directory of distinguished Ceylonese is preceded by twelve pages of abbreviations of titles used in the text. A note indicates that such titles as B.A., M.A., F.R.G.S., and D.D. "of course require no elucidation." The abbreviations range alphabetically from A.A.B.I. for Associate of the Book-keepers Institute of Australia to Z.S. for Zoological Society and include such honors as K.C.B., for the Knight Commander of the Distinguished Order of the Bath, and S.W., the Silver Wolf award of the Boy Scouts. This fascination with titles and prestige symbols is probably related to their tremendous importance under the feudal system, a predilection encouraged and exploited by the Dutch and, especially, the British, who sought successfully to win the loyalty of key individuals through the awarding of prestigious titles.

Despite the enduring remnants of the traditional value system, certain European conceptions have caused permanent changes in mental attitudes. A Ceylonese historian pointed out that even the Buddhist Commission report, *The Betrayal of Buddhism,* written during the 1950s by militant partisans of the traditional culture, was remarkable for the heavy European influence on its reasoning (see ch. 11, Religion; ch. 14, Political Dynamics). Western standards of historical proof were used to support the argument, and such traditional explanatory

222

concepts as *karma* (rebirth according to one's merit) were conspicuously absent.

Probably the most striking and enduring result of British colonialism was the creation of a pancommunal national elite trained in English, a group whose members are remarkable for their alienation from the traditional values and practices of their countrymen (see ch. 5, Ethnic Groups and Languages). Although the Ceylon Tamil (see Glossary) members of this class were somewhat less estranged from their tradition than their Sinhalese counterparts, they were so British-oriented that many Ceylonese referred to them as the Brown Sahibs—that is, brown Englishmen. This group adopted most British attitudes, including the colonial assumption of administrative superiority.

The privileged position of this elite allowed them to dominate many, if not most, aspects of national life, to the immense resentment of their more traditional countrymen. Since independence in 1948 this resentment has manifested itself in politics and in a resurgent Buddhist and Sinhalese nationalism (see ch. 5, Ethnic Groups and Languages; ch. 14, Political Dynamics; ch. 17, Political Values and Attitudes). During the 1950s and 1960s the symbols of traditional culture enjoyed a renaissance among the educated. By 1970 a citified version of the national dress was in vogue among politicians, and Sinhalese names were given to the children of the educated, unlike the English names of past generations. In addition, an intellectual interest in Sinhalese art, literature, and philosophy was developing (see ch. 10, Artistic and Intellectual Expression).

The residual effects of the colonial period and the increasing impact of modernizing industry are yearly bringing more and more persons into the orbit of the urban, market-oriented life of modern Ceylon (see ch. 6, Social Structure). An eminent Ceylonese social scientist has referred to urban life as the acquisitive society and noted that its values are at variance with those of the countryside. Urban life stresses competition, whereas rural life does not. The caste system assures every individual, if not prosperity, at least a secure place in the economic structure. Personal aspiration is limited by the relatively static nature of the rural society. Qualities of harmoniousness are valued rather than those of assertiveness.

Traditional village life is highly cooperative. Such institutions as fraternal polyandry presented no problems to the Sinhalese value system (see ch. 7, Family). Since inheritance was divided equally among all heirs, there was never a class of younger sons who had to make their own way in the world. Competition was neither expressed as a value nor manifested in sports or other forms of recreation. Competitive sports, which have gained considerable popularity, were introduced by the British and encouraged by the schools (see ch. 8, Living Conditions). Robert Knox observed, "Their chief play is to bowl cokernuts [coconuts] one against the other, to try which is hardest." In this game there is no comparison of the skill or ability of the participants, nor any element of competition. As the values of competitive life have gained, the popularity of British-style competitive sports has increased.

The self-assurance and freedom of action inherent in competition were not, however, entirely foreign to traditional Ceylonese culture. Buddhism and Hinduism do not emphasize fatalism or the helplessness of the individual before cosmic forces. Rather, the functioning of *karma* depends upon the interaction of the predetermined tendency of a life with the freely chosen actions of the individual. The Buddha enjoined his followers to "be lamps unto yourselves"; he believed in the ultimate efficacy of human striving (see ch. 11, Religion).

The value system of modern Ceylon is therefore an amalgam of elements, ancient and modern, derived from Asian and European sources. As the society itself is fluid and in a state of accelerating change, so are the values that support it. Although elements of alienation are present, the picture is not so much one of conflict of values as of reformulation. Various observers have noted that Ceylonese culture generally and Sinhalese culture in particular have elements of plasticity that permit the harmonious adoption of new cultural items and conceptions while retaining much of the old. Consequently, the introduction of profoundly foreign attitudes and conceptions has not destroyed the moral foundation of Ceylonese society but has brought about a new, if uneasy, form of dynamic equilibrium.

SECTION II. POLITICAL

CHAPTER 13

THE GOVERNMENTAL SYSTEM

The governmental system of Ceylon was based in 1970 on a constitutional document called the Ceylon (Constitution) Order in Council of May 1946, as amended by the Ceylon Independence Act of December 10, 1947, and the Ceylon Independence Order in Council of December 19, 1947. It provided for the British form of parliamentary and cabinet government and retained a nominal link with Great Britain by affirming the queen as Ceylon's symbolic head of state. The queen's formal authority is exercised in Colombo by a Ceylonese governor general appointed by the British monarch on the recommendation of the prime minister of Ceylon.

The governmental structure remained stable in 1970, with only minor modifications to suit the country's independent status. This stable and peaceful adaptation to the new political environment was assured by the presence of many British-trained Ceylonese administrators and professionals who could quickly fill the void created by British departure. These Ceylonese had little residual antagonism against the political system they inherited, largely because they had actually helped to run the system before independence.

The prime minister and his cabinet ministers, the nucleus of national leadership, are chosen by the political party or a coalition of parties that win the majority of seats in a parliamentary election held at least every five years. For purposes of cabinet formation, political parties must win the majority of seats in the 157-member House of Representatives, the lower house of Parliament. The pivotal figure in the governmental system is the prime minister, who is the leader of the majority party in the lower house. Under the Constitution, he serves as the minister of defense and external affairs and may hold additional ministerial portfolios as he sees necessary.

Changes in governmental leadership have been effected by the constitutional means of free choice at the polls. The Ceylonese were granted universal adult franchise in 1931 and have

225

exercised their right to vote and to be elected to public office in many national and local elections. All elections are conducted under the supervision of the Department of Elections, an impartial body provided for in the Constitution. Members of the civil service, the police force, and the armed forces are free to vote but are forbidden by law from participating in any form of partisan political activities.

For administrative purposes, the country is divided into provinces and districts; the provinces function mainly in coordinative and advisory capacity, whereas the districts serve as the basic units of field administration. Alongside the district administration is a system of local self-governing bodies catering to the needs and problems of urban and rural areas.

The judicial system is independent and is widely respected for its integrity. It consists of the Supreme Court at the top; district courts, magistrate's courts, and courts of requests (civil courts) in the middle; and rural courts and conciliation boards at the bottom. Appeals from decisions of the Supreme Court on criminal and civil cases can be made to the Judicial Committee of the Privy Council in London when such decisions are of major public importance. In the administration of justice, the rules and principles applied by the courts are based on three main legal traditions: the Roman-Dutch law, the English law, and a body of three customary codes.

THE CONSTITUTIONAL SYSTEM

The Constitution that was in force in 1970 was adopted originally by the British authorities in May 1946. The 1946 version was later amended and supplemented by other statutes to make it more compatible with independence (see ch. 3, Historical Setting).

The Constitution, sometimes referred to as the 1948 Constitution because it was put into effect on February 4, 1948, incorporates the British conventions of cabinet and bicameral parliamentary form of government and specifies the scope of checks and balances pertaining to the three branches of government—the legislature, the executive, and the judiciary. It provides for a unitary system of government, and its provisions may be amended by a two-thirds vote of the House of Representatives.

Ceylon is technically a monarchy by virtue of the retention of the British sovereign as the titular head of state. Thus, the executive and legislative authority of the government is vested in the British monarch. In actuality, however, this power is delegated to the governor general of Ceylon, and authority is exercised not by the governor general but, after the fashion of Great Britain, by the prime minister, who is accountable to the House of Representatives. Despite its retention of dominion status in the Commonwealth of Nations, Ceylon has, since independence, exercised unlimited sovereignty in its conduct of internal and external affairs.

Unlike the constitutions of other nations, the Ceylonese fundamental law does not contain sections dealing with preamble, directive principles of state, or the basic rights and liberties of citizens. The Constitution is explicit, however, in prohibiting the enactment of any law interfering with the right of religious worship or discriminating against persons on communal or religious grounds. According to the British conventions, even these provisions would have been left out, had it not been for the foresight of the drafters of the 1948 Constitution, who felt that Ceylon's minority groups needed such safeguards (see ch. 5, Ethnic Groups and Languages; ch. 14, Political Dynamics). The protection of individual rights is secured, as it was under British rule, by independent judiciary. Although Buddhism is the dominant faith of the country, the Constitution of 1948 makes no reference to the role of this religion. Thus, the separation of church and state is implicit, in line with British constitutional traditions.

THE CENTRAL GOVERNMENT

The Governor General

The governor general symbolizes the highest political authority in the country. Appointed by, and serving during the pleasure of, the British sovereign, he performs a constitutional role that is formal and advisory as in the case of the British monarch. The manner in which the governor general exercises his power and authority is thus determined by conventions, and he remains above partisan strife.

The governor general summons, suspends, or dissolves Parliament and may give or refuse his assent to bills passed by the legislature. He appoints as prime minister the person chosen by the majority political grouping in the lower house. He also appoints other cabinet members on the advice of the prime minister. The Constitution also vests in the office of the governor general the power to appoint the judges of the Supreme Court, members of the Judicial Service Commission, the Public (Civil) Service Commission, the commissioner of the Department of Elections, the attorney general, and certain senators and members of the lower house (see fig. 9). These appointments are made usually on the advice of the prime minister and the cabinet. Under the Ceylon (Office of Governor

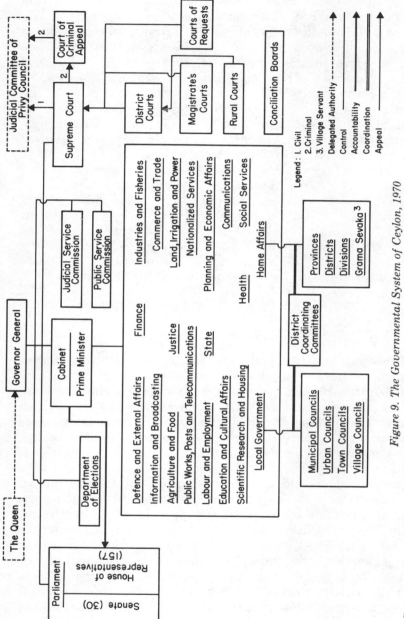

Figure 9. The Governmental System of Ceylon, 1970

Source: Adapted from *Appropriation Act, No. 30 of 1969: Estimates of the Revenue and Expenditure of the Government of Ceylon for the Financial Year, 1 October 1969 to 30 September 1970,* Colombo: *Ceylon Year Book, 1968,* Colombo, 1968, pp. 14–27; and *Ceylon Daily News,* January-March 15, 1970.

228

General) Letters Patent of December 19, 1947, and the Royal Instructions of December 19, 1947, the governor general serves as the commander in chief of the armed forces (see ch. 25, The Armed Forces).

Parliament

Parliament consists of the queen (represented by the governor general) and two houses—the Senate and the House of Representatives. The Senate has thirty members, of whom fifteen are elected by the House of Representatives according to the principle of proportional representation. The remainder are appointed by the governor general from among persons who had, according to the Constitution, "rendered distinguished public service or are persons of eminence in professional, commercial, industrial agricultural life, including education, law, medicine, science, engineering and banking." The Senate is a continuous body not to be affected by reason of a dissolution of the lower house. The senators serve for a term of six years, and one-third of them are retired every second year. Although the intent of the constitutional framers was to ensure that the Senate functioned as an effective restraining body against the lower house in legislative matters, experience since independence has shown that the legislative role of the Senate was overshadowed by the lower house.

The House of Representatives serves as the center of legislative and political reconciliation. Its members represent political organizations of varying orientations, and its legislative behavior is predictably along partisan lines. Until the general elections of 1960, the lower house was composed of 101 members, of whom 95 were elected by voters aged twenty-one and over on the basis of universal adult suffrage, and 6 were appointed by the governor general, on the advice of the prime minister, to ensure adequate representation of special groups that were believed to have been underrepresented.

For the 1960 election the voting age was lowered to eighteen and, to account for the increased electorate as well as the general increase in population after independence, the membership of the lower house was raised to 157, including 6 appointed members. The lower chamber must be elected once every five years, unless it is sooner dissolved. In dissolving the legislature, the governor general must announce a date for a new general election so that a new lower house can be convened not later than four months from the date of dissolution. In case an emergency arises after the announcement of dissolution, the governor general may, within three days of the dissolution, summon the Parliament so dissolved and keep it in session until the newly elected Parliament opens its session.

The House of Representatives elects its own speaker, the deputy speaker and chairman of committees, and the deputy chairman of committees. The privileges, immunities, and powers of both chambers are determined by Parliament and are to be exercised in the same manner they are enjoyed by the members of the British House of Commons.

The lower house is vested with broad powers to make laws "for the peace, order and good government" of the country. The Constitution does not enumerate legislative items, nor does it divide the lawmaking powers into central or provincial categories. It is explicit, however, in prohibiting Parliament from enacting any law that may discriminate against any communal or religious community.

The Constitution may be amended by two-thirds of the entire membership of the lower house, including those not present. A bill may originate in either chamber, except a money bill, which is under the exclusive jurisdiction of the lower house. A bill is deemed to have been passed by Parliament only when it has been passed by both houses; in case of conflict between the two chambers, the lower house usually prevails. A bill passed by both houses or by the lower house alone must be presented to the governor general for his assent and must be published in the *Government Gazette* to have the force of law.

Parliamentary procedures follow British conventions. The Speaker of the lower house, who generally stands above partisan politics once elected to that office by his peers in the House of Representatives, enforces rules and discipline. Parliamentary debates are conducted in English or Sinhala, the latter becoming more popular in recent years. Proceedings are open to the public with rare exception and are extensively reported in the press. Bills are deliberated in three stages before being put to vote.

The Cabinet

Under the Constitution, the executive power is vested in the British monarch and may be exercised, on her behalf, by the governor general of Ceylon. In actuality, this power is in the hands of the prime minister and his cabinet, operating under the supervision of Parliament or, more specifically, under the watchful eyes of the dominant political grouping that formed the cabinet. The cabinet is composed of the prime minister, ministers, and parliamentary secretaries.

The cabinet, which is collectively responsible to the House of

Representatives, is charged with the general direction and control of the government; it also exercises important legislative initiatives in consultation with the dominant political group in the lower house. The lack of parliamentary support for major cabinet decisions and policies occasionally results in the fall of the government, in which case Parliament must be dissolved and a new lower house must be elected. The vital but routine task of facilitating communication between the cabinet and Parliament is handled by a minister and a parliamentary secretary, both appointed by the governor general on the recommendation of the prime minister. The minister may be represented before the House by the parliamentary secretary if the minister is unable to attend session for any reason or if he is a member of the upper house. The minister is also assisted by a permanent secretary in the administration of departmental affairs.

In 1970 there were twenty ministries, of which two, the Ministry of Planning and Economic Affairs and the Ministry of Information and Broadcasting, were headed by the prime minister, who, in addition, was in charge of the Ministry of Defence and External Affairs. Other ministerial designations were finance; justice; state; agriculture and food; home affairs; land, irrigation and power; public works, posts and telecommunications; labor and employment; industries and fisheries; commerce and trade; education and cultural affairs; social services; health; communications; scientific research and housing; nationalized services; and local government. The Ministry of Nationalized Services handles such functions as transportation, port authorities, and petroleum distribution (see ch. 18, Character and Structure of the Economy).

Field Administration

The authority of the central government is extended down to the village level through government agents (*kachcherie*), each of whom is in charge of each of the nine provinces and each of the twenty-two districts; there are also a number of *grama sevakas* (village servants—see Glossary). For purposes of revenue administration, each district is divided into revenue divisions, of which there are 133. The field administration is under the control and supervision of the Department of Government Agencies in the Ministry of Home Affairs.

At the provincial level the government agent functions as the highest public servant. His role is more coordinative and supervisory than administrative. With a small number of assistants, he supervises district administrations and monitors the activities of field officers of various central ministries operating in his jurisdiction. Before independence the provincial administration under the government agent served as the most important unit of local administration but has since lost its former importance, especially since the mid-1950s, partly because of the devolution of power to the district level and partly because of the gradual evolution of local self-governing bodies.

The basic unit of local administration is the district, under a government agent appointed by the central government. A member of the civil service called the Ceylon Administrative Service (CAS), the government agent has general administrative and developmental responsibilities and is assisted by one or more land officers, a food controller, an assistant registering officer, a vital statistician, a financial officer, district revenue officers, and others concerned with developmental and public welfare activities. Subunits in a district are under the charge of officers known as district revenue officers (commonly abbreviated as DRO).

The district government agent is also responsible for coordinating the activities of field staffs from the technical and developmental departments of various ministries operating in his jurisdiction. In this effort he is assisted by the District Coordinating Committee composed of various departmental representatives, a DRO, and not more than two chairmen of village councils (the lowest unit of the local self-governing system). Members of Parliament from a particular district are invited to the committee meeting, which is presided over by the government agent and is usually held annually in October.

In mid-1968 Prime Minister Dudley Senanayake's cabinet sought to set up locally elected district councils in each of the twenty-two districts. The purpose was to promote a greater local participation in the government's developmental projects. The proposal was not implemented, however, because of Sinhalese opposition in and outside Parliament; the opposition contended that the decentralization measure would certainly encourage separatist tendencies in the Tamil-speaking areas, to the detriment of national integration (see ch. 5, Ethnic Groups and Languages; ch. 14, Political Dynamics). This proposal was actually a modified version of an earlier attempt in 1963 to replace the district administration with an elected body; the 1963 proposal had failed also because of the Sinhalese-Tamil controversy (see ch. 14, Political Dynamics).

At the base of the field administration is a *grama sevaka,* a locally recruited government official. The *grama sevaka's* duty is to help an assistant registering officer in the preparation of an electoral register that begins in June of each year and to help the police authorities in the maintenance of public peace in the village areas. The register is annually revised as a basis for conducting both parliamentary and local elections. The *grama sevaka*, who was called village headman until 1961, replaced the semifeudal village headman system.

LOCAL SELF-GOVERNMENT

In 1970 local government consisted of four types of elected bodies: 10 municipal councils in the major population centers; 36 urban councils in the urban areas; 76 town councils in the suburban areas; and 510 village councils in the rural areas. Local government is under the general supervision of the Department of Local Government (headed by a commissioner) in the Ministry of Local Government. The administrative limits of any of these bodies are defined and may be altered by the ministry to suit administrative convenience.

All local bodies are elected once every three years by the residents of their respective jurisdictions. Constituted as independent, statutory corporations with their powers and functions fixed by law, they have the power to own property, impose local taxes, and enact laws designed to increase revenues. Their functions relate to matters of public health, public utility services, housing, roadbuilding, water conservation, recreation, maternity and child welfare, libraries, firefighting, and the like.

Of the four types of local bodies, the village councils (known as village committees until August 1961) have the longest existence, dating back to the early kingdoms of the island, although not in their present form. Under the successive rules of the Portuguese, Dutch, and British colonial administrations, the village bodies administered by local elders and natural community leaders gradually weakened. In the latter half of the nineteenth century, however, the British administrators revived the ancient system, realizing that the traditional system, despite its semifeudal character, had certain democratic features comparable to modern practices of local self-government (see ch. 3, Historical Setting).

In 1970 nearly 90 percent of the country's total area of 25,332 square miles was being administered by the village councils, as compared to less than 10 percent of the areas controlled by the combination of municipal, urban, and town councils. Areas not serviced by any of these councils were under the jurisdiction of the River Valleys Development Board, created in 1949 to develop backward river basins. The board, supervised by the Ministry of Land, Irrigation and Power, had broad powers to promote agricultural, industrial, economic, and cultural progress in its designated areas (see ch. 19, Agriculture).

Each village council is in charge of two or more villages; a village is composed of one or more wards, each ward electing a council member. The chief executive officer of the council is called chairman, who also serves ex officio as the justice of peace during his three-year term.

A town council consists of three to eight elected members, who choose their own chairman. Until December 1946 the areas now administered by town councils were governed by what were then known as sanitary boards. The chairman of a town council is ex officio justice of the peace for his jurisdiction.

An urban council, known as the urban district council until January 1940, is composed of from four to twelve members, each representing a single ward. The council chairman serves as the chief executive officer and, as in other local bodies, may be removed by a two-thirds vote of council members in case of negligence, incompetence, or disobedience of rules and regulations.

A municipal council is established only in a large city. In 1970 there was a muncipal council in each of these municipalities: Colombo, Kandy, Galle, Jaffna, Kurunegala, Nuwara Eliya, Negombo, Dehiwala-Mt. Lavinia, Badulla, and Matale. The chief executive officer of this council is called mayor and is elected by the councillors of each city. In discharging his duties, the mayor is assisted by a municipal commissioner, who is responsible for the custody of books, deeds, contracts, accounts, vouchers, and other documents of the council. The commissioner directs and controls the activities of all municipal employees, who are members of the Local Government Service. The commissioner is forbidden, however, to act in contravention of any resolution, decision, direction, or order of the council, except with the permission in writing of the mayor.

Local government servants consist of two categories: those who are under the direct jurisdiction of the Local Government Service Commission and those who are outside the domain of the commission. The commission, established in 1945, is responsible for recruitment, appointment, transfer, and disciplinary control relating to employees at the higher end of salary scale. Low-ranking employees are controlled by the local bodies in whose jurisdiction they serve. The commission is composed of the commissioner of local government as ex officio chairman and eight members appointed by the minister of local government. It was reconstituted in late 1968 for the purpose of making the organization more democratic; details were not

234

readily available in early 1970 on the extent and nature of the reorganization.

The minister of local government is empowered to make general rules of operating procedures, to make recommendations concerning local policies, and to suspend or dissolve local bodies that are found to be incompetent, mismanaged, or disrespectful of the instructions issued by the ministry. The accounts of all local authorities are audited by the central government at least once a year. The degree of central control varies from one territorial level to another. There were indications in 1970 that the municipal councils were, according to an official publication, virtually autonomous, whereas the village and town councils were subjected to close ministerial guidance.

Local government undertakings are financed by three major sources: local taxation, which includes property taxes, entertainment taxes, and licensing fees and rents; central government grants; and loans and borrowings from the central government and commercial concerns obtained through the Local Loans and Development Fund. In terms of proportion, the local taxation amounts to about 5 to 6 percent of the total local revenues; the central government grants constitute about 40 percent of the total. Since these two sources are inadequate, it is usually the central government that has to make up the difference. In fact, in addition to its regular grants, the central government contributes substantially toward major water supply projects and other developmental undertakings being implemented by local self-governing bodies (see ch. 23, Finance).

In 1970 the inadequate local finances continued to be a major stumbling block in the evolution of a healthy local government. As the scope of developmental activities expanded in recent years, the need for financial resources increased proportionately and could only be met through greater central government contributions. An increased local dependence, thus, resulted in a greater central control through the district administration. Reports of tension between the district government agent and local self-governing bodies were not infrequent. This situation prompted one Ceylonese scholar to state in 1967 that the district administration "by dealing with problems of a purely local nature, has relegated the democratically elected local authorities to a role of comparative insignificance." The prevailing view in 1970 was that the parallel system of local government and field administration would have to continue until the local authorities could evolve into a more effective and viable entity.

THE CIVIL SERVICE

The civil service is officially known as the Ceylon Administrative Service (CAS); until May 1963 it was called the Ceylon Civil Service (CCS), established originally in 1801 as the nucleus of British colonial structure. Until it became an integral part of the CAS in 1963, the CCS had a total of 209 members. The 1963 reorganization swelled the ranks of the CAS to nearly 1,050 members. Although the CAS members are forbidden by law to engage in any form of political activities, they are free to join labor unions (see ch. 14, Political Dynamics; ch. 21, Labor).

The civil service inherited by independent Ceylon was generally regarded by foreigners as competent and disciplined. On the eve of independence it was composed of about 170 officers who had been trained, with rare exception, in the arts and humanities. Of this number, 32 were British officers holding senior positions. The number of British servants was reduced gradually after 1948, and by 1959 the last of the remaining British civil servants had been retired. Despite the complete Ceylonization, the civil service continued to retain the form and traditions of British administration. During the critical years of postindependence transition and adaptation, the CCS played an important stabilizing role; it was spared the ordeal of creating an entirely new structure, organizational procedures, and civil service staff (see ch. 14, Political Dynamics).

A career in the civil service has traditionally ensured security, prestige, and social status unrivaled by any other occupation. It has attracted the best educated and most talented youths of the island (see ch. 6, Social Structure). As a result, and because of the limited employment opportunities outside the public service for college graduates, competiton for civil service positions has been extremely intense. In 1963 alone some 2,700 applicants competed for only seventy openings in the upper grades of the service.

Under the Constitution, the civil service is regulated by an independent three-member Public Service Commission in respect to its recruitment, appointment, transfer, dismissal, and disciplinary matters. The members of the commission are appointed by the governor general on the advice of the prime minister for a term of five years and are eligible for reappointment. Since the commission is established to shield the public service from undue political interference and to allay minority fears of discrimination by the Sinhalese majority, its members are expected to act impartially in civil service matters. Members of Parliament must relinquish their seats when appointed to the commission. The commission members are ineligible for "further appointment as a public officer," a provision intended to remove the possibility of conflict of interest.

The Constitution allows the Public Service Commission to delegate any of its powers to ministerial authorities. As a result, although the commission still retains its control of the upper ranks of the civil service, the lower grade officers are placed under departmental heads within the ministries in respect to their appointments, promotions, and conditions of service. A lower rank officer may appeal directly to the commision, however, if he is dissatisfied with any decision handed down by his departmental superiors.

Despite the Public Service Commission, the civil service has not been entirely free of political as well as particularistic influences. Various ministries tend to exercise a large measure of discretionary powers in recruiting officials, with only nominal reference to the commission. The officials are chosen by either written examination or oral interview; recruiting procedures vary from one ministry to another and are sometimes criticized for alleged communal prejudices. Procedures relating to transfers and promotions are not infrequently attacked for being influenced more by political favoritism than the rational standard of merit. The more preferred civil service positions are those in Colombo and, to a lesser degree, Kandy, Galle, and Jaffna. Assignments outside these major cities are often considered by the civil servants as less prestigious.

The public service is divided into three broad categories: the staff grades at the top; the clerical and technical grades in the middle; and the minor grades at the bottom. The staff grade officers are usually university graduates who are recruited between the ages of twenty-two and twenty-six and who make up about 2 percent of the total number of the CAS. The middle level officers constitute about one-third of the total number; the minor grade officers form the remainder. All senior departmental positions in the central government ministries and government agents at the provincial and district levels belong to the staff grade category.

During the first decade of independence, the civil service was subjected to the strain of having to make necessary adjustments to new situations. Although the service was regarded as adequate for purposes of maintaining public peace, collecting revenues, and providing essential public and social services, it was considered obsolete for undertaking major developmental activities. Part of the difficulty encountered in the transition process stemmed from the training and educational background of the officers. In the British tradition of civil service, these officers had been trained mostly as generalists rather than specialists in developmental planning, coordination, and implementation. Since the mid-1950s the government has attempted to facilitate the transition, partly by an increased emphasis on the technical training of civil service cadres and partly by the establishment of public corporations in various fields requiring specialized attention (see ch. 18, Character and Structure of the Economy).

Because of the shortage of qualified technical and managerial personnel outside the government, however, members of the civil service continued to play a leading role even in the operation of public corporations such as the Ceylon Transport Board, the Port Cargo Corporation, the Ceylon Petroleum Corporation, and the Kantalai Sugar Corporation. In principle, these bodies are autonomous in matters of recruitment, discipline, and terms of service; they are not subject to public service regulations and are, hence, outside the jurisdiction of the Public Service Commission. Actually, various ministries exercise tight control over these corporations, especially in the appointment and removal of their governing board members. Most of these members are drawn from the senior ranks of the civil service on temporary loan status or from among retired civil service officers with good political connections. The salaries of these board members are usually higher than those for equivalent positions in the civil service.

THE ELECTORAL SYSTEM

In 1931 Ceylon became the first Asian country to adopt universal franchise for men and women of over twenty-one years of age. The first election under the franchise took place in 1932 (see ch. 3, Historical Setting). Since then many elections have been held to send representatives to national and local self-governing bodies. This experience with constitutional politics was largely responsible for the country's peaceful attainment of independence and for the decision to retain the British form of parliamentary government. The results of the general elections held in 1956, 1960, and 1965 have shown that the electoral system as currently constituted is functioning without stress.

Before the Donoughmore Constitution of 1931 was in force, the franchise had been restricted to only the 4 percent of the total male population that could meet property and educational qualifications. Moreover, the representation was on a communal basis in the proportion of two Sinhalese for every Tamil. After 1931 the ratio was changed to five Sinhalese for every Tamil, thereby giving greater representation to the numerically dominant Sinhalese group. The post-1931 scheme of territorial rather than communal representation was resented by the Tamil minorities. As a result, a new compromise formula was written into the Soulbury Constitution, which went into effect in 1946 and was later adopted as Ceylon's Constitution at independence (see ch. 3, Historical Setting).

As incorporated into the 1948 Constitution, the compromise calls for the delimitation of electoral districts into two categories: one based on population under which each district is to represent about 75,000 persons; and the other based on the size of territory at the rate of one district for each 1,000 square miles in those areas sparsely populated by minorities. The latter category of representation is aimed at enabling the minorities to win a higher number of seats than they could on the basis of population alone; the Constitution provides for twenty-five districts for this purpose.

As an additional safeguard measure, the Delimitation Commission, a statutory organization with constitutional status, is empowered to create one or more multimember electoral constituencies to assure adequate representation for one or more minority groups concentrated in an electoral district. The minority groups in this instance must be at least 10 percent of the total voting population of the electoral district.

There are two types of elections, parliamentary and local, but election procedures are nearly identical for both. The procedures are specified in the Ceylon (Parliamentary Elections) Order in Council of September 1946 and in the Local Authorities Elections Ordinance of 1946 as amended in 1949, 1953, 1955, 1963, and 1965. The administrative responsibility for the conduct of parliamentary and local elections lies with the Department of Elections, an independent statutory body headed by a commissioner of parliamentary elections. The commissioner is appointed by, and accountable only to, the governor general.

A voter must be at least eighteen years of age (twenty-one until 1960), a citizen of Ceylon, and a resident in the electoral district on the first day of June of an election year. One voter list, or register of electors, is used for both parliamentary and local elections. Convicts and the mentally unsound are not qualified to vote. The register of electors must be kept up to date every year. The registration of voters is conducted under the supervision of the Department of Elections, which maintains twenty-three registering officers. These officers are aided by assistant registering officers in the district administrations and also by *grama sevakas* at the village level. The registers of electors must be displayed for public examination.

An electoral district consists of polling districts, each containing not more than 1,500 eligible voters. The polling districts are divided into about 5,000 polling stations, each manned by eight to ten workers. For the general elections of 1965, the country was divided into 145 electoral districts. The number of eligible voters was, as of May 1965, a little over 5 million.

The register of electors for each electoral district and the lists prepared for the purpose of revising the register after public examination must be in the language of the majority (Sinhala) and, where the language of the majority of voters is not the official language of Ceylon as in the Northern and Eastern provinces, in Tamil. In the Tamil-speaking areas, however, Sinhala may be also used if this language is spoken by not less than 10 percent of the total electors of a given district.

When Parliament is dissolved by the governor general or when a notice ordering elections is issued by the commissioner of local government, candidates must be nominated within sixteen days to one month from the date the dissolution took place or the notice was issued. Candidates to public offices may campaign with or without party affiliation. They are provided with voting symbols on the ballot paper for the benefit of illiterate voters. To be treated as a "recognized" political party, a party must have returned at least two members to the House of Representatives in the previous general elections except in a case where the commissioner of parliamentary elections is satisfied, on application, that a given party has been engaged in political activity for a continuous period of not less than five years.

Electoral disputes or petitions are referred to a panel of election judges appointed by the governor general. The panel consists of not less than five judges chosen from among those holding office as judges of the Supreme Court, commissioners of assize, or judges of the district courts at Colombo, Kandy, Galle, and Jaffna. From this panel a trial judge is nominated by the chief justice of the Supreme Court. The decision of this panel is final and conclusive.

THE JUDICIARY

The Legal System

The administration of justice is based on the application of legal rules, codified and customary, which have evolved from the Roman-Dutch law, the English common law, and the three distinct customary codes observed, respectively, by the Sinhalese of the interior, the Tamils, and the Muslims (see ch. 3, Historical Setting). In the Central, North Central, Uva, and Saba-

240

ragamuwa provinces of the interior highlands, the traditional Kandyan customary laws, now partly codified, are applied to the Sinhalese in respect to inheritance, matrimony, and donations. In the Jaffna district of the north, Thesavalamai, a customary code originating in southern India, is enforced among the Tamil inhabitants in respect to persons and property. The Muslims are governed by their own personal and religious laws (see ch. 6, Social Structure; ch. 7, Family).

In the maritime provinces the Sinhalese are governed by the Roman-Dutch law as to the rights of property and inheritance, but in commercial matters and in criminal procedures the English law is applied (see ch. 24, Public Order and Internal Security). Until the early seventeenth century the Low-Country Sinhalese had been allowed to observe the same customary laws that had prevailed in the interior region; however, partly because of the conversion of some Sinhalese to Christianity and partly because of the exodus of many landowning Sinhalese families to the Kandyan interior, the traditional Sinhalese laws could not be sustained. As a result, the Roman-Dutch law of intestate succession came to be applied to the maritime provinces.

In the centuries of contact with both the Roman-Dutch law and the English law, the customary laws have been influenced considerably by foreign strains of legal principles, especially in cases where customs were silent or ambiguous. Thus, the law of succession, which was unknown to the Kandyans, is based on the Roman-Dutch law and the English law. The obligation of the husband to support his wife, ambiguous under the Kandyan law, derives from the Roman-Dutch law. In general, the attitude of jurists has been to apply the customary laws to personal relations unless these laws are silent on particular issues. The Roman-Dutch law is not to be applied before the customary laws or local enactments based on the English law are exhausted.

The Roman-Dutch law and the English law have also influenced each other. The two legal principles have not been mutually exclusive; instead, under the eclectic dictum that only so much of the Roman-Dutch law as suits the Ceylonese circumstances should be applied, the English-trained lawyers and judges have adapted the Roman-Dutch principles to new needs and conditions. The dual legal heritage has become an ingrained feature of the Ceylonese legal system.

Courts

The judiciary consists of a hierarchy of courts patterned after the British model that was introduced in the 1830s. It has been

241

widely respected in the country for its independence and integrity. The judicial service has functioned separately from the administrative service since the late 1930s. Under the Constitution, the authority relating to the appointment, transfer, dismissal, and disciplinary control of judicial officers, except for the members of the Supreme Court, is vested in the independent Judicial Service Commission rather than the Ministry of Justice.

The Judicial Service Commission consists of three members: the chief justice of the Supreme Court as chairman, a judge of the Supreme Court, and a third person who is, or was, a judge of the same tribunal. The latter two members are appointed by the governor general for a period of five years and are eligible for reappointment. In discharging its assigned duties, the commission may authorize the secretary to the commission to transfer judicial officers and make acting appointments within the limits of delegated power.

For purposes of judicial administration, the country is divided into five judicial circuits: Western, Midland, Northern, Southern, and Eastern. Each circuit is subdivided into districts or divisions. A district is administered by a district court, and a division is under the control of a magistrate's court.

The Supreme Court bench, composed of a chief justice and ten puisne judges (associate judges), all appointed by the governor general, holds office contingent on behavior and is not removable except on an address from both chambers of Parliament. The judges retire on reaching the age of sixty-two, unless the requirement is waived by the governor general for a period not exceeding twelve months. The governor general may also appoint a judicial officer known as a commissioner of assize to the Supreme Court bench; the commissioner of assize enjoys the same rights, powers, privileges, and immunities of a judge of the Supreme Court. In 1967 there were three commissioners of assize.

The Supreme Court has appellate jurisdiction in civil cases; as a rule, it does not assume original jurisdiction in civil cases except where it sits as the Court of Admiralty for maritime cases. In criminal cases, however, it is the court of first instance in respect to the more serious offenses, such as homicide and rape; these cases are tried before a jury and a single judge or a commissioner of assize. An appeal from decisions of the court is allowed, with the consent of the trial judge, to the Court of Criminal Appeal presided over by the chief justice of the Supreme Court and three puisne judges. In civil and criminal matters, an appeal may be taken to the Judicial Committee of the Privy Council in London, as was done occasionally in the 1960s. The appeal is disallowed unless there is a possibility of grave error or the issue under contention is of major public importance.

District courts are immediately below the Supreme Court. They have unlimited original jurisdiction in civil and revenue cases and criminal jurisdiction over cases not under the exclusive sphere of the Supreme Court. The number of presiding judges varies according to locations: five for the District Court of Colombo; two each for the courts at Kandy, Galle, Matara, Jaffna, Kalutara, Panadura, and Karunegala; and one each for other locations. The District Court of Colombo also handles maritime cases with limited jurisdiction.

Lower courts, below the district level, include the magistrate's courts, courts of requests, municipal courts, and rural courts. Of these tribunals, the courts of requests deal only with civil cases, whereas the others combine both civil and criminal jurisdictions. The courts of requests at Colombo, Colombo South, and Kandy are each presided over by a separate commissioner; the others are under the control of district judges or magistrates acting as commissioners of requests in addition to their court duties. Juvenile offenses are tried at the magistrate's courts, except in Colombo where there is a separate Juvenile Court presided over by a full-time judge.

Minor offenses are tried by the rural courts, and the more serious ones are reserved for superior courts, as specified in the Criminal Procedure Code of 1898 as amended. The primary responsibility for determining the competence of a court over a given criminal offense lies with the magistrate's court, which holds a pretrial hearing for this purpose (see ch. 24, Public Order and Internal Security).

A number of conciliation boards are established at the lowest level of the court hierarchy. They were set up in 1958 to bring expeditious justice to the rural areas. Minor civil and criminal offenses are brought before the boards for informal adjudication without reference to the regular criminal and civil procedures. Lawyers are not allowed in the board proceedings. When the informal proceedings fail to satisfy either contestant, the case must be brought before the rural courts.

CHAPTER 14

POLITICAL DYNAMICS

In 1970 politics continued to be dominated by two major blocs having sharply contrasting ideologies and programs. The pivotal organizations were Mrs. Sirimavo Ratwatte Dias Bandaranaike's left-of-center Sri Lanka Freedom Party (SLFP) and Dudley Senanayake's right-of-center United National Party (UNP). Between 1947 and 1970 the UNP had ruled for a total of thirteen years as compared to the SLFP's nine years.

In the general elections held in May 1970, the SLFP, which was allied with two Marxist parties, defeated the incumbent UNP by a lopsided margin and formed the coalition government under the premiership of Mrs. Bandaranaike. For independent Ceylon, the SLFP's ascension to power was the fifth in a succession of orderly transfers of power from government to opposition.

The SLFP-led coalition captured a total of 115 seats as against the UNP's 17 seats, with the SLFP winning 90 seats in its own right. Thus the coalition plurality, well above a two-thirds majority in the 157-member House of Representatives, gave Prime Minister Bandaranaike a virtually unlimited mandate, including the prerogatives to rewrite the Constitution and initiate sweeping changes in other areas based on the coalition's election manifesto.

Viewed in another perspective, however, the leftist victory appeared to be less overwhelming than its parliamentary plurality seemed to indicate; the UNP actually obtained more popular votes—about 1,877,000 votes, or 37.7 percent of the total valid votes—than the SLFP, which drew about 1,813,000 votes, or 36.3 percent of the total. This anomaly was explicable mainly by the electoral tactic of the leftist opposition called the no-contest pact. Under this pact, candidates of SLFP and its two Marxist allies—the Lanka Sama Samaja Party (LSSP) or roughly, Ceylon Equality Party, and the pro-Soviet wing of the Ceylon Communist Party, usually abbreviated as CCP (Moscow)—agreed not to compete with each other but to support instead a common, single anti-UNP candidate in any given electoral district, a tactic that helped to prevent the splitting of opposition votes.

Among the major issues confronting Prime Minister Bandaranaike's government were shortages of foreign exchange, an unfavorable balance of payments, the rising cost of living, unemployment, and the chronic shortage of essential foodstuffs (see ch. 18, Character and Structure of the Economy). After the mid-1960s popular grievances stemming from these economic issues became a focal point of partisan politics and, as a result, communal issues arising from the longstanding majority-minority controversy became less politically exploitable than they were during the decade beginning in the mid-1950s. The potency of communalism as a political issue declined mainly because the Sinhalese majority were able to restore their language and religion to the positions of preeminence that had obtained before Europeans, notably the British, arrive in the island.

In mid-1970 Ceylonese observers generally shared the view that varying degrees of political tension would confront the prime minister for a year or two. They assumed that, given the intractable nature of some of the economic problems, the moderately socialist SLFP would be subjected to conflicting pressures from its own Marxist allies, which were clamoring for radical remedies, on the one hand, and from the gradualist, conservative forces on the other.

Most politically influential persons were to be found in the House of Representatives and, particularly, in the cabinet. As elected members of the lower house, they represented not only territorial constituencies but also in many cases the interests of such groups as labor unions, businessmen, urban professionals, religious organizations, minorities, and landowners. By training and attitudinal orientation, most of the political leaders in 1970 were Sinhala educated, Buddhist, and hence more aware of indigenous cultural and political heritage than their counterparts who had dominated the political scene until the mid-1950s.

The 1970 election indicated that the party system was functioning as a central feature of politics. Political parties reflected the full range of the ideological spectrum from the far left to the far right. Furthermore, very few restrictions were imposed on party politics. With one or two insignificant exceptions, political parties as well as various interest groups continued to express their respective preferences and alternatives freely through the existing framework of parliamentary politics.

BACKGROUND

The assassination in September 1959 of Prime Minister Solomon West Ridgeway Dias Bandaranaike precipitated a period of instability, but the institution of parliamentary, multiparty politics proved to be viable enough to endure the resulting stresses and tensions (see ch. 3, Historical Setting). Leadership succession was resolved by orderly, constitutional means.

The premiership passed into the hands of Wijeyananda Dahanayake, then minister of education, who pledged his cabinet to carry on the socialist policies of his predecessor, but policy differences and personality clashes within the ruling circle forced him to dissolve Parliament in December 1959. The Dahanayake government was defeated in the March 1960 general elections by the UNP, which won only fifty seats but was the single largest parliamentary group in the lower house (see table 13).

In keeping with his previous pledge to stay in opposition rather than form a political alliance with leftist parties, Prime Minister Senanayake formed an all-UNP government. He was supported by other minor right-of-center parties, but his overall parliamentary majority was below the minimum of seventy-six seats required to defeat an opposition motion of no-confidence in the UNP cabinet. Less than a month after its formation, the UNP government fell, and new elections were ordered to be held in July 1960.

The July elections returned to power the leftist SLFP. The new government of Prime Minister Sirimavo Bandaranaike carried out its election pledges by taking over the management of nearly all Christian missionary schools receiving government assistance. It also nationalized the Bank of Ceylon and all life insurance businesses; pursued anticorruption measures; continued the policy of nonalignment in foreign relations; and initiated a series of austerity measures designed to halt the depletion of foreign exchange holdings (see ch. 9, Education; ch. 15, Foreign Relations; ch. 23, Finance).

The SLFP's promises to revise the Constitution and make Ceylon a republic were put aside, however, because of more pressing problems arising from the controversy over language, growing economic difficulties, and the government's attempt to widen its control over the press (see ch. 16, Public Information; ch. 18, Character and Structure of the Economy).

The Bandaranaike government's policy of making Sinhala the only official language of the land became a major source of political unrest in early 1961 when the Tamils of the Northern and Eastern provinces resorted to civil disobedience campaigns (see ch. 5, Ethnic Groups and Languages). The government had to declare a state of emergency, curtail the activities of Tamil political organizations in the disturbed provinces, and place the two Tamil-speaking provinces under virtual

247

Table 13. *Political Leadership in Ceylon, 1947-70*

Date	Prime Minister	Ruling party	General elections
September 1947-March 1952.	Don Stephen Senanayake	United National Party[1]	August-September 1947
March 1952-October 1953.	Dudley Senanayake	.. do .. [2]	May 1952
October 1953-April 1956.	John Kotelawala	.. do ..	....
April 1956-September 1959.	Solomon West Ridgeway Dias Bandaranaike.	People's United Front[3] (Mahajana Eksath Peramuna)	April 1956
September 1959-March 1960.	Wijeyananda Dahanayake	.. do ..	....
March 1960-July 1960.	Dudley Senanayake	United National Party	March 1960
July 1960-March 1965.	Sirimavo Ratwatte Dias Bandaranaike.	Sri Lanka Freedom Party	July 1960
March 1965-May 1970.	Dudley Senanayake	United National Party	March 1965
May 1970	Sirimavo Ratwatte Dias Bandaranaike.	Sri Lanka Freedom Party[4]	May 1970

[1] A coalition of non-Marxist, intercommunal political organizations.

[2] S.W.R.D. Bandaranaike's Sinhala Maha Sabha, one of the two major components of the United National Party coalition, broke away in July 1951 to form the Sri Lanka Freedom Party.

[3] The pivotal organization of this front was the Sri Lanka Freedom Party.

[4] Formed the leftist coalition government with Trotskyite Lanka Sama Samaja Party and the pro-Soviet wing of the Ceylon Communist Party.

military occupation (see ch. 24, Public Order and Internal Security; ch. 25, The Armed Forces). In April 1962, confronted with mounting Tamil antagonism, the government relaxed its emergency powers, but it was not until May of the following year that they were terminated.

A deteriorating balance of payments also troubled the government, which sought to cope with the situation by imposing stringent import controls and by producing more food grains at home. There were limits to what the government could do, however, because the conditions affecting the nation's export earnings, on which the government depended heavily for its annual revenues, were largely beyond the country's own control (see ch. 19, Agriculture; ch. 22, Trade).

The SLFP government was confronted with still another thorny issue, which concerned Prime Minister Bandaranaike's avowed policy of breaking up the country's two largest conservative newspaper chains. These chains had consistently opposed the socialist position of the SLFP government. The policy was aimed at imposing controls on the press in order to "ensure," in Prime Minister Bandaranaike's words, "the democratic character of newspapers" and prevent monopolistic abuses (see ch. 16, Public Information).

The government's attempts to pass restrictive press bills in November 1964 precipitated a crisis situation in which fourteen members of the ruling SLFP defected and joined the opposition in protest. The press controversy, coupled with the opposition charges that the government "miserably failed to solve such pressing problems as unemployment and the high cost of living," enabled the opposition to carry a motion of no-confidence in the government. As a result, the governor general dissolved Parliament in December 1964 and ordered new elections to be held in March 1965.

The Bandaranaike government was defeated by the UNP in the March 1965 elections. The UNP success was attributable in part to its electoral alliance with several minor opposition parties. In its election manifesto the UNP promised a policy of democratic socialism, a strengthened private sector of the economy, opposition to any form of press control, and the eventual modification of Ceylon's dominion status to that of a republic but still retaining its Commonwealth ties.

In contrast, the SLFP, which had formed an alliance with the LSSP in June 1964, declared a policy of widening the public sector and imposing controls on the press. In an attempt to draw Buddhist support, it also promised to enhance the role of Buddhism in national affairs.

Many observers attributed the electoral swing from left to

right in 1965 at least partly to the protest vote cast by many of the nearly 1 million young voters between the ages of eighteen and twenty; these youths were able to participate in national elections for the first time after the minimum voting age had been lowered from twenty-one to eighteen in 1959 (but not in time for them to vote in the 1960 elections). It was generally believed that the youths were disenchanted, as were many of the Sinhalese masses in urban and rural areas, with the failure of the government to solve unemployment among college graduates and with the general deterioration of the economy. Unlike the 1956 and 1960 elections, communal issues played a secondary role in the 1965 elections.

With only sixty-six seats, the UNP did not have an absolute majority in the House of Representatives. Thus it formed a coalition government (more commonly known as the national government) with the Tamil-serving Federal Party (FP). In exchange for its support, the FP was able to obtain assurances of certain political concessions from Prime Minister Senanayake. The new prime minister emphasized, among other priorities, the importance of increasing food-grain production as a prerequisite for the nation's economic development (see ch. 19, Agriculture). The new government also stated that it would restore fiscal integrity as soon as circumstances permitted.

Faced with what the UNP government called a bankrupt economy, the new government moved quickly to improve relations with the United States, which in early 1963 had suspended aid to Ceylon as a result of disagreements stemming from Prime Minister Bandaranaike's nationalization of foreign oil company facilities. The overtures led to the resumption of United States aid in July 1965 (see ch. 15, Foreign Relations).

The longstanding problems of majority-minority relations were once again dramatized in early 1966 when the UNP cabinet announced regulations providing for the "reasonable use" of Tamil for official purposes in the Tamil-speaking provinces (see ch. 5, Ethnic Groups and Languages). This announcement almost immediately aroused Sinhalese hostility and was followed by civil disorders. The state of emergency proclaimed in January 1966 lasted until early December of that year.

The communally inspired political tension was heightened further by the uncovering in February 1966 of an alleged coup attempt by a small number of military and police officers. More than twenty persons, including Major General Richard Udugama, then army chief of staff, were charged with anti-state conspiracy but were later acquitted by the Supreme Court (see ch. 24, Public Order and Internal Security; ch. 25, The Armed Forces). In the general elections of May 1970, Udu-

250

gama was elected to the House of Representatives as a member of the SLFP.

Meanwhile, the economy showed little indication of major improvement, partly because of the increase in import prices of rice by nearly 50 percent after 1965 and the steep fall in the prices of Ceylon's export crops. The food situation worsened abruptly in late 1966 because of the then-prevailing worldwide shortage of rice that made Thailand and Burma, the traditional suppliers, unable to supply their usual quota of rice. On December 18, 1966, the UNP government declared a state of emergency in an effort to avert possible food riots. Additionally, it announced the reduction of the subsidized weekly rice ration from four pounds to two pounds beginning on December 20, a reduction that remained in effect at the time of the 1970 general elections.

The UNP was able to manifest a measure of self-confidence after 1967 because of two consecutive bumper crops in 1967 and 1968, but even its much publicized food-drive success did not check its declining popularity. Moreover, after March 1968 the UNP's parliamentary strength was weakened by the breakaway of the FP from the coalition.

In an attempt to unite the anti-UNP opposition, the SLFP, LSSP, and CCP agreed in February 1968 on a common political program. This program was to form the common basis for their electoral competition with the UNP in 1970. Among other things, the leftist parties pledged themselves to seek governmental change through free and impartial elections and to establish the so-called people's government. According to the leftists, the people's government was to help the regular bureaucracy formulate economic plans, fight black-market activities, safeguard the popular interests, and promote the people's welfare.

Unlike the policy in 1965, however, the common program softened the leftist position on the press and economic issues. It dropped nationalization of the press and promised to safeguard freedom of the press by encouraging what it called independent newspapers (see ch. 16, Public Information). It also ruled out nationalization of commercial banks and private sector industries.

POLITICAL ISSUES AND GROUP ORIENTATIONS

Major Political Issues

Economic Grievances

For many years political stability and economic growth depended as much on favorable export prices as on the ability to supply rice at low retail prices. When after the early 1960s these two conditions ceased to prevail, successive governments sought to solve the resulting problems by reducing their food subsidies or by replacing the minister of finance. Although the reduction of the subsidies was fiscally imperative, it also entailed political risks because of its adverse impact on the average housewife's food budget.

In 1970 the country still relied heavily on unpredictable foreign markets for its essential foodstuffs, a reliance that not only placed a severe drain on scarce foreign exchange but also posed still another problem. Because rice is the staple food, the need for its stable supply at low consumer prices has always claimed a top welfare priority from governments. A higher consumer rice price meant a higher cost of living (see ch. 8, Living Conditions). Thus governments had to retail rice at prices considerably lower than import costs; in actual practice, the consumer had to pay only about one-fourth of the imported price, and the government had to subsidize the difference, which, depending on supply factor, ranged from 10 to 30 percent of annual budget expenditure (see ch. 8, Living Conditions; ch. 22, Trade; ch. 23, Finance).

Rice had emerged as a major political issue as early as 1953, when the food subsidies threatened to reach nearly 30 percent of government expenditures for the year. Under pressure, Prime Minister Senanayake saw no alternative but to withdraw the subsidies. This action almost immediately aroused a widespread public protest and was followed by public disorders and riotings, general strikes, and a sharp rise in the free-market price of rice. Resulting tensions led to the resignation of the prime minister in August and his temporary retirement from partisan politics. In the elections of 1956 the opposition SLFP effectively used this issue against the UNP.

Rice was again a focal point of crisis in 1962 when, under acute financial pressure caused by a steep drop in world market prices of the nation's export crops, Prime Minister Bandaranaike decided to reduce the subsidies by 25 percent. She described her decision as "painful but necessary" and explained that the reduction would considerably relieve fiscal pressures. The decision, which was opposed within the prime minister's own ranks, was met by hostile public protests, and the government retreated. Felix Reginald Dias Bandaranaike, then minister of finance, had to resign from his post since he found the retreat incompatible with his earlier public pronouncement that the reduction of the subsidies was the only economically feasible alternative in restoring fiscal integrity.

In December 1966 the UNP government reduced the subsidized weekly rice ration from four pounds to two pounds to avert fiscal collapse. This action was regarded as essential because the economy had suffered considerably during the year from adverse weather, labor unrest, a steep decline in its export earnings, and a deteriorating balance of payments. As the 1970 elections approached, the UNP hoped to take rice out of partisan politics, but the SLFP sought to capitalize on the issue by promising to restore the four-pound ration.

The steadily rising cost of living after 1967 was attributed in part to the reduction of food subsidies and the consequent rise in the free-market price of rice. The overall consumer price index jumped from 102 in 1966 (using 1963 as the base year) to 109 in 1967, 116 in 1968, and 122 in 1969. The situation took on critical proportions as unemployment among urbanites and especially among college graduates increased steadily in the late 1960s (see ch. 8, Living Conditions; ch. 21, Labor).

The UNP's vulnerability at the polls in 1970 thus appeared to be the fault of no single ruling group. The economic troubles that beset Prime Minister Senanayake dated back to the early 1950s and were attributable to many causes, some of which were beyond Ceylon's control (see ch. 18, Character and Structure of the Economy). Apart from the rice, these troubles included the more or less stagnant export earnings during the 1960s, the steadily expanding social welfare needs, the annual population increase at the rate of between 2.2 and 2.4 percent, and increasing numbers of college graduates entering the already tight job market each year. Ceylonese observers generally agreed that the cumulative unsettling impact of these adverse factors was probably responsible, at least in part, for the electoral swing from right to left in 1970.

Communalism

From about 1956 to 1965 the relationship between the Sinhalese majority and the Tamil minority was among the foremost concerns of most political leaders. But since the long-dormant Sinhalese-Buddhist community was able during that period to reassert its national dominance, communalism gradually receded into the background. In 1970 mutual suspicions and distrusts between the two communities, however, still remained a potentially explosive factor.

The so-called communal issues were carried over from generations past. The island is the home of four major world religions: Buddhism, Hinduism, Christianity, and Islam; the ethnic composition of its inhabitants shows similar diversity: Sinhalese, Tamils, Muslims, Eurasians, Burghers (see Glossary), and Malays. About 92 percent of the Sinhalese, who constitute nearly 70 percent of the total population, are Buddhists (see ch. 5, Ethnic Groups and Languages; ch. 11, Religion). The politics of the post-1947 years were a sequel to the historic antecedents of conflict and cooperation between these religious and ethnic communities (see ch. 3, Historical Setting).

Even before independence an attempt to foster communal peace had long been a major preoccupation of British authorities, who sought to give every community an access to the center of decisionmaking and power and a sense of participation in national affairs. In keeping with their promises to grant an increasing measure of self-government to the Ceylonese, the British administrators devised various constitutional schemes aimed at ensuring, as far as circumstances permitted, representation based on population as well as overall communal interests (see ch. 13, The Governmental System).

In the immediate postindependence years political leaders subordinated their communal differences to the common goal of striving for the working of parliamentary democratic institutions and solidifying the foundations of nationhood. They were primarily preoccupied with the moderately reformist, anti-Communist activities of the UNP and with seeking to foster a sense of Ceylonese nationalism based on territorial and intercommunal likes.

By the very nature of parliamentary politics, however, the ideals of reconciliation and harmony gradually gave way to community-oriented partisan competition. The shift was in tune with the essence of party politics in which, given a common basis of agreement, the numerically larger group could peacefully alter the power structure. Thus the Sinhalese-Buddhist majority, awakening to a new political awareness, was determined to regain the preemptive political power in order to establish a Sinhalese-centered nation.

The rising tide of Buddhist resurgence and the Sinhalese nationalist movement that followed independence was in reaction to, and directed against, the small numbers of Sinhalese Christians, Burghers, and Tamils who held favored positions as members of the upper layer of Ceylonese society. Under British rule, these minorities had been generally more receptive to Western influences than the culturally conservative Sinhalese-Buddhists, especially those of the Kandyan highland region. They had obtained an English education, dressed like Westerns, developed a taste for Western rather than indigenous culture, and moved into positions of prestige and influence in the bureaucracy (see ch. 6, Social Structure).

In their efforts to displace the religious and ethnic minorities, the Sinhalese took their case to the people through two channels, Buddhism and Sinhala, the language of the majority. Thus Buddhism was widely used as a popularly appealing ve-

254

hicle in forging a sense of nationalism based on the theme of Ceylon for the Sinhalese and in stressing the historic bonds between the Sinhalese and the faith. The All Ceylon Buddhist Congress and Bandaranaike's SLFP played major contributing roles (see ch. 3, Historical Setting; ch. 11, Religion; ch. 17, Political Values and Attitudes).

By the mid-1950s an attempt to make Sinhala the sole official language of the land had become the focal point of unity for the Sinhalese of various persuasions. The Sinhala Only movement aroused Tamil hostility and Sinhalese counterreaction during the decade that followed (see ch. 5, Ethnic Groups and Languages; ch. 24, Public Order and Internal Security).

The Sinhala Only movement, coupled with an active Buddhist involvement in partisan politics, had major sociopolitical consequences. The age-old schism between the Sinhalese and Tamil communities widened markedly, and responsible leaders in both communities found it politically damaging to seek reconciliation with each other, unless there were positive assurances of reciprocal benefits. In addition, the number of Sinhalese-Buddhist-oriented parliamentary members from rural areas, who until the mid-1950s had generally played a secondary role in national politics, increased sharply after the 1956 elections. The same process was also taking place in the Ceylon Civil Service (CCS).

The use of Sinhala as the medium of instruction in a reorganized school system helped to produce a generation of youth that became more conscious of Sinhalese-centered national identity. In a parallel process, Buddhism also gained in social and political importance as a principal determinant of social and political values (see ch. 12, Social Values; ch. 17, Political Values and Attitudes).

By the mid-1960s Ceylonese observers were generally agreed that the Sinhalese had succeeded in redressing what they called age-old injustices and discriminations. They also had predicted that passions aroused by language and religion would gradually subside. This assessment was borne out, at least in part, by the diminishing importance of communalism, as indicated by the parliamentary elections of 1965 and 1970.

Nevertheless, as of 1970 communalism was by no means a closed issue. The All Ceylon Buddhist Congress was still pressing the government and various political parties to adopt measures that had, even if not by design, anti-Tamil and anti-Christian undertones. Sinhalese groups were still seeking to restrict further the scope of various opportunities available for the Tamils of both Ceylonese and Indian origins.

There was also a persistent, widely shared Tamil desire for

a greater measure of internal autonomy in the Northern and Eastern provinces. The Tamils held the view that, so long as their demand for a federal type of constitution was not met, they had no means of elevating their position from the existing second-class citizenship status. They argued that the current unitary form of government that permitted little room for de-centralization of power in the Tamil-speaking areas would eventually bring about their extinction as a separate cultural entity. On the other hand, Sinhalese politicians remained adamant in their assertion that any concession to the Tamil demand for federalism would lead to a national disintegration (see ch. 17, Political Values and Attitudes).

Group Orientations

Events of the past decade indicated that, although it was possible to categorize the political activists according to various standards, this classificatory scheme often proved to be meaningless as a basis for understanding the complexity of political behavior. This difficulty was a result partly of deeply embedded social divisions within each identifiable segment and partly of the fact that the focus of political loyalty was generally diffused and thus no single major political party could exclusively enlist the support of any single group. An additional complication was that many voters tended to follow their leaders not so much for their ideological preferences or programmatic alternatives as for their personal and local influence.

In terms of functions, the electorate was divided into civil servants, members of the armed forces and police, organized labor, businessmen, urban professionals, Buddhist monks, youth and students, and the rural elite and peasants. Most of these political segments were also divided into communal blocs: Sinhalese, Tamils, Burghers, and Muslims. Based on geography, the Sinhalese majority was subdivided into Low-Country and Kandyan categories, each with its own traditions, political attitudes, and preferences (see ch. 5, Ethnic Groups and Languages; ch. 17, Political Attitudes and Values). In addition, urban-rural distinctions, caste standing, and family connections also affected the manner in which these groups reacted to public issues of both national and local importance (see ch. 6, Social Structure).

There were many channels through which these groups made their needs and problems known to the government. Some used informal, personalized contacts, whereas others relied on lob-bying through well-financed trade associations. Still others set up their own political parties to exert pressures on other more established parties. But the most common tactic was to attach allegiance to whichever political party seemed to be most responsive to their needs at any given moment. When none of these methods worked, the alternative was to resort to the time-honored practices of hunger fasting, general strikes, or civil disobedience, as was frequently the case in connection with the language dispute or labor-employer relations.

Civil servants and members of the military and police were forbidden by law to participate in partisan politics, but after 1956 they tended to reflect the changing political complexion of the country. Whereas until the mid-1950s top positions in these government services had been held for the most part by a small number of English-educated, upper middle class Low-Country Sinhalese Christians, Tamils, and Burghers, these subgroups were gradually replaced after the SLFP's ascension to power in 1956 by Sinhala-educated, middle class Sinhalese-Buddhists of both low-country and up-country origin. The process was hastened after the first abortive coup in 1962 by some senior military and police officers, most of whom were Roman Catholics (see ch. 25, The Armed Forces).

In 1970, by virture of their monopoly of coercive power, the military and police constituted potentially the most effective political group but, except for small numbers of senior officers implicated in the unsuccessful coup attempts of 1962 and 1966, they remained loyal to the civil authority and stayed outside the domain of partisan strife. Nevertheless, during the 1960s the potential military role in the political process became a lively subject of speculation (see ch. 25, The Armed Forces).

Labor union activities continued to have their impact on the political scene, even though organized labor could claim only 37 percent, or about 1,180,000 members, of the total of those employed and though labor unions were split into numerous politically partisan segments that were seldom able to unite into a single cohesive bloc (see ch. 21, Labor).

Labor union leadership came mostly from outside the ranks of labor and thus was more susceptible to manipulation and politically motivated strikes. Labor unrest and political tensions were usually interactive, sometimes forcing the government to call out units of the armed forces in an effort to maintain essential services (see ch. 24, Public Order and Internal Security).

Businessmen, lawyers, doctors, and newspapermen generally expressed their political views through their own trade associations. By training, many of them were British-educated, upper middle class urbanites with a general inclination toward parliamentary politics. Unlike the civil servants and senior military and police officers, relatively few persons in these groups were affected in their status by the language switch from English to Sinhala.

The affluent businessmen were inclined to support the UNP, whereas others who were unable to compete effectively with the well-established firms contributed to the SLFP. After the mid-1950s the business community was split along communal lines, with Sinhalese and Tamils supporting their respective political organizations.

During the years the SLFP was in power, many businessmen resisted efforts by the government to expand its economic role. Realizing this attitude, the SLFP-led coalition charted a cautious, moderate line during the 1970 campaigns. After the coalition assumed power in May, however, there were indications that the leftist government wanted to enlarge governmental controls over key sectors of the economy (see ch. 18, Character and Structure of the Economy).

Newspapermen and the leftist coalition frequently disagreed over the role of the press. At stake was the question of whether the nation's newspapers should be the continued monopoly of two major chains, which were generally against the SLFP and its Marxist allies. For years the SLFP attempted to impose some controls over the press. After the SLFP coalition assumed power in May 1970, some of the newspapers formerly under leftist attack sought to adjust to the new situation by changing the editorial staff and instituting a more balanced editorial presentation than had been the case in the past (see ch. 16, Public Information).

The students and youth in 1970 posed no immediate threat to the incumbent party or to the maintenance of public order. Their political relevance stemmed from growing indications that, given the financial burden of university education and the bleak prospect for gainful employment upon graduation, many students might opt for radical solutions to many basic socioeconomic issues. Student reactions to various political issues were also significant because they tended to reflect prevailing public sentiments.

The electoral behavior of students in 1965 and 1970 tended to support the view that youth was generally inclined to protest against what it regarded as ineffectual government. In 1965, for example, nearly 1 million students and youths aged eighteen to twenty were able to vote for the first time in a national election. Many observers attributed the upsetting of the incumbent SLFP by the UNP in 1965 to the protest votes of the young whom they believed to be disenchanted with the SLFP's ineffectiveness in stabilizing the economy and improving living conditions. In 1970, after the political swing from right to left, these observers offered a similar explanation for the UNP's debacle, implying that student unrest, political instability, and economic grievances were closely intertwined.

Buddhist monks (*bhikkus*) became active political participants from the early 1950s on and contributed to the rise to power of the SLFP-led coalition in 1956. Their participation was aimed at giving support to political candidates most sympathetic to the cause of Buddhist renaissance. Monks aided anti-UNP and anti-Marxist candidates in their campaigns by making favorable speeches about them.

After Prime Minister Bandaranaike was assassinated by a monk in 1959, the monks as a group became politically less conspicuous. Nevertheless, they continued to exert pressures through the All Ceylon Buddhist Congress and other splinter organizations by urging political parties to adopt a series of pro-Buddhist policies. Like other political groups, however, internal cleavages were also noticeable within the Buddhist clergy. In 1965 the Buddhist *sangha* (see Glossary) was split between those supporting the SLFP and those endorsing the UNP. In 1970 some monks also backed Marxist parties (see ch. 17, Political Values and Attitudes).

Despite sectarian differences, in 1970 the Buddhist monks were generally agreed that Ceylon should be a Buddhist state and that national priorities should be accordingly adjusted. The political manifesto issued by the All Ceylon Buddhist Congress in January 1970, for example, urged various political parties to consider: the establishment of a constituent assembly and the drafting of a new constitution; the prevention of monks from participating in party politics as a means of ensuring the dignity of the monastic order; the removal of discriminatory, anti-Buddhist laws passed during British rule; the abolition of private schools (meaning Christian missionary-supported schools); a public scrutiny of finances of all religious bodies; and "caution" in regard to family planning. Some Buddhists argued that any attempt at family planning was a conspiracy to reduce the Sinhalese-Buddhist majority to a minority; their contention was based on figures released in late 1969 by the nongovernmental, voluntary Family Planning Association that showed the decline in the birth rate to be greater among the Sinhalese than among the Tamils (see ch. 7, Family).

In the villages the vernacular schoolteachers, as well as specialists in indigenous medicine, heads of dominant castes, landowners, and shopkeepers, were still influential in 1970. Sometimes they are collectively referred to as the rural elite (see ch. 6, Social Structure). Their importance in the political process was especially enhanced after the mid-1950s when political parties sought to broaden their mass base and obtain electoral support through the networks of these individuals. Thus many of the local notables became intermediaries between party leaders in Colombo and the villages.

For the villagers, it was through men of local prominence that they could best hope to seek redress for whatever grievances they had. The peasants as a group had no representation, even at the local level. Repeated attempts by politicians to organize a peasant-oriented political force had been generally ineffective.

POLITICAL PARTIES

In 1970 the political parties still functioned as a central feature of the political system. Their ideological differences were sharp, as were the alternatives they offered for public approval in the national elections. But they tended to soften their rhetoric once they were voted into office. The parties were organizationally frail and lacked adequate financial resources. More often than not it was an individual leader who provided the focus of loyalty and solidarity; but it was evident, especially after the mid-1960s, that party labels and policy alternatives were also important as determinants of popular electoral behavior.

For purposes of parliamentary elections, political parties were classified by the government as either recognized or unrecognized. A recognized party enjoyed an advantage over those not so classified because it could use the same visual voting symbol that had been used in the previous general elections; the symbols—for example, a hand for the SLFP, an elephant for the UNP, and a key for the LSSP—are printed on the ballot and help illiterate voters identify the party affiliations of various candidates (see ch. 13, The Governmental System).

In order to gain recognition, political parties were required to apply to the commissioner, usually about two months before the election day. By law they could be recognized if they had been engaged in political activity for a period of at least five years up to the time of application or if they had returned at least two members to the House of Representatives at the previous general elections.

In early 1970 there existed more than twenty political parties, of varying popular following, of which seven contested the May elections as recognized parties. In terms of general popular appeal, the two principal parties were the SLFP and the UNP (see table 14).

Table 14. Party Representation in the House of Representatives, Ceylon, 1947-70[1]

Party[2]	September 1947	May 1952	April 1956[3]	March 1960[4]	July 1960	March 1965	May 1970
United National Party	42	54	8	50	30	66 (116)[5]	17 (128)[5]
Sri Lanka Freedom Party	....	9	38	46	75	42 (100)	90 (106)
Lanka Sama Samaja Party	9	9	14	10	12	10 (24)	19 (23)
Ceylon Communist Party	3	3	3	3	4	4 (9)[6]	
Tamil Congress	7	4	1	....	1	3 (15)	3 (12)
Federal Party	....	2	10	15	16	14 (20)	13 (19)
Total[7]	61	81	74	124	138	138	148

[1] Indicates the strength of various parties immediately after given parliamentary elections.

[2] Minor parties that failed to return any of their candidates in the 1970 parliamentary elections are omitted from this column.

[3] Until 1956 the House of Representatives was composed of ninety-five members, of which six were nominated members.

[4] Beginning in 1960, the membership of the House of Representatives was increased to 157, of which 6 were nominated members.

[5] Parenthetical figures indicate the number of seats contested by each party.

[6] Refers to the pro-Soviet group only.

[7] The difference between the total elected members of the House of Representatives and the figures shown here is accounted for by independents and those representing minor parties.

Sri Lanka Freedom Party

In May 1970 the SLFP stood left of center on most political and economic issues but not as far as the LSSP and the CCP (Moscow). As in the past, the SLFP maintained that it was not Marxist and that its goal was the establishment of a democratic socialist state through parliamentary means.

The SLFP had been established in mid-1951 by S. W. R. D. Bandaranaike after he withdrew the Sinhala Maha Sabha from the ruling UNP, which at that time was a loose coalition of several political associations. The Sinhala Maha Sabha, which Bandaranaike had organized in 1934 to promote the Sinhalese culture, was incorporated into the SLFP. The SLFP was intended to provide a non-Marxist, moderately reformist alternative to the UNP, and its first political manifesto pledged the party to the goals of reviving indigenous cultures, promoting the use of both Sinhala and Tamil as national languages, and establishing a welfare state responsive to the needs of the middle and lower classes. The manifesto promised to achieve the goals by peaceful parliamentary methods, rejecting the extremes of both Marxist and capitalist ways.

In an attempt to gain the broadest possible public support, the SLFP appealed to Buddhist groups, Sinhalese intellectuals and professionals, and lower middle class rural voters. It also modified its position on language by advocating a measure aimed at making Sinhala the only language of the nation. This Sinhalese-oriented policy paid off in 1956 when the SLFP ousted the UNP at the polls, but it also had the consequence of alienating the Tamil population.

The SLFP's favorite political tactic was to form the so-called no-contest pact with Marxist parties. This was used successfully against the UNP in 1956, in July 1960, and again in 1970. The no-contest pact led in turn to a coalition government when participating parties actually captured a majority of parliamentary seats. The coalition solidarity was cemented usually by assigning cabinet portfolios to the electoral partners. Events of the past two decades showed that, although the electoral alliance proved to be expedient, the coalition was seldom stable because of ideological incongruity and personal clashes between its participants.

In 1970 the SLFP's policymaking, executive functions were vested in its Executive Committee, known until 1963 as the Working Committee. Comprising more than eighty members, the committee met once a month to discuss the party's affairs. In point of fact, however, the parliamentary party caucus was the real center of decisionmaking. This situation sometimes caused a degree of friction between the organizational and parliamentary wings of the party.

In 1970, apart from Prime Minister Bandaranaike who has led the party since 1960, among the more prominent leaders of the SLFP were: Weligama Polwattege Ariyadasa (member of the House of Representatives and minister of health); Felix Reginald Dias Bandaranaike (member of the House of Representatives and minister of public administration, local government, and home affairs); Tikiri Banda Illangaratne (member of the House of Representatives and minister of foreign and internal trade); A. P. Jayasuriya (senator); Punchi Bandagunatilaka Kalugalle (member of the House of Representatives and minister of shipping and tourism); Badi-ud-in Mahmud (minister of education); Maitripala Senanayake (member of the House of Representatives and minister of irrigation, power and highways); and Tikiri Banda Subasinghe (member of the House of Representatives and minister of industries and scientific affairs).

The SLFP's election manifesto, as issued in April 1970, together with the SLFP's Marxist allies, called for the establishment of a "people's government of the three parties and other progressive forces"; the adoption of a new constitution that would make Ceylon a republic and of measures designed to make the government "more democratic" through the creation of so-called elected employees' councils, advisory committees in government offices, and people's committees; and the reorganization of the armed forces and the police in accordance with "the national and progressive aspirations of the people."

Economically, the manifesto called for nationalization of the banking system; governmental takeover of import trade; formation of "state agencies to guide and direct the plantation industries"; state ownership of heavy and other basic industires; and a review of the agreements that the UNP government had concluded with the International Bank for Reconstruction and Development (IBRD), and the International Development Association (IDA) (see ch. 18, Character and Structure of the Economy).

On other issues, the SLFP-led coalition promised to introduce a comprehensive scheme of social insurance; to eliminate unemployment and solve the problems of the unemployed youth; to reorganize the school system; and to find a solution to the language problem within the framework of the Official Language Act of 1956 and the Tamil Language (Special Provisions) Act of 1958. The SLFP also stressed the need of mobilizing internal resources by taxing the rich and by halting smuggling. According to the manifestò, a more effective antismuggling operation was expected to yield an annual revenue of about Rs1 billion (for value of rupee, see Glossary), which would be the equivalent of approximately one-third of the government's annual budget revenues (see ch. 23, Finance).

Among other pledges included in the manifesto were: effective implementation of the Indo-Ceylon agreement of 1966 concerning the status of Indian Tamils in Ceylon; a sweeping review of laws and regulations that restricted the "democratic rights of the people"; the safeguarding of press freedom by promoting "independent newspapers" and the ending of "the present domination of the daily press by capitalist monopolies"; the termination of activities by "all subversive imperialist agencies" in the country; the suspension of diplomatic relations with Israel until that country complied with the resolutions of the United Nations; and the extension of diplomatic recognition to East Germany, North Vietnam, North Korea, and the Viet Cong's Provisional Revolutionary Government (see ch. 15, Foreign Relations; ch. 16, Public Information).

United National Party

The UNP, which remained the standard bearer of conservative forces in 1970, was founded in 1946 by prominent nationalist leaders, such as D. S. (Don Stephen) Senanayake, who was soon to become the nation's first prime minister, and S. W. R. D. Bandaranaike, who later established the SLFP. The UNP was organized to compete in the country's first general elections scheduled for late 1947 and then to establish an anti-Communist, intercommunal, parliamentary form of government (see ch. 3, Historical Setting).

A coalition of several disparate political groups, the UNP was held together by its leaders' common ambitions. These men were for the most part British educated and, by Ceylonese standards, affluent. They came from various ethnic groups and were suspicious of Trotskyite and Stalinist organizations.

As the years passed, the party's internal differences gradually became evident, the first break coming in July 1951 when Bandaranaike's leftist bloc seceded to form the SLFP, the first major non-Marxist organization to oppose the UNP. Nevertheless, the centrist Senanayake was able to steer the UNP along the middle path, resisting conflicting pressures from the right and successfully projecting its image as the friend of private entrepreneurs and the champion of anticommunism. He also strove to maintain communal harmony; this attempt was considerably undermined when the SLFP was able to offer a non-Communist alternative to the Buddhists and Catholics alike.

264

After D. S. Senanayake's death in 1952, the UNP drifted toward the right under the influence of John Kotelawala. It was also outbid by the SLFP in their competition for Sinhalese support; thus, in a belated effort to attract Sinhalese votes, the UNP, shortly before the 1956 elections, promised to make Sinhala the sole official language and restore Buddhism to "its rightful place" in the nation. This attempt more or less formalized the Sinhalese-Tamil split.

After its electoral defeat in 1956, the UNP began to renovate its organization under Dudley Senanayake, who came out of retirement in early 1957. In an attempt to broaden its popular base and ideological appeal, it redefined its political and economic objectives in terms of democratic socialism, a program that the party adopted for the first time in 1958. Specifically, this plan proposed to make use, in judicious combinations, of three forms of economic initiatives: private, cooperative, and state.

In a series of organizational shakeups that followed, a working committee became the center of decisionmaking. Composed of about forty members, the committee intensified membership drives and formed two labor unions, the National Employees Union and the Lanka Jatika Estate Workers Union (see ch. 21, Labor). It also penetrated into the area of students and youth. By 1965 the UNP had developed the most extensive and effective network of party branches on the island.

During the 1970 election campaign the UNP promised to continue its policies of combining private and public ownership, attempting to make Ceylon self-sufficient in food grains and textiles, and working to solve the growing unemployment problem. Despite strong leftist protests, it decided to go ahead with the Mahaweli Ganga (river) diversion project, which had been approved by the IBRD. The thirty-year project, estimated to cost the equivalent of US$1 billion, was designed to double the present land area under cultivation, generate sufficient hydroelectric power to meet the country's maximum needs, and relocate about 1 million persons from densely populated areas.

In 1970 the UNP campaigned on what it called a record of achievements, which included: the restoration of racial and religious peace; steady economic progress, characterized by a marked increase in food-grain production; and the inducement of capital assistance from foreign sources. In an attempt to discredit the opposition, the UNP warned the public of the so-called "inherent dangers of totalitarianism enveloping the island" should the SLFP-led coalition return to power.

Among prominent persons in the UNP in 1970 were: Dudley

Senanayake, J. R. Jayewardene, second in command of the party and a former minister of state; M. D. Banda, former minister of agriculture and food; W. G. Montague Jayewickreme, former minister of public works, posts, and telecommunications; V. A. Sugathadasa, former minister of nationalized services; U. B. Wanninayake, former minister of finance; and A. F. Wijemanne, senator and former minister of justice.

Marxist Parties

In 1970 Ceylonese Marxists were divided into two main groups, one operating under the label of the Lanka Sama Samaja Party (LSSP), and the other functioning as the Ceylon Communist Party (CCP); a small number of more doctrinaire, militant activists from these two groups maintained separate splinter organizations. In addition there existed another Marxist group, the People's United Front (Mahajana Eksath Peramuna—MEP), which was headed by Philip Gunawardena, who in 1965 had supported the UNP and had later served in the Senanayake cabinet; in 1970 the MEP continued to support the UNP, but its own political impact was negligible.

Except for an insignificant number of militants, the Marxist parties tended to work within the framework of parliamentary politics. Their standard political tactic was to form electoral alliances with the more broadly based SLFP in their common opposition to the UNP.

The Marxists drew their support mostly from the densely populated southwest coastal areas that included Colombo; they had very little support from rural areas. Their strength came from among urban workers, lower caste persons, and minorities, most of whom traditionally resented the socially and politically dominant Goyigama caste along the southwestern coastal belt. Thus their popularity among the small number of urban discontented was based less on their ideological posture than on the fact that they could provide an organized channel for social protest.

Lanka Sama Samaja Party

The LSSP was launched in 1935 as a militant political movement by a group of young British-educated Marxists with the aim of bringing to Ceylon an immediate national independence and moderate socialism. These Marxists, who called themselves Samasamajists (a Sinhala term roughly equivalent to equalists or socialists), included, among others: Colvin Reginald de Silva, the party's first president; Nanyakkarapathirage Martin Perera;

S. A. Wickremasinghe; Leslie Simon Goonewardene; Vernon Gunaskera; and the Gunawardena brothers, Philip and Robert.

Among the objectives listed in its first manifesto were: the attainment of national independence; abolition of social and economic inequities; introduction of social reforms and various welfare measures for the working masses; socialization of the means of production, distribution and exchange; and a vaguely defined notion of class struggle.

From its very beginning, the LSSP was troubled by incessant ideological feuds and factional strife. The first major split came in 1939 when the Ceylonese followers of Leon Trotsky split with those of Stalin. In early 1940 the Trotskyites were able to expel the Stalinists from the LSSP. The Stalinists countered in late 1940 by forming the United Socialist Party and the Ceylon Trade Union Federation (CTUF) under S. A. Wickremasinghe and Pieter Keuneman. As a result of this division, the Trotskyites consistently refused to identify themselves with the Communist International (Comintern).

Another split came in 1945 when Colvin R. de Silva seceded and formed the Bolshevik-Leninist Party. In an effort to reunify the Samasamajist movement, he returned to the LSSP in 1950 but was opposed by Philip Gunawardena, who withdrew from the LSSP in protest and organized his own Viplavakari (Revolutionary) LSSP, or VLSSP, which after 1959 assumed the name Mahajana Eksath Peramuna.

Still another realignment took place in mid-1964 when Edmund Samarakkody, who had opposed the LSSP's policy of "responsive cooperation" with the SLFP, withdrew the radical wing of the party that he headed. He then established the so-called LSSP (Revolutionary). In contrast, the moderate wing of the LSSP, under N. M. Perera, generally agreed to cooperate with Mrs. Bandaranaike's SLFP.

In the general elections of 1970 the LSSP cooperated with the SLFP and the CCP in their common opposition to the UNP. It won nineteen seats in those areas where it agreed not to compete against the SLFP and CCP candidates. For this collaboration the LSSP leaders were rewarded with three cabinet posts in 1970; N. M. Perera was named minister of finance; Colvin R. de Silva, minister of plantation industries; and Leslie Simon Goonewardene, minister of communications.

Ceylon Communist Party

The CCP was formed in 1943 as an outgrowth of the United Socialist Party, which had been set up three years earlier. Up to 1970 the CCP was able to enlist limited support from among the discontented urban groups, workers, low-paid government clerical employees, and youth. The party continued to suffer the disadvantage of competing with other Marxist parties for membership and financial support. After 1947 the proportion of popular votes that the Communists obtained in national elections ranged from 3 to 5 percent; the bulk of the votes came from urban areas.

Beginning in 1950, the CCP collaborated with other anti-UNP and anti-Western political organizations because of the realization that continued disunity within the so-called progressive forces would only help the conservative UNP. At the same time, however, the Communists sought to maintain their own distinct identity and broaden their popular base of operation through a variety of auxiliary organizations, such as the CTUF, the all-Ceylon Federation of Communist and Progressive Youth League; the Ceylon Peace Council, the Afro-Asian Solidary Association, and the Ceylon-Soviet Friendship League.

The CCP's attempt to project its image as a Ceylonese, rather than a foreign-inspired, conspiratorial group was stepped up in 1960 when it proclaimed the goal of establishing "full democracy and socialism in Ceylon by peaceful means." Despite this stress on the parliamentary and electoral means of seizing power, however, the party in 1970 had yet to rule out the possibility of the so-called extraparliamentary struggles.

The Communists too had a long history of internal feuds. During the 1960s they were under pressure of events within the world Communist movement, notably the Sino-Soviet dispute and related issues affecting strategy and tactics. As a result, mutual recriminations between the pro-Soviet and pro-Chinese wings of the party became an open rupture in late 1963. In early 1964 the rival factions held separate party congresses. The split also caused reverberations among the party's ancillary organizations. In the 1970 elections the two separate groups competed against each other. The pro-Chinese organization, called the CCP (Peking), was headed by Nagalingam S. Sanmugathasan and Premalal Kumarasiri, whereas the pro-Soviet group, or the CCP (Moscow), remained in the hands of Pieter Keuneman, S. A. Wickremasinghe, and M. G. Mendis.

Other Parties

Among the parties that contested the 1970 elections were the Tamil Congress (TC), the FP, and the Sinhala People's Party (Sinhala Mahajana Pakshaya—SMP). The first two of these were generally known as communal parties because their objectives were to promote the general interests of the Tamil community.

The TC was the first political organization to be formed specifically to protect the welfare of an ethnic minority. It was founded in 1944 by G. G. Ponnambalam against the background of growing Tamil anxiety that, unless adequate safeguards were provided in the constitutional scheme of soon-to-be independent Ceylon, British domination would merely give way to domination by the Sinhalese majority.

After independence there emerged a dissident Tamil group, led by S. J. V. Chelvanayakam, which disagreed with Ponnambalam's policy of collaboration with the intercommunal but Sinhalese-dominated UNP. In 1949 the dissidents broke away and formed the rival Federal Party (FP) with the avowed purpose of establishing an "autonomous Tamil linguistic state within a Federal Union of Ceylon." The FP regarded this alternative as the only practical way to preserve Tamil identity from extinction.

In 1956 the FP emerged as the dominant Tamil political group as a result of its convincing victory over the conservative TC. Going into the election, the FP had a distinct advantage since the TC had suffered considerably from the stigma of its association with the UNP, which had abandoned its policy of making both Sinhala and Tamil national languages in an attempt to obtain the support of the numerically greater Sinhalese vote.

In 1965 the FP became a component of the UNP-led coalition government by committing its bloc of parliamentary seats to the UNP, which at that time needed the FP's support to form a stable parliamentary majority. In 1968, however, the FP withdrew from the UNP government because its leaders were convinced that the party could no longer derive any tangible benefit from further association with the UNP. In 1970, unlike the TC, whose leaders called on the Tamils to join hands with the Sinhalese to form a united front of equal partners, the FP campaigned independently.

The SMP was formed in 1968 by R. G. Senanayake, a leader of the UNP's liberal bloc until his defection in 1954. Later he joined the SLFP and became a vice president of the party but was expelled in 1968 on the grounds of having violated party discipline. Competing for the first time in the 1970 elections, the SMP pledged to: establish a democratic, socialist, and unitary form of government; "unite all races and communities under the Sinhala language"; nationalize foreign banks, estates, and enterprises; and implement a socialist economic plan aimed at ending capitalist monopolies. It also called for a series of measures with anti-Tamil undertones aimed at promoting Sinhalese welfare; among the measures was the demand for a separate electoral register for naturalized citizens (meaning Indian Tamils) so that the "due rights of the Sinhala people living in the hill country" could be safeguarded from the Indian Tamils.

THE GENERAL ELECTION OF MAY 1970

On May 27, 1970, the seventh general election, was won by the coalition of the SLFP-LSSP-CCP, which secured a total of 115 seats, as compared to the UNP's 17 seats. Thus the coalition, which in 1965 had had the combined total of only 55 seats, more than doubled its parliamentary strength. By virtue of its victory, it was able to claim additional seats by exercising the constitutional prerogative of nominating six members from among various underrepresented sociopolitical groups (see ch. 13, The Governmental System).

In May 1970 some 5.5 million persons over the age of eighteen, or about 45 percent of the total population, were eligible to vote. Approximately 4,948,000 persons, or 90 percent of the total electorate, actually went to the polls. The 1970 voter turnout was the highest ever in the nation's history, representing an increase of 9 percent over the 1965 election and about 20 percent over the 1956 contest. The lowest turnout, 49 percent, came in 1947 when the nation's first general election was held.

Elections held after 1947 indicated that the mass voters could freely exercise their franchise, making their choice of candidates from among numerous alternatives offered by political parties. They also proved that the transfer of power from one political group to another could take place in a peaceful and stable manner with a minimum of dysfunctional consequences. In mid-1970 all but a minuscule portion of the population accepted their electoral machinery as the most effective means of resolving political differences and as an essential feature of the parliamentary political tradition they inherited from the British.

Electoral results consistently indicated the existence of two major, more or less evenly split political tendencies in the country. These tendencies were represented, respectively, by the two principal political parties, the SLFP and the UNP. Since neither of these parties gravitated toward the extreme of either left or right, it could be inferred that the electorate was generally oriented toward the middle range of the ideological spectrum. Thus in 1970 the SLFP and the UNP together

270

accounted for more than 74 percent of the total valid votes (see table 15).

The continued dominance of these moderately left and right tendencies was expected, in the opinion of many Ceylonese analysts, to have a stabilizing influence on the working of electoral politics. This was borne out in part by the fact that it became increasingly difficult for splinter parties or independent candidates to win parliamentary seats because of competition from the relatively well established parties. As a result, the number of minor parties and independent candidates decreased considerably after the mid-1960s.

Given the effectiveness of this electoral scheme, it appeared in 1970 that political parties would continue to emphasize the importance of compromise and cooperation rather than the sterility of ideological formalism or exclusiveness. Thus the results of the 1970 election showed that the doctrinaire and rigid CCP (Peking) could garner no more than 3,500 votes; in 1965 this party had obtained 3,900 votes. By comparison, the CCP (Moscow) drew about 170,000 votes in 1970, about 60,000 more votes than it had received in 1965. The 1970 contest also suggested that a party advocating a program that had subtle anti-Tamil overtones could no longer draw as many Sinhalese votes as it had been able to do in the past. The SMP, which stood to the far left on economic issues but to the far right on measures relating to Indian Tamils, contested no fewer than fifty seats but failed to return a single candidate. It obtained only 20,500 votes.

Table 15. *Number of Votes and Percentage of Total Vote Won by Selected Political Parties, Ceylon, for Selected Years, 1947-70*[1]

Party	Percentage					1965		1970[2]	
	1947	1952	1956	March 1960	July 1960	Votes	Percent	Votes	Percent
United National Party..	39.9	44.0	27.4	28.4	37.5	1,590,929	[3]39.3	1,876,956	[3]37.7
Sri Lanka Freedom Party.	....	15.5	39.9	20.2	33.5	1,221,437	30.1	1,812,849	36.6
Lanka Sama Samaja Party.	10.8	- 13.1	10.4	10.5	7.3	302,095	7.4	433,224	8.7
Ceylon Communist Party.	3.7	5.7	4.5	4.6	2.9	109,754	2.7	169,229	3.4
Tamil Congress	4.3	2.7	0.3	1.2	1.5	98,746	2.4	115,567	2.3
Federal Party	....	1.9	5.4	5.5	7.0	217,914	5.3	245,747	4.9
Total	[4]58.7	[4]82.9	[4]87.9	[4]70.4	[4]89.7	3,540,875	87.2	4,653,572	93.6

[1]Votes for the elections held between 1947 and 1960 are not shown because of lack of space.
[2]Tentative figures as of mid-June 1970.
[3]This percentage is relative to the total number of valid votes obtained by all parties and independents and not to the total shown here.
[4]Percentage does not add up to 100; the difference is accounted for by minor parties and independent candidates.

Source: Adapted from Calvin A. Woodward, *The Growth of a Party System in Ceylon*, Providence, 1969, p. 244; and *Ceylon Daily News*, June 14, 1970, p. 7.

CHAPTER 15

FOREIGN RELATIONS

In 1970 the major diplomatic activities continued to take place within the context of three basic themes: maintenance of cordial relations with neighboring India; procurement of significant amounts of economic aid and assistance; and support of the special-interest activities and nonaligned policies of the Afro-Asian community. Foreign policy decisions are formulated and executed under the direct supervision of the prime minister who, by constitutional provision, also serves as the minister of defense and external affairs. Although various prime ministers have manifested a preference for a general pro-Western or proneutralist posture in international affairs, the conduct of foreign affairs remained remarkably constant between independence in 1948 and initial foreign policy statements by the newly elected socialist-coalition government in 1970.

Indo-Ceylon relations are cordial but are complicated by a number of major and minor issues, the only serious one being the citizenship status of over 1 million Indian Tamils (see Glossary) who reside in Ceylon. A 1964 agreement between the Ceylonese and Indian prime ministers provided for the repatriation of nearly one-half of the Indian Tamils to India and the granting of Ceylonese citizenship to about one-third over a fifteen-year period. By 1970 little progress had been made.

In addition to participation in the numerous Afro-Asian conferences during the 1950s and 1960s, Ceylon is an active member of several regional and international organizations. Those of significance in terms of economic aid and assistance are the Colombo Plan for Cooperative Economic Development in South and Southeast Asia, the British Commonwealth of Nations, the United Nations, the International Bank for Reconstruction and Development (IBRD, commonly known as the World Bank), and the International Monetary Fund (IMF).

RELATIONS WITH INDIA

Relations with India are complicated by a variety of geopolitical and domestic political factors. Ceylon, with a fine,

273

large, natural harbor at Trincomalee, is separated from the Indian mainland by the narrow, shallow Palk Strait. Possession or use of Ceylon air and naval bases by a force unfriendly to India would pose grave defense problems to that country.

On the other hand, nearly 23 percent of Ceylon's population of about 12.5 million are Tamils, who share the ethnic and linguistic origins and cultural values of more than 30 million of the over 500 million Indians. During the early years of independence many Sinhalese-Buddhists sincerely feared that their massive Indian neighbor might absorb Ceylon. In 1970 the crux of Indo-Ceylon relations continued to be the citizenship status of the Indian Tamils (see ch. 5, Ethnic Groups and Languages).

The Indian Tamils

In a 1947 meeting the Ceylonese and Indian prime ministers reached an agreement on the general principle that should be applied to those Indian Tamils who sought Ceylonese citizenship. They did not agree, however, on the required length of residency. Prime Minister D. S. (Don Stephen) Senanayake proposed that Ceylonese citizenship be acquired either by registration or by descent. The registration requirements would include proof of Indian origin and of continuous residence in Ceylon for seven years if married and ten years if unmarried. In order to meet the descent requirement, applicants would be required to prove residency of twenty years or more. Prime Minister Jawaharlal Nehru asserted that the proposal was too complicated and too strict.

In 1948 and 1949 the Ceylon Parliament enacted the Ceylon Citizenship Act and the Indian and Pakistani (Residents) (Citizenship) Act, respectively, both of which established provisions for eligibility on the basis of registration and descent. The registration requirement was basically the same as that set forth in the Nehru-Senanayake talks of 1947, but the descent was changed from a twenty-year residency requirement to proof of residency for three generations. Both of these laws were sharply criticized by the Indian press as both "complicated and discriminatory." The laws were later amended to ease the restrictions, but India still regarded them as too strict.

A significant problem still remained for those who failed to apply for citizenship or who did not meet the eligibility requirements. In 1953 Nehru and Senanayake again met to discuss a proposal of the latter that 400,000 Indian Tamils would be registered for Ceylonese citizenship and an additional 250,000 persons would be given permanent residency passes if India would compel the remaining 300,000 Indian Tamil residents to return to India. India, however, insisted on the principle of voluntary registration.

In 1954 at New Delhi the newly elected prime minister of Ceylon, Sir John Kotelawala, took up the discussion of the citizenship issue. A new dimension was added to the talks when the problem of illicit immigration was taken up, and both sides agreed upon steps to eliminate illegal traffic into Ceylon. The basic substance of disagreement between the two disputants precluded other progress, however. Ceylon took the position that all Indian Tamils were Indian nationals unless they were made Ceylon citizens; India, on the other hand, insisted that, unless Indian Tamils had passports showing express written intent to return to India, they would be regarded as "stateless."

Prime Minister Solomon West Ridgeway Bandaranaike opposed arbitration on the citizenship question and, from the time of his election in 1956 until his assassination in 1959, there were no formal discussions on the citizenship question. Unlike his predecessors, Bandaranaike regarded the matter of citizenship as solely a domestic issue, a position favored in Indian ruling circles.

When Mrs. Sirimavo Bandaranaike was elected prime minister in 1960, she reiterated the Ceylonese position taken at the New Delhi talks of 1954 that there were two classes of Indian Tamils. In the first category, according to Mrs. Bandaranaike, were those who had obtained Ceylonese citizenship, and in the second were those who had failed to pass eligibility requirements and who were Indian nationals. India persisted in its position that persons in the latter category were to be regarded as stateless.

In October 1964 Mrs. Bandaranaike met with Indian Prime Minister Lal Bahadur Shastri, and after considerable debate the two leaders concluded what became known as the Sirima-Shastri Pact. The pact called for the repatriation to India of 525,000 Indian Tamils plus their children born during the interval and the granting of Ceylonese citizenship to 300,000 Indian Tamils. These procedures were to take place over a period of fifteen years. The fate of the remaining 150,000 was to be decided at a later date. Ceylon's concession was the agreement to grant citizenship to 300,000 Indian Tamils in addition to the 134,000 Tamils who had already been granted nationality status under the Indian and Pakistani (Residents) (Citizenship) Act of 1949. India's concession was that for the first time it did not insist that those Indian Tamils who had not already secured Ceylonese citizenship were stateless.

In 1968 the Ceylon Parliament enacted legislation that allowed Indian Tamils extensive exemptions from currency regulations in transferring their financial assets to India at the time of repatriation. By January 1970, however, only about 4,000 Indian Tamils had been granted Ceylonese citizenship under the provisions of the pact, and only an estimated 66,130 had been repatriated to India.

The Kachchaitivu Issue

The status of the small uninhabited island of Kachchaitivu remained unresolved as of mid-1970. An island of less than one square mile, Kachchaitivu lies in the Palk Strait, approximately halfway between Pamban, off the southern tip of India, and Delft, off the northwestern coast of Ceylon.

In 1948 the British military in Ceylon used the island as a naval bombing area. In the following year, however, India used it for munitions tests. In 1956 the issue became a dominant theme of political debate between the political officials of both countries. The Ceylonese press announced its country's intention of using the island as an aerial bombing target. The Indian press countered by saying that the island had belonged to the Raja of Ramnad, who was alleged to have established an estate on the island during the reign of Queen Victoria. Ceylonese political officials claim, however, that during a meeting held in 1921 in Colombo, the Indian government tacitly admitted that the island belonged to Ceylon.

One of the major problems preventing accord on the issue is the fact that India recognizes a territorial limit of twelve miles, whereas Ceylon recognizes a six-mile limit. Should Ceylon change its territorial limit to twelve miles, as seemed possible in 1970, the two limits would meet in a line down the middle of Kachchaitivu, and the ownership of the island would still remain in dispute.

Ceylon and Sino-Indian Affairs

Although Ceylon maintained a neutralist attitude during the Sino-Indian conflict in 1962, relations with India were not severely strained, partly because Ceylon was instrumental in bringing together six nonaligned Afro-Asian nations in an attempt to mediate the dispute. Also, while the conflict was still raging, Dudley Senanayake, leader of the United National Party (UNP) opposition, sent letters of support to Prime Minister Nehru. In 1965, when the UNP came to power under Senanayake's leadership, the Indian government was still mindful of Senanayake's support, and relations between the countries improved throughout the middle and late 1960s.

RELATIONS WITH THE COMMONWEALTH

Since independence Ceylon has maintained close and harmonious relations with the members of the Commonwealth. As a nation that at independence had no armed forces, Ceylon concluded that membership in the Commonwealth offered protection of sorts. In June 1970 Mrs. Bandaranaike announced that Ceylon would terminate its dominion status and become a republic, but this decision would not, in and of itself, have any effect on Ceylon's ties within the Commonwealth (see ch. 13, The Governmental System).

Great Britain

British presence in Ceylon for approximately 150 years as a relatively benign colonial power made Great Britain a natural ally in the postindependence period. At the time of independence Ceylonese officials felt that British forces should remain at the naval base at Trincomalee and at the Katunayaka airbase to provide protection in the event of an intrusion by a hostile power into the Indian Ocean area (see ch. 25, The Armed Forces).

By the time S. W. R. D. Bandaranaike came to power in 1956, however, the situation had substantially changed. Ceylon had decided that India had no designs on making Ceylon part of an Indian federation. Also, British sea power had begun to wane. Bandaranaike felt that if Ceylon were to make good its commitment to a policy of nonalignment, it should end the defense agreement that allowed the British presence at Trincomalee and Katunayaka. At the request of the Ceylonese government, a phased withdrawal from the British bases was concluded in 1957.

Other Commonwealth Countries

Ceylon has maintained close relations with Pakistan, Malaysia, and Burma—the last a non-Commonwealth nation—as a counterweight of sorts to India's dominance. Through the Commonwealth and the Colombo Plan, Ceylonese-Australian relations have been particularly cordial. Numerous civil, police, and military officials have been trained in Australian schools (see ch. 25, The Armed Forces).

In 1970 Ceylon was allied with other Afro-Asian members of the Commonwealth in condemnation of a proposed sale by the British of military supplies to the Republic of South Africa. Ceylon's permanent representative to the United Nations has consistently supported African Commonwealth countries in their disputes with South Africa and Rhodesia.

RELATIONS WITH COMMUNIST CHINA

Shortly after the outbreak of the Korean conflict in 1950, the United Nations passed a resolution calling for an embargo on rubber shipments to Communist China and North Korea. At that time Communist China was buying rubber from Ceylon at a price significantly higher than the prevailing world price. In order to avert an economic crisis, Ceylon ignored the United Nations resolution. In 1953 Ceylon entered into a barter trade agreement with Communist China that involved the exchange of Chinese rice for Ceylonese rubber. The agreement was renegotiated in 1958, 1963, and 1969. In 1969 Ceylon shipped approximately 60 percent of its total rubber exports to China, receiving in return approximately 25 percent of its total rice consumption requirement (see ch. 22, Trade).

Relations with Communist China continued to be harmonious throughout the 1960s. When the Sino-Indian border conflict broke out in 1962, Ceylon took a neutral stand on the issue. Ceylon continued in 1970 to take a noncommittal attitude toward initiatives by the Soviet Union to form a region of collective security in Asia, an attitude that was not in conflict with Communist Chinese protestations that the Soviet proposal was designed to form an Asian defense pact aimed at Communist China.

In January 1970 Communist China announced that it intended to help Ceylon construct a cotton spinning and weaving mill. It also announced that it would finance the project from a grant equivalent to Rs75 million (for value of rupee, see Glossary) that it made in 1957.

RELATIONS WITH THE SOVIET UNION

In 1958 the Soviet Union concluded a loan agreement with Ceylon that made available the equivalent of approximately US$30 million specifically earmarked for use in the development of Ceylon's state corporations. Among other projects, Soviet aid made possible the construction of the Ceylon Tyre and Tube Factory, the Flour Mill, and the Iron and Steel Factory (see ch. 20, Industry).

Before 1958 relations had been strained because of differing approaches to world affairs. In 1955, at the Bandung Conference, the prime minister, Sir John Kotelawala, condemned communism as a form of imperialism. In 1957 the Ceylonese ambassador to the United Nations delivered a scathing criticism of the Soviet invasion of Hungary. Since 1958, however, relations between the two countries have rapidly improved. When Mrs. Sirimavo Bandaranaike's socialist coalition was elected in May 1970, Soviet Premier Alexei Kosygin sent a congratulatory message applauding her election as "a victory for the forces of socialism."

RELATIONS WITH OTHER COMMUNIST COUNTRIES

East German aid has been particularly helpful in the fields of science and technical education. As of mid-1968 thirty-five training courses had been set up under the sponsorship of East Germany. In addition, it had made available the equivalent of US$36 million, half of which had been used in constructing a textile mill at Thulhiriya (see ch. 20, Industry).

Ceylon has also had cordial relations with Czechoslovakia, and the Ceylonese government was openly critical of Soviet intervention in Czechoslovakia in 1968. Credit obtained from the Czech government has been utilized for the development of several technical and industrial projects.

RELATIONS WITH AFRO-ASIAN STATES

Ceylon's diplomatic contacts with most of the Afro-Asian nations are maintained through contacts at the United Nations, the British Commonwealth of Nations, the Colombo Plan, and the occasional meetings of nonaligned states. To the extent that Ceylon has taken a policy position critical of the Soviet Union, Communist China, or the Western states, the policy position has generally been in the mainstream of Afro-Asian opinion.

Ceylon's posture also reflects economic demands. The announcement in 1970 by the Bandaranaike government that it intended to sever relations with Israel was in harmony with the policy of many other Afro-Asian states, but it was also a function of Ceylon's increasing dependence on the Arab states as a market for Ceylon's major export, tea (see ch. 22, Trade; ch. 23, Finance).

RELATIONS WITH THE UNITED STATES

Relations with the United States have been complicated by the conflict of Ceylon's economic needs and the United States' cold-war legislation with respect to Communist China. Because of Ceylon's need to export rubber and other products at the highest possible price and to import rice at the lowest possible price, it became involved in the early 1950s both with the

United States economic situation and an embargo against trade with Communist China by a recipient of American economic aid.

Basically, in early 1952 the United States was a market for Ceylonese rubber and a supplier of rice. When the price of American rice went above the world market price and the price offered for Ceylonese rubber fell below the world market price, Ceylon followed the logical economic path of concluding in 1953 a rubber-rice barter agreement with Communist China that was advantageous to both parties. The United States in response curtailed economic aid to Ceylon.

In 1956 the United States resumed economic aid to Ceylon, but in 1963 the aid was again terminated when Ceylon nationalized aspects of United States petroleum-processing plants. Economic aid programs were resumed in 1965 when a settlement of the claims of the oil companies had been concluded.

During the late 1960s the United States extended economic assistance to Ceylon in many fields, such as health, irrigation, and transportation projects. Also, the United States supplied food assistance under Public Law 480 at the rate of about US$5 million per year. In 1970, however, the Ceylonese government requested a decrease in United States activities on the island through an early termination of the Peace Corps program and the Asia Foundation.

INTERNATIONAL AID

Ceylon receives monetary and technical assistance from a variety of sources, including the United Nations, the Cooperative for American Relief Everywhere (CARE), the Ford Foundation, the Asian Development Bank, the IMF, the IBRD, and the Colombo Plan (see ch. 23, Finance). The Colombo Plan began in 1950 as a strictly Commonwealth association but has expanded to include most of the countries of South and Southeast Asia, plus the United States, and Japan. Since its inception nearly 3,000 Ceylonese have received training abroad. Ceylon has contributed to the plan by providing facilities for the resident experts as well as the visiting trainees in the managing secretariat, which is located in Colombo. Also, Ceylon has provided assistance of approximately Rs206,000 to the Maldive Islands for the construction of an airstrip.

CHAPTER 16

PUBLIC INFORMATION

Although in mid-1970 the press was not under direct governmental control, the newly elected government of Mrs. Sirimavo Bandaranaike had appointed a committee to examine the advisability of establishing a press council to guide the press and to devise measures to curb or alter monopoly ownership of the press. The government announced, however, that it would not take over any newspapers. An attempt by a previous Bandaranaike government in the early 1960s to take over the press and to create a newspaper trust had contributed to the downfall of that government in December 1964 (see ch. 14, Political Dynamics).

The press plays an influential role in the life of the country. In the opinion of some observers, however, criticism of political figures and issues tends to be destructive rather than constructive. Most Ceylonese are said to consider the newspapers the most authoritative sources of information, especially on domestic issues. Although in the early 1960s three-quarters of the total number of newspaper readers resided in the western provinces, by 1970 circulation in other provinces was rising and newspapers even reached remote villages.

In early 1969 there were twenty daily newspapers with a combined circulation of nearly 600,000. The total circulation of the fourteen weekly newspapers approached 1 million. One hundred and fifty periodicals with a combined circulation of approximately 3 million catered to a population with a literacy rate estimated at above 80 percent. Four publishing houses—Associated Newspapers of Ceylon, Times of Ceylon, Ltd., Independent Newspapers, Ltd., and Virakesari, Ltd.—dominated the field. With the exception of one daily newspaper published in Jaffna, the other dailies were printed in Colombo. The Sinhala (see Glossary), Tamil (see Glossary), and English-language dailies owned by the same group often adopted different editorial policies to suit their readers.

Since 1966 Radio Ceylon has been operated by a public corporation called the Ceylon Broadcasting Corporation (CBC). It includes both a national and a commercial service. The commercial service specializes in light entertainment, in contrast to the more serious and educational programs of the national service. Both services broadcast in Sinhala, Tamil, and English. Although the CBC bans political broadcasts except during election campaigns, there have been charges that the government in power has influenced news reporting of political events. In 1968 there were an estimated 550,000 radios for a population of over 11 million, mostly in the southwestern provinces.

In 1969, 300 cinema theaters with a total seating capacity of 180,000 annually attracted an audience of just over 17 million. Locally made films made up only 22 percent of the total exhibited, the rest coming from India, the United States, and Europe. The Government Film Unit makes and distributes newsreels and documentaries.

Except for those in Colombo, Kandy, and Trincomalee, the few public libraries are small. A United Nations Educational, Scientific and Cultural Organization report in the 1960s stated that inadequate financing and a lack of trained personnel frustrated the obvious enthusiasm for better libraries. There is a modest private publishing industry, and the government prints textbooks.

Although in 1970 there was no censorship of books and newspapers, the registration of all books, newspapers, and periodicals printed in Ceylon was required. In addition, imported films were reviewed by a censorship panel, and public performances, such as concerts and theatrical productions, required official permits.

PRESS

A critical press emerged in the 1830s with the founding of the *Observer and Commercial Advertiser* (in 1970, known as the *Ceylon Observer*). An early editor, Christopher Elliott, was a frequent critic of government policies and was accused of fomenting the 1848 rebellion (see ch. 3, Historical Setting). British plantation and mercantile interests, the chief opponents of the governor in the mid-nineteenth century, started the *Ceylon Examiner* and the *Times of Ceylon* in 1846. During the latter half of the nineteenth century, the English-language press came increasingly into the hands of the Ceylonese, beginning with the acquisition of the *Ceylon Examiner* in 1859 by a group of educated Ceylonese. The *Ceylon Independent* was founded in 1888 by Burghers (see Glossary), although its editor was an Englishman. Both newspapers agitated for constitutional reform.

The first Sinhala-language newspaper dates back to 1862.

In the 1880s a number of vernacular publications appeared whose main purpose was to revive indigenous cultural and religious traditions. One of these, the *Sarasavisandaresa,* was edited by the Sinhalese (see Glossary) nationalist Anagarika Dharmapala and later by H. S. Perera. Perera's criticism of the government and of others in authority aroused charges of a "seditious native press," but he was supported by journalists and politicians in England. Perera also founded the *Dinamina* in 1909.

D. R. Wijewardene, founder of the powerful Associated Newspapers of Ceylon, came to journalism from politics. In 1913 he was elected secretary of the Ceylon National Association, which later, as the Ceylon National Congress, spearheaded the movement for independence. In 1918 he started the *Ceylon Daily News.* It was an immediate success and encouraged Wijewardene to buy the *Ceylon Observer.* After the death of Perera, Wijewardene bought the *Dinamina.* A succession of talented editors with close personal associations with nationalist leaders such as D. S. (Don Stephen) Senanayake (later, leader of the United National Party—UNP) enabled the Associated Newspapers group to achieve considerable influence.

During the 1956 election campaign, the alleged identification of the Associated Newspapers and, to a lesser extent, the *Times of Ceylon* groups with the interests of the UNP became an important issue. The Buddhist Commission of Inquiry in 1956 charged that the Lake House Press, publishers of the Associated Newspapers, was antagonistic to Buddhist culture, and the *sangha* (see Glossary) issued a leaflet entitled "The Enemies of Buddhism—the Lake House Press." In a policy statement immediately before his assassination in 1959, Solomon West Ridgeway Dias Bandaranaike, prime minister and leader of the Sri Lanka Freedom Party (SLFP), charged that if the people chose a government that the newspapers did not like, then the government could not carry on, and he suggested the appointment of a commission to inquire into the state of the newspapers.

As a result of the language riots of 1958 and the assassination of Bandaranaike in 1959, states of emergency were declared that involved varying degrees of press censorship, but it was not until the election of Mrs. Bandaranaike's government in 1960 that an attempt was made to place governmental controls on the press (see ch. 3, Historical Setting). The government announced its intention to appoint a commission to investigate the role of the press, especially with regard to the recent election, and to form a public corporation to run the

283

Associated Newspapers of Ceylon and the *Times of Ceylon* groups. Independent newspapers would be encouraged.

In September of the same year, the *Times of Ceylon* decided to form itself into a public company, keeping 28 percent of the shares for the existing shareholders and offering the rest to the public. Finance Minister Felix Reginald Dias Bandaranaike announced that the Ministry of Defence and External Affairs would soon draft a bill to be introduced in Parliament for the takeover of certain newspapers. There was immediate opposition to the proposed legislation both in Ceylon and abroad. The *Times of Ceylon* requested a press commission.

The government went ahead with the drafting of press legislation but was unable to come up with a draft acceptable to all factions of the government coalition until May 1962, when the government's fourth draft was accepted in principle by a government parliamentary group. In addition to enforcing the sale of shares of the two major newspaper chains to the public, the bill proposed the formation of a press council to handle the distribution of shares. Measures were included to force disclosure of sources of information, fines for publication of false news, and the appointment by the governor general of boards of trustees with the power to dismiss directors and editors.

Agreement could not be reached, however, on final details of the draft, and in August 1963 a press commission consisting of three members was appointed to examine the functioning of all newspapers. There were charges of bias against the appointment to the commission of Mrs. Theja Gunewardene, secretary of the Communist-oriented Afro-Asian Solidarity Association, and she later resigned. The terms of the commission were also revised in November, limiting the investigation to the major newspaper chains.

The commission's report was published in mid-1964. Its main recommendations included: conversion of the Lake House Press into the Newspaper Corporation of Ceylon; purchase of the *Times of Ceylon* group, to be run as a cooperative union; changing the newly formed Independent Newspapers, Ltd. into a public company; provisions for the Tamil-language newspapers to become public companies; and an insistence that the ownership of all newspapers be confined to Ceylon citizens. Also recommended was the establishment of a press council with broad powers to regulate standards, recruitment, prices and advertising. The report charged the press with a pro-western, anti-Buddhist bias and the "constant purveying of obscene pictures, cartoons, articles, and stories."

Two bills based on the press commission's report were introduced into Parliament, one to establish the press council and the other the press corporation. Both bills met with widespread opposition. Leading members of the *sangha* who had formerly favored press control came out against it. When it became clear that the bills would not pass, Mrs. Bandaranaike adjourned Parliament. Parliament reconvened in November but was dissolved in December when a minister and other government members went over to the opposition. In the election of March 1965, the SLFP lost to the UNP, and no further legislative attempts were made to control the press (see ch. 14, Political Dynamics).

Under the emergency regulations issued after the assassination of Bandaranaike in 1959, the press was forbidden to report "any matter suggesting or tending to bring the government into hatred or contempt, or to incite feelings of disaffection or hatred of the government, giving information about acts of violence or breaches of the peace and meetings, processions or demonstrations and matters relating to the disposition, condition or movement of the armed forces or police." During periods of partial press censorship, as in July 1958, the government reserved the right to approve information printed, although Parliament made its own reports directly to the press.

During the 1965-70 government of Dudley Senanayake, a state of emergency was declared in January 1966, under which certain opposition newspapers were suppressed. When the state of emergency terminated in June, press censorship remained in force. A month later, opposition papers were permitted to censor themselves, a privilege already exercised by progovernment newspapers. The emergency regulations were finally lifted on December 7, only to be reimposed on December 18. Under these new emergency regulations, *Janadina,* the newspaper published by the Lanka Sama Samaja Party (LSSP), was banned because of a report that was said to inflame communal passions. The state of emergency was not lifted until January 17, 1969. During the 1970 election campaign the SLFP charged that the UNP government had discriminated against opposition papers, both under emergency regulations and in its placement of advertisements principally with progovernment newspapers.

Other checks on press reporting in the 1960s were the libel laws and an amendment to the election laws under which a newspaper is required to provide proof of any statements it attributes to politicians. In 1963 Felix Dias Bandaranaike was awarded libel damages amounting to Rs50,000 (for value of rupee, see Glossary) against Associated Newspapers, and in 1967 the *Times of Ceylon* and its editor were fined for a statement concerning Mrs. Bandaranaike.

285

Freedom of the press was again an issue in the 1970 elections, supporters of the UNP charging that the SLFP would stifle press freedom. The new SLFP government, however, declared in a policy statement that "freedom of speech, organization, assembly and public procession will be guaranteed in law and in practice" and that independent newspapers would be encouraged to break any "capitalist" mcnopoly. Earlier the finance minister had announced the probable establishment of a press council. The *Ceylon Daily News,* whose offices were attacked by a mob shortly after the election, changed its chief editor and, in a June 6 editorial, declared that it was independent of all political parties and that it would follow the debates in Parliament as a "guide to its treatment of political news and opinions."

A national readership of the press has not developed, however. Family, community, language, and education determine a reader's interests. In consequence, the same newspaper chain varies its editorial comment according to the language and interests of one particular group. The Sinhala press, for example, has been described as provincial and parochial both editorially and in coverage. The English-language press gives greater attention to foreign affairs, and the Tamil press reports Indian, particularly South Indian, news. The rather free attitude toward sex in the Western-oriented English-language press is a constant target of criticism by the more conservative Sinhalese-Buddhists. The same press, however, has been active in promoting Sinhalese art, drama, and motion pictures (see ch. 10, Artistic and Intellectual Expression).

In addition to the daily and weekend press, weeklies and periodicals appeal to specialized audiences—for example, *Youth News, Ceylon Woman,* and *Financial Times and News of Ceylon.* Sinhala weeklies devoted to poetry, astrology, culture, and women's and children's interests have circulations ranging from 15,000 to 50,000. *Nava Yugaya,* published by Lake House Press, and *Rasavahini,* published by Times of Ceylon, Ltd., are the most popular general periodicals. The Tamil press also has specialized periodicals (see table 16).

The Moscow wing of the Ceylon Communist Party (CCP) publishes a weekly periodical in each of the three languages: in Sinhala, *Mawbima*; in English, *Forward*; and in Tamil, *Thesabimani*. The Ceylon Trade Union Federation (CTUF) publishes weeklies in Sinhala and Tamil, which are oriented toward the pro-Peking wing of the CCP (see ch. 21, Labor; ch. 14, Political Dynamics). The *Tribune* is Marxist-oriented with a reputation for well-written articles on current issues, and the *Young Socialist* is an intellectual English-language periodical that has appeared sporadically since 1937. The organ of the LSSP in English is the *Samasamajist*; in Sinhala, *Samasamajaya*; and in Tamil, *Samatharmam*.

In 1970 there was only one news agency, the Co-operative Press Trust of Ceylon, which was associated with Reuters of England and the Press Trust of India. The 1964 press commission recommended the establishment of a national news agency by taking over the shares of Lake House Press but, with the failure of the various press bills, no action was taken on the recommendation. The Associated Press (AP) and United Press International (UPI) of the United States, French Press Agency (Agence France Presse), German Press Agency (Deutsche Presse Agentur) of West Germany, and Telegraph Agency of the Soviet Union (Telegrafnoye Agentstvo Sovietskovo Soyuza—TASS) maintain offices in Colombo, and some Indian and British newspapers have correspondents. There is also a part-time correspondent for the United States-published *Time, Life,* and the *New York Times.*

RADIO

In 1970 radio broadcasting was the responsibility of the Ceylon Broadcasting Corporation (CBC), an independent corporation under the Ministry of Information and Broadcasting. The CBC was established by an act of Parliament in 1966 and began operating in January 1967. Previously, Radio Ceylon was administered as a government department. A commission appointed in 1965 to make recommendations concerning the quality and adequacy of broadcasting found that, financially and in terms of independent commentary, Radio Ceylon was seriously handicapped as a government department.

The commission recommended the establishment of an independent corporation, consisting of a board of five members under a chairman, to carry on and develop broadcasting services, to supervise program content, and to advise the minister. The board appoints a director general of broadcasting as its chief executive officer for a term of five years. Subject to the approval of the minister of finance, the board has power to buy and lease property and to borrow and invest funds. Annual reports and accounts are submitted to Parliament.

Background

A broadcasting service was inaugurated in 1925. The greatest expansion of radio, however, took place between 1950 and 1960, when the number of licensed sets rose from 32,000 to 352,000. Growth since 1960 has been slow because of the ban on the

Table 16. Selected National Newspapers of Ceylon

Title	Language	Year established	Approximate circulation	Publishers
Morning Dailies				
Dinamina	Sinhala	1909	101,500	Associated Newspapers of Ceylon, Ltd.
Lankadipa	..do ..	1947	51,800	Times of Ceylon
Dawasa	..do ..	1961	51,300	Independent Newspapers, Ltd.
Virakesari	Tamil	1930	23,000	Virakesari, Ltd.
Thinakaran	..do ..	1932	32,000	Associated Newspapers of Ceylon, Ltd.
Dinapathi	..do ..	1964	8,000-11,000	Independent Newspapers, Ltd.
Ceylon Daily News	English	1918	65,600	Associated Newspapers of Ceylon, Ltd.
Ceylon Daily Mirror	..do ..	1961	16,000	Times of Ceylon
Sun	..do ..	1964	18,000	Independent Newspapers, Ltd.
Evening Dailies				
Janata	Sinhala	1953	30,000	Associated Newspapers of Ceylon, Ltd.
Sawasa	..do ..	1963	34,000	Independent Newspapers, Ltd.
Mithiran	Tamil	1966	16,000-22,500	Virakesari, Ltd.
Thanthi	..do ..	1967	16,000	Independent Newspapers, Ltd.
Ceylon Observer	English	1834	13,000	Associated Newspapers of Ceylon, Ltd.

Times of Ceylon	..do..	1846	12,800	Times of Ceylon
Star	..do..	1967	43,000	Independent Newspapers, Ltd.
Poya Day Newspapers*				
Silumina	Sinhala	1930	170,000	Associated Newspapers of Ceylon, Ltd.
Sri Lankadipa	..do..	1951	115,000	Times of Ceylon
Rivirasa	..do..	1961	165,000	Independent Newspapers, Ltd.
Thinakaram	Tamil	1948	32,000	Associated Newspapers of Ceylon, Ltd.
Chintahamani	..do..	1966	27,000	Independent Newspapers, Ltd.
Observer (magazine edition)	English	1923	76,000	Associated Newspapers of Ceylon, Ltd.
Times Weekender	..do..	1923	31,000	Times of Ceylon, Ltd.
Weekend Sun	..do..	1965	43,000	Independent Newspapers, Ltd.
Sunday Mirror	..do..	1966	17,000	Times of Ceylon
Periodicals				
Nava Yugaya	Sinhala	1956	11,000	Associated Newspapers of Ceylon, Ltd.
Rasavahini	..do..	1956	14,000	Times of Ceylon
Sri	..do..	1963	28,000	Independent Newspapers, Ltd.

*Buddhist holiday, replacing Sunday.

Source: Adapted from *Ceylon Year Book, 1968*, Colombo, 1968, pp. 317-318; and *1969 International Yearbook*, New York, 1969, pp. 502-503.

299-639 O - 79 - 20

import of radio sets. In 1968 licensed sets were estimated at approximately 550,000. In 1966 the Commission on Broadcasting estimated that the number of sets would more than double within a short period after lifting the ban. Thirty-one percent of the sets are in the Colombo area, which has only about 16 percent of the entire population. The greatest demand exists in the rural areas, and this in part reflects technical shortcomings of CBC.

The Ceylon Broadcasting Corporation

The CBC is divided into national and commercial services. The national service is further divided by languages and the nature of programs. A complete service of news, commentary, interviews, discussions, drama, religious programs, and music is broadcast in each of the three languages—Tamil, Sinhala, and English (see table 17). In 1970 the national service broadcast more than seventy hours in Sinhala, about sixty hours iñ Tamil, and thirty-five hours in English. About twenty hours of school programs are broadcast each week in all three languages. In addition, a Sinhala service called the "Sandhya Sevaya" (Evening Service) was introduced in 1963 as an alternative Sinhala program for light entertainment. In the late 1960s school programs, which, according to a government official, were not being put to full use by the schools, were rebroadcast on the "Sandhya Sevaya" program, which brought the total hours broadcast in Sinhala to more than ninety a week.

In the late 1960s all programs originated in Colombo and were fed via cable and very high frequency (VHF) to mediumwave and shortwave transmitting stations at Ekala, Diyagama, and Welikada, which are all a distance of only about fifteen miles from Colombo. The range of the mediumwave transmitting stations does not exceed thirty miles, and for technical reasons the shortwave transmitter at Ekala cannot be utilized.

Regional transmitting stations have been set up at Senkadagala near Kandy and Anuradhapura. The Commission on Broadcasting recommended the use of VHF broadcasting in the Central and Southern provinces because of the mountainous terrain, but in 1970 this recommendation had not been followed. In 1968 West Germany agreed to provide two mediumwave transmitters with fifty kilowatt generating power and one with ten kilowatt. After installment these transmitters were expected to double the listening range and triple the number of listeners. One station was inaugurated in February 1970 at Maho in North Western Province.

Table 17. Radio Transmission by Ceylon Broadcasting Corporation in 1968

Service	Frequency (in kilohertz)*	Wavelength (in meters)	Power (in kilowatts)
National			
Sinhala	700	428	50
	4,900	61.22	10
	570	526.3	1
	3,385	88	10
	6,075	49.38	10
Tamil	870	344.8	20
	4,968	60.38	10
	6,005	49.96	10
English	920	326	10
	5,020	59.76	25
	6,130	48.94	10
"Sandhya Sevaya" (Sinhala)	1,030	294	10
	5,020	59.76	20
School	700	428	10
	6,075	49.38	50
	870	344.8	20
	6,005	49.96	10
External	17,830	16.83	35
	15,120	19.84	100
Commercial			
Sinhala	640	469	20
	4,870	61.60	10
	6,185	48.50	10
Tamil	920	326	25
	6,130	48.94	10
	5,020	59.76	10
	1,030	294	20
	5,076	59.10	10
English	920	326	25
	5,020	59.76	10
	6,130	48.94	10
	640	469	20
	4,870	61.60	10
All Asia			
Hindi	11,800	25.42	35
	9,720	30.86	100
	7,180	41.78	10
	6,075	49.38	10
Tamil	11,800	25.42	35
	9,720	30.86	100
	6,075	49.38	10
English	9,670	31.02	100
	15,120	19.84	100
	9,670	31.02	100

*Kilocycles; 1 kilohertz equals 1 kilocycle, or 1,000 cycles per second.

Source: Adapted from *World Radio-TV Handbook, 1970* (Ed., J. M. Frost) (24th ed.) Soliljevej, 1970, p. 147; and *Ceylon Year Book, 1968*, Colombo, 1968, pp. 319–321.

A rediffusion service was introduced in 1950. Ceylon Rediffusion Service, Ltd., was granted a license until 1970 to relay Radio Ceylon and other programs by a wired network. Development of this service was also adversely affected by the ban on radio imports. In the early 1950s the government distributed more than 2,000 free radio sets to community centers and public service institutions, but the scheme was discontinued a few years later because of the cost of maintenance.

Music programs in each of the three services have predominated, especially on the Sinhala service, which in 1965 accounted for more than 50 percent of the programs. Sinhala music is not well developed, and the criticism has been made that too much of the music played is Hindi (see ch. 10, Artistic and Intellectual Expression). The Sinhala service is considered of great importance culturally because no other sources of Sinhala programs are available to the public, as they are in English and Tamil. Efforts were made in the late 1960s to accent rural and development programs. The national service also broadcasts about twenty hours a week on its external service, both to Southeast Asia and Europe, but it has failed to attract many listeners.

Since its inception in 1950, the CBC commercial service has been an outstanding success in terms of money and popularity. It is primarily an advertising medium and serves not only Ceylon but many other countries in South Asia. The government has stated that the commercial service has the largest audience of any radio station in South Asia for its popular music, quiz and variety shows, and interviews with celebrities. There is evidence that the programs are listened to in southern portions of the Soviet Union, China, the Middle East, East Africa, and Malaysia. The programs are especially popular in India. According to CBC daily reports, the programs are also heard in several European countries, the United States, South Africa, Australia, and New Zealand.

Local programs on the commercial service are broadcast in Sinhala, Tamil, and English. Hindi programs are added to the external service. It has been recommended that more should be done on the overseas commercial service to promote Ceylonese culture and to attract tourism. The commercial service shares administrative and engineering facilities with the national service.

Although radio coverage of the population approximates that of the daily and weekend press, it is generally regarded as a less authoritative source of news. The broadcasting commission asserted that radio news bulletins tend to be "a rehash of items that have already appeared in the newspapers"; it described the content and presentation of news bulletins as poor and put the blame on inadequate staff and the absence of regional reporters for domestic news.

Radio Ceylon has also been charged with political bias. During the 1958 language riots, a Ceylonese observer criticized "the incursion of party politics" into the government-owned CBC. In 1964 the Speaker of the House of Representatives complained of the absence of opposition members' speeches on the radio. The director general of broadcasting and information is reported to have replied that "it was a long-standing practice not to report speeches by the Opposition or by government back-benchers."

The broadcasting commission was not in favor of political party broadcasts on CBC except for a taped broadcast for each political party before the elections "to explain its policies without any invective." The commission recommended balanced and restrained discussion of current issues. It also recognized that "all governments use the radio for official information and other governmental purposes."

During the 1965-70 period of UNP control, the portfolio of minister of information and broadcasting was held by the prime minister. In May 1970, during the election campaign, a group attacked the residence of the director general of broadcasting and information and demanded that a tape recording by a leading Buddhist *bhikku* (see Glossary) not be broadcast. In the recording, the Venerable Mahanayake Thero of Malwatte had stated his belief "that a socialist dictatorship fashioned according to Marxist philosophy will not guarantee democratic freedoms and protect national and religious interests." After the election of the SLFP coalition in May 1970, singers who had supported the UNP were kept off the air.

The broadcasting commission report recommended the introduction of television but recognized the heavy financial cost. In 1970 the government was negotiating with West Germany for setting up a station in Colombo.

The main relay station of Voice of America for South and Central Asia is located in Colombo. An agreement was signed between the United States and Ceylon in May 1951 by which the former would "furnish and install three shortwave broadcasting transmitters with power of not less than 35 KW" giving Ceylon priority use of one of the three transmitters and secondary use of the other two. In return, the Ceylon government would provide instantaneous or delayed relay of Voice of America programs in various languages. The Ceylon government retained the right to approve the schedule and content of the broadcasts, and the United States agreed not to sublet time on the transmitters. The agreement was extended in 1954 and again in 1962 until 1971. Use of these transmitters has greatly facilitated the broadcasts of Radio Ceylon.

LIBRARIES

In June 1970 the government announced that it intended to establish a national library system. Ceylonese and foreign observers have described the public library service as "thoroughly inadequate."

The oldest public library was established in Colombo in 1813 as the Ceylon United Services Library. In 1874 it became the Colombo Public Library. Another subscription library was started in Pettah in 1829 by a group of lawyers and civil servants. The Colombo and Pettah libraries were amalgamated in 1925 to become the largest public library in the country, consisting of a reading room, a lending library, and a reference section. In 1969 the book stock was estimated at 90,000 titles in Sinhala, Tamil, and English. Until the 1950s the titles were almost exclusively English, but the demand for books in Tamil and Sinhala rose steadily in the 1960s. For example, in 1960 just under 20,000 Sinhala books were borrowed, compared with over 80,000 in 1968. During the same period Tamil borrowings increased from 2,000 to 15,000.

The reference library contains special collections on Buddhism, Ceyloniana, Latin and Greek classics, and the fine arts. In 1968 more than 250 periodicals were subscribed to, the majority in English, and there were over sixty newspapers in English, Tamil, and Sinhala. An estimated 180,000 persons a year use the reading room facilities. A study room that was opened in 1958 has proved popular, especially at examination time, when students line up two hours before opening. In 1970 an expansion of staff and facilities was needed to keep up with the demand, and plans were underway for new buildings. The Colombo Public Library in 1969 had eight branch libraries, including two for children.

Public libraries are the concern of local governments. The eleven municipal councils on the island support public libraries, as do some urban and town councils. The Kandy municipal library, which was founded in 1841, has since been renamed the D. S. Senanayake Memorial Public Library. In 1970 the library contained more than 16,000 books with an annual book acquisition fund of Rs16,000. The public library in Anuradhapura is well organized and well used and is regarded as a model public library.

Apart from libraries in some of the other towns, such as Ambalangoda, Balangoda, and Chilaw, most so-called public libraries are only small collections of books in the charge of untrained clerks. Library services are even less adequate in rural areas. In the 1960s a mobile library unit served eight village communities in the Kandy area. It was run by the Department of Local Government and the Kandy Junior Chamber of Commerce.

There are a number of specialized libraries of varying quality. The Ceylon Scientific and Industrial Research Library has been described as excellently equipped and administered. Parliament, the Central Bank of Ceylon, and various government departments have libraries. Muslims and Catholics have their own religious libraries, and the Buddhists maintain temple libraries, a feature of Buddhism for many centuries (see ch. 10, Artistic and Intellectual Expression). The Colombo Museum receives all books under copyright. In addition to the major universities, some schools have good libraries.

PUBLISHING

The British Book-Development Council Mission that visited Ceylon in 1970 reported that the island, with its high literacy rate of approximately 80 percent, was an underdeveloped market of high potential. Books have not so far been an important medium of communication because of the poor supply of books in the vernacular languages. In 1954 there were more than 300 registered printing presses, but most were very small operations. Even the large publishing houses, such as Lake House Press, have a modest yearly output. Increasing attention is being paid to the publication of textbooks in the vernacular.

The Government Printing and Publishing Corporation was established in 1968 to print textbooks, but in 1970 it was heavily in arrears, and the printing of several school textbooks had to be transferred to private printers. In June 1970 the government announced its intention to set up a state publishing house to "free talented writers from exploitation by private publishers."

Development of an indigenous publishing industry is handicapped by the low purchasing power of the average reader. Paperback fiction with plenty of sex and violence has proved the most popular. There is, however, a good market for religious books among pious Buddhists and Hindus. Bookstalls are located throughout the island, and there are bookstores in nearly all the major towns. India, the United States, and the United Kingdom are the sources of most imported books, which gives an advantage to the English and Tamil readers.

FILMS

In early 1970 draft legislation was prepared to set up a national film institute. In the late 1960s there was increasing concern that Sinhala films needed protection against foreign competition. The great majority of imported films come from the United States, followed by Hindi and Tamil films from India and a smaller number from the United Kingdom.

Indigenous studios produce approximately twenty films a year, which in 1969 accounted for only 22 percent of screen time. In the late 1960s there were approximately seven film companies, all located in Colombo. Three companies had a monopoly on film distribution. Most of the approximately 300 cinema houses with a combined seating capacity of over 180,000 were situated in the southwestern provinces. In addition, there were some fifty mobile theaters operating with kerosine projectors. In 1969 an estimated 17 million attended the cinema, of whom about 50 percent were men, 25 percent women, and 25 percent children.

Fiscal measures for the promotion of new companies were approved by Parliament in February 1970. The newly elected government of Mrs. Bandaranaike declared its intention of carrying through additional film legislation, "especially in regard to the creation of State Studios and protection of the indigenous film industry from foreign competition." The government also announced plans to investigate the monopoly on film distribution.

INFORMAL CHANNELS OF COMMUNICATION

Although the traditional channels of communication, such as town criers, have largely given way to modern methods of disseminating information—newspapers, radio, telephone, and telegraph—and although the technical infrastructure for mass communications exists, most communication still takes place within family and caste rather than across community lines. Some civic clubs operate, but for the most part they play a marginal role in disseminating information except in the newly colonized areas. Family and village gossip is still a speedy and potent means of spreading news (see ch. 6, Social Structure).

CENSORSHIP

In mid-1970 there was no censorship of books and newspapers. There were, however, regulations for registering all books and newspapers printed in Ceylon and all printing presses. A copy of every newspaper published and four copies of every book had to be deposited with the registrar of books and newspapers. Public performances of films, concerts, circuses, and all stage entertainments are regulated by ordinances, the latest of which was enacted in 1951. The minister of defense and external affairs has the power to regulate the character of public performances, to issue and withdraw permits for shows, and to preview any show. The regulations, however, must be submitted to the House of Representatives. Every public performance must be certified by a board appointed by the minister. Some municipal councils have separate certifying powers. The maximum penalty for infringement is a fine of Rs1,000 or six months' imprisonment.

Censorship of stage performances and films has not been severe, but sensitive political or communal subjects cannot be treated with freedom, and there is a double standard for the treatment of sex in Western and local movies. In 1970 the English-language press openly discussed a director's plan to introduce nudity on stage in a private club.

GOVERNMENT INFORMATION PROGRAMS

In accordance with recommendations of the Commission on Broadcasting, in November 1966 the Department of Information was separated from Radio Ceylon and set up as a separate department under the Ministry of Information and Broadcasting. Both the Government Film Unit and the Government Publications Department were reamalgamated with the Department of Information, which was made responsible for "publicising Government policies, programmes and activities" at home and abroad. The department consists of press officers representing different government departments and of Sinhala and Tamil translators. The department has three main publications: the irregular monthly *Ceylon Today*, a glossy English-language magazine with features on various aspects of the economic, political, and cultural life of Ceylon; a newsletter for local distribution in Sinhala, Tamil, and English; and a weekly bulletin in English for overseas readers.

The Government Film Unit makes short documentaries on cultural, economic, and social aspects of island life, as well as frequent newsreels. The newsreels are shot on 35-mm film and distributed through the commercial cinema circuits. The Commission on Broadcasting criticized the newsreels for poor technical quality and "too obvious propaganda." The documentaries are made on both 16-mm and 35-mm film for showing in schools, rural development societies, community centers, and embassies abroad. Some films have won international awards, but others have been criticized for "amateurism" (see ch. 10, Artistic and Intellectual Expression). The Government Film Unit also makes its services available to local commercial and foreign film makers. These include sound dubbing, rerecording, and film processing.

OFFICIAL FOREIGN INFORMATION SERVICES

Cultural centers are maintained by France, West Germany, Japan, and the United Kingdom. The British Council, for example, arranges lectures, concerts, and other cultural activities; operates reading rooms with reference and lending facilities in Colombo and Kandy; and advises students on educational facilities in the United Kingdom. The United States Information Service (USIS) maintains a post in Colombo and a branch in Kandy. The Soviet Union and Communist China conduct active information campaigns, and in 1969 Communist countries broadcast 100 hours every week to Ceylon, most often in English.

CHAPTER 17

POLITICAL VALUES AND ATTITUDES

The dominant system of political beliefs, opinions, and attitudes, which is subscribed to by nearly three-fourths of the total population, has been influenced and shaped by the interplay of Buddhism and the liberal, democratic political tradition inherited from British rule. The institution of parliamentary government that emphasizes reconciliation and pragmatism and Buddhist precepts relating to the avoidance of extremes in human interactions have combined to produce a national frame of mind that is disposed toward the rejection of radical and doctrinaire alternatives. Non-Buddhist minorities, such as Tamils (see Glossary), Christians, and Muslims, are also affected by the persistence of this moderate political thinking, although in their case the Buddhist influence is less pronounced (see ch. 11, Religion).

Value and attitudinal orientations are also affected by the manner in which nationalism is perceived by different people. The Sinhalese-Buddhist majority generally regard the country as multiracial and multireligious, but their occasionally aggressive, exclusive posture has tended to arouse the hostility and suspicion of minorities, who generally favor a territorially rather than communally defined nationalism. Successive governments have sought to promote the emergence of a nationalism based on the oneness of Ceylon amid the diversity imposed on the country by history. Progress in this direction has been steady, yet in 1970, according to several prominent national leaders, the sense of oneness had yet to be achieved.

By and large the Ceylonese—Sinhalese (see Glossary) and minority groups alike—are alert to, and conscious of, various conflicting claims and ideological pressures. Although traditional family, caste, and village loyalties remain in varying degrees of animation, they are gradually being altered by a relatively mobile, literate, and issue-conscious population (see ch. 12, Social Values).

Ideological orientations are varied and changing. Since the mid-1960s there have been indications that the people are becoming more tolerant toward communism. This changing attitude is at least in part a consequence of the growing popular confidence in the efficacy of non-Communist alternatives and in the elasticity of the country's political and cultural heritage.

Political attitudes are translated peacefully into action through periodically conducted national elections, in which voter participation is consistently high (see ch. 14, Political Dynamics). On the whole, urbanites are more sensitive than their rural counterparts to sociopolitical stimuli, and coastal populations are generally more volatile than the peasants of the central highlands.

Attitudes toward the nation-state vary according to communal loyalties and political partisanship. The Sinhalese-Buddhists insist that Ceylon has the special historic responsibility of spreading Buddha's message of peace, tolerance, and compassion to other peoples of the world and thus should be a Buddhist state. Religious minorities have generally accepted the concept of a Buddhist-oriented nation-state insofar as this concept is not carried to its extreme by the Sinhalese.

Political party leaders generally subscribe to the view that the country is divided into socialist and capitalist camps. Actually these descriptions are used more for rhetorical effect than as a meaningful criterion for appreciating the intricacies of shifting political alignments.

In mid-1970 the nation-state concept was again being scrutinized as a result of a lingering question as to whether Ceylon could be regarded as sovereign and independent under the Constitution of 1948 (see ch. 13, The Governmental System). Many political leaders were asserting that, because of the country's acceptance of the British crown as its constitutional head of state, Ceylon was less than sovereign and that the new era of complete independence would be ushered in only when a new, Ceylonese-drafted constitution was adopted, making the country a republic and enabling the people to declare their allegiance to Ceylon rather than to Great Britain.

Unlike many other new and emerging nations, the concept of loyal opposition is firmly institutionalized in the country. Nearly every segment of the population rejects either authoritarian or totalitarian notions of rule, believing that government should be by a popularly elected body of officials and should be based on a program of priorities and policies popularly endorsed at the polls. The concept of responsive cooperation between government and the opposition has been occasionally put to test on a limited basis (see ch. 14, Political Dynamics).

SOURCES AND CHARACTER OF POLITICAL VALUES

The nation's political values are derived from heterogeneous sources—secular and religious, indigenous as well as foreign. Political organizations are free to espouse their widely differing ideologies, provided they are not seeking to subvert the existing political order. Buddhism is most commonly identified with the state, but the ideological foundation of the nation-state is essentially secular and diffuse. Since the mid-1950s successive governments have sought to remove residual elements of more than 450 years of European colonial bias against Buddhism and to restore the indigenous religion to its formerly prestigious place in the society. This effort was not undertaken because of any desire to make Buddhism the exclusive state religion or doctrine but rather because of the expediency of parliamentary politics (see ch. 3, Historical Setting; ch. 11, Religion; ch. 14, Political Dynamics).

For the Sinhalese majority, the tradition of British liberalism as reflected in the institutions of democratic, parliamentary government serve, along with Buddhism, as a major determinant of political orientations. The British heritage also conditions significantly the minorities, who are said to be under the influence of their respective religious beliefs relating to authority and power. In actual circumstances, however, value differences between religious communities, if discernible, are more nominal than real; attitudinal differences between the Buddhist and non-Buddhist communities, where they exist, are affected more by the manner in which religious issues have been subordinated sometimes to partisan purposes than by any doctrinal disagreement or incompatibility among the country's four religious systems (see ch. 11, Religion).

Generally speaking, for both the Sinhalese and the minorities, the Western, secular, democratic political ideals, rather than religious sentiments, served as guidelines in the management of national affairs. Beginning in the 1950s, national politics for a decade took on almost exclusively Buddhist characteristics, but few Buddhist monks questioned the soundness of the nation's constitutional framework, and the manner in which the Sinhalese-Buddhists sought to regain their historic role as the ruling group conformed to the spirit and substance of parliamentary politics.

Among the popularly held Western political ideals are the beliefs that the transfer of government leadership from one competing group to another should be through impartially conducted general elections, that political conflicts be resolved at the polls, and that the ordering of national priorities be entrusted to a body of public officials accountable to the electorate rather than to social or political groups claiming power that is not popularly consented to. Other firmly held political ideals relate to the equality of citizens before the law and the inviolability of fundamental rights.

Apart from giving the political system a strong democratic bent, the Western value system provides the nation, which is rent by divisive communal forces, with a common framework for political participation, facilitating political communication across communal barriers and aiding governmental efforts to integrate the diverse communities into a coherent whole.

Since the early 1950s Buddhism has become a powerful symbol of Sinhalese political reaction against the country's British-educated, urban, Westernized elite that embraced various non-Buddhist religions. Regarding this elite as representing an alien system of values, the Buddhists have pressed their demand for replacing it with the vernacular educated, whom they believed to be more representative of the mainstream of national thinking and culture. These efforts to redefine the country in a Buddhist and Sinhalese image at times bordered on exclusiveness, thus antagonizing the minorities (see ch. 14, Political Dynamics; ch. 24, Public Order and Internal Security).

Although some Buddhist monks tend to attribute governmental failures in dealing with economic and other problems to national leaders' disinclination to seek the advice of eminent Buddhist elders, they have not attempted to elevate their religion as the official doctrine or ideology of the state. Buddhism does not prescribe any form of polity that should be strictly observed by temporal governments. Buddhists, especially those of the *sangha* (see Glossary), have stressed that their faith cannot be imposed on others because to do so would violate the Buddhist precepts relating to self-reliance and self-purification (see ch. 11, Religion). Thus, in January 1970, in a continuing attempt to ensure the separation of church and state, the All Ceylon Buddhist Congress urged all political parties not to permit the participation of Buddhist monks in their partisan campaigns (see ch. 14, Political Dynamics).

In Buddhism secular rulers are urged to observe *dasajaradhamma*, or ten duties of a king. The ten duties call on the ruler to observe charity, high moral character, readiness to sacrifice for the good of the people, honesty, kindness, austerity, freedom from ill-will, nonviolence, tolerance, and nonopposition to the will of the people. Compliance with these duties is believed to be a necessary condition for a good and just government; noncompliance will be met by retribution under the Buddhist law of cause and effect (see ch. 11, Religion). In the contemporary context, the Buddhist doctrine of the Middle Way becomes immediately relevant and has been invoked by successive governments to justify their moderate political and economic posture that belongs neither to the extreme Left nor the extreme Right.

Many Buddhists believe that their faith is compatible with the Western political values and institutions as they are known in their country. Some maintain, for example, that what they call the ethic of a spiritual democracy was first proclaimed by Buddha, whereas others argue that "the world's first parliament" was convened by the founder of their religion. Still others assert that the founder of modern socialism was actually Buddha and that Lenin implemented a socialism that had been taken from Buddhism by Marx and Engels. A small number of Buddhists even contend that Buddhism and Marxism are essentially similar because both Buddha and Marx attributed the real cause of crime to poverty and the uneven distribution of wealth.

On the other hand, there are substantial numbers of Buddhists who would disagree with the position that Buddhism and Marxism are similar. They take the view that there is no common ground between their faith and what they call atheistic Marxism.

NATIONALISM

As a matter of national pride, Ceylonese readily point out that they won independence without the loss of a single life. Unlike other new nations emerging from colonial rule, Ceylon was not subjected to the frustration and bitterness that often accompany anticolonial nationalist struggles; there was little massive outburst of popular nationalistic fervor against foreign rule, and as a result, national consciousness was relatively slow in emerging. Independence came to the country by an act of the British Parliament as a result of cooperative efforts between British authorities and a small number of British-educated, Westernized Ceylonese, many of whom belonged to religious and ethnic minorities (see ch. 3, Historical Setting).

Thus nationalism is largely a postindependence phenomenon. During the first few years of independence, government leaders sought to build a nationalism based on a single geographical entity without regard to ethnic and religious factors, which they considered to be divisive and harmful. This attempt was frustrated, however, by the rising tide of Sinhalese-Buddhist protest reactions against the political and social domination of non-Buddhist minorities in the national power structure (see ch. 14, Political Dynamics).

During the late 1950s and early 1960s nationalism tended to be identified with, and a consequence of, intensified Sinhalese efforts to reassert their historic role as the original settlers and ruling race, a role that had been obscured by

303

nearly 450 years of European colonial domination. Nationalism, as belatedly aroused in the 1950s, served mainly as a
vehicle of Sinhalese attempts to realign the power structure
in their favor. Because most foreigners, the customary target
of nationalist attacks in new nations, had already departed,
Sinhalese nationalism instead turned on those who had been
closely identified with foreign rule—that is, the Westernized,
Christianized, or Tamil minorities. Until the mid-1960s the
Sinhalese drives for dominant social and political position
and the counterreactions they provoked took the form of a
language dispute (see ch. 5, Ethnic Groups and Languages;
Ch. 14, Political Dynamics; ch. 24, Public Order and Internal
Security).

Sinhalese nationalist assertion during the late 1960s was not
as anti-Tamil and anti-Christian as it was previously. This was
partly because the language dispute had shown signs of sub-
siding and partly because minorities had gradually reconciled
themselves to new situations.

In 1970 the function of fostering nationalism was mainly
the responsibility of the Ministry of Cultural Affairs. The prominent theme used in this effort was that Ceylon was the "Land
of Buddhism," and its history dated back at least to the day
when Buddha is said to have achieved *nirvana* (release from
the cycle of life—see Glossary).

Antiquity and Sinhalese-Buddhist conceptions of nationalism
are the dominant features of the nation's flag and offical em-
blem. On both of these the symbol of a yellow lion holding a
sword, copied from an ancient Sinhalese royal banner, is a
prominent feature. The lion (Sinha) is derived from the historic
name of the island (see ch. 3, Historical Setting). The flag is
framed in yellow to indicate the Buddhist character of Ceylon;
it also contains vertical stripes of green and saffron to represent minority groups.

POLITICAL CONSCIOUSNESS

The nation's socioeconomic and political variables are con-
ducive to a high degree of political awareness and participation. The country is geographically compact and has had a
relatively long period of preparation for self-government; its
cash economy has penetrated nearly every corner of the rural
areas, contributing toward the breakdown of the traditional
village system as a self-sufficient unit; and its system of free
compulsory education has produced a literate and increasingly
mobile population. In addition, a press relatively free from
official restraint, the persistence of communal tensions, and

the decreasing effectiveness of caste barriers make for a politically alert population.

Because of greater access to communications media, urbanites are on the whole more sensitive than rural dwellers to local, national, and even world affairs (see ch. 16, Public Information). They are also more susceptible to inflationary pressures, rising costs of living, and disruptions stemming from organized labor strikes.

Geographically, the inhabitants of the western and southwestern coastal areas and the Jaffna Peninsula are more politically aware than those of the central highlands, partly because of a higher literacy rate and high population density and partly because of job scarcity and vigorous leftist political activities. The preponderance of nuclear rather than joint families in the coastal belts has also contributed to a more acute awareness of political and other stimuli than might otherwise have been the case (see ch. 6, Social Structure; ch. 7, Family). Political consciousness and political tension tend to be mutually reinforcing where the Sinhalese and Tamils live in proximity as, for example, in the estate areas of the central highlands.

Political developments since the mid-1960s generally support the view that popular consciousness is stimulated more by mundane issues affecting daily routines than by ideological or doctrinal considerations. During the early years of independence, many Buddhists and other religious adherents were concerned about the potential threat of Marxism to their respective faiths and their democratic political system. Since that time attitudes have undergone discernible changes, however, partly because of their growing self-confidence in the resiliency and capability of their non-Marxist political leaders and partly because the Marxists and Communists, unable to attract broad mass support, have been forced to pursue a pragmatic, although sometimes erratic, alternative. Thus Marxist and Communist politicians have occasionally, and in many cases without the crisis of conscience, opted for expediency rather than doctrinal correctness by shifting party loyalty or aligning with parties of opposing ideologies (see ch. 14, Political Dynamics).

Some observers have suggested that the increasingly pragmatic political consciousness was a natural consequence of the progressive Buddhist teachings on tolerance; others have argued that the Buddhist precept of the Middle Way was sufficient to deter popular acceptance of an extremist political ideology. Still others have commented that such problems as the housing shortage, unemployment, and concentration of

305

wealth by the relatively few were practical matters that had to be dealt with by practical rather than doctrinal means.

The results of the 1970 general elections tended to support the view that issues instead of ideology determine popular political behavior so long as these issues are presented as problem-solving alternatives through popularly sanctioned channels of political activity. During the election campaign Prime Minister Dudley Senanayake's United National Party (UNP) described the forthcoming election as the all-important battle of life and death between democracy and Marxism. The UNP repeatedly asserted that, should Mrs. Sirimavo Banda-ranaike's leftist coalition win the contest, the outcome would be a Communist dictatorship, anarchy, destruction of religion, loss of fundamental rights, and the end of free elections. It turned out, however, that many voters were more concerned with the mundane issues of daily living. Indications are that the number of the traditionally conservative, anti-Communist Catholics and Muslims voting for the leftist coalition candidates in 1970 was measurably greater than in the previous elections.

NATION-STATE AND GOVERNMENT

Nearly every Ceylonese agrees that the country is multiracial and multireligious and that the government must preserve this national characteristic if various ethnic communities are to cooperate in the attempt to achieve national unity and progress. That communal harmony is a necessary condition of political stability has been manifested many times since the mid-1950s in connection with the language dispute (see ch. 5, Ethnic Groups and Languages; ch. 14, Political Dynamics; ch. 24, Public Order and Internal Security).

The multiracial and multireligious conception of nation-state is sometimes clouded, however, by the Sinhalese insistence that the country be identified more or less exclusively with Buddhism and ruled by the Sinhalese. Although this insistence has been tempered by the assurance that the fundamental rights and welfare of minorities would be safeguarded, in 1970 the minority communities remained suspicious of the Sinhalese. The Tamils in particular continued to demand the establishment of a federated governmental structure (see ch. 14, Political Dynamics). A sense of ethnic-religious separateness also continued to pervade the Christian and Muslim communities.

Leftist political leaders are prone to view the country in terms of a division between what they call socialist and capitalist camps; rightist politicians also draw a polarized picture of the polity as being split into the democratic and Marxist camps. These descriptions are quite misleading; popular political perceptions and behavior are affected more by ethnic, religious, caste, and kinship ties and the quality of political leaders than by the abstraction of ideology. Leaders who are considered to be fair and selfless are more appreciated at the polls than ideological labels or party affiliations.

Since the mid-1950s the Sinhalese efforts to upgrade the role of Buddhism have given the majority community a sense of uniqueness and a measure of national pride. These efforts have also significantly affected the popular attitude toward the nation-state and government. Typically, the Sinhalese assert that, although their country is small, it is unique and world famous because of its historic role as the preserver and carrier of Buddha's message of peace, tolerance, compassion, and love. They are disposed to arrogate to themselves the mission of spreading the message throughout a world troubled by sorrow, misery, and craving for materialistic gains and sorely in need of peace, reconciliation, and detachment. Some Buddhists would go so far as to regard the Sinhalese as a chosen people with the mission of maintaining Theravada Buddhism (see Glossary) in pristine purity, claiming that the decline of Ceylon would mean the erosion of Buddhism.

Many Sinhalese leaders are inclined to believe that they are qualified to play a world role as a mediator in power-conflict situtations. They would point out that their historic experience with the Buddhist teaching on tolerance, the Hindu universality in moral and world outlook, the Islamic precept of brotherhood, and the Christian spirit of charity would give them a distinct national advantage in seeking to reconcile conflicting claims.

Perhaps the most significant feature of Ceylonese political orientations is the firmly embedded concept of loyal opposition as an essential condition of parliamentary government. Opposition leaders are seldom silenced in their efforts to question the propriety of given policies and the conduct of the ruling parliamentary group. Sinhalese and minorities alike share the view that the government must be always answerable to the electorate and that conflicting partisan claims must be reconciled with a minimum of rancor and discord. Popular attitudes toward the expected role of government are fairly evenly split into moderately leftist and moderately rightist categories as indicated by the dominance of the Sri Lanka Freedom Party (SLFP) and the UNP as the two largest parties (see ch. 14, Political Dynamics).

SECTION III. ECONOMIC

CHAPTER 18

CHARACTER AND STRUCTURE OF THE ECONOMY

In 1970 the economy continued to be a classic example of an export economy. Until the mid-1940s and to a lesser degree through the late 1950s, an advanced, largely foreign-owned plantation export sector (consisting principally of tea, rubber, and coconuts) and a domestic, inefficient, mini-scale subsistence agricultural sector operated as separate entities, with only a minimum of direct connection or interaction. This high degree of separation derived from the fact that for practical purposes the exporters neither bought from nor sold to the indigenous sector. The subsistence economy was not prepared to provide the kind of labor the export sector required, and it was not sufficiently productive to create the necessary agricultural surplus with which to feed and clothe the export workers (see ch. 12, Social Values; ch. 21, Labor). As a result, the export sector imported its labor and its food and clothing supplies from abroad.

Ceylon's economy, however, has differed from many other export economies in that before independence the exporters were mainly of the same nationality as the colonial rulers of the country and that since independence the ownership and control of the export sector have been shifting to the Ceylonese. This has had the effect that the export sector has increasingly been visualized, both before and after independence, as an integral part of the overall economic framework manipulated by the government, and only within progressively narrower limits has it been permitted to segregate its welfare from that of the rest of the country.

During the colonial period and even until the mid-1950s, overseas demand for Ceylon's exports and efficient production methods at home resulted in a level of output and foreign sales that afforded Ceylon a higher standard of living than most of the neighboring countries. Since the mid-1950s the country has come upon more difficult times. Among the reasons for this have been a population growth of serious proportions, a persistent decline in the prices and foreign earnings of the country's main exports, and social welfare commitments on the part of successive governments that have taken the form of subsidizing consumption, rather than investment, imports. Another and increasingly significant factor has been the unwillingness of a progressivly more youthful population to accept the short-term sacrifices inherent in economic development under conditions of declining foreign income and wealth.

Although productivity and output in the domestic sector have greatly increased as a consequence of improved technological, marketing, and credit developments, they have not arrested or offset the decline in the export sector earnings. In the mid-1960s foreign aid was utilized in an attempt to redress the balance between decreasing export earnings and increasing imports, but it was unable to compensate for the import surplus.

For a variety of reasons, the role of government in the economy has been, and in 1970 continued to be, pervasive. The country acquired independence in 1948 from a paternalistic colonial government after an extended period of self-government in most domestic matters, without recourse to hostilities and within the protective framework of the British Commonwealth. The government inherited a full panoply of democratic rights and responsibilities, a framework of operating governmental organization, and a bias toward socialism (see ch. 13, The Governmental System; ch. 17, Political Values and Attitudes).

As of mid-1970 the export sector's prospects, for the near future at least, were depressed. The outlook for the domestic agricultural sector, on the other hand, gave reason for considerable optimism. For industry, which since independence had been going through a series of growing pains, the future seemed to hold promise of substantial development in a minor key. The principal economic problem was a shortage of foreign exchange.

STRUCTURE OF THE ECONOMY

Until independence, and more particularly until the establishment of the Central Bank in 1950, there were few statistics of any sort and fewer reliable ones. Since 1950 their number and coverage has increased apace; their dependability, however, in certain areas still leaves something to be desired. The Central Bank has assumed responsibility for the banking, national income, and balance-of-payments statistics. The banking statistics especially, where the Central Bank exerts a large measure of control over the collection as well as the processing of the raw data, are well considered. Where the Central Bank depends heavily on other agencies for the raw data, the series should probably be viewed with caution. In any case, data for periods later than 1966 should be taken as provisional.

In 1969 the island had an estimated gross domestic product (GDP), representing the value of all goods and services produced during the year, of Rs9.43 billion (for value of rupee, see Glossary) valued at constant (1959) factor-cost prices—that is, prices net of excise, sales, and other indirect taxes (see table 18). On the same basis, the GDP in 1963 totaled Rs6.95 billion and in 1959, Rs5.93 billion. The gross national product (GNP), which equals the GDP taken net of foreign investment income (interest, profits, and dividends from abroad, whether positive or negative), in 1969 was provisionally estimated at Rs9.37 billion, compared with about Rs6.9 billion in 1963 and Rs5.89 billion in 1959.

In 1969 the GNP per capita was estimated at Rs764, compared with Rs648 in 1963 and Rs612 in 1959. This represented an estimated increase in average per capita income, at constant prices, of about 1.68 percent per year during the first six years of the 1959–69 period and 3.25 percent during the last four, for an average of 2.48 percent over the period. This included increases of 5.72 percent in 1968 and 3.38 percent in 1969, compared with the widely prescribed average per capita growth norm for developing countries of 2.5 percent per year at constant prices. At that growth rate, per capita income would double in twenty-nine years; in order that it should double in twenty-five years, an average annual rate of 2.9 percent would be required.

Comparison of the GNP series at constant prices with that at current prices over the 1959–69 period suggests that, overall, the price level remained virtually stable from 1959 to 1965. It declined slightly in 1966 but thereafter rose sharply as a consequence of a 20-percent devaluation of the rupee in 1967, the increased cost of imports, and wage increases introduced by the government to mitigate the effect on low incomes of the rise in living costs. The high degree of overall stability reflects the use of imports to absorb excess purchasing power, the institution of price controls in the early 1960s, and the steadying effect of Central Bank activities (see ch. 23, Finance).

A breakdown of the GNP by sectors between 1959 and 1969 displays a gradual shift over the period away from agriculture toward industry and services. Nevertheless, agriculture (including forestry, hunting, and fishing) provided throughout the period by far the most important contribution to the GNP. It

Table 18. Gross National Product and Labor Force of Ceylon, by Economic Sectors, Selected Years, 1959-69[1]
(value in millions of rupees)[2]

Sector	1959		1963			1967	1968	1969	
	Value	Percent	Value	Percent	Percent of labor force	Value	Value	Value	Percent
Agriculture, forestry, hunting, and fishing.	2,302.4	39.1	2,846.0	41.2	52.9	3,039.9	3,248.4	3,312.0	35.4
Mining and quarrying	31.3	0.4	29.5	0.4	0.3	37.0	37.3	49.8	0.5
Manufacturing	682.1	11.6	853.0	12.3	9.8	1,052.0	1,540.0	1,220.8	13.0
Construction	282.9	4.8	271.8	3.9	2.7	350.8	446.0	526.9	5.6
Electricity, gas, water, and sanitary services.	9.5	0.2	11.4	0.2	0.3	14.7	15.0	17.7	0.2
Transport, storage, and communications.	540.9	9.2	591.8	8.6	4.2	781.6	823.9	922.6	9.8
Wholesale and retail trade ...	800.8	13.6	875.1	12.7	9.0	1,174.3	1,253.3	1,379.9	14.7
Banking, insurance, and real estate.	50.9	0.8	67.4	1.0		99.6	110.4	117.6	1.2
Ownership of dwellings	200.6	3.4	227.2	3.3	20.8[3]	265.4	274.7	281.0	3.0
Public administration and defense.	301.0	5.1	365.1	5.3		388.9	432.4	445.5	4.7
Services	727.6	12.3	812.3	11.8		1,021.4	1,104.8	1,152.1	12.3
Gross domestic product (GDP).	5,930.0	......	6,950.6	......	......	8,225.6	8,900.2	9,434.8	......

Net factor income from abroad.	-36.7	-0.6	-50.9	-0.7	......	-44.5	-38.7	-64.5	-0.7
Gross national product (GNP).	5,893.3	100.0[4]	6,899.7	100.0[4]	100.0[4]	8,181.1	8,861.5	9,370.3	100.0[4]
Percentage increase[5]	......	......	2.7	......	......	4.6	8.3	5.7	......
Midyear population (millions).	9.63	......	10.65	......	......	11.70	11.99	12.26	......
Percentage increase[5]	......	......	1.9	......	......	2.3	2.5	2.2	......
Per capita GDP (1959 prices).	616	......	653	......	......	703	742	769	......
Percentage increase[5]	......	......	0.9	......	......	2.3	5.5	3.6	......
Per capita GNP (1959 prices).	612	......	648	......	......	699	739	764	......
Percentage increase[5]	......	......	0.8	......	......	2.3	5.7	3.4	......
Per capita GNP index (1959 equals 100)[6].	100	......	106	......	......	114	120	125	......

[1]At constant (1959) factor-cost prices.
[2]Before November 20, 1967, Rs4.76 equaled US$1; thereafter, Rs5.95 have equaled US$1.
[3]Includes 5.3 percent "unallocated" because inadequately described.
[4]Columns may not add exactly, owing to rounding.
[5]Over the preceding year.
[6]Obtained by dividing the GNP for 1959 (in absolute figures) into each successive annual GNP (in absolute figures), and then multiplying by 100.

Source: Adapted from Central Bank of Ceylon, *Annual Report of the Monetary Board to the Minister of Finance for the Year 1969*, Colombo, 1970, tables 1 and 5; and Ceylon, *Statistical Abstract of Ceylon, 1966*, Colombo, 1969, p. 44.

represented, on the average, 36 percent of the total during the years 1967-69, compared with 37 percent in 1965, 41 percent in 1963, and an average of 39.5 percent during the years 1959-61.

In the early 1960s the value of output in the agricultural sector was more or less evenly divided between agriculture for export—mainly tea, rubber, and coconut products—and that for domestic consumption, of which rice represented about one-third. Subsequently, as the volume of domestic crops has risen and the prices of export crops have declined, the importance of domestic agriculture has tended to offset the export sector's decline in rupee terms, although not in terms of exchange earnings.

The slack left by the agricultural sector's relative decline was taken up on the one hand by manufacturing and construction and on the other by commerce, communications, and storage. Manufacturing and construction, which taken together might be considered in Ceylon as tantamount to industry, represented a combined 18.6 percent of total output of goods and services in 1969. This figure compared with 16.2 percent in 1963 and 16.4 percent in 1959; it reflected an expansion of 15 percent in industrial output in six years.

This growth contained qualitative as well as quantitative changes. The government, in the years since independence, has intervened in most areas of industry, establishing industries where none had existed before (see ch. 20, Industry). By 1969 the industry sector included a few large plants, mostly government owned, and a large number of privately owned small ones, with a production spectrum ranging from steel shapes and automobile assembly to tobacco, beverages, and foodstuffs. A number of the large production units had only recently come into production by 1969.

For many already established firms, for the most part in the private sector but sometimes including government plants, a chronic problem was obtaining the foreign exchange needed to import raw materials and spare parts. As a result, the industry sector has tended to show a ragged production schedule, with many firms, including the government-owned ones, operating below the optimum, or even the breakeven, point.

The increased relative growth of the trade, transport, and storage sectors over the 1959-69 period may be taken as largely a reflex of the increased output in the manufacturing, construction, and domestic agriculture sectors. Transport facilities had achieved reasonably satisfactory quantitative coverage for the existing needs of the economy. Policy, management, and maintenance, however, could still benefit from greater coordination and attention to the ratio between costs and benefits.

314

The remaining sectors mostly consist of services that, in one way or another, support the production and distribution sectors, such as banking, education, public health, insurance, public administration, and defense. In the aggregate they expanded along with the overall growth of the economy, although probably there was some shifting of relative importance of the components within the aggregate. Banking services for the export sector continued to be good, and there was expansion and some streamlining of the facilities for the rest of the economy.

In expenditure terms the proportion of the GNP devoted to investment (gross domestic capital formation) in 1969 was provisionally estimated at 19 percent, distributed between private and public investment as 14.4 percent and 4.6 percent, respectively, the balance of the expenditure being devoted to consumption. The 1969 investment level compared with an annual average rate of such investment of 15.4 percent for the period from 1961 to 1969, which in turn reflected an average of 10.4 percent per year in the private sector and 5 percent in the public sector. An average of around 20 percent is frequently taken as the level of investment necessary for a country to convert from subsistence agriculture to industrialization.

The labor force was estimated in the 1963 census at 30.2 percent of the total population. Estimates of the sectoral breakdown of the labor force in 1970 are based on the 1963 census and do not purport to be refined estimates. The 1963 estimates allotted 52.9 percent of total employment to agriculture, 9.8 percent to manufacturing, 2.7 percent to construction, 4.2 percent to the transport and communications sector, and 9 percent to the trade sector. Services, except the public utilities, were lumped into a residual item representing 20.8 percent of the total.

Allowing for the tentative nature of these data, a comparison of them with the sectoral breakdown of the GNP for the year 1963 affords some interesting insights. The proportion of employment engaged in agriculture was appreciably larger than the contribution of the agriculture sector to the GNP and suggests that average efficiency (productivity per worker) in that sector was below the average for the economy as a whole. On the other hand, the 9.8 percent of employment engaged in manufacturing, the 2.7 percent engaged in construction, and particularly, the 4.2 percent engaged in transport and communications, when compared with the 12.3, 3.9, and 8.6 percent, respectively, contributed by those sectors to the GNP, suggest a greater than average efficiency in those sectors and presumably reflected the greater amount of capital available to employees there. The remaining 20.8 percent of the gainfully employed closely paralleled the combined contribution of the remaining sectors to the GNP. This match, even if arrived at as a residual, suggests that efficiency in the service sectors taken together was about average for the economy as a whole, although it would probably be reasonable to expect the banking sector to display greater efficiency than the other services.

A tendency to underemployment is strengthened by widespread sharecropping and landlessness. It is probable, moreover, that both the religious taboos on eating different kinds of meat and the caste system, in which agriculturalists hold an elite position, act as impediments to a mixed occupation way of life. Unemployment, in contrast to underemployment, is apparently also widespread and on the increase, especially in the urban centers. Rapid population growth and migration to the cities have contributed to this situation. Furthermore, the government's emphasis on heavy industry tends to be capital, rather than labor, intensive. For these reasons and also because of the small size of the industrial market and the chronic shortage of raw materials for small industries, industrial development has failed to provide large-scale urban employment. The 1970 estimates of unemployment ranged between 350,000 and 750,000.

A particularly difficult aspect of the economic structure in recent years has been a persistently unfavorable ratio of its terms of trade (export prices divided by import prices and miltiplied by 100). The continued decline in export prices, along with the gradual worldwide rise in import prices, has meant a progressive decline in Ceylon's annual import capacity. Although the country is fortunate to have the sizable export markets it does have, the fact that it has to import all of its capital equipment, much of its raw materials, and a considerable amount of foodstuffs and other consumption goods makes the constant fall in the terms of trade a harrowing experience.

The necessity until the late 1960s to import up to one-half of the national rice consumption was only the most flagrantly difficult aspect of a general problem that has faced successive governments with an array of hard choices. For the first decade after independence, the government was largely able to sidestep this problem by depending on its accumulated foreign exchange reserves to finance the excess of imports over exports. By the mid-1960s, however, this recourse had largely been exhausted.

An important contributant to the decline in the foreign exchange reserves throughout the postindependence period was the excess of the government's rupee expenditures over its rupee revenues that led to increases in purchasing power and demand for imports. Until recently the banking system was quite restrained in adding to the private sector purchasing power, and the continuing decline in the reserves themselves served as an active depressant. Most of the increase in the money supply, which almost doubled between 1955 and 1970, thus resulted from the increase in the government indebtedness to the banking system. That this did not exert more upward push on prices than it did probably reflects, in addition to the inflow of consumption imports, some increasing monetization of the subsistence sector and the effectiveness of prevailing price controls.

During this period the government had adopted a policy of establishing industries such as paper, cement, plywood, and steel shapes, to replace imports, rather than supplement exports. These efforts were not universally successful, but invariably they added to the demand for raw materials, which had to compete for foreign exchange with foodstuff and other consumption imports and the plant and equipment for additional industrialization. At the same time, increasingly restrictive price and exchange control measures were put into effect in an attempt to plug unprogrammed sources of exchange leakage.

Beginning in the mid-1960s the international lending agencies, in collaboration with the United States and some of the Organization for Economic Cooperation and Development (OECD) and Commonwealth countries, undertook to help coordinate and finance a more concerted development effort. This was to be based on increasing diversification of exports and the achievement of self-sufficiency in foodstuffs, in addition to the earlier program of import substitution. The effort was to be organized around an internal development plan and a foreign exchange budget.

In mid-1970 appreciable headway had been made in the new direction, especially in connection with the self-sufficiency program. Nevertheless, the foreign exchange resources gap, in the context of an apparent tendency for the wealthy nations to contract their foreign aid programs, continued to confront the government not only with a seemingly intractable impediment to orderly economic development but also the promise of an undesirably large external indebtedness (see ch. 22, Trade).

ROLE OF GOVERNMENT

One of the most important of the rights that the government inherited from its predecessor at independence was the monopoly right to the still so-called crown lands (see ch. 19, Agriculture). These, for practical purposes, had for more than a century comprised all the existing unused land in the country, except lands belonging to the temples. The sale of the crown lands by the government at nominal prices had provided the base for the successive developments in the plantation sector. This monopoly position in relation to new land forced upon the new government the responsibility for providing the living space for the rapidly growing agricultural population and at the same time endowed the government with the means with which to do so. Because much of the available land was arid, the government also had to provide the necessary irrigation facilities to make the land productive. The government's ownership of most of the available land not only strengthened the government's socialist bias and sense of responsibility but also weakened the private sector by depriving it of a large reservoir of speculative wealth.

The government also either inherited or has asserted a monopoly position in the industrial sector. The government early staked out a claim to control of basic industries and has progressively intervened in most other areas of the industrial sector. This intervention frequently took the form of productive units sufficiently large, in relation to the small market for most articles, to monopolize the whole or a large part of several industries.

By 1969 state-controlled industrial corporations had intervened in industries producing or processing nineteen important foodstuffs, or other consumer or producer goods. In more than half of these the government corporation had assumed a monoply position. Upward of half the total value of industrial production in that year, as reported by the Central Bank, was apparently earned by government agencies and corporations.

Among the services supporting the commodity-producing sectors, the government's monopoly position also was far flung. At the end of 1969 the government directly controlled all major communication and transportation facilities, the major ports, the insurance industry, and most of the banking sector. Food and other strategic imports were state monopolies, and all exports and imports were subject to government licensing. After the 1970 national elections the government indicated that it intended to nationalize the remainder of the banking system and perhaps to take some parallel action in connection with the foreign-owned plantations.

The government has exerted further directive influence upon the economy through a network of subsidies and guaranteed price programs. These have mainly been in behalf of the in-

digenous sector, particularly the rural portion of it. The subsidies have been applied, for the most part, to various aspects
of rice production, with the double purpose of raising rural
incomes and inducing successive increases in the level of rice
production that would eventually eliminate the need for rice
imports. In 1967 and 1968 the successive devaluations of the
rupee were to a certain extent undertaken as part of a sub-
sidization program for the country's minor agricultural export
commodities. As the reverse of the same coin, the tax system
has been used, apart from its regular revenue purposes, as a
means of redistributing income from the plantation to the indigenous agricultural sector.

In its attitude toward foreign investment, the government
since independence has shown itself to be pulled in opposite
directions. On the one hand, there has been recognition of the
advantages and desirability of attracting foreign private capital
and technical expertise. On the other hand, nationalism has
served to reinforce the trend toward Ceylonization of the economy. This has taken numerous forms, including nationalization
of existing foreign investments, strict and direct limitations on
new investment, heavy dependence on import quotas and exchange controls, and bilateral trading arrangements.

The economic role which the government that took power in
May 1970 has foreseen for itself was set forth in some detail
in the government's official policy statement on June 14, 1970.
The government proposed to adopt a plan to Ceylonize the
economy and to advance further toward a socialist society. The
plan would include programs for rapid growth of the industrial
sector; reorganization of the rural sector, including fishing;
extension of irrigation and power resources, including cheap
electrification of the country; increased employment; and the
construction, repair, and maintenance of highways, housing,
and village irrigation reservoirs. The program of river valley
development projects would be expanded, but increasingly
under the control and direction of Ceylonese technicians. Agreements signed in 1969 and early 1970 with the International
Bank for Reconstruction and Development (IBRD) and its
affiliates in connection with power, irrigation, and highway
projects would be reviewed and, if it were deemed advisable,
revised.

The government also declared in its policy statement that it
would intervene in the operation of the plantation sector in
the interests of the nation. Cooperative societies would be reorganized and refinanced, and their functions would be expanded. In behalf of the small agricultural producers, the
government would redeem the very large indebtedness they

319

had accumulated, make cheap credit available, increase their subsidies for fertilizer and other agricultural input, make available more land for the landless, clear land titles in the villages, institute crop insurance, and raise the guaranteed prices for rice and other agricultural products (see ch. 19, Agriculture).

All heavy, basic, and capital goods industries would be state owned. Other industries would be assigned to cooperatives and private enterprise. The state would acquire shares in both foreign and domestic industries, and ownership of industries by Ceylonese would be actively pursued. Cottage industries would be fostered, and all industries would be protected from foreign competition.

The state would absorb the handling of all essential imports and would increase its participation in the export trade. Directly or indirectly, the state would take over the handling of the central wholesale trade of all imported essential commodities and of such domestically produced commodities as seemed necessary. The retail trade of the country would be Ceylonized. Foreign banks would be nationalized, and a series of specialized banks would successively be established to meet the special requirements of the agricultural, industrial, and other sectors.

DEVELOPMENT PLANNING

During the early years of independence, successive governments placed relatively little emphasis on development planning, in part, perhaps, because the immediate economic problems appeared to be small and manageable. This is not, however, to say that such planning aroused no interest or attention but, rather, that until the late 1950s and the 1960s development planning contributed relatively little to the country's progress.

In fact, official recognition of the desirability of planning under the independent government was given emphatic affirmation in the annual budget speech of the minister of finance in fiscal year 1947/48. The budget speech of 1948/49 launched the Six Year Plan for Ceylon, the first of a number of programming efforts that got bogged down in the play of forces that accompanied the economic boom and bust of the Korean conflict period and the tea boom of the middle 1950s that successively kept the export sector and, consequently, imports, the money supply, and prices off balance.

The preliminary efforts were followed in 1956 by the National Planning Council Act No. 40 of that year and the National Planning Council that, in accordance with the act's provisions, was set up in the Ministry of Finance. Between 1957 and 1959 the council and the Central Bank invited a number of prestigious foreign economists to visit Ceylon and to offer the government both their diagnoses of the country's economic problems and their prescriptions for the planning and implementation of recommended remedies. These studies have provided much of the scaffolding and rationale of economic planning and major economic measures since then, although not necessarily in any organized fashion.

Based on these studies, the National Planning Council in 1959 issued its Ten Year Plan, the most ambitious analysis of the economy and projection of planning that had yet been officially published. Unfortunately, its forecasts were based on quite faulty projections of population and labor force growth rates. Moreover, attempts to implement the plan collided with the exchange and price crunch of 1961 and 1962. Thus, although efforts were made to follow it up with a Three Year Short-Term Programme (fiscal years 1961/62-1963/64) and the subsequent Development Programme (1964-65) under a reorganized Department of National Planning, the plan became increasingly out of touch with a rapidly changing economic scene.

Development planning from 1966 to 1970 was carried out by the Ministry of Planning established in the combined Ministry of Planning and Economic Affairs (after May 1970, the Ministry of Planning and Employment). Both portfolios were held by the prime minister. The fact that the prime minister assumed responsibility for the planning portfolio bespoke the new government's acknowledgment of the growing relevance of planning to the increasingly serious economic condition of the country.

The work of the ministry was closely coordinated, moreover, with the active financial and technical support afforded by the IBRD, the International Monetary Fund (IMF), the United Nations Development Program (UNDP) and other United Nations agencies, the United States government, and members of the British Commonwealth, the Colombo Plan, and the OECD (See ch. 15, Foreign Relations).

The new approach to planning not only had the exceptional advantage of top-level decisionmaking and international support, but it also benefited from greater conceptual pragmatism and better organization. Under the new organizational setup the Ministry of Planning and Economic Affairs was divided into departments that were concerned with national planning, foreign aid, and plan implementation. Because the emphasis henceforth was to be upon sector planning, high-level committees on industry, economic infrastructure, domestic agriculture, and manpower were created. Their first task was to

321

review the current stage of progress of the several projects that were envisaged for inclusion in the four sectors. Thereupon they were to present their recommended priorities to the National Planning Council for review, coordination, and recommendation to the cabinet and Parliament for decision. Such decisions would provide the basis for five-year sector programs. In the course of these organizational changes, the Department of Planning was to be expanded, streamlined, and afforded enhanced responsibility; technical and mechanical assistance was to come from the UNDP.

The earlier concepts of planning had been based on long-term overall (aggregative) programs of progressively greater complexity. The new approach was geared to projects and economic sectors. These would be combined into coordinated one-year programs and gradually would be extended into coordinated plans designed around a moving five-year period. This type of plan is easier to visualize, more adaptable to change, if necessary, and easier to keep track of with limited human and mechanical resources.

The objectives of the new approach were succinct and clear: to achieve a substantial breakthrough in domestic agriculture, to step up the tempo of industrial development, to improve the economic infrastructure, and to train and orient the country's

Table 19. Gross Domestic Product of Ceylon[1], 1965 and 1971
(in millions of rupees)[2]

Sector	1965		1971		Average annual rate of growth[3]
	Price	Percent	Price	Percent	Percent
Agriculture	3,062	41.4	3,996	39.7	4.5
Production for export.	1,572	21.2	1,883	18.7	3.0
Production for domestic use.	1,490	20.2	2,113	21.0	6.0
Paddy (rice)	358	.....	643	.....	....
Fisheries	147	.....	294	.....	....
Others	985	.....	1,176	.....	....
Manufacturing, mining, and construction.	1,087	14.7	1,824	18.1	9.0
Services	3,255	44.0	4,240	42.1	4.5
Total[4]	7,404	100.0	10,060	100.0	5.2

[1] By economic sectors, at 1965 factor-cost prices; 1971 figures are projected.
[2] Before November 20, 1967, Rs4.76 equaled US$1; thereafter, Rs5.95 have equaled US$1.
[3] Compound average.
[4] Gross domestic product.

Source: Adapted from Ceylon, Ministry of Planning and Economic Affairs, *The Development: Programme, 1966-67*, Colombo, 1966, p. 10.

human resources toward development. The objectives were tentatively and quantitatively embodied in the following annual growth rates projected in the 1965-71 period: GDP, 5.2 percent per year; agriculture, 4.5 percent per year (export sector, 3 percent and domestic agriculture sector, 6 percent); industry (manufacturing, mining, and construction), 9 percent; and services, 4.5 percent (see table 19). These growth rates would depend on new investment averaging 13.5 percent annually.

CHAPTER 19

AGRICULTURE

In 1968, the most recent year for which figures are available, the agricultural sector (including forestry and livestock) accounted directly for about 40 percent of the gross national product (GNP), over 50 percent of the labor force, and 95 percent of the country's foreign exchange earnings. If account were also taken of the transportation, banking, and other services that immediately cater to agriculture, the overall contribution of the agricultural sector to the economy would have been well above 50 percent. Imports of foodstuffs, which in Ceylon are largely a function of the unusual organization of the agricultural sector, in 1966 constituted some 47 percent of total imports and could be viewed as being wholly responsible for the foreign trade deficit.

The agricultural sector is sharply divided between a clearly defined, geographically restricted, and mostly large-scale and technologically sophisticated plantation sector on the one hand and a countrywide, small-scale traditional subsistence economy on the other. The plantation sector, which produces mostly for export, is based on tea, rubber, and coconuts. The subsistence economy is organized around the staple foodstuff rice (paddy—see Glossary), subsidiary food crops, and garden vegetables and is domestically financed, in large part by government subvention.

From the 1840s until the early years of independence, the economy was shaped and powered by the export-oriented plantation sector. By the mid-1950s, however, the plantation sector was in trouble, and the situation had shown little improvement in 1970. World market prices were declining, but unit costs were rising because many of the trees were over age. Although new plant varieties, with twice the yield potential of existing plants, were available, the cost would be great, and it would perhaps not be easy to arrive at arrangements for financing that would be satisfactory to both the government and the planters.

Although the shortage of paddy land in the wet zone (see Glossary) did not promise to be immediately relieved, the malaria eradication program of the 1940s that had resulted in a population explosion in the wet zone had at the same time opened up to exploitation large sections of the dry zone, where the malaria infestation had been most virulent. Government experts have estimated that in the dry zone there are some 5.6 million acres of good land, plus an additional 1.5 million acres that could be made economically exploitable. Of this total, they estimated that over 3 million acres would be suitable for agricultural exploitation.

In 1966 the government introduced a five-year agricultural development program for the 1966–70 period that was designed to increase efficiency in both agricultural sectors. The government announced that there would be a followup six-year program beginning in 1971 (see ch. 18, Character and Structure of the Economy). Although the general parameters of the agricultural sector are more or less fixed, there is a good deal of flexibility and room for maneuver built into them. Given social stability in the subsistence sector and some improvement both in costs and prices of the export sector and in the attempts to contain the population explosion, the authorities seem justified in viewing the agricultural sector during the next period with some optimism.

PROGRESS OF AGRICULTURE IN CEYLON

The situation of agriculture in 1970 continued to be conditioned by three major historical developments. The first was the retreat of the Sinhalese kingdom after 1200 from the northern dry zone to the wet zone of the south and southwest (see ch. 3, Historical Setting). The introduction in the 1840s of large-scale plantation agriculture was the second development. The third was the conquest of malaria in the years immediately after World War II.

The subsistence farmer continues to carry on three traditional types of cultivation: the cultivation of *aswaddumized* paddy (rice grown on flooded flatland); the cultivation of supplementary household fruits and vegetables on those parts of his holdings not suitable for paddy; and stock grazing and *chena* (slash-and-burn cultivation—see Glossary) on areas beyond the village perimeter. For more than 1,000 years successive civilizations based on this sort of farming flourished in the northern dry zone, centered first on Anuradhapura and then on Polonnaruwa.

For a growing population geared to paddy, the northern dry zone region, with its limited rainfall, presented enormous problems of water logistics. Agriculture depended upon irrigation and, as the population grew, increasingly upon a massive network of canals and dammed-up streambeds and depressions, called tanks, to impound the waters of the short-lived rainy season. In the twelfth century, for a complex of reasons that are not entirely clear, the Sinhalese gradually moved south and west (see ch. 3, Historical Setting). They took with them their established social and land tenure relationships.

For the farming population, the movement into the hill country of the southwest meant the need to adapt to methods of cultivation based on monsoon-fed water abundance in lowland river valleys and mid- and low-country streambeds. This involved more effort in clearing the land and keeping it cleared but less dependence on a central government and more security and freedom of action at the village level. The general framework of farming practices, however, remained the same: production based on paddy grown on the flatlands, supplemented by garden and *chena* production of vegetables, fruits, curry spices, and tree crops on areas too high or too rough for paddy. It was into this traditional subsistence agriculture that rudimentary cash crop and plantation concepts were introduced by the Portuguese, Dutch, and British who, in the sixteenth through the nineteenth centuries, successively took control of the northern, southern, and western coastal plains and, ultimately, the interior.

In the 1830s and 1840s coffee, which had been introduced by the Dutch but had been unable to compete in the London markets with the West Indian product, was abruptly projected into an effectively competitive position by cost increases in the West Indies and tariff policy changes in London. Coffee as a plantation crop benefits from altitude and requires large amounts of capital and much hand labor. In order to stimulate production, the government made available on a virtually subsidized basis large amounts of unused land in the upland areas of the southwest, to which it had in theory fallen heir when the former kingdom of Kandy became part of the colony in 1815. In 1840, by means of the Crown Lands Encroachment Ordinance, the government established that all lands belonged to the crown to which title could not clearly be proved by other persons. Although this did not affect established village lands, it did absorb the communal lands that had previously been used for *chena* cultivation.

With this land bank at its disposal, the government laid the groundwork for the large-scale plantation agriculture in Ceylon that was to characterize that country's economy for the next century. When, from the 1860s to the 1880s, coffee was wiped out by a fungus, the government shifted its policy to tea and rubber and, to a lesser extent, to coconuts. By the 1920s the government had made more than 1 million acres available to plantation agriculture.

The rapid expansion of plantation agriculture was halted by the worldwide depression of the 1930s and further inhibited by World War II. After the war it was affected by the exhaustion of the rubber plantations during the war, the consequences of the wartime development of synthetic rubber, the changes that accompanied the shift from colonial to independent status, and the impact of a rapid population growth. The malaria control campaign in the mid-1940s precipitated a population explosion that, between 1946 and 1970, raised the population from 6.6 million to 12.5 million, one result of which has been an increasing pressure on the available land in the villages and a consequent reduction in the size of per capita holdings.

In the wet zone the effect has been to push the limits of the village holdings up against the holdings of the tea and rubber plantations, except in areas that are too rough for effective cultivation, and to create a critical shortage of arable land for the villages in the well-watered areas of the south and west. In the north, on the other hand, large areas that were unpopulated or underpopulated because of the previously high incidence of malaria still belonged to the government, and the malaria campaign had the effect of making such government lands available for colonization once they were cleared and irrigation facilities restored by the government. Extensive government efforts have been directed to this end, and large numbers of farmers from the more heavily populated areas of the south and west have been given holdings in rehabilitated regions of the northern dry zone.

LAND UTILIZATION

The Hunting Survey

Although agricultural censuses were made in 1946, 1952, and 1962, they were limited in purpose and did not provide an overall picture of the land and water resources and their uses. In 1961, however, as an aspect of Canada's technical assistance to Ceylon in the framework of the Colombo Plan, a survey of the use of the island's physical resources was drafted by the Hunting Survey Corporation Ltd., based on a 1956 aerial photographic survey of the whole country.

The survey indicated that, of the country's total area of 16.2 million acres, some 4.8 million (29 percent) were under permanent cultivation; 2.5 million, or 15.1 percent, under *chena* cultivation; 7.2 million, or 44 percent, under forest cover; and 1.1 million acres, or 6.4 percent, under various kinds of grasses (see table 20). Some 81,000 acres comprised swamp and marshland; about 155,000 acres, or 1 percent, unused lands; and almost 500,000 acres, or 3.2 percent, covered by water. Of the total area, approximately 23 percent was included in the wet zone, about 63 percent was in the dry zone, and the balance fell into an area that the survey labeled "intermediate," since it included both the wet and dry zones. The three-

Table 20. Land Utilization in Ceylon, by Zones, 1961
(area in thousands of acres)

Land Use	Zones			Total	
	Wet	Inter-mediate	Dry	Acres	Percent
Permanent Cultivation					
Cropland					
Paddy	384	249	630	1,262	7.8
Other	4	22	121	147	0.9
Subtotal	388	271	751	1,409	8.7
Tree Crops					
Tea	563	73	.....	636	3.9
Rubber	534	28	.....	562	3.5
Coconut	231	288	100	619	3.8
Other	53	8	72	133	0.7
Subtotal	1,381	397	172	1,950	11.9
Homestead gardens	842	327	280	1,448	9.0
Total	2,611	995	1,203	4,807	29.6
Slash-and-burn cultivation (*chena*).	247	625	1,583	2,455	15.1
Improved permanent pasture.	2	1	3	6	....
Unimproved grass and scrubland.	185	151	717	1,052	6.4
Forest					
High yield	29	.....	.....	29	0.2
Medium yield	117	19	376	512	3.1
Low yield	259	131	3,130	3,520	21.7
Nonproductive	158	171	2,692	3,021	18.7
Other	56	13	15	84	0.5
Total	619	151	6,213	7,166	44.2
Swamp and marshland	26	5	49	81	0.5
Unused land	37	9	109	155	1.0
Saltern (salt manufacture) ...	.....	.....	6	6	....
Water	40	33	424	497	3.2
Grand total	3,767	2,153	10,307	16,225	100.0

Source: Adapted from Ceylon, Department of Census and Statistics, *Census of Agriculture, 1962,* II, Ceylon, 1966, pp. 250–252.

way breakdown of water distribution was a refinement designed by the surveyors to make future planning of land resource utilization more exact and predictable.

Of the land under permanent cultivation in 1961, which included cropland (rice and other annual crops), land under plantation (tree crops), and homestead gardens, the survey indicated that some 75 percent was in the wet and intermediate zones and about 25 percent was in the dry zone. *Chena* cultivation, on the other hand, was predominantly in the dry zone, as were the grass, scrub, and forest lands. Although forest covered almost half the country, only about 0.2 percent and 3.1 percent of the forests were characterized as of high and intermediate yield, respectively. The study further indicated that approximately 70 percent of the land in the wet zone was under permanent cultivation, whereas in the dry zone only some 11.6 percent was in 1956 being cultivated on a permanent basis.

The Agricultural Census of 1962

The 1962 agricultural census was concerned solely with land under cultivation, which was divided into agricultural holdings. These were defined as the land included in the aggregate agricultural operations carried on by a single individual or enterprise, whether he was owner, lessee, or sharecropper, whether he operated one or more parcels of land, and whatever aspect of permanent agriculture he was engaged in. The lower cutoff limit of an agricultural holding was one-eighth of an acre, with the exception of a few cases of horticulture and livestock raising. There was no upper cutoff limit. The holdings were divided into estates (plantations containing more than fifty acres) and small holdings (having less than fifty acres). The estates were enumerated individually by mail, but the small holdings were handled by specially trained enumerators, on the basis of a carefully designed sample consisting of 10 percent of the small holdings.

The 1962 census showed a total agriculture area of 4,666,551 acres, 3.11 million in the wet zone and 1.56 million in the dry zone, distributed among 1,169,801 holdings (see table 21). The holdings were divided between 5,872 estates, with a combined acreage totaling 1,540,572 acres, and 1,163,929 small holdings totaling 3,125,979 acres.

During the sixteen-year interval between the 1946 and 1962 censuses, the total population increased by 3,785,661; the estimated area under cultivation, by 399,155 acres; and the estimated number of holdings, by around 300,000. In addition,

Table 21. Landholdings in Ceylon, by Number and Size, 1962

Size class of holding	Total number of holdings	Ratio to total holdings	Acres (in size class)	Ratio to total acres	Acres cropped	Ratio to total acres (in size class)	Cultivable (idle)	Acres Plantation crops[1]	Paddy
Holdings without land	3,490	0.30	.....	.....	.....	.....	.....	.....	.....
Under ¼ acre	91,780	7.85	14,160	0.30	8,520	60.17	800	4,760	660
¼ to under ½ acre	136,360	11.66	43,560	0.94	33,340	76.54	2,500	17,950	3,280
½ to under 1 acre	182,260	15.58	118,810	2.55	99,070	83.38	5,590	48,220	21,210
1 to under 2½ acres	350,262	29.94	541,190	11.62	477,991	86.69	27,950	210,611	147,780
2½ to under 5 acres	221,593	18.94	763,561	16.40	689,139	90.25	39,230	252,456	299,901
5 to under 10 acres	132,408	11.32	852,396	18.31	753,553	88.40	57,797	252,388	378,232
10 to under 25 acres	37,465	3.20	530,219	11.39	479,103	90.36	26,328	243,205	185,835
25 to 50 acres	8,311	0.71	262,083	5.63	234,467	89.67	12,574	170,561	50,816
50 to under 100 acres	2,811	0.24	192,024	4.12	172,181	87.62	7,922	150,561	14,669
100 to under 250 acres	1,654	0.14	246,632	5.30	216,103	84.25	10,244	194,292	13,490
250 to under 500 acres	643	0.05	224,230	4.82	188,907	75.10	8,356	175,800	7,474
500 acres and over	764	0.07	877,686	18.85	659,128	.....	34,757	602,511	11,841
Total	1,169,801	100.00	4,666,551	[2]100.23	4,011,502	.....	234,048	2,323,315	1,135,188

[1]Tea, rubber, coconut, cacao, and cinnamon.
[2]Column does not total 100 because of rounding.

Source: Adapted from Ceylon, Department of Statistics, Census of Agriculture, 1962, II, Ceylon, 1966, pp. 22-27.

although total agricultural land increased by only some 400,000 acres, agricultural land in the dry zone increased by about 955,640 acres. This suggested that the rapid increase of urban population in the wet zone absorbed sizable amounts of erstwhile agricultural land , that considerable amounts of land in the wet zone had, for other reasons, gone out of cultivation, and, perhaps, that the comparability between the two censuses was in this respect especially tenuous.

The most significiant finding was that, whereas total agricultural land had increased an estimated 9.4 percent between 1946 and 1962, the population had shot up practically 60 percent. The average number of acres of agricultural land per capita, therefore, had decreased from an estimated 0.64 acre per head in 1946 to an estimated 0.45 acre in 1962, and the size of an average agricultural holding had declined over the period from 3.3 acres to 2.7 acres. The proportion of agricultural land to the total area of the country was estimated at 29.2 percent.

Thus, in 1962 the wet zone, taking into consideration its topography, its population density, and the legal ban against putting under crops new land above 5,000 feet, was for practical purposes farmed up. By contrast, most of the dry zone area was still under forest or other uncultivated cover. The pronounced difference between the two regions in this respect reflected chiefly the relative availability of water in the two regions. It also reflected, however, the lack of training in, and experience with, dry farming on the part of the Sinhalese farmer and the circumstance that only in the late 1940s had the dry zone ceased to be one of the most malaria-ridden areas of the country and, therefore, to be the most avoided.

Of the 4.67 million acres of agricultural land tabulated in 1962, 4,013,502 acres (including those under grass) were actively being cultivated as follows: paddy rice, 1.1 million acres (28.3 percent); temporary crops, 0.2 million acres (4.2 percent); plantation crops, 2.3 million acres (57.9 percent); other crops, 0.4 million acres (8.8 percent); and grassland, 0.03 million acres. The actual distribution was probably less precise than the breakdown suggested, inasmuch as land that was under two crops at the same time (for example, grass or cassava being grown on the same land as coconuts) was only included under the heading of the principal crop. In the case of paddy rice land, land lying fallow or temporarily under some other crop was included in the paddy column. The census breakdown, thus, was somewhat of a misstatement, and it understated the production of minor crops.

The 1.17 million holdings tabulated in 1962 were distributed by size among graduated size classes ranging from less than one-fourth of an acre to more than 500 acres. Some 3,490 holdings engaged in horticulture or livestock and including less acreage than the one-eighth-acre lower limit were enumerated as holdings without land.

About 8 percent of the total holdings contained less than one-fourth of an acre each, and 35 percent of the total holdings had less than òne acre. More than 95 percent had less than ten acres, and 99.5 percent of all holdings contained less than fifty acres.

The census indicated that, of the total 4.67 million acres tabulated, 3.18 million acres were operated by the owner of the land or by his paid representative. Of these 3.18 million acres, 1.42 million were in the estate sector. In the small-holding sector 1.76 million acres were reported as owner operated. Some 280,000 acres were reported to be operated by share-croppers; 610,000 acres, under special grants of crown (public) land; 230,000 acres, under some other form of lease; and 250,000 acres, as squatters or under other form of rent-free arrangement.

Land Utilization Committee Report

In 1966, after publication of the soil and resource maps that derived from a survey conducted by the Hunting Survey Corporation Ltd. and the results of the 1962 agricultural census, the government created the Land Utilization Committee to study in detail the natural resources available for agricultural, livestock, and forestry exploitation and development. The committee was to determine how effectively the country's resources were actually being utilized and to recommend what measures should be taken in order to maximize the exploitation of land and water resources and what policy should be adopted regarding the future disposal of public lands, of which there were still in the government's possession more than 10 million acres.

The committee's report, which was released in 1968 under the title *Report of the Land Utilization Committee, August 1967*, laid down a long list of recommendations. These featured more precise planning and administration of all land and water resources; more careful protection and rehabilitation of those resources; and more intensive exploitation of, and greater productivity from, resources currently being utilized before undertaking the exploitation of hitherto unused resources. The committee advised concentration upon the dry zone and the return of marginal and unprotected areas of the wet zone to grass and forest. The committee recommended that more attention be given to the domestic production of substitutes for imported consumer foodstuffs and that closer coordination be developed between complementary activities of agriculture and industries based on agriculture.

The committee's report stated that there was "no general base of settled arable farming in Ceylon in the conventional sense of the word as used in other countries of Asia. . . ." From the 1920s on, various attempts had been made to explore the possibilities of replacing the *chena* method of cultivation with one based on settled dry farming, as in southern and central India. Up to the end of the 1960s these attempts indicated that the peasant farmer in Ceylon could not successfully farm small holdings (three to five acres) in the dry zone based on rainfall alone. The evidence, on the other hand, had indicated that large-area cultivation of rain fed grain crops, together with some pulses, soybeans, and castor beans, appears practicable in the major monsoon season. In the lesser monsoon season, some short-season crops, such as gingelly, sorghum, and cowpea, can be grown under rain fed conditions; however, this season is more efficiently used for onion, chilies, peanuts, pulses, soybeans, and cotton, all under irrigation.

LAND TENURE

The traditional Sinhalese agricultural system was based on small villages. These were apparently inhabited, at least in the first instance, by extended families or caste groups (see ch. 6, Social Structure). It was a subsistence economy, the staple of which was rice. Landholdings tended originally to be of a size that could be cultivated by a single family. Tenure appears to have been in the first instance either by right of seizure or as a reward for services to the feudal overlord.

The village usually lay on the down side of a pond or reservoir, an artificial body of water formed by damming a stream flowing (perhaps only during the rainy season) through a ravine or small valley. The cultivable land surrounding the body of water belonged to the village. Land lying below the level of the water was paddy land. It was leveled and divided by mud ridges into plots according to the ownership pattern of the village, and at the onset of the rainy season it was flooded, the soil broken up, and then planted to paddy rice. In the north usually only one crop of paddy rice was planted per year.

Areas adjacent to the reservoir that were too high for flooding but still fertile were also divided according to the ownership pattern of the village. There the villagers mostly had their house plots, with land for raising garden vegetables, fruits, coconuts, and other tree crops. In addition, the village enjoyed communal grazing and *chena* rights in the uncleared areas beyond the confines of the village proper. In such areas the cultivator could clear a plot of land, burn it over, raise some supplementary food or barter crops and, when the fertility of the plot was exhausted, move on to repeat the operation, leaving the first plot for a period of a dozen or more years to rejuvenate itself. Since neither the population nor the rate of population increase was great, this did not involve a major destructive intrusion upon the forest resources of the region.

Upon the death of a landowner, his land was generally divided equally among his children, whether male or female, and for the most part it was incumbent upon them not to sell the land outside the family, clan, or village. Each heir might crop his own portion of the land, or they might take turns cropping the whole of the inheritance in rotation. Alternatively, the land might be cultivated by a sharecropper. The relative shares of the production of the land were determined by negotiation, but the sharecropper was not likely to get more than half of the crop and, as the pressure of population increased, his bargaining position deteriorated. The owner might put up, as part of his share, seed and other inputs, depending upon the arrangement. As a third possibility, the land might be worked for wages by landless members of the cultivator class.

This traditional agriculture and land tenure system was transported by the Sinhalese as they slowly spread over the south and west. The system was perpetuated in the kingdom of Kandy until the 1830s, when various measures introduced by the British began the erosion of the system that in 1970 was still in process. The tempo of this process was greatly increased by the rapid population growth of the 1950s and 1960s, which had the effect of reducing the size of an average holding to approximately an acre. Because that figure is an average of holdings ranging in size from one-eighth of an acre to more than 500 acres, it conceals the existence of many holdings that are too small to engage the full efforts of the typical agricultural family or even to feed it.

Because of the social superiority of the cultivator caste, however, members of that caste who have very little land or none at all are loath to seek other occupations (see ch. 6, Social Structure). Consequently, in the Sinhalese farming communities of the wet zone, and especially in the ultraconservative hinterland, the increasingly numerous underemployed or landless agriculturists are seeking some or more land (see ch. 14, Political Dynamics). The situation has been less acute in areas of Tamil concentration because of the greater availability of cultivable land near at hand and because the technology of farming such dry zone land is one with which these cultivators are acquainted.

In earlier times a solution to the problem of population pressure on the land would have been sought in the communal land beyond the outskirts of the village. This recourse, however, was largely eliminated by the Crown Lands Encroachment Ordinance, by which more than 1 million acres were transferred to large-scale private ownership from what might be called the buffer area of the traditional subsistence sector of the wet zone.

This official land policy was reversed by the Land Development Ordinance of 1935, in favor of one actively devoted to benefiting the Sinhalese peasant. The new policy forbade the future transfer of crown lands for purposes of cultivation except to enlarge the landholdings of near-landless or totally landless peasant farmers.

Measures adopted by the government to implement the Land Development Ordinance have included emphasis on family planning, government subsidies to stimulate the production of foodstuffs, expropriation of foreign-owned estates for distribution to peasants, and colonization projects. The government has also provided explicit land reform measures to protect tenants and small owners from exploitation by landlords, moneylenders, and speculators.

The most successful of the government's measures have been the Guaranteed Price Scheme and the colonization efforts. Under the Guaranteed Price Scheme, the government has undertaken to purchase, at fixed and profitable prices, either directly or through cooperatives, all the rice and other foodstuffs offered to it. This scheme has been backstopped by measures by government agencies in cooperation with foreign agencies to make available to paddy farmers improved inputs (including credit, marketing, and storage facilities) and improved techniques of paddy cultivation. Concurrently, colonization projects have been undertaken to increase the amount of cultivable land, mainly by restoring or enlarging the irrigation facilities in the dry zone.

In 1958 the Paddy Lands Bill was enacted mainly to benefit the tenant-cultivators of some 400,000 acres of paddy land. The bill purported to assist tenants to purchase the land they worked, to protect them against eviction, and to establish a rent ceiling at around 25 percent of the crop.

The bill also established cultivation committees, composed of paddy farmers, to assume general responsibility for paddy cultivation in their respective areas, including responsibility for the direction and control of irrigation in minor irrigation projects. In its original form, the Paddy Lands Bill was in conflict with existing legislation and was, in effect, not administered. As subsequently amended, the bill in 1970 was believed to be achieving its purpose.

Although it is true that in most parts of the dry zone irrigation would be necessary for the cultivation of paddy and other food crops, it is also true that paddy is most efficiently grown under irrigation. Furthermore, in the case of rice, as of tea, rubber, wheat, and other crops, new varieties are becoming available that, if used, will appreciably increase yields. This would not only result in increased consumption, a major desideratum, but also, and scarcely less important from the overall viewpoint of the economy, in partial or complete elimination of rice imports.

CROPPING PATTERN

Agricultural production falls into four categories: major export crops, minor export crops, rice, and supplementary (minor) food crops. The annual food crops, especially rice, are further broken down into *maha* (big monsoon—see Glossary) and *yala* (lesser monsoon—see Glossary) crops; the former are sown between July and November and harvested five to six months later; the latter are sown between February and June and harvested about four months later.

Major Export Crops

Tea

Tea is the largest export crop, and Ceylon is second only to India in the free world's production of tea. Ceylon tea is a high-grade black tea. The plants, originally imported from Assam in India, are grown in the wet zone at low, middle, and high altitudes. The higher altitudes produce the best tea, and terracing is used to eke out the limited quantities of upper altitude land. In 1968 approximately 597,490 acres were planted to tea. Production totaled 496 million pounds for an average yield of 848 pounds per acre (see table 22). This yield compares favorably with an estimated average yield of 713 pounds per acre in 1959, reflecting the growing use of fertilizers over the intervening period. On the other hand, it compared unfavorably with yields of 2,000 to 4,000 pounds per acre available from newer varieties.

The 1962 census of agriculture concluded that some 82 per-

Table 22. Volume of Production of Major and Minor Crops in Ceylon, Selected Years, 1959-69

Major crops	1959	1962	1964	1965	1966	1967	1968	1969
Tea								
Production (million pounds)	413	467	482	503	490	487	496	512
Area (thousand acres)	580	591	592	594	596	599	597	n.a.
Average yield (pounds per acre)	713	790	814	814	873	829	848	n.a.
Rubber								
Production (thousand tons)	91	102	110	116	129	141	146	152
Area (thousand acres)	668	674	669	567	568	572	573	n.a.
Average yield (pounds per acre)	382	434	463	590	618	643	671	n.a.
Coconuts								
Production (million nuts)	2,306	2,811	3,000	2,681	2,486	2,421	2,643	2,800
Area (thousand acres)[1]	n.a.	1,152	1,152	1,152	1,152	1,152	1,152	n.a.
Average yield (nuts per acre)	n.a.	2,240	2,600	2,330	2,160	2,100	2,290	n.a.
Paddy (rice)								
Production (million bushels)	36	48	50	36	46	55	65	71
Gross area harvested (thousand acres).	1,203	1,492	1,535	1,243	1,512	1,567	1,634	n.a.
Average yield (bushels per acre)	35.0	37.9	38.6	34.1	35.9	40.8	47.5	51.2

Minor crops[2]

Chilies	n.a.	n.a.	n.a.	n.a.	13	32	75	128
Onions	n.a.	n.a.	n.a.	n.a.	422	516	680	843
Potatoes	n.a.	n.a.	n.a.	n.a.	53	147	209	600
Peanuts	n.a.	n.a.	n.a.	n.a.	150	173	298	n.a.
Manioc	n.a.	n.a.	n.a.	n.a.	5,693	7,544	8,550	n.a.
Milk (million pints)	n.a.	n.a.	n.a.	n.a.	285	276	295	n.a.
Eggs (millions)	n.a.	n.a.	n.a.	n.a.	384	385	396	n.a.
Cinnamon	n.a.	n.a.	n.a.	n.a.	54	61	79	n.a.
Tobacco	n.a.	n.a.	n.a.	n.a.	n.a.	127	119	n.a.
Cotton	n.a.	n.a.	n.a.	n.a.	35	32	35	n.a.

n.a.—not available.

[1] Because the year to year changes in the area under coconuts are difficult to determine, the area as tabulated by the 1962 agricultural census has been retained in subsequent years.

[2] In hundred-weight or tons unless otherwise specified.

Source: Adapted from Ceylon, Department of Commerce, *The Ceylon Trade Journal*, Colombo, June 1969, p. 305.

cent of the tea cropped in that year was grown on plantations of more than fifty acres in size. Tea cultivation is meticulous and time consuming, requiring constant and skilled attention of about one worker per acre. For these reasons tea is most efficiently grown on estates, based on large capital investment and having a highly organized and disciplined management and labor supply.

Because the Sinhalese peasant farmer has generally refused to engage in estate labor, the labor supply for the tea industry from its inception has been provided by Indian Tamil (see Glossary) immigrants residing on the estates. On the large establishments the tea is processed in the estate's factory; smaller estates use the large estates' factories. The finished product is sold at auctions, mainly in Colombo and London.

During the 1960s the world market demand for tea tended to rise at only around 1 percent a year. By the late 1960s most of the trees had passed their prime, resulting in higher production costs. At the same time, world prices continued to decline under the impact of the greater quantities being produced, with the increased use of fertilizers, in the struggle to reduce costs by raising output.

Increasingly available are new high-yielding clonal varieties that could produce perhaps twice as much as the existing trees. The drawback is the cost of replanting, which the large planters have been hesitant to undertake in the absence of assurance that the plantations would not be nationalized or taxed out of profitable existence before the investment has been recouped. The smaller growers, on the other hand, are not always fully aware of the new technology.

Since 1959 and 1962, respectively, the government has had plans for subsidizing the planting of new trees on tea lands and also on rubber lands not properly suited to rubber, but the subsidy was insufficient to overcome fully the reluctance of the large planters. During the late 1960s the government made available loans of up to Rs2,000 (for value of rupee, see Glossary) per acre on easy terms, in addition to a subsidy of Rs3,750 per acre in order to induce the large planters to shift to the high-yielding varieties. From 1959 until the early part of 1969, some 27,000 acres, less than 5 percent of the total tea acreage, had been replanted to the new varieties, but the government in 1969 expressed the hope that the rate could be increased to 12,000 acres per year.

Some credit and subsidy assistance is also given to planters for the modernization of their factories, many of which have been allowed to become antiquated. Small-holding tea estates are given a 50 percent subsidy on fertilizer purchases in order to increase its use as a means of increasing output and lowering the unit costs on the small estates. In 1967 the government's desire to help the tea industry was a major consideration in the devaluation of the rupee.

A bright spot in the generally gloomy tea picture of the late 1960s was an apparently successful technological breakthrough in the search for a commercially practicable quality instant tea, and exports have increased rapidly since 1966. In 1968 the Land Utilization Committee report recommended that the tea industry should focus its attention on the high-altitude, high-quality teas, for which a dependable market exists, and should develop a market, chiefly in the United States, for quality instant tea.

Rubber

Rubber is the second most important export crop, and in 1970 Ceylon was the world's fourth largest exporter of natural rubber. Rubber trees were introduced onto the island in the 1870s and became an important export item as a result of the demands generated by the new automobile industry and World War I.

Rubber does best under plantation conditions in the wet zone at lower altitudes. Although the 1962 census indicated that some 40 percent of the rubber was grown on small holdings, rubber yields were found to be much higher under plantation conditions. Unlike the tea estates, most rubber plantations are domestically owned.

In 1968 an estimated 146,400 long tons of rubber were raised on 573,000 acres, compared with 102,400 long tons raised on 674,300 acres in 1962 and 91,000 long tons on 668,000 acres in 1959. The yield in 1968 was estimated at 671 pounds per acre compared with an estimated 434 pounds per acre in 1962.

The increase in yields between 1962 and 1968 reflected the growing use of fertilizers and the introduction of new plant varieties, in order to offset declining prices with lower costs. Forced, or so-called slaughter, tapping of the rubber trees during World War II and the Korean conflict caused irreparable damage to many trees. Therefore, since 1953 the government has subsidized, at a rate of Rs1,400 per acre for estates and Rs1,500 per acre for small holdings, a replanting program intended to restore and increase the productivity of the rubber plantations by replacing existing plant varieties with new, high-yield, clonal types, which are disease resistant and have more than twice the productivity potential of the older varieties. By the end of 1968 some 264,000 acres had been replanted with the new kind of plants. The government also

341

subsidized the sales of seedlings and fertilizers to small holders.

As in the case of tea, the raw material is processed locally and, also as in the case of tea, the processing facilities have been allowed to deteriorate. The government is prepared to assist in the renovation of these facilities, preferably on the basis of introducing a new process, already underway in Malaya, for making the crumb type of rubber instead of the traditional forms of smoked sheets and latex crepe. The new type promises to be the form in which natural rubber will be demanded in the international markets, where Ceylon must compete both with the synthetics and with the natural product from Malaya, which has been cheaper because it is more efficiently produced.

In 1952 Ceylon and Communist China entered into the first of a series of five-year trade agreements, under which, in effect, Ceylon has exchanged rubber sheets for Chinese rice on terms favorable to Ceylon. The agreement was renewed in 1967 (see ch. 15, Foreign Relations). In 1968 some 60 percent of Ceylonese rubber went to Communist China under this agreement.

Coconuts

Coconuts, the third most important export, have been grown on the island for centuries. In 1968 about 1.15 million acres were under coconuts, an area nearly equal to the combined areas under tea and rubber, with an output estimated at 2.64 billion nuts, of which approximately one-half were exported. These figures compared with 1.15 million acres under coconuts and 2.8 billion nuts harvested in 1962. Estimated average yield showed little change between 1962 and 1968. The 1962 census estimated that almost 50 percent of the area in coconuts consisted of plots of less than 10 acres, but yields on estates appeared to run about twice those of the small holdings.

Coconuts are more widely grown geographically than tea or rubber. The principal coconut-growing districts in 1968 were Colombo, Kurunegala, and Chilaw; these districts, together with Kalutara, Galle, Matara, Hambantota, Puttalam, and Kegalla, accounted for approximately 90 percent of the total production.

In 1966 coconut exports included the following products: coconut oil, 57.5 percent; copra, 10.1 percent, dessicated coconut, 31.2 percent; and fresh nuts, 1.2 percent. In addition, the coconut is a household mainstay of the peasant, providing logs for construction, leaves for thatch and siding, coir for rope and rough textiles, shells for fuel and carving, and toddy and arrack for beverages.

Most of the island's coconut trees are more than fifty years old. Since 1956 the government has supported a two-pronged program to reduce costs and expand production. On the one hand, the government sells new high-yielding plant varieties at about 25 percent of cost; on the other, it provides fertilizers at about 50 percent of cost. In 1968 fertilizer sales, a government monopoly, were about evenly divided between estates and small holdings.

The Land Utilization Committee recommended study of the possibilities of combining the cultivation of other crops with that of coconuts. Experiments are being undertaken concerning the economic feasibility of planting coffee or cocoa or, alternatively, pasture under coconut trees and of intercropping coconuts with pineapples.

Minor Export Crops

Among the crops raised both for export and local consumption are cardamom, cinnamon, citronella oil, cloves, cocoa, coffee, nutmeg, and pepper. In 1968 the most important in export terms were cinnamon, cocoa, and cardamom. Accurate information in connection with these crops is difficult to come by, owing to the amount of intercropping. Data available in fiscal year 1965/66 indicated that acreage under cultivation of some crops was as follows: cocoa, 50,000; coffee, 3,000 to 5,000; cinnamon, 33,000; cardamom, 5,300; pepper, 10,600; and cloves and nutmeg, 2,000 to 3,000. Yields vary widely and are low. Some approximations, per acre, were as follows: cocoa, 100 pounds; coffee, 100 pounds of dried beans; cinnamon, 100 to 200 pounds; cardamom, 66 to 150 pounds; and pepper, 50 to 100 pounds.

With the exception of cocoa and coffee, these crops received little attention until the 1960s. In 1964 the Cocoa Planting Subsidy Scheme was introduced to underwrite replanting old and diseased cocoa plants with disease-free, high-yielding plant varieties. Initially, the project received little support from the planters, because of decreases in cocoa prices in the early 1960s. Subsequent changes in the program and upward movements in world prices increased the attractiveness of the scheme.

In connection with the other crops, an increasing amount of research is devoted to their disease problems, the development of high-yielding varieties, and the use of fertilizers. The development of these crops tends, however, to be determined by shortrun price movements, despite the fact that the crops are perennial rather than annual. The inclusion of most of these crops in the government's 1966 decision to subsidize minor exports tended to raise the prices received by the growers and will be likely to have the effect of inducing increased output. Output of crops, such as coffee, that are raised more for local consumption than for export and that are also imported will be affected by changes in basic import policies, as well as by world market prices.

Rice

The production of rice, the staple food of most of the population, is the core of the subsistence sector of the economy. Under the pressure of population growth, it was formerly the central focus of government preoccupation with agriculture. Rice is typically a small holder's hand-grown crop; nearly 85 percent of all paddy holdings contain less than two acres; 60 percent, less than one acre; and 31 percent, less than half an acre. It is generally sown by hand broadcast. After a month or so the seedlings are thinned and weeded by hand, under water, and thereafter allowed to grow to maturity without much further care, except against predators. Harvesting and threshing engage the family, plus all available friends and relations, and is attended and followed by ritual.

Because no completely perennial sources of water exist, there is some uncertainty regarding the adequacy of the supply each year. In the wet zone the uncertainty may show up in flooding and waterlogging, whereas in the dry zone even the irrigated areas are subject to the possibility of insufficient water. In the mid- and up-country wet zone areas, most of the available acreage is sown twice a year; in the dry zone, most holdings are sown only once; and in the low-country wet zone, the amount of flooding and waterlogging determines whether to plant once or twice.

In fiscal year 1967/68 the acreage planted to paddy totaled 1.74 million acres, of which 1.15 million acres were planted during the 1967–68 *maha* season and 595,511 acres during the 1968 *yala* season. Output totaled 64.6 million bushels, compared with a previous record of 50.5 million in fiscal year 1964/65 and 36.3 million in fiscal year 1965/66. Average yields in the *maha* season of 1967–68 and the *yala* season of 1968 were 47.5 and 44.5 bushels per acre, respectively, compared with 34.1 and 34.7 bushels per acre, respectively, in the *maha* season of 1964–65 and the *yala* season of 1965. Total output for 1969 was estimated at 71.3 million bushels, with a *maha* season yield of 51.2 bushels per acre. The targets for 1970 were 75 million bushels, with a *maha* season yield of 52.2 bushels per acre.

In the early 1950s Ceylon evolved its own high-yield hybrid, which in 1968 accounted for about 75 percent of the total area under paddy. Other varieties have been developed for certain areas of the country and to meet special demands. Experimentation begun in 1966 with the Philippine dwarf varieties has shown considerable promise. Concurrently with the increased use of improved seed, there has been more attention to improved cultural practices, including transplanting, row seeding, and mechanical tillage, as well as fertilization.

Since 1957 the government has maintained a Guaranteed Price Scheme for paddy, under which it has stood ready to purchase the farmer's entire crop at a price that was deemed to offer a profit to most producers. In addition, the government has increasingly made certified seed available to the farmer at prices that are virtually subsidized.

At the end of the 1960s the demand for fertilizers was growing rapidly but in usage was only about 25 percent of the amount recommended by the technicians. Shortages of storage and marketing facilities continued. Perhaps most important was the need of greater credit and administrative services and coordination of them. Given these services, however, and foreseeable improvements in plant materials, knowledgeable observers considered that the government's original rice production target of 70 million bushels in 1970 was not unduly optimistic.

Subsidiary Food Crops and Tobacco

Subsistence food crops include chilies, red onions, Bombay onions, potatoes, pulses, maize (corn), sugar, and curry spices, most of them imported. The desirability of increasing the production of these crops included the multiple purposes of diversifying the nonpeasant, nonplantation private sector, increasing the cash crops of the peasants, and reducing imports. Until the mid-1960s, however, a base for any rapid expansion of the subsidiary food crops had not been developed except on the Jaffna Peninsula where chilies, onions, and tobacco were grown under irrigation. Elsewhere these crops had been grown by *chena* cultivation.

In 1968 the Land Utilization Committee concluded that an estimated 300,000 acres throughout the country were devoted to nonsubsistence, non-large-estate cultivation. Of these, some 50,000 acres were in vegetables, tobacco, chilies, potatoes, and onions under settled farming conditions mainly in the mid- and up-country zones (Badulla, Nuwara Eliya, Kandy, and Matale) and to a lesser extent in Jaffna and Vanuniya. About 100,000 acres were in minor export tree crops. Most of the other 150,000 acres were under *chena* cultivation in the dry zone.

The Land Utilization Committee also concluded that it would be practicable to raise domestically, mainly under conditions of dry zone irrigation, the quantities of supplementary food crops that were imported in 1966. The committee estimated that to do so would require around 325,000 acres, of which 150,000 to 175,000 acres would be for pulses, 100,000 for sugar, and 36,000 for chilies. Sugar was the largest of the import items in terms both of value and volume. The cultivation of sugarcane has not been successful, but in 1970 it was hoped that the crop would prove adaptable to conditions in one or more of the river valley development projects.

In 1966 the government planned to bring 40,000 acres of irrigated land under subsidiary food crops by 1971. Some 20,000 acres would be added by lift irrigation to existing colonization and youth settlement projects, 15,000 acres would be under major reservoir projects, and 5,000 acres would be under minor projects. By 1970 the country had achieved self-sufficiency in tobacco and was rapidly increasing the production of chilies, onions, potatoes, peanuts, and sweet potatoes.

Animal Husbandry

Up to the mid-1960s the limited development of animal husbandry was on the basis of small-scale operations, with the exception of a few private companies and government farms. The livestock population, as reflected in the 1962 census of agriculture, with the 1946 census tabulations in parentheses, showed the following: cattle, 1,363,785 (1,166,909); buffalo, 596,481 (410,418); goats and sheep, 309,906 (296,151); and pigs, 56,184 (63,301).

The census and a survey conducted by the Hunting Survey Corporation, Ltd. provided information on the basis of which the government formulated a program of livestock development. Specific areas and plans for such development were for the first time set out in the book *Agricultural Development Proposals, 1966-70*. These plans emphasized expansion of the government livestock farms to increase the availabilities of upgraded breeding stock, particularly of beef and buffalo for draft and milk purposes, but also of poultry, pigs, goats, and sheep. Ancillary services, such as research and veterinary services, were also emphasized.

Concurrently, prices to milk producers were raised to attractive levels for milk delivered to government-constructed sterilizing, processing, and packaging plants. Between 1965 and

1968 the government Milk Board increased its daily purchases of milk from about 40,000 pints to nearly 100,000 pints. Milk production in 1969 was estimated at around 700,000 pints per day.

Forestry

The Hunting Survey indicated that, although almost half of the country's area was under some sort of forest, little of the forest consisted of high-yield timber stands. The survey did indicate, however, where many of the best stands were. In line with those findings and with technical assistance from abroad, the government streamlined its organization for dealing with its forest resources and embarked upon a program designed to meet the lumber requirements of domestic plywood factories and other lumber installations. A program of reforestation was also undertaken under which, by 1970, about 21,000 acres were being planted annually. Estimates are that the timber yield of such reforestation will exceed forty times the yield of natural forest.

ROLE OF GOVERNMENT

Since independence in 1948 governmental activity in the agricultural sector has tended to be increasingly pervasive. The export sector was accustomed to importing its capital goods, its labor, and the food and supplies for its labor, but the subsistence sector had only the government to turn to when rising population and declining land resources available to it broke down the sector's ability to fend for itself.

Rural Credit

At independence the money economy was still largely a function of the export plantation sector, in which export profits had traditionally been sufficient to permit importing a considerable proportion of the foodstuffs, including rice, required by the monetized sector. Nor, before independence, had it been imperative to give much thought to the needs of the subsistence sector. All this was changed by the shipping shortage caused by World War II, by independence, and by the population explosion. As it became increasingly necessary to expand domestic production of foodstuffs, especially rice, the demand for credit by the subsistence sector became a growing problem. The instrument chosen to meet this demand was government subvention of cooperative societies, backed by an agricultural credit program, under which the government

347

would annually provide, through the cooperatives, up to Rs175 per acre to subsistence farmers, repayable at harvesttime.

In 1969 the Central Bank of Ceylon embarked on an in-depth study of the rural credit situation. In mid-1970 there was scant exact information, but it was generally agreed that the situation was economically precarious. The information available was from sample studies made by government agencies in 1957 and 1962, the latter in connection with the census of agriculture. The study reports were in general but not in detailed agreement. The 1957 study estimated that rural indebtedness totaled around Rs500 million and that almost half of it was owed to "undesirable sources of credit," presumably moneylenders. The same study estimated the annual credit needs of the peasant sector at about Rs220 million.

The study made in connection with the 1962 census led to estimates of annual credit needs of the subsistence sector at about Rs178 million. It reached this calculation on the basis of 1.7 million acres of paddy land, requiring an annual outlay of Rs250 per acre, of which Rs175 was in the form of credit, in accordance with the government's agricultural credit program. In 1967 the upper limit of the agricultural credit program was raised from Rs175 to Rs262 per acre, for up to a total of ten acres per cultivator. This would raise the rural credit needs, as estimated on the basis of the 1966 paddy acreage, to around Rs400 million.

The 1962 census study estimated that some 65 percent of peasant farming families were members of the government-financed cooperative societies. Of the 35 percent who were not, some 5 percent indicated they had their own resources, and 4 percent had other sources of credit, such as relatives and friends, that were cheaper or easier than the cooperatives. The remaining 25 percent who were not members of cooperatives gave such reasons as distance, lack of confidence in cooperatives, poverty, or oversight in explanation of their non-membership. They admitted, however, that, except for the cooperatives, they had no alternative source of credit other than the local or itinerant trader-moneylenders, who charged very high interest rates. The moneylenders frequently insisted on an option to purchase the debtor's crops at harvesttime; if they took up the option, it was generally at a sizable discount by comparison with the government's guaranteed prices.

Even in the case of the cultivator who did have access to cooperative financing, such access was limited to production loans. If, for any reason, he needed a consumption loan—for example, for illness or marriage of his daughter, or for capital improvements or debt redemption—he would have to

348

turn to the trader-moneylender. The available information suggests that the subsistence cultivator has tended to get into debt and not to be able to get out.

In 1957 measures were adopted to combine the services offered by various separate cooperatives in the same community into multipurpose societies that would offer the farmer credit, storage, marketing, and sometimes even collection services, as well as implement the government's credit program. In 1963 the agricultural credit scheme was expanded in order to improve the operations of the societies. The Guaranteed Price Scheme for rice was restricted to cooperative members, some minor crops were included in the guarantee, and the beneficiaries of the government credit program were expected to sell enough of their crop to the cooperative to cover their borrowings.

In 1967 the upper limit of borrowings under agricultural credit was raised from Rs175 per acre to Rs262 per acre, up to ten acres. At the same time, the source of financing for the cooperatives was transferred from the government to the banking system, in order to raise the rate of recovery of loans, expand the credit limits of cooperative financing, and expedite the processing of credit scheme loans. In addition, the guaranteed prices were raised.

In fiscal year 1966/67 the rural cooperative movement consisted of some 5,000 multipurpose societies, providing an expanded group of services and expressly designed to implement both the agricultural credit program and the guaranteed prices for rice and subsidiary food crops. Under its reorganization schedule, the credit program was expected to show a gradual increase in annual credit disbursements from Rs30.1 million in 1965/66 to Rs56.7 million in 1969/70. In point of fact, disbursements in 1967/68, covering both the *maha* and *yala* seasons, totaled Rs72.7 million and were expected to keep rising. This reflected improved administration, as well as rising output, greater credit facilities, and price increases.

Irrigation

At the end of 1968 about 880,000 acres were under irrigation for rice; some 446,000 acres under major storage reservoirs and barrages, and 434,000 acres in minor irrigation projects. In addition, more than 13,500 acres of irrigated river valley land were in sugar, and some 700 to 1,000 acres of highland were under low-lift pump irrigation.

Major irrigation projects are associated with colonization programs, either under large reservoirs or in river valley developments. They are carried out and controlled by the Irrigation Department of the Ministry of Agriculture and Food. The beneficiaries pay irrigation rates for the use of the water. In early 1969 most of the major projects were in the North Central Province.

Minor irrigation projects are apparently constructed by the Irrigation Department and then turned over to the cultivation committees, created under the Paddy Land Act of 1958, which subsequently are responsible for maintaining them. The benefiting farmers provide labor services in lieu of paying irrigation rates.

During the Five Year Development Plan (1966-70) it was proposed to develop around 46,000 acres of irrigated land per year: by adding a total of 175,000 acres of new irrigated land, improving existing irrigation facilities on some 50,000 acres of land, and providing lift-pump irrigation on 10,000 acres of highland in existing settlement projects. It was anticipated that some 40,000 acres of new irrigated land resulting from projects undertaken during the 1966-70 period would not be completed until after 1970.

If, in addition, the areas necessary for reservoir beds and reservations for irrigation works and civic purposes, estimated at some 110,000 acres, are included, as well as some 100,000 acres of new land not under irrigation, the overall total of new land that it was proposed to develop in connection with irrigation projects under the Five Year Development Plan would be about 445,000 acres. From 1966 to the end of 1968 more than 100,000 acres had been provided with either irrigation or drainage. This was judged to be capable of increasing the annual output of paddy by an estimated 6 million bushels (that is, close to 60 bushels per acre per year).

Preliminary or more advanced studies of seven river-basin projects for development after 1970 have indicated a combined capability of nearly 700,000 acres of new land. The largest of these projects is the Mahaweli Ganga project which, in three stages over a period of perhaps twenty years, is expected to be able to irrigate some 650,000 acres of new land and to improve existing facilities on an additional 250,000 acres. Furthermore, this project, when completed, will have a hydroelectric capacity of some 900 megawatts, with an annual production of some 2.6 billion kilowatt-hours.

In addition, it is anticipated that various other major irrigation projects may be able to add up to another 55,000 acres to the irrigated area, plus some further acreage of highland. Minor irrigation projects will continue to be brought into production, although the annual rate is expected to decline from 10,000 to 11,000 acres to around 7,000.

The advent of the low-lift pump has made it possible to irrigate the highland sides of canals, reservoirs, and valleys. Pumps have also made tube-well (deep-well) water available in some parts of the dry zone areas of both the northwest and the southeast coast. Experiments are being conducted with both kinds of pumping, as part of an overall effort to increase the efficiency of both land and water use.

In the wet zone the irrigation problem has been one of drainage rather than of irrigation proper. Along the coastland there are sizable areas of low-lying marshland that have been lost to cultivation for want of effective drainage. Periodic flooding and salinity are additional problems. The government has projected a number of major drainage projects that would include sea-outfall works, rehabilitation of the canal network set up by the Dutch, and pumping where gravity flow is insufficient. It is estimated that perhaps 175,000 acres could be thus added to the country's cultivable area.

In 1968 the International Development Association (IDA) extended a fifty-year credit of US$2 million to help finance the installation of low-lift pumping facilities on some 6,500 acres of dry zone highland in four different colonization projects. The main crops will be chilies and onions. In 1969 the IDA extended a US$2.5-million credit to help finance the government's drainage and flood control program. The project will make dependable cultivation possible on about 13,200 acres of paddy land in six noncontiguous areas along the southwest coast. It will benefit some 10,000 farmers and reduce rice imports.

In January 1970 the International Bank for Reconstruction and Development (IBRD or World Bank) and the IDA extended US$14.5 million in loans and US$14.5 million in development credits toward the cost, estimated at the equivalent of US$50 million, of developing the first stage of the Mahaweli Ganga project. This initial stage will improve existing irrigation facilities on 127,000 acres of mainly paddy land and will enable 104,000 acres of new land to be developed later. It will make possible an appreciable increase in sugar production and a reduction in rice imports by 25 percent of the quantity imported in 1968.

Land Settlement

Land settlement, which has been a product of the same forces that placed great emphasis on irrigation, has gone through three stages. During the first, which embraced the early years after independence, government programs included, in addition to paddy, the increasing of domestic and even small-scale cultivation of tea, rubber, coconuts, and other tree crops. The second stage was focused on paddy and the landless cultivator and on the growing need to find employment for young men in other sectors of the economy. In the third stage, which paralleled the 1966–70 five-year plan and during which the paddy situation improved, the government tended to turn more of its attention to the production of subsidiary food crops, as well as to improving the productivity of the export sector.

Just as land settlement and irrigation programs have largely been joint responses to the same set of problems, the programs have experienced the same difficulties of policy, administration, coordination, and adjustment. By the same token, the land settlement program stands to benefit in the future by the same conditions of improvement that, other things being equal, in 1970 boded well for the development of irrigation.

By the end of 1966, in implementation of the various provisions of the 1935 Land Development Ordinance, the government had distributed approximately 1.26 million acres to some 587,000 settlers. About 435,000 acres were allotted to more or less the same number of paddy cultivators under the minor irrigation projects. Some 285,000 acres were distributed to 60,000 paddy farmers under major (reservoir and river valley) irrigation projects. Between 450,000 and 500,000 acres of upland and marginal land were granted to village farmers, middle class farmers, and commercially oriented individuals for tea, rubber, coconut, and subsidiary food crop cultivation. The remaining 60,000 to 100,000 acres were allocated for small-scale tea, rubber, or coconut cultivation, for expansion of mostly wet zone village highland garden plots, and for settlement of young men as part of an effort to absorb some of the growing unemployment among urban and educated youths (see ch. 21, Labor).

From 1966 to 1968, under major settlement projects, a further 57,000 acres were allotted to some 15,000 to 17,000 settlers. Between May 1966 and May 1969 about forty projects were established for around 2,500 educated youths for cultivation of subsidiary food crops and commercial highland crops, such as tea, coconuts, and cinnamon.

In addition to the settlements in the private sector and a number of state farms and agricultural experiment stations, the government maintains three state-operated settlement projects: the River Valleys Development Board, the Sri Lanka Sugar Corporation, and the Ceylon State Plantations Corporation. The river valleys project was established in 1949 as the Gal Oya Development Board and reorganized in 1965 to include a new project at the Walawe Reservoir. At Gal Oya the board has a multipurpose project containing about 105,000 acres of drained or irrigated land, mainly in paddy with some sugar, tobacco, fruits, and pasture; in 1966 it was settled by nearly 11,000 families. The Uda Walawe project, when completed, will also be mutipurpose and will contain some 60,000 acres of new irrigable land, of which about 26,000 are expected to be in double-cropped paddy, 15,000 in sugarcane, 15,000 in irrigated (*yala*) cotton, and 2,000 in citrus.

The Sri Lanka Sugar Corporation, established in 1957, has not been very successful. In 1966 it took over the sugar project at Gal Oya, giving it a total potential of some 10,000 to 12,000 acres. As of fiscal year 1967/68 it was still in the process of reorganization but planned eventually to have 50,000 acres under sugarcane in the two projects.

The State Plantations Corporation was established in 1958 to run state-acquired estates, mainly tea. In 1967/68 it was running four plantations totaling some 3,000 acres, mostly in high-yield tea. It runs three tea factories for tea growers not able to afford their own factories. It also has a 1,000-acre cashew plantation in Mannar District and a citrus plantation near Puttalam, both dependent on subterranean water.

CHAPTER 20

INDUSTRY

In mid-1970 the manufacturing sector continued to be dominated by the processing of agricultural produce for both the export and domestic markets. The most important manufacturing industries were those engaged in processing the principal export commodities—tea, rubber, and coconut (see ch. 19, Agriculture). Industrial activities accounted for only about 7 percent of the gross domestic product (GDP), and almost half of this 7 percent comprised food, drink, and tobacco products (see ch. 18, Character and Structure of the Economy).

In the late 1960s the manufacture of consumer goods for the domestic market began steadily to rise, largely in response to several years of government efforts to reduce foreign expenditures because of a constantly worsening foreign exchange position (see ch. 22, Trade). By 1970 the country was nearing self-sufficiency in such commodities as textiles; had achieved self-sufficiency in others, such as cement; and was making small exports in still others, such as salt.

In mid-1970 the industrial and economic policy of the newly elected government of Prime Minister Sirimavo Bandaranaike was not yet clear (see ch. 18, Character and Structure of the Economy). The government's policy, as enunciated in the June 14, 1970, speech by the governor general, provides for the establishment of state agencies under the new Ministry of Plantation Industry to regulate the tea, rubber, and coconut plantations, which to a great extent process their products as well as grow them. The government also will expand its control of the import and export of essential commodities, probably with the goal of encouraging import substitution manufacturing. In view of the campaign pledges and the governor general's speech, the Bandaranaike government appears to favor a policy of an intensification of effort in the public industrial sector and an increasing regulation of the private sector.

With the exception of a few large government-owned corporations and a few foreign-owned tea and rubber processing plants, most manufacturing and processing firms are characterized by small capital investment and few employees. In 1968 there were over 2,000 firms in both the public and private sectors with slightly more than 101,000 employees. Except for the process-ing plants on the tea and rubber estates, most of the firms are located in or near the larger cities, particularly Colombo.

THE CHANGING PATTERN OF INDUSTRIALIZATION

During the 1960s industrial development underwent a change of focus. A 1968 Central Bank of Ceylon study on the com-position of the industrial sector indicated that the value of production of consumer goods had been dropping, whereas the value of industrial production of investment (heavy capital intensive) goods had been steadily increasing. This change occurred partly as a result of the government's reliance on the public sector as the primary vehicle of development. Other contributing factors included the growing capability by large-scale state corporations to maximize their utilization of capac-ity, increased foreign exchange allocations, and a rise in in-comes after 1966.

In 1964 consumer goods accounted for 63 percent of the value of industrial production. By mid-1968 this category had dropped to 50 percent. In 1964 the proportion of intermediate goods, broadly defined as raw materials and spare and replace-ment parts, was 27 percent, and by 1968 it had risen to 34.2 percent. Investment goods have shown the sharpest increase, rising from a proportion of 9.5 to 16.1 percent over the same period.

The decline of consumer goods has been spearheaded by the falling trend of food, beverages, tobacco, and textiles as a percentage of total industrial output. On the other hand, the production of fabricated metals and electrical machinery has in-creased substantially. Since 1965 the government has approved over twice the number of projects in the base metal industries as in the food, beverages, and tobacco industries. The second largest number of projects that the government has assigned has been in the manufacture of machinery.

The government's rational restructuring of industry has also had an effect on the location of industries. Before 1965 most industries were located near large urban centers. Out of approximately 670 industrial projects approved for the 1965–69 period, nearly two-thirds were to be located in smaller pro-vincial towns.

Another manifestation of the changing focus of industrial-ization has been the emphasis on finding new sources of foreign exchange earnings. In the late 1960s the government sought to develop tobacco, textiles, cement, tires, coconut milling, minerals, fish products, and a variety of consumer goods as possible export commodities.

ROLE OF GOVERNMENT

The goal of government policy in mid-1970 was the attainment of a level of industry that would make the country self-sufficient in as many commodities as possible. In July 1966 the Ministry of Industries and Fisheries (changed in May 1970 to the Ministry of Industries and Scientific Affairs) enunciated the official policy with regard to expansion of industrial growth. The ministry report emphasized that the most important need was for the mechanization of agricultural production; included in the recommendation were plans for the mechanization of canning and the processing of fruits and vegetables. According to the report, second in importance were industries based on indigenous raw materials, particularly those capable of opening up a new export market. In rank order of priority, particular emphasis was placed on textiles, building and construction, engineering, and consumer goods. Import substitution of consumer goods was adopted in order to make it easier to concentrate on the importing of much-needed capital goods.

As of 1970 primary attention was being given to what the government regarded as "essential" industries; these included textiles, salt, cement, plywood, fertilizers, ceramics, steel, petroleum, tires, and cast-iron products. Government planners concluded that the primary export commodities—tea, rubber, and coconut—would have to remain at the center of economic growth. Because of the falling world market prices of these commodities, however, the government was forced to shift the focus of development toward new indigenous products that would fill domestic needs and, eventually, become exportable.

The government began taking an active role in promoting investment in the early 1950s. Because of a shortage of capital, the private sector was prone to invest in assured securities rather than in high-risk industrial ventures. The government tried to spur investment by launching a new phase of state participation in industrial investment. In the early 1950s the government began to identify industrial categories falling within the purview of the state sector, the private sector, or a combination of both. By 1957, however, it was clear that the government had turned to the public sector for the development of large-scale, investment-oriented industries; the government's policy of promoting the state sector was crystallized by a provision in the State Industrial Corporations Act of 1957 that removed from the Corporation Act of 1955 a clause promising that public enterprises would eventually be turned into private enterprises.

In mid-1970 there were twenty-three state corporations. Although they were autonomous in the conduct of their own daily affairs, their respective boards of directors remained responsible to the minister of industries and scientific affairs. The State Industrial Corporations Act provided that "the Minister may from time to time give the Board of Directors general directions and after consultation with such Board, special directions as to the exercise of the powers and discharge of the duties of such Board and such directions shall be carried out by the Board."

The United National Party (UNP) government of Dudley Senanayake (1965-70) issued statements urging the promotion of foreign capital investment, but by the time Mrs. Sirimavo Bandaranaike's coalition government came to power on May 28, 1970, few projects had been specifically set aside for foreign investment. Senanayake's government had expressed a desire to promote joint ventures but was reluctant to accept foreign enterprises that insisted on complete ownership. As of early 1970 those foreign enterprises that were operating were given remittances of profits, tax benefits, and dividends as incentives for investment.

PROCESSING INDUSTRIES

Tea

Tea is the source of nearly two-thirds of the country's revenue. In 1969 approximately 500 million pounds of tea were produced, 40 percent of which was "high grown," or the best variety of tea. Tea is generally considered to be in the agricultural sector of the economy, but many industrial analysts, recognizing that the processing of tea utilizes machinery as well as hired labor, prefer to designate tea as an industry.

Ownership of tea plantations is divided almost evenly among British-owned companies, Ceylonese-owned companies, and Ceylonese individuals (see ch. 19, Agriculture). In 1968 Great Britain was the leading importer of Ceylonese tea, importing 162.1 million pounds of tea; Iraq was second, with 41.9 million pounds, and the United States was third, with 38 million pounds. Tea was once marketed almost exclusively through the London market, but by 1970 nearly three-quarters of export-bound tea was marketed through the Colombo Tea Brokers Association.

Tea undergoes a five-step process before it is packed in chests and made ready for export. The first step involves a withering process, which consists of spreading tea leaves out on racks until the leaves become flaccid. They are then rolled through machines that extract the natural juices from the leaves. After the withering and rolling processes, the leaves are then fermented in humid storage; following fermentation, the leaves are heated until they reach a high temperature and begin turning black. The final stage occurs when the tea leaves are packed into chests.

The Tea Research Institute at St. Coombs conducts research in reducing the processing time as well as improving the methods of shipment. In an effort to gain new markets, Ceylon has also conducted research in the manufacture of instant tea, the marketing of tea bags, and the making of an oil from the tea seed.

Rubber

In the late 1960s rubber continued to be the nation's second leading export product, accounting for nearly 20 percent of the country's total export earnings (see ch. 22, Trade). In 1968, 328 million pounds of exported rubber were produced. Only a little more than 1 percent of rubber production was domestically consumed in the form of tires, mattresses, toys, and shoe heels and soles.

Ceylon manufactures various types of rubber. In 1968 ribbed, smoked sheet rubber constituted 59 percent of production; 25.4 percent comprised latex crepe; 13.8 percent, scrap crepe; 0.9 percent, sole crepe; and 0.5 percent, liquid latex. Nearly 90 percent of the ribbed, smoked sheet rubber, the highest quality, was shipped to Communist China under an exchange agreement between the two countries (see ch. 15, Foreign Relations; ch. 22, Trade).

Coconut

The equivalent of nearly half of the annual coconut crop of approximately 2,700 million nuts is exported in the form of copra, desiccated (shredded) coconut, coconut oil, fiber, poonac (a meal extract), and toddy. Copra and desiccated coconut are used as oils or as foods; coconut oil may also be used as a soap; coconut fibers are used in the manufacture of yarns or ropes; and poonac is used as an oil or food. The palm flower is also used in the production of intoxicating beverages.

In recent years the coconut industry has been adversely affected by an overabundance of old, low-producing trees. The government operates a coconut fertilizer subsidy project and a seedling subsidy program (see ch. 19, Agriculture).

PUBLIC SECTOR

Large-scale industries are those so designated by the Ministry of Finance. They are generally public-sector, investment-intensive industries, and most of them were incorporated under the State Industrial Corporations Act of 1957. As of early 1970 those industries considered basic to industrial development were the cement, sugar, chemical, paper, textile, tire and tube, flour, steel, plywood, salt, leather footwear, fertilizer, ceramics, roofing tile, and *ayurvedic* (herbal medicine) drug industries.

The cement industry was the earliest of the state-owned industries, beginning operations in 1950 with the opening of a factory at Kankesanturai. It has also been the most successful of the corporations, regularly producing annual profits. In fiscal year 1967/68 profits were estimated at Rs13.9 million (for value of rupee, see Glossary). Average annual output at Kankesanturai since 1965 has been 165,000 long tons per annum. In 1966 the Ruhunu Cement Works at Galle opened; the factory depends on imported clinker for grinding and by 1968 was producing 150,000 long tons per annum. As of mid-1970 the first stage of the cement factory on the west coast in Puttalam District was nearly completed; upon completion it is expected to produce an additional 220,000 long tons of cement annually. The addition of the Puttalam factory is expected to make Ceylon self-sufficient in cement by 1972.

In 1963 separate sugar factories at Kantalai on the Alut Oya in Eastern Province and on the Gal Oya due south of Kantalai in Eastern Province were placed under the Sri Lanka Sugar Corporation, which before 1963 was known as the Gal Oya Development Board. As of 1970 factories on the Gal Oya and at Kantalai and Uda Walawe on the Walawe Ganga in Southern Province were operating under the auspices of the state corporation. Because of an inadequate sugarcane supply, shortage of water for cane producing, and a shortage of labor, the sugar factories have been operating far below capacity. In 1968 the government instituted procedures to increase the supply of water on the plantations by enforcing strict conservation and by expanding irrigation projects. It was hoped that the increased supply of water would help produce a larger output of sugarcane (see ch. 19, Agriculture).

Most chemicals are manufactured by the Paranthan Chemicals Corporation. The corporation is headed by a board of five directors who are appointees of the minister of industries and scientific affairs. Most production is in the form of caustic soda, chlorine, or table salt. At the beginning of 1969 both caustic soda and chlorine were being produced below capacity while table salt was being produced above capacity. Since 1961 rising demands for chlorine and salt have resulted in increasing profits.

The Eastern Mills Paper Corporation at Valaichchenai in

Eastern Province is the country's supplier of material for bond paper, wastepaper, and rice straw. Incorporated under the State Industrial Corporations Act, the corporation steadily expanded its annual output from 3,750 metric tons in 1960 to 9,000 metric tons in 1966. Although the level of production has risen, demand has risen at an even faster rate, and in the late 1960s production was able to meet only about one-third of the country's demands. In 1967 plans were formulated to construct a paperboard plant as an addition to the Eastern Mills Paper Corporation. The new plant is scheduled to be in operation by 1971 with a capacity of 12,000 metric tons per year. During the late 1960s the government was also examining the possibility of establishing another paper factory in Nuwara Eliya District of Central Province with a production capacity of 15,000 metric tons per annum. The paper to be manufactured would be for packing and wrapping. As of mid-1970 work had not yet begun on the project.

The textile industry is characterized by large-scale plants in the public sector and small-scale and cottage industries in the private sector. In January 1958 the National Textile Corporation was set up, and since then the government has sought to meet consumer demands by utilizing domestic capabilities. Completion of the first stage of an integrated textile mill at Thulhiriya in September 1969 was expected to help the country meet its import substitution target of 150 million yards by 1970, which would supply 90 percent of the island's requirements. Although the industry continued to expand its weaving capacity, in 1970 it had fallen behind in its finishing and spinning capacity.

The Ceylon Tyre and Tube Corporation was established in 1962 at Kelaniya, a short distance from Colombo, as part of an economic agreement with the Soviet Union (see ch. 22, Trade). In May 1967 the corporation commenced production of tires, tubes, and mud flaps. Production of tires has increased since the corporation's inception, but production of flaps and tubes has decreased. In early 1970 blueprints were being prepared for the second stage of the corporation that would expand the annual capacity from 150,000 tires to a projected 360,000 tires.

The State Flour Corporation was established in 1964 on a grant from the Soviet Union. The factory, set up at Mutwal, a suburb of Colombo, has an annual capacity of 70,000 long tons; in 1970 it was operating at capacity.

The discovery of substantial deposits of iron ore in the western and southwestern sector of the island led to the setting up of steel-rolling mills in and around Colombo during World War II. The lack of modern machinery, however, eventually forced the plants to close down. In 1961 the Steel Corporation was set up; cooperation between the Soviet Union and Ceylon culminated in the commencement of operations of the Ceylon Iron and Steel Plant in 1966. The plant produces approximately 60,000 long tons a year of rolled steel and wire. The corporation aimed at a profit of Rs7.8 million in fiscal year 1968/69, but a decline in sales because of a relaxation of import restrictions caused it to fall short of its goal.

The Cast Iron Foundry and the Steel Foundry and Structural Shop at Oruwala were completed in 1968. These additions to the Steel Corporation have helped to reduce significantly dependence on imports. One manifestation of the expanding capabilities of the iron and steel industry has been a project that is designed to make Ceylon self-sufficient in bus and truck chassis.

The first plywood factory was established in 1941. Since its incorporation in 1957 the company has grown to an annual capacity of 25 million square feet of three-ply plywood and over 1 million tea chests. The corporation also manufactures doors, tables for table tennis, and veneers. In 1970 plans were being formulated for the creation of a second plywood and chipboard factory at Avissawella.

Salt is produced by solar evaporation by the National Salt Corporation at Elephant Pass in the southern sector of Jaffna District, Palavi in the northwest of Puttalam, and Hambantota in the southern portion of Hambantota District. The corporation had a total capital investment of Rs13.1 million at the end of 1969; in that same year it produced in excess of the country's demand by more than 16,000 long tons. The opening of a salt factory in the Jaffna lagoon in late 1970 should substantially enhance the export capability in salt.

In 1941 the first factory for tanning leather and manufacturing shoes was established. In 1957 the factory was incorporated as the Ceylon Leather Products Corporation. By the late 1960s another factory had been added to the corporation, which specializes in the production of leather and shoes. The corporation expanded its operations by establishing another tannery in 1969 in an effort to offset some of the stiff competition in the shoe industry by the private sector.

In 1964 the Ceylon Fertilizer Corporation was established as a means of carrying on the government's fertilizer subsidy projects for coconuts, rice, tea, and rubber. Through 1968 sixteen district fertilizer stores with a handling capacity of 23,750 long tons had been established. A price increase in April 1968 caused the corporation to show a sharp increase in profits for fiscal year 1968/69.

In 1968 the Ceramics Corporation had a total capital investment of nearly Rs20 million. With two factories, the corporation had an annual capacity of about 2,540 metric tons as of the end of 1968; as a result of the opening of a new factory in 1967, actual output of the corporation more than doubled from 1967 to 1968, expanding from 1,003 to 2,369 metric tons. Output is expected to increase further because of expansion of capabilities at the Negombo factory and expansion of the wall tile unit at Piliyandala in 1971.

The National Small Industries Corporation is responsible for the manufacture of bricks, roofing tiles, and *ayurvedic* drugs. The manufacture of bricks and tiles is conducted at six different factories, while *ayurvedic* drugs are prepared at a factory at Nawinna. At the end of the third quarter of 1969, the corporation had a total investment capital of Rs22.8 million. The greater demand for bricks and tiles, along with higher utilization of capacity, enabled the corporation to show steady increases, although there was a slight decline in the value of furniture and drug manufactures.

PRIVATE SECTOR

The private sector consists of over 2,000 light and intermediate consumer industries. These industries encompass everything from small automobile assembly plants to perfume factories. A very large portion of private sector industry, however, consists of food, beverage, and tobacco industries. In 1966, 65 medium-scale and 100 small-scale industrial units were involved in the production of food, beverages, and tobacco. Among these industries were: the biscuit, jam, and jelly industries; the meat preservation, packing, and canning industries; and the beer, cigarette, and match industries.

In the 1960s no clear government policy toward the private sector emerged; this lack of definition created an unwillingness on the part of investors to enter into what they felt were high-risk industrial ventures. In 1968 the government did release the equivalent of US$10 million of foreign exchange for industrial investment in the private sector. Most analysts are of the opinion that more foreign exchange will be needed; even more important, they feel, will be a clearer definition by the government of the limitation of public sector investments. Both of these steps are seen by most observers to be prerequisites of significant private sector involvement in industrial development strategy.

Despite the foreign exchange shortage, many private companies have been able to become powerful enough to rival similar companies in the state sector. The Bata Shoe Company, which began operations in Colombo in 1950, was able to surpass the output of the Ceylon Leather Products Corporation by concentrating on lighter and cheaper rubber shoes. The British Ceylon Corporation, Ltd. was the leading coconut-oil milling and shipping company in 1969, surpassing the state-owned Oils and Fats Corporation. The organization also manufactures different varieties of soaps and talcums.

There are a number of companies in the private sector that have no counterpart in the state sector. Ceylon Oxygen, Ltd., for example, is the only manufacturer of oxygen and acetylene in the country. The Ceylon Tobacco Company, the largest manufacturer of tobacco in the country, had a capital investment of Rs37.5 million at the end of 1968.

COTTAGE INDUSTRIES

During World War II cottage industries flourished, largely because they, unlike large-scale industries, were able to operate with limited capital. After the war, however, cottage industries were seriously affected by the resumption of a normal flow of imports.

In the early 1960s the government viewed the cottage industries as a means of absorbing the thousands of underemployed workers. In the mid-1960s the government, in an attempt to increase the value of cottage and small-scale industries to the economy, began offering cottage industries tax benefits and expansion of credit through state aid loans. In 1966 a program was launched setting up 1,000 hand loom centers at a cost of Rs9.9 million. The program opened employment opportunities to about 25,000 workers in 168 government-operated schools. Industrial training was offered to workers who specialized in pottery making, mat weaving, hand loom weaving, carpentry, jewelry manufacturing, wood carving, and coconut-fiber spinning.

The Department of Rural Development and Cottage Industries was responsible for the administering of loans to cooperative societies before July 1968; since that time the People's Bank and the Industrial Development Board have taken over the financial responsibility. The Department of Rural Development and Cottage Industries still helps in social and overall development matters. The government in the late 1960s was providing aid to the cottage industries in the field of sales promotion and management. The government has exempted industries that have an annual turnover of less than Rs100,000 from surrendering their foreign exchange entitlement certificates, thereby opening up more foreign exchange for cottage industries (see ch. 22, Trade).

364

POWER

The Department of Government Electrical Undertakings in 1927 took over the transmission of electricity throughout the country. In 1951 hydroelectric power came into use with the commissioning of the Laksapana project at the southwestern tip of Central Province. Demand for hydroelectric power increased from approximately twenty megawatts in 1951 to nearly seventy-three megawatts in 1963, 90 percent of which was met from hydroelectric sources.

Installed capacity in late 1969 was sufficient to meet the demand of nearly all the major towns and villages. In 1966 the Laksapana power station provided 50 megawatts of power; the Norton Bridge IIB project, just east of the Laksapana powerplant on the Kehelgama Oya, 50 megawatts; the Grandpass Thermal project at Colombo, 50 megawatts; the Gal Oya project in Uva Province, 10 megawatts; and other diesel and steam stations, 21 megawatts of power. In May 1969, with the introduction of the new Samanela power station as part of the Maskeliya Oya project at Polpitiya in Central Province, an additional 75 megawatts of power were provided. The Uda Walawe project on the Walawe Ganga in Southern Province supplied another 6 megawatts of power, bringing the total installed capacity to 262 megawatts.

The Mahaweli Ganga project, a multipurpose project scheduled for completion by about 1990, will have a hydroelectric capacity of 500 megawatts (see ch. 18, Character and Structure of the Economy). In 1965 a five-year program aimed at providing electricity for the rural areas was begun. It is expected that when this Rural Electrification Scheme is completed 510 villages will be included. By late 1969, however, only 150 villages had been covered by the project.

MINING

Mining is carried out in both the public and private sectors by roughly 5,000 miners and quarrymen. As of early 1970 Ceylon was the world's leading producer of amorphous graphite, producing nearly 10,000 long tons yearly. Almost all of the crude graphite, called plumbago, is found on the southwest coast; it is marketed to the United States, Great Britain, and Japan.

Rich deposits of ilmenite, rutile, and zircon—mineral sands used in the manufacture of paint and the fortification of metals—abound on the northeastern coast. Silica sand is found on the southwestern coast and is used in the manufacture of glassware. Also, quartz and feldspar are used in the manufacture of glass and ceramics.

Large deposits of limestone and clay are mined in the north-western sector of the island. Most mining of limestone and clay has been on a small scale with the exception of the government-sponsored mining operation at the Kankesanturai cement factory.

TOURISM

In May 1966 the government established the Ceylon Tourist Board, vesting in it the responsibility for invigorating the tourist industry. The board, operating as an autonomous corporation, was charged with promotional as well as organizational responsibilities. The board sees to it that improvements in transportation are met wherever deemed necessary and that prospective hotel employees are properly trained. Most provisions for tourists are in the hands of the private sector, but the board has established facilities in cases where private facilities are considered inadequate.

The government has offered a number of tax inducements to attract private and foreign investment in the hotel industry. Three hotels were in the planning stages in 1970, all of which were to be financed by foreign exchange allocations.

The Tourist Board operates many resthouses, but in recent years a private company has tended to take over operations of the resthouses. The board has effectively increased interest in bringing in tourists to the country, and it is estimated that an additional 1,800 rooms will be needed by 1971 in order to meet the expected demand.

The Bandaranaike government that won power in May 1970 included in the cabinet the Ministry of Shipping and Tourism. In mid-1970 it was assumed that the new ministry would seek to improve and expand tourist facilities.

CHAPTER 21

LABOR

In mid-1970 over half of the civilian labor force was engaged in agriculture or in industries based directly on agriculture. Of these, nearly 500,000 were Indian Tamils (see Glossary), who first came to Ceylon in the early 1800s to work the coffee plantations and later the tea estates.

The labor force was estimated to be approximately 3.5 million; there were roughly 850,000 self-employed workers, 77,200 employers, 160,000 unpaid family workers, 2,166,600 employed workers, and 266,200 unemployed persons. Government service was the second largest occupation group and was generally regarded as the most desirable career. Nearly 20 percent of those gainfully employed were women, who were found in all major occupation groups.

The labor situation continued to be characterized by a politically active trade unionist movement. Of the nearly 3.2 million who were gainfully employed in 1967, almost 37 percent were members of approximately 1,250 organized trade unions, most of which were very small. The bargaining power of even the large unions has never been forceful, however, because of the multiplicity and disparity of their interests, the communal and class antagonisms of many workers, and the wide social gulf separating the rank-and-file members from the leadership. Unions frequently resort to strikes as a means of articulating grievances.

In the 1960s working conditions improved considerably, largely because of surveillance by government inspectors of some factories and shops. Some small plantations and factories, however, were in 1970 still operating under what the International Labor Organization (ILO) described as substandard conditions. Wage scales varied widely according to the sector of the economy, the skill of the worker, and the duration of employment; wages boards and the Salaries and Cadres Commission, however, were required by law to review minimum wage rates periodically.

The rising number of unemployed persons has been a matter of growing concern to the government. According to official statistics, the number of unemployed has risen from about

160,000 in 1964 to over 260,000 in 1970. Experts cite as the primary reason for the rise in the unemployment rate the fact that the economy is not expanding fast enough to absorb the thousands of jobseekers who graduate from schools and colleges each year. In addition, land has become increasingly scarce, which has had the effect of creating a serious problem of underemployment—that is, workers who work less than a forty-hour week. The government, in cooperation with the ILO, has launched a number of vocational training projects aimed at leveling off the rising rate of unemployment and underemployment.

CHARACTERISTICS OF THE LABOR FORCE

Composition of the Labor Force

The bulk of the labor force comprised manual and clerical workers in the semiskilled and unskilled categories. Slightly over 660,000 employees had no schooling, and over 90 percent of these workers resided in rural areas. There were only 140,000 professional, technical, and related workers. Competition for the technical jobs is keen. It is highest among college graduates, as only 20 percent of the annual number of graduates are able to find employment.

The labor force comprises three distinct groups: the urban workers, the estate laborers, and the rural peasantry. Urban workers make up only 18.7 percent of the labor force, but they earn from 20 to 40 percent more than the estate laborers. The urban worker is often engaged in industrial activity; this usually includes coconut and rubber processing, engineering, and construction work (see ch. 20, Industry).

At the end of 1967 Indian Tamil estate laborers numbered about 500,000 (see ch. 5, Ethnic Groups and Languages). Approximately 86 percent of these estate laborers were the "stateless" Indian Tamils (see ch. 14, Political Dynamics; ch. 15, Foreign Relations).

The rural peasants are mostly landless workers and tenant farmers. Most of them are Sinhalese and are reluctant to work on the estates. Because of their close family attachment and deep sense of ethnic pride, they generally refuse to work as paid employees on the estates, which are mostly foreign owned and managed. Unlike the Tamils, who are known for their skill in heavy labor, the Sinhalese are noted for being artisans and craftsmen (see ch. 6, Social Structure).

Age and Sex Distribution

In 1967 nearly 2.5 million males and approximately 657,000 females were gainfully employed. Women constituted 13 percent of the rural labor force and an equal percentage of the urban labor force. If unpaid family workers were taken into account, there would be approximately 800,000 women in the labor force. Of these 800,000, nearly 67 percent are engaged in agriculture. The government employs the second largest percentage of women—nearly 17 percent; the industrial sector employs 8 percent, and the trade and financial services employ 2.5 percent. In the urban sector 63 percent of the employed women are on government payrolls, 12 percent are in manufacturing and industry, and 7 percent are in trade and financial services.

Children are legally permitted to work from the age of fourteen on. According to the 1963 census, however, there were 74,350 gainfully employed children between the ages of five and fourteen. This figure represented over 2 percent of the total for those gainfully employed.

In 1963 the largest percentage of workers in a five-year age span was 13.3 percent between the ages of twenty-five and twenty-nine. The age groups of twenty to twenty-four, twenty-five to twenty-nine, thirty to thirty-four, and thirty-five to thirty-nine were fairly evenly distributed, ranging between 12 and 13.3 percent. Except for the fifty-five to fifty-nine age group and older, the percentage of participants in the labor force does not drop below 5 percent. The average age for retirement of a worker in Colombo was fifty-five for men and fifty for women.

OCCUPATIONAL DISTRIBUTION

In 1967 agriculture and its related pursuits were the principal means of livelihood for an estimated 1,693,430 persons, nearly 53 percent of the gainfully employed. Of these, nearly 500,000 were descendants of Indian Tamils; most worked on the British-owned tea estates. In 1970 the major portion of the agricultural workers were engaged in work on tea, cardamom, pepper, rubber, and cocoa plantations (see ch. 19, Agriculture).

The government services were in 1967 the next largest employer, with approximately 495,270 people. Of these, about 4 percent were in technical or administrative jobs. The majority of these employed in government services consisted of clerical and manual workers.

In the nonagricultural labor force, over 142,000 were professional, technical, and related workers. Of these, teachers numbered about 90,160; physicians, surgeons, and dentists, 10,520; architects and engineers, 3,330; chemists, physicists, and geologists, 410; and biologists, 250.

There were nearly 33,000 administrative, executive, and managerial workers. Clerical workers totaled approximately

369

118,450, the largest percentage of whom were bookkeepers and cashiers. Of the 212,240 sales workers, 116,350 were working proprietors in the wholesale and retail trade. About 5,040 workers were in mines and quarries; transport and communications employed 101,130; craftsmen, producers, and process workers numbered 63,440; and service, sports, and recreation had 300,220 workers.

WORKING CONDITIONS

Working conditions continued to improve steadily during the 1960s, although they varied widely according to the type and size of employment activity. On the tea estates housing was clustered together in a series of long shacks, but almost every estate was equipped with its own medical facility. The larger estates had adequate sanitation facilities, but on many of the smaller plantations the facilities were less than adequate. Conditions were better in the larger mines, which had good ventilation and electrical equipment; the smaller mines, however, were often musty, and lighting was minimal. Some of the large factories had congested working conditions, but circulatory fans provided adequate ventilation. In the small factories, however, wash facilities were minimal, and inadequate plumbing and ventilation made working conditions difficult.

The Factories Ordinance No. 45 of 1942 set up guidelines for industrial safety and sanitation and made each factory liable to government inspection. Although the ordinance was passed in 1942, it did not become operative until 1950, and even in 1970 inspections were carried out in only a small percentage of factories. The Estate Labour Ordinance of 1889, the Mines and Machinery Ordinance of 1896, and the Diseases Ordinance of 1913 all aimed at raising standards of working conditions. These ordinances and numerous amendments since their original enactments have had the effect of making the Ceylonese worker highly conscious of the working environment. Strikes and boycotts very often take place because of inadequate meals at factories that have their own lunchrooms or because of a lack of coatrooms, lockers, or other facilities.

The length of the workweek varies. In the industrial sector the workweek is between 5½ and 6 days of eight hours. Overtime work is frequent and is rewarded with payment of 1½ times the average hourly rate. In the plantation sector the workweek is 6 days of eight hours, and overtime payment is 1¼ times the usual hourly rate. In mid-1970 there was discussion of eliminating one workday on the plantations. Some government officials assert that the rapid increase in the supply of labor over the demand for labor has created a situation wherein two people are doing the jobs that one person was formerly doing, and they contend that the number of workdays in the week should be shortened. The estate workers have expressed opposition to this suggestion, however, as they feel that a 6-day workweek is essential to their welfare.

Over the years a series of laws have been passed that restrict the working of children and women to designated time periods and places. The Factories Ordinance of 1942 prohibited work for women between the hours of 8 P.M. and 6 A.M. A 1957 amendment to the Shops and Offices Employees Act limited the length of time that a woman could work to nine hours in a day, and other laws were passed that prohibited children and women from working underground, especially in mines.

Holidays in the public sector are granted by executive decree, whereas those in the private sector are determined by legislative acts. As of early 1970 there were seventeen holidays in the calendar year; of these, two were bank holidays, at which time the banks took the day off to balance their books; the remainder were public and mercantile holidays. Workers in private enterprise did not have as many holidays as did public service workers, but legislative acts did provide for some of the same holidays as days off from work.

Unemployment

During the 1960s the labor force expanded at a rate of nearly 2.2 percent annually. At this rate over 200,000 persons per year will be added to the work force in the 1970s. Government officials frequently note that, unless this rapid expansion in the labor force is matched by an equal increase in labor demand, serious unemployment and underemployment will continue to plague the economy.

Until 1960 the economy generally had sufficient job opportunities to absorb the increased labor supply. During the 1960s, however, there were gradually fewer jobs for a greater number of people, and by late 1968, according to the ILO, 266,275 were unemployed.

Figures on unemployment are frequently subject to statistical error because they are based on projections from census and from figures on those registered at the various employment exchanges located throughout the country. These figures often exclude first-time jobseekers. Based on an analysis of a 1967 sample of 10 percent of the population, the experts estimated that, if first-time jobseekers were taken into account, the number of unemployed would have been nearly 500,000 in late 1968. In addition to the high number of unemployed, there is also a large number of underemployed persons. Underemployment figures include those people who work a short workweek, who are seasonal jobholders, and who form part of the excess labor force on small family farms (see ch. 19, Agriculture).

During the 1960s the government through the Ministry of Labour and Employment sought to cope with the problem of unemployment in a variety of ways. There were in 1969 twenty-three employment exchanges, one branch exchange, and forty-five registration centers that were designed to help people find jobs. In applying for a job, a person registers a card listing his or her aptitudes and skills and the type of employment that is most desired. When a vacancy occurs, the most qualified registrants are directed to the employer. The employer then decides whether the applicant is acceptable.

The Central Vocational Training and Trade Testing Centre at Urugodawatte operates under the auspices of the Department of Labour (see ch. 9, Education). Its goal is to make skilled craftsmen out of unemployed persons. The vocational school specializes in training men to be electricians, sheet metal workers, radio repairmen, machinists, mechanics, and a variety of other skilled workmen.

In 1965 the government launched a settlement program aimed at relieving the problem that educated youths were encountering in gaining entry into the labor market. The program allows two acres of cleared wasteland to be cultivated and another acre to be lived on in cottages provided by the government (see ch. 19, Agriculture).

Wages

In mid-1970 the minimum daily wage rate for the non-agricultural labor force was Rs4.72 (for value of rupee, see Glossary). The daily rate for the agricultural sector was Rs2.72. Daily wage scales for the agricultural sector were, in theory, roughly commensurate with those of the nonagricultural sector by payments in kind for food, clothing, and housing.

In the private sector wage scales are arrived at by wages boards that are set up for each industry. Each wages board included an equal number of employers' and workers' representatives and three members nominated by the Department of Labour. The board members usually are appointed for a three-year term, but this rule has never been rigidly adhered to. In the public sector wages are determined by salaries and cadres commissions that operate under the auspices of the treasury.

Real wage rates are determined by inputing a cost-of-living

index into the wage rate index. After 1952 the Colombo Consumers' Price Index was implemented in place of the cost-of-living index. The Colombo Consumers' Price Index rose from a base of 100 in 1952 to 105.2 in 1959 and to 121.5 in 1968. The minimum-wage rate index increased from a base of 100 in 1952 to 138.78 in 1968.

Tea and rubber estate workers earn an average of Rs2.68 per day. Although by 1968 the index of minimum wages on the estates had increased to 139.58 from a 1952 base of 100, the index of real wages for an estate worker had only risen to 103.7. In comparison to the real wage rate that an estate worker earned, an unskilled government worker earned a real wage rate index of 129.08.

Other wage scales for various occupations ranged widely according to the technical skill of the worker. For example, the printing industry paid monthly wages ranging from Rs247.6 for the most technically qualified employee to Rs132.66 for the unskilled worker; motor transport workers' salaries ranged from Rs178.42 to Rs123.82; and government manufacturing wages ranged from a daily rate of Rs7.32 to Rs4.72. The wholesale and retail trades offered monthly wages ranging from Rs600 to Rs820 after five years of service.

Differences in salaries between married and unmarried persons were slight as of the end of 1968. An unskilled married person earned an average of Rs180 a month, whereas an unmarried unskilled worker earned an average of Rs175 to Rs197.5. A highly skilled technical worker who was married earned an average of Rs282.5 to Rs360 monthly, as compared to an unmarried worker, who earned Rs270 to Rs330 monthly.

There are pronounced differences in the wage-earning potential of the male and the female. In urban areas the wage differential is considerable; in the rural peasant economy the difference is somewhat less but still significant; and on the estates the difference is approximately 50 percent. The average monthly wage of women in urban areas is Rs123, whereas that for men is Rs284. In the rural peasant sector women earn Rs72 as compared with Rs141 for men, and on the estates they earn an average of Rs51 monthly as compared to Rs77 for men.

THE GOVERNMENT AND LABOR LEGISLATION

Since the beginning of the importation of South Indian labor in the early 1800s, the government has played an active role in the labor movement as both an adjudicatory body and as the nation's second largest employer. The government concluded that it had to improve the lot of the Tamils in order to maintain morale on the tea estates, especially because tea was rapidly becoming the nation's leading cash crop. A series of ordinances were passed in the 1880s and 1890s establishing medical and wage benefits for the estate workers, but no uniform legislation emerged until just before independence on February 4, 1948.

In 1941 the government enacted the Wages Boards Ordinance, the first comprehensive piece of legislation regarding the payment of wages, the regulation of working hours, and sick and annual leave; the ordinance also empowered the then minister of labor to establish wages boards for any trade. The boards are composed of an equal number of representatives of workers and employers and three appointees by the commissioner of labor.

The factories ordinances No. 45 of 1942 and No. 22 of 1946 require all factories to be registered and establish minimum standards of health and safety. The ordinances also give the commissioner the right to send inspectors or to go himself to the factories and to judge whether a factory is meeting minimum standards. The Shops and Offices Employees Act of 1954 extended the provisions of the factories ordinance to small shops and made separate sanitary facilities for men and women mandatory.

The Maternity Benefits Ordinance of 1939, as amended in 1957, entitles a woman who works in a factory, mine, or estate to full compensation for a period of two weeks before her confinement and for four weeks after confinement. The employee must have worked for the employer 150 days before her confinement in order to be eligible to receive the benefits.

The Employees' Provident Fund Act No. 15 of 1958 established a national retirement program for people within the private sector, the government employees having their own pension plans. The Provident Fund requires an employer to contribute 6 percent of total earnings and an employee to contribute 4 percent of earnings exclusive of overtime pay. Upon retirement the employee is fully reimbursed for these contributions plus an additional 2.5-percent accrued interest.

The government has also enacted a series of ordinances aimed at limiting strikes, particularly in industries the government considers essential. Included in this category of ordinances are the Trade Union Act, the Industrial Disputes and the Public Security Act No. 25 of 1947 as amended by Act No. 8 of 1949, the Industrial Disputes Act of 1950, and the Public Security (Amendment) Act of 1959. The Industrial Disputes Act of 1950, the most widely used of the antistrike ordinances, provides that workers in an "essential industry" must give a twenty-one-day warning of an intent to strike; however, the two industries that government has always referred to as essential—fuel and transport—have had repeated unannounced strikes since the passage of the act. One observer suggests that a lack of disciplinary response by government officials in the past has caused unions to ignore the ordinances and to seek redress of grievances by means of strikes.

The government administers labor legislation through the Department of Labour of the Ministry of Labour and Employment. Under the Department of Labour there are six divisions each of which is headed by a deputy commissioner, who is directly responsible to the commissioner of labor, but his duty is so specialized that he has a high degree of autonomy. The six divisions are the Administrative Division, Industrial Relations Division, Employment Division, Enforcement Division, Factories Division, and Division of Occupational Health.

The Administrative Division is responsible for compiling vital statistics on labor. In addition, it audits and is responsible for the disbursement of funds to all branches of the department. Many members of the division are statisticians, economists, and accountants.

The Industrial Relations Division concerns itself with settlement of industrial disputes through implementation of methods of bringing disputants together for peaceful settlement, all of which are spelled out in the Industrial Disputes Act. These measures include conciliation, voluntary arbitration, compulsory arbitration, collective bargaining, decisions by wages boards, and judgment by industrial courts and labor tribunals.

The Employment Division periodically publishes information on the skills of the members of the labor force. Throughout the island the division operates twenty-three employment exchanges, one branch exchange, and forty-five registration centers. Records of each applicant are kept in the divisions' files, and copies are sent around to various employers. The Employment Division is also responsible for the operation of the Urugodawatte Vocational Training Centre, an unemployment relief program, and the training and placing of the physically handicapped.

The Enforcement Division is concerned with ensuring compliance with the provisions of the Wages Board Ordinance with respect to hours, leave, and payment of wages. The division also has an Employee's Provident Fund branch that keeps records of the claims of employees and sees that they receive their due amount upon retirement.

The Factories Division enforces compliance with the Factories Ordinance No. 45 of 1942. The division has numerous inspectors who are responsible for ensuring that factories meet minimum standards of health and safety.

The Division of Occupational Health makes sure that adequate medical facilities and medical personnel are provided by the employer as required by law. The division sees to it that the hospitals on the estates have sufficient equipment to keep running smoothly and safely.

LABOR RELATIONS IN MODERN INDUSTRY

A tradition of collective bargaining does not exist, primarily because of the diverse and overlapping interests of the numerous trade unions, the lack of cooperation between clerical and manual workers, and the immobility within the hierarchical structure of the unions (see ch. 6, Social Structure). Since World War II the government has assumed responsibility for settling the collective and individual labor disputes. In lieu of collective bargaining, there has evolved a tradition of compulsory arbitration with a government representative acting as the arbitrator; in some cases disputes are settled by wages boards, labor tribunals, or industrial courts.

The government also has promulgated a series of ordinances that establish regulations governing the proper dispensation of wages, holidays, and leave policies; the establishment of pension and social security benefits; standards of health and safety; and other uniform procedures of employment.

Industrial Relations

Under the Industrial Disputes Act of 1950, collective disputes can be settled by five legal methods: collective bargaining, arbitration by a single arbitrator, arbitration by an industrial court, conciliation, and action by wages boards. A labor tribunal adjudicates in cases of individual disputes. In industrial disputes the initial attempts at settlement are almost always by conciliation, the procedures of which are outlined in a 1958 report by the minister of labor. Essentially, conciliation takes place when a trade union submits a list of demands to the employer and the employer fails to respond to the demands within a week. The union then either calls for a strike or petitions the commissioner of labor for conciliation procedures. The aim of conciliation is for both parties to air their grievances and then to arrive at a peaceful settlement.

The conciliator is usually an appointee of the commissioner of labor but may in some instances be the commissioner himself. A two-week period is allotted for notification of the commissioner as to whether the recommendations have been accepted or rejected. If the union rejects the recommendations, they are then forced to seek arbitration. The government publishes the recommendations in the *Government Gazette* to demonstrate the efforts that have been made to arrive at a peaceful settlement.

Arbitration may either be voluntary or compulsory. In cases of voluntary arbitration the disputants pick their own arbitrator. More commonly, however, the minister of labor invokes the power to refer a dispute to a single arbitrator, a labor tribunal, or an industrial court.

Trade Unions and Federations

In 1915 A. E. Goonesinha, one of the first labor politicians, formed the Young Lanka League, which was affiliated with the Ceylon National Congress. In 1922 the Young Lanka League became the Ceylon Labour Union, the first enduring labor union in the country. The period between 1922 and 1931, when adult suffrage was granted, is sometimes referred to as the Goonesinha era, during which time Goonesinha succeeded in mobilizing the urban workers, a feat that had not been accomplished previously.

In the late 1920s the All Ceylon Indian Estate Labour Workers' Federation and the Ceylon Indian Workers Federation were formed by K. Nadesan in order to give representation to the large population on the estates. In 1929 the All Ceylon Trade Union Congress (ACTUC) was formed with a membership of twenty-two organizations, including Goonesinha's Ceylon Labour Union. The ACTUC was the first organization to press for minimum wages, maternity benefits, workmen's compensation, and a sophisticated means of peacefully settling disputes.

Upon the introduction of Marxist activity in 1932, the labor movement became more aggressive. The workers had become particularly amenable to a more radicalized movement because the major export commodities of tea, rubber, and coconut had fallen off considerably. The Marxists directed their displeasure with the economic situation at the owners of the tea and rubber plantations. Marxist union activity has continued to be in opposition to the parties in power (see ch. 14, Political Dynamics).

In 1935 the Trade Unions Ordinance was enacted, making it mandatory for trade unions to register publicly and to carry out certain legally recognized obligations as spelled out in the ordinance. Among these obligations was the provision that political funds and labor funds be kept separate. The ordinance also stated that "a union of public servants is forbidden to have any political objectives." This provision, however, has never been closely adhered to.

The passage of the Trade Unions Ordinance caused a rush of union registration, among them the Ceylon Mercantile Union, the Ceylon Labour Union, and the ACTUC. In the mid-1930s large numbers of the Tamil estate workers, fearing the aims of other unions, joined the Estate Labour Union or its affiliates.

It was not until after World War II and the 1947 election that unions became the dominant feature of the labor movement. In 1948 an amendment to the 1935 Trade Unions Ordinance allowed free association of unions in the public sector; by the election year of 1956 the estimated number of registered union members had reached 360,000. In that same year the Sri Lanka Freedom Party (SLFP) mobilized its affiliated unions under the Sri Lanka Independent Trade Union Federation, marking the initial attempt of a non-Marxist party to affiliate with a number of unions.

According to 1963 figures regarding trade union membership, the Ceylon Workers Congress (CWC) was the largest union in the country. It claimed a membership of approximately 325,000, nearly all of whom were the disenfranchised Indian Tamils (see ch. 3, Historical Setting). The CWC belongs to the anti-Communist International Confederation of Free Trade Unions. The second leading trade union in terms of numbers is the Democratic Workers Congress (DWC), which split off from the CWC in 1955. In 1963 the DWC claimed a membership of about 150,000. Both the CWC and the DWC have been able to stay free of political domination by any single party, a factor that has given both unions a wide degree of flexibility.

The trade union arm of the Lanka Sama Samaja Party (LSSP) is the Ceylon Federation of Labor (CFL), one of the major union federations. The CFL was registered in 1945 and, in 1963, claimed a membership of 112,610; in mid-1970 the CFL continued to be controlled by the Trotskyist wing of the LSSP (see ch. 14, Political Dynamics). The Ceylon Trade Union Federation (CTUF), with a 1963 membership of 35,271 members, is under the control of the Communist Party of Ceylon and is affiliated with the World Federation of Trade Unions. In 1963 a schism occurred in the Communist Party, and the CTUF was taken over by the pro-Peking group (see ch. 14, Political Dynamics).

Another major federation is the Central Council of Ceylon Trade Unions (CCCTU), which is politically aligned with the People's United Front (Mahajana Eksath Peramuna—MEP) and had 22,913 members in 1963. Over one-third of its members are from the All-Ceylon Harbor Dock Workers Union. The Sri

Lanka Trade Union Federation, the labor arm of the Sri Lanka Freedom Party, had a membership in 1963 of slightly over 20,000. The All-Ceylon Federation of Free Trade Unions is an independent organization that claimed a membership of 2,837 in the same year.

There are also two major government federations that, according to law, cannot be registered but have a large number of employees under their control. These are the Government Workers' Trade Union Federation (GWTUF) and the Public Service Workers' Trade Union Federation (PSWTUF), both of which claimed a membership of over 100,000 in 1963.

Trade unions have never been able to overlook class interests and political considerations in their efforts to present a solidified front. Many unions have a narrow range of interests and have not been able to engender broad support; this has often resulted in the formation of several small unions with largely identical interests.

The unions' leadership most often comes from the professional Western-educated and political elite (see ch. 6, Social Structure). In mid-1970 the president of the CFL was Nanyakkarapathirage Martin Perera, the political leader of the LSSP; Pieter Keuneman, general secretary of the Communist Party, was also president of the CTUF, and Philip Gunawardena, leader of the MEP, also served as secretary of the CCCTU. Some trade union constitutions require that 40 percent of the leaders actually work within the particular industry they represent, but enforcement has been rare. The rank-and-file members are often uneducated and unskilled and only rarely rise to an administrative position; most of them tend to regard union leaders as outsiders, and communication is often strained.

Employers' Organizations

There are a number of employers' organizations and associations that are responsible for articulating management views during negotiations. In mid-1970 the two most influential organizations were the Employers' Federation of Ceylon and the Estate Employers' Federation; the former was legally a federation and comprised employers from the industrial sector, and the latter, not registered as a federation, represented estate owners. Both organizations represent their affiliates in disputes before labor and industrial courts, and they often have members on wages boards.

The employers' associations were under the aegis of federations but usually were on almost an equal footing with the federations. The Low-Country Products Association, for example, composed mostly of coconut estate owners from the low country, has been able to exert much influence. Designated members have appeared before the National Wage Policy Commission to express management's position on wage scales for coconut growers, and representatives of the associations have sat on wages boards.

An ILO team of observers reported in 1959 that employees of the federations did not always treat the member association equally, and rivalries were often precipitated. The team also reported that employers who belonged to the federations also favored the multiplicity of unions because they saw any attempts at centralization as a threat to the federations. Other observations by the ILO team dealt with the need of employers' associations to improve managerial and personnel skills.

Strikes

Since the beginning of the labor movement, strikes have been the most frequently utilized method of articulating grievances. Even before the emergence of the Goonesinha-led Ceylon Labour Union in 1922, there were numerous strikes in workers' organizations.

Militant worker activity increased in the 1920s and 1930s with the emergence of Marxist-oriented opposition parties. The most famous strike of this period was the Mooloya Estate strike of late 1939 and early 1940. It involved the All Ceylon Estate Workers Union, organized by the LSSP, and was at first aimed at gaining wage increases. The strike widened, however, after a worker was dismissed from a plantation allegedly for organizing the original strike. The result of the strike was a violent clash between workers and the police, during which a bystander was shot and killed. The Legislative Council, under pressure from public opinion, requested postponement of action against the strikers. The governor's refusal caused all the ministers in the council to resign. The Mooloya Estate strike dramatized the effect of strikes on the political process (see ch. 3, Historical Setting; ch. 14, Political Dynamics).

Immediately after World War II, strikes were staged in reaction to rising prices. Transport and industrial workers led numerous walkouts to demonstrate against depressed wages. The strikes were also a means of giving notice of workers' grievances to the political parties before the 1947 election.

In 1953 the government reduced subsidies for rice, which resulted in a massive work halt staged by unions attached to leftist parties. The *hartal*, as the halt was called, resulted in the stoppage of all transport activities in spite of the provision in the Industrial Disputes Act of 1950 that proscribes strikes in essential industries.

In 1956 many labor unions struck in protest to the passage of the "Sinhala Only" language legislation (see ch. 3, Historical Setting). The strike paralyzed the port of Colombo, but when violence erupted many of the workers were forced to return to work.

In 1959 the Public Security Amendment was enacted that declared certain industries essential during an emergency period. Throughout the 1960s, however, strikes continued to occur in essential services. A fifty-one-day walkout began in the port of Colombo in late 1961 and continued into the beginning of 1962. The government responded by sending the army in to take over the operations of the harbor; this action, however, had the effect of arousing sympathetic unions, and on January 5, 1962, a general strike occurred throughout the country.

In the late 1960s strikes, most of which occurred on the estates, continued to plague labor-employer and union-government relations. In October 1969 eleven of the thirteen strikes that were staged were on tea estates. Strikes were carried out for a variety of reasons; a survey taken in 1968 revealed that nearly one-third of the strikes that took place that year were because of dismissals of workers, and almost as many of the strikes were in protest against poor working conditions.

CHAPTER 22

TRADE

In 1970 two distinct sets of trade continued to operate more or less side by side. The first was a sophisticated external trade in tea, rubber, and coconut products involving the plantations, foreign banking connections, and world markets. The other was semibarter trade, based on the production and a hand-to-mouth credit system of the rural sector but increasingly tied to the urban centers.

Because of rising incomes, improving means of credit and communication, and increasing monetization in the rural economy, the internal trade during the 1960s tended to expand. At the same time, the external sector was being buffeted by declining prices on the overseas market and by its feeling of political insecurity at home, In mid-1970 most economic indicators suggested further growth in the internal trade, but the future of the export trade was unclear, pending clarification of foreign market trends and domestic political developments (see ch. 14, Political Dynamics; ch. 15, Foreign Relations).

Despite sometimes quite rigorous foreign exchange controls by the government, successive external trade deficits since 1957 have created a foreign debt problem of growing dimensions. Efforts to meet this problem with increasing amounts of traditional institutional aid, bilateral agreements, suppliers' credits, and short-term commercial bank loans have proved only partially successful. These measures contain an inherent hazard of increasing significance as a consequence of shorter terms and rising interest rates.

INTERNAL TRADE

An overall measure of the size and shape of the internal market is provided by the Central Bank's breakdown of the national income in terms of expenditures by the several sectors of the economy. In 1968 gross domestic expenditure amounted to about Rs10.6 billion (for value of rupee, see Glossary), at current market prices. Approximately Rs7.5 billion represented private consumption; Rs1.4 billion was for government and other public sector consumption; and Rs1.7 billion went into fixed capital formation, of which a little more than half was in the private sector. The aggregate of private sector expenditures constituted almost 80 percent of total outlays.

Consumer Outlays

Because changes in private consumption depend largely on the distribution of the national income, the Central Bank in 1963 prepared a sample study of consumer finances, broken down by households and income receivers. This study indicated an average household of 5.75 persons, an average of 4.2 dependents per income receiver, and an average income per income receiver of about Rs1,510 before taxes.

The sample also revealed an appreciable measure of income inequality. The top 10 percent of income receivers received 39 percent of total income, whereas the bottom 10 percent received 1.1 percent. Eighty-four percent of all income recipients received 51 percent of the total. Sixty percent of total income was concentrated in the Rs1,200 to Rs4,800 income brackets, which accounted for about 36 percent of all recipients.

Income-level distributions of this kind promise heavy concentrations of expenditure for food, clothing, and household needs. Using the sample survey as a format, the Central Bank's estimated breakdown of total private consumption for 1968 showed approximately 50 percent of total private consumption devoted to food; 18.6 percent, household operation, including fuel, lighting, rent, water, and household equipment; 7.3 percent, clothing; some 5.6 percent, tobacco; and 2.7 percent, beverages. About 7.7 percent was spent on transport and communication, 5.4 percent on recreation, entertainment, and foreign travel, and 1.4 percent on miscellaneous services. Of total private consumption expenditures, around Rs6.4 billion, or about 85 percent, was for locally produced goods and services, and the remaining Rs1.5 billion was for imported consumption goods, of which rice, wheat flour, and sugar accounted for almost Rs600 million.

Commodity Market Framework

Most business activity is concentrated in Colombo, although there are secondary urban centers in Galle, Jaffna, Kandy, Nuwara Eliya, and elsewhere. The enterprises through which business activity is carried on include: the companies and agencies concerned with exports and the agency houses handling the import and distribution of consumer goods, mostly located in Colombo; private wholesale houses handling domestic consumer and producer goods in the urban sector; the

384

government's Cooperative Wholesale Establishment (CWE); and the retail sector scattered throughout the country.

The CWE is a state enterprise created during World War II to handle the import and distribution of essential foodstuffs. Subsequently, it was a part of the government's contribution to the development of the cooperative movement. In both instances it provided an instrument for controlling prices by serving as an alternative source of supply to private importers and retailers. In 1970 its major activities resided in its monopoly over the sale of imported sugar, canned fish, cemcnt, hardware, and other household requisites.

The retail sector comprises between 14,000 and 15,000 private shops, 5,000 cooperative societies, about 100 CWE retail outlets, and about 50 shops of the government's Marketing Department. The cooperative societies serve as distributing agencies for government-subsidized fertilizer, high-yielding plant varieties, and other agricultural aids and as purchasing agents for rice and subsidiary foodstuffs under the government's Guaranteed Price Scheme (see ch. 19, Agriculture).

The Marketing Department's shops are outlets for the department's purchases of domestic fruits, vegetables, and eggs. Such purchases are designed to even out the substantial fluctuation in the prices of those articles that result from alternating market gluts and shortages that reflect, among other things, inadequate cold-storage and marketing intelligence facilities.

Importers, agency houses, and wholesalers have their own warehouses in Colombo. In some cases they also have warehouses in the provinces; a few also operate their own trucking facilities. For the most part, wholesalers do not actively engage in trying to sell their wares but, rather, leave it to the retailers to take the initiative in seeking to fill their requirements. Although markup margins differ widely, the wholesale margin tends toward 3 percent, and the retail margin toward 20 percent. Inasmuch as traders are not generally in a position to obtain credit from institutional sources, sales tend to be on a cash basis, although at the wholesale end the agency houses and larger wholesalers do extend limited amounts of credit.

Although the government has undertaken to convert from the British to the metric system of commodity weights and measures, by mid-1970 no active steps had been taken in that direction. In 1970 the major units of weight were: the long ton (2,240 pounds); the candy (560 pounds), used for copra; the bale (392 pounds), and the hundredweight (112 pounds). A bushel of paddy (rice) weighed around 30 pounds, from 30 to

385

35 percent less than the same quantity of clean rice. The liquid gallon was the imperial gallon.

Transportation and Communication

In mid-1970 transport facilities in active operation ran the full gamut from train and jet plane to bullock cart. The first railway, completed in 1867, ran from Colombo into the upland coffee estates, was government owned, and was designed to cut the time and cost of moving the growing coffee output to the export terminus. After the collapse of coffee, the railway successively performed a similar function for tea, rubber, and coconuts.

At the end of 1968 the railway system totaled 925 miles, of which all but 87 miles were broad-gauge (5 feet, 6 inches). The broad-gauge system ran from Colombo to Galle and Matara on the south coast; to Negombo, Chilaw, and Puttalam on the west coast; and to Polgahawella, Kurunegala, Kandy, Matale, Nuwara Eliya, and Badulla in the highlands. From Kurunegala one line ran north via Maho and Anuradhapura to Jaffna, and another by way of Maho and Gal Oya to Trincomalee on one branch and to Batticaloa on another. The 87 miles of narrow-gauge (2 feet, 6 inches) line ran from Colombo to Avissawella, Ratnapura, and Opanaike. A train and ferry service connected Ceylon with India. In late 1969 the broad-gauge system was in the process of being fully dieselized.

The comparative abundance of foreign exchange available before 1955, together with the comparatively great flexibility of highway haulage in mountain country, led to rapid and unorganized growth of the bus and trucking industry between the two world wars. By 1934 highway haulage had broken the railway's long tradition of profitability. Thereafter, highway competition with the railway became increasingly acute.

Estimates made in fiscal year 1964/65 suggested that goods were hauled by rail some 185 million ton-miles, compared with 770 million ton-miles by highway. The estimates also indicated that in 1963/64 the railway operated some 1,453 million passenger-miles, compared with 3,780 million passenger-miles by the bus service, which had been nationalized in 1957.

At the end of 1965 the number of motor vehicles was estimated at around 148,600. Automobiles and taxicabs totaled about 82,500, and buses, close to 8,000, of which apparently only about one-half were in service. Trucks and vans numbered about 27,000; motocycles about 17,500; and bicycles, around 350,000.

In 1966 the highway network totaled an estimated 30,000 miles. Of these, about 10,000 were considered suitable for motor traffic, and about 70 percent were asphalt surfaced. The rest were earthen roads, some of them usable by motor vehicles in dry weather. Although the network spanned the whole country, coverage was limited in the dry zone (see Glossary), where until recently the demand for highway services was comparatively low. Even most of the roads labeled motorable, including the bridges serving them, were of low standard.

Until 1969 authority over the highway network was divided among four jurisdictions at various levels of government. In that year integrated control of the highway system was vested in the newly formed Highways Department as part of the government's economic development program. The new department was granted loans and development credits equivalent to Rs150 million by the International Bank for Reconstruction and Development (IBRD, commonly known as the World Bank) and the International Development Association (IDA) for renovation of roads and bridges.

Although the number of bullock carts was decreasing rapidly, in 1970 they continued to meet a widespread need that was unlikely to disappear in the near future. Their usage therefore could only be restricted to the extent of trying to protect the road surfaces and to keep carts off the main roads during rush hours.

In mid-1970 the government-owned airline, Air Ceylon, operated scheduled domestic flights to five points, a service to India, and a London-Colombo-Singapore route based on a blocked-space agreement with the British Overseas Air Corporation (BOAC). Additional air services, both internal and international, were to be inaugurated in connection with expanded hotel facilities for the growing tourist trade.

A proposed Ceylonese merchant marine, government-owned if necessary, has been under continuous study since independence in 1948. A growing argument for it has been the increasingly large expenditure of foreign exchange that has had to be paid on freight costs for exports and imports. A major difficulty that would face Ceylon's moving its own exports and imports would be that whereas the destination of exports to date has been limited to a few places, the sources of its imports have not. This would present formidable logistical, managerial, and financial problems for any new enterprise. In 1954 a private shipping venture was undertaken jointly with Norwegian interests. Despite efforts of the government to assist, the venture's shipping aspects were not successful, and emphasis was shifted to shipbroking and the provision of shipping agency services.

In early 1968 the country was estimated to have a total of

approximately 57,000 telephones, or around 1 per 200 inhabitants. At the end of 1969 arrangements for the installation of an intertelecommunication project for the Colombo area were agreed upon with Japan. The undertaking, which was expected to be completed by the end of 1972, will enable direct dialing between eighteen towns in the western, southern, and central portions of the country.

Market Patterns

An effort to define a sectoral breakdown of the market is difficult for a number of reasons in addition to lack of data. Among these reasons, perhaps the most important are the pervasive influence of government and the fact that the traditional patterns of goods exchange, where not limited to small-scale barter in the indigenous economy, tended to be vertically organized between internal portions of the market and their external counterparts, rather than horizontally between different portions of the internal market. This tendency had been strengthened by the orientation and rigidity of the railway, but during the 1960s it was being rapidly weakened by the shift from the railway to the highway. Despite these difficulties, however, it is probably not far off the mark to distinguish market subdivisions for at least the following sectors, among which there are greater or lesser degrees of overlapping: export, urban, and village.

A special case must be made of Colombo. It is the entrepôt for most of the movement of goods into and out of the country, and into it are crowded all the mechanisms, human and otherwise, required to perform that function. It is therefore the market par excellence, and in it all the other markets overlap.

A special case must also be made of the government's subsidized weekly rice ration program. Under this program the government, until December 1966, provided each low-income citizen two measures (four pounds) a week of heavily subsidized rice, a large part of which had to be imported. In 1966 an international rice shortage led the government to cut the ration in half, to eliminate all payment for the remaining ration, and to raise the guaranteed price for rice as an incentive to induce a larger production of it. In the latter respect the government was successful; the output of rice increased beyond expectations in 1967 and 1968. But in the 1970 general elections the opposition promised that, if elected, it would restore the second weekly two pounds of rice ration. It did win, and in late 1970 the cut was restored.

The export sector market embraces most of the tea and

388

rubber production and about one-half the coconut production, together with the facilities that service them. Such services comprise the transport, storage, agency, credit, and overseas marketing facilities, including the tea auctions in London and Colombo, that are needed to put the export commodities into the hands of those responsible for their sale and delivery abroad. This market is largely a wholesale market, using large amounts of credit, and mainly operates out of Colombo. At one time it monopolized much of the country's railway system and, subsequently, much of its automotive haulage activity. It is still a mainstay of the railways.

The urban market in 1970 was a byproduct of the automobile, the rapid population growth, the foreign exchange shortage, and the gradual monetization of the rural economy. It is thus a largely recent phenomenon, which probably may be expected to expand rapidly. The urban market is mainly a cash market, operating at both the wholesale and retail levels. The market provides a meetingplace for, on the one hand, the growing middle class (including tourists) and, on the other, the entrepreneurs representing the importers, domestic manufacturers (including the state corporations), and the owners of the surplus of the nonexport agricultural sector.

The indigenous rural sector market operates on at least three levels, based on the itinerant trader, the village fair, and the village shops. The itinerant trader moves around the countryside buying the available farm surplus of rice, minor crops, and poultry. He generally pays cash and has the reputation of striking a hard bargain. Most of the produce he collects goes promptly to the towns for sale in the shops and markets there.

The village fair is a weekly event, and the merchant trading there does his circuit weekly. There the villager offers vegetables, tobacco, poultry, eggs, goats, and honey, generally for cash. With the proceeds and such cash as may have been received from the itinerant trader in the past week, the villager buys textiles, dried fish, curry spices, rice, and miscellaneous manufactured and household articles. The merchant, having bought the best of the produce offered, will send his purchases to town for sale. Agricultural products not taken by the merchant will likely be sold or bartered to other villagers.

The village shopkeeper, unlike the itinerant trader and the merchant at the weekly fair, is a local resident, and he gives credit. He advances loans that can be repaid in rice, copra, coconut, or other produce. During the agricultural off-season he advances rice and other produce that can be repaid in kind. At both ends of the process the shopkeeper exacts a profit, often excessive. Until recently the villager had little defense against this mechanism and has tended to become enmeshed in debt (see ch. 19, Agriculture).

EXTERNAL TRADE

Balance of Payments

As an underdeveloped economy, the country continued in 1970 to lack the savings out of current income to create the investment in plant and equipment needed to expand income and consumption (and savings) for a rapidly growing population. Therefore it borrowed the means of investment, against future repayment. In the balance of payments such borrowing appeared as an excess of imports over exports and other (net) credit items in the goods and services account. The repayment was to take the form of exports of an excess of goods and services (including direct investment equities) over imports in the future. Thus one way of looking at the 1970 balance of payments was as a series of current items (services and grants) and capital items (loans and investments) that served to increase or decrease the government's capacity to maintain an excess of imports of goods and services over exports (see table 23).

In recent years, particularly during the 1960s, the main items in the goods and services (or current) account of the balance of payments that have tended to increase imports vis-à-vis exports have been port services in Colombo (listed as port expenditures) and foreign government grants (listed as transfer payments, official). In the capital (nonmonetary) account the items contributing to an increase in imports have been official foreign loans (central government, loans received), foreign suppliers' and trade credits (central government, short-term liabilities), and foreign short-term commercial bank loans (Central Bank, liabilities).

In addition to the decline in the terms of trade and the failure of the export sector to expand in line with the growth of the national income, a number of items have increasingly tended to restrict imports. Chief among these have been the rapidly growing interest costs of the government's foreign indebtedness (investment income, other), the increased repayments of foreign loans (which are netted out in the "central government, loans received" item), and the costs of foreign consultant and advisory services (other services, other), whether hired independently by the government or in connection with development projects being readied.

The other items in the balance of payments for the time

being tend to be neutral or not important. Freight and insurance tend to be insignificant. Foreign tourist expenditures (travel) are tending slowly to offset Ceylonese tourist outlays abroad and may reasonably be expected to become a net foreign currency earner in the future. Remittances of direct investment income (investment income, direct investment), mostly for the account of the plantations, were in fiscal year 1969/70 wholly or partially controlled: in the short run the item will probably increase somewhat, but in the longer run it will probably decline. Private remittances abroad (transfer payments, private) are declining and may be expected to continue doing so. Direct investment in the capital account represents plantation capital repatriation and probably will persist.

The "assets" items of the central government, the commercial banks (acting in this connection on account of the Central Bank), and the Central Bank taken together with the International Monetary Fund (IMF) have formed the residual item of the balance of payments, reflecting the ebb and flow of foreign exchange into and out of the official reserves as needed to eke out the provision of foreign currencies from other sources. (A minus sign in the balance of payment shows an increase in the official reserves.) The "errors and omissions" item is introduced to balance the accounts.

Between 1955 and 1969 exports were inflated from time to time by temporary price increases but showed a generally downward trend. Imports over the period showed an upward trend that reflected rising population and consumption requirements, growing government recognition of development needs, and increased prices. From 1955 to 1969 export surpluses occurred in 1955, 1956 and, for practical purposes, 1965. The other years displayed a long-term trend of mounting trade deficits. The surpluses reflected temporary bonuses in tea prices and special efforts on the part of the authorities to reduce the level of imports in order to protect the exchange reserves. A part of the exceptional upward movement noticeable in 1968 and 1969 reflected the 20-percent devaluation of the rupee in November 1967.

Over the 1959–69 period, particularly after 1965 and apart from the rupee devaluation, there were increases in the level of foreign loans, borrowings from the IMF, and short-term credit from foreign suppliers and commercial banks. These were not, however, sufficient to fill the growing gap between exports and imports, and the government had to run down its external assets as well.

The external assets are presented by the Central Bank and the IMF on both a gross and a net basis, the latter indicating

Table 23. Balance of Payments of Ceylon, Selected Years, 1959-69
(millions of rupees)[1]

Item	1959	1963	1964	1965	1966	1967	1968	1969 (provisional)
Goods and Services								
Exports f.o.b.[2]	1,773	1,708	1,767	1,909	1,674	1,650	1,976	1,909
Imports c.i.f.[3]	-1,958	-1,869	-1,960	-1,922	-2,018	-1,985	-2,356	-2,653
Trade balance	-185	-161	-193	-13	-344	-335	-380	-744
Nonmonetary gold	-2	-2	-1	-2	-2	-2	-3	....
Freight and merchandise insurance	3	....	....	4	2	2	2	1
Other transportation	77	75	67	87	91	113	102	103
Passenger fares	-19	-14	-14	-9	-9	-6	-16	-9
Port expenditures	96	88	84	96	108	122	129	124
Other	....	6	-3	....	-8	-3	-11	-12
Travel[4]	-31	-16	-9	-7	-9	-11	-10	-5
Investment income	-37	-35	-36	-15	-37	-53	-52	-104
Direct investment	-53	-47	-26	-3	-23	-31	-21	-60
Other	16	-6	-10	-12	-13	-22	-31	-44
Government expenditure n.i.e.[5]	13	....	1	4	12	12	14	2
Other services	-34	-25	-30	-40	-41	-36	-43	-46
Nonmerchandise insurance	-7	-10	-6	-8	-6	-2	-6	-6
Other	-27	-15	-24	-32	-35	-34	-37	-40
Total goods and services	-196	-182	-200	18	-327	-310	-370	-794
Transfer Payments								
Private	-56	-30	-36	-24	-26	-24	-13	-15
Official	44	44	76	64	63	46	28	46
Total current account	-208	-168	-160	59	-290	-288	-355	-762

Capital and Monetary Gold

Nonmonetary sector	95	78	167	93	71	163	199	423
Direct investment	-9	5	-1	.....	-14	-5	-12	-11
Other private long-term	3	.....	2	-3	-2	-2	-7	1
Other private short-term	10	-4	-9	-18	-18	-8	-7	-10
Central government	93	77	174	115	106	162	216	443
Loans received	15	75	7	37	153	167	235	285
Short-term liabilities[6]	42	4	35	26	-44	7	-14	164
Assets	36	-2	132	52	-3	-12	-4	-6
Monetary sector	109	86	1	-156	237	137	178	348
Commercial bank liabilities	.....	2	.....	9	8	12	3	1
Commercial bank assets	-13	-4	-2	16	-21	-7	-37	19
Central bank liabilities	-19	42	23	-70	32	141	13	249
Central bank assets	151	45	-22	-156	142	-118	25	70
IMF account[7]	-36	1	.....	56	75	109	174	9
Monetary gold	.....	.....	.....	.....	.....	.....	.....	.....
Errors and omissions	3	4	8	-6	-18	-12	-22	-9

[1] Before November 20, 1967, Rs4.76 equaled US$1; thereafter, Rs5.95 have equaled US$1.

[2] Free on board.

[3] Cost, insurance, and freight.

[4] Includes educational remittances and official travel. Passage collections by foreign shipping and airlines are included in passenger fares.

[5] Not indicated elsewhere.

[6] Credit entries refer mainly to an increase in liabilities resulting from imports under supplier's credits and other short-term trade credits, the debit entries in respect of which are in the merchandise accounts and are recorded on an arrivals basis. Debit entries refer to a decline in such liabilities and are recorded when settlements or payments are made in respect of such imports.

[7] The figures shown are the net of credit entries in respect of drawings from the International Monetary Fund (IMF), and debit entries in respect of repayments to the IMF in respect of earlier drawings. Gold contributions to the IMF, consequent to successive increases in Ceylon's quota, are also shown as debit entries.

Source: Adapted from Central Bank of Ceylon, *Annual Report of the Monetary Board to the Minister of Finance for the Year 1969*, Colombo, 1970, table 46.

external assets minus external liabilities. According to the gross-basis series, external assets totaled Rs1,154 million at the end of 1955, Rs458 million in 1960, Rs408 million in 1965, and Rs327 million at the end of 1969. According to the IMF net-basis series, external assets in 1955, 1960, 1965, and 1969 totaled Rs856 million, Rs220 million, Rs127 million, and Rs626 million, respectively.

Commodity Movements

Exports

The Central Bank uses two different sets of external trade figures. For its balance of payments purposes, including its breakdown by regions, the bank uses figures taken from the records of its Exchange Control Department; these are also the figures used by the IMF in its *Balance of Payments Yearbook*. For its yearly and monthly series on the terms of trade, however, and its several series on total export and import volume, prices, and value, as well as for its breakdown of trade by commodities, the Central Bank uses figures prepared by the Customs Department.

Between the two sets of figures for total annual exports and total annual imports, there is frequently a sizable spread, especially in the case of the import figures. Because it is not practicable to adjust for the spread, the two series are only precariously comparable. To the extent, however, that the series are used for different purposes and that the attempt is not made to use them interchangeably, the fact of their limited comparability need not cause confusion.

Traditionally, exports meant the plantation crops—tea, rubber, and coconut products. More precisely, the export sector includes two quite different parts. The first consists of the plantation exports, which in 1969 represented some 89 percent of the total export sector. Tea, rubber, and coconut products represented about 55, 22, and 12 percent, respectively, of total exports (see table 24). The second part of the export sector is composed of a group of minor exports that includes minerals, spices, and a number of agricultural products, such as cocoa beans, tobacco, citronella oil, and cinnamon leaf oil. Although these represent a small percentage of total exports, the government is fostering the cultivation of them, and their importance is growing.

During the colonial period the plantation export sector, responding to rising demand abroad and increasing effeciency at home, was able to supply most of the revenues needed to support the government, provide the transportation and other facilities required by the expanding export economy, and remit

Table 24. Ceylon's Major Exports[1], 1965-69

Commodity	Value in Millions of Rupees[2]					Percentage of total exports				
	1965	1966	1967	1968	1969	1965	1966	1967	1968	1969
Tea	1,210	1,027	1,061	1,162	1,062	62	60	63	57	55
Rubber	304	337	282	331	431	16	20	17	16	22
Major coconut products	275	196	167	331	221	14	12	10	17	12
Copra	49	25	18	34	26	3	2	1	2	1
Coconut oil	144	108	88	133	108	7	6	5	7	6
Desiccated coconut	82	63	61	164	87	4	4	4	8	5
Other domestic exports	127	116	121	152	161	6	7	7	8	8
Total domestic exports	1,916	1,676	1,631	1,976	1,875	98	99	97	98	97
Re-exports	33	24	59	60	41	2	1	3	3	2
Total	1,949	1,700	1,690	2,035	1,916	100	100	100	100	100

[1]Export earnings have been rounded off to the nearest million.
[2]Before November 20, 1967, Rs4.76 equaled US$1; thereafter, Rs5.95 have equaled US$1.

Source: Adapted from Central Bank of Ceylon, *Annual Report of the Monetary Board to the Minister of Finance for the Year 1969*, Colombo, 1970, p. 218.

a handsome return on the capital invested. As a result of growing pressures of competition from natural and synthetic substitutes abroad and of insecurity about taxation, nationalization, and future competitive possibilities at home, the plantation sector after 1958 faced a period of a downward trend in world prices for tea and rubber and of widely fluctuating prices for coconut products. In 1970 the outlook for rapid improvement was not considered bright (see ch. 19, Agriculture).

The trend of tea export volumes over the 1958–69 period was upward, although showing a tendency to decline in 1967 and 1968. For rubber, export volume over the same period increased, probably close to 50 percent. The export volume of coconut products over the period fluctuated sharply. Taking all exports together, including the minor exports, export volume appears to have increased about 20 percent over the period.

Imports

The nation's import list, as compiled from the customs returns, includes manufactured articles, both consumer and capital, as well as raw materials, such as cement, petroleum products, and chemicals; it also includes an extraordinarily large foodstuffs component (see table 25). In 1969 foodstuffs represented 38.4 percent of total imports, as shown by the customs returns: this compared with 47.1 percent in 1966 and 51 percent in 1964 and a 1966 average of about 17 percent for South and Southeast Asia. In 1969 rice represented 10.1 percent of imports (18.1 percent in 1966); wheat flour represented 10 percent (5.6 percent in 1966); and sugar represented 4.5 percent (9.4 percent in 1964). Milk products in 1969 accounted for 2 percent; fish and meat (mainly dried fish), 3.4 percent; and other foodstuffs—mainly pulses, onions, and chilies—8.4 percent.

The 1969 decline in the percentage of imports represented by foodstuffs resulted in part from decreases in the prices of rice and wheat flour and in part from the increase in total imports, as well, perhaps, as from a greater degree of import controls. In part, the decline also reflected the appreciably increased domestic production of foodstuffs (see ch. 19, Agriculture).

Among the remaining consumer goods imported in 1969, textiles, including clothing, represented 4.8 percent of total imports, compared with 7.3 percent in 1965 and 8.4 percent in 1964. All other consumer items in 1969 amounted to 4.7 percent of the total, showing practically no percentage change since 1964 and 1965.

Intermediate goods in 1969 included such items as petroleum products, fertilizers, yarn and thread, chemical products, and paper and paperboard, in that order of importance. Intermediate goods represented 23.3 percent of total imports in 1969; this compared with 29 percent of the total in 1968 and 28.1 percent in 1965. Like consumer goods imports, intermediate goods were also down somewhat in absolute figures from 1968 and thus represented a smaller percentage of a larger total imports category than in 1968.

Investment goods in 1969 represented 27.5 percent of total imports, compared with 17.6 percent in 1968 and 17.8 percent in 1966, both large import years. Even after allowing for the 1967 devaluation, the 1969 imports of investment goods category was by far the largest outlay for the purpose on record. The largest item in the category was for machinery and nontransport equipment, accounting for 14.5 percent of total imports, compared with 9 percent in 1968 and 6.8 percent in 1965. Transport equipment accounted for 8.4 percent of total imports in 1969, compared with 3.7 percent in 1968 and 6.5 percent in 1965; building materials were 3.9 percent in 1969, 4.5 percent in 1968, and 3.3 percent in 1965. The increase in the investment goods category accounted for most of the increase in total imports in 1969 over 1968.

Direction of Trade

In 1969 the most important outlet for exports was the United Kingdom with 23.3 percent, followed by the other sterling area countries (not including India) with 20.2 percent and Communist China with 11.5 percent (see table 26). In close order after Communist China were the United States and Canada (representing the dollar area), 10.6 percent; the other countries in the Organization for Economic Cooperation and Development (OECD), 10.4 percent; and the Soviet Union and Eastern European countries, 9.5 percent. India took 0.9 percent of Ceylonese exports in 1969, and 13.6 percent went to the rest of the world or were unallocated.

As a source of imports, the United Kingdom was also Ceylon's most important trading partner in 1969, accounting for 21.2 percent of the total imports in that year. After the United Kingdom, in order, were the other OECD countries (15.8 percent), the other sterling area countries (13 percent); and Communist China (10.3 percent). The United States and Canada together accounted for 9.7 percent of imports in 1969, the Soviet-bloc nations for 9.2 percent, and India for 7.8 percent. The balance, 13 percent of the total, was divided among the rest of the world or was unallocated.

In 1969 the only area to which Ceylon exported more than it imported was the sterling area, exclusive of the United Kingdom and India; with all other areas or countries the island had

Table 25. Ceylon's Major Imports, 1965–69

Category	Value in Millions of Rupees[1]					Percentage of Total Imports				
	1965	1966	1967	1968	1969	1965	1966	1967	1968	1969
Consumer goods	779	1,161	931	1,147	1,218	52.8	57.2	53.6	52.7	47.9
Food and drink	604	956	783	989	976	41.0	47.1	45.1	45.5	38.4
Rice	144	367	211	341	257	9.8	18.1	12.1	15.7	10.1
Flour	98	113	229	250	255	6.6	5.6	13.2	11.5	10.0
Sugar	71	103	74	97	115	4.8	5.1	4.3	4.5	4.5
Milk and milk products	77	77	66	74	52	5.2	3.8	3.8	3.4	2.0
Meat, fish, and eggs	61	101	56	70	87	4.1	5.0	3.2	3.2	3.4
fish (dried)	43	75	44	58	69	2.9	3.7	2.5	2.7	2.7
Food (other)	124	170	126	125	145	8.4	8.4	7.2	5.8	5.7
Potatoes	18	24	7	...	...	1.2	1.2	0.4	...	...
Grams and pulses	39	64	53	56	78	2.6	3.1	3.0	2.6	3.1
Onions	21	20	19	17	17	1.4	1.0	1.1	0.8	0.7
Chilies	30	43	29	34	26	2.0	2.0	1.7	1.6	1.0
Textiles (including clothing)	107	119	73	77	122	7.3	5.9	4.2	3.5	4.8

Other consumer goods	68	86	75	81	120	4.6	4.2	4.3	3.7	4.7
Intermediate goods	414	470	441	629	592	28.1	23.2	25.4	29.0	23.3
Fertilizers	88	91	80	110	66	6.0	4.5	4.6	5.1	2.6
Petroleum products	109	130	112	196	156	7.4	6.4	6.4	9.0	6.1
Chemical elements and compounds.	30	36	38	45	66	2.0	1.8	2.2	2.1	2.6
Paper and paperboard	28	50	41	37	55	1.9	2.5	2.4	1.7	2.2
Yarn and thread	41	42	45	71	80	2.8	2.1	2.6	3.3	3.1
Investment goods	261	361	330	383	700	17.7	17.8	19.0	17.6	27.5
Building materials	54	70	48	95	99	3.3	3.4	2.8	4.5	3.9
Transport equipment	96	116	89	80	213	6.5	5.7	5.1	3.7	8.4
Machinery and equipment	100	162	175	195	368	6.8	8.0	10.1	9.0	14.5
Total items[2]	1,454	1,992	1,702	2,159	2,510	98.7	98.2	98.0	99.3	98.7
Total imports	1,474	2,028	1,738	2,173	2,543	100.0	100.0	100.0	100.0	100.0

[1]Before November 20, 1967, Rs4.76 equaled US$1; thereafter, Rs5.95 have equaled US$1.

[2]Total of consumer, intermediate, and investment goods; totals not exact because of errors and omissions.

Source: Adapted from Central Bank of Ceylon, *Annual Report of the Monetary Board to the Minister of Finance for the Year 1969*, Colombo, p. 235.

Table 26. Ceylon's Major Trading Partners, by Country or Area, 1969
(values in millions of rupees)[1]

Area	Exports		Imports	
	Value	Percentage	Value	Percentage
United States and Canada	202	10.6	257	9.7
United Kingdom	441	23.3	562	21.2
India	19	0.9	208	7.8
Other sterling countries	387	20.2	343	13.0
Other European OECD countries[2]	199	10.4	418	15.8
Communist China	219	11.5	274	10.3
Soviet Union and Eastern European countries.	181	9.5	244	9.2
Other	259	13.6	346	13.0
Total	[3]1,909	100.0	[3]2,653	100.0

[1]Before November 20, 1967, Rs4.76 equaled US$1; thereafter, Rs5.95 have equaled US$1.
[2]Organization for Economic Cooperation and Development.
[3]May not add, owing to rounding.

Source: Adapted from Central Bank of Ceylon, *Annual Report of the Monetary Board to the Minister of Finance for the Year 1969*, Colombo, 1970, table 45.

a trade deficit. The largest deficit was with the European OECD countries, the next with India, and thereafter, in order, with the United Kingdom, the Soviet bloc, Communist China, the United States, and Canada.

At the end of 1969 Ceylon had bilateral trading arrangements with a number of nations, mostly in the Soviet sphere. The most important agreement, however, was with Communist China. In 1970 trade with China operated under a protocol to the Trade and Payments Agreement between the two countries that was originally signed in 1952 and most recently renewed in 1967. Under the terms of the protocol, Ceylon in 1970 was scheduled to export to China 41,000 metric tons of sheet rubber valued at about Rs124 million and to import from China 200,000 metric tons of rice valued at a like amount.

Terms of Trade

The commodity terms of trade, as published by the Central Bank with 1967 as the base year, in 1969 indicated that the purchasing power of the island's exports has been declining since 1955. Even if the index were hedged a little, it suggested that a given quantity of exports in 1969 would purchase less than two-thirds as much of its imports as it would have done in 1955. The accumulated loss in imports over the last fifteen years underlines the urgency of the government in trying to stem the downward trend in export prices, especially tea prices, because tea bulks so large in total exports.

FOREIGN EXCHANGE SYSTEM

As a member of the sterling area, Ceylon has arrangements for settlement of its accounts with other countries similar to those of other members of the sterling area. At the end of 1968 Ceylon had bilateral agreements with ten countries. Settlement of these agreements, as well as those operative under special arrangements with Pakistan and the United Arab Republic (Egypt), was made through special accounts provided for in the agreements, but only the rubber-for-rice agreement with Communist China contained specific commodity commitments. Settlements with other countries (except Rhodesia) could be made through the system of sterling and rupee external accounts of the sterling area or in the currency of the other country involved.

Ceylon entered upon independence with an essentially open-door policy on imports and a substantially optimistic outlook for its foreign trade relations. The collapse of the Korean conflict export boom, however, and a preview of the rapid rate of population increase foreshadowed by the malaria-control program led to second thoughts and, in 1953, to the Exchange Control Act. The tea boom of the mid-1950s temporarily relieved the pressure on the exchange reserves, but this also collapsed, while imports continued to rise.

In 1962 a rigorous system of exchange controls was instituted in response to continuing deterioration of the country's export earnings, the rising requirements for imports of food, raw materials, spare parts, and replacements, and the insistent demand by a growing urban population for imported consumer amenities. The controls are based on the Exchange Control Act of 1953, as subsequently amended, and are administered by the Exchange Control Department of the Central Bank, as the agent of the government, acting through authorized commercial banks.

The physical licenses corresponding to exchange permits are issued by the controller of imports and exports. The rationing activities of both departments are coordinated through the Foreign Exchange Budget drawn up annually by the Ministry of Planning and Employment. Under the existing legislation all exports and imports are subject to exchange controls, and foreign exchange entering the country, whether by way of exports, invisibles or the movements of capital, must be surrendered to the exchange control authorities.

Before 1968 import licenses were issued in three categories: trade quota licenses, issued to established importers on the basis of the highest annual imports made during the 1959–61 period, with special provision for Ceylonese newcomers in the

401

business; actual user licenses, issued to manufacturers for the import of raw materials, packing materials, and machinery; and direct user licenses, issued to private individuals and service agencies such as hotels and tourist transportation operators.

As of mid-1970 the exchange control system centered on the foreign exchange entitlement certificates introduced in May 1968 to replace the Export Incentive Bonus Voucher Scheme, which had been in effect since December 1966. Both procedures were part of the effort, sponsored by the IMF (which supported the move in 1968 with a US$19.5-million standby credit), to bring the overpriced rupee into line with other currencies. The effort also included the devaluation of the rupee in 1967.

The specific purposes of the procedure of foreign exchange entitlement certificates were several: to stimulate nontraditional exports; inhibit nonessential imports; and increase the economy's reliance on the influence of the price system rather than on bureaucratic discretion, by affording greater opportunities to importers to import (especially raw materials and replacement and expansion parts) where they foresaw the greatest profit advantage. It was also expected to: eliminate excessive middleman profits on imports; sidestep the need of a new devaluation; speed the process of nationalizing commerce and industry; and develop another source of revenue for the central government.

The foreign exchange entitlement certificates, in effect, were designed to provide a limited floating rate market for the rupee alongside the official market. The new market would be fed by exchange proceeds deriving from all exports except the big three (tea, rubber, and coconut products), as well as from tourism and inflows of capital, investment income, legacies, earnings, and the like. For all practical purposes, recourse could be had to this market for nearly everything except government imports.

Under the foreign exchange entitlement certificates, imports were divided into categories A and B. Inclusion in Category A carried with it the right to buy exchange at the overvalued official rate of Rs5.95 per US$1. Category A imports included essential foodstuffs and drugs, fertilizers, petroleum products, the imports of government and nonprofitmaking official corporations, and imports for small industries. These, for all practical purposes, were all imported by the government and represented around three-fourths of total imports.

Category B subsumed all imports at the floating rate. The imports were divided into two groups: imports admitted under individual license—that is, those which could be imported by private licensed importers—and imports admitted under Open General License (OGL). Imports admitted under OGL, although not requiring an individual license, did require the opening of a letter of credit.

When exchange having the entitlement privilege was surrendered, the official rate equivalent of the value of the exchange surrendered was paid in rupees. Accompanying the rupees were certificates having an identical face value. These were freely transferable for thirty days, by which time they must have been used or sold to an individual or to a bank. Exchange that enjoyed the entitlement privilege but that for some reason reached the Central Bank before the privilege had been utilized would be periodically auctioned off by the Central Bank to the highest bidder.

Importers in Category A did not have to deposit certificates when applying for an import license. Both groups of importers in Category B did have to accompany their applications with certificates.

Soon after the certificate scheme went into operation, the rate on certificates was fixed by the Central Bank at Rs44 per Rs100 of face value, closing out, in effect, the floating market and giving the rupee in the certificate market an effective value of Rs8.57 per US$1. In 1969 the certificate rate was raised to Rs55 per certificate of Rs100 face value, with an effective rate of Rs9.22 per US$1.

Also in 1969, with the beginning of the new fiscal year (October), most imports of government departments and corporations were transferred from Category A to the individual license group of Category B; within Category B a number of private import items were shifted from individual license to the OGL group. At the end of 1969 about 45 percent of all imports were included in the certificate market. In mid-1970, in the wake of the change in government in May, the operation of the foreign exchange entitlement certificate procedure was in abeyance pending an overall review of the program to determine whether it should be resumed, modified, or rescinded.

In a companion measure to the foreign exchange entitlement certificate procedure, the government canceled all previous registrations of importers, and new registrations were provided for. The new registration was to take two forms. Businesses that were 100-percent Ceylonese owned were to be given definitive registration. Other businesses were to receive provisional registration. This was part of a Ceylonization-of-business policy that in 1961 had limited new deposits by Ceylonese to the Ceylonese banks and in 1965 had provided that all importers, whether company or individual, should be Ceylonese (see ch. 23, Finance). Subsequently, Ceylonese traders were given the exclusive right to import from the "Ceylonized area," comprising almost twenty countries, mainly Communist or Eastern European but including Spain, West Germany, and Japan. Implementation of this policy proved difficult, however, and the requirement embodying it was relaxed.

EXTERNAL DEBT

Between 1957 and 1969 the balance of payments annually recorded foreign trade deficits, which were particularly large from 1966 on. By 1969 the cumulative total of the trade deficits had reached the equivalent of almost Rs3 billion. Although much of this had been financed more or less as it accrued, some of it had not. By 1970 this remnant, which tended to increase as the trade deficits grew larger after 1965, was placing increasing strain on Ceylon's credit facilities abroad, as well as on its foreign reserve position.

In 1965 the IBRD, which had made its first loan disbursements to Ceylon in 1955, sponsored an Aid-Ceylon group to help coordinate foreign financing for important development projects and the acquisition of intermediate goods (see ch. 15, Foreign Relations). In the meantime, assistance of various sorts was also being tendered by the United States, the sterling area countries, and Canada (all operating through the Colombo Plan), the Soviet bloc, and Communist China. Some of this, especially the dollar area component, was on a grant basis, but in the main it took the form of loans, which became increasingly onerous as the credit problems of 1969 and 1970 spread out from the United States and Europe.

At the end of September 1969 the outstanding official foreign debt stood at the equivalent of Rs1,375 million, compared with Rs910 million at the end of 1967, Rs489 million at the end of September 1965, Rs294 million at the end of September 1960, and Rs205 million at the end of September 1955. The official debt at the end of 1969 comprised the equivalent of Rs89 million of preindependence sterling loans, Rs504 million of project loans, and Rs845 million of commodity loans. Project loans are so called because they are explicitly designed and contracted for a specific project and, except as otherwise subsequently agreed, may be used only for the specific project. Commodity loans are more flexible, their purpose being largely to finance the import of raw materials and spare, replacement, or expansion parts to help the industrial projects already in existence. Sometimes commodity loans also include consumer goods, as in the case of the United States Public Law 480 food loans that have not only aided consumer imports but on accasion have also been wholly or partially repayable in rupees.

The official debt at the end of September 1969 was owed to thirteen countries, the IBRD, IDA, and the International Finance Corporation (IFC). Five of the creditors were socialist countries: Communist China, East Germany, Poland, the Soviet Union, and Yugoslavia. The other creditor nations were Canada, Denmark, France, West Germany, India, Japan, the United Kingdom, and the United States. The largest creditors were the United States (Rs350 million); the United Kingdom (Rs183 million); West Germany (Rs159 million); and the IBRD group, Japan, and East Germany (with Rs156 million, Rs94 million, and Rs89 million, respectively). Some of the official debt was on concessional terms—that is, up to fifty-year maturities at low or nominal rates of interest.

In addition to its official foreign debt, Ceylon at the end of 1969 had a debtor balance with the IMF of almost US$93 million which, except by special permission, for the time being exhausted its drawing power at the IMF. It also had an accumulated indebtedness in the form of short-term suppliers' credits, trade credits, bilateral credits, and foreign commercial bank credits that probably totaled more than Rs500 million. This additional indebtedness would have raised the government's total indebtedness abroad at the end of 1969 to probably not less than Rs2.5 billion.

Rapid increases in the external debt, by comparison with the domestic debt, present a double burden. Additions to the domestic debt involve only the problems of finding, through taxation, saving, or other means, the necessary additional local currency to meet the additional charges on the budget of the interest and amortization payments on the new debt. Increases in the foreign debt, however, require not only the same local currency to meet the enlarged budget item but also additional foreign currencies with which to transfer abroad the increased interest and amortization payments. To all intents and purposes, in the circumstances in which Ceylon found itself in 1970, this meant either a reduction in imports or still further borrowing abroad—from the international agencies, if possible, on concessional terms.

As such terms became decreasingly available in the late 1960s, and especially in 1969, the government was forced by unforeseen shortfalls in export earnings to resort to supplier and short-term commercial bank credit at a time when the cost of such credit was exceptionally high. This only served to aggravate the already difficult problem of transferring annually rising levels of interest and amortization without reducing the level of development imports. Estimates suggest that, unless means can be found of reducing the cost of such transfers, during the early and middle 1970s the cost will rise to 10 to 15 percent or more of export receipts, which represents a substantial drain on potential import flows.

CHAPTER 23

FINANCE

The central government's original estimate of its budget for fiscal year 1969/70 totaled Rs3.99 billion (for value of rupee, see Glossary), approaching one-third of the estimated gross domestic product (GDP) for the calendar year 1970. Total government revenues were estimated at Rs2.83 billion, of which about 60 percent were accounted for by taxation. The gap between expenditures and revenues was to be financed by credit of the Central Bank of Ceylon, domestic nonbank credit, and various forms of foreign credit. The self-financed expenditures of local government units were relatively insignificant.

Despite high tax rates on corporate and personal incomes, direct taxation accounted for only about 22 percent of tax revenues; the largest tax category was excise taxes, followed by customs duties. In 1968 the government-created Taxation Inquiry Commission, having subjected the tax system to a searching critique, set forth some far-reaching recommendations for updating the system and increasing its revenue-producing capacity. In mid-1979 several of these proposals either had been completed or were in the process of being carried out.

The monetary system is organized around the Central Bank and includes, in addition to a mixed Ceylonese and foreign private banking sector, a number of semipublic special-purpose financing institutions. The capital market is in the early stages of development. The money supply is composed of currency and private sector deposits. From 1948 to 1968 the money supply increased by about 215 percent, and since 1956 currency has anomalously represented a growing portion of it.

Between 1961 and 1968 the private banking sector was organized to benefit the Ceylonese component, and the Ceylonese banks assumed an imposing lead within the sector during that period. The Central Bank, although exerting an increasing degree of control over the private banks, has found itself persistently under the necessity of financing the government's budgetary deficits. As long as foreign exchange remained adequate, imports tended to absorb the inflationary tendencies. When the British pound sterling was devalued in November 1967, the Ceylonese rupee followed suit.

THE BUDGETARY PROCESS

The skeleton of the budgetary process is set out in the Constitution. The process is organized around the Consolidated Fund, into which are paid all taxes, duties, imposts (customs duties), rates, and other revenues of the central government that are not expressly earmarked by the legislature for specific purposes. Out of the fund are paid the current operating expenses of the government and any capital expenditures that are not financed by various types of borrowing.

Interest on the public debt, sinking fund payments, the costs of managing the Consolidated Fund, and other expenditures that Parliament may from time to time expressly determine are deemed to be statutory charges upon the Consolidated Fund and do not require annual permission of Parliament in order to be paid. No withdrawals may be made from the Consolidated Fund unless they are authorized by Parliament, either statutorily or expressly year by year, and unless countersigned by the minister of finance. An exception is made in the case where Parliament is dissolved before authorizing an Appropriation Bill for the current financial year (see ch. 13, The Governmental System). In this case the governor general may draw upon the Consolidated Fund to meet the requirements of current obligations. In addition to the Consolidated Fund, the Constitution allows, but does not require, Parliament to create a Contingencies Fund to meet unforeseen and urgent expenditures.

Money bills—that is, bills or motions that request authorization of withdrawals from the Consolidated Fund or other government funds, or that request the creation of new central government taxes or changes in existing ones, or bills dealing with the public debt—are established by the Constitution as being solely the jurisdiction of the House of Representatives. Such bills may only be introduced in the House. Before being introduced, these bills must have received the approval of the cabinet or other approval that the cabinet may have authorized.

Money bills may not be introduced in the Senate, and they do not require approval or authorization of the Senate to become law. After passage in the House of Representatives, the major money bills are sent to the Senate for information and comment. If the Senate fails to return a money bill to the House within a month, the House may then forward the bill to the governor general for his signature, and the bill thereupon becomes law.

The Constitution provides for the appointment of an auditor general to review the government accounts. He is appointed by the governor general for life and reports to the House of Representatives.

The two main money bills are the annual finance and appropriations bills. They are presented by the minister of finance to the House of Representatives early in August, along with the minister's annual budget speech. Of the two bills, the more important is the Appropriation Bill, for whereas the Finance Bill remains operative until repealed, the Appropriation Bill is good only for the year for which it is enacted. If a government could continue to operate on the proceeds of its existing taxes, it would not have to go back to Parliament for authority to keep on collecting those taxes. By contrast, constitutional prescription requires the government to return each year to Parliament for renewal of its power to spend the revenues it is collecting. The objects of its expenditures and their costs are explicitly spelled out in the Appropriation Bill, and their duration is limited to the year covered by that Appropriation Bill.

Although it is not inconceivable that the expenditures included in a given Appropriation Bill, even if somewhat increased, could be financed from existing taxes, it is more probable that there would be a need for new taxes or a reformulation and an increase in the rates of existing ones. Therefore a Finance Bill accompanies the Appropriation Bill. If it is so set forth in a given Finance Bill, the finance minister may subsequently modify the rates of the taxes included in the bill by an order in the *Government Gazette*, without previous consent of the House of Representatives. The minister must, however, go to the House for approval of his order within a specified interval. The House may approve by a resolution, rather than by enacting a bill. Should the House not approve the minister's change, the change is revoked but without affecting what transpired between the date of the order and the House's revocation of it.

The financial, or budgetary, year, to which the finance and appropriations bills refer, runs from October 1 through September 30, although the income tax year is April through March. The budgetary process usually commences in January with a circular from the Treasury Department of the Ministry of Finance to the various administrative departments of the government asking them to indicate by the fifteenth of March, on the basis of their estimates for the preceding year, their proposed new projects for the coming financial year, together with estimates of financial and personnel needs.

These proposals are subjected to resource availability, technical feasibility, and relative priority tests. Projects that survive these tests are returned to their respective departments to be drawn up in detail for inclusion in the budget. Differences between the Treasury Department and the other departments regarding the proposals are reconciled at the departmental level if possible; otherwise they are referred by the Treasury Department to the minister of finance for reconciliation at the ministerial level.

After such ministerial conferences, the budget takes its preliminary shape and goes to the Government Printer for the first print of budget estimates. This is then reviewed by the cabinet in terms of estimated domestic availability of revenue resources and the possibilities of borrowing at home and abroad. As cleared by the cabinet, the budget goes back to the printer, whence it emerges as the second print of budget estimates.

This version is placed before the House of Representatives on the day of the first reading of the Appropriation Bill. Two or three days later the second reading of the Appropriation Bill follows. This is introduced by the minister of finance's budget speech, in which he reviews the economic situation of the current fiscal year, previews the government's expenditure program for the next fiscal year, and sets forth the tax increases and additions he proposes to institute in order to finance the new expenditures. The second reading is thereafter devoted to a debate on the budget, which usually lasts at least ten days.

Upon conclusion of the second reading, the House of Representatives transforms itself into a committee of the whole and again considers the bill in terms of "cut motions" by the nonministerial members of the House. Nonministerial members may only introduce motions to cut budget items; motions to increase budget items or to introduce new ones must be introduced by ministers, and then only after clearance by the cabinet. After several days of "cut motion" debate, the bill, as modified, goes through the third reading and emerges voted by the House. Also provided by the vote are the revenues and borrowings necessary to finance the expenditures included in the bill.

Thereafter the minister of finance authorizes, by a series of warrants, the incurring of the expenditures authorized in the Appropriation Act. For the sake of convenience, a general warrant is obtained for all expenditure items over which the cabinet has no wish to retain further control. The items not included in the general warrant are subsequently released under special warrants to the corresponding departments.

At the end of the financial year the department heads present their accounts to the auditor general. He reviews them and sends his findings to the Public Accounts Committee of the House of Representatives, which in turn reviews the auditor general's findings and submits its own recommendations to the House. These are then studied by the Treasury Department. If the recommendations are not acceptable to the treasury, the House has the prerogative of pursuing the matter further. This process often requires eighteen months or more.

STRUCTURE OF THE REVENUE SYSTEM

The framework of the revenue system was retained from the colonial administration. Successive postindependence governments have increased the rates of taxation, expecially on the export sector, thereby absorbing most of the profits created there. The government has periodically sought to increase the effectiveness of the revenue system in the face of the decline of prices and revenues in the export sector (see ch. 22, Trade). In fiscal years 1953/54 and 1966/67 the government established taxation inquiry commissions to analyze the functioning of the system and to make recommendations for improvement. In addition, foreign specialists were asked for advice and recommendations, and on a more or less regular basis the government received suggestions from experts of the United Nations, the International Monetary Fund (IMF), the International Bank for Reconstruction and Development (IBRD), and the Agency for International Development (AID) of the United States government.

When the Taxation Inquiry Commission of 1966/67 was set up, the tax system proper (exclusive of such items as fees, charges, and sales) of the central government consisted of twelve separate revenue sources: personal income taxes, corporate income taxes, wealth tax, estate duty, gifts tax, stamp duty, excise duties, tea tax, business turnover tax, import and export duties, resale of automobiles, and transfer of property to nonnationals. The system was characterized by high taxes on major exports, by a miscellaneous collection of import taxes, and by extremely high rates of income taxation. The income tax on corporations was 50 percent, and the top marginal rate on individuals was 80 percent, with rapid rates of progression. The wealth tax on individuals was also high.

The Taxation Inquiry Commission started with the premise that in a developing country the primary function of a tax system was to produce revenue and that equity, within reason, should yield to the demands of revenue collection and the economic growth of the country. Because the corporation was the best mechanism for producing private sector savings, which in turn were the source of private sector growth, the commission concluded, on the one hand, that corporations should be fostered and, on the other, that they should also be taxed as far as it was to the best interests of the country to do so.

The corporate income tax was subject to periodic fluctuations, however, and to that extent was undependable as a revenue source. The commission therefore concluded that, for steady revenue flow, dependence should be placed on a broad-based set of consumption taxes, with differential rates to minimize the regressive tendency inherent in the consumption tax. This was also recommended on a strictly pragmatic basis because both incomes and exports were already being taxed to about the limit. There was thus no alternative to more and higher import duties and excises to secure the necessary additional revenue. Because taxable imports would in the future be replaced by domestically produced substitutes, consumption taxes would increasingly have to bear the brunt of the search for new revenues.

The commission advised the government to raise the exemptions, lower the top rates, and ease the progression rate on income, wealth, and gift taxes; to raise the excise taxes on tobacco, arrack, beer, and domestically consumed tea; and to increase the coverage and reduce the exemptions of the turnover tax. The commission also recommended that the personal income tax of employees should be on a pay-as-you-go basis and that import duties and tobacco taxes should be on an ad valorem, rather than specific, basis.

Furthermore, the commission suggested as essential to the purpose of streamlining and energizing the revenue system that all revenue departments should be placed together in the Directorate of Revenue within the Ministry of Finance. The directorate would be headed by a director general, who would have equal status with the treasury secretary.

By mid-1970 the government had put into effect many of the commission's recommendations. It raised the excises on tobacco and coconut arrack and put the tobacco excise on an ad valorem basis. Import duties and export duties on minor exports were placed on an ad valorem basis; imports were shifted from wholesale to c.i.f. (cost, insurance, freight) pricing; and the whole customs tariff was based on internationally accepted commodity categories in the Brussels Tariff Nomenclature. The government increased the rates of the business turnover excise on luxury and semiluxury articles, removed the exemption of cigarettes from the turnover tax, and lowered from Rs100,000 to Rs75,000 the level of annual output that entitled a business to exemption from the turnover tax. It also put the personal income tax for employees on a pay-as-you-go basis, effective in the summer of 1970. As a consequence, the revenue system in early 1970, although structured much as it had been before 1970, was differently weighted.

Direct Taxes

The income tax was one of those inherited from the pre-independence period. In mid-1968 an estimated 162,800 individuals paid income tax. For tax purposes, personal income in 1970 included income from all sources including that of one's spouse and children (except earned income of children), net of the expenses incurred in producing the income. Exemptions ranged from Rs3,000 to Rs5,700, depending on the existence of earned income and the number of dependents. The rate schedule began at 7½ percent and ran through twelve brackets to a top rate of 65 percent on taxable income above Rs48,000.

Individuals residing abroad pay a top rate of 65 percent on taxable income above Rs55,000 earned within Ceylon, and Hindu joint families pay 65 percent, plus 6 percent, on taxable income over Rs85,000 (see ch. 7, Family). Capital gains have a top limit of 25 percent; capital losses may be set off indefinitely against capital gains.

Corporations are treated as separate entities subject to a flat nonrefundable tax of 50 percent on their taxable income. A withholding tax of 33 1/3 per cent is levied on dividends distributed by resident companies. In the hands of shareholders the gross dividend is taxable, subject to a credit equal to the payment already made at the source by the company involved. Nonresident companies are additionally liable to a 6-percent levy in lieu of the estate tax. Tax incentives to business take the form of lump sum depreciation, indefinite carry-forward of losses against profits, and special treatment for new undertakings, small enterprises, and enterprises engaged in fishing. Usually cooperative societies are exempt from income tax. Charitable institutions are liable to a tax on their business and investment income. Closely held companies are penalized.

There are, in addition, wealth, gifts, and estate taxes with various rates and exemptions for residents and nonresidents. These taxes are all progressive, as is the rice subsidy tax that was introduced in 1967. The rice subsidy tax is payable by individuals having a taxable income of Rs12,000 and above.

Indirect Taxes

Customs duties were part of the revenue system Ceylon inherited from the preindependence period. Until 1950 import duties were consistently the government's major source of tax revenue. At various times, in addition to producing revenue, import duties were used to provide protection to domestic industry, grant incentives to new enterprises, discourage imports of nonessential commodities, and keep prices of essential commodities stable.

By the time the Taxation Inquiry Commission made its report, customs duties had become a confused multiplicity of rates that greatly needed rationalizing. In 1968 the government introduced a new customs tariff based on the Brussels Tariff Nomenclature. Under the new tariff, all categories of imports are specifically classified and the import duties standardized on the following basis: foodstuffs, chemicals, essential consumer goods, and industrial and agricultural machinery—duty-free; nonessential articles—10-percent preferential and 20-percent general; such articles as photographic goods, electric lighting, signaling equipment, and microphones—revenue-producing rates of 50 percent to 60 percent; articles under Open General License (OGL)—protective rates of 100 percent to prevent overimporting or to provide protection; such articles as liquor, tobacco products, luxury vehicles, and other luxury items—prohibitive rates ranging up to 300 percent. The new system involved putting imports on a c.i.f. basis and import duties on an ad valorem basis.

Export duties, also inherited, accounted for more than 25 percent of total government revenues in fiscal year 1955/56. By 1965/66 the proportion had fallen to about 14 percent. In the mid-1950s duties on exports averaged 18 to 20 percent of the total value of exports; from 1957/58 to 1965/66 that ratio declined to 14.4 percent.

For tariff purposes, exports are divided into the major exports—tea, rubber, and coconut products—and minor exports, which comprise all other export products and are insignificant in their tax contribution. The export duty on tea is the most important; it is divided into two parts: a specific tax on exports and an ad valorem tax that rises and falls with the tea auction prices in London and Colombo. The combined taxes in 1965/66 amounted to 18 percent of the value of tea exports.

The duties on rubber and coconut products are on sliding scales according to prices in the corresponding major international commodity markets. From 1959/60 to 1965/66 the export tax rates on coconut products were more stable and tended to average around 15 percent.

The excise duty category is misnamed to the extent that it includes rentals from arrack, toddy, and foreign liquor taverns; licenses; fees; and profits from the sale of arrack and salt.

414

Liquor rentals refer to auctions for the monopoly of the sale of the respective liquors in various parts of the country. Excise duties proper consist of the duties on country-made liquors (gin, brandy, beer, and other country spirits), tobacco, and matches. The duties are specific; as noted, the important ones have been, or are being, increased and expanded to include locally consumed tea.

The business turnover tax came into operation in 1963. It is a multiple stage tax on the turnover of all businesses other than those specifically exempted and those that had a turnover of less than a fixed amount during the taxable year. The tax had a large number of exemptions, different rates for manufacturing businesses and 1 percent on nonmanufacturing businesses, with an exemption of Rs100,000. The Taxation Inquiry Commission recommended making the tax shiftable, deleting most of the exceptions, lowering the exemption, and raising the tax rate on manufacturing businesses. By mid-1970 some of the recommendations had been implemented.

REVENUES AND EXPENDITURES

Governmental expenditures, which are divided into recurrent and capital (developmental), have consistently exceeded revenues, often by considerable margins. Total expenditures of the central government in fiscal year 1967/68, the last year for which actual figures were available in mid-1970, came to over Rs3 billion (see table 27). This figure was slightly more than 30 percent of the gross national product (GNP) of the calendar year 1968 and exceeded by about Rs829 million the government's revenue for fiscal year 1967/68 (see table 28). Estimated revenues increased by 83 percent between 1958/59 and 1968/69, and estimated expenditures rose by approximately 65 percent during the same period.

Revenues

Revenues are broken down into sixteen categories, of which the three tax categories of customs duties, excise taxes, and direct taxes on income and wealth were consistently the largest during the 1958/59 to 1968/69 period. As a group, they increased by 58 percent during the ten-year period, although excise tax revenue increased by some 185 percent. The other revenue sources increased by about 80 percent.

As preliminarily estimated for budget purposes, 1969/70 revenues were forecast at Rs2.8 billion (see table 29). This estimate was divided between more than Rs1.68 billion in taxes and nearly Rs1.15 billion from other revenue sources. The main

Table 27. Expenditures of the Central Government of Ceylon, Selected Years, 1958/59 to 1969/70
(millions of rupees)

	Actual						Estimate	
	1958/59	1960/61	1963/64	1965/66	1966/67	1967/68	1968/69	1969/70
Governor General, Prime Minister, Supreme Court, Parliament.	7.6	10.9	11.0	13.3	12.0	12.6	23.5	37.4
Ministries:								
Defence and External Affairs	98.2	129.2	112.2	121.7	129.1	135.5	159.3	164.6
Planning and Economic Affairs	0.3	0.3	0.3	0.8	2.1	3.2	4.9	5.4
Information and Broadcasting	...	...	...	...	...	1.6	10.0	5.6
State	16.8	17.9	20.6	27.5	28.1	31.8	34.5	38.4
Finance	418.0	284.0	637.2	435.3	502.5	632.4	585.9	1,029.3
Land, Irrigation, and Power	90.0	244.6	205.0	234.4	291.7	384.4	422.6	454.4
Home Affairs	39.9	40.0	47.2	55.6	65.3	63.5	75.5	73.7
Health	141.9	152.1	152.0	164.0	180.1	196.2	221.3	230.4
Nationalized Services	23.2	31.5	31.8	38.0	43.7	58.2	60.0	49.1
Industries and Fisheries	6.2	51.2	6.5	90.6	154.8	141.7	208.5	174.2

Commerce and Trade	21.5	96.3	54.6	14.4	5.6	2.2	2.8	4.8
Justice	23.4	24.8	24.2	25.4	25.2	25.5	27.6	29.5
Local Government	38.4	50.2	60.9	66.6	69.8	70.8	97.3	102.9
Agriculture and Food	237.0	317.0	452.1	390.0	334.2	448.9	507.9	571.4
Education and Cultural Affairs	250.6	302.1	360.5	367.6	385.8	404.8	479.8	506.1
Labor and Employment	8.6	10.1	9.7	10.5	11.5	11.6	11.9	13.2
Public Works, Posts, and Telecommunications.	93.3	123.8	149.6	151.4	191.7	195.9	228.0	285.2
Communications	114.4	142.7	143.7	171.4	167.1	167.4	187.9	180.6
Social Services	32.9	32.4	33.6	43.7	33.0	39.5	32.9	33.0
Scientific Research and Housing	....	....	....	....	....	3.5	8.5	9.8
Loan fund expenditure	286.5	....	....	....	....	....	....	....
Total	1,948.7	2,061.0	2,512.7	2,422.2	2,633.3	3,031.2	3,420.6	3,999.0

*Before November 20, 1967, Rs4.76 equaled US$1; thereafter, Rs5.95 have equaled US$1.

Source: Adapted from Ceylon, *Appropriation Act, No. 30 of 1969: Estimates of the Revenue and Expenditure of the Government of Ceylon for the Financial Year, 1 October 1969 to 30 September 1970,* Colombo, 1969, pp. 25-30.

417

Table 28. Revenues of the Central Government of Ceylon, Selected Years, 1958/59 to 1969/70
(millions of rupees)[1]

Revenue	Actual Revenue						Estimate	
	1958/59	1960/61	1963/64	1965/66	1966/67	1967/68	[2]1968/69	1969/70
Customs	674.2	659.8	687.1	682.7	692.7	709.9	760.8	616.0
Port, harbor, wharf, warehouse, and other dues.	26.8	26.6	29.6	33.8	33.8	36.3	38.3	37.3
Excise revenue	129.7	207.0	296.1	355.0	402.1	449.8	499.6	695.8
Income tax, estate duty, stamps, etc.	229.5	314.0	335.8	322.6	353.8	363.2	375.0	374.0
Licenses and internal revenue not otherwise classified.	18.6	28.7	49.7	51.1	68.0	102.7	41.9	48.0
Fees of court or office and payment for specific services.	16.3	28.5	29.7	34.3	35.7	27.3	30.0	30.7
Health services	3.9	4.2	4.8	5.7	6.5	6.5	6.8	7.0
Reimbursements	17.9	19.0	21.4	22.7	23.1	23.3	24.8	24.2
Postal and telecommunication services	40.1	46.0	50.4	54.8	56.9	64.6	67.0	78.0
Interest, annuities, and others	20.8	21.0	29.6	38.5	48.0	56.0	59.6	98.6

Miscellaneous receipts	34.2	34.4	68.7	109.0	64.7	102.5	68.1	78.9
Land revenue	4.8	4.4	5.9	6.5	7.6	7.2	7.3	7.5
Land sales	1.6	1.7	2.2	2.0	2.3	3.0	4.0	4.0
Receipts from sale of foreign exchange entitlement certificates.	...	...	...	...	...	77.0	265.8	540.0
Broadcasting department revenue	6.6	7.1	8.9	8.2	1.6	...	...	...
War loan interest	0.4	...	...	...	...	...	...	...
Subtotal (exclusive of railway and electrical department revenue).	1,225.2	1,402.2	1,620.0	1,726.9	1,796.8	2,029.5	2,249.2	2,640.1
Railway revenue	81.5	84.7	100.4	99.9	102.1	106.7	109.2	110.7
Electrical department revenue	23.7	27.1	37.3	50.7	55.9	65.8	77.1	83.2
Grand total[3]	1,330.4	1,513.9	1,757.6	1,877.6	1,954.8	2,202.1	2,435.5	2,833.9

[1]Before November 20, 1967, Rs4.76 equaled US$1; thereafter, Rs5.95 have equaled US$1.

[2]Revised.

[3]Figures may not add because of rounding.

Source: Adapted from Ceylon, *Appropriation Act, No. 30 of 1969: Estimates of the Revenue and Expenditure of the Government of Ceylon for the Financial Year, 1 October 1969 to 30 September 1970*, Colombo, 1969, p. 4.

Table 29. Estimated Budget Revenues of the Central Government
of Ceylon, 1969/70
(millions of rupees)[1]

Revenue	Amount
Tax	
Customs	616.0
Exports	297.0
Tea	(185.0)
Rubber	(41.3)
Coconut products	(40.2)
Other	(30.5)
Imports	319.0
Excise	695.7
Turnover	(282.0)
Tobacco	(220.0)
Profit from sale of arrack	(125.0)
Other	(68.7)
Direct taxes on income and wealth	374.0
Personal and corporate income[2]	(330.0)
Wealth	(11.0)
Estate	(9.0)
Rice subsidy	(2.0)
Gifts	(1.5)
Other[3]	(20.5)
Subtotal	1,685.7
Other	
Sale of foreign exchange settlement certificates	540.0
Railway revenue	110.7
Electrical department revenue	76.6
Postal, telephone, and telegraph revenue	78.0
Revenue from state-sponsored corporations	35.0
National lottery revenue	21.0
Miscellaneous: dues, fees, interest, licenses, receipts, sales, and service charges.	286.9
Subtotal	1,148.2
Total	2,833.9

[1]Before November 20, 1967, Rs4.76 equaled US$1; thereafter, Rs5.95 have equaled US$1.
[2]The revenue estimates do not distinguish between personal and corporate income.
[3]Includes Rs20 million in stamp sales, subsequently distributed among other categories.
Source: Adapted from Ceylon, *Appropriation Act, No. 30 of 1969: Estimates of the Government of Ceylon for the Financial Year, 1 October 1969 to 30 September 1970*, Colombo, 1969, pp. 7–17.

categories continued to be customs duties (Rs616 million), excise taxes (Rs695.7 million), and direct taxes (Rs374 million). Compared with the revised figures for 1968/69, however, the 1969/70 estimates showed some drastic changes.

Expenditures

In fiscal year 1969/70 the Ministry of Finance continued to disburse directly the largest amount of funds of the central government ministries. A large share of this expenditure was in pensions and public debt payments. The ministries involved in social services and economic development, such as education, health, communications, agriculture, public works, and irrigation, also made major expenditures. The Ministry of Defence and External Affairs continued to be a minor ministry in terms of funds expended (see ch. 25, The Armed Forces).

The government's estimated budgetary outlays in 1969/70 amounted to Rs4 billion (see table 30). Approximately 72 percent was for the recurrent costs of running the government; the balance was to provide for the government's outlays on new capital projects or on projects in process of completion. A breakdown of the 1969/70 estimates, on a functional basis, showed the three largest expenditure items to be for education, mainly elementary (almost Rs510 million); agricultural resettlement and irrigation, including produce subsidies, replanting programs, and animal husbandry (Rs480 million); and food subsidies (Rs362 million).

Finances of Local Government Units

The local governments have three main sources of revenue: local revenues, consisting mainly of the property tax, rates, and licenses; assigned revenues, which are collected by the central government on behalf of the local units; and grants from the central government, which assist the local units in financing capital outlays and help to fund the overrun of the local units that results from their only partially effective budgeting procedures.

A rough idea of the levels of income available to the local authorities is afforded by the fact that in 1964 the municipalities apparently had resources totaling somewhat more than Rs80 million; the urban councils apparently had an income of around Rs30 million, and the town councils had an income of about Rs6 million, both incomes excluding advances and deposits.

FISCAL ADMINISTRATION

At the time of the Taxation Inquiry Commission's report in 1968, fiscal policy was centralized in the hands of the Ministry of Finance, which was also responsible for monetary policy. Before fiscal year 1966/67, however, there had been little effort to integrate fiscal policy with the general economic and

Table 30. Estimated Budget Expenditures of the Central Government of
Ceylon, 1969/70
(millions of rupees)[1]

Purpose	Recurrent	Capital	Total
General administration	226.0	10.7	236.7
Justice and police	89.8	6.1	95.9
Defense	76.2	5.6	81.8
Education	463.1	46.8	509.9
Health	224.0	23.0	247.0
Housing	1.8	23.8	25.6
Food subsidies	361.8	....	361.8
Social welfare services	198.6	46.0	244.6
Land and agricultural resources (including forestry).	144.6	154.3 }	479.9
Irrigation	20.5	160.5 }	
Mineral surveys	1.3	0.2	1.5
Power (development and supply)	77.3	58.9	136.2
Roads and bridges	45.3	76.7	122.0
Ports, harbors, and airports	34.2	24.7	58.9
Industrial development (including fisheries).	22.8	183.4	206.2
Commerce and tourism development.	7.7	8.9	16.6
Postal services	93.2	21.3	114.5
Railway services	134.1	30.0	164.1
Other economic services	26.3	28.4	54.7
Interest on the public debt	238.3	....	238.3
Repayment of public debt	....	184.2	184.2
Purchase of FEECs by government[2] .	200.0	....	200.0
Other	195.6	23.0	218.6
Total	2,882.5	1,116.5	[3]3,999.0

[1]Before November 20, 1967, Rs4.76 equaled US$1; thereafter, Rs5.95 have equaled US$1.
[2]FEEC—Foreign exchange entitlement certificates.
[3]Does not agree with table, owing to rounding.
Source: Adapted from Ceylon, *Appropriation Act, No. 30 of 1969: Estimates of
the Government of Ceylon for the Financial Year, 1 October 1969 to 30
September 1970*, Colombo, 1969, pp. 31–33.

social policy of the government. The Treasury Department had
been responsible for making tax policy, even though this was
a task for which the treasury had insufficient personnel, and
those few had inadequate training and experience for the
purpose.

The administration of the revenue system was in the hands
of several independent and uncoordinated departments. Responsibility for customs duties and direct taxation lay with
two separate departments in the Ministry of Finance, whereas
responsibility for excise taxation was in the Ministry of Home
Affairs (in May 1970, changed to Ministry of Public Administration, Local Government, and Home Affairs). Responsi-

bility for the sale of foreign exchange entitlement certificates was vested in the Central Bank. The ministries of home affairs and finance shared responsibility for local unit budgets.

In the case of taxes on income and wealth, returns were filed each year for income, deductions, and allowances of the preceding year (the income tax year is April to March) and sent to the Department of Inland Revenue. There the returns were received, the tax was assessed, and the payment notice was sent to the taxpayer. Appeals from the assessment could be made to the commissioner of inland revenue and, if that failed, recourse could be had to the courts.

The Taxation Inquiry Commission recommended the establishment within the Ministry of Finance of the Directorate of Revenue with jurisdiction over all matters having to do with taxation, including policy, legislation, and implementation. Such a step, it was believed, would make practicable an effective coordination of tax and fiscal policy. It would furthermore place the minister of finance in a position to coordinate the whole realm of public finance, including the handling of the public debt, with the monetary and other activities of the Central Bank and with the objectives and activities of the development planning authorities. As of mid-1970 the government had not yet implemented this recommendation of the Taxation Inquiry Commission.

In 1970 review, audit, and if necessary, criticism of the implementation of the annual budget continued to lie with the auditor general, reporting to Parliament. Parliament, as it deems advisable, may take corrective or disciplinary action through its control over the appropriation process. Although the review process may take up to a year or more and thus tends to be self-diluting, it leaves the House of Representatives with the final voice in the whole matter of supply and use of government resources.

Public Debt of the Central Government

The gap between revenues and total expenditures has resulted in a rapid increase in the public debt (see table 31). The dimensions of the expenditure-revenue gap are difficult to arrive at by reviewing the expenditure-revenue data, inasmuch as for different purposes the gap may be presented as gross or net of interest and amortization payments, of sinking fund payments on certain domestic as well as foreign issues, and of the net position of semigovernment financial and industrial institutions. Increases in the domestic, or rupee, part of the public debt reflect, moreover, greater or lesser availability of

Table 31. Financing the Net Cash Deficit of the Government of Ceylon, Selected Years, 1958/59 to 1968/69[1]
(in millions of rupees)[2]

	1958/59	1960/61	1963/64	1965/66	1966/67	1967/68	1968/69 (estimate)
Current Payments							
Goods and services	886.5	977.1	1,053.4	1,139.6	1,206.5	1,357.8	1,469.2
Transfer payments							
Food subsidies	(146.5)	(248.0)	(375.4)	(290.0)	(193.0)	(297.5)	(334.5)
Interest on public debt	(44.0)	(68.6)	(113.7)	(123.1)	(143.4)	(166.4)	(191.9)
Grants to local authorities	(34.8)	(36.0)	(39.8)	(45.6)	(41.9)	(51.9)	(60.4)
Other (includes advances, net)	(168.4)	(155.8)	(155.2)	(204.1)	(275.1)	(205.6)	(228.0)
Total Transfer Payments	393.7	508.4	684.1	662.8	655.6	721.4	814.8
Total Current Payments	1,280.2	1,485.5	1,737.5	1,802.4	1,860.1	2,079.2	2,284.0
Total Capital Expenditures	463.6	490.9	483.2	596.9	701.5	792.8	945.4
Total Payments	1,743.8	1,976.4	2,220.7	2,399.3	2,561.6	2,872.0	3,229.4
Total Current Receipts[3]	1,330.4	1,513.9	1,759.0	1,833.3	1,954.8	2,156.4	2,338.5
Net Cash Surplus (+) or Deficit (–)	–413.4	–462.5	–461.7	–566.0	–606.8	–715.6	–890.9
Financing of Net Cash Deficit							
Foreign							
Grants	....	13.3	31.9	41.5	19.3	29.0 ⎫	403.2
Loans (net)	29.6	10.4	63.5	76.5	189.3	161.2 ⎭	

Domestic (net)							
Central bank	176.9	204.4	142.5	179.7	125.7	302.1 }	11.5
Commercial banks	-0.4	37.0	-27.3	-17.4	-74.4	1.4	286.5
Private nonbank	118.1	168.0	207.6	255.9	297.0	248.3	n.a.
Nonmarket borrowing	27.6	29.4	-1.9	112.2	72.3	9.8	n.a.
Government cash balances and commodity and counterpart funds.	61.7	....	45.4	-82.4	-22.4	-36.1	n.a.
Total Financing	[4]413.3	462.5	461.7	566.0	606.8	[4]715.7	890.9

n.a.—not available.

[1] The net cash deficit excludes: certain payments to international financial organizations and Central Bank special advances to finance them; contributions to sinking funds; direct repayment of public debt from revenue; and book adjustments arising from transfer to recurrent or capital expenditure of certain advances and losses incurred in previous financial years. Expenditure figures, therefore, may not agree with those published in the accounts of the government of Ceylon.

[2] Before November 20, 1967, Rs4.76 equaled US$1; thereafter, Rs5.95 have equaled US$1.

[3] Includes receipts from death, estate, and gift taxes; also includes principal repayments on account of government loans to local government units, government corporations, private sector enterprises, and others.

[4] Totals may not agree exactly with corresponding deficits because of rounding.

Source: Adapted from Central Bank of Ceylon, *Annual Report of the Monetary Board to the Minister of Finance for the Year 1968*, Colombo, 1969, tables 17, 19, and 22.

external financing. The domestic debt, as commonly presented by the Central Bank, on a net basis, totaled Rs4.9 billion at the end of September 1969, compared with Rs459 million in September 1950. In 1969 it was composed of Rs2.8 billion in government bonds, Rs1.75 billion in short-term treasury bills, Rs329 million in Central Bank advances (including special purpose loans and temporary financing), and Rs24.5 million in tax certificates. The domestic debt in 1969 was held mainly by the Central Bank (38 percent), provident and pension funds (21 percent), the various sinking funds (12 percent), savings institutions (11 percent), and insurance funds (8 percent).

THE MONETARY PROCESS

The monetary process in mid-1970 subsumed, on the one hand, the monetary apparatus and, on the other hand, the evidence of the workings of the apparatus as shown in the money supply, prices, and policy decisions.

The Monetary Apparatus

The monetary apparatus comprised the Capital market, the Central Bank of Ceylon, the commercial banks, and the savings, development, and other specialized institutions. In the absence of overall general banking legislation, unusually great dependence was placed on the discretionary powers of the Central Bank. At the same time, the Bank of Ceylon, the largest commercial bank, suffered from what were widely considered to be undesirable built-in constraints; as the first of Ceylon's indigenous banks, its ordinance of incorporation contained inhibitions and requirements that would probably have been considered less necessary had general banking legislation existed or had the Central Bank already been in existence. Neither the Central Bank nor the Bank of Ceylon, perhaps, could exert the restraining influence on governmental spending proclivities that might have been afforded by the existence of a general banking law.

Central Bank of Ceylon

The Central Bank of Ceylon was established in 1949 pursuant to the monetary law enacted in that year. The initial capital of Rs15 million was subscribed and paid up by the government and has not been increased.

The overall direction of the Central Bank rests with a three-member Monetary Board: the governor of the Central Bank, who is appointed by the governor general on the recommendation of the prime minister and is chairman of the board; the permanent secretary of the Ministry of Finance (ex officio); and a third member, also appointed by the governor general on the recommendation of the prime minister. The governor of the Central Bank and the third member are eligible for reappointment. The chief operating departments of the Central Bank are those dealing with exchange control, public debt, bank supervision, banking and currency, and economic research.

The objectives of the Central Bank are defined in the Monetary Law Act of 1949, as revised in 1956. The bank's task is to regulate the availability, cost, and international exchange of money, with the purpose of stabilizing domestic monetary values, preserving the international value of the rupee, and promoting high levels of production, employment, and real income in Ceylon through the full development of the country's productive resources.

The Central Bank has the sole right to issue currency in Ceylon. It is adviser to, and fiscal agent of, the government and is responsible for the management of the government debt. It is manager of the exchange control system, is the lender of last resort to the commercial banks, and is the guide and general warden of the monetary apparatus.

In pursuit of these objectives, the Central Bank has extensive monetary powers. It may alter the ratio of reserves the commercial banks must maintain against their deposits and the ratio of capital to assets. It may vary the bank rate, which is the rate of interest the Central Bank charges on advances to the commercial banks and which in turn serves as the cue to the commercial banks and other financial institutions to revise the whole structure of interest rates. The Central Bank may also engage in open market operations, making purchases and sales of government, or its own, securities to the public or the banking system in order to increase or decrease the quantity of money in the hands of the private sector, thereby inflating or deflating the economy as desired.

The bank is not bound by a fixed ratio between money supply and gold, dollars, sterling, or other monies, which in many countries serves as a statutory control over the amount of money that can be created at any given moment. On the other hand, the bank disposes of certain discretionary controls over the qualitative and quantitative composition of commercial bank credit that are far from universally granted to central banks. As in most other countries, however, it is the government that in the last analysis makes the decisions on the expansion or nonexpansion of credit, especially to the public sector, and thereby on the level of the money supply and prices.

The Central Bank is empowered to make short-term loans to commercial banks. Loans for 180 days may be made against promissory notes secured by liquid assets, and 270-day loans may be made for agricultural, animal, industrial, and mineral production. The bank is also allowed to make 365-day loans against securities to institutions dealing in mortgages, but only up to one-half of the value of the security tendered, and it may refinance production loans at long term. The bank may make direct provisional advances to the government to finance expenditures chargeable to the Consolidated Fund, provided such advances are repayable within 180 days and do not at any one time exceed 10 percent of estimated government revenue for that year.

At the end of 1968 the assets and liabilities of the Central Bank totaled Rs2.96 billion. The chief categories were: international assets, Rs235 million; loans and advances to government, Rs315 million, and to others, Rs89 million; and holdings of government and government-guaranteed indebtedness, Rs1.6 billion. Capital and surplus amounted to Rs69 million; notes in circulation, Rs1.1 billion; and coins, Rs66 million.

Commercial Banks

The commercial banks provide traditional short-term financing—bills, overdrafts, and loans—on which the export economy depends. The commercial bank system had its beginnings in the mid-nineteenth century. By the time of independence in 1948, there were seven exchange banks, three Indian and Pakistani banks, and two Ceylonese banks. At the end of 1969 there were still twelve commercial banks, but they included three Ceylonese banks, five exchange banks, and four Indian and Pakistani banks. The largest were the nationalized Bank of Ceylon and the People's Bank.

The exchange banks were all established before independence as branches of large British banks. Their original purpose was to finance the coffee planters and the two-way movement of the foreign trade that was the outgrowth first of coffee and subsequently of tea, rubber, and coconuts. This they initially did largely without capital or reserves, on the basis of local deposits and, in case of emergency, by having recourse to their head offices in London. The banks were mostly limited to their Colombo office and perhaps one or more offices in main towns, such as Kandy, Galle, and Nuwara Eliya, in the plantation districts. The bulk of their assets comprised liquid assets and government bills and securities. Their activity followed the movements of exports and imports, although through agency and brokerage firms they sometimes made short-term capital available to the plantations. Before the 1930s the banks also made substantial advances to the *chettiars* (Indian moneylenders).

The exchange banks usually kept their business with Ceylonese clients separate from that with Europeans. In charge of transactions with the Ceylonese clients was a *shroff*, or head cashier. He was a Ceylonese who personally guaranteed the loans the banks made its Ceylonese clients and was legally liable for the loans he guaranteed. The bank paid him interest on loans he brought to it, and the borrowers paid him a commission. His guarantee was secured by a mortgage on property of a least twice the value of the loan. This system was apparently in operation at some of the Indian and Pakistani banks as well as the exchange banks. After 1955 use of the *shroff* system was either restricted or abandoned entirely.

There were three Indian banks and one Pakistani bank in 1969; they were all branches of major banking institutions in their respective countries. With the exception of the State Bank of India, they had come to Ceylon after World War II; the State Bank of India, under earlier names (Bank of Madras and Imperial Bank of India), had been in Ceylon since 1867 and served as Ceylon's clearinghouse from 1885 until the establishment of the Central Bank. The Indian and Pakistani banks were primarily concerned with deposits, financing trade with their respective countires, and effecting remittances. The Pakistani bank also financed some local wholesale and retail trade.

In 1961 the foreign banks were forbidden by the government to accept new deposits from Ceylonese nationals, thereby opening the way for rapid expansion of the Ceylonese banks. In 1968 this constraint was partially removed; British banks that were prepared to broaden their ownership to include minority Ceylonese participation were permitted to resume accepting Ceylonese deposits, provided credit based on such deposits would only be made to Ceylonese nationals. On June 14, 1970, however, the newly elected government announced that, in keeping with its campaign promises, the foreign-owned banks would be nationalized.

At the end of 1967 the assets of the Ceylonese banks (Bank of Ceylon, People's Bank, and the very small Hatton Bank) totaled Rs1.56 billion (compared with Rs272 million in 1950); those of the Indian and Pakistani banks, Rs82.9 million (Rs82.3 million in 1950); and those of the exchange banks, Rs484 million (Rs504 million in 1950). The percentage of loans and advances—including bills discounted—to total deposits was 68.9 percent for the Ceylonese banks, 41.7 percent for the Indian and Pakistani banks, and 80.1 percent for the exchange banks.

Because in 1938 the banking facilities available to the Ceylonese community were considered inadequate, the colonial government established the Bank of Ceylon as a Ceylonese bank for the Ceylonese. The bank had an authorized capital of Rs7.5 million consisting of 30,000 preference shares (Rs1.5 million) and 120,000 ordinary shares (Rs6 million). The preference shares were from the start taken up by the government. Of the ordinary shares, 30,000 were initially issued; an additional 30,000 were issued in 1944. In 1961 the bank was nationalized.

Although the bank originally was created to provide commercial banking facilities to the Ceylonese community and was strictly limited as to the amount and kind of security required, it also engaged in some medium- to long-term lending activities after 1961. In 1970 the bank was increasingly interested in assisting the government's development efforts, provided ways could be found to improve its capital structure. At the end of 1968 the Bank of Ceylon was the largest commercial bank, having some forty-five branches and deposits of Rs892 million, almost 50 percent of the total commercial bank deposits.

The People's Bank was established in 1961, with the objective of combining short-term lending with medium- and long-term financing to shore up the cooperative movement, develop rural banking, and extend agricultural credit to small rural producers. It was capitalized at Rs6 million in ordinary shares (subject to increase by Parliament), half of which were taken up by the government and the balance were made available for purchase by cooperative societies. The Central Bank, as instructed by the minister of finance, is authorized to issue debentures on behalf of the People's Bank.

The activities of the People's Bank are more extensive than those of the Bank of Ceylon. To achieve the basic purpose of assisting in the rehabilitation and development of the cooperative movement, the powers of the People's Bank include: pawnbroking; the extension of short-, medium-, and long-term loans to cooperative societies and cultivation committees; the extension of loans to small-scale agricultural, industrial, and business undertakings, both rural and urban; the granting of small personal loans to rural residents; and the providing of technical assistance in those several spheres. By 1969 it had eighty-four branches and had become the second largest commercial bank.

The People's Bank channels funds to the rural sector through a number of devices. It provides funds to the cooperative movement through overdraft facilities to financially experienced multipurpose societies and by discounting the cooperatives' receipts from the government for goods, especially receipts for the delivery of rice to government purchasing agencies. These discounted receipts can be rediscounted at the Central Bank, and this process enables the cooperatives to keep up their purchases of rice from the small farmer under the Guaranteed Price Scheme when the government is slow in its commodity payments (see ch. 19, Agriculture). In 1967 People's Bank credit to the cooperative societies was between Rs150 million and Rs175 million.

After 1964 the People's Bank created a number of rural banks, by establishing in selected multipurpose cooperative societies rural credit departments to accept deposits and make loans. These proved successful and contributed to the efforts of the People's Bank to help incorporate the rural sector into the money economy. At the end of 1969 the bank's credit outstanding to the agricultural sector for cultivation, marketing, and consumer needs exceeded Rs200 million; the bank also had the best record of repayments of any institution engaged in the financing of peasant agriculture. In 1968 it also became involved in lending to industry, relieving government departments of that responsibility.

Specialized Financial Institutions

Although the government has increasingly sought to engage the commercial banks in development efforts, in 1970 the commercial banks, with the exceptions of the Bank of Ceylon and the People's Bank, continued to concentrate on their traditional role of short-term lending for business and commercial purposes. To provide the longer term financing that the development of both agriculture and industry required, the government since the mid-1940s has established various specialized institutions for financing development activities. A general characteristic of these institutions, in common with the nationalized commercial banks, has been an inadequacy of capitalization. Among the more important of the specialized institutions are the State Mortgage Bank, the Agricultural and Industrial Credit Corporation of Ceylon (AICC), the Development Finance Corporation of Ceylon (DFCC), the Insurance Corporation of Ceylon (ICC), the Cey-

431

lon Savings Bank, the Loan Board, and the National Housing Fund.

The State Mortgage Bank was established in 1931 to provide medium- and long-term credit to the agricultural sector, but in the mid-1930s its scope was expanded to include housing, urban as well as rural. Until 1968 the bank's business was confined to long-term credits, up to twenty-five years and up to Rs1 million, mainly secured on the primary mortgage of immovable property. Credit was available only to Ceylonese nationals. The bank did not accept deposits or engage in commercial operations, but it could act jointly in a loan operation with a bank that did lend on short term.

The bank's funds have come from government-guaranteed overdrafts at the Central Bank, from sale of debentures, and from government loans. Debentures could not exceed total outstanding loans secured by mortgages or otherwise as prescribed by the minister of finance. In the late 1960s most of the bank's debentures were held by government or semigovernment institutions. Repayments of loans had to be used to retire debentures. The limit on its operations in 1967 was Rs75.6 million.

In 1968 the bank's area of activity was enlarged to permit it to assume an increasingly important part in the development of agriculture, including tea plantations, the dairy industry, and subsidiary food crops. Simultaneously, the bank's security requirements were relaxed so that it could accept, in addition to primary mortgages, land with village title, suitable personal guarantees, life insurance policies, motor vehicles, bank guarantees, and promissory notes. Outstanding loans at the end of 1969 totaled Rs62 million.

The AICC was established in 1943 to provide long-term credit facilities to agricultural and industrial enterprises and cooperative societies for replanting existing plantations and opening new plantations, for factory expansion and the modernization of agricultural and industrial production facilities, and for the refinancing of debts incurred by such enterprises. Credit extended by the AICC takes the form of loans secured by primary mortgage of immovable property or by the pledging of livestock, standing crops, or permanently installed plant and equipment, provided the land they occupy can also be offered as security. This proviso is frequently a major obstacle because of the lack of assurance surrounding many land titles in Ceylon.

The AICC's own financing was originally a Rs10 million line of credit from the government. In 1950 the limit was increased to Rs30 million. In 1955 the line of credit was exhausted, and thereafter, until fiscal year 1969/70, its lending activities were limited to the annual income resulting from the repayment and interest from its outstanding loans. In 1969/70 the government determined that the AICC should take its loans to the Central Bank for refinancing and could raise its own limits on debt refunding and aggregate loans to any one borrower. By the end of September 1969 the AICC's outstanding loans totaled Rs31 million.

The DFCC was established in 1955 to undertake the numerous functions of development finance corporations: lending, investing in shares, underwriting, guaranteeing financial obligations, and providing technical assistance for most industries, including construction and transportation. The DFCC processes only those projects approved by the government. At the end of 1966 the government held 25 percent of the authorized share capital of Rs8 million; 39 percent was held by the domestic private sector, and 35 percent was held abroad. In 1967 the authorized share capital was increased to Rs24 million, and the corporation's powers were broadened, but as of the end of 1969 the distribution of paid-in capital had not changed.

At the end of March 1969 the DFCC's resources totaled Rs64.5 million, including capital of Rs8 million, reserves and surplus equal to Rs2.5 million, and a subordinated government loan of Rs16 million. In addition, the DFCC had a Rs4.5-million line of credit at the Bank of Ceylon and an indefinite amount of circumscribed refinancing facilities at the Central Bank, against which it had utilized some Rs9.75 million. In 1967 the corporation obtained a loan of US$4 million from the IBRD. In 1969 it obtained a further loan of US$8 million from the same source. The DFCC's outstanding loans and equities at the end of 1968 totaled Rs31.7 million.

In 1961 the ICC was established by the government with a monopoly over the writing of all new life insurance. Three years later the insurance business as a whole, which had been established in the nineteenth century, was similarly nationalized under the jurisdiction of the same corporation.

Before the new corporation was set up, there were 122 companies writing various kinds of insurance. Fifty-seven of them wrote life insurance, either exclusively or in combination with other forms of insurance; of these, 29 were foreign companies. There were 250,000 life insurance policies in effect, with a total value of about Rs750 million; 75 percent were in the hands of 7 foreign companies. The assets of all companies totaled about Rs410 million, of which foreign companies held about Rs344 million.

The ICC introduced group insurance and limited the amount of overseas reinsurance permitted in order to save foreign exchange. At the end of 1968 its premium income consisted of about Rs37 million from life insurance, Rs20 million from general accident insurance, and about Rs5 million and Rs4 million from fire insurance and marine insurance, respectively. Total investments amounted to almost Rs250 million in 1968.

The Ceylon Savings Bank, established in 1832 to promote thrift and mobilize savings, is the oldest financial institution in Ceylon. Originally a mixed bank, it was nationalized in 1869; it has subsequently been reorganized several times. In 1968 it had 171,437 depositors, savings deposits of about Rs98 million, housing loans of about Rs20 million, and investment in rupee securities of around Rs90 million.

The Loan Board was established by an ordinance of 1865, as amended in 1938. It receives deposits of suitors of the Supreme Court and district courts. The function of the Loan Board is to invest these funds to the best advantage of the suitors. All monies must be returned by the board to the respective suitors upon order of the courts. As a consequence, a high degree of liquidity must be maintained in the board's investments, which mostly are gilt-edged securities and house property loans with secure title. In 1966 the Loan Board had outstanding housing loans of approximately Rs11 million and investments in sterling, Indian, and rupee securities of around Rs75 million to Rs80 million.

The National Housing Fund was set up in 1954 to provide long-term (twenty to twenty-five years) financing ·for all aspects of residential development. It has had its funds from treasury loans and from the sale of debentures. In 1966 it was meeting about 20 percent of the apparent demand for the kind of financial services it offered. Inasmuch as it was apparently operating on a subsidized basis, however, the demand might be less if it were to charge enough to meet its costs. In 1968 it apparently granted loans of Rs14.3 million and had outstanding loans of about Rs114 million.

The Employees' Provident Fund, a mandatory government pension plan, was established in 1958 to include all employers of three or more persons not otherwise covered. Employee membership increased from 150,000 in 1959 to 1.54 million in 1967. The employer contributed 6 percent and the employee 4 percent of the gross wage. The fund's income was invested in government securities and, at the end of 1967, amounted to about Rs540 million. In addition to the official provident fund, there were some 400 other company funds with a combined membership of perhaps 50,000.

Savings facilities for small savers (the required minimum deposit is as little as 50 cents) are provided by the Ceylon Savings Bank, the Post Office Savings Bank, and the Ceylon savings certificates. The Post Office Savings Bank, established in 1885, had upward of 2,500 deposit offices in 1970. Savings certificates were introduced during World War II. Small savings are vigorously promoted through some 14,000 or more savings groups in all parts of the country, under the aegis of the National Savings Movement. At the end of 1968 the Post Office Savings Bank had deposits of Rs473 million, and the Ceylon Savings Bank, deposits of Rs100 million. Outstanding savings certificates totaled Rs91 million.

Capital Market

The capital market includes an unorganized indigenous market, which caters to the small rural or urban borrower and over which the Central Bank has little control, and an organized market, over which the Central Bank does have control and which may be subdivided into the call, short-term, and long-term money markets. Because at least 70 percent of the population depends on the land, the indigenous money market is largely, but not exclusively, a rural phenomenon. According to the Survey of Rural Indebtedness in 1957, less than 8 percent of rural credit was provided by government departments, cooperatives, and commercial banks taken together. Professional moneylenders, traders, and commission agents provided 25 to 30 percent, and relatives, friends, and landlords supplied more than 50 percent.

Professional moneylenders include Ceylonese and Indians—the latter of the *chettiar* caste—who mainly have their own December 1968, according to the index, were 106.4 and 127.4, rates from the commercial (mainly Indian) banks and reloan, often without security, at interest rates ranging from 12 to 18 percent and more.

The small village shopkeepers and itinerant small purchase agents lend on a very small scale. Because of their close association with their village debtors, the shopkeepers vary their terms to match the particular risk. Because they very often have to carry the borrower on credit from one harvest to the next, their terms are high, probably between 25 and 50 percent of the harvest. Important advantages from the viewpoint of the small rural borrower are that the creditors are available, the arrangement can be made rapidly, and they are willing to lend for consumption as well as for production.

The arrangements made by relatives and friends are not known. They probably vary appreciably from case to case and from one social group to another.

The call money market is confined mostly to interbank lending operations among the commercial banks in Colombo. Banks having surplus funds lend to those suffering from temporary shortages. Such lending is on very short term. After statutory reserves were established by the Central Bank and as the demand for credit rose, the excess reserves of the lending banks declined, and the cost of call money rose—from ½ percent in the early 1950s to 3½ percent after 1968. Call loans generally have been made without security.

Government treasury bills, redeemable within twelve months, were introduced in 1923 to meet short-term fluctuations in government revenue. The limit on treasury bills was successively raised from Rs10 million in 1941 to Rs25 million in 1948, Rs50 million in 1949, and Rs200 in 1953.

From the mid-1950s on, the government found itself increasingly in a financial squeeze. Under the pressure the treasury bills increasingly were used to help finance the annual deficits. The limit rose again in 1961, first to Rs750 million and then to Rs1,000 million. By stages the limit reached Rs1,750 million in 1968.

The treasury bill rate gradually rose from less than 1 percent in 1954 for public issues to 3 percent in 1963 and was at 3.64 percent at the end of 1968. The private market, however, was incapable of continuing to absorb rapidly increasing amounts of treasury bills, and the Central Bank has become the main depository for such bills. At the end of September 1968 the banking system held 96 percent of the total outstanding, with the Central Bank holding 91 percent. Since 1968 the yield to the Central Bank on treasury bills has been 2 percent.

Government securities have been marketed in Ceylon since 1892. In the post-World War II period, medium- and long-term loans were raised under the development loans acts, as well as under the annual appropriations acts. Up to 1958 the value of loans was not large, with a total of about Rs245 million from 1952 to 1958. After 1958, however, there was a sharp increase, with more than Rs1,100 million issued between 1959 and 1965. In September 1969 the total long-term government and government-guaranteed domestic debt, net of sinking fund holdings, stood at Rs2,798 million. The bulk of it was held by institutional investors.

There is no stock exchange in Ceylon, but since 1905 the Colombo Brokers Association, which is a commodity and share market, has served as a surrogate. In 1967 it had five members. It maintains a daily list of shares available and traded in the local market. In 1967, 230 shares were listed. In addition, there were preference shares and debenture issues of companies. The paid value of shares quoted in 1966 represented about 80 percent of the paid-up capital of all public companies at that time.

Turnover in the market has tended to be a function of the sale of foreign-held shares and the establishment of new companies. Because exchange control of remittances abroad in recent years restrained the sale of foreign-owned shares, there was a decline in the turnover in the market. This was compounded by tax measures introduced after 1958 and by the decline in the commodity markets.

Share prices also declined. On a 1952 base, prices reached a high of 103 in 1955, thereafter declining to 71 in 1963. In 1966 they had risen to 87 and then declined again to 74 by September 1969.

Cooperative Credit Societies

The cooperative movement officially dates from 1911, and until 1942 it was mainly a credit movement. Between 1942 and 1957 it went through a number of experimental changes; in 1957 it made an apparently permanent shift to multipurpose credit societies (see ch. 19, Agriculture).

In 1966, of 14,360 primary societies, those providing financing to agriculture comprised 3,621 credit societies and 5,158 multipurpose societies. The credit societies had a membership of 131,422, and the multipurpose societies had 944,782 members, out of a total of 1.8 million. The credit societies had working capital of Rs17 million, and the multipurpose societies, Rs123 million, out of a total Rs213 million.

The primary cooperative societies in 1966 were financed by seven cooperative provincial and district banks (Rs19.5 million), by the People's Bank (Rs34.4 million), and by the government through a number of its departments (Rs28 million). In 1966 the credit and multipurpose groups of societies had apparently granted loans of around Rs660 million to their members.

In 1967, in a move to improve the machinery for recovery of loans, the inadequacy in rural credit limits, and the length of time required for credit to reach the small farmers, the government designated the cooperative banks and the People's Bank as the sources of rural credit. By mid-1969 the rate of recovery had improved impressively, and the credit extended was more than 100 percent greater.

Money Supply

Currency

The money supply is defined as the sum of currency in the hands of the public and demand deposits held by the public in commercial banks. The standard unit of monetary value is the rupee, which is subdivided into 100 cents. Before 1952 the relationship between the rupee and the United States dollar was governed by the fact that the rupee was pegged to the pound sterling and moved in relation to third currencies in line with sterling.

On January 16, 1952, the government and the International Monetary Fund agreed on a par value for the rupee at the rate of Rs4.76 equal 1 United States dollar (1 rupee equaled US$0.21). On November 20, 1967, a new par value for the rupee was agreed on at the rate of Rs5.95 equal 1 United States dollar (1 rupee equals US$0.16615).

Since 1950 the currency issue has been the sole right of the Central Bank. As of the end of 1968 the Central Bank issued both notes and coins. The notes were denominated 10 cents, 25 cents, and 50 cents, and rupees, 1, 2, 5, 10, 50, and 100. The coins were denominated ½, 1, 2, 5, 10, 25, and 50 cents, and rupees, 1 and 5. The total currency issue at the end of 1968 amounted to Rs1,181.9 million, of which Rs9.1 million were held by the government, Rs106.6 million were in the banks, and Rs1,066.2 million were in the hands of the public. By comparison, currency in the hands of the public in 1950 had totaled Rs325.4 million and in 1960 had totaled Rs595.3 million.

Demand Deposits

Demand deposits held by the public at the end of 1968 totaled Rs847 million, compared with Rs585.4 million in 1950 and Rs613.6 million in 1960. In this connection, cooperative societies and state corporations, although in large part acting for the government and financed by it, were treated as part of the private, rather than the government, sector.

The money supply, therefore, at the end of 1968 totaled Rs1,913.2 million, compared with Rs910.7 million in 1950 and Rs1,208.9 million in 1960 (see table 32). In 1950 demand deposits represented 64.3 percent of the money supply; by 1960 that percentage had declined to 50.8 percent and in 1968 to 44.3 percent. The monetary authorities were inclined to attribute this rather anomalous trend to hoarding and tax evasion, as well as to the increased monetization of the rural sector.

The immediate causes of changes in the money supply are movements in the assets and liabilities of the various elements of the monetary apparatus. The underlying forces that induce these movements are broken down by the Central Bank into three main categories: external banking assets, private sector forces, and government sector forces; in addition there is a small balancing category called items in transit (see table 33).

Table 32. Money Supply of Ceylon, 1950–68
(in millions of rupees)*

| End of period | Held by the public | | Money Supply | Change (year-to-year) | Percentage Demand Deposits |
	Currency	Demand Deposits			
1950	325.4	585.3	910.7	303.9	64.3
1951	377.4	628.8	1,006.2	95.5	62.5
1952	356.6	539.2	895.8	110.4	60.2
1953	335.3	491.5	826.8	- 69.0	59.4
1954	341.8	615.3	957.1	130.3	64.3
1955	384.5	688.4	1,072.9	115.8	64.2
1956	401.1	725.7	1,126.8	53.9	64.4
1957	434.9	605.2	1,040.1	- 86.7	58.2
1958	529.8	546.9	1,076.7	36.6	50.8
1959	565.0	612.7	1,177.7	101.0	52.0
1960	595.3	613.6	1,208.9	31.2	50.8
1961	692.2	596.4	1,288.6	79.7	46.2
1962	712.6	630.0	1,342.6	54.0	46.9
1963	828.4	677.7	1,506.1	163.5	45.0
1964	853.0	768.8	1,621.8	115.7	47.4
1965	901.4	814.3	1,715.7	93.9	47.5
1966	882.5	776.4	1,658.9	- 56.8	46.8
1967	979.9	827.7	1,807.6	148.7	45.8
1968	1,066.2	847.0	1,913.2	105.6	44.3

*Before November 20, 1967, Rs4.76 equaled US$1; thereafter, Rs5.95 have equaled US$1.

Source: Adapted from Central Bank of Ceylon, *Annual Report of the Monetary Board to the Minister of Finance for the Year 1968*, Colombo, 1969, tables 1 and 2.

The external banking assets category is the net result of movements in the balance of payments. The private sector category comprises movements in commercial bank credit (net of changes in savings and fixed deposits) to the private sector proper by all the commercial banks, as well as credit extended by the People's Bank and the Bank of Ceylon to the cooperative societies and the state corporations. The government sector category consists of Central Bank credit to the government sector in the form of advances, treasury bills, and government and government-guaranteed securities; a smaller amount of commercial bank credit to the government in the same form, plus government import bills; and the changes in the government's cash balances with the banking system. Both private and government sectors include relatively minor items reflecting changes in noncredit, nondeposit items, such as capital, reserves, and the acquisition of physical assets.

Between December 1962 and December 1968, the money supply increased Rs570.5 million, some 42 percent. This increase reflected a net decline of Rs360 million in external

Table 33. Sources of Change in the Money Supply of Ceylon, 1963-68
(in millions of rupees)*

	1963	1964	1965	1966	1967	1968	Total
Net external banking assets	−53.2	+16.9	+79.8	−196.3	−91.5	−115.7	−360.0
Private sector (net)	+69.7	+25.5	−56.2	+ 57.6	−27.5	+ 98.6	+167.7
Cooperative institutions	....	....	− 9.0	+ 23.5	+ 5.9	+ 17.0	+ 37.4
State corporations	....	....	+ 9.2	+ 77.9	−39.8	+ 67.4	+114.7
Other private sector credit	+61.6	+30.4	−36.2	− 31.8	+37.4	+ 55.1	+116.5
Other commercial bank liabilities ...	+ 8.1	− 4.9	−20.2	− 12.0	−31.0	− 40.9	−100.9
Government sector	+147.2	+75.6	+67.1	+ 82.0	+267.8	+122.4	+762.1
Central bank credit	+146.5	+130.0	−10.7	+182.3	+122.6	+306.9	+877.6
Commercial bank credit	+19.7	+ 3.6	+92.3	− 62.6	+ 75.3	−114.9	+ 13.4
Government cash balances	− 8.3	− 3.2	−10.0	− 62.9	+ 56.0	− 69.4	− 97.8
Other net central bank liabilities ...	−10.7	−54.8	− 4.5	+ 25.2	+ 13.9	− 0.2	− 31.1
Items in Transit	− 0.2	− 2.3	+ 3.2	− 0.1	− 0.1	+ 0.2	+ 0.7
Change in money supply	+163.5	+115.7	+93.9	− 56.8	+148.7	+105.5	+570.5

*Before November 20, 1967, Rs4.76 equaled US$1; thereafter, Rs5.95 have equaled US$1.

Source: Adapted from Central Bank of Ceylon, *Annual Report of the Monetary Board to the Minister of Finance for the Year 1968*, Colombo, 1969, p. 126.

Table 34. Colombo Consumers' Price Index, Ceylon, 1955-68
(base 1952=100)

Period	All Items	Commodity					Sector		
		Food	Clothing	Fuel and light	Rent	Miscellaneous	Domestic	Import	Export
1955	100.5	105.1	80.5	102.3	101.5	94.6	98.4	102.8	102.2
1956	100.2	103.3	81.8	101.3	101.5	98.6	100.0	99.0	115.1
1957	102.8	104.9	84.4	97.3	101.5	106.9	104.9	98.1	126.8
1958	105.0	105.8	87.5	101.0	101.5	113.1	109.2	97.0	135.0
1959	105.2	104.7	92.1	102.4	101.5	115.3	108.0	97.1	153.1
1960	103.5	100.8	95.1	102.7	101.5	117.5	108.9	93.7	138.4
1961	104.8	99.8	103.9	104.4	101.5	122.8	112.3	94.6	119.1
1962	106.3	100.9	108.2	105.6	101.5	124.9	113.9	96.7	113.8
1963	108.8	103.0	118.2	103.0	101.5	126.6	113.4	102.5	117.7
1964	112.2	106.4	127.2	103.2	101.5	129.3	116.4	106.4	115.3
1965	112.5	107.3	126.8	100.7	101.5	128.3	116.4	106.4	127.2
1966	112.3	109.1	117.0	95.9	101.5	127.3	116.8	105.4	127.6
1967	114.8	112.7	116.7	96.5	101.5	128.9	117.1	111.2	123.9
1968	121.5	121.2	120.1	103.2	101.5	133.6	123.2	117.3	142.4

Source: Adapted from Central Bank of Ceylon, *Bulletin*, XX, No. 12, December 1969, Colombo, 1969, table 34.

441

banking assets, a net increase of Rs167.7 million in credit to the private sector, and an increase of Rs762 million in mainly Central Bank credit to the government sector. Each year during this period the major source of increase in the money supply was the central government, either directly or indirectly through its guarantee of other entities' securities absorbed by the Central Bank.

Prices

The chief measure of price movements in Ceylon is the Colombo Consumers' Price Index, based on 1952 prices and weights; it is probably restricted in its area coverage and outdated in its commodity coverage. The index is, however, the only regularly published measure of general price changes.

According to this index, the price level stood at 100.5 in 1955, at 106.3 in 1962, and at 121.5 in 1968 (see table 34). These are all yearly averages and show a rise in prices from 1955 to 1968 of 20.9 percent and from 1962 to 1968 of 14.3 percent. The end-of-year price levels in December 1962 and December 1968, according to the index, were 106.4 and 127.4, respectively, indicating an increase in the price level between those year-end dates of around 19.7 percent.

The change in prices between December 1962 and December 1968 compares with an estimated increase in real gross domestic product over that period of about 32 percent and an increase in the money supply of about 42 percent. The greater growth in income and money supply than in prices over the period would suggest, among other things, some increase in the use of money (especially currency) in the subsistence rural economy, the existence of a considerable degree of price control in the urban sector, and probably some deficiency in the index itself.

That the apparent divergence between the change in prices and the changes in income and money supply reflected some suppressed inflation is suggested by the fact that between the end of December 1967 and the end of December 1968 the price index rose from 119.3 to 127.4, or about 6.8 percent for the year. That the change in prices in 1967 and 1968 probably concealed inflationary tendencies is borne out by the fact that the Central Bank increased its interest rate from 5 percent to 5½ percent in 1968, thereby raising the whole pattern of interest rates, and established ceilings on commercial bank credit (see table 35). How strong the inflationary pressures were, however, was not easy to determine because of the relatively very large number of diverse influences affecting prices in 1967 and

1968. These influences included the devaluation of the rupee in November 1967; some wage increases in 1967 and 1968 to compensate for the rupee devaluation; increases in export prices of coconut products; the fact that some basic commodities, among them rice (which rose 50 percent in price in the 1965–68 period), were not included in the price index; the fact that other commodities were blanketed into the price control category in 1968 to keep them from rising further; and the multifarious effects of the introduction of the Foreign Exchange Entitlement Certificate plan in May 1968 (see ch. 22, Trade). In early 1970 the Central Bank further raised the bank rate to 6½ percent, implying that the pressures on prices were not yet entirely under control.

Table 35. Pattern of Interest Rates in Ceylon, 1968

Purpose	Rate (in percent)
Bank Rate	5.50
Central Bank Credit Fund Refinancing[1]	
Agricultural and industrial loans	4.00
Trade and commercial loans	5.50
Tea factory loans	5.00 - 7.00
Agricultural credit scheme loans or purchases	1.50
Commercial Bank Loans, Advances, and Discounts secured by:	
Government securities	5.75 - 8.50
Shares of joint stock companies	7.00 - 9.50
Stock in trade	7.00 - 9.50
Immovable property	7.00 - 9.50
Other forms of security	5.50 - 11.00
Unsecured advances	7.00 - 10.00
Bills bought or discounted	5.50 - 8.50
Deposits	
Fixed	
Less than Rs25,000 up to twelve months (maximum)[2]	3.50
More than Rs25,000 up to forty-eight months (maximum)[2].	4.25
Savings (maximum)	3.25
Government securities	
(more than twenty years' maturity)	5.50
Treasury bills	3.64

[1]Medium- and long-term loans of other credit institutions.
[2]Value of rupee—Rs5.95 equal US$1.

Source: Adapted from Central Bank of Ceylon, *Annual Report of the Monetary Board to the Minister of Finance for the Year 1968*, Colombo, 1969, p. 136.

SECTION IV.
NATIONAL SECURITY

CHAPTER 24

PUBLIC ORDER AND
INTERNAL SECURITY

During the years since independence in 1948, Ceylon has not been confronted with any popularly supported insurgency of either internal or external origin. In 1970, as during the late 1960s, the government expressed occasional concern that foreign-inspired Communists might resort to seditious activities in efforts to disrupt the public order and subvert the government. These elements constituted a minority, however, even within the Communist group, which was divided into warring factions (see ch. 14, Political Dynamics). At least partly because of tight police surveillance, these few extremists were unable to enlist broad popular support, and their activities were isolated and confined to propaganda and agitation.

In 1970 the foremost concern of internal security authorities continued to be focused on the latent danger of communal violence and resulting civil disorders such as had occurred in 1956, 1958, 1961, and 1966. Circumstances surrounding this communal tension are rooted in generations of mutual suspicion and mistrust between the Sinhalese and Tamil communities, especially over the issue of language (see ch. 5, Ethnic Groups and Languages; ch. 14, Political Dynamics).

In the 1960s there were two coup attempts by a handful of senior military and police officers. As far as is readily ascertainable, these officers did not attempt to rally any mass support, nor did they attempt to disseminate their political views outside their immediate circles. On both occasions the police and the armed forces remained loyal, and the coup attempts ended in the arrest and trial of those implicated. Most of the coup suspects were released on the ground of insufficient prosecution evidence, however, and those convicted by the Supreme Court were subsequently acquitted by the Judicial Committee of the Privy Council in London, the ultimate court of appeal in the judicial system (see ch. 13, The Governmental System).

The incidence of crime increased gradually in the 1960s in all categories of offenses and among all age groups. The authorities reported that juvenile crime was becoming a serious problem. They blamed growing economic difficulties among all classes of society, a general decline in the popular regard for law and authority, and an increased manufacture and consumption of alcoholic beverages.

Criminal courts, together with procedural and substantive laws, were based, with minor modifications, on British enactments of colonial times. The administration of criminal justice was widely regarded by the people as fair and impartial. When dissatisfied with the decisions of either the Supreme Court or the Court of Criminal Appeal, the Ceylonese citizens were able to appeal, in 1970 as in the past, to the Privy Council in London. Some politicians regard the role of the council to be an infringement on their country's exercise of unlimited sovereignty and have gone so far as to suggest that Ceylon should sever its dominion ties with Great Britain by becoming a republic under a new constitution. Other political leaders, however, disagree with such assertions, contending that the Privy Council serves effectively as an additional safeguard against the possibility of caprice or omission on the part of those in authority.

The organization and procedures of the Police Department in 1970 were based on British precedents that the country inherited. The department was under the direct control and supervision of the minister of defense and external affairs, who under the Constitution was also the prime minister. Directed by an inspector general of police, the department had an actual strength of more than 10,000 men in late 1960s. It also maintained an auxiliary force of about 2,200 reservists.

INTERNAL SECURITY

Since independence the country has not been forced to cope with any serious internal security problem resulting from insurgency, nor has it been confronted with any external threat to its territorial integrity or any popularly supported subversive movement aimed at overthrowing the lawfully constituted government. In 1956, for example, the decision of Prime Minister Solomon West Ridgeway Dias Bandaranaike's cabinet to exchange diplomatic missions with Communist China was based, at least in part, on the official assessment that there was no danger of foreign-supported Communist subversion in Ceylon. As a result, the primary concern of the police authorities has been focused on the prevention of civil disorders precipitated by communal passions (see ch. 14, Political Dynamics).

Antistate Activities

In the years since independence Ceylon has not outlawed any political or social organization for reasons of subversive threat, although there were instances where certain organizations were temporarily banned because of their menace, actual and potential, to the maintenance of public peace. The authorities maintained a strict distinction between the two types of law enforcement problems arising, on the one hand, out of antistate activities and, on the other, civil disobedience. Whether an offense constitutes a treason or a mere breach of public tranquillity is determined by the presumed intent of the offender, rather than by the fact of participation in a mass riot situation.

Until 1970 there had been at least two instances where charges of antistate crime were proffered by the government. These charges related to two coup attempts made by small numbers of senior military and police officers, the first in 1962 and the second in 1966. In mid-1970 the limited information available concerning these attempts indicated that the persons implicated on both occasions had neither a popular following nor an articulate political program or ideology that could serve as an effective framework for mass action. The attempted coups had no discernible disruptive consequences on internal security, partly because they were uncovered before the conspirators could actually carry out their schemes and partly because the motivations behind the plots, whatever they might have been, were known only to a limited circle of officers in the armed forces and the police.

The first coup attempt was reported to have been made in late January 1962. According to the initial government announcement, some senior officers of the police and the armed forces conspired to arrest an undetermined number of cabinet ministers and some leftist politicians. Twenty-nine persons, many of whom were Roman Catholics, were arrested on suspicion of complicity in the plot to overthrow the government and establish a new one of their own chosing.

In the following month Parliamentary Secretary for Defence and External Affairs Felix Reginald Dias Bandaranaike stated before the House of Representatives that it was essential to inflict "deterrent punishment of a severe character" on those responsible for the coup plot; he declared that the conspirators were pursuing "reactionary aims and objectives." His statement was followed almost immediately by the introduction in the lower house of the Criminal Law (Special Provisions) Bill, which was aimed at covering, with retroactive effect, offenses committed after January 1, 1962.

The bill made conspiracy against the state a capital offense punishable by death; until that time this category of offense had carried the maximum penalty of imprisonment for a term of twenty years at hard labor. The proposed bill also contained provisions allowing for detention incommunicado of suspected persons for sixty days, trial without a jury before three Supreme Court judges to be appointed by the minister of justice, and denial of the right of appeal to the Court of Criminal Appeal. The right of appeal to the Privy Council was not affected, however.

Despite a storm of angry protest from opposition members, the bill was passed by Parliament and was signed into law in March 1962. The following month the International Commission of Jurists in Geneva publicly took exception to many provisions of the law on the ground that the provisions were "entirely contrary to the generally accepted principles of the rule of law . . . ."

The coup suspects were brought to trial in July 1962 before a three-judge bench on charges of having conspired to "wage war against the Queen"—as phrased in Section 114 of the Penal Code of 1883—and to overthrow the government by unlawful means. In October of that year, however, the judges, in response to defense applications, disqualified themselves on the ground that they had no jurisdiction to try the case because they should have been appointed by the chief justice of the Supreme Court rather than the minister of justice; they declared that the power to appoint trial judges was the constitutional prerogative of the judiciary alone. At the time this ruling was widely acclaimed; the International Commission of Jurists, for example, commended the decision as "bold, fearless and independent."

As a result, the Criminal Law (Special Provisions) Bill was amended in November 1962 so that the bench could be nominated by the chief justice. In January 1963 the trial was reopened, but the court was again dissolved on a technicality. By the time the proceedings resumed in June 1963, the number of the accused had been reduced from twenty-four to eleven. The trial dragged on until April 1965, when the eleven defendants were found guilty and were sentenced to ten years of imprisonment at hard labor. They appealed to the Privy Council and were acquitted on the ground that the laws under which they had been tried were unconstitutional.

According to the security authorities, another coup was to be attempted in February 1966 this time by a small number of senior military officers. In July 1966, an intensive police investigation culminated in the arrest of the commander of the

Ceylon Army, Major General Richard Udugama, on suspicion of complicity in a conspiracy. A total of twenty-eight officers and men and a Buddhist monk were arrested in this connection. Of these, twenty-two suspects were brought to trial in January 1968. In the course of the trial, charges against ten of them were dropped, and the remaining defendants were acquitted in January 1970 by a unanimous verdict of the jury.

There were indications after the mid-1960s that the security authorities were concerned about the possibility of foreign-supported Communist subversive activities. In October 1966, for example, the Police Department was checking into what was described as a plan by foreign-trained Communists to launch a wave of subversive activities with financial support from unnamed foreign sources. There was, however, no public evidence of such activities.

In late April 1970 the Ministry of Defence and External Affairs was reported to have uncovered a Communist plot to sabotage the general election set for May 27. According to the ministry, the police authorities had seized documents purporting to show that leaders of the plot, said to be admirers of Che Guevara and Mao Tse-tung, had received guerrilla training in China and Albania and that some 10,000 persons, mostly youths from rural areas and including "some policemen," were involved in the subversive scheme.

Shortly before the ministry's statement, the Police Department had warned that a group of university graudates working independently of established Communist parties might attempt to create what the *Ceylon Daily News* (April 12, 1970) reported as "a revolutionary situation in which power could be forcibly wrested from a capitalist government and vested in a true, socialist leadership." The department also revealed that some of these extremists were believed to have surveyed several sites in the up-country interior for possible use as guerrilla-training centers. At the end of May 1970, however, there were no reports of any antistate activities attributed to the Communists.

Communal Disturbances

By far the most serious problem confronting the law enforcement authorities since independence has been the continuing danger of communal violence between the two major ethnic communities, the Sinhalese and the Tamils (see ch. 5, Ethnic Groups and Languages; ch. 14, Political Dynamics). The first serious communally inspired riot broke out after the passage in July 1956 of the Official Language Bill, which made Sinhala

449

the sole official language of the country and provided for a transitional period of five years (see ch. 3, Historical Setting).

In 1958 far more violent communal disturbances occurred over the same language issue. In May of that year the government declared a state of national emergency throughout the country, ordered units of the armed forces to assist the civil police in restoring law and order, and banned temporarily the activities of the Tamil-supported Federal Party and of the National Liberation Front (Jatika Vimukti Peramuna), a Sinhalese communal organization (see ch. 3, Historical Setting).

In an attempt to cope more effectively with civil disturbances, the government in March 1959 amended the Public Security Ordinance of 1947. The ordinance empowered the governor general to issue, on the recommendation of the prime minister, emergency regulations aimed at: maintaining public peace; preserving public order; suppressing mutiny, riot, or civil commotion; and ensuring the continuance of supplies and services essential to the life of the community. The amended version, called the Public Security (Amendment) Act, strengthened the previous ordinance and made it more specific for purposes of application. It enabled the governor general to impose a state of emergency in a limited area without its being applied, as under the 1947 ordinance, to the rest of the country. The amended act also empowered the prime minister to call out units of the armed forces for the maintenance of public order in a given area if he found that the civil police were in need of additional coercive power (see ch. 25, The Armed Forces).

In addition, the 1959 amendment authorized the prime minister to impose a curfew on any disturbed area and to prohibit labor strikes in any sector declared by him to be an "essential service" for the maintenance of life of the public. The latter restriction, however, was not to be applied to legitimate strikes undertaken by a registered union under the terms of the Industrial Disputes Act of 1950 (see ch. 21, Labor). The statute exempted public officials from criminal or civil liability for acts done in good faith in the course of enforcing emergency regulations; however, the law made it mandatory for the prime minister, within ten days from the date of issuance, to report emergency regulations to Parliament for appropriate action by Parliament.

In a related development, the government of Prime Minister W. Dahanayake set up in January 1960 a new agency called the Ministry of Internal Security. The purpose of the ministry was to strengthen the Police Department for a more effective and concerted action in matters relating to public order and security. The measure was unpopular with the opposition, and the ministry was not revived by the successor cabinet after the prime minister's party lost in the general election held in March 1960 (see ch. 14, Political Dynamics).

In early 1961 public peace was again disturbed after Sinhala became the official language as of January 1, 1961. The Tamils in the Northern and Eastern provinces dramatized their displeasure by resorting to *satyagraha* (civil disobedience) and *hartal* (work stoppage). By April 1961 the situation became so critical that the governor general had to proclaim a state of emergency for the whole country. Volunteer and reserve units of the armed forces were mobilized to maintain public order and essential services, and a new emergency regulation was issued to impose the death penalty or life imprisonment on those convicted of offenses relating to arson, sabotage, looting, or unlawful assembly. The Federal Party, the Tamil political organization, was also temporarily banned for its leading role in the civil disobedience drive.

Partly as a result, the government in July 1962 also temporarily banned three Tamil organizations located in Colombo: the Ceylon Progressive Society (Ceylon Munnethra Kazhagam); the Ceylon Dravidian Progressive Society (Ceylon Dravida Munnethra Kazhagam); and the All-Ceylon Dravidian Progressive Federation (see ch. 14, Political Dynamics). The three organizations were suspected of being inspired by the Madras-based Dravida Munnethra Kazhagam (Dravidian Progressive Society), the principal South Indian politicocultural organization devoted to the promotion of Tamil interests in cultural, political, and economic matters. Government officials declared that the propaganda activities of these groups were prejudicial to public safety and could potentially spread "discontent and disaffection among the inhabitants of Ceylon or any section, class or group of them."

Another contributing factor in the government's action was believed to be Ceylon's growing dissatisfaction with India's position over the question of what to do with the stateless Tamil estate workers residing on the island. In mid-1962 the banned Tamil organizations were actively advocating positions that were deemed unacceptable by the Ceylonese government (see ch. 15, Foreign Relations).

The long-smoldering language dispute again erupted into massive riots in Colombo in January 1966. A general state of emergency was imposed, and the police had to use tear gas to disperse the mob of some 3,000 Sinhalese demonstrators who were protesting against the government regulations to implement the Tamil Language (Special Provisions) Act of 1958 beginning in January 1966. Units of the armed forces were called out to aid the civil force; strikes, public processions, and unlawful assemblies were banned; and press censorship was imposed as a precaution against publicity aimed at arousing communal passions. The rioters asserted that the Tamil Language (Special Provisions) Regulations, passed by Parliament in January 1966, would encourage Tamil separatism and prejudice national unity; these regulations allowed, among others, the use of Tamil for administrative purposes in the Tamil-speaking Northern and Eastern provinces but without altering the status of Sinhala as the sole official language of the country (see ch. 5, Ethnic Groups and Languages).

THE POLICE SYSTEM

The Police Department is organized and functions under the Police Ordinance of 1865 as amended by subsequent statutes. At independence it retained the British precedents relating to organization, training, and procedures. The department is headed by an inspector general of police (known as the IG), who reports directly to the minister of defense and external affairs (see fig. 10). The functions of policymaking and control and supervisory powers are centralized in the Police Headquarters in Colombo; the department has a wide latitude in directing its operational functions.

In December 1965 the government appointed a police commission, the first one to be set up after 1947, to review the activities of the department in the years after independence and to submit a report outlining measures needed to keep the service up to date and in line with the country's new status as an independent nation. The commission was also asked to recommend measures for the improvement of effectiveness and performance relating to a wide range of law enforcement functions. The report was issued in the late 1960s but was not readily available in early 1970.

As of late 1967 the Police Department had an actual strength of over 10,000 men, as compared to the authorized strength of over 11,000 men (see table 36). The actual strength was almost double the force level of 1947. These men were posted at nearly 260 stations throughout the country, except in the so-called unpoliced areas in parts of Northern, North Western, Eastern, Central, and Uva provinces. In those areas the police functions were being performed by village officials (*grama sevakas*) and by divisional revenue officers; serious crimes were investigated, however, directly by the regular police of the nearest jurisdiction (see ch. 13, The Governmental System). The government's plan to establish police stations in the unpoliced areas was hampered by financial limitations.

452

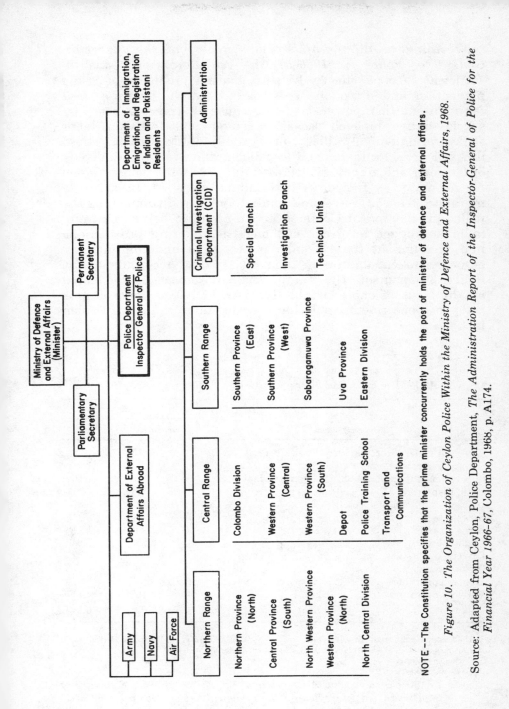

NOTE --The Constitution specifies that the prime minister concurrently holds the post of minister of defence and external affairs.

Figure 10. *The Organization of Ceylon Police Within the Ministry of Defence and External Affairs, 1968.*

Source: Adapted from Ceylon, Police Department, *The Administration Report of the Inspector-General of Police for the Financial Year 1966-67*, Colombo, 1968, p. A174.

According to the *Administration Report of the Inspector-General of Police for 1966-67,* the 1967 force level was insufficient to cope effectively with routine problems of crime prevention and detection. The report cited the growing need for additional manpower, largely because of strains imposed by special duties on such occasions as religious festivals, labor strikes, and political rallies. During the Buddhist Wesak festival in April 1967, for instance, the police authorities had to deploy 3,000 men (or about 30 percent of the total police force) for as many as five days in Colombo alone in an effort to maintain peace and avert communal violence. Inasmuch as the police jurisdiction of Colombo had a strength below the minimum authorized level of 2,600 men, neighboring jurisdictions had to augment the Colombo police, thus undermining law enforcement capabilities in their own areas. According to the Police Department, the manpower requirement is calculated on the basis of one constable for every 1,000 persons; at this ratio the department would have needed more than 11,700 men in 1967.

Table 36. *The Rank and Strength of Ceylon Police, September 1967*[1]

Rank designations	Strength	
	Authorized	Actual
Inspector general	1	1
Deputy inspectors general	5	2[2]
Superintendents and assistant superintendents	120	109[3]
Chief inspectors	11	11
Inspectors and subinspectors	889	865
Sergeants major	20	19
Sergeants	1,256	1,118
Constables	8,253	7,340
Drivers	588	522
Women sergeants	3	3
Women constables	47	43
Wireless operators	130	111
Total	11,323	10,144

[1]The actual strength might have increased, by mid-1970 to more than 12,500 (excluding clerical staff); this figure is tentative, and breakdown by rank was not available as of mid-1970.
[2]One under suspension.
[3]Five under suspension.

Source: Adapted from Ceylon, *Appropriation Act, No. 30 of 1969: Estimates of the Government of Ceylon for the Financial Year, 1 October 1969 to 30 September 1970,* Colombo, 1969, p. 37; Ceylon, Police Department, *The Administration Report of the Inspector-General of Police for the Financial Year 1966-67,* Colombo, 1968, p. A137; and *Ceylon Daily News,* May 22, 1970, p. 1.

As of late 1968 the police establishment consisted of a special unit called the Criminal Investigation Department (CID), an administration unit, and three territorial units: Central Range, Northern Range, and Southern Range. The Central Range was additionally in control of specialized functions, such as the Depot, Police Training School, and transport and communications. A deputy inspector general (DIG) of police was in charge of each of the five major subdivisions.

On the territorial level the department was divided into provinces, divisions, districts, and stations. The more densely populated Western, Central, and Southern provinces each had more than two subdivisions; the thinly populated Eastern and North Central provinces were designated as divisions instead of provinces. The Colombo jurisdiction was also a division instead of a district because of its special status as the national capital. As a rule, provinces and divisions are each headed by a superintendent; districts, by assistant superintendents; and stations, by inspectors.

Recruitment and Training

An applicant for a police service career must have completed at least a senior secondary school, equivalent to a tenth-grade education in the United States. Until 1965 recruitment was handled by the Police Training School, which continues to serve as the only institution for the professional preparation of police officers. Since 1966 all ranks have been recruited to the police service through a four-stage screening process. Candidates are first interviewed in provincial towns by a provincial board composed of three senior police officers. Those passing the first test are then subjected to a second interview by a central board in Colombo consisting of three senior officers, including a DIG. At the third stage applicants must take a written examination given by a panel of examiners appointed by the inspector general of police. The fourth and final step is again an interview before a panel of three DIGs.

New recruits are sent to the Police Training School for six months of resident instruction. Transferred to Colombo from Kalutara in 1967, the school is headed by a director with the rank of superintendent. Classes are held in three languages— Sinhala, Tamil, and English. Special emphasis is placed on police-community relations, practical police work, and general knowledge. The school maintains eight training stations in Colombo to give practical experience to new constables, probationary subinspectors, and probationary assistant superintendents. Upon completion of this instruction, trainees are posted to the provinces and divisions for further inservice experience.

In addition, the Police Training School offers courses for those interested in promotion and refresher courses for those selected for advanced training. Outstanding police officers are sometimes sent abroad for more advanced instruction; since independence most of them have been sent to Great Britain for this purpose. The teaching staff of the school is drawn from the police service and is given instruction at the Government Teacher Training College at Maharagama; senior instructors are sent to the Academy of Administrative Studies, the center for the basic training of civil servants located in Colombo.

Specialized Units

The Criminal Investigation Department (CID) is divided into a Special Branch and an Investigation Branch. The former handles information-gathering activities, and the latter conducts criminal investigation relating to immigration, currency violation, forgery, and criminal misappropriation. The CID is supported by an array of support functions: the Fingerprint Bureau, Crime Record Office, Photographic Bureau, and Counterfeit Currency Bureau, all under the supervision of the superintendent heading the CID. The CID maintains its own administrative section.

In an effort to prevent the illegal entry of Indian nationals, the CID works closely with the police authorities of South India and frequently holds coordinative working sessions with the Indian police. The CID also cooperates closely with units of the Ceylon Army, the Royal Ceylon Navy, and the Royal Ceylon Air Force and with customs officials in connection with antismuggling and the anti-illicit immigration operations. Because of the shortage of police officers assigned to these operations during the 1960s, units of the armed forces were frequently called upon for assistance (see ch. 25, The Armed Forces).

Police stations in thirty-four major provincial towns are linked through a system of radio communications that is operated from the Radio Control Room in the Police Headquarters in Colombo. The Radio Control Room also monitors the operation of the police emergency system in Colombo; under this system any person in distress can dial "3333" for assistance. All police patrol cars are connected to this emergency network.

Emergency duties are performed by a specially trained task

force of about 450 men called the Depot Police. Located at Bambalapitiya, a suburb of Colombo, the Depot Police may be dispatched to any trouble spot in the country to render assistance to local police, especially in situations involving strikes, labor disputes, riots, communal clashes, or natural calamities. In addition, they escort important public officials, perform traffic and crowd control duties, guard government office buildings at Colombo, and provide honor guards at important ceremonial state functions.

The Police Department maintains in various subdivisions an auxiliary task force called the Special Police Reserve. At the end of 1967 there were about 2,200 reservists, as compared to the authorized strength of 3,000 men. The reservists may be called out locally to assist the regular police in the maintenance of law and order, as the need arises. The recruitment was temporarily halted in 1961 because of financial shortages but was resumed in 1966 because of the useful function performed by the reserve, especially in times of serious public disturbances. Appointments are made locally from among employees of the government and the government-owned public corporations. The reservists are provided with uniforms, living allowances, and free rail transportation when called into service.

An important function of the Colombo jurisdiction is to safeguard the port facilities of Colombo and perform regular law enforcement duties within the port area. This task is the primary responsibility of the Colombo Harbor Division, whose chief, an assistant superintendent, reports directly to the superintendent of the Colombo Division.

THE PENAL CODE

Various categories and subcategories of offenses and punishments are defined and enumerated in the Penal Code of 1883. In 1885 this code, which was patterned after the Indian Penal Code of 1860, replaced the Roman-Dutch criminal law in force at that time and was made applicable to every person on the island. The 1883 code has been retained by independent Ceylon with relatively few modifications.

Offenses are listed in general categories, and each category is in turn subdivided into specific violations. The general categories include abetment of, and conspiracy for the commission of, any offense and crimes against the state, public tranquillity, public officials, or a person or property. Other offenses are related to the armed forces; elections; administration of justice; coins and stamps; weights and measures; public health, safety, and morality; religion; forgery of documents, trade marks, and banknotes; defamation; criminal intimidation, insult, and annoyance; and unlawful oaths.

The scale of punishments consists of death by hanging, imprisonment, whipping, forfeiture of property, and fines. The imprisonment may be "simple" (ordinary) or "rigorous" (at hard labor). The death penalty may not be imposed on persons under the age of sixteen or on pregnant women; minors may be detained any length of term as may be specified by the governor general, and pregnant women may be sentenced to imprisonment for life. In meting out the sentence of imprisonment, the court has a degree of latitude in deciding whether the confinement should be ordinary or at hard labor.

Female convicts and persons sentenced to death or to imprisonment for more than five years may not be punished by whipping. The sentence of whipping must state whether the convicted is above or under the age of sixteen and must specify the number of lashes or strokes to be administered but not exceeding twenty-four. For adults whipping must be inflicted in the presence of a medical officer; minors are punished with a light cane or rattan switch, the maximum number of strokes being six.

An attempt by the government to eliminate capital punishment has received mixed reactions. In April 1956 the Bandaranaike government proposed the suspension of capital punishment for murder and abetment of suicide for a trial period of three years; this experiment was to be reviewed thereafter with the aim of abolishing capital punishment from the statute book. Parliament passed the Suspension of Death Penalty Bill in May 1956.

In October 1958 the government appointed a commission on capital punishment to examine the question of whether the suspension had contributed to any increase in the incidence of murder. Shortly before Prime Minister Bandaranaike was assassinated in September 1959, the commission released its report with the conclusion that the record through the end of 1958 showed nothing to justify the reimposition of capital punishment and recommended that the suspension be continued until April 1961 to permit a more extensive and conclusive study of causal relationship.

The commission's recommendation was set aside, however, because of the Bandaranaike assassination. In October 1959 the government decided to restore the death penalty, and a bill giving effect to this decision was passed in November 1959.

The Penal Code provides for certain extenuating circumstances. A child under the age of eight is not criminally responsible for any act as is a minor between the ages of eight and twelve, because of their "insufficient maturity of understanding." Self-defense, an act by a person who is mentally unsound, or an involuntary offense by an intoxicated person may be leniently considered in the courts of law. The act of a law enforcement officer performed in good faith in the course of discharging his duty is not held criminally liable, nor is the act of a judge done in judicial capacity.

CRIMINAL COURTS AND PROCEDURES

Offenses under the Penal Code are tried according to the provisions contained in the Criminal Procedure Code of 1899, as amended. Major statutes relevant to the administration of criminal justice are: the Courts Ordinance of 1890, which defines the powers and jurisdiction of courts; the Rural Courts Ordinance of 1946; the Court of Criminal Appeal Ordinance of 1940; the Appeals (Privy Council) Ordinance of 1910; the Ceylon Courts of Admiralty Ordinance of 1892, for maritime cases; the Evidence Ordinance of 1896; the Prevention of Crimes Ordinance of 1929; and the Public Security (Amendment) Act of 1959.

Juvenile cases are administered under the Children and Young Persons Ordinance of 1939, as amended. Irregularities involving judges, members of Parliament, law enforcement officers, and civil servants are tried under the Bribery Act of 1954. All offenses relating to defense secrets are punishable under the Official Secrets Act of 1955.

In early 1970 a law reform committee was examining the question of whether the existing statutes, substantive as well as procedural, should be simplified and changed. The purpose of this exercise was to eliminate longstanding problems of judicial delays and to secure expeditious, inexpensive, and effective justice for the public. Ceylonese observers have long asserted, especially since independence, that procedures for penal proceedings were too complicated and unwieldy.

There are five types of ciminal courts: the Supreme Court, district courts, magistrate's courts, municipal courts, and rural courts. The jurisdiction of each of these courts and the procedures concerning warrant, bail, and punishments are enumerated in a tabular statement called the First Schedule, which is attached to the Criminal Procedure Code.

The original jurisdiction of the Supreme Court covers any serious offense punishable by death, imprisonment for a term exceeding two years, or a fine exceeding Rs1,000 (for value of the rupee, see Glossary). Criminal sessions of the court are held before a jury of seven members and a puisne (associate) judge or a commissioner of assize, who is assigned by the chief justice to any one of the five judicial circuits (see ch. 13, The Governmental System). In certain cases such as anti-state crimes, the chief justice may, under the Criminal Procedure Code, order a trial by jury before a three-judge bench in Colombo. The same code also empowers the minister of justice to direct that trials involving sedition, civil disorders, or "disturbance of public feeling" be held without a jury before three Supreme Court judges. It does not, however, authorize the minister to appoint any trial judge. To be binding, the verdict of the jury must be either unanimous or by a majority of not less than five.

A district court hears any case committed to it by a magistrate's court, which has the principal responsibility for the determination of jurisdiction and venue. The district tribunal may impose a sentence of imprisonment for a term not exceeding two years, a fine not exceeding Rs1,000, whipping, or a penalty combining any two of these sentences. The trial is presided over by a single judge who, at his discretion or upon the application of any party to a litigation, may seek the aid of three assessors or lay assistants; the opinion of the assessors is not binding, however, on the presiding judge.

A magistrate's court is summary in nature and tries lesser offenses punishable by imprisonment not exceeding six months; a fine not exceeding Rs100; whipping, if the offender is under sixteen years of age; or any two of these sentences combined. This court is probably the busiest of all criminal courts, since more than 80 percent of all those convicted and committed to penal institutions are tried at this level.

Criminal courts in municipalities are presided over by municipal magistrates and try offenses listed in nearly thirty ordinances enumerated in Section 163 (1) of the Municipal Council Ordinance of 1947. Municipal courts are governed by the same rules, forms, and procedures prescribed for, and observed by, magistrate's courts; they may not impose sentences exceeding those authorized for the magistrate's courts.

A rural court, formerly known as a village tribunal, tries minor offenses punishable by imprisonment ranging from seven days to fourteen days or a fine not exceeding Rs50. Where the offender is a minor, up to six lashes of whipping with a rattan switch may be administered in lieu of confinement or a fine. The rural court is presided over by a president or additional president appointed by the Judicial Service Commission (see ch. 13, The Governmental System).

Proceedings before the rural courts are informal and not subject to the provisions of the Criminal Procedure Code, unless exceptions are allowed by the Rural Courts Ordinance.

Prosecutors and defense attorneys are not permitted to appear in this court. The ordinance directs that wherever possible the rural court should "endeavor to bring the parties to an amicable settlement, and to remove, with their consent, the real cause of grievance between them; and for this purpose the Rural Court shall have power, on the application of the parties, to refer the matter in issue to arbitration. . . ."

Procedures governing search, arrest, pretrial hearings, rules of evidence, and trial proceedings closely follow British practice. The accused are presumed innocent until proven guilty. Minor offenses are handled summarily on complaint, oral or written; serious offenders are arraigned on the indictment served on them. Prosecution in the magistrate's court is usually conducted by a police officer and in higher courts, by the attorney general, solicitor general, crown counsel, or a prosecutor authorized by the attorney general.

Appeals from the rural court are taken to the district court, where the decision is final. Judgments of the district or magistrate's court may be referred to the Supreme Court; appeals are disallowed in these circumstances if the accused has pleaded guilty and has been convicted by either of the courts, unless the penalties are relatively severe.

Under the Court of Criminal Appeal Ordinance, any aggrieved person may seek relief from the Court of Criminal Appeal against his conviction by the Supreme Court or directly from the Judicial Committee of the Privy Council in London, the ultimate court of appeal in the judicial system. Appeal may be on any ground involving a point of law or fact, or both. The Court of Criminal Appeal consists of an odd number of Supreme Court judges, the minimum being three, nominated by the chief justice; it is presided over by the chief justice or, in his absence, by the senior member of the Supreme Court. The decision of the appellate tribunal is by a majority of the bench hearing the case.

The Privy Council may entertain any appeal from the decision of the Court of Criminal Appeal or the Supreme Court if the disputed case is certified by the Supreme Court as being of "great general or public importance." In this connection, the Appeals (Privy Council) Ordinance provides certain rules to be observed by all parties concerned, but the council also reserves the right to hear a case on the personal petition of an aggrieved party without reference to the provisions of the ordinance.

In early 1970 court proceedings were recorded, as in the past, in English, although the Language of the Courts Act of 1961 directed that they be recorded in Sinhala as soon as this switch was practicable; under a subsequent regulation, this transition was to begin in August 1963. In February 1970, however, a cabinet officer acknowledged that, as far as he could ascertain, no district or magistrate's court conducted its business in Sinhala. In the Northern and Eastern provinces Tamil continued to be the medium of legal proceedings under the Tamil Language (Special Provisions) Act of 1958.

According to Ceylonese sources, the lack of progress in the use of Sinhala is largely attributable to the confusion created by a variety of Sinhala equivalents for English legal terms. Many ordinances and legal documents, including the Criminal Procedure Code and the Civil Procedure Code of 1890, have been already translated into Sinhala, but the Sinhala versions have been subject to interminable criticism by legal scholars and jurists alike for their ambiguity and inconsistencies. As a result, a thirteen-member committee of specialists was appointed by the government and met for the first time in March 1970 to discuss the general principles to be adopted in formulating standardized Sinhala legal terms.

THE INCIDENCE OF CRIME

In the postindependence years the incidence of crimes decreased considerably from approximately 28,300 cases reported in 1947 to 18,100 cases in 1951, a decline of 36 percent. The 1951 level remained more or less stable for a decade, except during the communally disturbed years of 1956 and 1958. After the early 1960s, however, the rate of what the government calls grave crimes increased steadily, from about 19,500 cases during fiscal year 1962/63 to 28,800 cases during 1966/67, a rise of around 44 percent. For statistical purposes the government lists fifteen categories of offenses as grave crimes: abduction, arson, burglary, cattle stealing, abandonment of children, grievous hurt, homicide, attempted homicide, injury by knife, rape, unnatural offense, riot, robbery, theft over the value of Rs20, and theft of bicycles.

According to the annual reports issued by the inspector general of police, the main contributing reasons for the rise in crimes include population growth, the general decline in discipline causing a widespread lack of regard for law and authority, economic hardships accentuated by rising living costs, and an increased consumption of illegally manufactured liquors containing a high alcohol content.

Over the years the six most common crimes have been, in descending order of frequency, thefts over Rs20, injury by knife, burglary, grievous hurt, robbery, and theft of bicycles.

Together they accounted for an annual average of 85 percent of the total. Of the six categories, crimes against property claimed an annual average of 63 percent, and crimes against person, 57 percent. Government sources show that the crimes of violence (homicide, attempted homicide, injury by knife, and grievous hurt) were caused by, in descending order of frequency, "sudden quarrels," longstanding grudges, land disputes, intoxication, and jealousy over women.

In the commission of crimes against person, by far the most common weapon used has been a knife; the use of firearms has been negligible. As a result, the carrying of a knife is strictly controlled under the Dangerous Knives Ordinance of 1906, as amended. Under this statute, "prohibited knife" means any knife more than two inches long, sword, dagger, or similar sharp-edged instrument. Carrying a prohibited knife is punishable by a fine not exceeding Rs50; a fine of less than Rs100 may be imposed if the same person is convicted on a second offense.

According to official reports issued in 1966 and 1967, juvenile crime was becoming a serious problem. These reports suggested the establishment of a special unit in the Police Department, to be staffed by trained specialists working closely with juvenile courts and interested social organizations. They listed 11,500 cases of juvenile violation for fiscal year 1965/66 and 13,300 for 1966/67. The 1966/67 figure represented a 15-percent increase over 1965/66. Between the two final years, offenses by "children" under thirteen years of age increased nearly 43 percent; by "young persons" between the ages of fourteen and sixteen, 18 percent; and by "youthful offenders" between the ages of seventeen and twenty, 12 percent. The incidence of crime varied according to age group; the more common juvenile crimes included violence, theft under Rs20, theft over Rs20, and offenses relating to liquor and narcotics.

PENAL INSTITUTIONS

All correctional institutions are administered by the Department of Prisons under the Ministry of Justice. Staffed by about 2,000 employees in charge of a commissioner, these institutions are regulated by the Prisons Ordinance of 1878, as amended.

In late 1968 there were fourteen prisons, four open prison camps, and two training schools for youthful offenders (commonly abbreviated as TSYO). During fiscal year 1965/66, the latest period for which information was available in mid-1970, some 10,000 persons (97 percent of them males) were committed to these institutions as convicted prisoners; in addition, about 23,500 persons were admitted to them to be held in detention pending trial. After independence the number of convicts admitted each year ranged from a low of 7,000 during 1961/62 to a high of 10,150 during 1965/66; the number of detainees awaiting trial ranged from 14,300 in the calendar year 1951 to 23,500 during 1965/66.

During 1965/66 the daily average size of the prison population (the balance of detainees entering and leaving prisons each day) was 6,350, of which the convicted inmates accounted for 70 percent and the unconvicted, 30 percent. This seventy-to-thirty ratio remained fairly stable after independence. Taken as a whole, about 91 convicts for every 100,000 persons were admitted to prisons during 1965/66. In mid-1966 the Welikada Prison, the largest penal center in the country, had nearly 1,500 inmates, or about 23 percent of the total prison population at the time.

According to the *Administration Report of the Commissioner of Prisons for 1965–66*, nearly 29 percent of the 10,150 convicted prisoners were charged with excise offenses—that is, violations involving liquor, import and export regulations, or licensing regulations. The next largest category of offense was theft, accounting for about 17 percent; and the third category was grievous hurt, 4 percent. Of the convicts admitted during 1965/66, 62 percent were first offenders, and 38 percent were repeaters. By districts, Colombo accounted for nearly 34 percent of the total committed; Kalutara, in Western Province, was a distant second, with about 9 percent of the total.

Of the total of 10,150 convicts, 75 percent were Sinhalese (most of them Buddhists); 16 percent were Tamils (most of them Hindus); and the balance was accounted for by other minorities. By occupations, farmers topped with 26 percent, followed by unskilled workers, 24 percent; skilled workers, 9.5 percent; and unemployed, 7.8 percent. Twenty-six percent of the total convicts were illiterate. Based on the length of confinement, 33 percent of the total were to serve less than one month; 31 percent, one to three months; 17 percent, three to six months, and 8 percent, six to twelve months. Of the remaining, 10 percent were sentenced to terms ranging from one year to ten years, and only 1 percent were to serve for more than ten years.

In the late 1960s the Department of Prisons maintained one open-type correctional house for juvenile convicts at Wathapitiwela. This institution, called the Training School for Youthful Offenders, was patterned after a residential school, being divided into a number of houses, each in charge of a house master. It offered vocational training of various types.

Juveniles sentenced to less than one month of imprisonment are committed to local prisons, which are equipped with segregated facilities for this purpose. Those serving terms of more than one month are sent to either Wathapitiwela or another training school at Negombo; the latter institution, a closed type, is reserved for more troublesome juveniles requiring strict supervision.

The Department of Prisons also runs four open prison camps at Pallekelle, Anuradhapura, Kipay, and Taldena, for good-behavior inmates. These camps are provided with facilities for agricultural training; the Department of Agriculture is cooperating closely with the prison authorities.

299-639 O - 79 - 31

CHAPTER 25

THE ARMED FORCES

In mid-1970 the defense force of less than 10,000 officers and men continued to be oriented toward internal security matters, although the navy and air force were actively engaged in operations to curb smuggling and illicit immigration from India. From the time of independence in 1948 to 1970, the island had faced no foreign threats to its security.

The Constitution of 1948 designated the governor general as the commander in chief of the three services—the Ceylon Army, the Royal Ceylon Navy, and the Royal Ceylon Air Force. In mid-1970, however, the Constituent Assembly was engaged in the drafting of a new constitution that will, among other things, change Ceylon from a British dominion to a republic (see ch. 13, The Governmental System). When the new constitution is implemented in early 1971, the navy and air force will discontinue the use of the designation "Royal," and the office of the governor general will cease to exist.

Although the governor general in emergency situations has exercised his prerogatives and discharged his obligations as commander in chief, he has done so with the advice and approval of the prime minister, who is constitutionally required to serve as the minister of defense and external affairs (see ch. 13, The Governmental System; ch. 24, Public Order and Internal Security). The prime minister makes major policy and personnel decisions for the armed forces, and there has been a tendency for each new government to replace some of the ranking military officers.

In 1970 the armed forces, which were composed exclusively of volunteers, continued to be very closely patterned on their British equivalents in such matters as procedures and protocol, military justice, uniforms, ordinance and equipment, and training. Since independence many middle- and senior-level officers have been sent abroad for training. The service schools most frequently attended have been those in the United Kingdom, India, Pakistan, Australia, and the United States. Shortly after assuming office in May 1970, the government of Mrs. Sirimavo Bandaranaike decided that in the future officers would not be sent to the United States.

In 1962 and again in 1966 a few military officers, police officials, and civilians were arrested and charged with conspiracy to overthrow the government. Although all of those charged either were released without trial or were acquitted on technical grounds, several of the military officers were forced to leave the service on "compulsory leave" (see ch. 24, Public Order and Internal Security).

One of the first official acts of Prime Minister Bandaranaike on assuming power in 1970 was to reinstate the fourteen military officers who had been forced to retire in 1966. One of those reinstated was made commandant of a new special unit of the army that was established to provide protection for the prime minister. The prime minister also announced that the armed forces would be reorganized "so as to identify them with the national and progressive aspirations of the people and to reflect their interests."

DEVELOPMENT AND COMPOSITION

At the time of independence there were no Ceylonese armed forces, and it was not until 1949, over a year after independence, that legislation to establish an army, navy, and air force was enacted. The legislation envisaged a very small total force, with the army originally limited to 3,000 officers and men. Until these forces were raised and made operational, British military elements were the sole armed forces on the island.

Ceylon Army

The army came into being on October 10, 1949. A few of the officers and senior noncommissioned personnel had served with units of the British army during World War II, and these individuals formed the core of the small professional force. The primary army mission in 1970 continued to be that of internal security.

The army has had a slow but steady growth, but in 1970 only about 6,000 men were on active duty in the regular force. There were perhaps an equal number in the volunteer force (active reserve), the regular reserve (retired personnel), and the volunteer reserve (inactive reserve). The army is basically an infantry force organized into companies and battalions. The weapons are of British origin of World War II vintage. There are a few armored vehicles, but there is no artillery.

An important but relatively unpublicized army activity during the 1960s was community action and developmental work. Army personnel and equipment assisted both in the preparation of new agricultural settlement areas and in the transfer of families into the projects. Army units also participated in road, irrigation, and related construction work.

Royal Ceylon Navy

The navy was formally established on December 9, 1950. In 1970 it was composed of less than 2,000 officers and men and approximately thirty vessels, including a frigate and numerous patrol boats.

The main naval base was at Trincomalee, but the navy's main operational mission was to patrol the northern, northwestern, and western coastlines. The navy patrol was part of the Task Force Illicit Immigration Branch (known as the TFII), but the patrols had the related function of conducting antismuggling operations. The Bandaranaike government announced in 1970 that the antismuggling campaign would be expanded and intensified because of the very large sum of money believed to have been diverted from taxation.

Royal Ceylon Air Force

The air force became operational on October 10, 1950, and by 1970 was composed of approximately twoscore aircraft and about 1,500 officers and men. Its main bases were at Katunayaka near Colombo and at China Bay near Trincomalee.

The primary missions of the air force were to assist the navy's antismuggling operations by coastal reconnaissance flights and to provide air support to the army in its internal security functions. The air force also provides occasional transport throughout the island for cabinet ministers and other senior government officials.

MILITARY TRADITION AND RECRUITMENT

The basic philosophical tenets of Buddhism and Hinduism contain explicit condemnations of force and violence and extended praise of pacifism and nonviolence (see ch. 11, Religion). A military career is, to a considerable extent, antithetical to the values and mores of the majority of the population, and a military or warrior caste or class has never developed on the island. The folk histories and myths, for example, praise the various ancient kings far less for their military feats than for their patronage of Buddhism and the arts and their sponsorship of irrigation projects (see ch. 3, Historical Setting).

This latent antipathy for a military career has not resulted, however, in any lack of volunteers. Although this has been true in part because the armed forces have not, since their formation, been engaged in combat or other violent activity, the very considerable prestige of a career as a government servant and the high value attached to titles, ranks, and uniformed ceremony make a career in the armed forces a desirable one (see ch. 12, Social Values).

FOREIGN INFLUENCE

In 1970 the most pervasive foreign influence continued to be that of the British. Several of the senior officers received their military education in British military academies and served in British units. Although a governmental commission in the 1950s recommended various changes in the military uniforms, in 1970 both the fatigue and dress uniforms for all services were in all basic aspects identical to their British counterparts. During the late 1960s the British service schools and academies were utilized more extensively than those of any other foreign nation. British concepts, both as to military procedures and gentlemanly conduct, continued to dominate the patterns of behavior in the officer corps, and reliance was placed on the United Kingdom for logistical support.

These behavioral patterns were particularly significant because of the heavy concentration of English-speaking, Christian Burghers (see Glossary) in the officer corps. During a parliamentary debate in 1962, evidence submitted indicated that, although 70 percent of the population was Sinhalese-Buddhist, Christians and Hindu Tamils (see Glossary) constituted a majority in the officer corps, with the Christian Burghers alone accounting for from 55 to 75 percent of the officers in the three services (see ch. 11, Religion; ch. 14, Political Dynamics; ch. 17, Political Values and Attitudes).

MILITARY JUSTICE

In common with most other significant aspects of military conduct, the code of military justice that defines offenses, limits punishments, and provides regulations governing the various types of military courts either is patterned directly on or is an amended version of the British military court system. As of 1970 legislation had been passed, but had not yet been implemented, to alter in some respects the administration of military justice; the nomenclature and composition of the military courts, however, generally conform to the British model.

Although in theory a general court-martial, the highest of the three-tier military court system, may try any military person for any offense and pass any sentence including death or imprisonment, charges of mutiny or of conspiracy to engage in mutiny and civil offenses punishable by death or life imprisonment have been tried in the first instance by civil courts. A civil offense of this nature is one, such as murder, culpable homicide, or rape, committed by a military person against a civilian.

Because the officers and men of all services are volunteers and because military service offers both relative economic security and prosperity and an element of social prestige as a government servant, the threat of dismissal from the armed forces serves as a powerful deterrent to misconduct. The large number of qualified volunteers for the few yearly openings enables the military commands to demand and secure a high standard of conduct from all personnel.

THE ARMED FORCES AND THE ECONOMY

During the 1960s the funds spent on the three services never exceeded 4 percent, and were usually about 3 percent, of total central government expenditures. The budget estimates for fiscal year 1969/70, for example, provided about Rs81.3 million (for value of rupee, see Glossary) for defense purposes, which was about 3 percent of total estimated expenditures. Slightly more than half, Rs44.1 million, was allocated to the army, and Rs20.7 million and Rs16.5 million were for the navy and air force, respectively.

Because of the small number of military personnel relative to an estimated population of 12.5 million, the services do not deprive the labor force of needed personnel. By the same token, however, only a relatively few military personnel acquire skills that are readily applicable and valuable when they leave the military service.

THE ARMED FORCES AND POLITICS

The professional officer corps adopted as part of its creed the British tradition of military neutrality in political affairs. Because of the two attempted coups, however, and because the military possesses a near monopoly of force, it is viewed by the political leaders as, at least, a powerful interest group. During the 1970 elections, for example, Mrs. Bandaranaike and two other leaders of the united opposition formally informed the governor general of their fears that, should their parties defeat the ruling United National Party (UNP) in the elections, the armed forces would, with police assistance, seize control of the government. Spokesmen for the armed forces denied the allegations, and, in the event, the UNP defeat, the subsequent reinstatement by Prime Minister Banda-ranaike of officers forced from the service by the previous UNP government, and the designation of new senior military officers occasioned no immediately observable opposition by the armed forces.

BIBLIOGRAPHY

Section I. Social

RECOMMENDED SOURCES

Ames, Michael M. "Ideological and Social Changes in Ceylon," *Human Organization*, XXII, No. 2, June 1963, 45-53.
_____. "The Impact of Western Education on Religion and Society in Ceylon," *Pacific Affairs*, LX, Nos. 1 and 2, Spring and Summer 1967, 19-42.

Arasaratnam, Sinnappah. *Ceylon*. Englewood Cliffs: Prentice-Hall, 1964.
_____. "Nationalism, Communalism, and National Unity in Ceylon." Pages 260-278 in Philip Mason (ed.), *India and Ceylon: Unity and Diversity*. New York: Oxford University Press, 1967.

Banks, Michael, "Caste in Jaffna." Pages 61-77 in E. R. Leach (ed.), *Aspects of Caste in South India, Ceylon, and North-west Pakistan*. (Cambridge Papers in Social Anthropology, No. 2.) Cambridge: Cambridge University Press, 1969.

Bareau, Andre. *La Vie et l'Organisation des Communites Buddhiques Modernes de Ceylon*. Pondichery: Institut Francais d'Indologie, 1957.

Basham, A. L. *The Wonder That was India*. New York: Grove Press, 1954.

Brohier, R. L. *Seeing Ceylon*. Colombo: Lake House Investments, 1965.

Cartman, James. *Hinduism in Ceylon*. Colombo: M. D. Gunasena, 1957.

Ceylon. Registrar General. *Report of the Registrar General of Ceylon on Vital Statistics for 1963*. Colombo: Government Press, 1968.

Ceylon. State Council. Select Committee on Sinhalese and Tamil as Official Languages. *Sinhalese and Tamil as Official Languages*. Colombo: Government Press, 1946.

Conze, Edward. *Buddhism: Its Essence and Development*. Oxford: Bruno Cassirer, 1953.

Cook, Elsie K. *Ceylon: Its Geography, Its Resources, and Its People*. London: Macmillan, 1951.

Coomaraswamy, Ananda K. *Mediaeval Sinhalese Art.* Gloucestershire: Essex House Press, 1908.

de Alwis, E. H. "The Growth of Secondary Education," *Ceylon Today*, XVII, Nos. 2-4, February-April 1968, 54-58.

Demographic Yearbook, 1967. New York: United Nations Educational, Scientific and Cultural Organization, 1967.

de Silva, S. F. *The New Geography of Ceylon.* Colombo: Colombo Apothecaries, 1943.

Egan, E. W. *Ceylon in Pictures.* (Visual Geography Series.) New York: Sterling, 1967.

Farmer, B. H. *Ceylon: A Divided Nation.* New York: Oxford University Press, 1963.

_____. "The Social Basis of Nationalism in Ceylon," *Journal of Asian Studies*, XXIV, No. 3, May 1965, 431-440.

Farquhar, C. N. *A Primer of Hinduism.* London: Christian Literature Society for India, 1911.

Ferguson's Ceylon Directory, 1966. (108th ed.) Colombo: Associated Newspapers of Ceylon, 1966.

International Bank for Reconstruction and Development. *The Economic Development of Ceylon.* Baltimore: Johns Hopkins Press, 1953.

Jaspers, Karl. *Socrates, Buddha, Confucius, Jesus.* New York: Harcourt, Brace, and World, 1962.

Jayasuriya, J. E. *Education in Ceylon Before and After Independence, 1939-1968.* Colombo: Associated Educational Publishers, 1969.

Kearney, Robert N. *Communalism and Language in the Politics of Ceylon.* Durham: Duke University Press, 1967.

_____. "Sinhalese Nationalism and Social Conflict in Ceylon," *Pacific Affairs*, XXXVII, No. 2, Summer 1964, 125-136.

Leach, E. R. *Pul Eliya—A Village in Ceylon: A Study of Land Tenure and Kinship.* Cambridge: Cambridge University Press, 1961.

Ludowyk, Evelyn F. C. *The Footprint of the Buddha.* London: Allen and Unwin, 1958.

_____. *The Modern History of Ceylon.* New York: Praeger, 1966.

Malalasekera, G. P. "Development of University Education in Ceylon," *Ceylon Today*, XVII, Nos. 2-4, February-April 1968, 59-63.

_____. "Social Tensions in Ceylon: Government and Students," *Pacific Community*, I, No. 4, July 1970, 743-754.

Mendis, G. C. "The Causes of Communal Conflict in Ceylon," *University of Ceylon Review*, I, No. 1, 1943, 41-49.

_____. *Ceylon Today and Yesterday: Main Currents of Ceylon*

History. (2d ed.) Colombo: Associated Newspapers of Ceylon, 1963.

Navaratnam, C. S. *A Short History of Hinduism in Ceylon.* Jaffna: Sri Sanmugantha Press, 1964.

Nicholas, C. W., and Paranavitana, S. *A Concise History of Ceylon.* Colombo: Ceylon University Press, 1961.

Obeyesekere, Gananath. "The Buddhist Pantheon in Ceylon and Its Extensions." Pages 1-26 in *Anthropological Studies in Theravada Buddhism.* (Cultural Report Series, No. 13.) New Haven: Yale University, Southeast Asia Studies, 1966.

———. "The Great Tradition and the Little Tradition in the Perspective of Sinhalese Buddhism," *Journal of Asian Studies,* XXII, No. 2, February 1963, 139-154.

Phadnis, Urmila. "The Indo-Ceylon Pact and the 'Stateless' Indians in Ceylon," *Asian Survey,* VII, No. 4, April 1967, 226-236.

Pieris, Ralph. "Character Formation in the Evolution of the Acquisitive Society," *Psychiatry,* XV, 1952, 53-60.

———. *Sinhalese Social Organization: The Kandyan Period.* Colombo: Ceylon University Press Board, 1956.

———. "Society and Ideology in Ceylon During a 'Time of Troubles,' 1795-1850," *University of Ceylon Review,* IX, June-September 1951, 79-101, 171-185, and 267-279.

Ross, Nancy Wilson. *Three Ways of Asian Wisdom: Hinduism, Buddhism, Zen.* New York: Simon and Schuster, 1966.

Ruberu, T. Ranjit. *Education in Colonial Ceylon.* Kandy: Kandy Printers, 1962.

Ryan, Bryce F. *Caste in Modern Ceylon.* New Brunswick: Rutgers University Press, 1953.

———. "Status, Achievement and Education in Ceylon," *Journal of Asian Studies,* XX, No. 4, August 1961, 463-476.

Ryan, Bryce F., and Straus, Murray Arnold. "The Integration of Sinhalese Society," *Research Studies of the State College of Washington,* XXII, No. 4, December 1954, 179-228.

Ryan, Bryce F.; Jayasena, L. D.; and Wickremesinghe, D. C. R. *Sinhalese Village.* Coral Gables: University of Miami Press, 1958.

Sarathchandra, E. R. *The Folk Drama of Ceylon.* Colombo: Department of Cultural Affairs, 1966.

———. *The Sinhalese Novel.* Colombo: M. D. Gunasena, 1950.

Sarkar, N. K. *The Demography of Ceylon.* Colombo: Government Press, 1957.

Schecter, Jerrold. *The New Face of Buddha: Buddhism and Political Power in Southeast Asia.* New York: Coward-McCann, 1967.

475

Singer, Marshall R. *The Emerging Elite: A Study of Political Leadership in Ceylon.* Cambridge: Massachusetts Institute of Technology Press, 1964.

"Sinhalese Buddhists Castigate Family Planning Move," *Sunday Pakistan Observer*, October 7, 1969, 9.

Siriwardane, C. D. S. "Buddhist Reorganization in Ceylon." Pages 531-546 in Donald E. Smith (ed.), *South Asian Politics and Religion.* Princeton: Princeton University Press, 1966.

Siriwardena, B. S. "The Life of Ceylon Women." Pages 150-174 in Barbara E. Ward (ed.), *Women in the New Asia.* Paris: United Nations Educational, Scientific and Cultural Organization, 1965.

Snodgrass, Donald R. *Ceylon: An Export Economy in Transition.* Homewood: Richard D. Irwin, 1966.

Straus, Murrary Arnold. "Child Training and Child Personality in a Rural and Urban Area of Ceylon." (Unpublished doctoral dissertation, University of Wisconsin, 1956.)

Tambiah, Stanley J. "Ethnic Representation in Ceylon's Higher Administrative Services, 1870-1946," *University of Ceylon Review*, VIII, No. 2, 1955, 113-134.

––––––. "Kinship Fact and Fiction in Relation to the Kandyan Sinhalese," *Journal of the Royal Anthropological Institute*, XCV, No. 2, July-December 1965, 131-173.

––––––. "The Process of Secularization in Three Ceylonese Peasant Communities." (Unpublished doctoral dissertation, Cornell University, 1954.)

Tresidder, Argus John. *Ceylon: An Introduction to the "Resplendent Land."* (Asia Library Series.) Princeton: Van Nostrand, 1960

United Nations. "Population and Vital Statistics Report," *Statistical Papers*, XXI, Series A, No. 4, October 1969, 6.

U. S. Agency for International Development. *Population Program Assistance.* Washington: Population Service, Office of the War on Hunger, 1968.

U. S. Department of Labor. Bureau of Labor Statistics. *Labor Law and Practice in Ceylon.* Washington: GPO, 1962.

U. S. Department of the Army. International Relations and Government Department. *Nations of the World.* Fort Benjamin Harrison: Defense Information School, 1969.

Vittachi, Tarzie. *The Brown Sahib.* London: Andre Deutsch, 1962.

––––––. *Emergency '58: The Story of the Ceylon Race Riots.* London: Andre Deutsch, 1958.

Wanninayake, U. B. *Economic and Social Progress, 1965-69.* Colombo: Ministry of Finance, Government of Ceylon, 1969.

Weston, Christine. *Ceylon.* (World Background Book Series.) New York: Scribner, 1960.

Wijesekera, Nandadeva D. *The People of Ceylon.* Colombo: M. D. Gunasena, 1965.

Wriggins, W. Howard. *Ceylon: Dilemmas of a New Nation.* Princeton: Princeton University Press, 1960.

Wright, Nicholas H. "Recent Fertility Change in Ceylon and Prospects for the National Family Planning Program." Reprinted from *Demography,* V, No. 2, 1968.

Yalman, Nur. "The Flexibility of Caste Principles in a Kandyan Community." Pages 78-112 in E. R. Leach (ed.), *Aspects of Caste in South India, Ceylon, and Northwest Pakistan.* Cambridge: Cambridge University Press, 1969.

_____. "On the Purity of Women in the Castes of Ceylon and Malabar," *Journal of the Royal Anthropological Institute,* XCIII, No. 1, January-June 1963, 25-58.

_____. "The Structure of the Sinhalese Kindred: A Re-examination of the Dravidian Terminology," *American Anthropologist,* LXIV, No. 3, June 1962, 548-574.

_____. *Under the Bo Tree.* Berkeley: University of California Press, 1960.

OTHER SOURCES USED

Ames, Michael M. "Ritual Prestations and the Structure of the Sinhalese Pantheon." Pages 27-50 in *Anthropological Studies in Theravada Buddhism.* (Cultural Report Series, No. 13.) New Haven: Yale University, Southeast Asia Studies, 1966.

"Assistance to National Film Industry," *Ceylon Today,* XVIII, Nos. 7 and 8, July and August 1969, 30-33.

Bandaranaike, Yasmine Dias. "The Literature of Ceylon." Pages 100-114 in A. L. McLeod (ed.), *The Commonwealth Pen.* Ithaca: Cornell University Press, 1961.

Basnayake, S. R., et al. "Sinhalese Technical Terms in Physiology and Biochemistry," *University of Ceylon Review,* XX, No. 1, 1962, 138-155.

Bonney, Harold V. *Library Services for Ceylon.* Colombo: Government Press, n.d.

Buddhist Paintings. (A Mentor-UNESCO Art Book.) New York: New American Library of World Literature, 1964.

Ceylon. Department of Cultural Affairs. *Administrative Report of the Director of Cultural Affairs for the Financial Year 1963/64,* IV: Education, Science and Art, by Palitha Weeraman. Colombo: Government Press, 1965.

_____. *Administrative Report of the Director of Cultural Af-*

fairs for the Financial Year 1964/65, IV: Education, Science and Art, by S. B. Senanayake. Colombo: Government Press, 1966.

Ceylon. Minister of Health Services. *Administration Report of the Director of Health Services*. Colombo: Government Press, 1966.

Ceylon. Ministry of Planning and Economic Affairs. *Economic Development: Review and Trends, 1966-68*. Colombo: Government Press, 1967.

Ceylon Association for the Advancement of Science. *Report of the 24th Annual Session (14-17 December 1968)*. Colombo: 1969.

Ceylon Calendar of Festivals and Other Events. Colombo: Ceylon Tourist Board, 1968.

Ceylon Year Book, 1967. Colombo: Government Press, 1967.

Ceylon Year Book, 1968. Colombo: Government Press, 1968.

Changalvaraya Pillai, V. S. *History of Tamil Prose Literature*. Madras: South Indian Saive Siddhanta Works Publishing Society, 1966.

Christian Workers Fellowship. *Social Change in Ceylon: A Study in Outline*. Colombo: 1967.

Coates, William Ames. "The Languages of Ceylon in 1946 and 1953," *University of Ceylon Review*, XIX, No. 1, 1961, 81-92.

Coomaraswamy, Ananda K. *History of Indian and Indonesian Art*. New York: Dover, n.d.

Cooray, Percival Gerald. *An Introduction to the Geology of Ceylon*. Colombo: National Museums of Ceylon, 1967.

Da Cunha, J. Gerson. *Memoir on the History of the Tooth Relic of Ceylon*. London: W. Thacker, 1875.

Dayaratne, D. G. "Development of the Theater in Ceylon," *Ceylon Today*, XVII, Nos. 2-4, February-April 1968, 91-94.

de Lanerolle, Julius. "The Future Official Languages of Ceylon," *University of Ceylon Review*, III, No. 2, November 1945, 35-43.

de la Vallée Poussin, Louis. *Buddhisme: Opinions sur l'Histoire de la Domatique*. Paris: Gabriel Beauchesne, 1925.

de Silva, Mervyn. "Lead, Kindly Stars," *Far Eastern Economic Review*, XLVII, No. 15, April 9, 1970, 23-25.

Devendra, D. T. "The Archaeological Survey of Ceylon, 1890-1960," *Ceylon Today*, IX, No. 7, July 1960, 13-18.

Dharmadasa, K. N. O. "Purism and Linguistic Authoritarianism," *Ceylon Daily News* (Colombo), January 18, 1970, 7.

Dubois, J. A., and Beauchamp, H. K. *Hindu Manners, Customs, and Ceremonies*. London: Oxford University Press, 1924.

Durand, John D. (ed.) *The Annals of the American Academy of Political and Social Science*, CCCLXIX, January 1967, 19.

Economist Intelligence Unit. *Quarterly Economic Review: Ceylon; Annual Supplement, 1969*. London: 1969.

"Exhibition of Tissa Ranasinghe's Sculpture," *Ceylon Today*, VIII, No. 12, December 1959, 8–13.

Far Eastern Economic Review Yearbook, 1969. Hong Kong: FEER, 1969.

Fernando, Chitra. "Contemporary Drama in Ceylon," *Hemisphere*, VIII, April 1964, 35–36.

Fernando, P. T. M. "Factors Affecting Marital Selection: A Study of Matrimonial Advertisements by Middle-Class Sinhalese," *Ceylon Journal of Historical and Social Studies*, VII, No. 2, July-December 1964, 171–188.

Geiger, Wilhelm. *Culture of Ceylon in Mediaeval Times*. Wiesbaden: Otto Harrassowitz, 1960.

––––––. "The Linguistic Character of Sinhalese," *Journal of the Ceylon Branch of the Royal Asiatic Society*, XXXIV, No. 90, 1937, 16–44.

Godakumbura, C. E. *The Literature of Ceylon*, IV: Arts of Ceylon. Colombo: Government Press, 1963.

Goetz, Hermann. *Five Thousand Years of Indian Art*. New York: McGraw-Hill, 1959.

Gogerly, John Daniel. *Ceylon Buddhism*. London: Kegal Paul, Trench, Trubner, 1908.

Goonetilleke, L. P. "Contemporary Painting and Sculpture in Ceylon," *Ceylon Today*, XVII, Nos. 2–4, February-April 1968, 76–90.

Goonewardene, James. "Dance Magic in Ceylon," *Ceylon Today*, IX, No. 1, January 1960, 10–13.

––––––. "Dances and Present Trends," *Ceylon Today*, IX, No. 6, June 1960, 27–29.

Green, T. L. "Education and Social Needs in Ceylon," *University of Ceylon Review*, X, No. 4, October 1952, 297–316.

Gunasinghe, Siri. "The Sinhala Cinema," *Ceylon Today*, XVII, Nos. 2–4, February-April 1968, 95–99.

International Bank for Reconstruction and Development. *Press Tour of Ceylon, October 15-26, 1969*. Washington: 1970 (mimeo.).

Jayawardan, Ben. *Living Buddhism; Containing Some Comments on the Sangha of Ceylon*. London: Buddhist Lodge, 1937.

Kanakasabhai, V. *The Tamils Eighteen Hundred Years Ago*. (2d ed.) Tiruneveli: South India Saiva Siddhanta Works Publishing Society, 1956.

Kanapathi Pillai, K. "Tamil Publications in Ceylon," *University of Ceylon Review*, XVI, Nos. 1 and 2, 1958, 6–16.

Kanthi, M. Sri. "Sri La Sri Arumugar Navalar: Reformer, Revivalist, and Scholar," *Ceylon Today*, XVIII, Nos. 7 and 8, July and August 1969, 28–29.

Kearney, Robert N. "New Directions in the Politics of Ceylon," *Asian Survey*, VII, No. 2, February 1968, 111–116.

Leach, E. R. "Introduction: What Should We Mean by Caste?" Pages 1–10 in E. R. Leach (ed.), *Aspects of Caste in South India, Ceylon, and Northwest Pakistan*. Cambridge: Cambridge University Press. 1969.

McClelland, Donald R. "The Paintings and Drawings of Justin Pieris Daraniyagala," *Ceylon Today*, XVIII, Nos. 3 and 4, March and April 1969, 28–30.

Majusri, L. T. P. "Victoria on Temple Walls," *Ceylon Daily News* (Colombo), April 5, 1970, 11.

Navaratnam, C. S. *Tamils and Ceylon*. Jaffna: Saive Prakasa Press, n.d.

Nesiah, K. "The Status of Tamil in Ceylon," *Tamil Culture*, VII, No. 2, April 1958, 183–196.

―――. "A Tamil University," *Ceylon Daily News* (Colombo), January 13, 1970, 9.

Obeyesekere, Gananath. *Land Tenure in Village Ceylon*. Cambridge: Cambridge University Press, 1967.

―――. "The Ritual Drama of the Sanni Demons: Collective Representations of Disease in Ceylon," *Comparative Studies in Society and History*, II, No. 4, October 1969, 174–216.

O'Malley, L. S. S. *Popular Hinduism*. New York: Macmillan, 1935.

Pakeman, S. A. *Ceylon*. New York: Praeger, 1964.

Passé, H. A. "The English Language in Ceylon," *University of Ceylon Review*, I, No. 2, 1943, 50–66.

Pathirana, Jayatissa. "Anagarika Dharmapala: A Great National Hero," *Ceylon Today*, XIII, No. 9, September 1964, 15–18.

Peiris, William. "The Kandy Perahera," *Ceylon Today*, VIII, No. 8, August 1959, 7–10.

Pieris, Ralph. "Caste, Ethos, and Social Equilibrium," *Social Forces*, XXX, 1951–52, 409–415.

―――. "Speech and Society: A Sociological Approach to Language," *American Sociological Review*, XVI, 1951, 499–505.

Raghavan, M. D. *Handsome Beggars: The Rodiyas of Ceylon*. Colombo: Colombo Book Center, 1957.

―――. *India in Ceylonese History, Society and Culture*. New York: Asia Publishing House, 1964.

Rajasundaram, C. V. "Western Influence on Modern Tamil Poetry," *Ceylon Today*, XV, No. 11, November 1966, 11–14.

The Report of the Commission of Inquiry into the Film Industry in Ceylon Appointed by His Excellency the Governor-

General on September 10, 1962. Colombo: Government Press, 1965.

Ross, Floyd H. *The Meaning of Life in Hinduism and Buddhism.* Boston: Beacon Press, 1953.

Ryan, Bryce F. "The Ceylonese Village and the New Value System" *Rural Sociology,* XVII, 1952, 9–28.

―――. "The Female Factory Worker in Colombo," *International Labour Review,* LXIV, 1951, 439–461.

―――. "Primary and Secondary Contacts in a Peasant Community," *Rural Sociology,* XVII, 1952, 311–321.

Sena, Devar Surya. "Folk Songs of Ceylon," *Ceylon Today,* II, No. 7, August 1953, 18–21.

―――. "Music of Ceylon, II," *Ceylon Today,* X, No. 4, April 1961, 19–23.

―――. "Music of Ceylon, III," *Ceylon Today,* X, No. 5, May 1961, 19–21.

Shanmugam Pillai, M. "A Tamil Dialect in Ceylon," *Indian Linguistics,* XXIII, 1962, 90–98.

―――. "Tamil—Literary and Colloquial," *International Journal of American Linguistics,* XXVI, No. 3, July 1960, 27–42.

Singer, Marshall R. "Group Perception and Social Change in Ceylon," *International Journal of Comparative Sociology,* VII, 1966, 209–226.

―――. "National Government in Ceylon: A Year of Reconciliation," *Asian Survey,* VI, No. 2, February 1966, 90–95.

Siriwardena, R. "The Contemporary Sinhalese Theater," *Ceylon Today,* VIII, No. 2, February 1959, 23–28.

Smith, Donald E. "The Political Monks and Monastic Reform." Pages 489–509 in Donald E. Smith (ed.), *South Asian Politics and Religion.* Princeton: Princeton University Press, 1966.

―――. "The Sinhalese Buddhist Revolution." Pages 453–488 in Donald E. Smith (ed.), *South Asian Politics and Religion.* Princton: Princeton University Press, 1966.

Spate, O. H. K. *India and Pakistan: A General and Regional Geography.* London: Methuen, 1957.

Stamp, L. Dudley. *Asia: A Regional and Economic Geography.* London: Methuen, 1957.

Straus, Jacqueline H., and Straus, Murray Arnold. "Suicide, Homicide, and Social Structure in Ceylon," *American Journal of Sociology,* LVIII, 1953, 461–469.

Straus, Murray Arnold. "Family Characteristics and Occupational Choice of University Entrants as Clues to the Social Structure of Ceylon," *University of Ceylon Review,* IX, No. 2, April 1951, 125–140.

―――. "Mental Ability and Cultural Needs: A Psycho-Cultural Interpretation of the Intelligence Test Performance of Ceylon

481

University Entrants," *American Sociological Review*, XVI, 1951, 371–375.

———. "Subcultural Variation in Ceylonese Mental Ability: A Study in National Character," *Journal of Social Psychology*, XXXIX, 1953, 129–141.

Subramanyan, Ka Naa. "Tamil Writing Today: The Wasted Heritage," *Journal of the Royal Society for India, Pakistan and Ceylon*, II, No. 3, April 1969, 203–214.

Sumanasuriya, K. T. U. "Founder of Buddhist Schools," *Ceylon Daily News* (Colombo), February 17, 1970, 8.

Tambiah, H. W. *The Laws and Customs of the Tamils of Ceylon*. Jaffna: Tamil Cultural Society of Ceylon, 1954.

———. *Sinhala Laws and Customs*. Colombo: Lake House Investments, 1968.

Tambiah, Stanley J., and Ryan, Bryce F. "Secularization of Family Values in Ceylon," *American Sociological Review*, XXII, 1957, 292–299.

"Tamilnad Prepares for Rehabilitation," *Ceylon Daily News* (Colombo), January 24, 1970, 5.

Tilakasiri, J. *Puppetry in Ceylon*, I. (Arts of Ceylon.) Colombo: Government Press, 1961.

———. "A Vanishing Art: 'Rukada'," *Ceylon Today*, II, No. 10, November 1953, 11–16.

"Twenty Years of the Government Film Unit," *Ceylon Today*, XVII, Nos. 9 and 10, September and October 1968, 22–27.

U. S. Department of Health, Education and Welfare. *Social Security Programs Throughout the World, 1964*. Washington: GPO, 1964.

Vithiananthan, S. "The Tamil Folk Drama," *Ceylon Today*, XII, No. 10, October 1963, 19–23.

Vogel, J. *Buddhist Art in India, Ceylon and Java*. Oxford: Clarendon Press, 1936.

Ward, Barbara E. "Men, Women, and Change: An Essay in Understanding Social Roles in South and South-East Asia." Pages 26–99 in Barbara E. Ward (ed.), *Women in the New Asia*. Paris: United Nations Educational, Scientific and Cultural Organization, 1965.

Wickramasinghe, Martin. *Aspects of Sinhalese Culture*. Colombo: Associated Newspapers of Ceylon, 1958.

Wijesekera, Nandadeva D. *Ancient Paintings and Sculpture of Ceylon*. (Arts of Ceylon.) Colombo: Government Press, 1962.

Williams, Harry. *Ceylon, Pearl of the East*. London: Robert Hale, 1963.

Wilson, A. Jeyaratnam. "Buddhism in Ceylon Politics, 1960–1965." Pages 510–530 in Donald E. Smith (ed.), *South Asian*

Politics and Religion. Princeton: Princeton University Press, 1966.

Yalman, Nur. "Dual Organization in Central Ceylon." Pages 197–224 in *Anthropological Studies in Theravada Buddhism.* (Cultural Report Series, No. 13.) New Haven: Yale University, Southeast Asia Studies, 1966.

Zimmer, Heinrich. *Art of Indian Asia.* (Bollingen Foundation Series.) Princeton: Princeton University Press, 1960.

(Various issues of *Ceylon Daily News* [Colombo], January-May 1970, were also used in the preparation of this section.)

Section II. Political

RECOMMENDED SOURCES

Ames, Michael M. "Ideological and Social Change in Ceylon," *Human Organization*, XXII, No. 1, June 1963, 45–53.

Arasaratnam, Sinnappah. *Ceylon*. Englewood Cliffs: Prentice-Hall, 1964.

———. "Nationalism, Communalism, and National Unity in Ceylon." Pages 260–278 in Philip Mason (ed.), *India and Ceylon: Unity and Diversity*. New York: Oxford University Press, 1967.

Bandaranaike, S. W. R. D. "Buddhism and World Peace," *Ceylon Today*, XIII, No. 5, May 1964, 9–14.

Ceylon. Ministry of Planning and Economic Affairs. *Foreign Aid*. Colombo: Government Press, 1968.

"Ceylon-India: The Kachchativu Island Dispute," *Keesing's Contemporary Archives*, XVII, January 11–18, 1969, 23131.

Collins, Charles. "Ceylon: The Imperial Heritage." Pages 444–549 in Ralph Braibanti (ed.), *Asian Bureaucratic Systems Emergent from the British Imperial Tradition*. Durham: Duke University Press, 1966.

Far Eastern Economic Review Yearbook, 1970. Hong Kong: FEER, 1970.

Fernando, Edgar. *Local Government Elections in Ceylon*. Ja-Ela: 1967.

Fretty, Ralph E. "Ceylon: Election-Oriented Politics," *Asian Survey*, IX, No. 2, February 1969, 99–103.

Guruge, Ananda, "Ceylon's Contribution to Buddhism," *Ceylon Today*, XIII, No. 5, May 1964. 32–34.

"India and Ceylon," *Ceylon Daily News* (Colombo), June 29, 1970, 6.

Jupp, James. "Constitutional Developments in Ceylon Since Independence," *Pacific Affairs*, XLI, No. 2, Summer 1968, 169–183.

Kearney, Robert N. "Ceylon: The Contemporary Bureaucracy." Pages 485–549 in Ralph Braibanti (ed.), *Asian Bureaucratic Systems Emergent from the British Imperial Tradition*. Durham: Duke University Press, 1966.

———. *Communalism and Language in the Politics of Ceylon*. Durham: Duke University Press, 1967.

485

———. "The Marxists and Coalition Government in Ceylon," *Asian Survey*, V, No. 2, February 1965, 120–124.

———. "New Directions in the Politics of Ceylon," *Asian Survey*, VII, No. 2, February 1967, 111–116.

———. "The Partisan Involvement of Trade Unions in Ceylon," *Asian Survey*, VIII, No. 7, July 1968, 576–588.

———. "Political Stresses and Cohesion," *Asian Survey*, VIII, No. 2, February 1968, 105–109.

———. "Sinhalese Nationalism and Social Conflict in Ceylon," *Pacific Affairs*, XXXVII, No. 2, Summer 1964, 125–136.

Kodikara, S. U. *Indo-Ceylon Relations Since Independence*. Colombo: Ceylon Institute of World Affairs, 1965.

LeGro, William E., Jr. *Expropriation of American Owned Properties in Ceylon: A Case Study in Retaliation*. (Unpublished doctoral dissertation, American University, 1964.)

Mendis, G. C. *Ceylon Today and Yesterday: Main Currents of Ceylon History*. (2d ed.) Colombo: Associated Newspapers of Ceylon, 1963.

Myrdal, Gunnar. *Asian Drama*. 3 vols. New York: Pantheon, 1968.

Phadnis, Urmila. "The Indo-Ceylon Pact and the 'Stateless' Indians in Ceylon," *Asian Survey*, VII, No. 4, April 1967, 226–236.

"Re-Organize Foreign Service," *Ceylon Daily News* (Colombo), July 7, 1970, 1.

Siriwardane, C. D. S. "Buddhist Reorganization in Ceylon." Pages 531–546 in Donald E. Smith (ed.), *South Asian Politics and Religion*. Princeton: Princeton University Press, 1966.

Smith, Donald E. "The Political Monks and Monastic Reform." Pages 489–509 in Donald E. Smith (ed.), *South Asian Politics and Religion*. Princeton: Princeton University Press, 1966.

———. "The Sinhalese Buddhist Revolution." Pages 453–488 in Donald E. Smith (ed.), *South Asian Politics and Religion*. Princeton: Princeton University Press, 1966.

Tambiah, H. W. *Sinhala Laws and Customs*. Colombo: Lake House Investments, 1968.

"Text of Throne Sppech," *Ceylon Daily News* (Colombo), June 15, 1970, 3.

Thalgodapitiya, W. *Portraits of Ten Patriots of Sri Lanka*. Kandy: T. B. S. Godamunne, 1966.

van der Kroef, Justus M. "Cehlon's Political Left: Its Development and Aspirations," *Pacific Affairs*, XL, Nos. 3 and 4, Fall and Winter 1967–68. 250–278.

———. "Many Faces of Ceylonese Communism," *Problems of Communism*, XVII, No. 2, March and April 1968, 48–60.

Wilson, A. Jeyaratnam. "Buddhism in Ceylon Politics, 1960–

1965." Pages 510-530 in Donald E. Smith (ed.), *South Asian Politics and Religion*. Princeton: Princeton University Press, 1966.

Wood, Arthur L. "Political Radicalism in Changing Sinhalese Villages," *Human Organization*, XXIII, No. 2, Summer 1964, 99-107.

Woodward, Calvin A. *The Growth of a Party System in Ceylon*. Providence; Brown University Press, 1969.

––––––. "The Trotskyite Movement in Ceylon," *World Politics*, XIV, No. 2, January 1962, 307-321.

Wriggins, W. Howard. *Ceylon: Dilemmas of a New Nation*. Princeton: Princeton University Press, 1960.

OTHER SOURCES USED

Abeyesinghe, E. F. Dias. *Administration Report of the Commissioner of Elections for 1966-67*. Colombo: Government Press, 1968.

Amerasinghe, Chittharanjan Felix. *Aspects of the Actio Iniuriarum in Roman-Dutch Law*. Colombo: Lake House Investments, 1966.

Ceylon, Laws, Statues, etc. *The Legislative Enactments of Ceylon*, I. (Rev. ed.) Colombo: Government Press, 1958.
1967 Supplement to the Revised Edition of the Legislative Enactments of Ceylon, I. Colombo: Government Press, 1967.

Ceylon Year Book, 1968. Colombo: Government Press, 1968.

Christian Workers Fellowship. *Social Change in Ceylon: A Study in Outline*. Colombo: 1967.

Cooray, L. J. M., and Jupp, James. "The Constitutional System in Ceylon: Notes and Comments," *Pacific Affairs*, XLIII, No. 1, Spring 1970, 73-83.

David, René, and Brierley, John E. C. *Major Legal Systems in the World Today*. London: Free Press, 1968.

de Silva, Colvin R. *Ceylon Under the British Occupation, 1795-1833: Its Political and Administrative Development*, I. Colombo: Colombo Apothecaries, 1953.

de Silva, Mervyn. "Blue Breasts in Green Valleys," *Far Eastern Economic Review*, LXVIII, No. 19, May 7, 1970, 26-28.

Ferguson's Ceylon Directory, 1967. (109th ed.) Colombo: Associated Newspapers of Ceylon, 1967.

George, T. J. S. "Ceylon: Sirimavo Slays 'Em," *Far Eastern Economic Review*, LXVIII, No. 23, June 4, 1970, 5-6.

Gupta, Babu Lal. *Political and Civil Status of Indians in Ceylon*. Agra: Gaya Prasad, 1963.

Jennings, Ivor. "Politics in Ceylon Since 1952," *Pacific Affairs*, XXVIII, No. 4, December 1954, 338-352.

Kearney, Robert N. "The Ceylon Communist Party: Competition for Marxist Supremacy." Pages 373-398 in Robert A. Scalapino (ed.), *The Communist Revolution in Asia: Tactics, Goals, and Achievements*. Englewood Cliffs: Prentice-Hall, 1965.

―――. "Militant Public Service Trade Unionism in a New State," *Journal of Asian Studies*, XXV, No. 3, May 1966, 397-409.

Lerski, George Jan. *Origins of Trotskyism in Ceylon: A Documentary History of the Lanka Sama Samaja Party, 1935-1942*. Stanford: Hoover Institution on War, Revolution and Peace, 1968.

Ludowyk, Evelyn F. C. *The Modern History of Ceylon*. New York: Praeger, 1966.

Malalasekera, G. P. "Social Tensions in Ceylon: Government and Students," *Pacific Community*, I, No. 4, July 1970, 743-754.

Minattur, Joseph. *Martial Law in India, Pakistan, and Ceylon*. The Hague: Martinus Nijhoff, 1962.

Namasivayam, S. *Parliamentary Governments in Ceylon, 1948-1958*. Colombo: K. V. G. De Silva, 1959.

1969 International Yearbook. New York: Editor and Publisher, 1969

Peaslee, Amos J. *Constitutions of Nations*, II: Asia, Australia, and Oceania. (3d ed., rev.) The Hague: Martinus Nijhoff, 1966.

Saddhatissa, H. "A Teaching for All," *Ceylon Today*, XIII, No. 5, May 1964, 6-8.

"Senanayake's Visit: Joint Communiqué," *Asian Recorder*, XV, No. 4, January 22-29, 1969, 8727-8728.

Singer, Marshall R. *The Emerging Elite: A Study of Political Leadership in Ceylon*. Cambridge: Massachusetts Institute of Technology Press, 1964.

Tambiah, Stanley J. "Ethnic Representation in Ceylon's Higher Administrative Services, 1870-1946," *University of Ceylon Review*, XIII, No. 2, 1955, 113-134.

United Nations. "Economic Development and Regional Cooperation in Southeast Asia," *Economic Bulletin for Asia and the Far East*, XX, No. 2, September 1969, 1-8.

U. S. Department of State. Bureau of Intelligence and Research. *World Strength of the Communist Party Organizations*. (Department of State Publication 8455.) Washington: GPO, 1969.

Weerawarana. *Government and Politics in Ceylon (1930-1946)*. Colombo: Ceylon Economic Research Association, 1951.

Wickramasinghe, Martin. *Aspects of Sinhalese Culture.* Colombo: Associated Newspapers of Ceylon, 1958.

World Radio-TV Handbook, 1970. (Ed., H. M. Frost). 24th ed.) Soliljevej: H. P. J. Meakin, 1970.

(Various issues of Economist Intelligence Unit, *Quarterly Economic Review: Ceylon* [London], January-May 1970, were also used in the preparation of this section.)

Section III. Economic

RECOMMENDED SOURCES

Central Bank of Ceylon. *Annual Report of the Monetary Board to the Minister of Finance for the Year 1967.* Colombo: 1968.

Ceylon. *Report of the Committee of Inquiry into the Law and Practice of the Trade Unions Ordinance.* Colombo: Government Press, 1967.

Ceylon. Department of Census and Statistics. *Census of Population,* I. Colombo: Government Press, 1967.

Ceylon. Department of Labour. *Ceylon Labour Gazette,* XXI, No. 1, January 1970.

Ceylon. Laws, Statutes, etc.

"Appropriation Act, No. 7 of 1965," *1966 Supplement to the Revised Edition of the Legislative Enactments of Ceylon,* II. Colombo: Government Press, 1966.

"Inland Revenue Act, No. 4 of 1963," *1966 Supplement to the Revised Edition of the Legislative Enactments of Ceylon,* II. Colombo: Government Press, 1966.

"Monetary Law Act (1956 Revision)," *1966 Supplement to the Revised Edition of the Legislative Enactments of Ceylon,* I. Colombo: Government Press, 1966.

Ceylon. Ministry of Labour and Employment. *Administration Report of the Commissioner of Labour for 1950,* I. Colombo: Government Press, 1951.

———. *Interim Report of the Salaries and Cadres Commission, 1969.* Colombo: Government Press, 1969.

Ceylon. Ministry of Planning and Economic Affairs. *The Problem of Foreign Exchange and Long-Term Growth of Ceylon.* (Report of an IBRD mission to Ceylon.) Colombo: Government Press, 1968.

Ceylon. Taxation Inquiry Commission. *Report, 1966–67.* Colombo: Government Press, 1968.

The Ceylon Trade Union Movement. Colombo: National Welfare Association, 1968.

Ceylon Year Book, 1968. Colombo: Government Press, 1968.

"Ceylonese Plantation Workers Demand Wage Increase," *International Trade Union News,* February 1968.

Economist Intelligence Unit. *Ceylon Investment Guide: Rub-*

ber, Leather, Wood and Non-Metallic Mineral Products Kent: Robert Stace, 1968.

───────. Ceylon Investment Guide: The Agricultural Processing Industry. Kent: Robert Stace, 1968.

───────. Ceylon Investment Guide: The General Economic Environment. Kent: Robert Stace, 1968.

───────. Ceylon Investment Guide: The Light Engineering Industry. Tunbridge Wells: Robert Stace, 1968.

───────. Quarterly Economic Review: Ceylon; Annual Supplement, 1968. London: 1968.

Ferguson's Ceylon Directory, 1967. (109th ed.) Colombo: Associated Newspapers of Ceylon, 1967.

Gunasekera, H. A. "Ceylon." Pages 279–302 in W. F. Crick (ed.), Commonwealth Banking Systems. Oxford: Clarendon Press, 1965.

Hicks, J. R. "Reflections on the Economic Problems of Ceylon." Pages 9–21 in National Planning Council, Papers by Visiting Economists. Colombo: Government Press, 1959.

"Industrial Development and Its Contribution to the National Economy," Ceylon Today, XVII, Nos. 2–4, February-April 1968, 29–36.

International Labor Organization. "Monthly Salaries and Normal Hours of Work per Week of Employees in Selected Occupations," Bulletin of Labor Statistics, 2d Quarter, October 1968, 131.

───────. Reports on the Visit of a Joint Team of Experts on Labour-Management Relations to Pakistan and Ceylon. (ILO Labour-Management Relations Series 10–11A, September-November 1959.) Geneva: 1961.

Jennings, Ivor. The Economy of Ceylon. Calcutta: Oxford University Press, 1951.

Kaldor, Nicholas. "Observations on the Problem of Economic Development in Ceylon." Pages 24–33 in National Planning Council, Papers by Visiting Economists. Colombo: Government Press, 1959.

Kannangara, Imogen. "Women's Employment in Ceylon," International Labour Review, XCIII, January-June 1966, 117–122.

Karunatilake, H. N. S. Banking and Financial Institutions in Ceylon. Colombo: Central Bank of Ceylon, 1968.

Kearney, Robert N. "Militant Public Service Trade Unionism in a New State," Journal of Asian Studies, XXV, No. 3, May 1966, 397–409.

───────. Trade Unions and Politics in Ceylon. (Paper Prepared for the University of Wisconsin Seminar on Comparative Governments.) Madison: University of Wisconsin Press, 1967.

Lange, Oskar. "The Tasks of Economic Planning in Ceylon." Pages 73–91 in National Planning Council, *Papers by Visiting Economists*. Colombo: Government Press, 1959.

Myrdal, Gunnar. *Asian Drama*. 3 vols. New York: Pantheon, 1968.

Naylor, G. W. *Report of Reconnaissance Mission to Ceylon in Connection with State Industrial Corporations, February 16-March 16, 1966*. Colombo: Ministry of Planning and Economic Affairs, 1966.

Orde-Brown, Granville St. John. *Report on Labour Conditions in Ceylon*. Colombo: Government Press, 1943.

Snodgrass, Donald R. *Ceylon: An Export Economy in Transition*. Homewood: Richard D. Irwin, 1966.

Tambiah, Stanley J. "Ceylon," Pages 45–125 in Richard D. Lambert and B. F. Hoselitz (eds.), *The Role of Savings and Wealth in Southern Asia and the West*. Paris: United Nations Educational, Scientific and Cultural Organization, 1963.

"Unemployment," *International Financial News Survey*, XX, No. 23, Jun 14, 1968, 125.

United Nations. *Industrial Developments in Asia and the Far East*, II, (Country Studies.) New York: 1966.

U. S. Department of Commerce. *Basic Data on the Economy of Ceylon*. (Overseas Business Reports, 66–87.) Washington: GPO, 1966.

U. S. Department of Commerce. Bureau of International Commerce. *Foreign Economic Trends and Their Implications for the United States*. Washington: 1969.

U. S. Department of Labor. Bureau of Labor Statistics. *Labor Digest No. 6*. Washington: GPO, 1963.

––––––. *Labor Law and Practice in Ceylon*. Washington: GPO, 1962.

Wanninayake, M. D., and Thehon, U. B. *Economic and Social Progress, 1965-69*. (Supplement to the Budget Speech, 1969.) Colombo: Department of Government Printing, 1969.

Weston, Christine. *Ceylon*. (A World Background Book Series.) New York: Scribner, 1960.

Wriggins, W. Howard. *Ceylon: Dilemmas of a New Nation*. Princeton: Princeton University Press, 1960.

OTHER SOURCES USED

Agarwala, Omar, and Singh, Sampat. *Economics of Underdeveloped Areas*. London: Oxford University Press, 1959.

Asian Development Bank. *Asian Agricultural Survey: Regional Report*, I and II. Manila: 1968.

_____. _Regional Seminar on Agriculture, Papers and Proceedings._ Hong Kong: 1969.

Balance of Payments Yearbook, XXI: Ceylon. Washington: International Monetary Fund, 1970.

Balasingham, C. "Government Budgeting and Accounting in Ceylon." Pages 51–108 in _The Constitution and Public Finance in Ceylon._ Colombo: Institute of Chartered Accountants, 1964.

_____. _Parliamentary Control of Finance._ Colombo: Government Press, 1968.

Central Bank of Ceylon. _Annual Report, 1968._ Colombo: 1969.

_____. _Annual Report of the Monetary Board to the Minister of Finance for the Year 1968._ Colombo: 1969.

_____. _Annual Report of the Monetary Board to the Minister of Finance for the Year 1969._ Colombo: 1970.

_____. _Bulletin_, XVII, Nos. 7 and 8, July and August 1967; and XX, No. 12, December 1969.

_____. _Report on the Sample Survey of Consumer Finances_, I. Colombo: 1964.

Ceylon. Chamber of Commerce. _Annual Report and Accounts, 1965._ Colombo: Colombo Apothecaries, 1966.

_____: _Annual Report and Accounts, 1966._ Colombo: Colombo Apothecaries, 1967.

_____. _Annual Report and Accounts, 1967._ Colombo: Colombo Apothecaries, 1968.

_____. Commission of Inquiry, 1968. _Report_, I. Colombo: Government Press, 1968.

_____. Department of Census and Statistics. _Census of Agriculture, 1962._ 4 vols. Colombo: Government Press, 1965–67.

_____. _Statistical Abstract of Ceylon, 1966._ Colombo: Government Press, 1969.

_____. _Statistical Pocket Book, 1968._ Colombo: Government Press, 1969.

_____. _Statistical Pocket Book, 1969._ Colombo: Government Press, 1970.

_____. Department of Commerce. _Administration Report of the Director of Commerce, 1961/62._ Colombo: Government Press, 1964.

_____. _Administration Report of the Director of Commerce, 1962/63._ Colombo: Government Press, 1965.

_____. _Administration Report of the Director of Commerce, 1963/64._ Colombo: Government Press, 1966.

_____. _Administration Report of the Director of Commerce, 1964/65._ Colombo: Government Press, 1967.

_____. _Administration Report of the Director of Commerce, 1965/66._ Colombo: Government Press, 1968.

———. *Administration Report of the Director of Commerce, 1966/67*. Colombo: Government Press, 1969.

———. *The Ceylon Trade Journal*. Colombo: June 1969.

———. Department of National Planning. *The Development Program, 1964-1965*. Colombo: Government Press, 1964.

———. Governor-General. "Text of Throne Speech," *Ceylon Daily News* (Colombo), June 15, 1970, 3, 5.

———. Land Commission. *Interim Report*. Colombo: Government Press, 1957.

———. Land Utilization Committee, 1966/67. *Report*. Colombo: Government Press, 1968.

———. Laws, Statutes, etc.

Appropriation Act, No. 30 of 1969: Estimates of the Revenue and Expenditure of the Government of Ceylon for the Financial Year, 1 October 1969 to 30 September 1970. Colombo: Government Press, 1969.

———. Marketing Department. *Administration Report of the Commissioner for Development of Marketing, 1967/68*. Colombo: Government Press, 1969.

———. Ministry of Agriculture and Food. *Agricultural Development Proposals, 1966-1970*. Colombo: Government Press, 1966.

———. *Agricultural Development Proposals, 1966-1970: Implementation Programme and Targets, 1970*. Colombo: Government Press, 1970.

———. Ministry of Finance. *Budget Speech, 1968-69*. Colombo: Government Press, 1968.

———. *Budget Speech, 1969-70*. Colombo: Government Press, 1969.

———. *Economic and Social Progress, 1956-62*. Colombo: Government Press, 1963.

———. *Economic and Social Progress, 1965-69*. Colombo: Government Press, 1969.

———. *Six-Year Plan for Ceylon*. Colombo: Government Press, 1948.

———. Ministry of Land, Irrigation, and Power. *Plan of Development, 1966-1970*. Colombo: Government Press, 1966.

———. Ministry of Planning and Economic Affairs. *Albert Waterston: Recommendations on Economic Planning in Ceylon*. Colombo: Government Press, 1966.

———. *The Development Programme, 1966-67*. Colombo: Government Press, 1966.

———. *Economic Development: Review and Trends, 1966-68*. Colombo: Government Press, 1967.

———. *Economic Indicators, 1968*. Colombo: 1969.

———. *Foreign Aid*. Colombo: Government Press, 1966.

———. *Foreign Exchange Budget, 1969.* Colombo: Government Press, 1969.

———. *Report of a Bank (IBRD) Transportation Mission (to Ceylon).* Colombo: Government Press, 1966.

———. National Planning Council. *First Interim Report.* Colombo: Government Press, 1957.

———. *The Ten-Year Plan.* Colombo: Government Press, 1959.

———. People's Bank Commission. *Report.* Colombo: Government Press, 1966.

———. Transport Commission. *Report of the Transport Commission.* Colombo: Government Press, 1967.

Colombo Plan Bureau. *Progress of the Colombo Plan, 1964.* Colombo: 1965.

Cooray, J. A. L. "Some Aspects of the Constitution of Ceylon." Pages 1-50 in *The Constitution and Public Finance in Ceylon.* Colombo: Institute of Chartered Accountants, 1964.

de Silva, S. F. *The New Geography of Ceylon.* Colombo: Colombo Apothecaries, 1943.

Economist Intelligence Unit. *World Outlook, 1970.* London: 1970.

Egan, E. W. *Ceylon in Pictures.* (Visual Geography Series.) New York: Sterling, 1967.

Far Eastern Economic Review Year Book, 1969. Hong Kong: FEER, 1969.

Far Eastern Economic Review Year Book, 1970. Hong Kong: FEER, 1970.

Farmer, B. H. *Ceylon: A Divided Nation.* New York: Oxford University Press, 1963.

Galbraith, John Kenneth. "Industrial Organization and Economic Development." Pages 95-103 in National Planning Council, *Papers by Visiting Economists.* Colombo: Government Press, 1959.

Greenberg, Michael. "Central Banking in Ceylon," Pages 9-27 in S. Gethyn Davies (ed.), *Central Banking in South and East Asia.* Hong Kong: Hong Kong University Press, 1960.

Gunasekera, H. A. *From Dependent Currency to Central Banking in Ceylon.* London: G. Bell, 1962.

Hicks, Ursula K. *Development from Below.* London: Oxford University Press, 1961.

———. "Local Government and Finance in Ceylon." Pages 108-118 in National Planning Council, *Papers by Visiting Economists.* Colombo: Government Press, 1959.

Higgins, Benjamin H. *Economic Development.* New York: W. W. Norton, 1959.

Hunting Survey Corporation. *A Forest Inventory of Ceylon.* Colombo: n.pub., 1961.

International Bank for Reconstruction and Development. *The Economic Development of Ceylon.* Baltimore: Johns Hopkins Press, 1953.

―――. *Press Tour of Ceylon, October 15-26, 1969.* Washington: 1970 (mimeo.).

International Monetary Fund. *International Financial Statistics,* XXIII, No. 6, June 1970.

―――. *Twentieth Annual Report on Exchange Restrictions.* Washington: 1969.

Jayawardene, N. V. "Public Finance in Ceylon." Pages 110-271 in *The Constitution and Public Finance in Ceylon.* Colombo: Institute of Chartered Accountants, 1964.

Kaldor, Nicholas. *Comprehensive Reform of Direct Taxation.* (Sessional Paper IV of 1960.) Colombo: Government Press, 1969.

Kearney, Robert N. "The Partisan Involvement of Trade Unions in Ceylon," *Asian Survey,* VIII, No. 7, July 1968, 576-588.

Leach, E. R. "Land Tenure in a Sinhalese Village, North Central Province, Ceylon," *Man,* LV, No. 178, November 1955, 166-167.

―――. *Pul Eliya—A Village in Ceylon: A Study of Land Tenure and Kinship.* Cambridge: Cambridge University Press, 1961.

Levin, Jonathan V. *The Export Economies.* Cambridge: Harvard University Press, 1960.

Loganathan, C. "Some Aspects of Deposit Banking in Ceylon." Pages 48-129 in *Banking in Ceylon.* Colombo: Institute of Chartered Accountants, 1963.

Ludowyk, Evelyn F. C. *The Modern History of Ceylon.* New York: Praeger, 1966.

Mendis, G. C. *Ceylon Today and Yesterday: Main Currents of Ceylon History.* (2d ed.) Colombo: Associated Newspapers of Ceylon, 1963.

Morgan, Theodore, and Spoelstra, Nyle (eds.). *Economic Interdependence in Southeast Asia.* Madison: University of Wisconsin Press, 1969.

Myrdal, Gunnar. "Comments on Planning and Related Matters." Appendix in National Planning Council, *Papers by Visiting Economists.* Colombo: Government Press, 1959.

Obeyesekere, Gananath. *Land Tenure in Village Ceylon.* Cambridge: Cambridge University Press, 1967.

Onslow, Cranley (ed.). *Asian Economic Development.* New York: Praeger, 1965.

Pakeman, S. A. *Ceylon.* New York: Praeger, 1964.

Robinson, Joan. "Economic Possibilities of Ceylon." Pages 39-71 in National Planning Council, *Papers by Visiting Economists.* Colombo: Government Press, 1959.

497

Sarkar, N. K. *The Demography of Ceylon.* Colombo: Government Press, 1957.

Sarker, N. K., and Tambiah, Stanley J. *The Disintegrating Village.* Colombo: Ceylon University Press, 1957.

Senewiratne, S. T., and Appadurai, R. R. *Field Crops of Pakistan.* Colombo: Lake House Investments, 1966.

Shannon, L. W. *Underdeveloped Areas.* New York: Harper, 1957.

Spate, O. H. K. *India and Pakistan: A General and Regional Geography.* (2d ed.) London: Methuen, 1957.

Stamp, L. Dudley. *Asia: A Regional and Economic Geography.* London: Methuen, 1957.

Statistical Yearbook, 1968. New York: United Nations, 1969.

U. S. Department of Commerce. *Ceylon.* (Foreign Economic Trends, ET69-67.) Washington: GPO, 1969.

Uswatte-Aratchi, G. "Why Ceylon Needs Foreign Aid," *Asian Review* (London), I, No. 2, January 1968.

Wijesekera, Nandadeva D. *The People of Ceylon.* Colombo: M. D. Gunasena, 1965.

Yearbook of International Trade Statistics, 1966. New York: United Nations, 1968.

Yoxall, W. T. "Development Banking in Ceylon." Pages 131–174 in *Banking in Ceylon.* Colombo: Institute of Chartered Accountants, 1963.

(Various issues of Economist Intelligence Unit, *Quarterly Economic Review: Ceylon* [London], August 23, 1968-May 1970, were also used in the preparation of this section.)

Section IV. National Security

RECOMMENDED SOURCES

Ceylon. Department of Prisons. *The Administration Report of the Commissioner of Prisons for 1965-66.* Colombo: Government Press, 1967.

Ceylon. Police Department. *The Administration Report of the Inspector-General of Police for the Financial Year 1966-67.* Colombo: Government Press, 1968.

Jupp, James. "Constitutional Developments in Ceylon Since Independence," *Pacific Affairs*, XLI, No. 2, Summer 1968, 169-183.

Kearney, Robert N. *Communalism and Language in the Politics of Ceylon.* Durham: Duke University Press, 1967.

Leonard, John D. (comp.) *The History and Development of the Ceylon Police System.* (Prepared for the International Cooperation Administration, Public Safety Division.) Colombo: 1959 (mimeo.).

Myrdal, Gunnar. *Asian Drama*, I. New York: Pantheon, 1968.

Smith, Donald E. (ed.) *South Asian Politics and Religion.* Princeton: Princeton University Press, 1966.

Wriggins, W. Howard. *Ceylon: Dilemmas of a New Nation.* Princeton: Princeton University Press, 1960.

OTHER SOURCES USED

Arasaratnam, Sinnappah. "Nationalism, Communalism, and National Unity in Ceylon." Pages 260-278 in Philip Mason (ed.), *India and Ceylon: Unity and Diversity.* New York: Oxford University Press, 1967.

Blackman, Raymond V. B. (ed.) *Jane's Fighting Ships, 1969-70.* London: Haymarket Publishing Group, 1970.

Ceylon. Department of Census and Statistics. *Statistical Abstract of Ceylon, 1966.* Colombo: Government Press, 1969.

_____. Department of Prisons. *The Administration Report of the Commissioner of Prisons for 1964-65.* Colombo: Government Press, 1966.

_____. Laws, Statutes, etc.

The Legislative Enactments of Ceylon in Force on the 30th

Day of June 1956, I-IV. (Rev. ed.) Colombo: Government Press, 1958.

1966 Supplement to the Revised Edition of the Legislative Enactments of Ceylon, I and II. Colombo: Government Press, 1966.

1967 Supplement to the Revised Edition of the Legislative Enactments of Ceylon, I and II. Colombo: Government Press, 1967.

———. Ministry of Justice. Department of Covernment Analyst. The Administration Report of the Government Analyst for 1965-66. Colombo: Government Press, 1967.

———. Police Department. The Administration Report of the Inspector-General of Police for the Financial Year 1961/62. Colombo: Government Press, 1963.

———. The Administration Report of the Inspector-General of Police for the Financial Year 1963/64. Colombo: Government Press, 1965.

———. The Administration Report of the Inspector-General of Police for the Financial Year 1965/66. Colombo: Government Press, 1967.

Ceylon Year Book, 1968. Colombo: Government Press, 1968.

Cramer, James. The World's Police. London: Cassell, 1964.

Ferguson's Ceylon Directory, 1967. (109th ed.) Colombo: Associated Newspapers of Ceylon, 1967.

Hanning, Hugh. The Peaceful Uses of Military Forces. New York: Praeger, 1967.

Kearney, Robert N. "New Directions in the Politics of Ceylon," Asian Survey, VII, No. 2, February 1967, 111–116.

———. "Sinhalese Nationalism and Social Conflict in Ceylon," Pacific Affairs, XXXVII, No. 2, Summer 1964, 125–136.

Ludowyk, Evelyn F. C. The Modern History of Ceylon. New York: Praeger, 1966.

Pretty, R. T., and Archer, D. H. R. (eds.) Jane's Weapon Systems, 1969-70. London: Haymarket Publishing Group, 1970.

The Reference Handbook of the Armed Forces of the World. Garden City: Robert C. Sellers, 1968.

Ryan, Bryce F., and Straus, Murray Arnold. "The Integration of Sinhalese Society," Research Studies of the State College of Washington, XXII, No. 4, December 1954, 179–228.

Schecter, Jerrold. The New Face of Buddha: Buddhism and Political Power in Southeast Asia. New York: Coward-McCann, 1967.

Stateman's Year Book, 1969-70. (eds., S. H. Steinberg, and John Paxton.) London: Macmillan, 1969.

U. S. Department of State. Bureau of Intelligence and Research. World Strength of the Communist Party Organiza-

tions. (Department of State Publication 8455.) Washington: GPO, 1969.

Worldmark Encyclopedia of the Nations, IV: Ceylon. (Ed., Louis Barron.) New York: Harper and Row, 1967.

(Various issues of the following periodicals were also used in the preparation of this section: *Asian Recorder* [New Delhi], January 1963–December 1969; and *Keesing's Contemporary Archives* [London], January 1965–December 1969.)

GLOSSARY

ayurvedic—System of healing based on homeopathy and naturopathy, with an extensive use of herbs. There are *ayurvedic* doctors, hospitals, and colleges, all recognized by the government.

bhikkus—Buddhist monks. When capitalized, an honorific title. The *bhikkus* are not priests, rabbis, or reverends in the Western sense of the terms.

Burghers—Small Christian community of Eurasians and Europeans constituting perhaps 1 percent of population. Eurasians are generally descendants of Portuguese or Dutch colonialists and local women.

CAS—Ceylon Administrative Service.

CCP—Ceylon Communist Party.

CCP(Moscow)—Ceylon Communist Party (Moscow).

CCP(Peking)—Ceylon Communist Party (Peking).

Ceylon Tamils—*See* Tamils.

chena—Slash-and-burn agriculture. Forest or shrub undergrowth is cleared by cutting and burning. Land is farmed until its productivity falls, then new area is cleared. This type of agriculture is usually associated with shifting cultivation.

crown lands—The equivalent of federal public lands in the United States. The crown lands were for the most part secured as state succession or as inheritance from the king of Kandy.

dry zone—North-central and eastern portion of island receiving from fifty to seventy-five inches of rain per year.

grama sevaka—Literally, village servant, but functioning as a village chief or headman. In addition to his role as the chief administrative officer of a village, he assists the police in maintaining public order and helps also in the annual preparation of the electoral register.

IBRD—International Bank for Reconstruction and Development.

IDA—International Development Agency.

IFC—International Finance Corporation.

IMF—International Monetary Fund.

Indian Tamils—*See* Tamils.

jaggory—A sugar confection made from palm sap.

karma—Religious doctrine that each rebirth in the cycle of lives represents the sum of the merit accumulated by an individual during his previous lives. *Karma* establishes the general tendency of a life but does not determine specific actions. In each life the interaction between individual character and previously established *karma* forms the *karma* of succeeding lives.

LSSP—Lanka Sama Samaja Party or, roughly, Ceylon Equality Party.

maha—The main growing season under rain-fed conditions for paddy (rice) and most other annual crops. Sowing is around August to October, depending on the time of the monsoon, and the crop is harvested around February to March.

nibbana—The release from the cycle of rebirths and the annihilation of the individual being that occurs on achievement of perfect spiritual understanding. More commonly known in the West as *nirvana*.

nirvana—*See nibbana.*

paddy—Threshed, unmilled rice, which is the basis of the subsistence economy of much of South and Southeast Asia. It is grown on flooded or heavily irrigated flatland.

Pali—The language of the Theravada Buddhist sacred scriptures. A Prakrit, or a language derived from Sanskrit.

rupee—Monetary unit of Ceylon. The official exchange rate (par value) from January 16, 1952, to November 20, 1967, was Rs4.76 per US$1; since November 21, 1967, Rs5.95 have equalled US$1.

sangha—The total community of *bhikkus*, or Buddhist monks, in the broadest and most abstract sense; the *sangha* is composed of all sects and residential communities.

Sinhala—An Indo-European language of the Indo-Iranian group. It was derived from a Prakrit, or dialectical form of Sanskrit. Majority language of Ceylon.

Sinhala Maha Sabha—Literally, the Great Committee of Sinhala. It was founded in 1934 to represent the interests of Sinhala-language speakers in the Ceylon National Congress.

Sinhalese—The Sinhala-speaking majority ethnic group, constituting approximately 70 percent of the population. Over 90 percent of them are Theravada Buddhists. Their ancestors probably came from North India several centuries B.C.

SLFP—Sri Lanka Freedom Party.

swabasha—Local language.

Tamils—Speakers of a Dravidian language and of South Indian origin, preponderantly Hindu. Ceylon Tamils are descendants of settlers and invaders; the Indian Tamils are descendants of estate laborers imported into the island mostly in the nineteenth century.

tank—Local word for artificial water storage and irrigation system.

Theravada Buddhism—Literally, the Buddhism that is "the way of the elders." This branch is sometimes called Hinayana (Lesser Vehicle) in contradistinction to Mahayana (Greater Vehicle) Buddhism. The Ceylonese, with rare exception, speak only of Theravada.

UNP—United National Party.

wet zone—Area of southwest side of hill country and southwestern plain receiving from 100 to 200 inches of rain per year.

yala—The secondary growing season for paddy (rice) and most other annual crops. Sowing is in March and April, and the crop is harvested around July to September. For some foodstuffs and cotton, when grown in the dry zone under irrigation, the yala crop is more important that the maha crop.

INDEX

283, 284, 285, 305, 468, 471; government (1960), 247-249; government (1970), 3, 151, 246, 279, 281, 296, 355, 358, 366, 467, 469

Bandaranaike, Solomon West Ridgeway Dias: 2, 31, 56, 58, 59, 60-63, 81, 197, 246, 248, 262, 264, 275, 277, 283, 446

Bank of Ceylon: 48, 247, 426, 428, 429, 430, 431, 439

banks and banking (see also Bank of Ceylon; Central Bank; nationalization; Peoples Bank): 312, 315, 316, 317, 325, 349, 391, 403, 407, 426, 428-435, 436, 438-442, 443

Barnes, Edward, Governor: 47

Basawakkulam: 17, 18

Bata Shoe Company: 364

Batticaloa: 16, 85, 386; history, 40, 41

Bay of Bengal: v, 7, 19

beaches: 10

Bell, H. C. P.: 186

bhikkus (see also sangha): 2, 88, 104, 105, 112, 181, 192, 195, 196, 210; and politics, 53, 61, 63, 259, 301

birds: 24-25

birth control (see also family planning): 67

birth rate: 65, 66, 67, 71, 73, 259

Bo Tree, Sacred: 79, 163, 165, 190-192, 193, 199, 208

Brahmins: 38, 97, 107, 193, 212

British bases: 56, 58, 63, 72, 277

British Ceylon Corporation: 364

British East India Company: 42, 43

British Overseas Airways Corporation (BOAC): ix, 387

British rule (see also British Sovereign; cultural influences; taxation): v, 1, 5, 9, 10, 29, 30, 43, 80, 81, 82, 86, 87, 88, 149, 168, 221-222, 223, 227, 233, 254, 309, 310, 327, 335; (1796-1833), 42-46; (1833-1900), 46-49; constitutional reform and independence movement, 49-58; religion, 189, 192, 194-197, 214

British Sovereign (see also Queen Victoria): vii, 44, 58, 225, 226, 227, 228, 229, 230, 300

broadcasting commission: 290, 292, 293, 297

Brownrigg, Robert, Governor: 195

Buddha: images, 165-166, 168; life and teachings, 190, 192, 202-205, 208, 209, 224, 303, 304; relics (see also tooth relic), 163, 190, 192, 208

Buddha Jayanti: 61, 90, 197, 198

Buddhaghosa: 170

Buddhism and the State: 30, 31, 32, 45, 48, 192, 194-195, 198, 227, 249, 259, 300, 302

Buddhist Commission of Inquiry: 197-198, 283; Report, 197-198, 222-223

Buddhist Sasana Council: 61

Buddhist Temperence Movement: 51

Buddhists and Buddhism (see also Buddhism and the State; pansala; pirivena; sangha; Sinhalese Buddhist nationalism; Theravada Buddhism): vii, 1-2, 31, 51-55, 61, 74, 76, 77, 84, 87-88, 97, 106, 116, 140, 141, 146, 147, 154, 161, 163, 174, 178, 181-183, 187, 189-210, 215, 218, 222, 224, 253, 259, 262, 264, 283, 294, 295, 299-307, 469; concepts and teachings, 200-205; development of religion, 190-198, 205; history, 9, 32, 33, 34, 36, 37, 38, 40, 44; popular Buddhism, 198-200, 207-210

budget: 407, 423; system, 408-411

Burghers (see also communalism): vii, 1, 5, 41, 46, 53, 66, 77, 78, 85-86, 88, 89, 98, 115, 122, 189, 215, 253, 282

cabinet: viii, 225, 227, 230-231, 410

Canada: 328, 397, 400, 404

canals: 18, 28, 351

capital investment: 315; foreign, 47, 319, 358, 366; repatriation, 391

capital market: 407, 426, 435-437

capital punishment: 448, 451, 458, 459, 470-471

carts and cart tracks: 8, 16, 386, 387

caste system: 4, 37, 38, 77, 78, 97-113, 115-119, 138, 168, 218, 219, 221, 223, 256, 259, 299, 305, 306, 316, 335; Sinhalese, 37, 96, 97-106, 206, 334; Tamil, 38, 82, 97, 99, 101, 107-110, 111, 211-212

cement: 22, 317, 355, 357, 360, 396

censorship (see also press): 63, 296-297; press, 282, 285, 296

census: 69; (1871), 66; (1911), 102; (1946), 146; (1963), 65, 66, 69, 71, 153, 315, 369; agricultural, 328, 330-333, 337, 341, 342, 348

Central Bank: ix, 295, 310-311, 318, 321, 391, 394, 400, 401, 403, 423, 426-428, 429, 431, 433, 435, 438;

credit operations, 390, 407, 427–428, 432, 436, 439, 440, 442, 443; surveys and studies, 348, 356, 383, 384, 391, 392–393, 438
Central Council of Ceylon Trade Unions (CCCTU): 378, 379
ceramics: 357, 363, 365
Ceylon Administrative Service (CAS): 219–220, 232, 236
Ceylon Agricultural Society: 49
Ceylon Army (see also armed forces; reserve forces): 6, 453, 468–469
Ceylon Association for the Advancement of Science (CAAS): 185
Ceylon Broadcasting Corporation (CBC): 281, 287, 290–294
Ceylon Chamber of Commerce: 54
Ceylon Civil Service (CCS): 43, 45, 46, 47, 51, 55, 236, 255
Ceylon Communist Party (CCP): 58, 245, 251, 261, 262, 266, 267–268, 270, 271, 272, 286, 378, 379
Ceylon Daily News: 283, 286, 288, 449
Ceylon Indian Congress: 58
Ceylon Institute of Scientific and Industrial Research (CISIR): 186
Ceylon Labour Union: 377, 378, 380
Ceylon League: 50
Ceylon National Congress: 53, 54, 58, 283, 377
Ceylon Observer: 282, 283, 288
Ceylon Rediffusion Service Ltd.: 292
Ceylon Savings Bank: 139, 432, 435
Ceylon Trade Union Federation (CTUF): 267, 268, 378, 379
Ceylon Transport Board: 63
Ceylon Workers Congress (CWC): 378
Ceyloniana: 294
Chelvanayakam, S. J. V.: 59, 62, 63, 269
chemicals: 360, 396, 399
chena (see also slash and burn agriculture): 8, 23, 326, 327, 328, 329, 334, 335, 345, 346
chettiars: 429, 435
Chilaw: 12, 77, 294, 386
children and childhood (see also infant mortality; juvenile crime; school children): 121–122, 124, 125, 126, 132, 141–142, 147, 148, 150, 160, 220–221, 223, 413; handicapped, 142; labor, 369, 371
China and the Chinese (historic): 9, 34, 35, 38

Chitra Sena: 179
Christians and Christianity (see also Protestantism; Roman Catholicism): vii, 1, 2, 30, 39, 40, 45, 51, 61, 77, 80, 82, 86, 88, 91, 106, 119, 120, 140, 147, 173, 175, 181–182, 193, 194, 195, 196, 197, 198, 214–215, 241, 253, 254, 255, 299, 304, 306, 307; schools, 145, 147, 149, 150, 151, 154–155, 195, 259
cinema (see also films): 141, 282, 296
cinnamon: viii, 38, 40, 41, 43, 45, 49, 343, 394
citizenship: 59, 239, 256, 301; Act (1948), 274; Indian and Pakistani Act (1949), 274, 275; Indian Tamils, 2–3, 59, 68, 82–83, 274–276
citronella: viii, 24, 343, 394
civil disobedience: 62, 247, 257, 447, 451
civil disorder (see also civil disobedience): 249, 250, 252, 257, 445, 446, 460
civil rights (see also censorship; citizenship; disenfranchisement; suffrage): 97, 227, 230, 264, 286, 301, 306
civil service (see also Ceylon Administrative Service; Ceylon Civil Service; employment; Public Service Commission; trade unions): 2, 5, 59, 81, 94, 98, 112, 149, 219–220, 221, 226, 236–238, 257, 459
climate: vii, 4, 7, 18–20
clothing. See dress
cocoa: viii, 343, 394
coconut (see also customs duties; plantation economy): viii, 10, 13, 21, 27, 49, 327, 329, 332, 335, 338, 342–343, 359
coffee (see also plantation economy): 46, 47–48, 327, 343, 346
Colebrooke-Cameron Commission (1831–1832): 45, 46, 195
Colombo: vii, ix, 4, 7, 16, 27, 72, 85, 138, 148, 156, 361, 384, 388, 464; history, 39, 41; local government, 50, 142; port, 27, 63, 381, 390, 457; public information, 281, 282, 287, 290, 293, 296, 298
Colombo Academy (see also Royal College): 50, 149
Colombo Brokers Association: 436
Colombo Plan: ix, 273, 277, 279, 280, 321, 328
Colombo Seminary: 148

511

112, 149, 159; financing, 146, 157; free, vii, 5, 131, 145, 151, 304; higher, 220; vernacular, 50, 149, 161, 172

Eight-fold Path: 204, 206

Eksath Bhikku Peramuna: 61

Elara, King: 35

elections: viii, 225-226, 229, 238-240, 248, 260, 272, 285, 300, 301, 306; (1931), 1; (1932), 55, 238; (1936), 56; (1947), 58, 264, 270, 380; (1952), 60, 61; (1956), 2, 60, 61, 62, 206, 238, 250, 252, 255, 265, 270; 283; (1960, March and July), 229, 238, 247, 250, 451; (1965), 238, 240, 249, 255, 258, 270; (1970), 245, 253, 255, 260, 267, 269, 270-271, 286, 306, 318, 388; local government, 233

electricity (see also hydroelectricity): 131, 138, 312, 319, 365

elite. See Western oriented elite

Ella gap: 14

Elliot, Christopher: 282

Employees Provident Fund: 374, 375, 434

employers organisations: 379-380

employment (see also civil service; Employees Provident Fund; employers organisations; labor force; trade unions; unemployment; wages): 68, 319, 355, 364; conditions, 367, 370-371, 376, 380; exchanges, 371, 375; government, 367, 369, 373

endogamy: 116, 117

English language (see also education; newspapers; press; Western oriented elite): vii, ix, 2, 45, 46, 61, 62, 76, 77, 86, 89, 92-94, 112, 146, 151, 153, 172, 195, 291, 292, 294, 295, 297, 298, 455, 461

ethnic groups (see also Burghers; communalism; Eurasians; Europeans; Muslims; Sinhalese Tamils): 75-96

Eurasians (see also Burghers): vii, 66, 75, 78, 85, 86

Europeans: vii, 53, 55, 75, 78, 85, 149

Exchange Control Act (1953): 401

Exchange Control Department: 391, 401, 427

excise taxes: 407, 412, 415, 418, 422

Executive Council: 54

expenditure: 407, 415, 416, 421

export (see also coconut; custom duties; rubber; tea): viii, 3, 251, 309, 310, 314, 316, 317, 318, 319, 320, 322, 325, 337, 343-344, 347, 355, 356, 383, 388-389, 391-397, 400, 401, 411, 443; agencies, 384

external affairs. See foreign relations

Fa Hsien (A.D. 400): 9, 34, 147, 167

family (see also marriage): 5, 98, 100, 115-129, 218, 299, 334, 413

family planning: 65, 66, 72-74, 134, 259, 336

Federal Party (FP): 59, 62, 63, 261, 268, 269, 272, 450, 451; alliance with U.N.P. (1965), 250, 251

Fernando, Marcus: 185

fertilizers: viii, 4, 320, 341, 343, 345, 357, 396, 399; government subsidies, 340, 362; production, 362

festivals and holidays (see also Buddha Jayanti; Perahera; Poya day): 140-141, 190, 191, 199, 213-214, 371, 454

feudal system: 102-105, 168, 169, 174, 192, 196, 217, 218, 220, 222, 334

films (see also cinema): 162, 179-181, 282, 296, 297

finance (see also balance of payments; banks and banking; budget; expenditure; public debt; revenue): ix; administration, 421-423

fishing and fisheries (see also pearl fisheries): 7, 8, 16, 136, 311, 312, 319; villages, 8

flooding: 16, 131, 142, 334, 344, 351

foodstuffs (see also imports; rice): 317; production, 314, 318, 325, 347, 356, 363; shortage, 246, 251; subsidies, 253

Ford Foundation: 280

foreign exchange (see also Exchange Control Department): 246, 247, 314, 316-317, 355, 356, 363, 364, 386, 387, 389, 394, 407, 423; control, 317, 319, 383, 427, 437, 443; earnings, 253, 310, 325, 356; system, 401-404

foreign relations (see also defense; Communist China; Great Britain; India; Ministry of Defence and External Affairs; Soviet Union; United States): viii, 3, 62, 264, 273-280

forests and forestry: 8, 12, 21, 23, 24, 311, 312, 325, 329, 330, 332, 333, 334, 335, 347

"43 Group": 162, 169

Four Noble Truths: 203, 204

France and French (historic): 42

franchise. *See* suffrage

Freedom From Hunger Campaign: 136

Gal Oya: 62, 353, 360, 365, 386; Board, 352, 360

Galle: ix, 10, 27, 50, 72, 139, 142, 152, 360, 384, 386

gansabhas: 50

gems (*see also* pearls): 8, 12, 20, 34; trade, 9

geology: 8, 10, 12

gods and demons: 198-199, 208, 209-210, 213

Goonesinha, A. E.: 377, 380

Goonetilleke, Sir Oliver: 63

Goonewardene, Leslie Simon: 58

government, organisation and administration (*see also* government role; local government): viii, 225-243

government agent: 231-232, 235

Government College of Fine Arts: 170, 187

Government Film Unit: 180, 282, 297, 298

Government Gazette: 230, 377, 409

government role (*see also* credit operations; economic development; housing; land; language; nationalization; power; prices; public corporations; settlement; state corporations; tourism): agriculture, 325, 336, 340, 341-342, 343-344, 346-347; culture, 186-188; economy, 317-323; industry, 314, 317, 318, 320, 355, 357-358; labor, 373-377; trade, 385, 388; transportation, 387

government service. *See* civil service

governor: 42-43, 44, 46, 49, 57, 58

governor general (office and functions): vii, viii, 58, 157, 225, 226, 227-229, 230, 231, 236, 239, 240, 249, 284, 408, 426, 427, 450, 451, 467

Goyigama caste (*see also* caste system): 207, 266

grama sevaka: 231, 232-233, 239, 452

graphite: 8, 20, 365

grassland (*see also patana; talawa*): 24, 329, 330

Great Britain (*see also* British rule): 225, 277, 295, 296, 298, 300, 397, 400, 456, 467; trade, 358, 365

gross domestic product (GDP): 311, 312, 322, 323, 407

gross national product (GNP): 159, 311, 312, 313, 315, 316, 325, 415

Gulf of Manar: 7, 10

Gunawardene, Philip: 58, 266, 267, 379

Gupta Empire of India: 165, 167

Guaranteed Price Scheme: 318, 336, 345, 349, 388

Guerrilla training: 449

Guevara, Che: 449

Hambantota: 12, 19, 362

Haputale gap: 14

Harijans. *See* untouchables and outcastes

Hatton plateau: 14, 26

health (*see also* diet; disease; life expectancy; malaria; medical care; tuberculosis): vii-viii, 5, 131, 132-137; education, 132, 133, 134, 136; public programs, 67, 132

Hinayana Buddhism. *See* Theravada Buddhism

Hindus and Hinduism: vii, 1, 2, 38, 71, 76, 77, 84, 87, 107, 116, 122, 126, 140, 141, 147, 153, 154, 183, 187, 189, 190, 194, 195, 196, 198, 199, 208, 210-214, 222, 224, 253, 295, 307, 413, 469; concepts and teachings, 200-205

holidays. *See* festivals and holidays

honours and titles: 222

hospitals: 131, 133-135

House of Representatives (*see also* parliament): 225, 226, 227, 229, 230, 231, 240, 245, 409, 410, 423

housing, 131, 138-139, 305, 370, 432, 434; government schemes, 131, 138, 319

Hunting Survey Corporation Ltd.: 328, 333, 346, 347

hydroelectricity: 18, 265, 350, 365

ilmenite: 22, 365

immigration: 68; illicit, 275, 456, 467, 469

import (*see also* consumer goods; customs duties): viii, 311, 316, 317, 318, 320, 355, 384-385, 394, 396-400, 401-404; agency houses, 384, 385; foodstuffs, 316, 317, 318, 325, 345, 347, 351, 396, 398, 401; licences and quotas, 319, 401-404; raw material and capital equipment, 314, 316, 396, 401; substitution, 355, 361, 362, 412

513

income (*see also* wages): 140, 319, 356, 383, 384, 390, 411, 427, 442; per capita, 140, 311; tax, 411, 412
independence: 1, 29, 30; movement and achievement, 46, 50-58, 89, 283
Independent Newspapers Ltd.: 281, 284, 288, 289
India (*see also* Indo-Ceylon agreements): 3, 51, 60, 68, 87, 91, 273-276, 277, 295, 296, 386, 397, 400, 451, 456; historical, 30, 31, 35, 37; Indian Tamil issue, 3, 68, 91
Indian Ocean: v, 7
Indo-Ceylon agreements: (1964), 3; (1966), 264
Industrial Development Board: 364
industry (*see also* cottage industry; private sector; public corporations; public sector; state corporations): viii, 112, 310, 311, 314, 315, 316, 323, 334, 355-366; government intervention, 314, 317, 318, 320, 357-358
infant mortality: vii, 5, 67, 69, 132
information (*see also* newspapers; press; radio): 281-297, 305
inheritance: 115, 123, 124, 125, 126, 223, 241, 335
inland navigation (*see also* canals): 18
insurance: 247, 312, 318, 431, 433-434, agricultural, 320
Insurance Corporation of Ceylon (ICC): 431, 433-434
intercropping: 332, 343
internal security: 6, 445-465, 467, 469
International Bank for Reconstruction and Development (IBRD): ix, 60, 263, 265, 273, 280, 319, 320, 351, 387, 404, 405, 411, 433
International Commission of Jurists: 448
International Confederation of Free Trade Unions (ICFTU): 378
International Council of Scientific Unions: 185
International Development Association (IDA): 263, 351, 387, 405
International Labor Organisation (ILO): 367, 368, 371, 380
international memberships agreements and treaties (*see also* aid (foreign); individual organisations; Indo-Ceylon agreements; trade agreements): ix, 273, 405
International Monetary Fund (IMF):

ix, 273, 280, 320, 391, 394, 402, 405, 411, 438
iron and steel: 357, 361-362
iron ore: 8
irrigation works (*see also* tanks): 4, 16, 17-18, 20, 26, 27-28, 32-33, 37, 50, 55, 318, 319, 326-327, 337, 346, 349-351, 352, 360
Islam: 153, 187, 189, 194, 195, 215-216
Israel: 264, 279

Jaffna Peninsula: 8, 13, 20, 22, 24, 26, 70, 81, 88, 91, 139, 148, 152, 175, 183, 214, 281, 345, 362, 384, 386; history, 40, 41; town, 27, 281
Japan: 280, 365, 388, 404
jataka: 162, 167, 171, 174, 176
Jayamanna, brothers: 176
Jayasena, Henry: 176
Jayatilaka, D. B.: 53
Jayawardene, J. R.: 266
Jennings, Sir Ivor: 56
journalists and journalism (*see also* newspapers): 172, 257, 282, 283
Judicial Service Commission: 227, 228, 242, 460
judiciary: viii, 45-46, 226, 240-243
jury trial: 43, 46, 242, 448, 459-460
justice (*see also* judiciary; law): 446; military, 470-471
Juvenile Court: 243
juvenile crime: 243, 446, 458-459, 463, 464-465

Kachchaitivu: 276
Kandy (*see also* Kandyan Kingdom): 20, 22, 45, 50, 72, 85, 141, 142, 152, 156, 384, 386; plateau, 15, 16; public information, 282, 290, 295, 298
Kandyan Kingdom: 29, 33, 34, 40, 41, 44, 51, 85, 102, 161, 168-169, 178, 189, 194, 327, 335
Kandyan Law Commission: 123
Kandyan Peasantry Commission: 100
Kandyan Sinhalese (*see also* caste system; customary codes; family; marriage; social structure): 9, 26, 41, 50, 53, 59, 62, 71, 79, 81, 82, 88, 89, 97, 100, 102-105, 116, 117, 120, 122-125, 128, 240, 254, 300
Kankesanturai: 27, 360
kaolin: 22
Karava caste (*see also* caste system): 193, 214, 221
karma: 199, 201-202, 209, 211, 223, 224

against, 5, 67, 132, 185, 325, 328, 401; epidemics, 67
Malayarata: 179
Malays: vii, 75, 78, 85, 215
malnutrition: 136
Malwatu Oya: 17-18
Maname: 176, 188
manufacturing (*see also* labor force): 312, 314, 322, 355, 356
Marketing Department: 385
marriage (*see also* divorce; polyandry; polygamy): 4, 5, 37, 69-71, 73, 77, 98, 106, 109, 111, 115-129, 152, 199, 218, 220, 241; intermarriage, 77, 84, 193, 216
marshland: 329, 351
Marxists and Marxism. *See* Communists and communism
Matale: 20, 22, 386; valley, 15, 16
Matara: 27
McCallum, Henry, Governor: 51
medical care (*see also* hospitals): vii-viii, 5, 67, 131-137, 143, 370, 374
medical personnel: vii-viii, 131, 133, 134, 152
Medical Research Institute: 136
Medical School: 50, 134, 156, 185, 220
Menik Ganga: 11, 16
mica: 20-22
middle class: 111-112, 121, 152, 169, 173, 176, 182, 257
Middle Way: 302, 305
migration: 67-68, 86, 91, 112
milk: 136, 346-347, 396
minerals (*see also* gems; graphite; ilmenite; mica): viii, 8, 20-22, 365-366, 394
mining: 8, 20, 28, 312, 322, 365-366; labor, 370
ministers and ministries (*see also* cabinet; individual ministries): 230-231, 410, 416-417
Ministry of Agriculture and Lands: 136
Ministry of Defence and External Affairs: 6, 228, 231, 284, 449, 453; minister, 225, 273, 297, 446, 452, 467
Ministry of Education and Cultural Affairs: 146, 159, 160, 187, 304
Ministry of Finance: 320, 359, 409-410, 412, 421, 422, 423, 427; minister, 408, 409, 410, 423
Ministry of Health: 73, 133, 134, 135
Ministry of Home Affairs: 231, 422

Ministry of Industries and Fisheries: 357
Ministry of Industries and Scientific Affairs: 357; minister, 358
Ministry of Information and Broadcasting: 231, 287, 297; minister, 293
Ministry of Justice: 242, 463; minister, 448, 460
Ministry of Labour and Employment: 372, 375
Ministry of Land Irrigation and Power: 233
Ministry of Local Government: 233, 295; minister, 234, 235
Ministry of Nationalized Services: 231
Ministry of Planning and Economic Affairs: 231, 321
Ministry of Planning and Employment: 401
Ministry of Plantation Industry: 355
minorities (*see also* Burghers; communalism; Hindus; Muslims; Tamils): 246, 253, 302
monetary system. *See* finance
monks. *See* bhikkus
monsoons: 4, 7, 9, 19, 23
moonstone: 164, 166
Moors (*see also* Arabs; Muslims): vii, 1, 66, 75, 78, 82, 84, 193, 215, 218
mountains: 4, 7, 10, 12, 13-16
mudaliyar: 41, 42
Mullaitivu: 13
municipalities: 142, 233, 234, 297, 421, 460
Museum of Modern Art, New York: 180
museums: 187, 295
music: 153, 161, 162, 174, 178, 292
Muslim (*see also* Islam; Malays; marriage; Moors): vii, 1, 39, 40, 41, 50, 51, 54, 55, 56, 75, 77, 83-85, 97, 100, 115, 116, 117, 126-129, 140, 154, 189, 193, 199, 240, 241, 295, 299, 306
mythology and folklore: 1, 31, 469

nadagama: 162, 175, 176, 177, 178, 184
Nadesan, K: 377
National Council of Higher Education: 157
National Employees Union: 265
National Housing Fund: 432, 434
national languages. *See* official language; Sinhalese language; Tamil language

National Liberation Front (Jatika Vimukti Peramuna): 450
National Planning Council: 320-321, 322
National Savings Movement: 139
National Science Council: 163
national symbols: 304
nationalism (see also Sinhalese Buddhist nationalism): 87, 254, 299, 303-304
nationalization: 63, 247, 250, 251, 263, 318, 319, 320, 336, 396, 428, 433; schools, 146, 151, 155, 247
navy. See Royal Ceylon Navy
Nehru, Jawaharlal, Prime Minister of India: 274, 276
neutrality policies: 273, 276
news agencies: 287
newspapers (see also advertising; censorship; journalists and journalism; press): 92, 94, 134, 141, 151, 161, 172, 182, 200, 230, 249, 257, 258, 264, 281, 288, 292, 296, 297
nibbana. See nirvana
nirvana: 31, 61, 79, 90, 197, 203, 206, 208
Nissankamalla, King (A.D. 1187-96): 37, 166
North, Frederick, Governor: 43, 149
nurtiya: 175-176, 178, 180
nutrition. See diet
Nuwara Eliya: 14-15, 18, 19, 23, 361, 384, 386

Obeyesekere, Gananath: 185-186
official language (see also Sinhalese language; Tamil language): vii, 94-95, 247, 262, 265; Act (1956), 263
Olcott, Henry Steele, Colonel: 182, 196
Open General License: 403, 414
opposition in politics: 245, 249, 251, 252, 293, 300, 307
Organisation for Economic Cooperation and Development (OECD): 317, 321, 397, 400
outcastes. See untouchables and outcastes

paddy. See rice
Paddy Lands Bill (1958): 63, 196, 336-337, 350
Pakistanis (see also citizenship): vii
Pali: 31, 34, 95, 170, 171, 190, 205
Palk Strait: 7, 276
palmyra: 10, 26

pansalas: 146-147, 150, 153
paper: 360-361, 396, 399
Parakramabahu 1, King (1153-86): 37, 166, 181
Paranavitana, S.: 171, 186
parliament (see also House of Representatives; Senate): viii, 226, 227, 228, 229-230, 322, 408, 409, 450; dissolution, 229, 231, 240, 247, 249; members, 232, 236-237, 245, 246, 410, 459
patanas: 14, 21, 24
pattus: 26
Paynter, David: 169
Peace Corps: 280
Peace of Amiens treaty (1802): 43
pearls: 10, 34; fisheries, 10, 38
Peiris, Harry: 169
Peiris, Lester James: 180
penal institutions: 463-465
pension schemes (see also Employees Provident Fund): 143
Peoples Bank: 364, 428, 429, 430, 431, 437, 439
Peoples United Front (Mahajana Eksath Peramuna, MEP): 62, 248, 266, 267, 378, 379
Perahera: 141; Esala, 52, 104, 198
Perera, H. S.: 283
Perera, J. D. A.: 169
Perera, Nanayakkarapathirage Martin: 58, 266, 267, 379
petroleum: 231, 357, 396, 399; nationalization, 250
Pidurutalagala: 14, 15
Pieris, Sir James: 111
pirit: 210
pirivenas (see also Vidyalankara Pirivena; Vidyodaya Pirivena): 34, 146-147, 150, 153, 155, 196
plantation economy (see also coconut; rubber; tea): 14, 30, 44, 46-47, 82, 107, 153, 185, 309, 318, 319, 325, 326, 327-328, 330, 347, 355, 383, 386, 391, 394-396, 428-429, 432; labor, 47, 59, 68, 82, 370, 373, 374, 377
Planters Association: 49
plumbago. See graphite
plywood: 357, 360, 362
Point Pedro: 7
police (see also coup attempts): 6, 226, 257, 445, 446, 447, 448, 449, 450, 452-457, 463; recruitment, 455-456; training, 277, 455-456
political parties (see also elections;

517

reserve forces: 53; army, 451, 468; police, 446, 457

revenue (see also taxation): 264, 394, 402, 408, 411-420; administration, 411-415, 422

rice (see also agriculture; rubber-rice barter): viii, 4, 12, 21, 41, 48, 251, 252, 279, 280, 314, 319, 325, 396; cultivation, 26, 326, 327, 329, 330, 334, 338, 344-345, 349, 352; ration and subsidy, 60, 135, 251, 252-253, 380, 388, 413

riots and rebellions (see also civil disorder; strikes): 2, 6, 30, 31, 42, 44, 62, 90, 91, 457; (1818), 44; (1848), 48, 282; (1915), 52; (1956), 449; (1958), 2, 31, 63, 283, 293, 450; (1966), 451-452

rites and rituals: 100, 101, 121-122, 140, 162, 169, 174, 178, 179, 198, 205, 210, 211, 213, 214, 219, 344

river valley development (see also Gal Oya; Mahaweli Ganga): 319, 349, 350, 352-353; Board, 233-234, 352

rivers (see also individual rivers; river valley development; waterfalls): 4, 10, 11, 12, 13, 14, 16-18, 28

roads and highways (see also carts and cart tracks): ix, 8, 9, 16, 17, 26, 28, 46, 48, 49, 319, 386-387, 388

Rodiya: 97, 100, 105

Roman Catholicism (see also Christians and Christianity): 80, 86, 106, 175, 193, 194, 198, 214, 257, 264, 295, 306, 447; schools, 147-148, 155, 197

Roman-Dutch law: viii, 30, 41, 43, 46, 115, 226, 240, 241, 457

Royal Ceylon Air Force: 6, 456, 467, 468, 469

Royal Ceylon Navy: 6, 456, 467, 468, 469

Royal College (see also Colombo Academy): 151-152

rubber (see also customs duties; export; plantation economy; rubber-rice barter): viii, 9, 14, 21, 27, 49, 60, 327, 328, 329, 338, 341-342, 355

rubber-rice barter: 60, 278, 279-280, 342, 359, 400, 401

Ruhuna Park: 25

rupee: 427, 438, devaluation, 311, 319, 394, 397, 407, 443

rural society (see also schools): 90, 113, 220, 223, 259-260, 295, 299, 304, 320, 460; culture, 161-162; economy, 319, 383, 388, 389-390; education, 145, 146, 149, 153, 192; intelligentsia, 80, 89-90, 217; labor, 368, 369, 373; living conditions, 131, 138, 139, 140, 365; local government, 50, 233-234; politics, 90, 112, 300; population, 67, 79, 70, 71-72; social structure, 4-5, 98, 99, 105, 107, 122, 218

Russia. See Soviet Union

Sabaragamuwa ridges: 12

Salaries and Cadres Commission: 367, 372

salt: 329, 355, 357, 360, 362

Sangam: 184

Sangamankande Point: 7

sangha (see also bhikkus): 32, 34, 161, 162, 178, 181, 182, 192, 193, 194, 195, 205-207, 302; and politics, 30, 48, 194, 195, 197, 259, 283, 285, 302

sanitation: 131, 134, 370

Sanskrit: 147, 176, 177, 180

Sao Paolo Biennial (1963): 170

Sarathchandra, E. R.: 176, 188

sari: 122, 137

sarong: 137

savings institutions (see also Ceylon Savings Bank): 426, 434, 435

school children: 136, 137, 141, 146-147, 148, 150, 152

schools (see also Government College of Fine Arts; Medical School; nationalization; pansala; pirivena; teachers; universities): 2, 61, 145-160, 255, 263, 295; British, 149-151; curriculum and textbooks, 146, 147, 150, 151, 153, 159-160, 282, 295; Dutch, 148; elementary, 145, 146, 153; enrollment, 154, 157; Portuguese, 147; private denominational, 145, 146, 148, 149, 150, 151, 154-155, 259; public, 145, 150, 153-154; secondary, 145, 146, 152, 154; vernacular, 88, 89, 145, 148, 149, 150, 259

sculpture (see also Buddha): 161, 164, 166, 170, 178

Senanayake, Don Stephen: 53, 55, 56-57, 58, 81, 248, 264, 265, 274, 283

Senanayake, Dudley: v, 59-60, 91, 151, 198, 210, 232, 245, 248, 252, 265, 266, 276, 306; government

519

trade unions: 58, 236, 246, 257, 265, 367, 376, 377-379, 381, 450; teachers, 158-159
Trade Unions Ordinance (1935): 377-378
transportation (*see also* air transportation; carts and cart tracks; communications; labor force; railways; roads and highways): ix, 8, 16, 139, 231, 318, 325, 375, 380, 386-388, 389; equipment, 397, 399
Treasury Department: 409, 410, 411, 422
Tribune: 286
Trincomalee: 10, 16, 19, 22, 27, 56, 63, 72, 274, 282, 386, 469; history, 40, 41, 42
Tripitaka: 205
Trotskyites. *See* Lanka Sama Samajists Party
tuberculosis: 5-6
tires and tubes: 361

Uda Walawe. *See* Walawe Ganga
Udugama, Richard, Major General: 250-251, 449
unemployment: viii, 4, 67, 105, 140, 249, 250, 253, 263, 305, 316, 352, 367-368, 371-372
United Kingdom. *See* Great Britain
United National Party (UNP): 30, 58, 59-61, 62, 245, 248, 249, 252, 253, 254, 258, 259, 260, 261, 262, 263, 264-266, 267, 268, 269, 270, 272, 283, 285, 286, 306, 307, 358, 471-472; government (1960), 247; government (1965), 250-251, 252-253, 276, 293
United Nations (*see also* specialized agencies): ix, 264, 273, 277, 278-279, 280, 321, 411; Development Programme, 321, 322; Special Fund, 156
United Nations Educational, Scientific and Cultural Organisation (UNESCO): 187, 282
United States: 282, 287, 292, 293-294, 295, 296, 298, 467; aid, ix, 250, 280, 317, 321, 404; relations with, 250, 279-280; trade, 341, 358, 365, 397, 400
United States Board on Geographic Names: v
United States Information Service (USIS): 298
universities: vii, 2, 92, 145, 146, 154,

155, 156-158, 160, 207, 220, 295; foreign, 88; graduates, 4, 5, 112, 119, 140, 158, 237, 368, 449
University of Ceylon, Colombo and Peradeniya: 56, 120, 134, 156-157, 158, 176, 185, 186
University of Leyden: 148
University of London: 156, 185
untouchables and outcastes (*see also* Rodiyas): 108, 109
urban society (*see also* family; municipalities): 4, 5, 8, 153, 223, 253, 305, 316; economy, 388, 389; ethnic composition, 86, 93; industry, 356; labor, 368; living conditions, 131, 138; local government, 71; politics, 30, 58, 266, 268, 300, 305; population, 66, 67, 69, 70, 71-72, 86; social structure, 98, 100, 110-113, 116, 119, 121
Uva: 86, 87; basin, 14

values (*see also* caste system; social status; social structure): political, 299-307; social, 217-224
Vedas: 210, 211
Veddhas: vii, 31, 75, 78, 86-87, 178, 190
vegetation (*see also* forests and forestry; *patanas*; *talawas*): 21, 22-24
Vellala caste (*see also* caste system): 38, 213
Vidyalankara Pirivena: 155, 157
Vidyodaya Pirivena: 155, 157, 158
Vietnam. *See* foreign relations
vihara. *See* temples
Vijayabahu 1, King: 36, 37, 171
village councils: 233-234, 235
villages (*see also* rural society): 8, 27, 79-80; fishing, 8, 27; plantation, 8
Virakesari Ltd.: 281, 288
vocational and technical education: 142, 149, 152, 154, 155-156, 368, 372
Voice of America: 293
volunteer organisations: 142

wages (*see also* income; Salaries and Cadres Commission): 311, 367, 372-373, 374, 375, 376, 377, 380, 443
Walawe Ganga: 12, 13; project, 353, 360, 365
waterfalls: 13, 16, 18
water supply: 131, 135, 138, 235
West Germany: 290, 293, 298, 404
Western oriented elite: 2, 30, 46, 51,

75-76, 81, 88, 89, 90, 91, 98, 107, 111, 115, 119, 122, 145, 161, 173, 182, 194, 196, 197, 217, 223, 254, 257, 302, 303, 304, 379
wet zone: vii, 4, 8, 20, 23, 326, 329, 330, 333, 351; agriculture, 325, 328, 335, 337, 341, 344
Wickramasinghe, Martin: 162, 173-174, 180, 182
Wickremasinghe, S. A.: 267, 268
Wijewardene, D. R.: 283
wild life: 8, 24-26; preserves, 8, 25
Williams, Tennessee: 176-177
Wilpattu: 25
women (see also children and childhood; marriage): 5, 69, 70, 71, 73, 116, 120-122, 123, 127, 139, 152,

175-176, 179, 206, 215, 238, 458; education, 120, 152-153, 157; labor, 367, 368-369, 371, 373, 374
workmen's compensation: 143, 377
World Federation of Trade Unions: 378
World Health Organization (WHO): 132
World War I: 156
World War II: 22, 56, 58, 72, 468

Yapa, Sugathapala Senerat: 180
Yapahuwa: 168, 178, 186
Young Lanka League: 377
youth (see also school children; universities): 258, 265, 310, 346, 352, 372

PUBLISHED AREA HANDBOOKS

550-65	Afghanistan	550-81	Korea, North
550-98	Albania	550-41	Korea, Rep. of
550-44	Algeria	550-58	Laos
550-59	Angola	550-24	Lebanon
550-73	Argentina	550-38	Liberia
550-20	Brazil	550-85	Libya
550-61	Burma	550-163	Malagasy Republic
550-83	Burundi	550-45	Malaysia
550-166	Cameroon	550-161	Mauritania
550-96	Ceylon	550-79	Mexico
550-159	Chad	550-76	Mongolia
550-77	Chile	550-49	Morocco
550-60	China, People's Rep. of	550-64	Mozambique
550-63	China, Rep. of	550-35	Nepal, Bhutan and Sikkim
550-26	Colombia	550-88	Nicaragua
550-67	Congo, Democratic Rep. of (Zaire)	550-157	Nigeria
		550-94	Oceania
550-91	Congo, People's Rep. of	550-48	Pakistan
550-90	Costa Rica	550-46	Panama
550-152	Cuba	550-156	Paraguay
550-22	Cyprus	550-92	Peripheral States of the Arabian Peninsula
550-158	Czechoslovakia		
550-54	Dominican Republic	550-42	Peru
550-155	East Germany	550-72	Philippines
550-52	Ecuador	550-162	Poland
550-150	El Salvador	550-160	Romania
550-28	Ethiopia	550-84	Rwanda
550-29	Germany	550-51	Saudi Arabia
550-153	Ghana	550-70	Senegal
550-87	Greece	550-86	Somalia
550-78	Guatemala	550-93	South Africa, Rep. of
550-82	Guyana	550-95	Soviet Union
550-164	Haiti	550-27	Sudan, Democratic Rep. of
550-165	Hungary	550-47	Syria
550-151	Honduras	550-62	Tanzania
550-21	India	550-53	Thailand
550-154	Indian Ocean Territories	550-89	Tunisia
550-39	Indonesia	550-80	Turkey
550-68	Iran	550-74	Uganda
550-31	Iraq	550-43	United Arab Republic (Egypt)
550-25	Israel	550-97	Uruguay
550-69	Ivory Coast	550-71	Venezuela
550-30	Japan	550-57	Vietnam, North
550-34	Jordan	550-55	Vietnam, South
550-56	Kenya	550-99	Yugoslavia
550-50	Khmer Republic (Cambodia)	550-75	Zambia

U.S. GOVERNMENT PRINTING OFFICE : 1979 O—299-639